Selected Letters of W. D. Howells

Volume 1

1 8 5 2 – 1 8 7 2

HOWELLS EDITION

David J. Nordloh, *General Editor*
Christoph K. Lohmann, *Associate Editor*

HOWELLS EDITION EDITORIAL BOARD

George Arms, *Executive Committee*
Louis J. Budd
Edwin H. Cady, *Executive Committee*
Everett Carter
Don L. Cook, *Executive Committee*
William M. Gibson, *Executive Committee*
Ronald Gottesman, *Executive Committee*
Christoph K. Lohmann
David J. Nordloh, *Executive Committee*
James Woodress

GENERAL EDITORS OF THE SELECTED LETTERS

George Arms
Richard H. Ballinger
Christoph K. Lohmann

Howells Collection, Harvard College Library

William Dean Howells
ca. 1860

W. D. HOWELLS

Selected Letters

Volume 1: 1852-1872

Edited and Annotated by
George Arms, Richard H. Ballinger,
Christoph K. Lohmann, and John K. Reeves

Textual Editors
Don L. Cook, Christoph K. Lohmann,
and David J. Nordloh

TWAYNE PUBLISHERS

Boston

1979

This volume of Selected Letters is also published as
Volume 4 of A Selected Edition of W. D. Howells

Editorial expenses for this volume have been supported by grants from
the National Endowment for the Humanities administered through
the Center for Editions of American Authors of the Modern Language Association

Copyright © 1979 by G. K. Hall & Co.
and the Howells Edition Editorial Board
All rights reserved

Published in 1979 by Twayne Publishers, A Division of G. K. Hall & Co.,
70 Lincoln Street, Boston, Massachusetts 02111

Printed on permanent/durable acid-free paper and bound in
the United States of America

First Printing

Library of Congress Cataloging in Publication Information

Howells, William Dean, 1837–1920.
Selected letters.

(His A Selected edition of W. D. Howells; v. 4–)
Includes index.
CONTENTS: v. 1. 1852–1872.
1. Howells, William Dean, 1837–1920—Correspondence.
2. Novelists, American—19th century—Correspondence.
I. Arms, George Warren, 1912–
II. Title.
PS2020.F68   vol. 4, etc.   [PS2033.A4]   818'.4'09 [B]   78-27247
ISBN 0-8057-8527-2

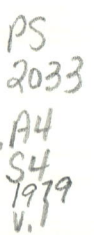

Acknowledgments

The editors and the Howells Edition Center have accumulated many debts in the preparation of this and subsequent letters volumes. We are grateful for the support of John W. Ryan, President, and officers of research administration at Indiana University, and for the gracious assistance and cooperation of Professor William White Howells and the heirs of W. D. Howells. On a more practical level, these volumes could not have been completed without the conscientious labors performed by members of the Howells Edition staff, especially Lia Sayers Barnes, Christy Brown, Velma Carmichael, Barbara Clarke-Mossberg, Jane Clay, Sarah Craft, John Fitzpatrick, Sydelle Grant, Jerry Herron, Norman Mark Klein, David Kleinman, Gary Milsark, Carol Robertson, Daniel R. Rubey, Don R. Smith, and Gregory Sojka.

So many persons have been helpful to us in so many ways—foremost among them the staff of the Houghton Library, Harvard University, W. H. Bond, Carolyn E. Jakeman (retired), and Marte Shaw—that the following list is necessarily incomplete; the late Frederick Anderson, the Mark Twain Papers; Margaret B. Andrews and Robert L. Voltz, University of Rochester Library; Ellen B. Ballou, Dublin, New Hampshire; Mary A. Benjamin, Hunter, New York; Scott Bennett, University of Illinois; Dorothy W. Bridgewater, Beinecke Library, Yale University; John C. Broderick and Kate M. Stewart, Library of Congress; Harry Brown, Michigan State University; Vinton Chapin, Cambridge, Massachusetts; Mrs. Vinton Chapin, Dublin, New Hampshire; Fanny G. Clark and Mrs. Lawrence K. Miller, Pittsfield, Massachusetts; Giuseppe Gadda Conti, Rome; Cynthia Cook, Los Angeles; George W. Corner, American Philosophical Society; Martin Duberman, Herbert H. Lehman College; Elizabeth S. Duvall, Northampton, Massachusetts; Clark A. Elliott, Harvard University Archives; James P. Elliott, Clark University; Anne Freudenberg and Elizabeth Ryall, University of Virginia Library; Ulrich Halfmann, Universität Mannheim; Irving Halpern, New York; James D. Hart, University of California, Berkeley; Virginia R. Hawley, Western Reserve Historical Society; Elinor S. Hearn, Church Historical Society; Mrs. George S. Hellman and Geoffrey T. Hellman; Robert W. Hill, Gerald D. McDonald, Paul Myers, and Lola Szladits (Berg Collection), New York Public Library; John Noyes Mead Howells, Kittery Point, Maine; Kathleen Jacklin, Cornell Regional Historical Collection; Rudolf Kirk and the late Clara M. Kirk, San Marcos, Texas; the late John S.

ACKNOWLEDGMENTS

Van E. Kohn, New York; Mrs. Charles W. Lundgren, Lancaster County Historical Society; Watt B. Marchman, Rutherford B. Hayes Memorial Library; Michael Millgate, University of Toronto; George Monteiro, Brown University; Irene Morgan, Bancroft Library; Roger Dean Paulson, Urbana College; Polly Pierce, Stockbridge Library Association; Wanda M. Randall, Princeton University Library; Gordon N. Ray, Guggenheim Memorial Foundation; Diana J. and Kenneth B. Rendell, Somerville, Massachusetts; Lyon N. Richardson, Case Western Reserve University; Judith Schiff and Richard B. Sewall, Sterling Library, Yale University; Elwyn E. Seelye, Lake George, New York; the late Phillip A. Shelley, State College, Pennsylvania; Anthony Shipps, Indiana University Library; James Stronks, University of Illinois, Chicago; Kermit Vanderbilt, San Diego State University; Lewis H. Webster, Century Association; James Woodress, University of California, Davis; Thomas Wortham, University of California, Los Angeles. We apologize to those who have been inadvertently omitted from this list. We shall endeavor to make corrections and acknowledge additional debts in later volumes.

Permission to print complete letters or excerpts from letters has been graciously given by the following institutions and individuals:

The Century Association

Columbia University Libraries

Concord Free Public Library

Cornell University Library

Essex Institute

Rutherford B. Hayes Library

Houghton Library, Harvard University

The Henry E. Huntington Library

King Library, Miami University

William Blake Dean and Family Papers, Minnesota Historical Society

United States National Archives and Records Service

Henry W. and Albert A. Berg Collection, The New York Public Library; Astor, Lenox and Tilden Foundations

Martha Kinney Cooper Ohioana Library Association

Historical Society of Pennsylvania

Allison-Shelley Collection, Pennsylvania State University Libraries

Charles Patterson Van Pelt Library, University of Pennsylvania

McGill University Libraries

Princeton University Library

Professor Gordon N. Ray, Department of English, New York University

University of Rochester Library

Rutgers University Library

Sophia Smith Collection (Women's History Archive), Smith College, Northampton, Massachusetts

ACKNOWLEDGMENTS

American Literature Collection, University of Southern California Library

Clifton Waller Barrett Library, University of Virginia

Collection of American Literature, Beinecke Rare Book and Manuscript Library, Yale University

Individually, the editors also wish to acknowledge personal indebtedness not only to many of those named earlier but also to the following for immediate assistance: George Arms, for grants from the American Council of Learned Societies, the American Philosophical Society, the Center for Editions of American Authors, and the University of New Mexico, and for extended research assistance from Becky Bustamente, Maria Greer, Mary Maxine, and Sarah Nagel; Richard H. Ballinger, for grants from the American Philosophical Society, the Center for Editions of American Authors, and Texas A & M University, and for assistance from Mrs. William A. Jackson, Cambridge, Massachusetts, Mrs. Maria Grossman, Andover-Harvard Theological Seminary Library, Divinity School, Harvard University, H. Gilbert Kelley, Rutgers University Library, Robert H. Land, Library of Congress, Mrs. Sally Leach, Humanities Research Library, The University of Texas at Austin, and B. Joseph O'Neil and J. A. Monahan, Boston Public Library; Christoph K. Lohmann for continued support from the National Endowment for the Humanities and from Kenneth R. R. Gros Louis, Dean of the College of Arts and Sciences, Indiana University, Bloomington.

Finally, we wish to recall our obligations to former editors, who through either death or new academic commitments did not remain with the project until its completion: the late Frederic C. Marston, Jr., whose files form the nucleus of those at the Howells Edition Center and to whom this volume is dedicated; and Edwin H. Cady, Duke University, whose association was of shorter duration, but who as founding editor of "A Selected Edition of W. D. Howells" and a continuing member of its Executive Committee, has a long and generous association with the editing of the letters.

Contents

GENERAL INTRODUCTION		xiii
A NOTE ON EDITORIAL PRACTICE		xxii
I.	From Ashtabula to Venice (1852–1861)	1
	Introduction	
	Letters and Notes	
II.	The Venetian Consulship (1861–1865)	91
	Introduction	
	Letters and Notes	
III.	The Early *Atlantic* Years (1866–1872)	243
	Introduction	
	Letters and Notes	
TEXTUAL APPARATUS		
	Introduction	415
	Textual Record	421
	Word-Division	457
FAMILY GENEALOGIES		
	Genealogical Tables	462
	Biographical Notices	465
LIST OF HOWELLS' CORRESPONDENTS		469
INDEX		473

General Introduction

THE aim of *W. D. Howells: Selected Letters* is to present in six volumes the career of Howells in his many roles—as poet, novelist, editor, literary and social critic, son-brother-husband-father, and friend (or occasionally, enemy) of the major literary figures of his period. Covering almost seventy years, from 1852 to 1920, these volumes provide not only a close view of the nuances of Howells' personality and experience but also a panorama of his era. They reflect a life dominated by the art and business of literature and shaped by deep personal and social commitments. At the same time they provide a chronicle of the changes in the cultural life of the nation between the age of Hawthorne, Emerson, and Longfellow and that of Crane, Norris, and Frost. During these seven decades Howells knew, corresponded with, and wrote about most of the major and many of the minor figures of the literary world. Friend and sponsor of Mark Twain, Henry James, Bret Harte, Hamlin Garland, he also assessed the importance of Walt Whitman, Emily Dickinson, Booth Tarkington, George Ade, Robert Herrick, Havelock Ellis, George M. Cohan, and brought to the consciousness of American readers an awareness of Flaubert, Turgenev, Tolstoy, and Ibsen. His life *was* the life of the mind and of letters in America from before the Civil War until after World War I.

His public role as dean of American letters is of course well known, and his voluminous published essays, columns, and memoirs document his critical positions. But it is chiefly in his letters that we penetrate the public manner characterized by grace, polish, and conscious craftsmanship and see instead the day-to-day management of Howells' literary career and the personal store of shrewdness, compassion, insecurity, ambition, and moral determination upon which he built that career. Instead of the public performance at which Howells became so adept, these volumes present the personal and "working papers" of a professional writer. The letters communicate news, advice, editorial judgments, private opinions and confidences, and show him attending to the practical concerns of writing and publishing, of sensing and shaping public response to literature, and of directing American civilization to what he strongly believed to be the higher ground. But there is also a fine reflection of Howells' sense of audience, even an audience of one. Without consulting the salutations or specific references, one can, for instance, soon distinguish among Howells' letters to James Russell Lowell, Henry James, and Mark Twain on the basis of their tone alone. Though Howells' letters reach neither the heights of polished circumlocution that characterize James' nor the breadth of rollicking hyperbole of Clemens', they are forceful and sensitive communications and give us more explicit information about the American literary scene than do the letters of any other figure of the period.

These volumes are designed for use by both the specialized scholar, for whom rigorous textual accuracy is a professional necessity, and the more casual reader, who may find greater interest in the explanatory annotations that follow each letter. Both kinds of readers of course depend upon the scholarly accuracy and conscientiousness with which the texts are prepared, and it is the function of the Textual Apparatus at the end of the volume to present the evidence for the decisions made in establishing the text. The letters are, therefore, presented in clear text; that is, the use of editorial symbols within the text has been entirely avoided, all textual matters being dealt with in a separate section of each volume. A general description of the textual principles and of the policy of annotation is provided in A Note on Editorial Practice, following this General Introduction. A more detailed discussion of the process of textual editing and the presentation of the results of that process for these volumes of letters will be found in the Textual Apparatus at the end of each volume.

Each volume is provided with one or more chronological introductions providing a brief outline of Howells' situation and his activities during a particular period of his life. In the first volume, for instance, the editors have chronicled Howells' apprenticeship in journalism, his period as consul at Venice, and his growth in responsibility and authority at the *Atlantic Monthly*. These introductions suggest the personal and professional concerns that dominate his letters and mention the friends and professional associates with whom he was corresponding during a particular period. Used with the index, they will enable the reader to locate not only letters to individual correspondents but letters that address Howells' persistent concerns.

As one would expect, during his long and active literary career Howells produced a voluminous correspondence. In a letter to Maurice Thompson in 1874 he wrote, "You will forgive me, I hope, for not answering your letter sooner, when I tell you that I have written about four hundred letters to contributors during the last four months...." While he edited the *Atlantic* his correspondence was of course particularly heavy, but his statement suggests the enormous quantity of letters that left his desk. Any attempt to calculate the total number must be a guess, but even an approximate estimate might serve to put in perspective the number of letters known to exist and the problem of selecting letters for inclusion in a collection of limited size. Recognizing that his correspondence diminished when he left the *Atlantic,* one must still guess at a figure somewhere between forty and seventy thousand letters written between 1860 and 1920. Whatever the actual number written, the editors have examined for themselves or received detailed information about all of the known extant letters, almost ten thousand of them, of which some 1,650 will eventually appear in the six volumes of this edition. Many of the extant letters are of course business notes, or acceptances or refusals of invitations, preserved for their autograph value. These are sometimes useful to researchers in establishing dates, and therefore should be preserved but not published. How many other letters are extant but still unknown cannot even be guessed. Each year about a dozen are offered in the catalogs of autograph dealers and probably at least that many more are sold directly to collectors without listing in such catalogs. In 1971, twenty letters by Howells to the Indiana poet Maurice Thompson which were previously thought to have been destroyed were sold at auction. The originals of a number of printed letters may still exist unrecorded in family papers or in the collections of individuals.

The Houghton Library at Harvard University has the largest collection of letters by and to Howells. It first purchased 2,700 letters from Howells' literary executors in 1937 and since then has received many others, by gift and purchase, including the letters of Howells to his father and sisters. Before the first acquisition, Harvard already had many letters by Howells in the collections of his Cambridge friends, and since then it has acquired more letters by Howells in the papers of other correspondents. In all, the Houghton Library collection now contains about 4,000 letters by Howells and about 3,000 letters to him. The letters to Howells in the purchase of 1937 are listed and described in Richard H. Ballinger, "A Calendar of the William Dean Howells Collection in the Library of Harvard University."[1] In that work, Ballinger has summarized and indexed 2,698 letters to Howells, 62 letters by Howells to Horace E. Scudder and members of his family, and a miscellaneous group of 107 letters including some to Mrs. Howells. The Houghton Library has also compiled a 214-page typescript catalog of its Howells family letters, diaries, and related material under the title "The Howells Papers." While the letters are listed in groups without individual dates, i.e., "Aldrich, Thomas Bailey, 1836–1907. 24 letters; 1878–1906 & [n.d.]," there is a complete index of correspondents, and the

---

1. Ph.D. dissertation (Harvard, 1952).

papers of Elinor Mead Howells, Winifred, Mildred, and John Mead Howells are listed separately.

Though small in comparison with the Harvard collection, the holdings at other libraries are often of surprising size and of great interest. Libraries having at least 200 letters are the American Academy of Arts and Letters, the American Antiquarian Society, the University of California at Berkeley (mostly in the Mark Twain Papers), the Library of Congress, the Huntington Library, the National Archives, the New York Public Library (including the Berg Collection), Princeton University, and the University of Virginia. Other libraries, including the Hayes Memorial Library, Fremont, Ohio, and the libraries of the University of Southern California and Yale University, fall only a little short of 200, and many of the smaller collections contain very informative correspondence. In all, letters have been located at about 140 libraries (including the libraries of publishers) and in about 60 personal collections.

The largest single collection of copies of Howells' letters, poetry, articles, and books in various editions has been gathered at the Howells Edition Center at Indiana University. While there are very few holograph manuscripts in this collection, the files do contain photocopies of the Howells correspondence in most of the major collections in the United States and England, as well as transcriptions and editorial work sheets for all the letters being printed in this edition and for many which are not. These working materials—except those photocopies and transcriptions which are restricted to the use of the editors of the letters and which must be destroyed or returned to the original owners—are available for the use of scholars who wish to consult them. At the completion of this selected edition, the files of the Howells Center will remain accessible in a suitable public depository.

In his own lifetime a few personal letters by Howells appeared in print, such as his letter to Mrs. Cora Crane in the *Academy*[2] or his early letter to J. J. Piatt in *The Hesperian Tree*.[3] These seem to have been published with his tacit or open consent. As volumes of letters of friends were published, such as those of Lowell, Norton, Mark Twain, and Henry James, Howells lent letters that he had received from these men, though he withheld or perhaps even destroyed some letters from Samuel Clemens because, as he mentions in *My Mark Twain*, they had an "Elizabethan breadth of parlance": "I could not bear to burn them, and I could not, after the first reading, quite bear to look at them."[4]

---

2. 59 (18 August 1900), 123.
3. Edited by John James Piatt (Columbus, Ohio: S. F. Harriman, 1903), pp. 425–29.
4. "My Mark Twain," in *Literary Friends and Acquaintance*, ed. David F. Hiatt and Edwin H. Cady (Bloomington: Indiana University Press, 1968), p. 256.

But with few exceptions the letters printed during Howells' lifetime were those he had received rather than those he had written.

About a year after the death of her father, Mildred Howells began to ask his friends for his letters, and by 1925 had collected the major part of the letters she edited as *Life in Letters of William Dean Howells*.[5] The two volumes contain about 800 letters, the great majority by Howells. Though Miss Howells noted in her preface that she had "neither training nor experience to help me in editing these letters," she produced an extraordinarily fine collection for which every biographer and scholar is grateful. Typescripts, notes, and correspondence (now in the Howells Papers at the Houghton Library) bear witness to her indefatigable energy in finding letters and to her thoroughness. But there are shortcomings in *Life in Letters*. Many of the correspondents, or their widows or children, were still alive when Miss Howells was working, and as a result she omitted letters that otherwise might have been printed. She also generally refrained from presenting her father in his less endearing moments. More is removed than the "trivial and tiresome things" that she, in her preface, admitted to deleting. She regularized the styling in a fashion that would not be acceptable in our day, though she deserves praise for having regularized less than standards of her own time would have allowed. Finally, she occasionally misread, misdated, and misannotated, though when one considers that she worked alone, her accuracy is remarkable.

The appearance of *Life in Letters* did not cause much stir. The *Book Review Digest* for 1928 and 1929 lists only thirteen reviews, and the newly established scholarly journals *New England Quarterly* and *American Literature* took no note. In *The New Republic*, F. O. Matthiessen, a recent Harvard Ph.D., concluded that "Perhaps the next generation will see more than we do in his cool, classic pages. At least social historians will discover nowhere else such a complete picture of every-day American existence in the last half of the nineteenth century. But for the time being these two volumes of Howells' letters stand as a monument to what Stephen Crane called his 'kind, benevolent life,' unhappily with no more meaning for us than most monuments have."[6] Carl Van

---

5. Garden City, N. Y.: Doubleday, Doran & Co., 1928.
6. For this review and others, see *Booklist* 25 (January 1929), 162; *Cleveland Public Library Open Shelf*, March 1929, p. 41; *Nation and Athenaeum* 45 (22 June 1929), 404; *New Statesman* 33 (29 June 1929), 378; *Among Our Books* 34 (February 1929), 10; *St. Louis Public Library Monthly Bulletin* 27 (March 1929), 100; *Times Literary Supplement*, 6 June 1929, p. 450; Katherine Canby Balderston, New York *Times Book Review*, 25 November 1928, pp. 3, 22; Oscar W. Firkins, *Saturday Review of Literature* 5 (16 March 1929), 775; Bradley Gilman, Boston *Evening Transcript* (Book Section), 1 December 1928, p. 2; C. E. Lawrence, *Bookman* (London), 76 (August 1929), 266; F. O. Matthiessen, *New Republic* 58 (24 April 1929), 284–85; Carl Van

Doren, writing in *Books* (New York *Herald Tribune*), praised the letters, especially those to Henry James and Mark Twain, but pointed out that "it will still be necessary to turn again to his books, creative and critical, by which he made himself an American academy before there was an American Academy for him to be president of."

By the time the second major collection of Howells letters appeared in 1960—the two-volume *Mark Twain–Howells Letters*, edited by Henry Nash Smith and William M. Gibson[7]—Howells' reputation had undergone a tremendous change. James Woodress aptly named it "The Dean's Comeback" in an account of what had happened during the previous four decades.[8] As Woodress observed, thirty-eight dissertations on Howells had been announced or completed between 1939 and 1959, and between 1950 and August 1959, seventy-nine articles and thirty-four introductions or parts of books had been devoted to Howells. A great many of the articles contained new letters by or to Howells, as did some of the books. Among books of the period prominent in reassessing Howells were Clara M. and Rudolf Kirk's *Howells: Representative Selections*,[9] with a long introduction that in effect constitutes a critical biography, Everett Carter's *Howells and the Age of Realism*,[10] Olov Fryckstedt's *In Quest of America*,[11] George Bennett's *William Dean Howells*,[12] and, with a reversal from his earlier attitude toward Howells, Van Wyck Brooks' *Howells*.[13] Most impressive and most influential of all was the two-volume life of Howells, still the only definitive biography we have, Edwin H. Cady's *The Road to Realism* and *The Realist at War*.[14]

With the revival of interest in Howells, it is not surprising that the Mark Twain–Howells volumes received more than twice as many reviews as did *Life in Letters*. A large part of the interest was in Mark Twain rather than Howells, but the fact that five of the thirty-five reviewers were Howells "specialists" who expressed serious and informed interest in Howells' letters suggests that the "Dean" had indeed

---

Doren, *Books* (New York *Herald Tribune*), 25 November 1928, pp. 1–2; Raymond Weaver, New York *Evening Post* (Magazine Section), 22 December 1928, p. 8; Edith Franklin Wyatt, *Yale Review* 18 (June 1929), 809–11.

7. Cambridge, Mass.: Harvard University Press, Belknap Press, 1960.

8. James Woodress, "The Dean's Comeback: Four Decades of Howells Scholarship," in *Howells: A Century of Criticism*, ed. Kenneth E. Eble (Dallas: Southern Methodist University Press, 1962), pp. 236–47; first printed in *Texas Studies in Literature and Language* 2 (Spring 1960), 115–23.

9. New York: Hill and Wang, 1950. In nearly all their many articles and books on Howells, the Kirks have published hitherto unprinted Howells letters.

10. Philadelphia: J. B. Lippincott, 1950.

11. Cambridge, Mass.: Harvard University Press, 1958.

12. Norman, Okla.: University of Oklahoma Press, 1959.

13. New York: E. P. Dutton, 1959.

14. Syracuse, N. Y.: Syracuse University Press, 1956 and 1958.

come back. In the *Nation* Howard C. Horsford observed that "Howells emerges a warmly friendly, acute intelligence, a restrained strength to match the volatility of Twain."[15] The reviewer for the *Times Literary Supplement* spoke of the correspondence as "composing in the whole a detailed and altogether engaging record of two affectionate and admirable men, devoted to each other and to the craft of writing." Howells' letters to Mark Twain are some of his most charming and lively, and there is a great temptation to include all of them in any collection. But given the mass of extant letters and the availability of the 1960 edition of this correspondence, it has been thought wiser to avoid extensive duplication of contents and to devote the available space primarily to letters not presently available in print.

It was perhaps inevitable, given the personality of Samuel Clemens, that even Howells, upon whom he relied heavily for literary advice and emotional support, should occasionally find himself playing end man to Mark Twain's Mr. Interlocutor. With other literary acquaintances Howells' role and tone varied according to the sympathy, encouragement, guidance, or severity he felt would most benefit them. Howells was quick to recognize Henry James' literary gifts, writing to Clarence Stedman in 1866, eleven years before the publication of *The American*,

---

15. For this review and others see *Booklist* 56 (1 May 1960), 538; *Bulletin from Virginia Kirkus Service* 28 (1 April 1960), 312; *New Mexico Quarterly* 30 (Winter 1960–1961), 422; *Times Literary Supplement*, 12 August 1960, p. 512; *Yale Review* 49 (June 1960), viii, xii; Howard G. Baetzhold, *American Quarterly* 13 (Spring 1961), 102; Walter Blair, New York *Herald Tribune Book Review*, 8 May 1960, p. 1; D. W. Brogan, Manchester *Guardian*, 1 July 1960, p. 6; Louis J. Budd, *Mississippi Valley Historical Review* 47 (September 1960), 342–43; Edwin H. Cady, *Virginia Quarterly Review* 36 (Summer 1960), 473–76; James B. Colvert, *Dalhousie Review* 40 (Winter 1960–1961), 567–71; H. S. Commager, New York *Times Book Review* (24 April 1960), 40–41; Pascal Covici, Jr., *Southwest Review* 45 (Summer 1960), 277–79; L. G. Crossman, *Queen's Quarterly* 68 (Spring 1961), 201; E. H. Eby, *Modern Language Quarterly* 23 (March 1962), 90–91; DeLancey Ferguson, *American Scholar* 29 (Summer 1960), 410, 412, 414; John T. Flanagan, *Journal of English and Germanic Philology* 60 (April 1961), 342–44; Granville Hicks, *Saturday Review* 43 (23 April 1960), 20; Hamlin Hill, *Modern Philology* 58 (November 1960), 142–44; Howard C. Horsford, *Nation* 190 (14 May 1960), 426–27; Dan Jacobson, *Spectator* 205 (5 August 1960), 219–20; Fred W. Lorch, *American Literature* 33 (March 1961), 78–80; Kenneth S. Lynn, *New England Quarterly* 35 (March 1962), 110–11; Michael Millgate, *Modern Language Review* 56 (July 1961), 417–18; Robert Peel, *Christian Science Monitor*, 21 April 1960, p. 11; Stow Persons, *American Historical Review* 66 (October 1960), 177–78; Gordon Roper, *Canadian Forum* 41 (April 1961), 22–23; James B. Stronks, *Commonweal* 72 (8 July 1960), 355–56; Edward Wagenknecht, Chicago *Sunday Tribune* (Magazine Section), 24 April 1960, p. 2; Hyatt H. Waggoner, *Criticism* 3 (Winter 1961), 62–65; Frank J. Warnke, *New Republic* 142 (13 June 1960), 24–25; Earle F. Walbridge, *Library Journal* 85 (15 April 1960), 1590; Margaret Willy, *English* 13 (Spring 1961), 153–54; Karl-Heintz Wirstberger, *Zeitschrift für Anglistik und Amerikanistik* (East Berlin), 9, no. 4 (4 November 1961), 431–33; James Woodress, *Nineteenth-Century Fiction* 15 (December 1960), 268–71.

that James was "gifted enough to do better than any one has yet done toward making us a real American novel." Though the *Atlantic* had printed a story by Sarah Orne Jewett as early as December 1869, Howells continued for several years to give her detailed instructions for revision; in 1871 he wrote, "make a sketch of your story if you don't feel secure of your powers of invention. . . . develop character very fully—much more fully than you have . . . ." To the very popular Lucy Larcom he wrote, "You take rejection so sweetly that I've scarcely the heart to accept anything of yours," and to Hjalmar Hjorth Boyesen, "This notice is so far inferior to that you printed in The Nation that I shall not be able to use it." But the following month he was encouraging Boyesen to remain in America and to continue his career in literature: "You have met with generous recognition, and you have an audience not mean in taste or numbers which I'm sure will rapidly increase. *Pray send me all the poems you write.*"

Stephen Crane also enjoyed Howells' encouragement and sponsorship. In 1896 Howells wrote, "I am glad you are getting your glory young. For once, the English who habitually know nothing of art, seem to know something.—For me, I remain true to my first love, 'Maggie.'" But even while attempting to find a publisher for Crane's poems, Howells frankly confessed his dissatisfaction with them. "I wish you had given them more form, for then things so striking would have found a public ready made for them; as it is they will have to make one." Hamlin Garland, with whom Howells maintained one of his closest friendships among the younger generation of writers, also enjoyed the alternate praise and prodding that characterized Howells' letters of encouragement. In 1894 he tried to buttress Garland's lagging confidence, telling him, "You are getting plenty of abuse from the critics these days, but you are getting respect, too. They all know there is an honest man inside your book, and a strong one." Three years later he was attempting to improve Garland's language. "You have got some newspaper diction in your penpoint, and you must shake it out. . . . Here and there a word, a phrase, jarred on me. Be plain as you please; there is nothing better than homespun . . . ." And in 1910, after reading Garland's *Cavanagh*, Howells wrote, "One day, I hope you will revert to the temper of your first work, and give us a picture of the wild life you know so well on the lines of 'Main Traveled Roads.' You have in you greater things than you have done . . . ." Howells was sensitive to more than the craftsmanship of literature; he saw also the cultural milieu in which an author wrote. In a letter to Henry Blake Fuller he spoke of Charles Chesnutt's *Marrow of Tradition,* saying, "he writes of the black and white situation with an awful bitterness. But he is an artist almost of the first quality; as yet too literary, but promising things hereafter.... Good lord! How such a negro must hate us. And then think of the Filipinos and the Cubans and Puerto Ricans whom we have added to our happy family." Whatever despair he felt over the way his youthful dreams of literature and democracy were turning out, he could hardly fail to be comforted by the letters he received from young writers to whom he had given his praise and his strength. Frank Norris wrote to Howells about his review of *McTeague*, "It has encouraged me more than anything that has ever been said of my work." And Paul Laurence Dunbar's response to Howells' public recognition was similar: "Now from the very depths of my heart I want to thank you. You yourself do not know what you have done for me. I feel much as a poor, insignificant, hopeless boy would feel to suddenly find himself knighted." Howells' receptivity to serious young writers, his copious and incisive criticism, and the honesty with which he held authors, fledgling or established, to the highest standards help to account for the influence on American literature that gradually accrued to him. Sympathy, tact, and his ready response to what is best in each individual nature underlay all of his literary work, and these qualities show nowhere more clearly than in his letters.

G. A.
R. H. B.
C. K. L.
J. K. R.

A Note on Editorial Practice

Two basic principles inform the treatment of the texts of the Howells correspondence which have been selected for publication in these volumes: one, the contents of the original documents are reproduced as fully and correctly as possible; and, two, all physical details of the manuscripts necessary for accurate reconstruction of the text are reported, though without encumbering the reading text itself. Consistent with these principles, the printed versions of the letters which form the body of these volumes retain the eccentricities of Howells' spelling, punctuation, and occasionally elliptical epistolary style, and are presented without such editorial appurtenances as brackets, arrows, virgules, and *sic*'s. The printed text is, insofar as possible, that of the finished letter, after Howells revised it either locally or generally by writing over, crossing out, and interlining. Howells' errors, except for inadvertent repetitions of words or syllables, are printed as they appear in the holographs, so long as the sense of the text can be discerned.

In accordance with the principle of reporting significant manuscript information, each letter is represented by a full itemization of cancellations, interlineations, the unusual placement of postscripts and marginal comments, and the presence of nonauthorial notes and comments believed to be contemporary with the composition or receipt of the letter, as well as of those editorial revisions necessary to insure comprehension. The reader should be aware, therefore, that some few words, letters, and marks of punctuation printed in this text are not in the original letters (or in transcriptions which have been employed when the originals are no longer extant or accessible). The full record of emendations, editorial comments, textual details, and Howells' revisions is provided in the Textual Apparatus, the introduction to which explains the symbols and abbreviations used to allow for the printing of the maximum of evidence in a minimum of space. Several exceptions, however, should be noted. Howells frequently failed to lift his pen when moving from one word to the next; thus, he often joined words that were not meant to be joined. Occasionally, though not always, he would repair such errors by separating these inadvertently joined words with a vertical line. Conversely, he sometimes lifted his pen while writing a single word, or he disconnected compounds that appear elsewhere as one word. In such cases, no notation of these irregularities has been included in the apparatus, while an attempt has been made, through comparisons among the letters, to render Howells' texts as nearly as possible in the form that he seems likely to have intended.

Given the wealth of references to personal and public events in the letters and the relevance of the letters to the shape and movement of Howells' career, annotation is potentially endless. The policy of these volumes is to present only the basic information which will make the context of the letters understandable and the letters themselves useful to both scholar and general reader. Annotation is thus restricted to explanation and clarification of references to people, places, events, literary works, and other such primary data. Interpretive comment is excluded.

Since the letters in this series represent only a portion of the extant Howells correspondence, it is also important that their relationship to each other and to letters not printed in these volumes be indicated. Cross references to other letters printed in the series simply identify correspondent and date: e.g., "Howells to Comly, 7 July 1868"; references to annotation accompanying letters add to this citation the specific footnote number: e.g., "Howells to Comly, 7 July 1868, n. 4." Manuscript letters not printed in this edition but cited or quoted are identified by correspondent and date, followed by the library location or collector's name in parentheses: e.g., "(MH)" for Harvard University or "(Ray)" for the collection of Gordon N. Ray.[1] Special collections within libraries are not indicated. When manuscripts of texts cited are also available in major printed collections (e.g., *Mark Twain–Howells Letters*), publication information follows the library symbol. Publication information appearing without notation of manuscript location should be assumed to designate texts extant only in published form. Quotations from letters in annotations follow the final, revised forms, and do not include a record of internal revisions. In addition, to avoid the proliferation of annotation, information necessary to the understanding of such quoted letters is provided within brackets at appropriate points within the quotations.

To further reduce the bulk and duplication of annotation, several other conventions have been adopted. People, events, and literary works are identified in footnotes at the points where their first significant mention appears in the whole series of letters. Further annotation of these same details is provided only where the context of a specific letter demands elaboration. The basic information can be located by using the indexes to the individual volumes or the cumulative index in

---

1. Libraries are indicated by the abbreviations detailed in *Symbols of American Libraries*, 10th ed. (Washington: Library of Congress, 1969).

xxiv A NOTE ON EDITORIAL PRACTICE

the final volume of letters, where major references are distinguished by the printing of the appropriate page numbers in italic type. References to books give the year of first publication; however, books reviewed in dated articles should be assumed to have been published in the same year as the review, unless information to the contrary is provided. Whenever possible, references to books by Howells identify volumes published in "A Selected Edition of W. D. Howells," signaled by the abbreviation "HE" immediately following the title; references to works not available in this form generally cite the American first edition, which is identified by date of publication.

The editors have followed a consistent policy in the use of ellipses in quotations. If the first period is close up to the word preceding it, it stands for an end-of-sentence period in the original, with the omission following it. Thus, "invention.... develop" indicates that there is a period in the original after "invention," with the omitted portion of the text following it. However "hereafter .... Good lord!" indicates that there is more text in the same sentence after "hereafter."

Titles of most secondary sources are given in full, but a number of them are cited so often in this series that the following list of short titles has been adopted.

Cady, *Howells*, I	Edwin H. Cady, *The Road to Realism: The Early Years, 1837–1885, of William Dean Howells* (Syracuse, N. Y.: Syracuse University Press, 1956)
Cady, *Howells*, II	Edwin H. Cady, *The Realist at War: The Mature Years, 1885–1920, of William Dean Howells* (Syracuse, N. Y.: Syracuse University Press, 1958)
James Letters	*Henry James Letters*, ed. Leon Edel, 2 vols. (Cambridge, Mass.: Harvard University Press, Belknap Press, 1974–1975)
Gibson-Arms, *Bibliography*	William M. Gibson and George Arms, *A Bibliography of William Dean Howells* (New York: New York Public Library, 1948; reprinted, New York Public Library and Arno Press, 1971)
Life in Letters	*Life in Letters of William Dean Howells*, ed. Mildred Howells, 2 vols. (Garden City, N. Y.: Doubleday, Doran & Co., 1928)

Lynn, *Howells*	Kenneth S. Lynn, *William Dean Howells: An American Life* (New York: Harcourt Brace Jovanovich, 1971)
Norton, *Lowell Letters*	*Letters of James Russell Lowell*, ed. C. E. Norton, 2 vols. (New York: Harper & Brothers, 1894)
Transatlantic Dialogue	*Transatlantic Dialogue: Selected American Correspondence of Edmund Gosse*, ed. Paul F. Mattheisen and Michael Millgate (Austin: University of Texas Press, 1965)
Twain-Howells	*Mark Twain-Howells Letters*, ed. Henry Nash Smith and William M. Gibson, 2 vols. (Cambridge, Mass.: Harvard University Press, Belknap Press, 1960)
Woodress, *Howells & Italy*	James L. Woodress, Jr., *Howells & Italy* (Durham, N. C.: Duke University Press, 1952)

C. K. L.
D. J. N.

I

From Ashtabula to Venice

1 8 5 2 – 1 8 6 1

Introduction

WHEN on 7 December 1861 Howells wrote his family, "At last, I am arrived," he was speaking literally of his reaching Venice after the long journey through Europe. But he might well have been using the phrase metaphorically. In less than ten years the printer's apprentice from Ashtabula had achieved something of a reputation as poet and journalist, and now his campaign biography of Lincoln had secured him an appointment as U. S. consul to Venice—a political sinecure, but one that would allow him to supplement and polish his homemade education.

The journey that took Howells to Venice began twenty-five years earlier with his birth in the village of Martinsville, Ohio. In his first extant letter, written in 1852, he records that his family had already moved four times: to Hamilton, the "boy's town," then to Dayton, Eureka Mills, and Columbus. His father—Swedenborgian, utopian, and Free-Soiler—had repeatedly found his opinions unwelcome; only in the editorship of the Ashtabula *Sentinel* in the more liberal Western Reserve of Ohio did he find a permanent and profitable vehicle for his views. William Cooper Howells' support of the congenial political policies of Congressman Joshua R. Giddings and Senator Benjamin F. Wade provided him entrée into state politics, and when he became clerk of the state legislature in 1857 he took young Will with him and soon had him writing a "Letter from Columbus" for the Cincinnati *Gazette*. So well were these reports received that at the conclusion of the legislative session the young correspondent was offered the position of city editor of the *Gazette*.[1] Howells accepted the position, but after a month gave it up out of a combination of homesickness and an inability to face what he saw as the sordidness of the life he was to report.

Howells' early years reveal a curious combination of strengths and weaknesses, both displayed obliquely in *A Boy's Town* and *Years of My Youth*. In 1856 he was so obsessed with hydrophobia that he could neither work in his father's print shop nor pursue his studies of languages and literature. In 1858 and 1859 his letters often speak of his sicknesses, his hypochondria or "hippo" as he called it, his vertigo, his malaise at home in Jefferson matched by his miserable homesickness

---

1. Here and elsewhere for most of the biography not in the correspondence itself we are indebted to Cady, *Howells*, I.

when away. And yet with relatively little formal instruction Howells not only became acquainted with the major figures of English literature and the currents of contemporary culture revealed in the English reviews, he also taught himself to read Spanish and German, wrote and translated extensively, and, after repeated appearances of his verse in local and regional publications, broke into the sacred precincts of the *Atlantic*. The publication of "Andenken," accepted for the *Atlantic* in July 1859, was delayed until the following January while James Russell Lowell searched the poetry of Heine, fearing that so polished a contribution might be a translation rather than an original composition.

The surviving letters through 1858 (one in 1852 and seven each in 1857 and 1858) provide only a sketchy account of these years, and one must turn to *A Boy's Town* and *Years of My Youth* for a fuller, though of course reconsidered, narrative. But beginning in 1859, perhaps because of his only half-joking suggestion to his sister that his correspondence might be of value to future biographers, the family began to save more letters, and from that year nearly thirty items survive, with greater numbers in 1860 and 1861. There would be more had not Howells burned a "half bushel" in 1861. So while the account of this early period that emerges from his autobiographical writing is more complete, the letters provide a sense of specific incident and exact date and do so in a personal and contemporary tone.

Throughout his letters one has a keen sense of Howells' attractiveness to those around him. Even during periods of hypochondria and malaise, he continued to form close friendships, with Jim Williams and Harvey Green in Jefferson and later in Columbus with Artemas Fullerton, James Comly, Samuel Reed, and Samuel Price. John J. Piatt, whom he first came to know in Columbus in 1852, became his coauthor in *Poems of Two Friends* eight years later. But it was not only youthful companions with whom he formed such ties. He also enjoyed and profited from the close friendship of two older women in Columbus, Mrs. Francis Carter and Mrs. Samuel Smith, whose husband became Howells' physician and temporary financial backer;[2] he met Hawthorne and Emerson during his first trip to New England in 1860; and he interested Holmes and Lowell in his literary talent and its development. But he did not neglect to form acquaintances with contemporaries—John Hay, Richard Henry Stoddard, and Edmund Clarence Stedman in New York, for instance—which were to contribute to his eventual position as mentor to and dean of the writing fraternity.

In spite of his strong commitment to the world of letters and his own professional ambitions, in spite of an often uneasy relationship with

---

2. *Years of My Youth*, HE, pp. 141–42, 150.

his parents, Howells had a deep and abiding love for his family. In these early years at least, the family letters give a sense of natural intimacy and frankness that makes them stand out from the rest. With all his enjoyment of his new experiences and with his literary successes as well as disappointments, his thoughts constantly turned toward home. Everyone is included: his parents, the older brother, Joe, his favorite sister, Victoria; Sam, Aurelia, Annie, Johnnie, and even the deranged Henry. Sometimes he could be defensive, patronizing, and critical, but even then one senses his warm affection.[3] It is uncertain how much he told his family about his love for Elinor, since letters about this delicate matter may have been destroyed, but his later roundabout announcement of their engagement (22 July 1862) suggests that he may have felt that this normal development threatened the family's solidarity. Still, an early letter from Europe (24 November 1861) demonstrates the intensity of his ties with the "Dear folks at Home," ties that had at least in part developed out of the family's shared enjoyment of literature. "How I languished," Howells wrote, "to have each and all of you with me, as I recognized one after another all the beautiful features of the scenery, of which we have read so much in books." Literature, friendships, family: these were the materials of his life until 1861. His arrival in Europe opened an even broader world than any of these had yet revealed to him.

G. A.

---

3. Cady, *Howells*, I, and Lynn, *Howells*, explore these tensions fully, though with somewhat different diagnoses.

25 JULY 1852, ASHTABULA, TO WILLIAM C. FRENCH

Ashtabula, July 25, 1852.[1]

Dear Sir:[2]

I have delayed writing to you this long, in order that I can give you a few particulars of our office, place, lake, &c. The office is in a building owned by Mr. Fassett,[3] father's partner, and is divided into two rooms, one of which is the editorial room, and the other contains the press, cases, stands, and all the other necessaries of a country printing-office, not to mention a very noisy apprentice boy. My brother acts as foreman, and I and our boy get up the paper. Sammy does what folding of papers and rolling there is to do.[4] We work off 6 tokens of papers; which is one more token than the edition of the other office.[5] We have pretty plenty of job work since father has got here. We get off about noon on Saturday's, and then we all go to the lake.

I cannot describe to you my delight on seeing the lake. I would willingly walk to it every day. It is a thing which never loses its interest. Yesterday when we were there the waves were running about three feet high, and the lake was covered with white-caps, and the shore was one continuous line of foam. It was fine swimming, I can assure you. The waves come floating over you, and knocking you about, lifting you off your feet, and placing you in water knee deep, and then come roaring back, covering you all over. After the late hard storm, our harbor presents rather a dilapidated appearance. When the waves are high, they cannot get out to the light-house to light the lanterns; and so when a light is most needed, there is none at all. By the side of the light-house is a very lonely looking "grocery," stood up on four sticks. This, with the light house, a row of sticks extending into the lake, the custom-house, a few rusty old buildings, lots of rotten timber, (once part of the harbor) buried in the sand, and a very great deal of drift, comprises our harbor! I suppose it might be made a very good harbor, if the goverment would appropriate the necessary sum, but all I know now is, that it is not a good one.

The country about here is very hilly. I like it all the better for that. It is something new to me to stand at the base of one of these hills, and glance up, and see far, far above me, the little springs come dancing over their beds of rock till they mingle at my feet with the lazy waters of the creek. All along the hill-sides these springs of now pure crystal water, have worn deep gulches and ravines, so that when there is the least rain these come thundering down, filling their channels, and carrying off huge masses of rock, shrubbery, and sometimes trees. In some places the sides of these hills are perpendicular, and are covered with mountain-growth—pine, hemlock, cedar, &c. It is indeed a strange sight for one who has always lived in a flat country, and seen nothing but oaks, maples, ashes, and hickorys to stand over top of a hill some 200 feet high, and see the tops of pines, whose roots are at the base, spreading their tops before him. The hills are covered with mountain raspberries, gooseberries, and all sorts of wild fruits and flowers. The timber on the uplands, back from the hills, is mostly chestnut. There promises to be a great crop of the nuts this year, as the trees are now full of burrs. Of these, I hope, to have the pleasure of sending you a little box in the fall. We are just now begining to have new potatoes here, and peas have been fit for use only about 2 weeks.

We are all well at this time, and the health of the place is pretty good, though there is some talk of small-pox in the country. I'd love dearly to see you all again. Remember me to Frank, and give my respects to Gamaliel.[6] I believe this is all at present,

Yours, respectfully,
W. D. Howells.

Rev. W. C. French.

1. According to Howells' 21 July 1852 diary entry (MS located at MH), the family had moved from Columbus to Ashtabula about 1 July. Howells' father was printer-editor of the Ashtabula *Sentinel* which, beginning 15 January 1853, was published in Jefferson.

2. William C. French (1818–1893), Episcopal clergyman, had been Howells' print-shop foreman in the *Ohio State Journal* office. He was rector of St. John's Church in Worthington, near Columbus (1852–1854); secretary of the Diocesan Convention of Ohio (1852–1887); and, after moving to Oberlin, editor of an evangelical periodical, *Standard of the Cross* (1868–1892).

3. Henry Fassett (b. 1817) was "Editor & Proprietor" of the *Sentinel* until W. C. Howells' arrival, after which the two names appear together without titles.

4. Joseph A. Howells was the foreman. Sammy was Samuel D. Howells, then a boy of twelve.

5. Usually a "token" was 250 impressions. The "other office" refers to the *Sentinel*'s competitor, the Ashtabula *Telegraph*.

6. Frank and Gamaliel were probably Howells' friends in the *Journal* office. His 1852 diary about Columbus (entry for 22 March) mentions Frank Barnes, and Gamaliel Scott is listed as a printer in the Columbus directories of 1850 and 1855.

10 April 1857, Cincinnati, to Joseph A. Howells

Cincinnati, April 10, 1857.

My dear Brother—

As this is merely a letter of congratulation, you will not expect it to be of any great length. I think it peculiarly fortunate that your *son* should be a *boy*[1]—which is a sad bull, but may serve to express my delight that your *boy* is not a *girl*. (Girls are not the thing till they get to be about seventeen or eighteen years old.) Let me felicitate you upon your fatherhood, while I beg to be most warmly and affectionately remembered to your wife *and family*. (And family! sir, dont that make you expand a little?) You must name the young gentleman *entirely* for me. I wont share the honor with father.

For myself, here, I am as little settled, yet, as a house that is partly moved out of, and partly moved into. I lodge in Mr Babb's chambers for the present, and eat at a restaurant.[2] I like this mode of living very well; but it will of course be better to go to a hotel or boarding-house, after while. I find that I can board myself at a restaurant for about three dollars a week; and for my lodgement, why as long as I use Mr Babb's room, bed and *blacking*, it is not likely to cost me much. B. has been untiringly kind and attentive to me; and I believe I shall like my place very well. Already, I am grown fond of this big bustling city. The everlasting and furious rushing up and down, and to and fro, pleases me, and I like nothing better than to stroll about the streets alone; and stealthily contemplate the shop windows and orange stands, and speculate on the people I meet. I have been down to the river nearly every day; but have not seen any of our uncles' boats.[3] The Ohio is pretty well up; but there are not a great many boats at the north.

So far, I have been engaged on the news department, helping Babb. I suppose they will gradually work me into the local's place.[4] Already I have done some little itemizing; and have *corrected* the Mss. of the present incumbent, whose writings have all to be reviewed before they go into the paper.

I will write you often. Give my love to all our folks, and tell Harvey that he will hear from me soon.[5] Write to your affectionate brother.

Will.

1. William Dean Howells II (1857–1954), the first child of Joseph and Eliza Whitmore Howells, eventually succeeded his father as editor of the Ashtabula *Sentinel*.

2. Edmund B. Babb was with the Cincinnati *Gazette* (1856–1860). In a friendly letter of 7 September 1857 to Howells (MH) he renewed the "Letter from Columbus" contract for 1858; but later the friendship seems to have ended. See Howells to Victoria Howells, 2 January 1859; and Howells to W. H. Smith, 7 February 1860.

3. Of the several Dean uncles who were river pilots, Howells' favorite was William Dean. See *Years of My Youth*, HE, pp. 12–13.

4. Howells' title on the staff of the *Gazette* was "city editor" and his salary $1,000. He was offered the job because of his "Letter from Columbus," *Gazette* (7 January–20 April 1857), but he suffered from homesickness and disliked reporting sordid incidents at the police station. See *Years of My Youth*, HE, p. 123; *My Literary Passions* (1895), pp. 166–67.

5. Harvey Green, sometimes J. H. Greene, was one of the printers in the *Sentinel* office and lived with the Howells family. He later served as captain in the Union Army and in 1869 became editor of the Medina *Gazette*, a position he still held in 1881. See *Years of My Youth*, HE, pp. 105–6.

20 APRIL 1857, CINCINNATI, TO VICTORIA M. HOWELLS

Gazette Office, ...
Cincinnati, April 20 1857

Dear Vic—

I suppose your are motherless as well as brotherless, at home, about now. Our dear family circle has been sadly broken up during the present year; but I hope we shall all be united again within a few weeks. I expect maybe I will be at home the last of next week, but the thing is quite uncertain. I will leave Cincinnati, then, at any rate, unless I should get further advices from Brown to the contrary, which I do not expect.—I hardly know how I shall like to be in Farmer office.[1] Somehow, I don't feel exactly right toward a man who wants me to do so much for so little as Brown does. But I hope I do him injustice; and doubtless I ought to be thankful, for his offer was like a God-send to me, a few ago. Did you have a very fine time at Prentice's?[2] I guess my dancing days are about over. I did so miserably at the last Goodale House hop that I was ashamed of myself.[3]

There is too much going on here for me to be descriptive of anything, but when I see you, I can tell a thousand things.—

I should like to have seen the performances by Jim, at the dance.[4] They must have been funny. I wrote to the scamp. Tell him to answer me.

I have received two letters from Harvey this week. Poor, homesick soul! he's twice as "bad took" as I—and after all the tossing about in the world that he has done, too![5] It's ridiculous. I should like well enough to be at home, but I dont want to go back to live at Jefferson any more—which sentiment, were it known in that village, would ruin me. Wanting to see you very badly I am affectionately your brother

Will.

Don't use any more of Joe's horrible envelopes

1. The offer from Thomas Brown (1819–1867), editor of the *Ohio Farmer*, published in Cleveland, either was not extended or was rejected. On 19 April Howells had also written to his father about the job there (MH). In 1854–1855 and in 1857–1858 he contributed infrequently to that newspaper.

2. Perhaps Noyes B. Prentice, formerly mayor of Jefferson (1846–1848 and 1851); but many other Prentices lived in Jefferson and nearby towns.

3. The Goodale House was a hotel in Columbus.

4. Possibly Jim Bloss, who with his sister Clara is mentioned in Howells' letter to Aurelia and Annie Howells, 21 February 1858 (MH). Jim Williams, mentioned in Howells' letter to Victoria, 18–24 April 1859, lived in Jefferson before this time.

5. Harvey Green's being "bad took" probably refers to the love affair that eventually led to his marriage. See *Years of My Youth*, HE, pp. 105–6.

9 AND 11 SEPTEMBER 1857, JEFFERSON, TO DUNE DEAN

Jefferson, Sept. 9, 1857.

Dear Cousin[1]—

If I am frightfully prompt to answer your letter, it is for the reason already explained, and so I have no reason to enlarge upon that subject. Which does not, however, as I hope, prevent me from enlarging upon any other that may suggest itself.

This present scripture is being written at the house of Joe, *fratermeus*, with whom I am briefly sojourning; his *frau* being gone beyond the pale of civilization—I mean, into Pennsylvania. She is to be gone several days; and to prevent a relapse into bachelorhood, Joe keeps house, and has me stay with him o'nights, to drive away the lonesomes. Which being fully explained, reduces me to the same estate of having nothing to say in which I set out to say nothing.

Do you know I have found a treasure? Not, verily, one of gold nor yet silver, but of books, classics, German classics! Was denkst du? He is a book binder, and a learned and well read man—thoroughly Teutonic, and an enthusiast about German literature.[2] He has lent me a work of Heinrich Heine's—in which I have not read much—beyond this sublime sentiment, which Heine quotes from another German. Isn't it fine?—listen:

"Nothing is continual, but Change; nothing eternal but Death. Every beat of the heart gives us a wound, and Life were an endless bleeding, if it were not for Poetry. Poetry gives us what nature denies us: a golden times that rusts not; a spring that fades not; unclouded fortune and everlasting Youth."[3]

Without knowing or thinking whether this would please you as much as it has pleased me, I have given you the benefit of the greatest thought that I have yet read outside of our own language. The sweet German of it runs in my head all the while, and like

"The phantom of a silent song
That went and came a thousand times,"[4]

is unceasingly repeated to me—"Nichts ist dauernd als der wechsel, nichts beständig, als der Tod."[5]—Don't get mad that I write in foreign tongues and barbarous—it is a vice of mine, which you can't cure—very impolite, illbred and all that, but then, a great satisfaction.—But say, isn't my Dutch bookbinding acquaintance a treasure if he possesses books with things in them like that? Hey now, seriously?

The dull pool of my life stagnates again. The few pebbles that you dropped into it woke ripples on its surface, which have subsided; and all is as if nothing had happened. I have so long lived *by* myself and *in* myself, and my unhappy disposition has clung to me so steadfastly through good and evil entreatment, that I think I would rather be lonesome and miserable than not. As I pass up and down the streets of this not-to-be-sufficiently-detested village, and consider that there is not one in it (saving my own kin) for whom I care a hands turning, and that all in it are about that much interested in me, I feel a kind of selfish content that I would not exchange for the sensations of gratified vanity. After all, my dear, (since I have begun to preach I may as well go on,) it is in oneself that one finds the true filicity. If my tooth aches, my friend doesn't lessen my pain by groaning in company with me, let his exertions be never so disinterested and sincere. Neither shall I, by taking snuff, make him to sneeze. As it is with pain so it is with pleasure. No one surrounded by the perfectest happiness feels one happy sentiment unless something has occurred to him to put him in good humour. There are those who will tell you an atmosphere of any emotion, joy or grief will fill you with sympathetic feelings. Gammon and stuff! A death causes (the thought is horrible, but true, as I know by observation) nothing but jesting and merriment outside the circle whom it affects immediately; and there are some scenes of happiness that enrage and disgust the beholder. It is my belief that since there can be no effect without a cause, there cannot be a cause in one soul and an effect in another. Truly, if the principle of felicity has not been excited in me, I don't care how good humoured all the world is; I am still sulky. *Ergo—O Puella!* this is my consolation in my present loneliness—If I dwelt in a king's house, and breakfasted every morning upon the tenderest beefsteak, and had nothing to do but to read new poems by Tennyson, I would not be content, if I had not schooled myself *to be happy on my own hook. All the busy moments are honey-laden bees. Let me steal their sweetness from them ere they pass me forever.* Amen! That is the genuine philosophy of living.

Of all the arrogant, provoking ones, you are the arrogantest and provokingest!—I used to think that heaven had gifted me with a fair share of impudent assurance, but when I find you pretending to have conquered *me*, and to have driven me to take refuge in flight, I begin to believe that I am a remarkably modest and unassuming young person. You know that upon the only occasion when we had a decisive battle I came off victorious, and actually dictated terms to you! And in the thousand and one ceaseless skirmishes, who was obliged to surrender me sticks, plums, rose-seed-bulbs, stones, stocks, etc.? Who was tied to a tree? Who, when I said Do it, did it? Who, when I said come, came? O your memory, believe me, is utterly unworthy to be trusted!

I am rejoiced that you are obliged to learn Latin—partly because it will do you good, and mostly because it is disagreeable to you. I wish you had to learn Sanscrit and Hebrew. Are you going to take lessons in German? You had better.

Last Sunday I took a walk down the river road almost to the bridge where you saw the ghost. It was a charming day, and I couldn't help wishing that I was taking a ride with you upon that road—it would have been such a grand time to shew off its beauties. Have you pleasant weather in Pittsburgh? It is delightful here.

Looking over your letter I find that you have asked me with genuine feminine recklessness, no less than—a great many unanswerable questions. Of the perfidious schoolmarm I know nothing, and I am reduced to that state of desperation in regard to her, that I do not care whether I hear about her any tidings more. I did not cry at the wedding, and consequently was not affected to tears because it was not I was being married.—I am going to be simply a good uncle to my nephew who is to inherit my virtues and talent and wealth (slender legacy!). I am growing fat and my moustache is turning gray. Look here! if you don't quit using that offensive term of compassion—"poor little fellow"— I'll never come to see you. So you can choose between the pleasure of my future acquaintance, and your natural disposition to be contrary— you incorrigible!

I attended a "whisk"[6] party since you left—at Ellen Holman's, and was beaten—all because you were not there to play with me. There is nothing else of news. When do you expect Vic at P?

We will be most glad to hear from your mother—to whom remember me, with all rest.—Which is all at present from:

Your cousin,
Will.

Post Scriptum—Sept. 11. After two days' lapse I have read the foregoing, and find it to be twaddle—which I am specially gifted to write, indeed. I despair of doing anything better at present, however, and so will mail this! A letter from Cincinnati, received yesterday, assures me of passing the coming winter at Columbus.

Yours very elatedly
Will.

1. Probably a cousin, Dune Dean, the daughter of Samuel Dean, who lived in Pittsburgh.
2. Otto Limbeck (b. 1824), with whom Howells studied German, especially Heine, may have worked with W. R. Allen, who advertised weekly in the Ashtabula *Sentinel* as bookbinder, bookseller, and stationer. See *My Literary Passions*, pp. 166–69.
3. At the beginning of *Reisebilder* (*Werke und Briefe*, ed. H. Kaufmann [Berlin: Aufbau-Verlag, 1961–64], III, 17) Heine quotes this passage from Karl Ludwig Börne (1786–1837).
4. Tennyson, "The Miller's Daughter," lines 71–72.
5. The German of the first sentence from Börne, quoted earlier in the letter.
6. "Whisk" was by this time a dialect or vulgar term for the card game whist.

27 OCTOBER 1857, JEFFERSON, TO VICTORIA M. HOWELLS

Jefferson Oct. 27, 1857.

Mein Liebes Schwesterchen—

If you'll excuse that much German—your letter to father and mother was received to day; your letters to me, a frightfully long while ago.

I write to you now more from a sense of duty than from a conviction that I have anything to say. That I have nothing to say, is partly owing to the fact that nothing has happened, and chiefly to the fact that if any thing had happened I would n't know it. For I have not darkened the door, nor straddled the threshhold of any one in this place since you left, but upon one notable occasion when I called on Kate.[1] That was when your absence was a week old. She then told me to give you her love, and remind you of your promise to write, which I of course forgot to do, and the command laid upon me has set as easily as old shoe till this moment. Ecce Signeur! Some little gossip I have, however, as that Mary Hart is married to George Loomis, and that the felicitious couple have gone to reside at Columbus.[2] They will board at the Goodale House.—That's all.

I'm in such a state of mind, not to say sin and misery, as hardly to be able to write. In the morning I get up in a stew, and boil and simmer all day, and go to bed sodden, and ferociously misanthropical. An hundred times a day, I give myself to the devil for having come back to Jefferson, when neither sickness nor starvation drove me; and as often I take myself to task for a discontented fool. For I know very well that had I remained in Cincinnati or Cleveland, I would have discovered as clearly as I have here, that I was in the worst possible situation, the most uncomfortable, the most unprofitable and unpromising. It's a taint of the blood. Here I am, *at home*,—to me the dearest of all places on earth—to begin with. I have books—the best friends. I have time—the most precious thing. No one molests me nor makes me afraid. I sit under my own vine and fig tree (figurative) and cock up my feet on my own secretary (reality.). Yet I am not happy. I am not reasonable. They are fools or humbugs who say man *reasons*. Gammon! He wishes for, he grumbles at. The horse who shakes himself free of the wrinkles and recollections of his harness, and gratefully crops the grass, *reasons* more.

The present question with me, for instance, is, how am I to make a living? I bore myself continually about, conjuring up possible unpleasant predicaments, and give myself no rest. I am proud, vain, and poor. I want to make money, and be rich and grand. But I don't know that I shall live an hour—a minute! O it was the loftiest and holiest wisdom that bade us take no thought for the morrow and to consider the lilies of the field! If a man were to pray for the *summum bonum*, he would pray; Give me heart to enjoy this hour. Alas for me! Here I might be happy, yet here I am wretched. I want to be out in the world, though I know that I am not formed to battle with life. I want to succeed, yet I am of too indolent a nature to begin.—I want to be admired and looked up to, when I might be loved.—I know myself, and I speak by the card, when I pronounce myself *a mistake*.

This is chiefly sermon. Don't be bored, Vic. It has cleared my mind a good deal to write all this trash.

Have you written to Cousin Joe since you have been gone?[3] He wrote me some time since, complaining of neglect by us all. I answered him immediately, and promised that you should. He lives at New Albany, Ind., and will probably be married this winter to a lady in Greenville—the one of whom he used to talk.

Joe got a letter from Harvey, not long ago.[4] H. is a good deal discouraged. They feel the hard times severely in lithograph cities. He has had to discharge two hands already.

I sincerely hope you may get to visit New Orleans—tho' I don't know what father and mother may dicide about it.

My love to all, and the sincerest affection accept for yourself. Tell my good aunt I will write to her as soon as I am in a good humour.[5]

Your affectionate brother
Will.

Are you reading "What will he do with it?" in Blackwood. It is Bulwer's best—which is the highest praise.[6]

1. Probably Kate A. Jones (1839–1868), a Jefferson girl and niece of Joshua R. Giddings, who may be the K. J. referred to by Howells in his Venetian diary for 1861–1862 (MS located at MH) as "my first love"; however, in a letter to Joseph A. Howells, 22 March 1908 (*Life in Letters*, II, 251) he likewise designates two other girls. Her marriage to Josiah D. Ensign was reported in the Ashtabula *Sentinel*, 9 September 1858. See Lynn, *Howells*, p. 218.

2. George M. Loomis (b. 1822) is listed in the 1870 census as a Jefferson butcher. His marriage to Mary E. Hart was reported in the *Sentinel*, 29 October 1857.

3. Joseph Howells, a cousin at New Albany, Indiana, may have been the son of William C. Howells' brother Joseph (1814–1896), a physician.

4. Joe was Howells' brother; and Harvey was Harvey Green, who had left the *Sentinel* and become a journeyman printer.

5. Probably Anne Cooper Howells (1809–1868), the sister of Howells' father.

6. Edward George Earle Bulwer-Lytton, "What Will He Do with It?" *Blackwood's*, June 1857–January 1859.

30 NOVEMBER 1857, JEFFERSON, TO HARVEY AND JANE GREEN

Jefferson, Nov. 30, 1857.

Dear Harvey and Jane—

Before you suffer any exclamation as of terror or amazement to escape you at sight of the formidable dimensions of this sheet, I beg to state that in all epistolary probability, I shall not more than write it half full. At any rate, I promise not to cross-write any of the pages.

I got your husbandandwifely and exceedingly welcome letter, more than a week ago: last Friday night but one. I "swore a very wicked oath" that I would answer it as soon as I got done work—making the mental reservation that I would first, however, "do" my German Lesson. Now for two or three days there had been a villainous hint of rheumatism in my shoulders; and on that same evening, being vexed and goaded on by a strong draft from the kitchen door, this hint of rheumatism threw off all disguise, and racked my joints till I was almost crazy. I spent the night in an armchair by the stoveside. The next day and the next my right arm was so full of pain and so stiff that I could not handle my knife and fork deftly, let alone a pen. The next day I had a horrible cold in addition, and yet the next and the next a fever. So it is no lie, as most of epistolary excuses are, to say that the present is the first time I have had, when time was of any use to me.

And now, do you expect an invalid—as I set up to be—to give you any village gossip? I know you do, such is the unreasonableness of people away from home; but I couldn't tell you anything of people without throwing in seasonings of the very unchristian sentiments I cherish towards most of folks; and I shall be obliged, if I give you any news at all, to so harrass and guard myself that, I will end in abusing you. Truth to tell, there is little enough going on here. ("That," says Jane, is a speech that has been in the mouth of every Jefferson body, for the last three years. Do you call that news?" I didn't say it *was* news, did I? Don't be so fast.) There has been, in the way of amusements within the last two weeks, a lecture on Mormonism by Dr Richmond (and a very good lecture the Doctor made,)[1] a troupe of circotheatricals, who indefinitely postponed on account of weather; a genteel operatic niggershow (very select, performing chiefly to members of the press,) and to-morrow night we are advertised a panorama—the same I think, whose painting of Abraham sacrificing Isaac, was of such unmittigated atrocity as to extort from the Doctor the confession that he didn't wonder Abe was going to kill that boy! No matter—these are the public diversions of our charming hamlet. The private ones I know nothing of—by reason of adhering to my old habit of not going any where.— There is now and then I believe a surreptitious tea party, and occasionally a latent party of whist. Rumour, nothing definiter, is my authority.

For personal gossip, you have to know the Gid. family are going to spend the coming winter at Washington.[2] Possibly the old lady will remain at home; but the old "warhorse" is not to be trusted with his equine atrophy so far from home alone. I do not wonder at their solicitude; for he certainly is very feeble, for all his present accession of health. Laura is now in Jefferson, and all the family are busily preparing for their flitting.—"We shall miss Maria very much in the choir," was the remark of a lady whose story style Jane will recognize. I was malicious enough to chuckle at it. It *was* good, eh?

Stiles Jones, you will have heard, has passed through this place on his way east—to be wedded, gossip hath it, to Ell-n G-ll-tt.[3] I cannot, not knowing, "tell so long beforehand" how much truth there may be in the report. But I should not be surprised, Should you?

Clara Bloss spent the last week here. I was not so fortunate as to be able to see her, but I have the most solemn assurance from mutual friends that she is just the same as ever.

You of course know that Mollie Hart is married, and now lives at Columbus.[4] Ensign was down there not long since, and dined with her.[5] She is keeping house.—I suppose I shall see her, this winter, as I have made an engagement with the *Cin. Gaz.* to correspond for that paper—a much better engagement than I had expected to make.[6] Mrs Cadwell, I hear, will spend part of the winter at the Capital, and so we shall have quite a little community of Jeffersonians there.[7]

After the close of the session, I have the avuncular promise of a trip up the Mississippi to Saint Paul,[8] and you may be sure, that I will make you a visit if there is the remotest and minutest possibility of doing so. You wouldn't believe how much I want to see you, if I told you, and so I *wont* tell you.

I suppose no one doubts my being a competent person to give advice on the conduct of matrimonial life? I would like to say a few words to you young people in private, but you probably would n't mind what I say. I will therefore refer you to Tupper for the substance of my views.[9] (Now, I don't know whether Tupper says anything about marriage, or not. But one is safe in predicating anything of Tupper, for there is no one will be such a fool as to examine his works for authority, on any consideration.)

I tell you, I'm charmed with the "Atlantic." "The Autocrat of the Breakfast Table," "Illusions," "Florentine Mosaics" and "Douglass Jerrold" "are alone worth the price of subscription," as we say in despair of Godey.[10] Don't you think, though, it's a little too *Bostony* in its flavor? And after all the "Atlantic" isn't "Putnam," is it? Poor, old, peagreen Putnam! We shall not look upon thy like again.[11] I don't believe a catholic-toned magazine possible outside of New York.

Vic. will probably go down to New Orleans in a week or two, and possibly may not go at all, for rivers freeze and steamboats are fallible. Vic. is enjoying herself hugely. I had a letter from her tonight.

I hope you have felt the severest pressure of the hard times—that is, that they are over with you now. This is a little eddy, you know, in the rushing stream of American life, and we hardly know how it is with people in the current.—In the office, we get along in the old fashion; plenty to do, but little to collect. The farmers hold on to their cheese, and so there is no money in the county.—I declare, I have talked myself down, and have only breath left to assure you that I am with mothers love to both,

Ever yours,
Will.

Write—write.

1. The lecture may have been by Dr. B. W. Richmond, whose resumption of practice was reported in the *Sentinel*, 11 March 1858.
2. Joshua R. Giddings (1795–1864) was the congressman (1838–1859) who lived in Jefferson and who was "corresponding editor" of the *Sentinel* after it was moved to Jefferson in January 1853. Laura Ann (1839–1884) and Lura Maria (1825–1871) were his daughters.
3. Stiles Jones and "Ell-n G-ll-tt" have not been identified.
4. Mollie was the nickname for Mary E. Hart.
5. Josiah D. Ensign (1833–1923) served as clerk of courts in Ashtabula County (1857–1863), became county auditor in 1857, and practiced law in Jefferson until 1868 when his wife died and he moved to Rochester, Minnesota. Later he became a prominent attorney and judge and mayor of Duluth.
6. Howells' second engagement with the Cincinnati *Gazette* was largely for

writing "Letter from Columbus," mostly reports on the legislature, as had been the first engagement (January–March[?] 1857).

7. Mrs. Cadwell was the wife of Darius W. Cadwell (b. 1821), a prominent Jefferson lawyer. In 1857 he was elected state senator and appointed a general in the Ohio Volunteer Militia. Clara G. Cadwell, described as a close friend of the Howells family, was probably her daughter. See William Coyle, *Ohio Authors* (Cleveland: World Publishing Co., 1962), p. 96.

8. See Howells to Joseph A. Howells, 10 April 1857, n. 3.

9. Martin F. Tupper (1810–1889) published *Proverbial Philosophy* (1838 and 1842), a subliterary and didactic work of great popularity.

10. "The Autocrat of the Breakfast Table," by O. W. Holmes; "Illusions," by R. W. Emerson; "Florentine Mosaics," by J. L. Motley; "Douglas Jerrold," by James Hannay, *Atlantic*, November 1857. *Godey's Lady's Book* was published from 1830 to 1898.

11. Begun in 1853, *Putnam's Monthly Magazine* ceased publication in 1857, but it was later briefly revived as *Putnam's Magazine* (1868–1870).

21 SEPTEMBER 1858, JEFFERSON, TO GAMALIEL BAILEY

Jefferson, Sept. 21, 1858.

Dr G. Bailey[1]—

Dear Sir—

I enclose a copy of verses, changing my nom de plume from that used with "The Doubt,"[2] to one under which I have done considerable scribbling, and which I have the vanity to hope will be known to some of your readers.

With an amount of leisure upon my hands that I don't well know what to do with, and a reading that has been discursive and varied, if not extensive, (not to mention a seated infirmity of scribbling,) I have been wondering whether I might not contribute to the Era a series of papers to be called "Desultoria," and, (this is the chief matter,) whether you might not pay me for them.[3] The papers would embrace those little notes in a sketchy, biographic and critical way, which would be so well set afloat each by itself.—After I have heard from you in regard to the matter, however, I will send you, if you desire it, some Desultoria, and then you can test the pudding by the tasting. May I venture to count upon a reply from you? whether you want me to write or not.

Respectfully,
Will. D. Howells.

1. Gamaliel Bailey (1807–1859) was a doctor and abolitionist. Chosen editor of the *National Era* at its founding in 1847, he moved from Cincinnati to Washington, D. C., where he made it one of the most important organs of the abolitionist movement. *Uncle Tom's Cabin* first appeared serially in the *National Era* (1851–1852).

2. The enclosed poem was probably "Gone," *National Era*, 21 October 1858. However, like "The Doubt," *National Era*, 16 September 1858, it is signed Wilhelm Constant. The two poems also appear in *Poems of Two Friends* (1860).

3. "The Bird Song," *National Era*, 2 December 1858, was Howells' only other contribution. While no columns titled "Desultoria" have been located, his first "News and Humor of the Mails" appeared in the *Ohio State Journal*, 22 November 1858, the approximate date of his joining that paper's staff.

9 OCTOBER 1858, JEFFERSON, TO MARTIN D. POTTER

Jefferson, Ashtabula. co., O. Oct. 9, 1858.

M. D. Potter[1]—

Dear Sir—

I would like to furnish Legislative Correspondence, the coming Session, for the Daily "Commercial."[2] Two winters' experience at Columbus as the correspondent of the "Gazette," of your city, would enable me to serve you better than one new to the business and unacquainted at the capital. My letters as "Chispa," are the reference I give, literarily. It may be worth while to state that I have not applied to the "Gazette," for my last winter's berth, and therefore do not come to you after a failure with that journal.

I would write for the same pay I received from the Gazette—ten dollars a week. I believe that sum was also given to your correspondent, Mr Smith.[3]

An early answer will oblige me greatly.

Respectfully,
Will. D. Howells.

If you should not wish to employ me, it is perhaps needless to say that I would desire the present application to be considered confidential.

1. Martin D. Potter (1819–1866) entered the Cincinnati *Commercial* office in 1846 and later became principal editor and owner.
2. Howells did not finally undertake the correspondence for the *Commercial*, but began working for the *Ohio State Journal* in November.
3. Probably William Henry Smith, who commenced as editor of the *Odd-Fellows' Casket* in Cincinnati, November 1858. That publication died December 1859.

26 DECEMBER 1858, COLUMBUS, TO VICTORIA M. HOWELLS

Columbus, Dec. 26, '58.

Dear Sister Vic—

I wish you were here with me to-day, sitting with your eyes upon the cheerful coal fire—and listening to the rain dropping from tower to tower, with musical irregularity. I am in the most charming state of animal comfort. I have just eaten the heartiest dinner, have accomplished without disaster, three flights of stairs, and am embraced by the arms of a great split-bottom chair. It is entirely dismal out of door, and its dismalness makes it more pleasant indoors. Directly, when I have finished this letter, my roommate Fullerton will drop in,[1] and we will chat away the time over some favorite author, with frequent reading of select passages aloud; or else we will throw ourselves upon the beds, and let the rain sing us to sleep. In the evening, I will go up to old Jones'es room, and we make our Sunday call at our German friend's house.[2] But is their no shadow in this bright picture? Assuredly. There is a shadow and a skeleton. I have an abominably sore nose, which to my diseased imagination and impracticable vision seems monstrous. As nearly as I can describe it, it appears about the size of a sugar-bowl, and is of a dull mahogany color. Could you see it, I am sure you would find it quite a consolation. What can ail the unfortunate feature, I am at a loss to know.

I got father's letter this morning, though a short note had previously relieved my mind in regard to John.[3] You can well imagine, I think, how much trouble my dream gave me. I dream almost every night something about home. But so long as I continue to improve in health, I shall not be homesick. I am going to send some presents home, for New Years. I am sorry about that watch business; but sometime it will be made all right. I am going to write for the Odd-fellows Casket,[4] to which I have been invited to contribute, and anything I can make in that outside way, shall not be used selfishly. The Casket pays $2.00 a page. I think I can earn eight or ten dollars in that way every month.

Babb is going to be in town next week, and then if the thing can be done honorably I will be reconciled to him. I may need his friendship.

You saw that I printed "Bobby" in the Journal.[5] Benedict of the Cleveland Herald said he would copy my things and designate me as the author,[6] and Coggeshall will also help to bring me out.[7] I am not satisfied with the New Years Address I have written, but I will suffer it to be printed any way.[8]

During the past week, I have[9]

1. Artemas Thomas Fullerton (1834–1901), Howells' roommate at the boardinghouse that had formerly been Starling Medical College, was admitted to the bar in 1855 and later became a Presbyterian minister. The *Atlantic* published three of his poems before accepting any by Howells: "By the Dead," March 1858; "The Birth-Mark," September 1858; and "Two Years After," May 1859. See *Years of My Youth*, HE, pp. 159–60.

2. Thomas D. Jones (1811–1881) was a portrait sculptor and medallionist, best known for his sculptures of Lincoln and Salmon P. Chase. The German friend was the "Madame R." mentioned again in later letters. See *Years of My Youth*, HE, pp. 185–87.

3. John Butler Howells was sick with the measles.

4. Howells made four contributions to the *Casket* in 1859. See Gibson-Arms, *Bibliography*, pp. 81–82.

5. *Ohio State Journal*, 14 December 1858.

6. George A. Benedict (1813–1876), Cleveland lawyer, city official, postmaster, and journalist, became one of the editors and proprietors of the Cleveland *Herald* in 1848 and remained with it until his death.

7. William Turner Coggeshall (1824–1867), state librarian at Columbus (1856–1862), was author or editor of several books and newspapers. He edited *The Poets and Poetry of the West* (1860) in which biographical notices and poems by Howells appeared.

8. "The Old and the New Year," *Ohio State Journal*, 1 January 1859. In the same issue appeared Coggeshall's "Pay as You Go: A Story for the New Year."

9. The rest of the manuscript letter has not been located.

2 JANUARY 1859, COLUMBUS, TO VICTORIA M. HOWELLS

(For Vic)

Columbus, Jan 2, 1859,

My dear Sister—

I got your doleful little letter by Mr Cadwell,[1] and was very sorry to hear of the poor Childie's sickness.[2] Of course it is painful to know of his suffering; but I really think that his having the measles will be all the better for him. Kiss the dear little soul for his brother. I quite enter into your feelings of sympathy for him.

Well, my dear sister, I have not much to write you—though I believe that is an excuse I make in every letter. I wish it were so that you might be here with me. I miss your companionship so much. I think we were as nearly confidants as it is possible for brother and sister to be; and then with my home habits, we were so constantly together. We said many things to each other that we would not have breathed to anybody else, and sort of comforted each other in our hard task of making bricks without straw for those Jefferson Egyptians. Some day I hope to rescue my kindred out of the bondage.

I must tell to you all my little triumphs. I have sold to Smith of the Odd-Fellow's Casket at Cincinnati, that little story—you remember I read to you early last summer. I called it "Not a love story."[3] He gives me six dollars for it; and he says that as soon as I have time to dress up the translation that Babb rejected, he will buy that.[4] At the rate of two dollars a page, it will bring me sixteen or eighteen dollars. "Bobby" is going the rounds of the country papers.[5] Aston,[6] the bookseller here, told our local editor that it was enough to make anybody's reputation —that he and his family laughed prodigiously over it. Dear to me— O how unspeakably sweet are these little flattering speeches, and I can repeat these, I thank heaven! to those who will prize them equally.

O, how genially I come out in this ray of sunlight, after being frozen up so many years in Jefferson. All my faculties expend, and the gloom leaves me, that haunted me forever. I have the assurance that I shall succeed, but, O God! sometimes, I tremble lest something should happen to destroy my hopes. I think, though, that my adversity came first, and now it is prosperity lies before me. I am going to try and get up a poem fit to be printed in the Atlantic.[7] They pay Fullerton $25 a page. I can sell, now, just as much as I will write.

New Year's is gone again. I took dinner at Coggeshall's and supper at Lynch's.[8] I made no calls. Fullerton, my roommate, made *fifty-one*. About ten last night, I went to the governor's on business,[9] and on his asking me if I had called anywhere, I told him I fortunately knew nobody. He said that I could not make that excuse in regard to them, and I felt quite caught and guilty. I must go Tuesday night to Miss Chase's reception and make my "abologies."[10]

Love to all from
Will.

1. Darius W. Cadwell.
2. John Butler Howells.
3. "Not a Love Story," *Odd-Fellows' Casket*, February 1859.
4. The translation was not published in the *Casket*; it may be one of several translations that appeared in the *Ohio State Journal* in 1859. See Gibson-Arms, *Bibliography*, pp. 81–83.
5. Howells' sketch, *Ohio State Journal*, 14 December 1858, was evidently being widely reprinted.
6. Isaac C. Aston, of Randall & Aston, booksellers. Although the firm emphasized religious books in its advertisements, "Bobby" is flippant and secular.
7. "Andenken" eventually appeared in the *Atlantic*, January 1860. See *Years of My Youth*, HE, p. 155.
8. Probably Isaac Lynch's boardinghouse at 48 North High.
9. Salmon P. Chase (1808–1873) was U. S. senator from Ohio (1849–1855, 1860), governor (1855–1859), secretary of treasury (1861–1864), and chief justice of the U. S. Supreme Court (1864–1873).
10. Katherine Chase (1840–1899) began to serve as her father's official hostess at sixteen. In 1863 she married William Sprague, governor of Rhode Island (1860–1863) and U. S. senator from that state (1863–1875). See *Years of My Youth*, HE, pp. 133–34.

23 JANUARY 1859, COLUMBUS, TO VICTORIA M. HOWELLS

Columbus, January 23, 1859.

Dear Vic.

You at last advices, were the sick one, and so I write my letter to you. I hope it will find you well. I did not get father's package till Thursday, not knowing that any was come for me, and Mr Cadwell not having taken the trouble to tell me. When I read the letter my heart somewhat smote me, for I had not thought so much about home lately, as I ought to have done. I pictured the disappointment of my dear mother, looking for me in vain, that Saturday night, and I could have—well, acted very foolishly. My dormant homesickness awoke, and I longed to be with you. But I was going to hear Grace Greenwood, and so did not give way so much to that feeling. After the lecture, I was introduced to her, and paid her a compliment, very prodigious, and slightly insincere. She has been a beautiful woman, and she has now fine eyes, but she is *agée* and faded.[1]

Tuesday night I attended Miss Chase's reception, and had a delightful time, making the acquaintance of a young New Church lady from Urbana,[2] where her family, Cincinnatians, are residing, to give their children the benefit of the University. We had chat, and music, and I made my first appearance in the *Lanceurs*, Miss Wright (daughter of the State Auditor,)[3] kindly putting me through.

Friday evening, my particular friend, Mrs Dr Carter[4] invited a number of young folks, to meet me at her house, advertising me I fear with a flourish, which my after-appearance could not justify. The evening passed away very pleasantly, but I confess, that though the young ladies were all very beautiful, and intelligent, and aristocratic, I cared most to talk with Mrs Carter, who was obliged to scold me for my inattention to the *demoiselles*. When they left, I went home with Miss Wright. You see I tell you this foolish gossip, not because you care for such things, but because there is nothing else to say. The other evenings of the week were spent at theatre, etc.

All the time, I say to myself, you fool, don't let all this elate you. You have achieved your present little notoriety without desert, and you may suddenly lose it the same way. It is difficult to keep acting absurdly, sometimes; but I believe that I have my share of common sense after all. Reed[5] (one of our editors) says we Journal-ists are as greedy of compliments, as school-girls, and derides himself and me for being tickled with them.

I called on Mrs Cadwell, Friday, and spent half an hour in chat with her. Even she had something pleasant to say to me.—Vic, don't breathe to anybody, the absurd things I write you.

If I can possibly get off, I will come home at the end of the present week. But do not expect me too confidently; for it may be I cannot come.

My health continues good. Tell "Bobby" I wont forget his gun-flints.[6] And so with dearest love to all I am your affectionate brother

Will. D Howells.

1. Grace Greenwood, pseudonym for Sarah Jane (Clarke) Lippincott (1823–1904), who became most famous as the author of *Greenwood Leaves* (1850), was one of the earliest women newspaper correspondents and published many travel sketches and biographies. Her Columbus lecture is mentioned in the *Ohio State Journal*, 21 January 1859, and an earlier advertisement refers to it as her "celebrated lecture" on "The Children of Today—the Men and Women of Twenty Years Hence."

2. Possibly the Miss Graham mentioned in the letter to Victoria and Johnny, 15 February 1859.

3. Francis M. Wright was state auditor (1856–1860). The lancers was a popular dance, a set of quadrilles.

4. Isabella E. Carter, mother of Annie Carter, was married to Dr. Francis Carter (1814–1881), a graduate of King's College in Dublin and a founding trustee of Starling Medical College (1847), where he was professor of obstetrics. See *Years of My Youth*, HE, pp. 150–51.

5. Samuel R. Reed (1820?–1889) later joined the staff of the Cincinnati *Gazette*. See *Years of My Youth*, HE, pp. 128–31.

6. See the letter to Victoria and Johnny, 15 February 1859, on hunting together. John Butler Howells and "Bobby," a character in Howells' recently published sketch, have nothing in common except their age.

15 FEBRUARY 1859, COLUMBUS, TO VICTORIA M. AND JOHN B. HOWELLS

Columbus, February 15, 1859.

My dear Sister—

I have but just read your sad little letter, and I answer it at once. I have been invited to a large party at the Deshler's,[1] tonight, but I prefer not to go. You know I don't care much about society; and I begin to find that a very large acquaintance in Columbus would embarrass my purposes. A few intimate, or familiar friends, will be all that is desirable to me; for I have but little time, and that I do not feel like wasting on people for whom I care nothing. Tonight, I am especially unfit to go out. What with having been more or less depressed all day, and the added feelings of melancholy with which I read your letter, I am quite in the dumps doleful.

Still I am going to try and write you an encouraging reply. It would of course be foolish for me to pretend that there is not much to make you discontented and even unhappy at times; but still your cloud has its silver lining too. You live with our dear father and mother, and your brothers and sisters are about you all the time. You have books, and music; and when the spring comes, there will be gardening and all that to do. The great trouble with all of us has been, that we had no definite purpose; and I think that what you want is an *object*, no matter how insignificant. Would not the study of something—geology, botany, a language—even pursued at disadvantage, as you must do it—occupy you to the exclusion of gloomy thoughts? I am stumbling in the dark, I dare say, for a man cannot understand a woman—even his own sister; but you will forgive my awkwardness for my good intention's sake. Why don't you *write*, dear Vic? If you will write a little story or sketch of any kind, I will engage to sell it for you. Did you see my "Not a Love Story" in the last Casket?—If this is a little incoherent, I have to plead in excuse that it is written while Fullerton blacks his boots, and keeps up a running fire of talk with a friend who is come to accompany him to the party.

—I was sorry that I could not bring you down with me, when I left home; but the truth is, that economise as I will, I can barely manage to live upon my $10 a week. My clothes wear out, and I have no one to do any repairing for me, and save the nine stitches by one in time. I shall before long, *apply* for an increase of salary. Ah! we all have our rows to hoe. The other day I let my watch drop—that it will cost a dollar to repair; my coat is out at elbows, and I must get it mended; my pantaloons are treacherously giving way in every quarter.

So poor little Mollie J. called upon you. I suppose you owe that to my civility. She was very sad and silent, I dare say. Give my regards to Mrs Pub. J. I haven't hunted up Miss Greene, yet.[2] I am afraid I wont, either.

Sunday night, I spent as usual, at Mrs Carter's. She has a very intelligent, and quite pretty young lady visiting her—a Miss Graham from Cincinnati.[3]

This week, I must try to make some calls. It will be a great effort, but I will make it.

> Affectionately,
> Will.

Dear Brother Johnny—

I read your letter with a great deal of pleasure. It was very good of you to write, when I know it must be a trouble to you. How do the rabbit-traps flourish? Have you caught any since I left? Were you lonesome when I comeaway? The next time I come home I'll stay a week, and then we'll have a grand time, hunting. I'll think about that shot gun. Wouldn't you rather have a pistol? You know we've got two guns already.

> Your affectionate brother
> Willie.

---

1. Possibly David Waggoner Deshler (1792–1869), the owner of the Clinton Bank, and his wife Betsey Green Deshler; or more likely their son William Green Deshler (1827–1916), founder of the Deshler National Bank, and his wife Ann Eliza Sinks Deshler.

2. "Mrs. Pub. J." was probably the wife of Publius V. Jones (b. 1819), a pros-

perous farmer and occasional officeholder in Jefferson. They were the parents of Kate Jones, mentioned in an earlier letter, and apparently also of Mollie. Miss Greene has not been identified.

3. Probably the daughter of Dr. James Graham (1818?–1897), Professor of Materia Medica and Therapeutics, Medical College of Ohio, Cincinnati (1854–1874).

4 MARCH 1859, COLUMBUS, TO JOHN J. PIATT

Columbus, March 4, 1859.

My dear Piatt:[1]

When I got your letter this morning, I upbraided myself that I had neglected you. But you know how I live—in a continual strife with time and fate, and always being beaten—and I think you can forgive me.

As often as we have published your poems, I have sent you copies of the paper.[2] With regard to the ms. I have still unpublished, I will do as you ask.[3] I was so glad and proud that you had got into the *Atlantic*, though a mean little pang of envy was felt at first. I "noticed" the fact of *The Morning Street* being from your pen.[4] Ah! if I only could write something worthy of the *Atlantic*! To whom did you send your poem, and who replied announcing its acceptance, and—do tell me all about it.

I have not latterly done a great deal of scribbling for the *Journal*—running chiefly to translations and news.[5] I do not understand what story you refer to as being a decided case of falling in love. I have seen a very charming sonnet of yours to certain beautiful-eyed Indiana cousins. *Hab' acht*! Cousins are very dangerous. I've tried it.

Dear old Jones is gone to Cincinnati, and I don't haunt the Neil House any more.[6] It is quite lonesome without him. He promised to write me, but hasn't.

Had I bought Schiller before you left? I got that pretty edition we looked at in Randall's.[7] I am not so much in love with him as with Heine. Ah! dear, wicked Heine! I have read *Das Lied von der Glocke*—the Bell Song, you know. Of course it has *gefallen* me, but I can't say anything very rapturous about it, which is not to my credit, I suppose.

I have not been at the governor's house since you were here; but am going to call shortly. The governor lent me a curious book, *Future Life*, by the author of *Peter Schlemihl in America*.[8] I read it and could not give any opinion of it. He says he wants to convert me, and has asked me to call some evening. He expressed himself to Jones as much pleased with your poetical success *Atlantic*-ward. You lucky boy!

I have just been reading a foolish life of Sir Philip Sidney by a silly woman.[9] If you want to laugh, read it—a new book, Boston published. A lady friend lent it me with the expectation that I would admire it. Dear heaven!

If you should ever find any German Volksbücher, read them.[10] I have newly finished one. They are very poetical, and so simple in diction that the poorest Germanicist shall understand them.

I am writing more than you want to read. Here are two poemlings. I send them in manuscript because I would rather have them printed in your *Journal* than ours. "Should you think them worthy," please say they are by me, giving the *National Era* credit of original publication.[11] Will you?

Yours always,
Will. D. Howells.

1. John J. Piatt (1835–1917) first met Howells at the printing office in Columbus in 1852. At the time of this letter he was on the staff of the Louisville *Journal*. After the publication of *Poems of Two Friends*, Howells continued to extol Piatt's poetry and to secure reviews of his books, but in later years became less sure of his merits as a poet. Still, upon Piatt's death, Howells devoted an "Editor's Easy Chair," *Harper's Monthly*, July 1917, to him, calling him a poet of "rare," and "genuinely Western, quality."

2. In February 1859 two poems by Piatt appeared in the *Ohio State Journal*: "The Unmended Bow," subtitled "After Mrs. Hermans's 'Bended Bow'" (18 February); "Parting and Meeting" (28 February), introduced as "another charming lyric from the pen of our friend, J. J. Piatt."

3. Perhaps Piatt had sent Howells the manuscript of his poem "The Church Path," asking him to forego original publication. It was reprinted from the Louisville *Journal* in the *Ohio State Journal*, 23 April 1859.

4. There is no "notice" of Piatt's "The Morning Street," *Atlantic*, February 1859; only a seven-line item on the February *Atlantic* appeared in the *Ohio State Journal*, 28 January 1859.

5. Howells' column "News and Humor of the Mails" was appearing at this time, as well as many translations, mostly from the *Courrier des Etats-Unis* and *La Crónica*.

6. Jones was Thomas D. Jones. Howells later described the Neil House as "then the finest hotel in the West." See *Years of My Youth*, HE, pp. 112–13.

7. Possibly the edition of Schiller he purchased at Randall & Aston's was *Gedichte* (Stuttgart, 1859). "Das Lied von der Glocke" is among the best known of Schiller's poems.

8. Governor Salmon P. Chase lent Howells *Future Life, or Scenes in Another World* (1858) by George Wood.

9. Mrs. Sarah Matilda Henry Davis, *The Life and Times of Sir Philip Sidney* (1859). A brief notice appeared in the *Ohio State Journal*, 10 February 1859.

10. German Volksbücher are the equivalents of chapbooks, pamphlet editions of popular literature. These were widely distributed in the United States during the first quarter of the nineteenth century. Gothic tales, jokes, marvelous tales, etc., were included in them.

11. "Gone," *National Era*, 21 October 1858; "The Bird Song," *National Era*, 2 December 1858.

13 March 1859, Columbus, to Victoria M. Howells

Columbus, March, Sunday.

O dear Vic—

You don't know how much I am denying myself for your sake. This is one of the divinest days—just such days, I think as they must have in heaven. There is not a cloud in the sky of perfect blue; the sun shines warm, and the air is crystal-clear, and fresh and crisp. Everything is so beautiful, that my heart aches with rapture. The buds are bursting to the music of the robins and the blue-birds, and I almost

"Hear the growing of the grass,"[1]

so green and rank is it already. The streets are full of people, and the great vault of heaven with the voice of chiming bells.

You can guess how much I long to be out every moment—but you can't rightly estimate the sacrifice after all.

I know well enough what you and the other dear "grils" are doing this morning—and of you "my eyes make pictures when they're shut."[2] I am so glad to think I have such sisters to love; and every day's separation endears you to me more and more. I see no other girls whom I think half so good and wise as you. Indeed my heart flows out to you all, forever and forever.

I am glad you have begun to take music lessons again. Has Anne resumed *her* music lessons?[3] Make the "beast" practice every day. I think music is her speciality. If you want any books, send to me for them. I have some seven or eight pieces of sheet music here, which I will send home by father when he returns—he wrote me that he would probably come to see me before long.

I have been to so many places, and had so many adventures, socially speaking, since I saw you, that I cannot begin to give you a strict account of those things. Mrs Carter took me to Mr J. W. Andrews,[4] where I attended the pleasantest sort of a party, and spent the whole evening in talking with Miss Lallie Swain.[5] She is so intelligent and sprightly, that we kept up a fire of badinage and repartee the whole time. It was peculiarly delightful to me, for she is one of those women who provoke you to say good things, and then seem to enjoy them so heartily. Do you remember her? I think you used to go to school together, but I don't recollect.—The same week of the party I have mentioned, I attended one at Col. Swains, where I enjoyed myself greatly likewise, flirting desperately with a very fast young lady, who as a great dancer of the "Lanceurs," I promenaded with her, and talked her dumb saying all manner of stupid things with the air of being very witty. I don't know, but if I didn't enchant the damsel, I bewildered her considerably. She is a Kate Jones kind of a girl.

The last pow-wow I was at, was one of the Esther Institute Receptions.[6] The "Lanceurs" were there my chief delight.

—Dear Vic, of course this nonesense is merely for your private eye. Don't even read it to the folks at home, and never breathe it to anybody else. But I needn't charge you.

Are you applying yourself to literature? I wish you would write something. Steal time, and make a little sketch to be printed in the Journal. I think your letters are so admirable, and if you could only have a chance to write, I am sure you would succeed.—O, I am so ambitious for every one of us!

Try to pacify Sam on the subject of my not writing to him. I am going to do so shortly. His "locals" are very good. But he must remember the sage criticism on painting in the "Vicar of Wakefield."[7]

I want father to bring me several things when he comes down—a razor and shaving-box—you have duplicates at home—those shirts mother is getting ready, and "Lazarillo de Tormas," with whatever other books he may think I'll want.[8]—I sent the sweet potatoes. The half bushel cost $1, and the expressage was 50 cts.—that he may charge to the man in partnership with him.—The "Sentinel" was "a large twelve-page paper" I noticed last week.[9] I see the Telegraph keeps barking now and then.[10] If I were father I would take no notice of it.

I wrote to grandmother and aunt Anne last week.

How is dear mother's health now? She did not seem well when I was last at home. Kiss her for me, as I would like to do this morning.

Give my best love to all. Has Aurelia forsaken her brother? Her sister Annie writes me that she was quite "gay" on the occasion of a certain sleghride, when she rejoiced in the company of one of the three Charles. Remember me to the good Ellen Holman,[11] and to whom else you like.

Affectionately
Will.

Do you ever hear from Ellen Smith? I have not answered her letter, that I received before I went home. If I had a pass on the Little Miami Road, I would like to go see her, but I can't pay $10 for the luxury.[12]

Does *somebody* write you ever?

1. Wordsworth, "The Idiot Boy": "The grass you almost hear it growing" (line 285).
2. Coleridge, "A Day-Dream": "My eyes make pictures, when they are shut" (line 1).
3. Annie was learning to play the melodeon, as Howells mentions in a letter to Aurelia and Annie, 21 February 1858 (MH).

4. Dr. John W. Andrews (b. 1805) first practiced medicine in Jefferson and later became a bank president there and in Columbus. His administration of the Lyne Starling estate suggests his close association with Starling Medical College. See *Ohio State Journal*, 23 March 1860.

5. Mary Llewellyn (Lallie or Lillie) Swayne (1840?–1913) was the daughter of Noah H. Swayne (1804–1884), associate justice of the U. S. Supreme Court (1862–1881). He is the "Col. Swain" mentioned later in this letter.

6. The Esther Institute, a private school, occupied a large building on Broad Street.

7. At this time Sam may have been writing local notices for the Ashtabula *Sentinel*. In Goldsmith's *The Vicar of Wakefield* (1776) George Primrose's cousin says that one of the rules for becoming a *cognoscento* in art is "always to observe that the picture might have been better if the painter had taken more pains" (chapter 20).

8. At this time Howells wanted to translate *Lazarillo de Tormes* (anonymous, 1553) because he admired the "simplicity of design" of the Spanish picaresque novel and considered it "one of the best forms for an American story." See *My Literary Passions*, pp. 142–44.

9. The Ashtabula *Sentinel*, 10 March 1859, consisted of twelve pages, and the editor announced that he expected to expand it to this size often, though not regularly. It is on the basis of this information that the date of this letter can be exactly established as 13 March.

10. The *Telegraph* was the rival of the *Sentinel*.

11. Neither "the three Charles" nor Ellen Holman, all presumably of Jefferson, have been identified.

12. Only one partial letter by Howells to Ellen Smith, of Hamilton, is extant; it is dated 3 April 1858 (MH). Her name appears again as one of the guests at a reception in Howells' honor given upon the occasion of his visit to Hamilton, 26 November 1899. See "Howells' Last Visit in 1899," Hamilton *Journal-Daily News*, 22 July 1963, p. 10.

18–24 April 1859, Columbus, to Victoria M. Howells

Journal for Vic.[1]

Monday. Columbus, April 18. A cold day, eminently disagreeable, that relented, before night, and smiled a sunset.—Went down to the depôt with four "fellows" to see-off *Comly*, who goes to New Orleans, to settle up an uncle's estate.[2] Comly, you know, is my present Jim Williams.[3] I was mighty sorry to see him go.—It seems to me I have done nothing but open exchanges, today. The mails were mercilessly heavy. Finished reading a pamphlet on The Claims of Swedenborg, and commenced to read his life.[4] Read a little German—Göthe. Wrote nothing. Called at Foster's, to learn if my Spanish books were not come—not.[5] Mem. To ask father to send me my large Spanish dictionary by express.—Forgot to mail for home, the letter I wrote yesterday, until about four, this afternoon.—10½ P.M. Have just returned from making a long call upon Mrs Cooke[6] with Mrs Smith and Miss Anthony.[7] Had a delightful evening. Everytime that I talk with Miss Anthony, my regard for her increases. She is so quiet, and kind and earnest. After a shower of Mrs

Carter she is as serene and pleasant as a rainwashed summer evening. I like women best, who are older than myself.—I got a letter a day or two since from Miss Ransom.[8] Good night, my dear sister. My heart kisses you.

Tuesday, 11 P.M. Just *inroomed* after attending a he-party at the governor's, given in honor of old Gid, I suppose.[9] The old gentleman sought me out, and shook hands very cordially. I was glad to see him, for he seemed to have that sentiment toward me. The evening passed very pleasantly—I taking possession of poor Herr Croissant, the editor of our new German "Republican," who cannot talk English.[10] He is a very pleasant man, and I had a long chat with him and gave my limited German vocabulary a thorough airing. Besides I talked to a dozen others in English.—Previous to going to the party, I called upon Miss Carter,[11] and had a very pleasant little time. She is a good and common-sensible girl, just now terribly determined upon "improving her mind."—Was much disappointed at not getting a letter from home. Feel so uncomfortable about the Oliver business.[12]—To-day worked harder, I think, than usual, and consequently feel better.—Am at peace with all the world, and the rest of mankind, tonight. Would not kick the editor of the Ashtabula Telegraph, even, if that blessed boon were offered me.[13] Good night.

Wednesday, 9½ P.M. Received a letter from father today. Wonder why I did not get one from the "grils?"—Not an eventful day at all. Took tea at Mrs Carter's, and talked aesthetics. Jones, the sculptor, there. Told some of his precious old yarns, which are so hard to listen to, after you have heard them a dozen times.

The weather has been beautiful, especially this afternoon. Took an abbreviated stroll, but did not much enjoy it, Comely missing. He and I used to do our walking together—after breakfast, a long saunter, just before supper, short walk; at midnight, extended and romantic ramble. Ah me! *Er ist fort! "Ich bin allein—ganz allein."*[14] Good night.

Thursday, 9 P.M. Last night, I had a regular turn of "hippo,"[15] being nervous I think from drinking coffee at supper. Nothing at all has happened to-day. It was very pleasant in the morning, and I took a long lonesome stroll out to the Idiot Asylum, where I saw the poor little creatures at play, and made myself sad with thinking of Henry.[16]— It has rained almost steadily since noon. Goodnight.

Friday. Why haven't the girls written to me?—A most cold and unfriendly day. Rain, and just now wind that shrieks like a wild thing in the towers and gables.—Commenced reading Goethe's Elective Affinities.[17]

Sunday.—Nothing of particular note occurred yesterday. Was miserably tired by night. After supper I intended to make some calls, but compromised the matter with myself by going to the office, where I had a long metaphysical conversation with a German friend, of whom I think you may expect to hear much in these pages.[18] Came to room, and read Wahlverwandschaften a little; and certain stories of chivalry a good deal. In bed by 10.—This morning, after a walk, I went to Catholic church (for Easter Sunday's sake) but could not get inside of the door more than a step or two, for the press. While there, I beheld *A Being*, with whom I instantly fell in love. I suppose I shall never see her again, and therefore I shall never wed. Went walking this afternoon. Weather fine, but coolish.

1. In a letter to Victoria, dated "Sunday" [24 April 1859] (MH), Howells writes of enclosing this journal, which "may one day be useful to my biographers."

2. James M. Comly (1832–1887) became editor and proprietor of the *Ohio State Journal* in 1865 and, after serving as minister to Hawaii (1877–1882), part owner of the Toledo *Journal*. See *Years of My Youth*, HE, pp. 195–97.

3. Jim Williams had been a boon companion in the *Sentinel* print shop; he boarded with the Howells family, and left, probably about 1856, to become a professor of modern languages in a Wisconsin college. He was probably the James E. Williams listed in official army records as having been killed in action near Baton Rouge, 4 March 1864. In *Years of My Youth*, HE, pp. 86–90, Howells refers to him as "J. W.", but the full name appears in the 1851 diary MS (located at MH).

4. *The Three Principal Objections Against the Claims of Emmanuel Swedenborg to Supernatural Communications Stated and Examined*, an anonymous 23-page pamphlet published by Otis Clapp, Boston, 1848.

5. Frank E. Foster and his father-in-law, Oran Follett (1798–1894), a former editor of the *Ohio State Journal*, founded the publishing firm of Follett, Foster & Co. in 1857. The firm ceased operating probably in 1865, after it had moved from Columbus to New York.

6. The wife of Henry D. Cooke (1825–1881), editor of the *Ohio State Journal* (1856–1861) and governor of the District of Columbia (1871–1873), who was later closely associated with his brother Jay Cooke, the financier.

7. Mrs. Smith was the wife of Dr. Samuel M. Smith (1816–1874), a founder of Starling Medical College and professor of theory and practice, who was Howells' own physician. Miss Anthony was Mrs. Smith's sister. In *Years of My Youth* Howells often mentions the family with affection; see, for example, HE, pp. 141–42.

8. Possibly Caroline L. Ransom (1838?–1910), a well-known portrait painter, who grew up near Jefferson.

9. Governor Chase's party was apparently given for Joshua R. Giddings.

10. The appearance of the first number of the "German Columbus Republican," edited by Philip Croissant, was noted in the *Ohio State Journal*, 18 April 1859; but the paper appears to have been short-lived.

11. Annie Carter was the daughter of Dr. Francis Carter and his wife Isabella.

12. In October 1854 Joseph A. Howells bought out James L. Oliver's interest in the Ashtabula *Sentinel*. Thomas Oliver, a Methodist clergyman, was for several years clerk of Jefferson township, his reelection being announced in the *Sentinel*, 7 April 1859. Whether either of these Olivers was the cause of Howells' discomfort remains speculative.

13. James Reed (b. 1819) became proprietor of the Ashtabula *Telegraph* in 1856.

14. German for "He is gone! 'I am alone—all alone.'"

15. Howells suffered much from hypochondria, especially during his Columbus years. See Cady, *Howells*, I, 24, 54–56.

16. Howells' younger brother Henry sustained an injury in a childhood accident that stopped his mental development.
17. The English title of *Die Wahlverwandtschaften* (1809).
18. The German friend was most likely the "Madame R." mentioned in the following letter.

25 APRIL AND 1 MAY 1859, COLUMBUS, TO VICTORIA M. HOWELLS

Journal for Vic.

Monday 25. The usual nothing occurred at the office. In the afternoon, I carried home to Madame R. a volume of Heine I had borrowed several months ago. I thought to be received with coolness and reproaches for not having come to see her for so long a time (she is the German lady at whose house I used to visit so much with Jones when I first came to Columbus,)[1] but instead of this, she treated me with the greatest cordiality, and complimented my German immensely.

In the evening, I called upon Miss Wing, a *Dickens*-girl, with whom I spent an hour in very pleasant talk.[2] I liked her, for her freedom and heartiness put me in mind of my dear sister. When I rose to go, she said "Don't go, Mr Howells,—I'm about to sing for you, though you haven't asked me." She is a glorious singer. I had heard her at Dr Smith's, when she sang "Excelsior" in a manner that made my heart ache. I ought to have remembered to ask her to sing, but I really didn't think. I excused this, and declared that I should be delighted to hear her. So she sat down, and sang "Morning, Noon and Night," "Here's a double health to thee, Tom Moore," (a beautiful thing that Dune was perpetually huming last spring when I was at Pittsburgh,) "Kathleen Mavourneen," and Schubart's "Seranade."[3] I was charmed, and exceedingly provoked when two young fellows came and interrupted us. Wasn't this a different way of spending an evening from that of Jefferson, where the girls seem so stiff and constrained, that a call is painful to them and everybody else?—It was then nine o'clock, so went and got a book which I had promised to Miss Carter, and carried it to her. Sat down and had an hour's chat—pleasant, of course—about books and people. The Misses Carter had been spending the evening at Baldwin's.[4] Mrs Carter came in, and the talk centering upon religions (she is a very devout Swedenborgian) she said she did hope that Mr Howells would never do anything bad to make her dislike him. Is it possible for a fellow with such friends, to be wicked?—Came home, and read "The Initials,"[5] till twelve: Sleep.

Sunday, May 1st. I have to-day, a whole week's work to bring up. The coming of dear Joe broke in upon the regularity of my habits, and I have neglected the diary until to-day. I enjoyed Joe's visit so much, but he seemed "kinder not to take no interest." Why I don't know, but I felt so dissatisfied and disappointed when he went away that if I had been a girl, I suppose I should have taken "a good cry."

The same evening that Joe came, after he had imbedded himself, I went to a party at Judge Swan's, where I had a very desolate time.[6] Fate consorted me with a very young lady, whose talk was of the thrilling and momentous occurrances of school life.[7] I wanted to spread myself and flirt a little, but it was impossible to do so under the circumstances. I said numbers of stupid things to numbers of people, and came away gnashing my teeth. Afterwards I learned from Mrs Dr Smith, that I ought to feel immensely flattered at being asked there, as no young gentlemen but those of the first-chop-est description were invited, and that the party was extremely aristocratic. I was presented to Mrs Parsons, who, I am told, affects the *bon*-est possible *ton*; but who was extremely gracious to me.[8]

Joe went home Thursday morning, and that evening, I called at Dr Smith's, and had a long and delightful chat with madame and with Miss Anthony, whom I regard with the deepest respect. I don't know,— everybody, even those who have been mentioned as entirely different, seem to me single hearted and sincere—perhaps because I am so myself, and I enjoy me in nearly all companies. Mrs S. is said to be a flatterer and deceitful, which I told her I had heard. She explained that when she liked people she let them know it, for it seemed to make them feel pleasant; but she was equally ready to exhibit her dislike. Not a bad defence.

Last night, I walked the twilight up, and was about lounging in at the College post, when I heard a flutter and twitter, and was aware that Mrs Carter was at her gate. She was going to call upon Miss Lellie Swain.[9] Would I go with her? I pleaded dusty boots, but she said, nobody would look at my boots, I was so agreeable—that the dress of stupid people was alone subjected to criticism. I knew that not so, but I went with her. Fortunately Miss L. was at home, and she shewed me some books on German literature that she had been reading, and our talk, fortunately for me, fell in that channel. She is extremely lively and *picturesque*, and so I enjoyed myself mightily, and Mrs Carter was obliged to say twice that she was sorry to hurry me away, before I consented to move.

I came to my room, and read "Wahlverwandtachaften," after which I made an unsuccessful attempt to write some poetry, and then went to bed.

The weather, to-day is indescribably glorious. Everything is so beautiful that my heart aches with a höchst angenehmer Schmerz.[10] There is no news. Dearest love to all. Will write during the week to father and mother.

Affectionately,
Will.

1. Madame R., whom Howells and Thomas D. Jones visited, has not been identified.
2. Miss Wing has not been identified; Howells apparently thought of her as resembling a character in one of Dickens' novels.
3. The songs are "Excelsior," by H. W. Longfellow, music by the Hutchinson family; perhaps three sonnets, "Morning," "Noon," and "Night," words and music by James Hook; "My Boat Is on the Shore" ["To Thomas Moore"] by Byron, music by H. R. Bishop; "Kathleen Marvourneen," by L. M. J. M. Crawford, music by F. W. M. Crouch; "Serenade," by Ludwig Rellstab, music by Franz Schubert. Dune Dean was the Pittsburgh cousin, to whom Howells probably wrote on 9 September 1857.
4. Probably William J. Baldwin (1822–1889), lawyer and Yale graduate, his wife Margaret Hoge Baldwin, and their only child Clara.
5. Baroness Jemina (Montgomery) von Tautphoeus, *The Initials* (1850), a novel about life in Bavaria.
6. Joseph Rockwell Swan (1802–1884) was justice of the Ohio Supreme Court (1855–1859) and chief justice (February–November 1859). See *Years of My Youth*, HE, pp. 147–48.
7. The young lady could conceivably have been Isabelle Moodie (1844–1900), the mother of the poet Robert Frost. Beginning in 1853 she lived with an uncle in Columbus, later taught school there, and recalled meeting Howells in the 1860s. See *Selected Letters of Robert Frost*, ed. L. Thompson (New York: Holt, Rinehart and Winston, 1964), p. 191. In a letter to his mother, 30 June 1861 (MH), Howells mentioned a Miss Moodie.
8. Perhaps the wife of Dr. Samuel Parsons, president of the Franklin Bank; but there were other important Parsons in Columbus.
9. See Howells to Victoria M. Howells, 13 March 1859, n. 5.
10. Heinrich Heine, *Reisebilder*, III, 18: "Vergnügen ist nichts als ein höchst angenehmer Schmerz" (*Werke und Briefe*, ed. H. Kaufmann [Berlin: Aufbau-Verlag, 1961–1964], III, 231). Translation: "Amusement is nothing other than a most agreeable pain."

16–22 MAY 1859, COLUMBUS, TO VICTORIA M. HOWELLS

Journal for Vic.

Monday, May 16. I saw Sam off this morning, about nine o'clock.[1] He intended to go to Hamilton, remain there one day and then on to New Albany. I was very sorry to part with the poor fellow. I wish to heaven I were someway situated, that we could both be together. It does seem hard that our family must be scattered; but the putting asunder *has* to come, sometime, I suppose. This afternoon, Reed[2] asked me what was my brother going to do? I said, go into a store; and then he asked, "Why doesn't he cultivate his newspaper propensities?" I mean that he shall. I have advised him as to a course of reading, and he is to write to me regularly every week. I will have him make his letters general, and occasionally print extracts from them. I don't believe any of us are intended for shop-keepers, and it may be that after a while I shall be in a position to take Sam into the newspaper business along with me. I dont regard the Journal as my finality.

It has rained this afternoon, and settled the stifling dust for a few hours again.—O, I wish that I were at home this evening. I know that it must be very lonesome with your three oldest brothers out of the house.—I would sally forth with you, this fragrant open hour before supper, and take a good slow saunter toward the old Judge's,[3] and tell you of all my plans of which you know, I have thousands. The robins would be singing in our maples, and on the Irish-house sycamores, as I hear them singing now, in the trees; we should smell the sweet smell of the growing leaves and grass, and the perfume of the earth, and see rising before us, in pensive stateliness, that grand old melancholy elm. As I write this, it seems to be the Me of a year ago, and the You of then, and we are really together. Ah me! if it were not for these pleasant delusions, with which we cheat pain and absence, and care, and toil—how could we live?

I hear the soft bells of the Catholic church ringing Six, and if I shut my eyes, they sing me back to my dear home. I am sitting, not in my lonesome room, here, but on our little stoop; and I hear you and talking together.[4] Aurelia is making a C of herself over a book. Mother has been sewing, but her hands and work have dropped into her lap, and she looks up thinking,—as she often does. Henry plays all over the yard. Father is just come in sight at Horkins's,[5] and John runs on before him, like an uncontrollable locomotive, announcing the arrival of the train, with piercing shrieks. Well, well:

Tuesday.

The record of to-day is not much—indeed, nothing but work; and to-night, for the first time in a long while, I have made no calls. Last night, I went with Miss Anthony to call upon Miss Sullivant, whose father is the eminent geologist, and one of "the Sullivant family."[6] I was pleased; and the call accomplished, returned to Dr. Smith's. Directly Ferguson (the droll of our company, "a fellow of infinite jest,") dropped in,[7] and after a while, Comely. We all went off up town together, had some supper at a restaurant, and then started on a stroll. It was half past one, by the time I returned to my room.

Thursday.

I am exceedingly uneasy and annoyed at not having received any letters from home, this week. I can't understand what it means. Is it very likely to be mere neglect; and I am sure if you only knew how much I counted upon hearing from home every week, you would not forget me again. I have not heard yet from Sam, though he promised to write to me from Hamilton. I suppose he is in New Albany by this time.

This morning I was awakened by Fullerton's exclamation of "Hello! whose bouquet is this?" He was standing near the slop-bucket, and directly picked up a card from it, inscribed to me. I got up and looked. There was a most beautiful bouquet most ignominiously soused in the dirty water. When it came, or how it got into that bucket I don't know. I can only account for it by supposing that it was brought while I was out last evening, and laid upon my washstand, which is near the door, and afterwards tumbled into the bucket. A little funny, wasn't it?—and provoking?—that so sentimental a gift should be presented in so unromantic a manner,—in a bucket! Horrid! However.

There has nothing happened to-day worth telling; and at any rate I am so much discouraged at not having heard from home, that I cant write. *Mem.* Have father bring down my *summer raglan* when he comes to the convention.

Thursday. Still no letter from home. What the deuce *can* it mean? I have not heard from Sam yet, either. I hope that if father attends the fire-eating at Cleveland,[8] and there is anything like a rescue of the prisoners attempted, he will keep on the Howells side of danger and responsibility.

This morning, in accordance, with permission given me while I was at home, I invited Comly to pay you a visit at the time I do in June. He promised to do so, conditionally, and I think you may expect him.

This afternoon, I visited the Catholic Orphan's Home.[9] I think you would have been greatly interested, as I was, in Sister Felicitas, who has charge of it. She is of noble birth, and bred a protestant, but was converted to Catholicism, became a nun, and now, like another Evangeline, devotes her life to doing good.

Sunday. Took breakfast this morning with Reed, and after that went to Catholic Church with Ferguson. It was very crowded, and we came away in about ten minutes. Then we took Tennyson's poems, and went to the woods and read. Last evening, I supped at Dr. Smith's. We had strawberries and a pleasant time. I have given you all the news there is. I have not heard from Sam yet. Got father's letter on Friday. To-day, two weeks, I hope to be at home.

Dear love to all.

---

1. Howells had tried to obtain a place for his brother Sam as a book agent for Follett, Foster & Co., and as a reporter for the Sandusky *Register*. See Howells to Victoria M. Howells, 3 July 1859 (MH).

2. Samuel R. Reed, an editor on the staff of the *Ohio State Journal*.

3. Probably Benjamin F. Wade (1800–1878), U. S. senator (1851–1869), with whom Howells read law for a month in May 1855. See *Years of My Youth*, HE, pp. 93–94.

4. Since the copy-text used is a typed transcription of the lost holograph, it is not known whether Howells or the original typist left the blank space.

5. The copyist of the lost holograph must have misread "Hoskins." Noah Hoskins (b. 1817) served frequently as a trustee of Jefferson between 1847 and 1860.

6. Miss Sullivant was the daughter of the foremost American bryologist, William Starling Sullivant (1803–1873), author of *Icones Muscorum* (1864).

7. [Thomas?] Ferguson was the "blithe young Irish bank clerk," who is described in the manuscript of *Years of My Youth*, HE, p. 160 and Emendations, 160.25–27. The quotation in parenthesis is from *Hamlet*, V, i, 203–4.

8. A large meeting in Cleveland, held to protest the arrests of persons who had violated the Fugitive Slave Act, was reported in the *Ohio State Journal*, 26 May 1859. W. C. Howells had officiated at a similar meeting in Jefferson. See *Ashtabula Sentinel*, 12 May 1859.

9. Howells described his visit in the *Ohio State Journal*, 21 May 1859, under the heading "Local Affairs."

24 MAY 1859, COLUMBUS, TO MARY D. HOWELLS

Columbus, May 24, 1859.

My dear mother—

I got Sissy's[1] letter this, Tuesday, morning, and now I write this, in my leisure hour, just before dinner. I would have written promptly in reply to all your letters, but I was keeping a journal for Vic, and tho't that would suffice for the whole family. You mustn't think me neglectful, mother? It is of you I think most, whoever I write to. Last night I took a walk with Comly, and told him how I knew you were sitting upon our little front porch, and counting up the days until I should be with you. I tell you, it seems a long time since I saw you, and I can hardly wait, now, that the time of meeting again is so near.—I have asked Comly to go home with me, and he has conditionally promised to do so. He is a nice fellow, and my "dearest friend." You know you told me to invite him. I think it will be pleasant for you all to know him.

I have heard nothing from Sam yet, though he promised to write to me from Hamilton. I can't imagine what is the reason.—When he was here, he told me that some of you, Joe particularly, thought I ought to send money home occasionally, help pay for the house, etc. Now, mother, I had better have left off this explanation until I saw you, but the suspicion that you tho't me perhaps neglectful of my duty, has been rankling ever since Sam told me this. I have never failed to send you money whenever you asked for it; and I have certainly wanted to do everything for you. But you know what a slender salary mine is; and I have to meet many expenses here that you don't know of. I live more frugally than any other young fellow of my acquaintance, and I aim to economise all the time, but it is a continual struggle with me to save anything. I must dress well—I can't go about the city streets looking as shabbily as Joe does at home. My boarding must be promptly paid; then

I buy a book occasionally—and so the money goes. By dint of hard scratching I have saved about thirty dollars, and that I will give you when I come home. The magazine for which I wrote in Cincinnati owes me $15, which I suppose I'll never get.[2] I must soon buy new clothes— boots, socks, shirts, handkerchiefs, everything. Clothes cost more here than in the country. When I come home, I will tell you all about my affairs, and business matters which I would rather not write about. But a little more than a week now, and I shall see you. Till then goodbye, with dear love to all.

>Affectionately
>Your son
>Will.

1. "Sissy" is Victoria. Howells refers to her by some variation of this nickname in letters of 13 November 1859, 12 September 1860, and elsewhere.

2. Howells received $6 from the *Odd-Fellows' Casket* for "Not a Love Story." The $15 may have been for "A Summer Sunday in a Country Village," and "A Perfect Goose," both in the April number; and for "Romance of the Crossing," in the May number.

14 AUGUST 1859, COLUMBUS, TO JOSEPH A. HOWELLS

>Columbus, Aug. 14, 1859.

Dear Joe—

As the lady justly remarks in the play, "How swiftly the time flies!"[1] It is mid-August, and the summer is nearly wasted away. I have been sitting at my window, (having lately risen from a delightful post-prandial nap,) and looking out on the sweep of land-and-chimney-scape it commands. All afternoon the sun has been bland and warm, and the summer wind has borne innumerable thistle down through the soft light. In the vacant lot on the east of the college, the thistles grow luxuriantly, and the place is forever haunted by twittering yellow birds—do you mind them, in the old "Dayton Lane?"[2] And so the autumn comes, and fills my heart as it always does with a passionate pain that is sweeter in its sourness than pleasure—in other words, a psychological lemonade.

> "Tears, idle tears, I know not what they mean,
> Tears from the depth of some divine despair,
> Rise in the heart and gather to the eyes,
> When looking on the happy autumn fields,
> And thinking of the days that are no more."[3]

Do you remember one August afternoon, near the close of a grass-hopper-eaten summer, when you and I rode to Rock Creek,[4] and I repeated these lines?—I don't know why, but I think of many things that happened to you and me; and I am happy in believing that as we have grown to be men, we have not grown apart. As boys, and members of the great evil brotherhood of boys, we had many fights and quarrels; the first are now become impossible, and the latter, I hope we have left behind us forever. It seems a foolish superfluity to write this, but I have never yet told my brother in words how dear he was to me.

I feel particularly light hearted, to-day. For two months, my familiar devil, Hypochondria, had tormented me, so that I sometimes thought that death would be a relief. Yesterday, I could bear it no longer, and went Dr Smith, telling him my trouble, and receiving for answer that there was nothing the matter with me.[5]—You may mention this to father.

I hope that you and father will keep me posted in regard to politics. Remember that my anxiety is just as lively as your own. I notice by the Telegraph that Krum declines to be a candidate for the Board of Equalization.[6] How will that affect matters?

If you send a package of quoins here, of course they will be noticed. I will attend to it myself.

I believe there is nothing more to write. Only take that small *Vevie*,[7] and kiss him on both eyes, after his uncle's favorite method. My love to Eliza, and all at home. Tell Vic I will write to her during the week.

Affectionately
Will.
"Unc Vevie."

1. The play has not been identified.
2. "Dayton Lane" may be a reference to the road leading from the mill near Xenia to Dayton, the memory of which is reflected in *New Leaf Mills* (1913).
3 Tennyson, *The Princess, A Medley*, lines 1–5 See *Years of My Youth*, HE, pp. 85–86.
4. Rock Creek is about five miles southwest of Jefferson.
5. See *Years of My Youth*, HE, p. 144.
6. See Ashtabula *Sentinel*, 18 August 1859. Abel Krum was, however, elected to the Ohio House of Representatives (1860–1863), having defeated W. C. Howells for the county nomination. See *Sentinel*, 1 September 1859.
7. The nickname for William Dean Howells II. Later it was used for Anne Howells Fréchette's daughter, Marie Marguerite.

10 SEPTEMBER 1859, COLUMBUS, TO JOHN J. PIATT

Columbus, September 10th, 1859

Dear Piatt—

Getting a Louisville Journal yesterday containing a poem of yours, made me lament again that I could not see you.[1] So many things constantly happen to one, you know so many curious revelations of self are made to one—that I, feeling my growth, want to talk of these things to some one. They bore most people, I think, but I believe you could stand it; if I listened patiently in turn. The trouble is—I have plenty of acquaintance, and friends, who would do much—I can't tell you what the trouble is—only I wish you and I were together. Don't you think the thing could be brought about, by—fasting and prayer, say? Try. You fast and I'll "chop up the whiners," a piece of blasphemy learnt out of "Pelham."[2]

I have been reading a vast deal lately—"Idyls of the King" "Montaigne" "Erinnerungen von Heine"—a book that makes me cry almost; all Thackeray's lesser works, and "Klosterheim" by de Quincey; and many books to please the fair. One has lent me "Adam Bede," with request to mark passages that I thought re-markable.[3] And I never mark books!—you know.—I think it impertinent, dont you? What can I do? Withal, I have scribbled much; and last month it happened to me, to receive notice from the *Atlantic*, that a poem of mine was accepted by that great periodical, "Andenken" hight—to appear when there is room;—I read the rhymes to you, when you were here last; and if you should come again, I would cheerfully repeat the lection. If you can't come, oblige me by reading them in the Atlantic.[4]

—For many months before Heine's death, hardly any of his Parisian friends came to see him. At last one was announced. "Ah!" said the moribund "he was always original!" At another time he commanded his wife to marry as soon as he was dead—that one man might truly lament him. Prostrated, he wished he could walk on crutches. Where would he go? To church—if he could walk without them, he would go upon the boulevard. He described a crack-brain as "quite a madman with lucid intervals when he was only stupid."—"You will find me dull this morning. Blank and I have had a friendly interchange of ideas." Et cetera. All garnered for you out of the "Erinnerungen" and no extra charge.[5]

I have copied your "Night Train," which quite carried me off. Write soon to

yours, ever,
Wm. D Howells.

How is that "Tigerrizzerin" of your head?[6] I have been sick abed.

---

1. Possibly "The Night Train," mentioned later in this letter. In "News and Humor of the Mails," *Ohio State Journal*, 12 September 1859, Howells reprinted the poem with a complimentary introduction.

2. In Edward George Earle Bulwer-Lytton, *Pelham, or The Adventures of a Gentleman* (1828), the underworld expression, "to chop up the whiners," is explained as meaning "to say prayers" (chapter 82).

3. Tennyson, *Idylls of the King* (1859); it is unclear whether "Montaigne" refers to the *Essays* or to a book about the author; Alfred Meissner, *Heinrich Heine: Erinnerungen* (1856); Thomas DeQuincey, *Klosterheim* (1832); George Eliot, *Adam Bede* (1859).

4. The editors accepted the poem in a form letter, 25 July 1859 (MH); "Andenken" appeared in the *Atlantic*, January 1860. Mildred Howells explains that "It was probably this poem that, as Lowell told Howells years after, was held for some time to make sure it was not a translation from Heine...." See *Life in Letters*, I, 24; also *Literary Friends and Acquaintance*, HE, p. 27.

5. Howells' quotations are from Meissner, *Heine*, pp. 241, 167, 155, and 125.

6. Howells' reference has not been identified.

19 SEPTEMBER 1859, COLUMBUS, TO JOHN J. PIATT

Columbus, Sept. 19, 1859.

My dear Piatt—

Excuse the shabbiness of this paper and the conveniency of pencil. You know—and if you don't, it is time you learned—that I am lazy.

I have a new sensation. I have Uhland—*der süßte der deutschen Dichtern!*[1] I am boring everybody to death about him, and I must mention him to you. I was afraid, when I had finished Heine, that "now the wine of life was drawn," but I was mistaken. Uhland pleases me quite as well—perhaps better. He is purer, and dreamier. You of course have read him Longfellow-ed;[2] but the honey of his poetry has not the genuine taste, even when strained through the silver net of *our* poet's thought.—I really don't know what I shall do! If I go on admiring Uhland at this rate, and swelling with unexpressed sentiments, I am afraid I shall *burst*.

Here is something, I wrote the other evening. It is not for publication, but for you to laugh at, if you find it sufficiently unjust.

The Poet's Friends.

The Robin sings in the elm—
The Cattle stand beneath,
Sedate and grave with great brown eyes,
And fragrant meadow-breath.

They listen to the flattered bird,—
The wise looking, stupid things!
And they never understand a word
Of all the Robin sings![3]

What do you think?, "Strictly private and confidential."

I think you are right about Coates Kinney;[4] there is but *one* poet in the west, and the first letter of his name is Piatt.—While I am on the subject of *you*—I had a talk with Foster the other day. I am going to get him up a holyday book—Selections from Percy's Reliques, with an essay on ballad poetry. He will print the book in beautiful style—green and gold[5]—and will issue your poems uniform with it, if you feel like publishing. I think it would pay you.—You are known and popular throughout the west. You have friends at Cincinnati, Louisville, and Columbus—and I would spread myself on a review of you for the "Saturday Press." (They published some notices of Aldrich I made,—the first thing under their editorial head.)[6] Or you and I might make up a book of prose sketches and sleep together under the same covers.[7]

Write about it.

The note I got from the *Atlantic* was printed, and signed "The Editors."

I suppose we shall all be put in Mr Coggeshall's book. A prodigious man, with a fine faculty for feeding the public on sawdust.[8]

Now I am ashamed to write you that your "Ada" was printed in our paper that contained Lincoln's speech and every copy was sold before I could send any to you.[9] I will have it published in the weekly, and mail you copies. Thank you for remembering the *Journal*. Several persons have already spoken in compliment of "Ada." *Who* is it? *Any*one?

Yours ever
Will D Howells.

P. S. Where is she? *Any*where?

1. *Gedichte*, by Johann Ludwig Uhland, a fourth edition of which was published in Stuttgart and Augsburg in 1856. Howells' German sentence is incorrect; it should read: "der süßeste der deutschen Dichter" ("the sweetest of all German poets").

2. Longfellow's *Hyperion* (1839; reissued by the Riverside Press, 1857) contains translations of two poems by Uhland: "The Castle by the Sea" ("Das Schloss am Meere") and "The Black Knight" ("Der Schwarze Ritter").

3. "The Poet's Friends," *Atlantic*, February 1860.

4. Coates Kinney (1826–1904), then living in Cincinnati, was the author of *Ke-u-ka & Other Poems* (1855). Howells later corresponded with him and wrote about him in the "Editor's Study," *Harper's Monthly*, May and September 1888.

5. Follett, Foster & Co. never published the projected book.

6. Review of Thomas Bailey Aldrich, *Ballad of Babie Bell and Other Poems*: "A Book Read Yesterday," *Saturday Press*, 30 July 1859.

7. The coauthored "prose sketches" became *Poems of Two Friends*.

8. Coggeshall's *The Poets and Poetry of the West* (1860) contains six poems by Howells and seven by Piatt.

9. "Ada" appeared in the *Ohio State Journal*, 17 September 1859, with a complimentary introduction.

22 SEPTEMBER 1859, COLUMBUS, TO JOHN J. PIATT

Columbus, Sept. 22, 1859

Now there! There is absolutely nothing to hinder me from telling you that I think we had much better put off laying anything to Foster, (except that you are in a Barkis-ean state of willin'ness)[1] until you come to Columbus in the flesh. There are reasons why. I am a deuced bad hand at making arrangements for myself, and I am afraid I should only blunder for you. Moreover, when you are here, we can look your poems over together; and I constituting myself an awful judge of what you propose to print, could be a sort of pre-public to you.[2] There, too, we might decide about publishing our verses together. I am dreadfully beset with the temptation of having you to come and go upon in a first book. All this by way of suggestion. Remember that your friendship can ask no service of me which I will not willing perform.—I thank you very much for your kind expressions about me. It does me good to have such things said, even if one's own heart contradicts them. Come to Columbus whether the Dunce writes dis-or-encouragingly.[3]

Business, however, is base. Let us talk about Uhland. It happens that I have read all the poems you referred to; and I have un-Germaned "The Dream" as follows.[4] I suppose my translation differs somewhat from that you read—it is more literal I think:

> "In the beautiful garden wandered
>   Two lovers, hand in hand—
> Two souls all sick and languid:
>   They paused in that Flower land.
>
> They kissed each other in anguish,
>   Both lip and cheek, in pain—
> They cling in fast embraces,—
>   They were whole and young again.
>
> Two bells rang loud and clearly,—
>   The dream was broken that hour:
> She lay in her cell in the cloister—
>   He far in his prison tower.

I enclose you, also, the rough draught of a translation made for a lady friend. It is a poem which I don't think has been *overset* before. Heine quotes it in his Romantische Schule, and relates that he used to declaim it in his callow days.[5] Isn't it exquisitely tender and beautiful? I have several things of my own, I would like to show you, if you were here "already".—Those confounded Atlantic people haven't printed my verses in their October number.[6] O, if they knew how agonizing it is to wait!

There is nothing else—only a little more pigtail—Come, come!

Ever yours,
Will. D. Howells

1. An allusion to Barkis in Dickens, *David Copperfield* (1850).
2. Apparently the coauthored prose sketches (see Howells to Piatt, 19 September 1859) were still in mind, along with a volume of Piatt's own poetry; but the idea of a joint volume of poetry emerges in the sentences that follow.
3. In context, the "Dunce" is Frank E. Foster, the publisher.
4. Howells had earlier published a poem of this title in the *Ohio Farmer*, 18 September 1858. Though "Der Traum" appears in Uhland's collected poetry, it is now generally attributed to Heine. See *Werke und Briefe*, ed. H. Kaufmann (Berlin: Aufbau Verlag, 1961–1964), X, 180.
5. Uhland, "Der Schäfer."
6. "Andenken," *Atlantic*, January 1860.

5 OCTOBER 1859, COLUMBUS, TO JOHN J. PIATT

Columbus, Oct. 5, 1859.

My dear Piatt—

The little things you sent me are *very* pretty—"Living and Dead," and "In Autumn" are *wunderschön*. The latter I am going to print, *te volente* or not.[1] Indeed you are a poetical brick of the very first burning. By the way, here is something of my own—a mere conceit, that I thought nice when it came into my head first.

"From dainty rose-bud lips in pout,
Lo kiss the perfect flower out."

You see I insist upon making two syllables of "flower," in spite of you. Why *did* you criticise my rough translation at all? You know I told you it was the first draft merely. Remember the saw, of which the teeth never grow dull.—The other day, looking over the Journals, I came upon a stanza I had quoted from a poem of yours, in which occurred the lines:

"They have left the *ghosts of their silence*
Walking in my brain."[2]

The verses are beautiful, but it made me shudder to read them; for I had just written, a week or two before, the following, with which I was greatly in humor:

"In the wainscot, ticks the Deathwatch,
Chirps the Cricket in the floor,
In the distance dogs are barking,
Feet go by outside my door.

"From her window's honeysuckle,
Stealing in upon the gloom,
Spice and sweets embalm the Silence
Dead within the lonesome room.

> "And the *ghost of that dead Silence,*
> Haunts me ever, thin and chill,
> In the pauses of the Deathwatch,
> When the Cricket's cry is still."[3]

Isn't there a fearful similarity of phantoms here? And can there be any doubt that I stole your ghost? Believe me, that I carried it away in the mouth of my sack, as innocently as any Benjamin. Take it again, O Joseph.[4] But look you! Don't you attempt to claim the embalming process. Keep your *fresh* silence ghost; but remember that the pickled article is mine. Yours will soon spoil; mine wont.

I take it very kindly of you to damn our printers so effectually. If you have got any more indignation on hand at the same price, you may let me have the whole lot. For my part, I have become so used to having my best intentions stabbd to death, that I rather enjoy the slaughter. For you, however, I am sorry.[5] What would you? Our forman passes my expostulations by as the idle wind, which he regards not.[6]

I suppose you do not see my occasionalities in the Saturday Press?[7] I do not observe a diseased eagerness on the part of editors to copy them. Ah, me!

The John Smith of your affectionate inquiry is a spectacled person, who abides chiefly in the State Library, and as a contributor, has the gift of continuance in a remarkable degree. Was there really anything in "Lines of Life"?[8] I gave it an editorial, not a poetical perusal.

I have commenced to take lessons in German composition, of a professor who diets on onions and beer, and smells accordingly.[9]

It is really no dream that you are to publish, for I had a waking conversation with your publisher about you this morning. (Our Publisher! Think, O dear Heaven!) Can't you see me before three weeks? My "suffering is intolerable."

Have you ever read a translation of Uhland's "Love of the Singers."? Beautifully sad it is.[10]—Heine's old mother is dead at Hamburgh.[11] Do you remember—

> "Denk ich an Deutschland in der Nacht"?[12]

Your budget of poetry came safely to hand, and was eagerly read. Wouldn't it be a good plan for you to print something at the east?—say in the N. Y. Post, the National Era, and Boston Courier, the Century, etc. When "the book come out" the editors would be sure to mention you as a contributor.

There is nothing more for me to write except that I am

Ever Yours
Will. D. Howells.

1. It appeared under the new title, "In the Orchard," as part of "News and Humor of the Mails," *Ohio State Journal*, 10 October 1859.

2. From "Ghosts." reprinted in *Poems of Two Friends*; the quotation in the *Ohio State Journal* has not been located.

3. Part 3 of "Pleasure-Pain," *Atlantic*, April 1860, contains these lines slightly changed; but in *Poems* (1873) they were omitted.

4. Howells refers to the story of Joseph's placing a silver cup in Benjamin's sack (Gen. 44).

5. Since *Poems of Two Friends* was to be published in less than three months, Howells may refer to its typesetting, though a later paragraph in this letter suggests the book had not yet reached that stage.

6. Shakespeare, *Julius Caesar*, IV, iii, 68–69: "... they [your threats] pass me by as the idle wind, / Which I respect not."

7. In 1859 Howells contributed nine "occasionalities" to the *Saturday Press*.

8. John Smith, "Lines of Life," *Ohio State Journal*, 26 September 1859.

9. The German professor remains unidentified. It has been suggested that he is the prototype of Lindau in *A Hazard of New Fortunes*. See R. and C. Kirk, *Journal of Rutgers University Library* 4 (1941), 39; but see also Howells' comments in *Years of My Youth*, HE, p. 117.

10. Uhland's "Sängerliebe" is a cycle of five poems.

11. Howells reported the death of Betty Heine (1770–1859) in "News and Humor of the Mails," *Ohio State Journal*, 3 October 1859.

12. "I think of Germany in the night" is the first line of Heine's "Nachtgedanken," a poem printed in Meissner's *Erinnerungen*, pp. 157–59, which Howells had been reading.

26 October 1859, Columbus, to William C. Howells

Columbus, Oct. 26, 1859.

My dear father—

I have just spoken to Mr Cooke about the Senate Clerkship; and he tells me that so far he has heard of no applications for that post. Many apply for searg. at arms-ships, and one man from Newark wants an assistant clerkship. The field seems to be open, and you know what to do. Cooke thinks the best plan would be to get the W. R. Senators pledged, as there might be some Corwin prejudice against you. Parish, of Sandusky City is an old Freesoiler.[1] I will make inquiries from time to time in regard to this matter, and write you. Meanwhile, you'd better pitch in at once.—I got Sam's and Vic's letter this morning. I am sorry that I can't help you monywise. There is nearly $100 coming to me, of which I can't get a cent.[2] O dear!—Foster will get out my poems in about a month.[3] I don't suppose I shall make anything out of them.—I am heartsick with waiting and disappointment. Dear heaven! the way is *so* rough and hard.—The "Atlantic" has not published my poem yet.[4] I don't know what to think. I'm afraid it wont at all.[5]—Tell dear mother I'll write to her soon, and I'll go home as soon as I can raise the money to do so. Good bye.

                                Your affectionate son,
                                Will.

    1. Unable to secure the clerkship in 1860, W. C. Howells was nominated for official reporter of the Ohio House of Representatives. See *Ohio State Journal*, 7 January 1860. Thomas Corwin (1794–1865), formerly U. S. senator (1845–1850) from Ohio, served in the U. S. House of Representatives (1859–1861). Francis D. Parish (1796–1886), lawyer, abolitionist, and farmer, was state senator from Erie County (1860–1862). Both were from the Western Reserve, referred to by Howells as "W. R."
    2. Howells had written to his father on 7 August 1859 (MH) that he thought the *Ohio State Journal* was "on its final leg," for Cooke had no money to meet the compositors' bills or to pay Howells' weekly salary of $10.
    3. *Poems of Two Friends* appeared about 23 December 1859, the date of the first printed notice.
    4. Howells was still waiting for the appearance of "Andenken."
    5. In a letter to Victoria, 5 October 1859 (MH), Howells had expressed a similarly mixed mood of despondency and hope about his future: "I am working very hard—reading, studying, and scribbling constantly—aside from the drudgery I perform on the Journal.... O, it's such a long way up! But I have my eye on the temple that 'shines afar,' and I will fall uphill, if I must succumb."

6 NOVEMBER 1859, COLUMBUS, TO WILLIAM C. HOWELLS

                                Columbus, Nov. 6, 1859.

Dear father—

I had a talk with Russell[1] about your Clerkship, and he thinks you can get it without any great trouble. He did not make any suggestions of value—that is, beyond what you are already doing. Your opposition to Corwin and your extreme antislavery views will not injure you.[2] He said that if you got a few Senators who would go for nobody but you, the case was pretty safe, but you know that, already.

My life drags on here, in the accustomed way, and there is little to tell you. Old John Brown is the prevailing thought and talk.[3] Everybody—nearly—deprecates, while he sympathises.

I send you to hand to young John Brown a copy of Wendell Phillips' glorious lecture.[4] Mr Reed and I desire to be remembered to him in the heartiest sympathy.—He comes of a noble stock. If I were not your son, I would desire to be Old John Brown's—God bless him!

I did hope to see something violent in the Sentinel on the subject of Harper's Ferry. I trust that old Gid stands firm. There was something in his speech, I didn't like; and I was glad when a Boston man in a lecture hit him for it. He had said: "The history of this event will occupy but a brief page in the history of country."[5] "If this be true," said Thoreau (he is author of Walden, by the way,) "how long will be the paragraph that records the history of the Republican party?"[6]—Brown has become an idea—a thousand times purer and better and loftier than the Republican idea, which I'm afraid is not an idea at all.[7]

The weather here, is beautiful—genuine Indian Summer, days of dream, that lose themselves in delicious nights.

I don't know what to write. I think Brown all the time. Give my dear love to all at home. I don't know how long it will be till I see you.

Good night, with love.
Will.

Bad-breath Hutchins (Uriah) of Warren will be a candidate for the Senate Clerkship.[8]

1. Addison Peale Russell (1826–1912), Ohio secretary of state (1857–1861) and financial agent for Ohio in New York City (1862–1868), probably helped Howells secure the position on the *Ohio State Journal*. See *Years of My Youth*, HE, pp. 187–88.
2. The senior Howells' opposition probably resulted from Corwin's milder antislavery position.
3. John Brown (1800–1859), the abolitionist, had taken possession of the U. S. arsenal at Harper's Ferry, Virginia, on 16 October 1859.
4. "Harper's Ferry," by Wendell Phillips, was first delivered on 1 November 1859.
5. The speech by Joshua R. Giddings, the former congressman, appeared in the Ashtabula *Sentinel*, 10 November 1859.
6. See *The Writings of Henry David Thoreau* (Boston: Houghton Mifflin, 1906), XII, 439.
7. The change in Howells' view of Brown from that expressed in his letter to his father, 20 October 1859 (copy at MH), is complete: "I suppose you are all dredfully [sic] stirred up about the Harper's Ferry business. Reed and I are getting off any amount of [writing?] on the subject. In some respects, it is the most absurd and laughable event of the age; but I'm sorry for poor crazy Brown." The lead editorials in the *Ohio State Journal*, 19 and 20 October 1859, are not sympathetic to Brown; however, they cannot with certainty be attributed to Howells. "Another Invasion," *Ohio State Journal*, 22 October 1859, is critical of the Virginians' treatment of Edmund B. Babb of the Cincinnati *Gazette*. But by 3 November 1859 the lead editorial had become thoroughly pro-Brown. W. C. Howells' immediate response to his son's suggestion for "something violent in the *Sentinel*" was a balanced editorial, "John Brown," 10 November 1859. But soon his attitude toward Brown became more favorable. See *Sentinel*, 1 December (a special John Brown issue) and 8 December 1859; also Cady, *Howells*, I, 43.
8. Uriah H. Hutchins, brother of John Hutchins (1812–1891) the congressman (1859–1863), was a lawyer and mayor of Warren and later a clerk in the Patent Office.

13 NOVEMBER 1859, COLUMBUS, TO ANNE T. AND AURELIA H. HOWELLS

Columbus Nov. 13, 1859.

My dear sisters Annie and Lelie[1]—

I owe you both letters and apologies. I'll write the first, and you can excuse the last.

We are in the lap of winter this morning, and a very cold and slippery lap the old gent has. After rainy buckets and hogsheads full continually yesterday, the weather changed its mind suddenly last night, and snowed. Which I suppose is just as it happened with you.

I am glad that you girls are so warlike. Remember what Mr Wendell Phillips says—"Insurrection is the lesson of the hour." (By the way, have you both read Phillips' speech?)[2] Insurrect against somebody—invade the pig or Henry, if you can't do better. Be treasonable. Be virtuous and you'll be happy.—I feel dreadfully pugnacious. I think if I could find a very small proslavery orphan boy, I would beat him. Here's to old John Brown, and many returns of the same! Who deniges it, Betsy Prig?[3] Who deniges it?—I read Annie's letter to Mr Reed, who enjoyed it much, and laughed heartily, at my brave little sister's valor; then I read it to Mr Ruess—our German editor, who said I was gome of a refolutionary vamily; and last night I regaled Dr Smith's family with the much perused epistle.—Mr Ruess has been teaching his children the stories of Schiller, the good poet of Freedom, of Robert Blum, the martyr to liberty, and of our glorious old John Brown. He says "My little girl, ven I deach dem do her—she *veeped.*"[4] Ruess is an old revolutionist—and carries about with him in a small pocket in his left leg, a little leaden present, the soldiers of the king of Prussia gave him, one fine day, when he stood behind the barricades in Berlin.

You may count certainly upon seeing me Thanksgiving Day, and then I'll tell you all the things it's such a bore to write. I'm preparing a nice surprise for you *gril's*—something you don't think of at all. You'll be delighted.—How are all the detested *beasts* in Jeff, anyway? Has anybody sassed you lately? Just wait till I'm there, and I'll put them to death.—How does Henry get on—and Vevie, and Dodda? Tell Sam, Mr Hurd was inquiring about him yesterday. I hope the poor fellow is getting better. Is the beloved Georgius with you still?[5] Cherish him girls, and be kind to him. You dont know what a treasure you've got. Have you heard from Sissie?

Dear love to all. Write soon. No more at present from your loving brother,

Will.

1. Lelie was Howells' nickname for Aurelia.
2. See Howells to W. C. Howells, 6 November 1859, n. 4.
3. Betsy Prig is a character in Dickens' *Martin Chuzzlewit* (1844).
4. Herman Ruess was editor of the short-lived *Ohio Republican Press*, begun in 1858. Robert Blum (1807–1848) was a German journalist who was executed in the 1848 revolution. See *Years of My Youth*, HE, p. 164; and *Ohio State Journal*, 10 November 1859, which contains an article on Blum, comparing him twice to John Brown.

5. Dodda was Joseph A. Howells; Hurd was probably William T. Hurd, an assistant clerk in the state auditor's department, who may have been trying to get Sam a job there; Georgius was presumably a household pet or servant.

31 JANUARY 1860, COLUMBUS, TO WILLIAM H. SMITH

Columbus, Jan. 31, 1860—

My dear Smith[1]—

I am sorry I did not get to see you this morning, but I suppose I can do the business on hand, epistolarily; so I enclose to you a review, from the New York Saturday Press, of the "Poems of Two Friends," in which you will see I am very flatteringly spoken of.[2]

Some extended notice of the book ought, in decency, to have appeared first in a western journal, and I need not conceal from you the expectation I cherished, (from my acquaintance with its editors, and former connection with the paper,) that it should receive consideration at the hands of the Gazette. As you know, it has not, and it is disgustingly probable that every copy sent to your city, will rot upon the booksellers' shelves. I write all this to you, without the least fear of misconstruction, for you know me. I am the more gratified at the notice of the *Press*, because of the perfectly independent-and-don't-care character of that paper, which is not in the habit of reviewing books at all. While, however, I have nothing to urge against what the Press says of me, I don't think its estimate of J. J. Piatt is at all just; and I would be sorry if the article re-appeared without some protest to that effect. A remark that the book is on sale at all your bookstores would be useful to it, in connection with this review. It is not properly my business to make this request of you, but you are my friend, and so I thought I would not leave it to my publishers. If you don't use the enclosed, please return it to me, for it is the only copy I have.

Regards to madame and the little one.

Yours ever
Will.

1. William Henry Smith (1833–1896), formerly editor of the *Odd-Fellows' Casket*, was on the editorial staff of the Cincinnati *Gazette*. He was secretary of state of Ohio (1864–1866) and became general manager of the Western and New York Associated Press after their merger in 1882.

2. Henry Clapp (1814–1875), founder and editor of the *Saturday Press* (1858–1860, 1865–1866), wrote the review (28 January 1860), which disparages Piatt but contains the following comments on Howells: "Mr. Howells is a man of genius.... His genius is not, indeed, of the highest order, but it is genius, nevertheless.... A striking indication of genius in this poet, is the intense compression of his style. In

his better poems there is no laborious detail—nothing of the agony of inefficient art." See also Cady, *Howells*, I, 78, and *Literary Friends and Acquaintance*, HE, pp. 62–66.

7 FEBRUARY 1860, COLUMBUS, TO WILLIAM H. SMITH

Columbus, Feb'y 7, 1860

My dear Smith—

I am sorry to have been indirectly the author of any unpleasantness in the Gazette office; and particularly regret to have agitated the bosom of Mr Perry.[1] It is of course a mystery to me how he could have misrepresented me to the Gazette authorities, or how *any* misrepresentations could affect them toward my literary aspirations. I thank you for sustaining me so well; and ask you to forget the mortification, I may have innocently caused you as my friend. I suppose, now, that I ought not to have asked the favor I did; but I was naturally elated on reading the flattering criticism of the Press, and more with a desire that it should be read by my old friends in Hamilton (where the Gazette extensively circulates) than anything else, I requested you to republish it. Of course, the refusal to do so, is painful to me—or my vanity, which is most concerned, I believe. Yet there is consolation in it, too. I knew I had lukewarm friends, (not you, you kind soul,) this occurrence shews me that I have at least *one* enemy. I embrace him. I hope you wont do anything for me that will affect yourself unpleasantly—business-wise or otherwise. I would not take Mr Perry's position on the Gazette if it were offered to me. It is not one to my taste, and I have no desire to supplant such a person.

You may read this letter, if you like, to Mr Glenn.[2]

Yours ever
Will.

1. John T. Perry was associated with the Cincinnati *Gazette* (1860–1882).
2. Joseph Glenn (1826–1874) was on the *Gazette* staff (1859–1874).

27 FEBRUARY 1860, COLUMBUS, TO GAIL HAMILTON

Columbus, February 27, 1860.

Gail Hamilton[1]—

My danger is now that I shall overdo my repentance, as before I overdid my indignation.[2] I wish I could destroy the recollection of the unfortunate communication I sent to you, as readily as I destroy the paper itself. I am aware that I cannot say anything more than this in reparation; and yet it seems that I should say something to prove myself not wholly insensible of the kindness you intended to me.

I appreciate your peculiar relation, in friendship, to our wretched little book;[3] but the very fact (to which Mrs Piatt referred,) that it had received nothing but notices,—except a very kind and flattering review in the N. Y. Saturday Press—made me anxious that whoever spoke of it in the Era should do so critically—treating the book not with the least leniency as a first book, but justly and *equally*. I have never been so foolish, I believe, as to defy criticism; yet I believe I could have borne censure without a murmur. The patronizing manner you (no doubt unconsciously,) assumed toward us, stung me into the expressions which I fear may have given pain.

I can only renew my very sincere regrets.

Respectfully
W. D. Howells.

1. Gail Hamilton was the pseudonym for Mary Abigail Dodge (1833–1896), author of many books; she was at this time associated with Dr. Gamaliel Bailey, editor of the *National Era*; in later years (1865–1867) she was an editor of *Our Young Folks*, a children's magazine. In his letter to Piatt, 4 August 1861, Howells mentions that he destroyed her reply to this letter or to an earlier one.

2. In her review of *Poems of Two Friends*, *National Era*, 16 February 1860, Gail Hamilton had poked fun at the sentimental anguish in the poetry, and referred to the two poets as "a pair of stout-limbed, ruddy-cheeked, corn-fed country boys."

3. This clause suggests that Gail Hamilton was a friend of J. J. Piatt's mother, Mrs. Emily Scott Piatt. Piatt's marriage to Sarah Morgan Bryan did not take place until 1861.

1 APRIL 1860, COLUMBUS, TO ARTEMAS T. FULLERTON

Columbus, April 1, 1860.

Dear Fullerton[1]—

Coggeshall has asked me to write you for the facts of your life, death, and Christian sufferings in the cause of western literature, in order that you may be decently handed down to oblivion in his forthcoming book.

Tell me where you were born, and where you expect to be buried, and make a selection, please, of such pieces as you would like put in the "Poet's and Poetry." If you like, I will frame your facts together in an introductory essay, or you can arrange the matter any other way you please.[2]

I suppose the April *Atlantic* is creating a tremendous sensation out in Peoria. You have seen it and read the remarkable poems it contains, as well as that admirable notice of recent book of poems?[3]

I attended a small-sized party at Frank Muigs', the other night, where I saw "the dearest girl in the world."[4]

I have no gossip, and wouldn't write any if I had, because you have never writen to me.

Yours
Howells.

1. Howells' former roommate was now practicing law in Peoria, Illinois, but was to enter Princeton Theological Seminary in October 1860.

2. Fullerton's poetry did not appear in *The Poets and Poetry of the West*; but Howells wrote biographical notices for other poets in the volume. See Gibson-Arms, *Bibliography*, item 60–E.

3. Howells' two poems, "Pleasure-Pain" and "Lost Beliefs," and a review of *Poems of Two Friends* by James Russell Lowell, *Atlantic*, April 1860.

4. Neither Muigs nor the girl has been identified.

21 APRIL 1860, COLUMBUS, TO WILLIAM C. HOWELLS FAMILY

Columbus, April 21, 1860

Dear folks at home—

I don't remember exactly which one I ought to write to, and so I will write to you all.

I was very glad indeed to hear from dear mother, and I wish that she could find time to write to me oftener. It always seems to me that I feel a little kindlier toward myself and everybody else after reading one of her letters.

As Columbus grows old to me, it seems to contract, and I begin to feel here the gnawing discontent that I felt in Jefferson. Father need not be afraid that I should be seduced by Bohemianism in New York.[1] I confess that a life which defies usage has its charm for me; but I chiefly long now for change from a comparatively narrow to a wider field of action. Men must sort with their kind; and since Mr Reed is gone, there is no strictly literary person here with I can associate. I received a very kind letter from Reed the other day, inviting me to visit him at Cincinnati.[2]

On Thursday I walked over the greater part of the city with a person who brought a letter of introduction from father.[3] I did my duty, I hope; but—

Last week I saw Freyer and Sheriff Hendry, a few minutes.[4]

In regard to my autograph for Redpath's book:[5] I do not feel like furnishing it. My sentiments with regard to John Brown remain unchanged; but I am as yet a person of too little consequence to confer celebrity on a work by my connection with it; and, at any rate, I do not seek notoriety in any but a purely literary way. What I said of Brown came from my heart; and was never intended as a literary achievement.

Tell Aurelia that her friend Mrs Carter is on a visit at Urbana. Why doesn't Aurelia write to me?

As the summer approaches, I begin to feel touches of hypochondria, but I hope not to go crazy.

Tell Joe and Vic to write to me. I have a perfect mania for getting letters; and I have rented a box at the post office, that I look at twenty times a day. I was disappointed in only getting one letter from home last week.

Wrote a long article to day for the O. S. J.[6] slept the whole afternoon, and went to church this evening. The sermon was wretched, and made me worse.

With regard to my business affairs there is nothing new to write. I begin to like my place at Foster's very well.[7]

Tell Johnny that there is not a copy of Capt. Riley's Narrative at any bookstore in the city, and I suspect it is entirely out of print. Why doesn't he read "The Greek Soldier"?[8]

Goodnight and dear love to all.

Affectionately,
Will.

1. Howells contributed fourteen poems and one review to the New York *Saturday Press* between 18 June 1859 and 26 May 1860. See Gibson-Arms, *Bibliography*, pp. 82–84. Later, however, he became disenchanted with the magazine and its Bohemianism, as is suggested in a letter, 3 March 1861 (MH), to Howells from William Winter (1836–1917), a journalist associated with the Bohemian group: "As to Bohemianism—n'importe! You are right enough, probably, in your views of it.... For the 'S. P.', Bohemianism worked very well. Personally, I agree in your view that it absorbs identity." See also *Literary Friends and Acquaintance*, HE, pp. 61–68.

2. At the time of Samuel R. Reed's move from the editorship of the *Ohio State Journal* to the Cincinnati *Gazette*, Howells already knew James M. Comly well, but apparently did not consider him a strictly literary person. See *Years of My Youth*, HE, pp. 195–97.

3. The person has not been identified.

4. E. L. Freyer was U. S. marshal, and William Hendry became sheriff of Ashtabula County in 1857.

5. *Echoes of Harper's Ferry*, ed. J. Redpath (published about 12 May 1860), contains Howells' "Old Brown." Many signatures, as for example those of Emerson, Thoreau, and Whittier, appear in facsimile.

6. Possibly "Literary Gossip," *Ohio State Journal*, 26 April 1860.

7. For Howells' connection with Follett, Foster & Co., and his work for the *Ohio State Journal* at this time and during the summer of 1860, see Lynn, *Howells*, pp. 89–90, 102.

8. James Riley, *An Authentic Narrative of the Loss of the American Brig "Commerce"* ... (1817) was frequently reprinted. "The Greek Soldier" has not been identified, but Howells describes both books in *A Boy's Town* (1890), pp. 173–74.

29 APRIL 1860, COLUMBUS, TO JOSEPH A. HOWELLS

Columbus 29, 1860. April.

Dear Joe—

I wish it were possible for me to go to Chicago with you, but it is not. I have neither the passes nor the time. I couldn't get the former, and I don't feel like taking the latter. I am very glad to hear that dear mother and father are going to Washington, and I hope they will enjoy the trip.[1] I received no invitation, and should not have gone if I had; for I have not the least curiosity to see that part of the country.

The fact is I want now to go home above all things. It seems to me that I am growing away from whatever was gentle and good in the influences of my life. Sometimes I shudder to think how nearly beyond them I am; and I believe if I can be with you all a few weeks, I shall renew and better myself. I *do* nothing bad, I hope, but my habit of thought is harsh and skeptical, and I am the victim of an *ennui* which I cannot escape. While I work, I am comparatively content, but the moment I throw off the harness, I am languid, weary of myself and everything else. How it is all to result, I do not know. I have ceased to look forward with much comfort—

"I have but an angry fancy, what is it that I should do?"[2] I know well enough that if I live, I shall succeed in the ambition of my life, but that I shall be a happy man I do not believe. Religion seems such a fabulous far-off thing; and if I should taste all the pleasures and excitements of the world, I should be tired of them all, and then—what? To die at bay, entering the future backwards.—I suppose this bores a married man like you, with his child at his knee, and his dear wife to love and live for; and it is not the custom for one to make one's brother the confident of dyspeptic wretchedness. Yet I let what I have written, remain—for it speaks my mind more than half my time.

Columbus, just now, is most beautiful. I do think that to walk by an orchard in the suburbs, where every tree is a sphere, a little world of fragrant bloom, inhabited by drowsy honeybees—while the wind comes in light breaths, and blows you a dream of the happy, uncareful life of the flowers and the insects—is the most delicious bit of sensuous intoxication that I ever experienced. Then as the clangor of the bells breaks the broad golden calm of the Sunday morning, my heart fills with

"Tears from the depth of some divine despair."³

I wish I had the habit of going to church.

You will excuse four pages of nothing, when I tell you that was all I had to write, and I am sure that you can refrain from laughing at my dolefulness, for I am not often melancholy in your presence.

Give my dear love to all, and kiss Vevie for me. Write, telling me when mother and father are to return, and I will make arrangements to be home about the same time.

Your affectionate brother
Will.

1. Howells' parents left for Washington on 1 May, participating in an excursion of editors sponsored by the Baltimore and Ohio Railroad. They returned on 13 or 14 May, and some of their impressions are reflected in a series of letters published in the *Sentinel*, 9–30 May 1860.
2. See Tennyson, "Locksley Hall," line 102.
3. Tennyson, *The Princess, A Medley*, line 2.

3 AUGUST 1860, BOSTON, TO WILLIAM C. HOWELLS FAMILY

of travel and literature. I was delighted.) Well we all met at Parker's, and had a glorious time.¹ I think I never heard so much delicious wit and wisdom and drollery, as when Lowell and the Autocrat got started. I was only too glad to sit still and do the laughing, on which I come out strong.

The dinner lasted four hours—from three till seven, and involved an intoxication to me, as entire as that of Rhine wine, which you know I am in the habit of getting drunk on. Lowell and Holmes both seemed to take me by the hand, and the Autocrat,² about the time coffee came in, began to talk about the apostolic succession.³ Tomorrow evening, I am to take tea with him;⁴ and next day, I am off for the White Mountains.⁵

Goodbye,

Affectionately
Will.

1. The beginning of the manuscript of this letter has not been located; for the establishment of its date, see n. 5 below. There is a detailed description of the Boston dinner in *Literary Friends and Acquaintance*, HE, pp. 35–38.
2. Oliver Wendell Holmes, the author of *The Autocrat of the Breakfast Table* (1858).
3. Howells later recalled Holmes' comment to Lowell: "Well, James, this is something like the apostolic succession; this is the laying on of hands" (*Literary Friends and Acquaintance*, HE, p. 36).

4. Howells recounts the tea with Holmes in *Literary Friends and Acquaintance*, HE, pp. 41-44.

5. The trip to the White Mountains appears to have been a euphemism for a visit to Elinor Mead and her family in Brattleboro, Vermont. The chronology of the events mentioned in this letter remains uncertain. The editors of *Literary Friends and Acquaintance*, HE, pp. 324-25, predicate their analysis on the date of Lowell's note to Hawthorne, which they give as Sunday, 5 August 1860; but in Norton, *Lowell Letters*, I, 305, the note is dated "Monday, Aug., 1860," and his letter to Howells conveying the note bears the dateline "Cambridge, Monday" (MH). Lowell used this occasion to give his "dear young friend" some kind words of advice: "Don't print too much & too soon, don't get married in a hurry, read what will make you *think* not *dream*, hold yourself dear & more power to your elbow! God bless you!"

22 AUGUST 1860, JEFFERSON, TO JAMES T. FIELDS

Jefferson, O., August 22, 1860

My dear Mr Fields[1]—

I ought to have written you from New York, that my application to Mr Bigelow was not entirely successful.[2] He objected to my youth, and rather deferred the decision of the matter, giving me some writing to do. I was obliged, however to come home at once, and could not finish the work. So he said that I should drop him a letter from Columbus, occasionally, and we should keep our eyes upon each other. That was about the result. So I am now at my father's and shall leave for Columbus, this afternoon. I do not know exactly what lies before me there, but I shall do, for the present, whatever I can find to do. My regret at not getting the place on the Post, was softened by the fact that the more I saw of New York, the more I did not like it.

"Better fifty years of Boston than a cycle of New York," if one may so dilapidate "Locksley Hall."[3] The truth is, there is no place quite so good as Boston—God bless it! and I look forward to living there some day—being possibly the linchpin in the hub. I wonder if I could not find enough writing there, on different journals, literary and otherwise, to employ me, and support me in comfortable poverty? I know that the pen is a feeble instrument with which to keep the wolf from the door, but then, what will not youth dare—to hope?

I am very glad the correction was made in the poem, and I trust the expense did not fall altogether upon the publishers.[4] Have you seen what the N. Y. World said about "The Pilot's Story?"[5] The World is a journal of taste. If possibly in looking at the notices received you should send me some (if there are any) that are favorable, I would be very glad.

I will write up the story of which I spoke to you, and submit it to the *Atlantic* as soon as possible.[6]

Regards to Mr Ticknor,[7] to the dear "Professor" and to Mr Lowell. Pray remember me to Mrs Fields, and please do write me a line at Columbus, if you can think of anything comforting to say.

Very sincerely yours
W. D. Howells.

1. James T. Fields (1817–1881) was publisher of the *Atlantic* at this time; serving as its editor (1862–1870), he appointed Howells to the assistant editorship in 1866. Howells had met Fields on his visit to Boston in August 1860, and described his breakfast at the Fields' in *Literary Friends and Acquaintance*, HE, pp. 38–41.

2. John Bigelow (1817–1911) was managing editor and joint owner with William Cullen Bryant of the New York *Evening Post* (1848–1861). In 1861 he was appointed consul general at Paris, and afterwards served briefly (1865–1866) as minister to France.

3. See Tennyson, "Locksley Hall," line 184.

4. Howells described the costly correction of a change made by a final reader in "The Pilot's Story," *Atlantic*, September 1860, in *Literary Friends and Acquaintance*, HE, pp. 33–35.

5. The review of the September *Atlantic*, probably by E. C. Stedman, praises the poem as being "simple, strong, true, and full of feeling" (New York *World*, 18 August 1860).

6. Howells later remembered having asked Fields for the assistant editorship of the *Atlantic*, but his reminiscences do not mention anything in regard to a story. See *Literary Friends and Acquaintance*, HE, p. 60.

7. Howard Malcolm Ticknor (1836–1905), son of the founder of Ticknor & Fields, became assistant editor of the *Atlantic* with James Russell Lowell. He was also an editor of *Our Young Folks* (1864–1869).

27 AUGUST 1860, COLUMBUS, TO EDITORS, CINCINNATI *Gazette*

Columbus, August 27, 1860.

Editors Gazette—

I have already written to Mr Glenn requesting, if letters I wrote from Haverhill, Salem, Boston, New York and elsewhere (which were not published,) were received by you, that would return them to me here. Of course I have received no reply. I want the letters, for they will be useful to me. At the same time you return them, you may fix your price upon those published, and send me the money.[1]

W. D. Howells.

1. Seven letters were published in the *Gazette* under the title "Glimpses of Summer Travel" (21 July–9 August 1860). See Gibson-Arms, *Bibliography*, p. 85.

31 August 1860, Columbus, to James R. Lowell

Columbus, August 31, 1860.

Dear Mr Lowell—

I have yet to thank you for making me acquainted with Mr. Hawthorne, whom I liked very much, and came nearer to, than I at first believed possible.[1] I was two days in old Concord; and look back to the time I spent there with a pleasure only less hearty than that with which I remember Boston. At New York, I spent four days, and was glad to come away. Indeed, the metropolis disappointed me—which was sad for the metropolis, and annoying to me.[2]

Finally, I am not sorry to be again in Columbus—for I find myself willing and able to work, which only another locution for willingness and ability to be happy. To the young poet at least, a little immediate applause is grateful, if not necessary, and I get this in Columbus. The whole dear town seemed glad to see me; and one of my particular triumphs was that an acquaintance, a violent proslavery physician, (the worst possible combination, you know,) should stop me, to shake hands and tell me that he thought my "Pilot's Story" was very good.[3] The poem has been copied into a Cincinnati paper at length, and the praise of the Boston papers has found its echo here.

Well, it was not wholly of myself that I meant to speak. Indeed, the volume which this accompanies will suggest that I had something else to mention. A glance at the title-page will reveal the nature of the book, and a glance at the preface will make known its peculiar constitution. It is only your attention to the work that I write to secure; for I have neither the wish nor the space to tell you all my own feeling in regard to it. It is the work of a very industrious literateur, and an enthusiastic believer in the merits and sufferings of western poets.[4] For myself, I believe that so far as Western Poetry has deserved recognition, it has received it. The sad error has been on the part of its friends, the belief that cockle and cheat with sufficient cultivation will turn to grain, and they have delved and dug about in fields, that would never have yielded anything but weeds, whether upon the Ohio, or the Charles. Nevertheless I fondly believe that there is some poetry in this book, and that it will have its uses. There are dreary wastes of trash in it which I would not have set down in the map of Western Literature; but the purpose of the editor was candor and fidelity to all that existed; and the historical value of the book is not to be forgotten.

I hope, Mr Lowell, that you will understand me only to direct your attention to the book. It is foolish, I think, to deprecate just criticism; for nothing is finally so mischievous. It is the wish of the publisher and editor alike, I believe, who submit through me the volume to you, that it shall be judged according to the merits of the plan—but after all this is only impertinence, for you will know how to judge, and we have confidence that you will be just.

> Very sincerely yours
> W. D. Howells.

1. Lowell's note of introduction to Hawthorne says in part: "But he wants to look at you, which will do you no harm, and him a great deal of good.... If my judgment is good for anything, this youth has more in him than any of our younger fellows in the way of rhyme" (Norton, *Lowell Letters*, I, 305–6).
2. See *Literary Friends and Acquaintance*, HE, pp. 61–70.
3. The proslavery physician has not been identified.
4. Lowell wrote to Howells on 1 December 1860 (MH) that he could not write a notice of *The Poets and Poetry of the West* because "To be perfectly honest, your own was wellnigh the only poetry I found in it, & the amount of rhyme-&-water was prodigious" (Norton, *Lowell Letters*, I, 306–7).

1 SEPTEMBER 1860, COLUMBUS, TO OLIVER W. HOLMES, JR.

Columbus, September 1, 1860.

Dear friend—

You must not be astonished, to begin with, if I write each succeeding letter in a hand different from the last. It is a part of my unsteadfast nature, and haphazard education to do so. The only thing in which I am chirographically confirmed is cacography—for which grasp of Hellenism, I needn't of course apologize to a famous Grecian like yourself. Out West you know, they make fencing out of any material—rails, stumps, brush, hedges—but nevertheless they raise great crops of corn and wheat—and so I have grown to thinking that a settled hand writing is not a great virtue. If I fence in a bit of paper that bears ideas, I don't mind much how I do it.

So much for nothing—or for a start. Of course since my return, I have bragged immensely, about the evening I spent at your father's;[1] and the post-caenal talk (at the house of a friend where I was drinking tea,) glided through the impulses I received in that memorable conversation with the "Professor," when we advocated the excellence of gooseberry fact—glided (I'm a fearful distance from the beginning of that sentence,) into the same supernatural, or super-usual vein. Now, did you ever have an absurd picture of the position of the months, or numerals, in that mere world of names where they exist? Did it ever appear to you that *June* was a month not intended for everybody; but was rather an exclusive thing, intended for the enjoyment of aristocratic people who could afford it? Or that the numerals, in tens, describe a wild and frantic zigzag from one to an hundred? This is nonesense, but what shall one do with one's nonesense, unless one writes it?

I am not so religious as I am superstitious, I fear, but I have an adoration for everything that depicts, or suggests the passion of the saviour. I stop at the catholic shop-windows, and pay a devoir to the print of the Holy One, shewing his pierced and bleeding heart. The other day, I met an Italian, who had plaster images to sell; and I bought a medallion, having the thorn-crowned head of our Saviour in bas-relief, and to me inexpressibly beautiful. I forget from what painting it is copied. I have it over my mantel now, between a small bust of Shakespeare, and a cast of Goethe; and I do not mean a blasphemy, by this location.—By the way, speaking of crucifixion-passion-art, I would have you borrow or buy Heinrich Heine, and read that part of his *Romantische Schule*, in which he attributes the glorious anguish of Christian art to the abnegation and self-sacrifice of the genius that produced it. He says: "Therefore, in sculpture and painting, those hideous themes [remember that Heine is a Hellenist, and Greek in his belief of earthly pleasure,] martyrdom, crucifixions, dying saints, mortification of the flesh. The work itself was a martyrdom of the artist, and whenever I see one of those distorted pieces, through the lamb-patient heads, thin arms, meager limbs, and anguished, helpless forms of which, Christian abstinence and mortification is expressed—I am seized with an infinite pity for the artists of that time."[2]

I don't quote Heine on any subject anymore, if I can help it. I have wearied a little of his brillance and subtlety—both partly false. Just now, I have commenced reading a translation of Dante, with an ashamed conviction that I ought to be reading the original. You see I am perfectly desultory. Let us be so, I beg. Life is so, and why not talk—friendship?

Yours always
W. D. Howells.

Send me the Magazine. I inclose a few articles of mine.[3]

1. Howells' description of the evening, which ended in a walk with O. W. Holmes, Jr., appears in *Literary Friends and Acquaintance*, HE, pp. 41–44. There is no evidence of continued correspondence with the younger Holmes, the distinguished associate justice of the U. S. Supreme Court (1902–1932), after 1860–1861.
2. The passage that Howells translated appears early in Book I. See *Werke und Briefe*, ed. H. Kaufmann (Berlin: Aufbau Verlag, 1961–1964), V, 22.
3. The magazine Howells requested was probably the *Harvard Magazine*; the articles may have been those on his eastern trip, which appeared under the title. "Glimpses of Summer Travel," in the Cincinnati *Gazette*, 21 July–9 August, and as "En Passant" in the *Ohio State Journal*, 21 July–7 August 1860. See Gibson-Arms, *Bibliography*, p. 85.

12 SEPTEMBER 1860, COLUMBUS, TO ANNE T. HOWELLS

Columbus, Sept. 12, 1860.

My dear Annie—

If you conclude to write to me in French, have the goodness to spell the name of that language with a capital "F;" and not again to say you are "studing" anything. It is quite as bad as to say "rebublican," which I see you repented of and scratched out. (That's the way, I take you brats down!) Annie, never try to come the flourishes over a brother so much your superior. I ought to be constantly near you in order to correct your tendency to "imperence." Ask mother to give you a good talking to.

I believe there is nothing particularly new in this section of the moral vineyard, except that I received a letter from cousin Dune,[1] the other day, in reply to one which I wrote asking for some verses I once contributed to her album. She gave no news, and was chiefly reminiscent of the summer she spent at our house. I have not yet answered her letter.

You are a very foolish girl (if you will permit me to say so,) for studying arithmetic. There is no earthly necessity that you should do so, and I am surprised that father lets you. I am going to write a book some day on The Absurdity of a Female knowledge of Figures—except those figures which they make when well dressed. But that is a secret.

The Carters are all very well. I astonished Annie the other night, by going to Church with her, and I believe she thinks I am not so near the brink of the Bottomless, as she used to.[2] They always send love to you all.

I enclose a slight token of esteem to you "grils"—one for you, and one for Sis, and one for Aurelia, flying over the cuckoo's nest.[3]

"Yours respectfully"
W. D. H.

You can each buy you a nice apple-peeling machine with the money, in order to prepare Applebutter for my thanksgiving visit

1. Dune Dean, of Pittsburgh.
2. Annie Carter, daughter of Dr. Francis Carter, was frequently mentioned by Howells during his Columbus years.
3. See the American counting rhyme, "One, two, three, four, five, six, seven,..." in *The Annotated Mother Goose*, ed. W. S. and C. Baring-Gould (New York: New American Library, 1962), p. 249.

14 November 1860, Columbus, to Oliver W. Holmes, Jr.

Columbus, Nov. 14, 1860

Dear Holmes—

I was very glad to get your letter, for I began to be afraid our pen-and-paper acquaintance was come to an end. The truth is, I always exact, from my friends, the appearance of friendship. Our sentiments of esteem and affection amount to very little, you know, unless expressed in some way. (That's dreadfully didactic—I'll leave that branch of the subject.)

Yes, I received your maga, and read it, with I hope profit—with pleasure certainly. I want to hand your article on Durer to a young artist here, who is also a witty and charming girl, and as good as anything she paints.[1] When she has read it, I will write you my opinion. By all means send me your article on Plato.[2] You know we talked chiefly about psychics, and I shall enjoy your essay for many reasons.—I am going largely into skepticism at present. Cultivating my incredulity on a course of Voltaire and the Westminster Review.[3] Of course, I was delighted with the last chapters of the "Professor's Story"—a thing you ought to read.[4] There are some good ideas in it. I said of it, "noticing" the *Atlantic*, that Dr Holmes had the gift of always touching upon what you have just been thinking about, and I had the satisfaction of seeing the sentiment stolen by every country editor who noticed the magazine afterwards. Otherwise I have been doing a little French Revolution, Milton, Leigh Hunt's Autobiography, Italian Poets, and Faust.[5] Politics and criticism not counted.

The other Sunday I wrote a long poem, half-fun and half-earnest—of which perhaps, I may send you passages in my next. I call it "Bopeep: A Pastoral."[6]

This much for literature.

Now for sentiment.

I have fallen in love with a white-faced being in a blue dress. Good heaven! I met her three times yesterday, and died three several divine deaths. She has one of those lily-pale faces—that pale aspèct superb,—night-black eyes,—light straw hat, mantle indescrible, a blue dress, and an angelic glide. She goes by the office nearly every day, and plays the deuce with the editorials. I am acquainted with her, but haven't the least desire to go and see her, for I have no doubt that I should see some fault in her beauty if I did, and experience a blight of the affections. So I stop away, and content myself with making these misanthropical verses in the most abominable German—

SELECTED LETTERS 1860

I

Das blaugekleidste Mädchen,
Sie geht und kommt vorbei,
Sie ist meine Herzallerliebste—
Doch bin ich kalt und scheu.

II

Ich denke die Engelinen
Sind besser in dem Ferne—
Nein, was sind, als Erdematerie,
(Im Nahe,) selbst die Sterne?[7]

You see what I am come to? But it will all blow over in a little while—as soon as the blue dress is put off.

In the meantime, yours for the peaceable secession of South Carolina.

W. D. Howells.

1. "Notes on Albert Durer," *Harvard Magazine*, October 1860. The "young artist" was probably Caroline L. Ransom.
2. "Plato," *University Quarterly*, October 1860.
3. There are no notices on Voltaire or the *Westminster and Foreign Quarterly Review* in the *Ohio State Journal*; but at this time Howells had charge of the literary section of the *Ohio State Weekly Journal*. Since only scattered issues of the weekly edition have been preserved, such notices can no longer be identified.
4. O. W. Holmes, Sr., "The Professor's Story," *Atlantic*, November 1860. Howells' notice in the *Ohio State Journal*, 23 October 1860, reads in part: "Dr. Holmes has the rare gift of nearly always touching just what you have been thinking about; and the acknowledgement which we make for the excellence of the November chapters comes as much from gratitude as admiration." For book publication, the title was changed to *Elsie Venner* (1861).
5. Perhaps Howells was reading Thomas Carlyle, *The French Revolution* (1837); and *Faust* is presumably Goethe's. Whether "Italian Poets" was a collection or merely an area of interest is uncertain.
6. See Howells to Holmes, Jr., 25 November 1860, n. 4.
7. No publication of this poem, in either German or English, has been located. A literal translation of Howells' rather faulty German reads as follows: "I. The maiden dressed in blue / She comes and passes by / She is the dearest to my heart— / But I am cold and shy. II. I think that female angels / Are more perfect far away— / What but earthly matter / Are the stars when seen up close?"

25 NOVEMBER 1860, COLUMBUS, TO OLIVER W. HOLMES, JR.

Columbus, Nov. 25, 1860.

My dear Holmes—

I would rather have taken you than your letter to breakfast with me this morning. But the letter was very good. My fellow editor and I have hired lodgings together,[1] and have our meals at an eatinghouse, not far beyond the post-office. So I got your epistolary presence out of "Nineteen, please!" and brought it with me to the matutinal mutton-chop. Believe me, the breakfast was much the better for a sprinkling of Attic salt. You kept me long over the coffee, and at last I carried you, magnificently accompanied in the same pocket by the "Harvard," to my friend, the charming little paintress. To her I read aloud a part of "Durer," and we both rejected with infinite scorn the idea of Emersonism.[2] Afterwards, being provoked to it, by your philosophical analysis of art, we fell into discourse upon the analytical tendency of the mind—the critical, uncreative nature of modern thought. She regards (somewhat sadly) art—painting and the like—as an anachronism at present; and I thought that all literature tended to the development of the philosophical speculation, the subjective poem, and the analytical fiction—the fiction as written by Hawthorne, Thackeray and Bulwer, and "The Autocrat." I do not know in what degree I may be influenced to this opinion, by the story which I am now writing,[3] and which grows so frightfully analytical, that I sometimes think it bears the same relation to a romance, that an accurate print of the human heart would bear to the picture of a soul-illuminated face.—

My new poem of which I spoke to you, is a revolt against this analytical tendency. I have made it the simplest and foolishest love-story, related to no probability nor reason. It is so much of this nature, that I hesitate about sending it to the Atlantic, because I doubt if it would pass the editorial ordeal, and because I think it would not be favorably received by the Atlantic readers if published. I enclose you some random stanzas.[4]

I am glad you happen to have read the Westminster's "Neo-Christianity." It is an article which interested me intensely, and I briefly noticed it in our paper.[5]

I send you this comment of mine—which on re-perusal, I find does not go to a sufficient length, though it fairly indicates what I would have said.—The editor-in-chief did not altogether like to admit the article—for you know anything that does not noisily denounce skepticism, is looked upon as anti-Christian.

Sometimes, I think it would be well to cast this subject of religion wholly aside—it bores me to death. And yet it has a fascination about it that I cannot resist, and every interest of life presses it upon me. Lately, I have become acquainted with a young Scotchman who is a great metaphysician, and we have long walks and talks together upon the nature of the soul, and "the ways of God to man." He has read Sir William Hamilton, whose book is so tremendously big, that I look upon my friend as a sort of metaphysical paladin, who can slay any work upon the subject no matter how huge, or defended by obscurities.

He has lent me Young's criticism upon the Bampton Lectures, in which The Province of Reason is discussed, and the mention in that, has set me to reading Heine's resumé of German philosophy.[6]

—The blue dress has been taken off, and I am all right again.—I met the "party" the other evening at a festivity, and my passion dashed itself to death against a sharp and poignant shoulder blade—she being in that condition described by the ladies as low-necked. It is the old story, adapted to modern life, of the nightingale piercing its breast with the thorn.

Adieu!

W. D. Howells

I am going home to Thanksgiving this week. Would that you were in my company.

1. The fellow-editor was Samuel Price (d. 1870). He soon went to Cleveland and then, beginning in 1862, edited the Toledo *Commercial*, with which he was associated until his death. See *Years of My Youth*, HE, pp. 179, 204–6.
2. See Howells to Holmes, Jr., 14 November 1860, n. 1.
3. In a rejection from David Masson, the editor of *Macmillan's Magazine*, 31 December 1862 (MH), the story is referred to as "Geoffrey: A Study of American Life." For a discussion of the manuscript of "Geoffrey Winter," see J. K. Reeves, "The Literary Manuscripts of W. D. Howells," *Bulletin of the New York Public Library* 62 (1958), 350. Howells described his efforts to get the story published in *Years of My Youth*, HE, p. 180.
4. The stanzas are part of "Bopeep." Only six lines (in stanza 18) appear in the printed versions (stanza 14) of the *Atlantic Almanac* (1870) and *Poems* (1873), and the plots are totally different. The manuscript of stanzas 18–28 (MH) is described in Reeves, "Literary Manuscripts," p. 273.
5. The only reference to "Neo-Christianity," *Westminster and Foreign Quarterly Review*, 1 October 1860, in the *Ohio State Journal* appears 14 January 1861. There is also an extended notice of the January 1861 number of the *North American Review* and its comments on *Essays and Reviews* (a volume of controversial essays on theology mostly by Oxford clergymen, published in 1860) and Sir William Hamilton's *Lectures on Metaphysics* (1858). The author of the *Journal* article was probably the "young Scotchman" mentioned later in this letter rather than Howells.
6. Hamilton's "tremendously big" book may have been *Lectures on Logic* (1860), which was noted in "Literary Gossip," *Ohio State Journal*, 28 August 1860. The other books mentioned are John Young, *The Province of Reason: A Criticism of the Bampton Lecture on "The Limits of Reason"* (1860), a discussion of Henry L. Mansel's 1858 Bampton Lecture, "The Limits of Religious Thought"; and Heinrich Heine, *Salon II: Zur Geschichte der Religion und Philosophie in Deutschland* (1835).

14 December 1860, Columbus, to James R. Lowell

Columbus, Dec. 14, 1860.

Dear Mr Lowell—

I thought to have thanked you before this for a letter which gave me great pleasure—but deferred my reply to you until I could accompany it with my poem.¹ And now the poem (in the light of your praise,) does not altogether please me, and so I do not send it. I think I learned from you more than any other man I have seen, a virtue of patience, that I did not have before I found how calm and self-contained one could be. A little time, therefore—the Atlantic will ebb and flow for a while without my slender tribute.

I have permitted myself—such is the weakness of human nature—to be announced for a lecture here, and am even now engaged every moment I can steal from the newspaper in writing and reading up the genius of Heinrich Heine.²

The publishers of the *Atlantic* wrote asking if I could furnish a number of articles on The West. I think I could, if I knew what kind of articles were wanted.³—I am afraid that you are right about the Poets and Poetry of the West.⁴ But no feeling of mine is hurt (you took care of that so kindly that you make me incredulous). I have never believed in a sectional literature as some people here would have it. The conditions in the west are rather against poetry, I think. It is hardly possible to assimilate and poetize the crude, harsh life we live. Sometimes I doubt,—but vade retro Sathanas!⁵

Well, your word of cheer came all the more gratefully that I happened to be in rather an arid spot, and was thirsty. Will it surprise you to learn—or will you laugh a wise laugh at my innocence?—that I am already subjected to considerable personal abuse in the newspapers, because I have happened to do a not unsuccessful thing? Already, every newspaper clown, who is offended with me as an editor, pitches into my poetry. I confess it gives me pain. You know, it doesn't greatly matter who strikes a blow, if the blow is a wanton and cruel one. Do you chance to know any balsam of fierblas?⁶

Piatt was here, and spent Sunday with me. I wish you could see him, and through him—which latter I can't altogether.

Forgive me that I have laid even a foolish trouble before you. It was chiefly to show you how much your letter touched and encourged me.

Very sincerely
W. D. Howells.

1. Lowell had written Howells a complimentary letter, 1 December 1860 (MH), in which he praised "The Pilot's Story," calling it "a really fine poem." He then continued: "Accordingly, I am glad to hear that you are to send us another—glad also that you are *making yourself scarce*. That is not only wise but worldlywise too" (Norton, *Lowell Letters*, I, 306–7). The poem Howells meant to send was probably "Bubbles."

2. A series of "Atheneum lectures" was announced in the *Ohio State Journal*, 12 December 1860, with an untitled one by Howells for 14 January 1861. The first lecture was indefinitely postponed (*Journal*, 25 December), and there is no indication that any of them were ever delivered.

3. Howells wrote in a letter to Ticknor and Fields, 10 June 1861 (CSmH) that he was still considering the possibility of touring the West for a series of three articles. See *Life in Letters*, I, 35.
4. See Howells to Lowell, 31 August 1860, n. 4.
5. "Get thee behind me Satan" (Luke 4:8).
6. "Fierblas" may combine words used by Quixote and Sancho in *Don Quixote*. See Samuel Putnam's note on part 1, chapters 10 and 15, in his *Portable Cervantes* (New York: Viking Press, 1951), p. 812, explaining Quixote's "Fierbras's balm" and Sancho's "a couple of draughts of that ugly Bras."

24 DECEMBER 1860, COLUMBUS, TO JAMES R. LOWELL

Columbus, Dec. 24. '60

Dear Mr Lowell—

I send you for the *Atlantic,* some verses made upon a theme of which we talked as we stood beside your meadow-stream at Cambridge. It may be that the bubbles have really a cheerfuller significance, but I could not make it out.[1]

Mr Ticknor, the younger, wrote to me before he went to England that a certain poem of mine called "The Empty House" was accepted.[2] It is so long since I sent it—June I think was the month—that I am sometimes anxious about its fate.

Very sincerely yours,
W. D. Howells.

1. "Bubbles," *Atlantic,* April 1861.
2. See Howells to Holmes, Jr., 24 February 1861, n. 2.

6 JANUARY 1861, COLUMBUS, TO OLIVER W. HOLMES, JR.

Columbus, Jan. 6, 1861.

My dear friend—

I hope the verses I sent to you, have not been too much for your friendship, for I do not wish that the detestation I now feel for my poem[1] should be increased by a chance so melancholy. I am in that state with regard to the production from which the verses were extracted, that anything shall make me disown it.

Meantime, I have read your article on Plato,[2] and liked it with an impartial affection. You presented the subject to me very originally, and I think your analysis of the Socratian method admirable—indeed the whole thing was admirable. Thank you for the "Quarterly." Don't fail to send me everything you write. I fancy that in every word there is a flavor of your personality, and I am constantly reminded of the charming evening I spent at your father's, and of the after-walk in the Common.

They were going to have a course of "domestic" lectures here, this winter, and I was down for one, but the course is already run without the first step, and my lecture will probably never be delivered. I wrote on "Boston Notions,"[3] which I treated esthetically, politically and civilly, and launched out tremendously in glorification of your city. Yes, if I had eaten your chowder-hashush from infancy, I could not have pictured a Boston more incredibly magnified. But that is past. At present I am chiefly journalizing, and intent upon parties of which (since Columbus is the capital) there are many here every winter. A little while ago, I had a touch of metaphysics, but recently, nothing but the diptheria and secession.

What are you doing with the Harvard Magazine? I see by one of the Boston paper's that the periodical alluded to has criticised "Miss Gilbert's Career," and I would like to read the critique.[4] Yours? I have no business to doubt Dr Holland's genius, but I do.

I gave up Voltaire after a volume's trial of the Philosophical Dictionary. I thought it idle to read a man who was not disposed to question anything more than I. Do you find time to read anything out of your study? About's "King of the Mountains" is capital, and the author does us occidentals—of the cornfields here—justice in the character of John Harris.[5] I am amazed that a Frenchman, at that a Parisian, could have so truthfully delineated, so felicitously colored an American character. It is a miracle.

Let me hear from you only when you are interested in writing. This is my two-ahead.

          Yours faithfully and relentlessly
          W. D. H.

 1. "Bopeep: A Pastoral."
 2. "Plato," *University Quarterly*, October 1860. See Mark A. DeWolfe Howe, *Justice Oliver Wendell Holmes* (Cambridge, Mass.: Harvard University Press, Belknap Press, 1957), I, 54–57.
 3. In a letter, 16 September 1861 (MH), sixteen friends of Howells requested that before leaving for Venice he deliver a lecture on Boston that they heard he had prepared. Evidently having changed the subject of his undelivered Columbus lecture from Heine to Boston (see Howells to Lowell, 14 December 1860, n. 2), Howells was scheduled to speak at the Town Hall on 28 September, according to the Ashtabula *Sentinel*, 25 September 1861.
 4. *Miss Gilbert's Career*, a novel by Josiah Gilbert Holland, was reviewed in *The Harvard Magazine*, November 1860, by Wendell Phillips Garrison, who criticized Holland's bias against professionally ambitious women.
 5. A review, presumably by Howells, of Edmund About's *King of the Mountains* appeared in the *Ohio State Journal*, 10 January 1861.

17 January 1861, Columbus, to James R. Lowell

Columbus, Jan. 17, 1861

Dear Mr Lowell—

Need I make excuses for sending the enclosed attempts directly to you? You know it affords me each time the pleasure of speaking with you; and beside I have now really something to say, and that is with regard to a longer poem which I mentioned having done. It came so easily to words at first, that I was much delighted with it, and on the joyous impulse mentioned it in my letter to Mr Fields.[1] I am not sorry that I did so, now, for it brought a word from you, in response. But on looking over the poem critically, it does not seem to bear the internal evidences of inspiration, and I will not therefore offer it to the *Atlantic*.

Of the accompanying poems, I have only to say that I hope the one called "Drowsihed" will be perfectly clear to you as one of those just-before-dropping-asleep visions, in which one identifies himself with the object of his doze-dream, and suddenly wakes.[2] If you do not think it will have this definiteness—it cannot be successful. I confess that I like it.

I remember every word that you said to me, and particularly all that touching my Heine-leeshore, and I try to write always outside of my affection for that poet.[3] But what with the German blood I have, and my intense love for German poetry, it is hard for me to avoid the German manner. My intropection (which goes on unconsciously all the time) has, however, brought me this fact plainly in view: that if I let myself become a part of my own reading, I relinquish every reasonable claim to become the reading of anybody else.

The other day, I got Sir William Hamilton's metaphysics,[4] and am alternating that with a witty book of Alphonse Karr's.[5] For the rest, I am taken up with journalizing, and walking and altogether too much talking,—for it must be confessed that I very often find other people's company pleasanter than my own.

—I speak of myself with a freedom which will perhaps not seem altogether consequent when you remember how little you have seen of me.

—I lament very much the prospect of war in this country—not indeed for its present disaster and desolation, but for the future of barbarism which it must compel. It seems to me that not only will all the humanities be retarded in their growth, but that war will create a military ambition among the people, and turn them from their dawning knowledge of true greatness to the worship of that beast, military glory. But I have no right to trouble you about all this.

Very sincerely,
W D Howells.

1. The poem has not been identified.
2. The *Atlantic* did not accept "Drowsihed," nor was it ever published. For a description of the manuscript see J. K. Reeves, "The Literary Manuscripts of W. D. Howells," *Bulletin of the New York Public Library* 62 (1958), 277.
3. Much later, in a letter of 28 July 1864 (MH), Lowell wrote Howells: "I don't forget my good opinion of you & my interest in your genius. Therefore I may be frank. You have enough in you to do honor to our literature. Keep on cultivating yourself. You know what I thought. You must sweat the Heine out of you as men do mercury. You are as good as Heine—remember that." See Norton, *Lowell Letters*, I, 338, and *Literary Friends and Acquaintance*, HE, p. 182, where Howells tentatively dates the advice as having been given in 1865–1866.
4. *Lectures on Metaphysics*.
5. Of the many books by the French journalist and author, Jean Baptiste Alphonse Karr (1808–1890), only two appear to have been translated into English: *The Alain Family* (1853), a novel, and *A Tour Round My Garden* (1855 and 1859), an essay. The latter is probably the "witty book" mentioned by Howells.

24 FEBRUARY 1861, COLUMBUS, TO OLIVER W. HOLMES, JR.

Columbus, Feb. 24, 1861.

My dear Holmes—

Actually a hesitation befell me after writing that address! I have been writing nothing, reading nothing, thinking nothing for the last two months, and as I always want to report progress to you in my letters, it occurred to me that I had no business to write the present one. I am quite a fatalist. I accept every event, every fact of life with a belief that no possibility could have prevented it; but I never can help being ashamed of idleness. I always shiver with the doubt: Is this indolence a pause in the scheme of my developement? Have I come to the end? For you know I forget that I am young, and being very anxious to do a great deal, I question my powers, as a man does who resentfully acknowledges the approaches of age.—Horror! I failed so detestably in that stupid poem of which I sent you verses[1]—failed not only in execution, but in judgment, for I was in good humor with it at first—heaven forgive me! I have a certain final confidence in myself—but these blunders—ach!—Then, I was not pleased with my last *Atlantic* poem. By some error of taste, the title of the thing was changed by the editors from "The Empty House," to "The Old Homestead,"[2]—a title which seemed to me utterly insignificant and commonplace. The change destroyed all the pleasure I would have taken in the printed poem, and so evilly enchanted the verses, that I do not know them.—I would rather you gave over looking at my printed—hardly published—copartnership volume. Somethings in it, I am not ashamed of, but others are sadly *young* and jejune. However, I may survive my present desolation, and send you the book. I don't think it is to be had in Boston.[3]—Tell me, about that friend who died suddenly—or rather how the event affected you. Are you like myself, in leaving death altogether out of the scheme of life? I have a small salary, on which I live with the splendor of a lord, and the generosity of a vagabond.—Recklessly I squander my mortality in the same way. I think from the nature of things that I cannot be long-lived, but yet I live as if no night lay between this and eternity. I take my eternity at once, in fact—and if there *should* happen to be nothing after death—why, I have had my eternity, you know.—Some lives seem to be perfectly accomplished before existence ceases—that is, no fortuity can suggest new possibilities for them. Example: Some five or six years ago, a young girl came to learn the printing-business in my father's office. She had a strange kind of beauty—yes, a very peculiar beauty. You know that engraving of Evangeline to be seen in a million shop windows—where she is represented as she—

"Sat by some nameless grave, and thought that perhaps in its bosom He was already at rest, and she longed to slumber beside him."[4]

Well, this young girl's face looked like that Evangeline's; and she had those *glowing* dark eyes,—so different from the glitter and shallow twinkle of most black eyes. They had a divine languor in them, a richness and warmth ineffable. Then her complexion was of that opulent tint which I have never seen except among the women of the lake-shores. This girl had intelligence, taste, culture—she had read a great deal, with the deep inner sense of the beautiful, belonging to so few readers. All sumptuous books she loved, in poetry and prose, and she had that rare gift in women of understanding humor. She was cruelly, mercilessly sarcastic—I confess I was afraid of her tongue, for my vanity is thin-skinned, and she knew very well where to strike. She was a woman who could have shone most brilliantly in any society—she would have graced the highest position. And now behold one of the contradictions that tempt one to atheism! She was poor, and must work for her living. Her genius, purely feminine, was not creative or positive, and could not have lifted her to a higher vocation. In that desolate little village, no rich man came a-marrying. So she worked at her trade three years in our printing-office. At last a very honest person, every way but in age, her inferior fell in love with her and was to have been her husband. If you understand anything of her character from my way of talking about it, you discern how wretched she must have been in a union with such a person, had not the good death forbidden.—She fell ill, and through cruel pain and long agony, died. I recounted to myself the facts of her character and the facts of her life, when she was dead, and it seemed to me that everything had been accomplished for her even before the close. It seems a hard and cruel thing to say that the only thing one can do is to die. But for her, what else remained? Either a monotonous drudgery through life at the trade she detested, or a domestic round of tasks and stupid little duties. She could not have been religious. She did not believe enough.—She could not write well enough, or would not write ill enough to achieve that doubtful splendor and distinction of female authorship. From her nature, I think, motherhood would not have made her happy, for though passionate, I do not think she had much affection—though here I may wrong her. What then? Only death.—Have I made this idea clear to you, or does my long story go for nothing?

Many things suggested by your letter remain unattended to, but I cannot write any more just now, unless I write on the subject which I ought not to have touched. For I feel it wrong—dissecting that dead girl's nature.

Write to me soon.

> Yours always
> W. D. H.

1. "Bopeep: A Pastoral," about which Holmes had commented in a letter to Howells, 4 February 1861 (MH): "I would thank you very heartily for the last verses[.] They had a real poetic flavor to them though they wanted boiling down[.]—"

2. In *Poems* (1873) Howells reverted to the original title. Holmes' comment about the poem in his letter of 4 February was somewhat critical: "I liked your last piece in the Atlantic though not equally with the *Pilot's Story* wh. I have told you was very remarkable—Your last is rather Tennyson-ish—& I prefer pure Howells to any foreign flavored productions[.]—"

3. Holmes' request, in his letter of 4 February, for a copy of "Poems by 2 Friends" may have helped Howells overcome his reluctance to present copies of *Poems of Two Friends*.

4. Longfellow, "Evangeline," lines 697–98. The popular engraving may be an etching made by James Faed (1821–1911), a Scottish painter and engraver, of a painting by his brother, Thomas Faed (1826–1900). See *The Letters of Henry Wadsworth Longfellow*, ed. A. Hilen (Cambridge, Mass.: Harvard University Press, Belknap Press, 1972), III, 489–90, 533. The young girl of whom Howells writes has not been identified.

13 MARCH 1861, COLUMBUS, TO JOHN G. NICOLAY

Columbus, O., March 13, 1861

Dear Sir[1]—

To-day a letter was enclosed to Senator Wade for the President, asking my appointment to the consulship of Munich in Bavaria. The letter was signed by various persons of prominence in our State government, and drawn up by one of our Senators.[2]

May I hope that you will interest yourself in my cause? I want to go Munich to pursue the study of German literature, and to have four years' opportunity. I do not conceive that I have any claims upon the president, superior to those of other Republican journalists, but have thought that the rank I held in the "noble army of" biographers might at least commend me to his notice.[3]

I regret not seeing you, when in Columbus,—not altogether for selfish reasons, I believe.[4]

May I hear from you in response to this application—if only a line?

Trusting that you will pardon the liberty I have taken in addressing you, and asking your good offices, I am,

Very truly yours
W. D. Howells.

Mr John G. Nicolay.

1. John George Nicolay (1832–1901) and John Hay were Lincoln's private secretaries. They later collaborated on *Abraham Lincoln: A History* (1890), which Howells reviewed in "Editor's Study," *Harper's Monthly*, February 1891.

2. Writing to B. F. Wade, 13 March 1861 (DNA), W. C. Howells enclosed a letter to Lincoln with the request that Wade endorse it or add his signature. The letter to Lincoln, 12 March 1861 (DNA), is signed by W. Dennison, W. T. Bascom, W. T. Coggeshall, John J. Janney, R. W. Taylor, H. B. Carrington, A. P. Russell, W. B. Thrall, J. A. Garfield, J. D. Cox, Ed A. Parrott, James Monroe, R. C. Parsons, B. R. Cowen, S. E. Browne, C. P. Wolcott, and H. E. Parsons. Wade did not sign but apparently passed the letter on to Lincoln. The state senator who drew up the letter was probably James A. Garfield (1831–1881), "an old family friend of mine," as Howells calls him in *Literary Friends and Acquaintance*, HE, p. 176. Howells wrote Garfield's obituary for the *Atlantic*, November 1881. See also *Years of My Youth*, HE, pp. 175–77.

3. The first edition of Howells' campaign biography, which makes up the first part of *Lives and Speeches of Abraham Lincoln and Hannibal Hamlin* was published by Follett, Foster & Co. on 5 June 1860. It was the ninth such biography to appear. See Ernest J. Wessen, "Campaign Lives of Abraham Lincoln," *Papers in Illinois History and Transactions for the Year 1937*, 44 (1938), 188–220.

4. Howells had not been invited to the party given for Hay and Nicolay when they stopped in Columbus on their way to Lincoln's inauguration, 13–14 February. See *Years of My Youth*, HE, pp. 181–82.

24 MARCH 1861, COLUMBUS, TO VICTORIA M. HOWELLS

Sunday March 24, 1861.

Dear Vic—

It is a much longer time since I wrote to you, than I ever meant it should be; but you know how it is with those flighty purposes, that have not the pleasure of the company of deeds. I am afraid indeed that I have the habit of taking things too much for granted and of thinking that you can understand. I think about you when I am not writing to you. And then, it cannot be denied that I grow indolent and selfish, and wait for humors of writing, which never come.

But it seems to me if ever I went back to Jefferson to live (and distant be *that* fate!) we should be just as much confidants as if long absences and long silences had not intervened between this and the times we walked and talked together. Dear Vic, after I began to see thoroughly the meanness and hollowness of that wretched little village-life, and narrowed the circle of my days to the limits of home, you made me many a dreary Sunday evening pleasant. You were always kind and full of sympathy, and believed in me, often when I could not believe in myself. And sometimes looking back, I fear lest I may have ever seemed ungrateful to you, or forgetful of you,—when I did not know. I am aware of the "finer female sense," which is easier hurt than any feelings of a man—but I have always tried to be the same to you that I used to be. I am sure, when I think of the good, unselfish life you live, devoting yourself to poor little Henry, I am quite ashamed of myself, and want to do something better than achieve reputation, and be admired of young ladies who read the "Atlantic." I take myself quite sharply to task, and go on being just as "languid and base" as before.

I am engaged now, every leisure moment in copying and dressing up that story of which I read you part last summer.[1] In some respects I like it, but I encounter so many faults, that I have to struggle continually against impulses of disgust. The hopes of the money for which it will sell, and the thought of the pleasure I can give in several ways with that mony, lure me on.—I have been working on a poem of some length,[2] but it is another failure, and is finally thrown aside.—Otherwise, I don't know much in a literary way to tell you about myself—and I don't know whether you will be even interested in this.

How did you enjoy your Bowling-green visit? If I should go to Germany, (which is improbable,) I will start sometime in June, and before I leave, I will make a tour of the Howells family, and so will visit grandmother.[3] I think I will go to see her at any rate, as I go home this spring.

I presume, you have heard from father, by the word Mrs Carter sent, of a violent flirtation which has been going on here this winter. Father is very curious about it, but masks his anxiety under a pretence that you girls would like to know.[4] I said I thought your opportunities of information were somewhat limited; but I don't mind telling you that nothing very serious has occurred. Tell Annie the subjects of her sketches were admirable, but I could not admire them as works of art.

I understand both of the "grils" are down on me because I have written them letters of salutary reproof. I am very sorry—but such is the ingratitude of people you make yourself disagreeable to.

I had not much news to write you, Vic, and indeed only wrote this letter in order to resume our correspondence. We have heard from Sam, who says (it is rather short notice) that he likes dentistry very well.[5] Sam made the best impression here.

Give my dear love to mother and all the family.

Your affectionate brother
Will.

  1. The unpublished "Geoffrey Winter."
  2. "Bopeep: A Pastoral."
  3. Earlier Howells' paternal grandmother, Anne Thomas Howells (1785?–1863), widow of Joseph (1783–1858), and her daughter Anne Cooper Howells (1809–1868), had lived in Jefferson; the date of their move to Bowling Green has not been established.
  4. Howells may refer to his acquaintance with Elinor G. Mead, as the earlier phrase about "young ladies who read the 'Atlantic'" also suggests. See *Years of My Youth*, HE, p. 194, and *Life in Letters*, I, 24.
  5. Sam may have served as a dental apprentice with his uncle Henry C. Howells in Hamilton. Later he was looking for further training in New York (see Howells to Mary D. Howells, 6 November 1861), and in subsequent years he intermittently practiced dentistry in Jefferson.

21 April 1861, Columbus, to Victoria M. Howells

Columbus, April 21, 1861.

My dear Sister—

Your reproach that I neglect you at home is hardly deserved. The past week I have been so very busy, I really could not write, if the excitement had permitted me to write anything. I knew that father was writing, and I thought that would do, until I got time.

Everything is in an uproar here, and the war feeling is on the increase, if possible.[1] There has been a sort of calm to-day in the city, but down at the camp the carpenters were busy building barracks, and the troops were drilling and the mad and blind devil of war was spreading himself generally. The volunteers seemed to be in very good spirits, and to look upon campaigning as something of a frolic. A good many of them are young boys—not over eighteen; but some are men past their prime. Poor fellows! I pitied them but being at work on a patriotic paper, I tried to see some sense in the business they had undertaken, but couldn't. It is a sad fact that after the war has been fought out, the government must treat upon the basis of disunion at last. I don't see that the war could have been avoided, but it is not the less a stupid and foolish war on that account. War is always stupid and foolish.[2]

Father has doubtless told you that we received a letter from Sam. He wont volunteer, and I wont, so long as there are people more eager to go.

There is not much to write but war news. I am quite well. Dear love to all. Write soon,

Your affectionate brother,
Will.

1. Five days earlier, on 16 April, Howells had written about his reaction to the war in "From Ohio," New York *World*, 22 April 1861. It was the first of five such reports by Howells to appear in the *World* (see Gibson-Arms, *Bibliography*, p. 86), and there is evidence that Howells tried to get a position on that paper about this time. On 16 May 1861 he wrote to Edmund Clarence Stedman (1833–1908), then a staff member of the *World*: "I have journalized for four or five years, and know something of political and other writing; and it occurs to me that perhaps the *World* is not so full, but that I could sell occasional articles to it, or even make some regular engagement. You see, the fact is I want to live in New York...." See *Life and Letters of Edmund Clarence Stedman*, ed. L. Stedman and G. M. Gould (New York: Moffat, Yard & Co., 1910), I, 248. Stedman's reply of 20 May 1861 (MH) reads in part: "In relation to your coming to N. Y.—The fact that I find time to write you even this brief note, is at this time the strongest evidence I can show of a genuine desire to see you and know you as a N. Y. literary man.... And as for The World. We think it a success, but as a new journal, encountering a virulent jealousy, it has of course suffered more & been obliged to contract more than the other leading sheets. So there is no place open here at present." For Howells' later comments on his friendship with Stedman, see *Literary Friends and Acquaintance*, HE, pp. 74–78.

2. In his report of 22 April, Howells adopts a different attitude toward the war preparations as he describes with apparent pride the confidence "the loyal citizens of Ohio" have in "the ability and general intentions of the present administration, and in the justice of the cause."

22 MAY 1861, COLUMBUS, TO OLIVER W. HOLMES, JR.

Columbus, May 22, 1861.

My dear Holmes—

It is my shame and punishment that I have so long deprived myself of the pleasure of hearing from you. I really meant to have written that Next Week which is now so long lost in the past, that I can't remember how it came or went.

I hear by a circuitous route that you have enlisted. Is that true?[1] If so,—how? why? when? For myself, I have not yet gone in. But who knows himself now-a-days? I seriously contemplate a Zouave company now forming here of my young men friends, who offer me a privacy, on favorable terms.[2] But as I said, who knows himself? The hot weather comes on. The drill will be very hot and oppressive. And whatever valor I have had in earlier years, has been pretty well metaphysicked out of me, since I came of thought.

Your New England fellows, by Jove! are glorious. And you've heard how Ohio has done? It *is* a great country, isn't it? And what a magnificent age—for throat-cutting. Bon dieu! how sad was the error of the people that died last year!

You see, this is merely an excuse to get to hear from you again.

Write to me soon, please, and tell me all about yourself.

Yours always
Howells.

1. Holmes enlisted on 25 April 1861. See Mark A. DeWolfe Howe, *Justice Oliver Wendell Holmes* (Cambridge, Mass.: Harvard University Press, Belknap Press, 1957), I, 70.

2. See Howells to Mary D. Howells, 26 May 1861.

26 MAY 1861, COLUMBUS, TO MARY D. HOWELLS

Columbus, May 26, 1861.

My dear Mother—

Again I must write instead of going to see you; but I will not delay my visit home much longer. Day after day, week after week I have waited for Mr Cooke's return, fearing to go away in his absence lest he should come to Columbus, and leave again without my seeing him.[1] I have no earthly means of telling when he will be back here, and I will not wait for him any longer. Mr Price has promised to dun him for me in the most solemn and impressive manner, and I couldn't do more than that if I remained. I have returned an obsolete *pass* to Cleveland, in order that it may be changed to one of present effect, and when I get that I will start for home—probably the latter part of this week. I'm very anxious to see all—doubly so to see you in particular.

The other evening, Selden Day came to see me.[2] He was in Columbus on army business—trying to get a company which he had raised, accepted for the three years' service. He told me he thought I could be elected lieutenant, if I chose to go into his company, and I was greatly tempted. Besides the natural curiosity and willingness to see military service, the fact that all kinds of business and especially literature, will be dull for the next year, formed an inducement to enter upon the adventure. I have not yet wholly relinquished the idea, but from my natural tendency to have spells and to get over them, I presume I shall recover from this. Captain Day is very ardent—and he's rather a nice boy—a good deal like Sam.

I thought of going to Bowling-Green before visiting home, but now I've concluded to stop there on my way back to Columbus.

Love to all.

Your affectionate son,
Will.

1. Howells had written to his mother on 5 May 1861 (MH; *Life in Letters*, I, 34–35) that he might lose both his job and the two hundred dollars Henry D. Cooke owed him when F. W. Hurtt (with Dr. Isaac J. Allen) took over the *Ohio State Journal*. In his letter to his father of 7 August 1861 (MH), Howells wrote that he still had not received the money.

2. Selden Allan Day (b. 1836) did not secure his captainship; he began service as a private in 1861 and remained in the army until his retirement as a lieutenant colonel in 1902. In a letter to W. C. Howells, 17 November 1872 (MH), Howells called Day "a good fellow, but an awful braggart and swell—in an innocent, unconceited way, however."

24 JUNE 1861, COLUMBUS, TO JOHN G. NICOLAY

Columbus, June 24, 1861.

My dear Sir—

I am sorry that Munich seems impossible; but I am glad to have heard from you, and to have received the assurance of your interest in me.

I wanted to go to Munich, you know, not only because it was a German city, but because it was also a city of literature and art, and because I should there be in the atmosphere for which I have always longed.[1] Vienna does not seem to me to be such a place; but the idea of four years' opportunity at Europe, and four years' release from an occupation which I never liked, makes the place a great temptation. Vienna, I notice, is a consulate of $1,500 while Munich is only $1000. I would rather have had the latter at the lesser salary, for though I am certainly poor enough, money was not at all what I wanted. Indeed, I would rather go to almost any other German city than Vienna.[2] Leipzig—is that spoken for?

But you intimate that even a degree of uncertainty attaches to Vienna. Then I give you a carte blanche and—there is the Blue Book![3] You see I am perfectly reasonable, and will take anything, so that the salary is not too large.—I suggest: I am acquainted with the Spanish language. Is Cadiz gone the way of Munich?

You are very kind, and I am very sorry about Munich. I have despaired all along, but still it is desolating to find that the place is at last denied me. Is there really no hope?

Anything you can do for me will be gratefully appreciated.—And I shall hope to hear from you of the prospect, when you can find time to write.

Very truly yours,
W. D. Howells.

Please don't misconstrue what I have said into an unwillingness to accept the Vienna consulate, unless there should still be some chance of Munich.

Mr John G. Nicolay.

    1. In his letter to Howells, 18 June 1861 (MH), John Hay, who also served as Lincoln's private secretary, had written that although the applications for the "Munich consulate...are somewhat numerous, none seem so well supported as yours. Besides, you have in Gov. Chase a sincere and earnest advocate. Still, though I think your chances hopeful, you know that it is easier to predict the destination of a thunderbolt than of an office." John Hay (1838–1905) was later secretary of state (1898–1905). He maintained a close literary and personal relationship with Howells that is reflected in his 70 extant letters to Howells. On Hay's death, Howells wrote "John Hay in Literature," *North American Review*, September 1905.
    2. Howells wrote Nicolay the next day, 25 June 1861 (DLC), that he would take the consulship at Vienna by all means if the position at Munich should become unavailable.
    3. The Department of State issued a blue-bound *Register of Officers and Agents* listing all positions in the department.

4 AUGUST 1861, COLUMBUS, TO JOHN J. PIATT

Columbus, August 4, 1861.

My dear Piatt—

Looking over my letters today, in order to burn a half bushel of those I did not value, I carefully laid yours aside for preservation.[1] "Piatt will be a great man—or the world will find out that he is great one of these days," I said to myself. It was not a noble motive for keeping your letters; but it was one that among others actuated me. Is it comfort to know that I have faith in you? Be comforted then, even now, when—the hopes of literature lie dead. It filled me with a kind of sadness to read these letters which you wrote me abroad, the time The Book was coming out.[2] I have hoped so much since then, and done so little—and then, I thought with some bitterness how even the little good there was in the poor little book had never received justice. It was droll—the whole affair—but we were so honest, so foolish, so audacious in the venture—that I have never regretted it! Have you? Have you ever met Gail Hamilton?— I found her letter among the rest, but had not the countinance to read it.[3] E——! I did not come out first in that encounter, I fear, and yet the right was on my side; and she was most unfair. But she was a woman and not to blame for that.

You attribute my failure to send my poem to the wrong motive.[4] It is already copied; and I was sincere in giving the reasons I did. Indeed, I am quite out of hand with whatever I do, or have done. Vaulting ambition! and so forth.

Aren't you sorry the Atlantic goes so gun-powderfully into the war?

It's patriotic; but do we not get enough in the newspapers? I would rather have the honey of Attic bees.

In a short time I'm going to New York to live. I'm out of the State Journal,[5] and Munich seems extremely improbable. By the way, could you learn when the consular appointments will probably be made, and write me some account of the matter immediately?

If I were you, I think I would try to make Mr. Hay's acquaintance. From the letter he wrote, and from all I have heard about him, he must be a fine fellow. I have nothing very interesting to say, and write principally that I may hear from you again.

I understand that a new critical and art journal is to start in New York by — —, who used to be on the poor dear S. Press.[6] I don't see how such a thing could succeed now. However!

Adieu—and write me soon.

W. D. H.

1. Only one earlier letter from Piatt to Howells has been located; it is dated 15 November 1860 (MH). Half a dozen later ones are extant.

2. *Poems of Two Friends.* There is no further evidence of Piatt's having gone abroad in 1859–1860.

3. Presumably the letter Howells destroyed was Gail Hamilton's reply to his letter of 27 February 1860, or to an earlier one.

4. Possibly "Louis Lebeau's Conversion," *Atlantic,* November 1862, the first major poem published after this letter.

5. Just when Howells left the *Ohio State Journal* is uncertain. His last recorded publication there for this year is "Literary Gossip," 23 February 1861. A letter of 6 May 1861 (MH) from Henry D. Cooke suggests that Howells' resignation was submitted on 30 April, but Howells' letters to his mother on 5 May (MH) and 26 May indicate that he remained in Columbus, hoping to collect the money due him for past services. Later Howells remembered that his departure took place either in late July or early August. See Howells to Comly, 7 July 1868, and *Years of My Youth,* HE, pp. 204–6.

6. The *Saturday Press* stopped publication in 1860, and briefly resumed it in 1865. Probably Howells was referring not to the editor, Henry Clapp, but to another member of the staff.

7 September 1861, WASHINGTON, TO WILLIAM C. HOWELLS

Washington, Sept. 7, 1861.

Dear father—

I suppose you are anxious to hear from me, and my success in office-seeking. After spending a day and a half in New York, I came on to this city, and arrived in a rain that sank my heart into my boots—it was so dismal.[1] But I set to work at once. I found that the law did not permit the increase of the pay of any but sea-port consulates, and I found that

Rome was worth but a trifle over $500, and very uncertain at that.[2] So I went to see Mr Nicolay, the President's private secretary. He said he would see if the Consulate of Venice were vacant. I should call again next day. I called, the place was vacant, he thought I could have it. I am told by him that President has signed my commission, and that it only awaits some formality at the State Department. Nicolay thinks I will get it on Monday.[3] Venice is now worth $750 a year—*in salary*, and N. says, that being a seaport can be raised to $1000. I am pleased with my luck, and consider the change a fortunate one. When I get my commission in my pocket, I shall feel perfectly satisfied.

I am well, and full of hope. I have seen poor Hinton,[4] who is neither, and in truth Washington is a most heart-sickening place—the Disappointed throng the streets like uneasy ghost, and refuse to believe themselves hopeless.—There is nothing to make a letter about for the paper. The place is dull and quiet, and you hear nothing of war.

I don't know exactly when I'll be home, but soon I hope. I'm staying with Piatt,[5] and am managing cheaply. Love to all,

Affectionately
Will.

1. For a somewhat different account of this trip, see *Years of My Youth*, HE, p. 205.
2. Howells had written to J. J. Piatt on 23 August 1861 (location of manuscript unknown) that he had received an appointment to the consulate at Rome.
3. As expected, Howells received his appointment on Monday, 9 September 1861.
4. Richard J. Hinton (1830–1901), a London-born journalist and author, was associated with John Brown in Kansas and served in the Union Army (1861–1865).
5. Piatt was at this time a clerk in the Treasury Department (1861–1867); he had married Sarah Morgan Bryan on 18 June 1861 and was living in Georgetown.

28 SEPTEMBER 1861, JEFFERSON, TO MRS. SAMUEL M. SMITH

Jefferson, Sept. 28, 1861.

Dear Mrs Smith—

Your kindness has reached me even here,—remote from man, with cheese I spend my days.[1] I know it will pursue me to Venice, and cause me to add the tears of gratitude to the brine of the canals. I promise to name my gondolas (for I shall have several) after the members of The Smith Family. I am a thousand times obliged to the Doctor—and please say to him, that I will be very glad if he can raise me the $200, and send them to me here directly, in New York exchange. If it had not been for going to Washington, I could have managed with $100, but that expedition destroyed the efficiency of a similar sum so badly, that

I am obliged to—not to put too fine a point upon it—borrow $200.[2] The Doctor has been very kind in this matter, and has conferred a favor upon the Consular service that it will ever remember.

If it were possible, I'd tell you about my experiences in Washington—but Washington, like the most subtle varieties of emotion is more easily imagined than described. When you've been at Washington, you know somethings that you didn't know, before you'd been there. For instance, you find that office, like osculation, goes by favor; and that a re-iterent and long-continuing friend at court, is much better than many virtues and services. But I don't wish to unveil the dreadful mysteries of Republican government to your trustful vision. Only, if you ever have an opportunity of going to Washington, improve it by keeping away. (This is a sacred aside—delivered in a hoarse whisper, audible only to the orchestra, and the front seats of the pit.). From Washington, I went to New York, and after concluding an engagement to write occasional letters to the N. Y. Times, I went on to Boston.[3] There I met my last summer friends, and enjoyed them greatly. Their friendship had suvived a year—it will be eternal! I dined with Mr Lowell, at his house a little out of Cambridge, and had a dinner of vegetables and poultry, which he thought had a peculiar excellence because they were all raised upon his place. I saw his wife—and his daughter—the latter a little younger than your Fanny; the former, bearing a striking resemblance to Miss Annie Swan—as was.[4] In the evening, Mr Sturgis,[5] who is attending law school at Cambridge, called upon me at the Parker House, and we drank a bottle of Catawba to the glory and prosperity of Ohio, and declared, as we drew near the heel, that there never was a place worthy to be compared to Columbus, and that C. was inhabited by a race of beings—females—who would certainly fly, if they did not know it was more graceful even for angels to walk.—Next morning I breakfasted with Mr Fields, who told me among other things that the story of "The Haunted Shanty" was founded upon facts current in Summit co. O. Eber Nicolson is now in one of the Illinois regiments; Rachel Emmons died at Toledo.[6] Isn't that curious?—I ran in a moment after breakfast to see Dr Holmes, who lives only a few doors off, and suffered myself to be beguiled out of all recollection of a train which I was to take, until the very last moment. Dr Holmes is always delightful—I think there's nobody like him. He gave me his carte de visite, and wrote his name upon it. His son, with whom I corresponded, is a lieutenant in one of the Massachusetts regiments at Washington. After seeing Boston I re-turned to N. Y. and so came home.[7] Since my arrival here, I have visited my grandmother in Wood co.; today I've just got back.[8] I've sent my bond on to Washington,[9] and I now only wait my passport (and the $ $ $) before sailing. I wont go out in the Great Eastern[10]—your

letter has determined me. My love—if you please—to all your family.—
Remember me to Miss Anthony, when you write her. I shall never forget
our delightful little picnic.

Very sincerely yours
W. D. Howells.

Please express my gratitude to Mrs McMillan,[11] whose letter I shall use all the same as if I had gone to Rome.

1. A humorous misquotation from Thomas Parnell, "The Hermit": "Remote from man, with God he passed the days" (line 5).

2. Dr. Smith sent Howells $150 on 1 October 1861 (MH), promising $50 more; the letter is annotated in Mildred Howells' hand: "lent three hundred dollars to W. D. H. when he went abroad." Howells thanked Smith for $150 on 3 October 1861 (OHi). See also *Years of My Youth*, HE, p. 144.

3. The arrangement with the New York *Times* did not result in contributions. Three "Letters from Europe" appeared in the *Ohio State Journal* in January 1862; "Letter from Europe" and "From Europe" were published in the *Sentinel*, 14 May and 30 July 1862 respectively; and "Letters from Venice" began in the Boston *Advertiser*, 27 March 1863. See Gibson-Arms, *Bibliography*, pp. 87–89.

4. Lowell's second wife was Frances Dunlap; Mabel, the daughter of Lowell's first marriage to Maria White, was born in 1847. Fanny Smith may be "the youngest daughter of the house" mentioned in *Years of My Youth*, HE, p. 142, and Annie Swan the daughter of Judge Joseph R. Swan.

5. Charles Matthews Sturges (b. 1838) was a law student at Harvard (1861–1862); beginning in 1863 he practiced law in Chicago.

6. Bayard Taylor, "The Haunted Shanty," *Atlantic*, July 1861. Eber Nicholson and Rachel Emmons are characters in the story.

7. By means of a long curved line connecting "re" and "turned," Howells here suggests a detour via Brattleboro to visit Elinor Mead. See Cady, *Howells*, I, 91.

8. See *Years of My Youth*, HE, pp. 7–8.

9. See Howells to Seward, 28 October 1861, n. 2.

10. The *Great Eastern* was the longest ship built until 1899, but it attracted few passengers.

11. Probably the wife of Dr. William L. McMillen (1829–1902), active in civic and political affairs, and editor of the *Columbus Review of Medicine and Surgery*.

6 OCTOBER 1861, JEFFERSON, TO OLIVER W. HOLMES, JR.

Jefferson, Oct. 6, 1861.

My dear friend—

I'm very sorry I just missed seeing you at Boston. The same thing happened last summer, and I thought once was enough. However, I've no doubt fate will arrange matters better on another occasion. In general, my destiny is good to me—almost incredibly good in this Venetian business. I feel that I shall now have for the first time in my life, *a chance* —and if I don't improve my opportunity of Europe, of money, of leisure, I shall not look forward to a continuation of those blessings, for I certainly wont deserve them.

As to the poor little poems sent back: I was certainly disappointed in the rejection of *one*.[1] It seemed to me the best thing I ever did; and the worst effect is that I wont dare, hereafter, to send anything, that *I* like, to the Atlantic.

Please remember me to your father and to Mr Fields. If it ever occurs to you to write me, be sure that the U. S. Consul at Venice will be glad to hear from you.

And goodbye, with thanks for good wishes, and the heartiest reciprocation of them.

Yours very sincerely,
W D Howells.

1. One poem rejected by the *Atlantic* was "Bereft," which probably became "Forlorn," *Nation*, 16 August 1866. See *Literary Friends and Acquaintance*, HE, pp. 75–76.

28 OCTOBER 1861, JEFFERSON, TO WILLIAM H. SEWARD

Jefferson, Ashtabula county, Ohio
October 28, 1861.

Hon. Wm H. Seward,[1]
Secretary of State—

Sir—

In transmitting my bond as Consul at Venice to the Department of State,[2] I omitted, in thus requesting my passport, to communicate the facts of personal description, etc., usually furnished to the Department by applicants for passports. I now communicate these facts, as follows:

Name, William D Howells; place of birth, Martinville, Belmont county, Ohio; last place of residence, Columbus Ohio; profession, journalist. Age 24 years; stature, five feet and five inches; forehead, medium height; eyes gray; nose nearly straight; mouth medium size; chin somewhat short, hair brown; face oval; complexion rather dark.

I am, sir, very respectfully

Your obedient servant,
W D Howells,
U. S. Consul at Venice.[3]

1. William Henry Seward (1801–1872) served in a number of public offices beginning in 1830. An unsuccessful candidate for the presidential nomination in 1860, he became secretary of state in 1861, remaining in that office until 1869.

2. Howells first sent his bond to Seward on 18 September, but it was lost, and

he sent another on 25 October (DNA). Dated 22 October 1861, it is for $3,000, signed by Howells, Joseph A. Giddings, Stephen McIntyre, witnessed by W. C. Howells and P[?]. W. McIntyre, and certified 23 October by R. F. Paine, U. S. district attorney at Cleveland.

3. For a full record of official endorsements of consular reports and correspondence see Textual Apparatus. George J. Abbott, mentioned in the endorsement, is listed in the Department of State *Register of Officers and Agents*, 1861, as clerk of the fourth class in the office of the secretary of state.

31 OCTOBER 1861, NEW YORK, TO WILLIAM C. AND MARY D. HOWELLS

New York, Oct. 31, 1861.

Dear father and Mother—

I've got so far, you see, on my outward bound journey; but I shall not be afloat for a week, yet. The gentleman who is going out as Consul to Civita Vecchia,[1] has concluded a bargain with me, to the effect that if I will wait one week for him, he'll go through Germany with me, so that we shall be compagnons du voyage the whole way. He's a good, whole-hearted fellow, whom it will do me good, in more ways than one, to be with. I don't find my spirits rise with the distance between me and home, and I feel like clinging to something American as long as possible. Moreover, this consul to C. V. is an adept in Italian, and can be useful to me in my study of the grammar going across the Atlantic.—I have not found cousin Henry in town here,[2] but he leaves me a note directing me to make his boarding house my home, so that my week's stay here, will not cost me much.—While I think of it, let me ask you to disintegrate my "Atlantics" and taking out my poems, have Otto[3] bind them up in a little flexible backed book, with some twenty blank pages. Please do this immediately, and express the book to me at Mr Ward's.[4] I got your letter, this morning, having arrived here at 4 A.M.

In Washington, I enjoyed myself very much indeed, with French, Piatt, "Harrington" O'Connor, Eldredge (Thayer & Eldredge) Stedman of the *World*, and last and best, Charley Howells.[5] He *is* a capital fellow, and did everything he could—which was a good deal—to make my stay in Washington pleasant. I succeeded so well in my affairs, that I felt well, and could take advantage of the good society I had. Among other feats of mine, was eating a *peck* of steamed oysters.—Charley and his wife desired to be most kindly remembered to you, and gave many invitations for you to visit them.

Tell Sam, that cousin Charlie has given me a letter to a Dentist here in N. Y. with whom he thinks Sam can get a place.[6] I'll deliver the letter tomorrow, and then write Sam immediately. Dearest love to all.

Affectionately your son
Will.

You see I've got the *thinnest* paper that could be bought for money. Write me as soon as you get this, care of Ward.

I suppose you've received my passport from the Dep't. I got one in Washington, but you may send the other here. I can't have too many passports.

1. Harry B. Brown, better known as Harrison B. Brown (1831–1915), a painter, became consular agent at Civita Vecchia, the chief port of Rome, on 28 December 1861. He was dismissed shortly afterwards, allegedly for issuing American passports for spies in Italy. Howells later remembered him in "Overland to Venice," *Harper's Monthly*, November 1918. See *Years of My Youth*, HE, p. 209.
2. Henry C. Howells, Jr., son of Howells' uncle, Henry C. Howells, Sr., the Hamilton dentist.
3. Otto Limbeck, the Jefferson bookbinder.
4. John Quincy Adams Ward (1830–1910), the sculptor, knew Howells well in Ohio; they saw each other occasionally throughout their lives. See *Years of My Youth*, HE, pp. 184–85, 187.
5. Mansfield French (1810–1876), clergyman, was a teacher and founder of several Ohio colleges in the 1840s and 1850s; in Washington he was engaged in plans for freeing and educating the slaves. William Douglas O'Connor (1832–1889) had his abolitionist novel, *Harrington* (1860), published by Thayer and Eldridge and by Follett, Foster & Co. A review, possibly by Howells, appeared in the *Ohio State Journal*, 26 November 1860. Charles W. Eldridge was a partner in this company, which also published the 1860 edition of Whitman's *Leaves of Grass*. Charles E. Howells was probably the brother of Henry C. Howells, Jr.
6. See Howells to V. M. Howells, 24 March 1861, n. 5.

6 NOVEMBER 1861, NEW YORK, TO MARY D. HOWELLS

New York, Nov. 6, 1861.

Dear Mother—

I certainly hope you have by this time got some of the many letters I have written home. The last one which came to me was from father, who stated that you had not yet heard from me. I write again, today, and shall write once more on Friday, for you know I sail on Saturday. Dear mother, I need not distress you by telling what a pang it is, to leave you so far for so long—no, I cannot write of it without tears. I have had more things to bear than you know—but I believe I am coming out of all a better man, and that my trouble has done me good. At least, it will always do me good to think of you and those at home, and I shall not despair of myself until I cease to think of you—which can never be.

In a business point of view, my office is a very fortunate thing just now, for literary people are by no means prosperous in New York, and if I came here to seek my fortune, it would be hard to find it. Then I am going abroad for my pleasure as much as profit—you must think of this, and of the fact that hundreds envy me this chance of livelihood and self-improvement.

Since my last, I have seen father's cousin Dora—who is a very nice girl a little older than Vic.[1] She had many inquiries to make about my sisters, of whom she had heard a great deal one way and another. I soon gave her to understand that they didn't amount to a great deal, but received a sort of reflected lustre from their brother. Perhaps I was somewhat vexed to find her as much interested in them as in me. The people Dora lives with are abolition and Swedenborgian, and they know a great deal more about the anti-slavery experiences of you ones at home than I did. At any rate they talked a great deal about them.—The N. Y. Howellses are by no means a disgrace to the family. Henry (with whom I am stopping,) will visit you the next time he goes west, and then you can judge for yourself. In the meantime, he wants you to have that medallion of mine photographed, and to send him two copies of the photograph exactly similar, so that he can have them arranged for a stereoscope. Just send them on the photograph paper—*not* mounted on cardboard. I hope that you have got my letter requesting my poems to be torn out of the "Atlantics" and bound up for me.

I do not think of any further news to tell you, but something may turn up to write about on Friday. I called again to see that Dentist for Sam, but did not find him. I'll try this morning. Goodbye for the present.

Your affectionate son,
Will.

I have seen that Dentist, and he tells me that there is nothing now doing in the profession here; but that he will keep Sam in mind, and give him the benefit of the first chance. That Preterre, in the Bowery, makes mere servants of his assistants, and no dentist can work for him without loss of reputation.[2] So if Sam *could* go back to uncle for a little while, until something turns up, it would be all the better for him. The Dentist of whom I speak has his address, and will write him, the first occasion.

I'm not going by the Hamburgh steamer—the first cabin is too dear, and the second too dirty. I'll go out by the Liverpool line, and through Belgium and Bavaria.[3] Tell Otto, I'll either see his parents next summer, or send the letters to them immediately.[4] I'll write again.

Affectionately
Will

1. The first mention of Theodora Howells, daughter of Israel, appears in a letter of 3 November 1861 (MH), in which Howells wrote his father that he had tried to look up "your cousin Dora" but did not find her at home. In a letter to

"Cousin Dora," 27 May and 12 June 1879 (MnHi), Howells sent a card of introduction to Larkin Mead, Jr., for her European trip. She was then living in Chicago.

2. Eugene and A. Preterre had offices at 159 Bowery as well as in Paris and later in Nice. The other dentist has not been identified. See also Howells to V. M. Howells, 24 March 1861, n. 5.

3. Howells sailed on 9 November 1861 on the *City of Glasgow*.

4. Otto Limbeck.

II

The Venetian Consulship

1 8 6 1 – 1 8 6 5

Introduction

HOWELLS arrived in Venice by train from Vienna on 7 December 1861, but he did not officially take charge of the consulate until 24 February 1862. The small number of American ships entering Venice made his consular duties very light, even for a conscientious public servant, and thus he enjoyed abundant leisure—a luxury he had never known except in periods of illness. At first he was the wide-eyed American tourist on his first European trip, noting the "wonders and novelties" of the city. "I am crushed flat beneath them—" he wrote his sister, "pounded to powder by pure astonishment." But Howells was already enough of a realist and sturdy American democrat to note as well the "mournfullest decay" and the "Squalor herding with vice in palaces...."

Much of his time was devoted to learning Italian, and his earlier practice in teaching himself languages enabled him to make rapid progress. Before long he could read Italian literature and enjoy theater performances, especially of the comedies of the eighteenth-century Venetian dramatist Carlo Goldoni, who was to be a major influence in the development of Howells' realistic fiction. His enthusiastic study of Italian literature, while pleasurable, was also a conscious step toward establishing himself as a professional critic and writer. He explained to his father on 27 April 1865: "I'm now reading up all the Italian literature of this century which I can, in order to make some articles for the N. American [Review]."

Howells' study of Italian culture included making friends and seeing famous places and art treasures. At first his social life was rather restricted by what he considered to be the generally unfriendly nature of the Italians. He particularly missed the company of young ladies for intellectual pleasures, as he had enjoyed it in Columbus. But gradually he made a number of friends who introduced him to the culture. Among them were G. A. Tortorini, who not only nursed Howells during a period of illness in early 1862, but lent him money and entertained him at his country home near Padua, and the much younger Eugenio Brunetta, who advised Howells in his studies of Italian literature and was his companion on many visits to the theater.

Nothing, however, was as effective in dispelling Howells' sense of social tedium and homesickness as his marriage to Elinor Mead of Brattleboro, Vermont, whom he had met in Columbus some time during the winter of 1859–1860. They had planned to marry in the summer of 1863 in America, but, unable to absent himself from the consulate for more than ten days at a time, Howells arranged to meet Elinor in England. Accompanied by her brother Larkin, they traveled to Paris, where they were married on 24 December 1862. The remaining years in Venice were blissfully happy ones for the young couple who fondly called one another "ducks." They rented first an apartment in Casa Falier and later the Palazzo Giustiniani, both overlooking the Grand Canal. They explored the city and its treasures of art and architecture, Elinor with her sketchbook and Howells with a sharp eye for manners and customs. Trips to Florence, Arquà, and Padua yielded additional material for literary treatment, but the birth of their first child, Winifred, on 17 December 1863 put a temporary end to their travels and focused their lives on domestic matters. Elinor soon began the custom of having "a little coffee and cake and cards Saturday evenings."

Howells' literary career did not advance as rapidly as he had hoped it would. He arrived in Venice with a desire to be a poet; he left three and one-half years later generally disappointed in his poetic endeavors but with a new respect for what he might accomplish in prose. One of his disappointments in poetry was the failure to find an English publisher for a volume of poems, even though his friend Moncure D. Conway, who had agreed to act as an informal literary agent, did manage to secure from Robert Browning a favorable written comment on the verse. Howells was also exasperated with Frank E. Foster, who reneged on his earlier agreement to publish the long poem "Disillusion." The *Atlantic*'s rejection of all Howells' offerings, after the publication of "Louis Lebeau's Conversion" in November 1862, finally forced him to work up his impressions and observations into a series of "Letters from Venice," which ran first in the Boston *Advertiser* and later developed into *Venetian Life*. As Lowell put it succinctly in his review of that volume, "Venice has been the university in which he fairly earned the degree of Master."

Howells' letters from Venice often express a somber mood about being far from home; he was anxious about his failure to find publishers for his poetry and about the discouraging news of the Civil War and the disruption it threatened to the lives of his brothers; he also experienced deep sorrow over the death of his brother John and the assassination of President Lincoln. Yet his letters convey an increasingly confident tone about his developing literary abilities. He was eager to put them to the test, and for that he felt he must return to America. When Howells and his young family disembarked at Boston on 3 August 1865 he was ready to begin earning his living with his pen.

R. H. B.

24 NOVEMBER 1861, LONDON, TO WILLIAM C. HOWELLS FAMILY

> Golden Cross,[1] Charing Cross, London.
> Nov. 24, 1861.

Dear folks at Home—

I mailed you a long and illegible letter at Queenstown, Ireland, on Friday morning. The following day, about 5 a.m. we landed at Liverpool, and by nine had passed scathless through the Customhouse. The examination of baggage, which I had thought of with annoyance, was a very cursory business,—the officer merely *feeling* through my valises, and not even looking at the title-pages of my books, which I told him were not reprints. So having my dear old Tennyson in my coat-pocket, I smuggled that through with a clean conscience. In a little while the passengers were all scattered, and I parted very regretfully with two or three—especially those pleasant New Englanders, of whom I spoke. They went on to Hamburg, by a direct route; and at half past ten I took the train for London. The day at Liverpool was wretchedly dismal, and I had made up my mind not to stop there, though there were of course many things to be seen.— (I shall have to stick to this plan throughout, if I wish to reach Venice with as much money in my pocket as I want. I did not prepay the letter I mailed at Queenstown, for I had to send it from the ship, and the purser told me that the money I sent might not be applied to postage by the messenger.) Liverpool, what with the muddy banks of the Mersey River, and the smokiness and grime of everything, made me think of Pittsburg—and this is all of Liverpool. But, that Rr. ride between Liverpool and London, was delicious. The English cars with their narrow, snug little compartments, are so much nicer than ours, and the road was so smooth that there was no jolting at all. And Oh! the English country landscapes! How I languished to have each and all of you with me, as I recognized one after another all the beautiful features of the scenery, of which we have read so much in books. Here was Dickens and Tennyson over and over again. It was like a fair dream of England that I once had—a gracious peaceful land, with sloping meadows, and long hedgerows, and groves of oaks; with canals and "slow barges"; with pretty country roads winding through the unfaded fields, and with cosy farmhouses, snugly set among the trees. Like all beautiful things, this lovely landscape filled with "joy hidden in sorrow,"[2] and it was as often, I think the tears in my own eyes, as the breath of the engine upon the window, that obscured the scene. I am sorry that I have said anything about it; for I cannot picture it, and can only provoke your curiosity. You must have herds feeding in those little vales, and windblown flocks of rooks rising from the fields; you must have glimpses of stately mansions, crowning distant, bosky knolls; you must imagine a continuous village along the whole route, nearly; then you must plunge into the many-chimnyed grime and darkness of Wolverhampton, of Birmingham, and the other great manufacturing towns through which we passed. Do not forget to clear up your weather, and shine softly upon the landscape with a sun that sets redly at a little after three o'clock.—It was five o'clock and quite dark, when we reached London.—Now everything seems so secure and well-cared for in England, that I had no tremor in reaching the greatest city in the world, such as nervous people usually experience in strange places. The railroad men are models of politeness—one old Tony-Weller-guard coming to our window at each stoppage,[3] and chatting cheerfully about our progress, etc., and at one eating-station, running to call my compagnons du voyage lest "the three foreign gentlemen" should ignorantly get left?[4] (First time, by the way, that I ever heard an American called a "foreigner.") As soon as the train stopped in London, we got out, and one of the railroad porters got us a cab,—which brought us hither to the heart of the city, for about 27 cents each—very cheap. After I got my dinner, I fell into chat with a very intelligent Englishman in the coffee-room, who had once been in Canada, and who was delighted to talk about America. (You may be sure that I did not omit to spread the Eagle.)— one's patriotism rises, the further one gets from home, I find. After while I went out and made some purchases—getting some linen handkerchiefs for an English shilling apiece which would have cost 75 cents in America—but it is the belly, not the back, which costs in this country. On my return, I found the young man with whom I came over—he is in the sewing machine line,—waiting for me with his principal, an American, who has just started his business in London. With these two, today, I have seen something of the outside of London, and a little of the inside. We went through part of Westminster Abbey—O, girls! *such* a sensation! We saw the Parliament Houses, St Jameses Palace, Buckingham Palace, passed through St Jamese's Park, Hyde Park, and Kensington Gardens, and saw the vast buildings which they are putting up for the World's Fair. It is of no use for me to exclaim about each one of these places, and so I leave all that off—only you know everything was great, and vast and old, and the parks were full of people, and I was mightily interested.—Mem. The English women do not know how to walk, but have a plunging gallop. Mem. The men wear the most atrociously ill fitting clothes, and boots that can be bought for money.—Mem. The Devil is not so black as he is painted. I saw the sun to-day through the London smoke. Mem. That the day, nevertheless has been very raw and cold—there having been a heavy frost last night.

I feel very well, except for a slight cold, which I hope will have passed off by tomorrow.—I do not expect to be in London more than a day or two now, and I shall hardly write you again from this point; but I think you will hear from me at Munich, where I expect to spend next Sunday. This letter (with my dearest love,) ought to reach you in about two weeks, before which time, I hope to be in Venice.

O, is it possible that I am in England? Do you believe it or shall I wake presently, with the cry of father calling Sam? Goodnight. Kisses and hugs all around.

Affectionately,
Will.

1. Howells stayed at the Golden Cross because David Copperfield had stayed there. See "Overland to Venice," in *Years of My Youth*, HE, p. 213. The events related in this letter are described in greater detail in "Letter from Europe," *Ohio State Journal*, 9, 30, and 31 January 1862, but none of Howells' fellow passengers have been identified.

2. Tennyson, "The Dying Swan," stanza 3, lines 2–3.

3. Tony Weller is a character in Dickens, *Pickwick Papers* (1837).

4. Howells' company did not include Harrison B. Brown, with whom he had originally planned to travel, because Brown had missed the ship in New York. See *Years of My Youth*, HE, p. 209.

7 DECEMBER 1861, VENICE, TO WILLIAM C. HOWELLS FAMILY

Venice, December 7th, 1861.

Dear folks at home—

At last, I am arrived in this wonder-city to which it seems as if I had been coming all my life—so long, so wearisome has been the journey. Don't let the map of Europe deceive you. If the continent is small, the railroads are slow, and one spends as much time in traversing a little German State as it takes to go from home to New York.—I wrote you the last from London,[1] where I stopped three days, and then pushed on to Paris. I intended indeed to have written you from each point on my route, but I found myself often without the leisure, and often without the humor, for I knew that you did not want a *short* letter, and I could write no other. Making very brief pauses, where I halted at all, I was naturally eager to see the most that I could of each place, and I would be so tired after sight-seeing that I had not energy to take up a pen.—Let me tell you now of my travel, and you can look out the route on the map, if you like. From London, I went to a little seaboard town called Folkstone, arriving at eleven in the evening, and waiting three or four hours for the little steamer which was to take me to France. About five o'clock in the morning, we landed at *Boulogne sur Mer*, and were immediately boarded by some twenty frantic little old women, who in B. s. M. are the porters. They furiously possessed themselves of our baggage, and rushed up to the customhouse, where the officers scanned my modest traps with an eagle eye, and passed them unopened. (Note well that here in Boulogne, I got my first cup of French coffee, which is the most delicious drink in the world, and is successfully emulated by the German and Italian coffee. It is quadroon-colored, rich as Croesus, and bland as June.) I had the good fortune to be in company with some English people, who could speak French, and went with them to their hotel in Paris, where I bought a day's experience of Paris for eleven francs. (Don't expect me to tell you of cities, and that sort of thing. This is merely a little selfish record for your perusal alone). Of course Paris is wonderful—I'm going to write about it for the State Journal.[2] I left that city at eight o'clock in the evening, and instead of going to Marseilles, as I first intended, I went to Strasbourg, and so pursued my journey hither, overland. We stopped about an hour only at Strasbourg, and I made no other halt until I reached Stuttgardt, the capital of Würtemberg. I had on my way the company of a little old lady from London, who got in at Paris, and who was so delighted at my speaking English to her, that she executed a little comical pas de seul in the car.[3] She was going to Heidelberg to see her son, who was sick, there, and she told me nearly all her family history. I was equally confiding, and the dear old creature took pity on me so far from home, and was as tender of me, as could be. And when we got to the German frontier, where I could use the honest, good *sprache*, then I was at home, and managed magnificently for the old lady, settling her route, and doing everything for her. I got to Stuttgardt at ten o'clock, Friday night, and intended to go on the next day at four p.m., but calling on our consul there, I found him a gentleman from Cincinnati, living in such good American fashion with his mother and sisters, that I couldn't resist staying three days in Stuttgardt.[4] It is quite a wonderful little city, full of palaces full of pictures, and I saw everything—even the little village where Schiller was born.[5] Leaving these good friends on Monday afternoon, I went so far as Munich, where I stayed all night. The next morning at ten, I took the cars for Vienna, which city I reached Wednesday morning at 5 o'clock. Here I stopped two days, leaving Thursday. At Vienna, too, I enjoyed myself greatly, for there I found the consul a German from Illinois, and he went all about with me, and was extremely kind and good.[6] I took supper at his house, and he went with me to restaurants, where they have the most delicious coffee imaginable. And good beef-steak.—It was excessively cold, travelling from Vienna to this place, until we reached the southside of the mountains, when the most surprising change of temperature took place. On Thursday night the frost stood on our window panes nearly an half-inch thick, but Friday night there was none. It was five o'clock Saturday morning when I reached Venice. There at the depot, I took a gondola, and glided up the Grand Canal, with its sad old palaces on either side, and through an hundred secret, winding streets of water, to the door of the Hotel Danielli.[7] You cannot imagine how weird and strange this little ride was. A perfect silence reigned, except for the starlit-silvered dip of the oars, and the groaning of the gondoliers. The lofty houses, white and grand, lifted on either side, and the lamps burning at intervals only made the night more solemn and mysterious. I confess to you that I did not feel altogether comfortable. I had a little mony about me, and my gay gondolier might have dipped me into the water, and let me stay there, without my being able to make anybody understand the facts of the situation. However, they didn't, and I went to bed at the hotel, and slept till ten o'clock.—Now you know, I have just arrived in Venice, and I write you without being able to enter into particulars; but I can tell you that the city is as beautiful as ever it was dreamed, and that my heart if beauty could satisfy it, would be at peace. But exile is so sad, and my foolish heart yearns for America. Ah! come abroad, anybody that wants to know what a dear country Americans have!—We tremble here, the outgoing Consul and I, lest there should be a war with England, which would be most disastrous in every respect. God avert it!—En passant, this Ex-consul has acted in the kindest manner, and does everything to assist me in learning the way to do things.[8] But for his protection, I should already have been grievously cheated in one hundred ways.

Now I bring the letter to a close, hoping to write again in a few days. If father will do this for me, he will save me writing to all these people, and consequently many heavy postages. Let him write, please to C. F. Brown of Vanity Fair, and request him to prepay each copy sent to me, and charge to my account.[9] The postpaid postage is frightful. Write also to Mr John Swinton of the New York Daily Times, and tell him to send me the Weekly Times prepaying as aforesaid.[10] Write to cousin Henry in N. Y. and tell him that the letter I sent him from London was not prepaid through an error of the hotel people, and that I am ashamed, and will write him soon. If you like you can send this letter to Mrs Carter, to whom I'm going to write before long.[11] Goodbye. I hope to hear soon from home, for I have as yet received no letters. Dearest love to every one.

Most affectionately,
Will.

1. The letter of 24 November 1861.
2. The description of Paris, if it was written, did not appear in the *Ohio State Journal*.
3. The English lady has not been identified.
4. William Frederick Nast (1840–1893) was U. S. consul at Stuttgart until 1864. He was the son of William Nast (1807–1899), founder of "German Methodism" in America, and became the father of Condé Nast (1874–1942), publisher of *Vogue*.
5. Marbach on the Neckar River.
6. The consul at Vienna was Dr. Theodore Canisius, to whom Lincoln had written a widely reprinted political letter on 17 May 1859, and for whom he had purchased the *Illinois Staats-Anzeiger* to enable Canisius to become its editor.
7. The Hotel Danieli, founded in 1822, was famous as the favorite of royalty and distinguished authors.
8. John Jacob Sprenger (1825–1902) served as U. S. consul at Dresden before his Venetian appointment. Principally a brewer, he lived in Lancaster, Pennsylvania. until he moved to Atlanta about 1872.
9. Charles Farrar Browne (1834–1867), better known by his pseudonym "Artemus Ward," began his literary career with his series of "Sayings" in the Cleveland *Plain Dealer* (1857); he was editor of *Vanity Fair* in 1860, when Howells contributed an unidentified poem to it. See *Literary Friends and Acquaintance*, HE, pp. 72, 110; and *Years of My Youth*, HE, p. 183.
10. John Swinton (1830–1901) was an editor of the New York *Times* (1860–1870) and of the New York *Sun* (1875–1883). With increasing interest in labor causes, he published *John Swinton's Paper* (1883–1887), but later rejoined the *Sun* and remained there until 1897.
11. Howells' projected letter to Isabella Carter has not been located.

19 DECEMBER 1861, VENICE, TO ANNE T. HOWELLS

Venice, December 19, 1861.

My dear Annie—

I got your most welcome letter just a few minutes ago, and now I hasten to reply—somewhat briefly,—for before this, you will have received three letters from me, and you can read all the letters which accompany this, if you like, except the one sealed. That page addressed to "Sammie" is for Mr Price, which you must mail to him, wherever he is, with the explanation that it came in a letter to you. The letter addressed "dear Cousin" is for H. C. Howells jr., 359 Broadway, N. Y. care of G. L. & J. B. Kelty.[1] Miss Platt's letter according to superscription.[2] —I'm suited very well in Venice. No city could be more to my mind—it so quaint, so old, so beautiful, so sad. If no war with England occurs to interrupt communication with America, and all things go well at home, I foresee that the four years I shall spend here will, D. V., be very happy ones. In a former letter—written a week ago, I told the folks of my arrival here, etc. I would like now to tell you of all the wonders and novelties that I have encountered during the two weeks that I have been here; but how can I, Annie? I am crushed flat beneath them —pounded to powder by pure astonishment. Imagine a city with ninety splendid cathedrals full of exquisite paintings, with hundreds of beautiful palaces in the mournfullest decay. Fancy a city in which the streets are water—for, as Rogers says poetically, so is it most true of Venice, that

> "The sea is in her broad, her narrow streets,
> Ebbing and flowing, and the salt sea weed
> Clings to the marble of her palaces."[3]

There is not a horse nor mule, nor any beast of burden in the whole wonderful city, and only the black, slender gondolas steal through the streets. Everywhere are thousands of little, narrow crooked lanes, threaded through lofty palaces, and curious shops, and curious old houses, expanding now and then into a broad square before some church, always with a marble cistern in the center of it. The sun never shines in these sad little lanes that wander about so blindly, and thousands and thousands of the people never see the sun's blessed face, unless they come into the piazza to look at it. In this strange city, innumerable beautiful bridges cross the little canals, and they are full of grace and art. Statues are everywhere—so profuse indeed, as if here they quarried art out of the ground, as elsewhere they quarry the rough rock. All round the city lie charming little islands on the breast of the Adriatic, as serene and blue as heaven. To look down upon all this marvel, from the top of the lofty Campanile, is such a wild surprise as almost takes your breath away. It is more like a dream than a reality, and you wonder that it does not dissolve away before your eyes. Ah! Annie—Venice is everything that the poets and the painters have told us; but they have not always put the ruin and the melancholy desolation in their pictures, and yet this strikes me more even than the transcendent beauty. Everywhere decay, rust, rot, damp, dirt. Squalor herding with vice in palaces once beautiful enough for saints to live in; and the most painful stillness brooding over the poor old mistress of the sea. God grant that the pride of our own dear republic may have no fall like hers,—though sometimes I can hardly keep the tears back, when I think what perils threaten our country. At this distance, one sees them more clearly I think than when at home.

I have been very well here, since my arrival. The winter is no winter at all—nothing, but a Reserve May called December for fun.

When you write to grandmother, give my best love to her and to aunt Anne. Tell them I don't forget them, and am meditating a long letter to them.

I don't prepay the postage on my letters, because the money is not too abundant with me, just now;[4] and I can make it all up in a lump to father some day.

Dearest love to all. Write whenever you get my letters. I'll write again soon.

Your affectionate brother,
Will.

1. Cousin Henry was working for the Keltys, who were dealers in window shades and curtain goods.

2. Laura Platt, a cousin of Elinor Mead, had introduced Howells to his future wife in Columbus. She later married John G. Mitchell (1838–1894), a brigadier general in the Union Army and later a lawyer in Columbus. See *Years of My Youth*, HE, p. 202.

3. See Samuel Rogers, *Italy*: "Venice," lines 2–4.

4. Howells did not begin to receive his salary until he officially assumed office on 24 February 1862. Probably little or nothing remained of the loans from Dr. S. M. Smith and Joseph A. Howells, alluded to by Howells in his letter to his father, 22 March 1862 (MH). He wrote a draft for $91.69 on the secretary of treasury soon after his arrival in Venice (signed document, 10 December 1861; DNA); some time before he received his salary for the first quarter he wrote another draft for $259.00 (autograph document, 30 June 1862; DNA); and G. A. Tortorini lent him twelve gold sovereigns (about $90).

18 AND 21 JANUARY 1862, VENICE, TO VICTORIA M. HOWELLS

Venice, January 18, 1862.

Dear sister Vic—

I've just read through your letter, which the postman brought to me ten minutes ago. I answer while the impression is yet fresh upon my mind—an impression only less delightful than that I should receive from hearing you talk all that you wrote. I think your letter was too short—that's all; and I do not see why all the family do not send something each time. As for my own letters, I do not think you have to complain of their brevity; for since I have been in Venice, I have not only written you folks at home long letters, but have given you the benefit of numerous enclosures to other people. There are two in the present letter: one for "Richard M Stoddard, Corner 10th street and 4th Avenue, N. Y.,"[1] and the other for "Mr John Swinton, Care of the Scottish American Journal[2] or N. Y. Times, N. Y." I wish you'd send them, Vic, and accept the accompanying photographs, as a slight token of my gratitude, and a faint intimation of the glorious things I see in Venice every day. As for describing the place, and its novelties, the task is simply hopeless; it's as much as any one can do to enjoy them. Only you may well believe that Venice is as wonderful and beautiful as it is "cracked up to be." By this time, you will have read accounts of my London sensations in the State Journal,[3] if they publish my letters, and I do not know that I can say anything more than I have said about England.

You know that I was only there three days, and had not more than twelve hours daylight, put it altogether. Besides I felt so bitter toward the English, that I was glad to get out of England, where I was constantly insulted by the most brutal exultation at our national misfortunes. I tell you Vic, no one knows how much better than the whole world America is, until he tries some other part of the world. Our people are manlier and purer than any in Europe; and though I hope to stay here my full four years, and know I shall profit by my experience and enjoy it, I still hope to go back and engage in the strife and combat, which makes America so glorious a land for individuals.

Not but what I like the Italians and the Germans with their gentle and amiable ways. You would like them even better, and would undoubtedly pronounce them preferable to the best of Yankees. (By the way, that fair New Englander, was from Massachusetts, middle-aged and married.)—Last night I attended a lecture at the Schiller Casino (an Austrian club, here,) and met again the Russian gentleman of whom I spoke in my letter to Mrs Carter.[4] We fell into the pleasantest chat,—as Americans and Russians always do—and watched the people dancing, after the lecture was over. Your being present at a dance in Europe is sufficiant warrant that you are a proper person; and a gentleman does not require an introduction before asking a lady to dance; but though I was greatly tempted to dance, I refrained, for I was in my frock coat, and had only dark gloves. People are so punctilious here about such matters; and in order to stamp myself as respectable I've been obliged to buy and wear a "plug" hat, and have my boots blacked in the most regular manner. This latter service is performed for me at 25 soldi (about 10 cents) a week, by the most filthy and fascinating old wretch imaginable. It is a part of Venetian nature to cheat, and this excellent man tried to have me pay him in advance, urging a large, interesting, and suffering family in justification. I affected the extremest indignation, and declared that he could either do what I said, or leave my boots. Then he complied, and now every morning takes off his greasy old cap, and calls himself my servant, with a brazen humility that is worth twenty times the money I give him.—Of course beggars abound, but if you do not give, you say simply, *Altrovolle*! (another time,) when they bless you all the same, and you save a soldo. —The gondoliere are a droll race, much decenter than hackmen (to whom they correspond) in other cities. They have a charming vein of swindling and romance in their nature, and still cheat the *Inglesi* and chaunt the songs of Tasso. I have mustered enough Italian to talk to them, when I have business to; but I cannot wander about the city, seeking such base and unique conversation as I would like to do, for nothing on the part of a Consul would astonish the punctilious Italians so much, as curiosity that would take the form of actual inquiry. In fact I'm forced to be "respectable"—and am to that extent miserable. However, people become habituated to anything, and I've no doubt I shall get used to "living cleanly like a gentleman."[5]—You tell me of a mild winter. Here it has been unusually cold, and today, the weather is freezing. I just walked through the court of the Doge's palace on my way to get those photographs at a shop on the Riva Schiavoni, and I found it a mass of ice around the beautiful bronze fountains in the court. On New Years we had snow, to the depth of several inches; but that was soon disposed by the poor people who are paid for shoveling it up and throwing it into the canals. That couldn't be done in Jefferson, could it? However, of course the winter has been absolutely nothing to me, northern born to six month's freezing. The temperature for the most part has been that of those first frosty days in the fall, when you begin to make fires and think of chestnuts. In a few weeks now the spring will open. I rather dread the coming of summer, for I have been so well, up to this time, and in such good spirits, whereas the hot weather always makes me hypochondriacal. But I wont anticipate evil. I am so glad and contented to be here, and the future is all bright.—I study Italian every day, and spend my time in reading and writing. I have already sketched a poem—a love-story, which I call "Louis Lebeau's Conversion."[6] The scene is a camp-meeting one, and I think the poem will be successful. Tell father and mother I first thought of it that night they told me of camp meetings, when we sat out on the porch last September.

[Vic, if Aurelia is not glad to hear from Mrs Hinton, I'm glad of her indifference. You needn't say anything, but I do think Hinton is about the last person I'd want her to like. And for reasons.]

I hope father will succeed in his attempt on the Ohio Legislature, though I shouldn't think from the way he went in on the fusion people, that he could have a great number of hopes.[7]

To morrow, I'm going to see the Italian friends with whom I became acquainted. I wish you could know the lady, who is Russian by birth, and only Italian by marriage.[8] I called to see her husband, the other Sunday, and she was obliged to act as interpreter, speaking German with me, and translating into French for her husband.—She asked me all about my family, and how many sisters I had, and whether they were pretty. (I made you out *syrups*, every one.) Then she wanted to know whether I intended to marry in Italy, or had some beloved in America, and many other droll question, concluding by asking me whether I was of a very cheerful temperament, or not. She also promised to me acquainted with Italians, and bade me come often to her house.

Tuesday.—On Saturday night, I fell in with my Russian friend at the caffè, and we went to the opera together. The opera was "I Puritani," and it was beautifully sung. When it was about finished, there was a slight commotion in the crowd, and then a general clapping of hands, and the people rose to greet the Emperor who appeared in his box.[9] He is a rather handsome young soldier, and looked much more like royalty, than the old King of Wurtemberg, whom I saw at Stuttgardt. After bowing slightly to the audience, he sat down, stroking his blonde beard, and presently took his opera glass and engaged in the somewhat despiriting occupation of contemplating the hard-favored German ladies who were present.—On Sunday, I went to see Signor Borrozzi again, and had a very pleasant little half-hour's visit.[10] I send you his card, on which is his coat of arms, for his family is noble, and their name was written in the Golden Book of the Republic.[11]—The weather has taken a new and unfavorable turn, and after blowing cold has compromised by snowing again. But after January, we shall have no more cold weather, until the last of October.—Have none of you heard from Mrs Carter since I've been gone?

You see, I'm rather straining myself to make out this letter. It's got cold, somehow, and at any rate, I must reserve part of my strength for a letter to Joe. When you write next, specify some things you'd like to know about, and don't, dear, leave me to the hopeless task of telling about everything. *You* must write to me always, Vic. And now give my dearest love to all, and so good bye,

> Your affectionate brother,
> Will.

1. Richard Henry Stoddard (1825–1903), the poet and literary reviewer for the *World* (1860–1870), was a prominent member of the New York literary group. Howells met the Stoddards in October 1861, occasionally reviewed their books, corresponded with them, and speaks of them in *Literary Friends and Acquaintance*, HE, pp. 77–78. See also Howells to Taylor, 23 September 1862, n. 3.

2. The *Scottish American Journal*, on which Swinton apparently held a position, was a semiweekly New York newspaper.

3. "Letter from Europe," *Ohio State Journal*, 31 January 1862.

4. The "fair New Englander" may have been a member of "the American party" of which Howells writes in his Venetian diary (MH) on 15 December 1861: "They all had money—they were nouveaux riches, I think. The young gentleman—a good fellow—had a taste for brandy; his sister had a taste for cathedrals, and his pretty little cousin, a taste for travelling." The "Russian gentleman" may be one of the several foreigners Howells met "at the house of the painter Mr. de Nerly, a Prussian," also described in his diary under the date of 25 December 1861.

5. See Shakespeare, *Henry IV, Part I*, V, iv, 168–69.

6. "Louis Lebeau's Conversion," *Atlantic*, November 1862.

7. W. C. Howells apparently hoped for an appointive office, having lost the nomination for state representative in the October 1861 primary election to Abel Krum.

8. Possibly Mrs. Baleormini, the wife of the Russian consul at Venice. See Howells to Piatt, 15 February 1865, n. 2.

9. Franz Josef I (1830–1916), emperor of Austria (1848–1916). At Stuttgart Howells had seen William I of Württemberg.

10. According to Woodress, a "scholar-friend named Barozzi" was engaged by Howells to help J. L. Motley, the American minister at Vienna, in his archival research on Venice. See *Howells & Italy*, p. 21, and Motley to Howells, 7 August 1862 (MH).

11. The Golden Book has not been further identified.

27 JANUARY 1862, VENICE, TO JOHN J. PIATT[1]

Venice, January 27, 1862.

My dear Piatt,—

Have n't you noticed that when you have nothing at all to do, you become absorbed in that occupation to the exclusion of everything else? This is my experience, and let me add further, in excuse for not having written you before, that I have the most fatal disposition to take advantage of any affection or forbearance that my friends have for me, and to try it to the utmost. I do n't want to seem ungrateful or forgetful of people to whom I am indebted in affection and favor; and so, if I have been in Venice two months without writing to you, it is to be understood that I am not so basely recreant to friendship as another person would be under the same circumstances. I assure you that I 've remembered you every day, and that the hours I spent at your house in Georgetown return to me with a freshness that almost vivifies the dull loneliness of my life here. I think those fellows who took supper with us at my cousin's[2]—that is, O'Connor, Eldridge, Stedman, and yourself —were all delightful people, and I heartily wish that they were here that I might

> "Welcome the coming, speed the parting *jest*"[3]

with them, and make these sad old echoes of Venice listen to some American fun.

It comes hard on a social nature like mine, that delights in talk and laughter, to be thrown with people in whose language I am as yet incapable of expressing anything but the simplest sentiments of the phrase-books, which, though improving, can not be called lively. I like the Italians, so far as I have seen them, and I have made some friends already; but American life and American things are, after all, the best. You must come to Europe to understand this, though whether it is worth while to go through so much for so little is questionable enough. When I tell you that intellectual life is cheap in America and dear in Europe, perhaps you 'll catch a glimpse of my meaning. Of course, you find culture, and all that, here, but it is so hedged in by conventional and social and political tyranny that you are slow to get at it. You do not find here, as in America, cultivated minds and simple, humble ways together; or, if you do, you behold them unrespected, and that makes the pain. I look back upon the careless, independent life I led at Columbus as something too good to be altogether true, and when I remember it I bow to the European conventionalities with a groan of profound regret. O, my easy-going brother poet, be happy in America, for in Europe you would be most wretched! Though you made much of the pictures, and the palaces, and the ruins, I doubt if they would console you; for I assure you that our American freedom, social, intellectual, and political, is better than all the past and present slavery of Europe, however glorious in art and history that may be.

Do n't let me disgust you with myself, or give you a false idea of my state of feeling here.

"If the sense is hard
To alien ears, I did not speak to these;
No, not to thee, but to myself in thee."[4]

I have been writing so many letters home that it seems to me I must have told you about my ocean voyage and my Continental progress hither. The ocean trip was not pleasant; it began with sea-sickness, and ended in England. It was foggy and cold and cheerless, and I did not begin to feel that I had got my money back until I reached Germany, through which I lounged one happy week, coming within thirty miles of Uhland (who is still alive at Tübingen), and actually seeing the little village where the good Schiller was born.[5] I was in Paris one sunny day, dawdling up and down the boulevards, deliciously lost and incapable of the slightest French, and thinking all the while of poor Heine, whose sensuous ghost, I 'm sure, must haunt the many-peopled asphalt of those promenades, and constantly flatten its nose against the windows for a glimpse of the charming little shop-girls within. The phantom pursued me as far as Munich, and I actually took my coffee at one of those drinking-places for which the new Athenians have as many names as the French have for love—which is to say a thousand. I was also greatly pleased with Vienna; but it was cold there, and I hurried to Italy, and found a dream of winter this side of the Tyrol which, after two months, is just now letting poor, sad Venice awake to the most joyous and exuberant spring.

To-day I walked along the Riva dei Schiavoni, and found happiness in giving two soldi to a beggar, in watching some vagabond boys stoning the bowsprit of a ship, and in the fresh wind that blew over "the azure, and green, and purple" of the bay, and brought in the gentle tide of the Adriatic. Then, after I had feasted my eyes on the glories of the snow-crested Tyrolese mountains, I looked backward athwart the crescent of the bay, and saw Venice more beautiful than I ever saw it before. O ships that lie so idle at the breasts of the poor old Mother of Commerce, I marvel not that you linger there! O clouds, that kiss so lovingly the domes and spires of her hundred churches, I wonder not that you hang so low and droop so tenderly toward her! No, there is no place like Venice—so beautiful, so sad—and I could be unlimitedly sentimental here, and melancholy and wretched, with no one to molest me or make me afraid. It is a city that disappoints no one—it can not; for, however differently fair you may have figured it, you will find the reality better than your fancy, a hundred times. The gondolas are more black swanlike than you could have thought, San Marco and the Doge's Palace are more glorious, the Bridge of Sighs more impressive, and the Titians and Tintorettos more gorgeous and magnificent than your gayest dreams of them. Each morning the golden angel on the crest of the Campanile looks in my drowsy eyes and makes me glad and proud to be here, and it is only when I remember how utterly alone I am that I feel at all downcast.

I have greeted the winged lions and the bronze horses for Mrs. Piatt, and pumped several laborious inspirations for you on the Bridge of Sighs. The only thing I regret is that you are not here with me, so that we might stroll everywhere together, by gondola and on foot, and you might, in the proper clime, learn how *"dolce"* it is to *"far niente."*[6] My life is a round of eating, sleeping, studying Italian, making verses, lounging in the café and thinking about America.... I have not yet received my exequatur, and so am not yet installed in my office; but everything comes at last, even death, and I do not look for the suspension of a natural law in the case of an exequatur.

My dear Piatt, I hope you will write to me very soon, and give me news of my friends in Washington, to whom also I beg you to remember me; particularly to my cousin Charley, to O'Connor, to French, to Gangwer,[7] and all the rest. Tell me any literary gossip you know, and what you yourself are doing in that way. Have you got into the *Atlantic* yet? or *Vanity Fair*? or *Harper*? Did that new magazine, *The Continental*, go off at Boston, or "go up?" The publisher owes me twelve dollars, and I hope he will be attended to in a future state for his refusal to liquidate that small obligation.[8]

It *is* pretty dull here; but if I get through the first six months, I 'll know enough Italian to begin to talk fluently, and then I shall do splendidly.

The war in America at last seems to move on, and I hope to hear of great victories soon. *Galignani*[9] has been very dismal reading since I 've been here, and the English press is by no means flattering yet on the subject of the resumption of specie payments.

I have written, or rather sketched, a poem in hexameters, which I call "Louis Labeau's Conversion."

Remember me to Mrs. Piatt, and do n't neglect, my dear fellow, to write me very soon. Use thin paper, and write a great deal on it. Send the letters to my father, at Jefferson, and he 'll inclose them to me here, which will save you a half-dollar's postage.

Always yours,
W. D. Howells.

Another time, when my purse is fuller, I 'll send you some photographs. They are better than any description of Venice I could write, and so I have n't done any word-painting in this letter. There 's an opera, which I attend sometimes; but I see nothing of Venetian society there, as only the Austrians go. I know one Italian author here, and a Prussian painter, both pleasant people, and comprising my entire circle of acquaintance, almost.[10]

1. The printed and only extant version appeared in *The Hesperian Tree*, ed. J. J. Piatt (Columbus: S. F. Harriman, 1903). In the process of planning his next "Annual," Piatt wrote Howells, 20 June 1900 (MH), that he had recently come upon "two or three sketches & letters of yours" which he thought of using in the projected volume. He refers specifically to this letter, though he dates it "Dec. 1861."

2. For Howells' comments about his cousin Charles Howells, see his letter to his parents, 31 October 1861.

3. Howells substitutes "jest" for "guest" in Alexander Pope's translation of the *Odyssey*, XV.

4. These lines have not been identified.

5. See Howells to his family, 7 December 1861, n. 5.

6. Italian for "Sweet to do nothing."

7. Probably A. M. Gangewar, who was associated with the *Ohio State Journal* (1856–1858), private secretary of Governor Chase (1859), and, after 1861, for many years in the U. S. Treasury Department.

8. The Boston *Continental Monthly* (1862–1864) contains no contributions identifiable as Howells' in its first volume (January–June 1862). Its publisher was James Roberts Gilman, and Charles Godfrey Leland was the first editor (1862–1863).

9. Howells is referring to reports of the war published in *Galignani's Messenger*; see Howells to M. D. and E. D. Conway, 18 September 1863, n. 11.

10. The Italian author has not been identified; for the Prussian painter, de Nerly, see Howells to V. M. Howells, 18 January 1862, n. 4.

7 March 1862, Venice, to William C. Howells

Venice, March 7, 1862.

Dear father—

I wrote a little short letter to mother, the other day, telling her that I'd been sick. I have to tell you now that I am quite well again, with good spirits and good appetite, though I was down for nearly a week with fever—billious, I suppose it was. The people with whom I lodge were very kind and attentive to me, and I did not lack for anything during my sickness.[1] For anything? O surely, for home, and home, and home! For voices, for steps, for touches, for tenderness that made sickness an empire, when I was with you. We are so eager to fly away from the nest, (God forgive us,) when we get our wings fledged, and when we cannot fly back again with our poor broken plumes—that is the sad time. Do you know, I thought all through this fever, of a fever that I had in Hamilton when I was a very little child, and used to doze upon the old settee, and mother would come and kiss me, and ask me if I had slept. But I never could tell her; and I could not answer myself now if I had slept, after the dreamful intervals of not-awaking.—I remember that I had been all day ranging with the boys up down the hydraulic in the cold winter sun and wind, and came home chilled and dizzy; and mother did not know I was sick at first, nor I either, till the print of my book swam under my heavy eyes.[2] So the other Saturday, I walked all day in the damp weather, and sat late over a German translation of Euripides that I have found at a bookstall.[3] I rose at last with aching shoulders, dull brain, and a cold shuddering from the heart out. There was no one to ask me if I were sick; but I stated the fact very clearly to myself, and had confirmation of it by ten days' illness. I think it was only my determination to not give up that saved me from a very long illness—my determination, and my old friend, Tortorini, and these good people of the house here.—You ask me how I live in Venice? Until now, in this way: I had a room at ten florins a month, and then I took my *meal* (for they only eat dinner at Venice) at a restaurant, and coffee, three or four times a day at different caffè. In spite my utmost economy, my living (with lodging) alone cost me two florins (exactly $1) a day. When anybody speaks to you again of cheap living in Europe, shrug your shoulders, and show the palms of your hands. If that isn't enough, wag the forefinger of your right hand back and forth, and at last scrape the bottom of your chin with the back of your hand outwards, and tell him, "Lies, lies, lies!" You can live cheaper in America than anywhere else, and better, far better,—for no American would diet himself in the manner to which the beggarly bellies of Europe are accustomed. I don't speak of the poorer people—they live upon a kind of food for cattle,—coarse fish, mush, and a tough filthy looking decoction formed of old boots in slices, I should think. But even well-to-do people know nothing of abundance—a dish of soup—a plate of cauliflower—boiled beef,—figs,—this is dinner, and, remember, the only meal of the day. The rest is coffee and expectation. Meat is dear, vegetables are dear, rents are high. I'm talking of Italy—the cheapest place in Europe. A friend who had been spending the winter in Hanover,[4] because he expected to find Germany very cheap, paid $11 a week for board that we could get for $3.50 in Columbus. I'm mad when I think of the monstrous lies I used to swallow about cheap living in Europe.—The folks with whom I lodge have taken me in *pension,* or boarding for a week, and if we can agree upon terms, and I like it, we shall come to some arrangement, and I can live cheaper at least than I have been living, so far.—While I think of it: Have you followed the Congressional proceedings attentively enough to know whether my appointment has been confirmed in the Senate? I suppose it has; but if it hasn't, wont you please write to Wade, or to Mr Sumner (who is head of the foreign af. com.) not to let it be overlooked.[5] It's possible such a thing might be neglected through oversight, you know.—You asked me sometime since to tell you of country-life in Italy, and I replied that I knew nothing of it. In June, I'm to go Mr Tortorini's "Cawntree" as he calls his country-seat, Mont Sedici, near the old city of Padua.[6] Then I shall have an opportunity of telling you all that you wish to know, and will probably write something for the Sentinel about it. I quit writing for the State Journal, because I found I couldn't avoid politics, and then I'm forbidden to touch. I'm very sorry you made so pointed an allusion to the anti-Anglican feeling of my letter—such a thing might cause my removal from office, if properly worked up by a judicious enemy.[7] It was a poor, flippant letter, and it wasn't necessary to parade my consular dignity in connection with the authorship.—One of these days I'm going into the printing-offices here, and I'll write you some account of them. They do beautiful printing in Venice, and I fancy they must have well arranged offices. I don't know whether I've ever sent you my card. I enclose two—one done at Vienna, and the other (the smaller) here. As for newspapers, there are no Italian journals worth sending, except those printed in the kingdom of Italy, and they are not permitted to come to Venice. But I'll send you a copy of the "Gazetta di Venezia," a hightoned, conservative sheet, edited by the police, the calm and judicious tenor of whose articles would delight the soul of Mr Cooke.—I wish, father, if you have any trade, by which you could get a first-quality gold pen, you'd send me one. Let it be rather soft, but not *too* soft. I want to make a present of it to my old friend Tortorini, who never saw a gold pen till he saw mine, for they are not in Italy, nor elsewhere in Europe, except perhaps England. You can send the pen in a letter, well enveloped in soft paper.—Did you get the poem I sent you for the *Atlantic*?[8] Did you like it.—I write a good deal, here, and after the first confusion of ideas, consequent upon the novelty, begin to think somewhat—which is better than writing. I take it that if I do nothing in literature publicly until the war is over, it will be just as well.—Very glad to hear the news of those three victories, and everybody here has been congratulating me. There's no doubt about the current of Italian sympathy.—If you ever write to Reed, please tell him how glad I was to see the "good old Gazette," and to observe that that gunboat controversy with the Commercial was raging as furiously as ever.[9]—Your article on the abolition of the franking privilege was excellent.[10] I'm anxious this letter should go at once, and as I don't think of anything more to write at the moment—here's goodbye, with dearest love to all.

> Your affectionate son
> Will.

1. In Howells' earlier letter to his mother, 4 March 1862 (MH, printed in part in *Life in Letters*, I, 51–52), he described the nursing he had received at the hands of G. A. Tortorini (b. 1806?), a retired apothecary and mayor of Monselice, who had studied English with the former consul, J. J. Sprenger, and had lived for several years in England. See "An Old Venetian Friend," in *Years of My Youth*, HE, pp. 225–37.

2. In *A Boy's Town*, pp. 45–52, Howells describes the "Hydraulic" and its construction.

3. Probably C. T. Gravenhorst, *Griechisches Theater* (1856). For Howells' acquaintance with *Medea*, see "Introduction," *A Modern Instance*, HE, and Gerard M. Sweeney, "The Medea Howells Saw," *American Literature* 42 (1970), 83–89. See also the reviews, possibly by Howells, *Ohio State Journal*, 24 March 1859 and 25 January 1861.

4. The friend has not been identified.

5. Benjamin F. Wade, the senator from Ohio, who lived in Jefferson; and Charles Sumner, the senator from Massachusetts, who may have known Howells through the *Atlantic* circle and who wrote W. H. Seward a brief letter of recommendation, 24 March 1861 (DNA), though Howells discovered later that "he was not a very gracious person." See *Literary Friends and Acquaintance*, HE, p. 120.

6. When Howells wrote "Mont Sedici," he misunderstood Tortorini's pronunciation of "Monselice." He actually did not visit Tortorini's country place until 1865. For a description and recollection of the visit, see Howells to W. C. Howells, 6 June 1865, and "An Old Venetian Friend."

7. W. C. Howells had introduced the author of "Letter from Europe," reprinted in the Ashtabula *Sentinel*, 5 February 1862, as U. S. consul at Venice, and commented that "The writer in this letter, seems to have conceived no very high idea of the English."

8. Howells had sent "Louis Lebeau's Conversion" to his father, 12 February 1862 (MH), for submission to the *Atlantic*. In the letter he asked his father to check on two historical points, proposing a possible footnote.

9. The Cincinnati *Gazette* had just published a series of articles, presumably by Samuel R. Reed, which harshly criticized the *Commercial* on its remarks about the Union use of gunboats.

10. W. C. Howells defended the franking privilege in his editorial in the Ashtabula *Sentinel*, 29 January 1862.

26 April 1862, Venice, to Victoria M. Howells

Venice, April 26, 1862.

My dear sister—

You don't know how sorely you tempted me by saying—come home. I thought just one minute of the joy of meeting you, and of being in America again, and then I stopped resolutely, and put the thought away. It isn't for me, now, sweet and dear as it is; for nothing is further from my purpose than to return now. I shall not accomplish here, just what I expected to do; but I shall accomplish somethings. I shall save a little money to begin life on when I get back, and I shall have time here to go on with studies that I interrupted five or six years ago, by a too impatient plunge into the world. My health is perfectly restored, and though I am often lonesome, I'm not homesick, nor low-spirited. I am studying Italian quite earnestly and I am going to take up French, and read the Latin and Greek classics, either in the original, or in German translations. I have commenced another poem, and keep a journal from which I hope to make a book about Venice.[1] I hope the "Atlantic" will accept my poem, for the reason that I dont want the "Atlantic" public to forget me, but I shall not let its rejection discourage me. With a new access of earnestness, I have won new self respect, and look forward to all the chances of literary success or failure with reasonable calm. I hope, dear Vic, that if father was hurt by anything I said to him of the correction of my poem,[2] which he so kindly, and so unwisely undertook, that you excused me all you could. Father knows nothing of the principles of the verse in which the poem is written, and I'm afraid his correction has been the death of it. But give him my dear love. I would rather lose the poem twenty times over, than cause him pain. I dreamed of living in America last night, as I have done so many, many times since I have been here; and in my dream I said to myself—looking round on the low houses nestling in the beloved trees on either side of the wide streets—"Well this at last, is no dream, and I'm at home and awake." But a pang of regret for Venice went through my heart, for I thought I had left it too soon, and before I knew perfectly all the glorious and beautiful things that are in it. So comfort mother, dear, and beg her to spare me a little while longer. If the salary of this consulate has not been permanently increased, and is only fixed at $1500 during the war, I'll resign directly the war is over; for it wont pay to stay here for $750. If, however, mother should be sick, or her health become so feeble as to alarm you, you must write to me at once, Vic, and let me come home without delay.

I suppose that before this reaches you, father will have received my letter containing something to be used for the Sentinel.[3] I intended also to send something in this letter which he could use, but shall defer it now till another time. Tell father that the pen came safely to hand, and that I will give it to Sig. Tortorini as soon as he comes to Venice;—he is now at Padua with his sick son. I'm greatly obliged to father. It is quite right to send the letters as you do by way of Bremen; I haven't lost any, yet, and they come with reasonable dispatch.—I do wish you'd always write me long letters from home, and make them come up to the full half ounce. It cost me 69 soldi (or 34 cents) to send each letter of a quarter of an ounce, and I have always taken all the law allowed me in the weight of letters sent.—The weather is inexpressibly delightful here, now, and it is spring without being summer—a thing we can't quite understand in the American climate. All day long, the little campo where I live, rings with the music of the canaries and finches hung in their cages at the balconies of an old palazzo opposite.[4]

I presume I shall be quite as much alone throughout my whole stay in Venice, as I am now. Society is so entirely different in its constitution here from what it is in America, that much as I want to study Italian life, it is difficult for me to do so. What with their political discontents, and the natural effect of their mode of education, the Venetians are eminently unsocial. There are no parties, nor anything of that kind. The ladies have a certain day in the week on which they receive company—that is, people who call from five to fifteen minutes. The men meet and talk in the caffè. As for seeking women's society for intellectual pleasure, as I used in Columbus, it is a thing so far from their knowledge, that they could not understand it. Young ladies *never* receive calls, and a young lady cannot go upon the street unless accompanied by her mother or brother. If she went alone she would lose her character. Where they happen to be in company, they are startled and stupefied if you talk directly to them, and not through the medium of the mamma. The natural consequence of which is that the young men are beasts, and the women what you might expect them. O Vic, Vic! prize America all you can. Try not to think of the American's faults—they are a people so much purer and nobler and better than any other, that I think they will be pardoned the wrong they do. I'm getting disgusted with this stupid Europe, and am growing to hate it. What I have told you of society here in Italy, is true of society throughout the continent. Germany is socially rotten—and the Germans have a filthy frankness in their vice, which is unspeakably hideous and abominable to me. The less we know of Europe, the better for our civilization; and the fewer German customs that take root among us, the better for our decency. You will read the lies of many people who say that life in Europe is more cheerful and social than ours. Lies, I say—or stupidities, which are almost as bad.

There is no life in the whole world so cheerful, so social, so beautiful as the American. You see people talking and laughing, here, at the caffè; but do you know that this is their only social amusement. The pleasure which we have innocently in America, from our unrestrained and unconventional social intercourse, is guilty in Europe—brilliant men and women know something of it; but they are also guilty men and women. Are you getting tired of my lecture, dear? I think these things over a great deal, with sorrow for errors into which I fell regarding my country; and the most earnest, earnest prayer that my heart can conceive that America may grow more and more unlike Europe every day. I think when I return home I will go to Oregon—or Dorset[5]—and live as far as possible from the influences of European civilization. While I write on this theme, I scarcely can have patience with my former impertinent and stupid ideas.—I'm not going to make you a very long letter this time, my dear sister; but that's no reason why you should shorten your reply. How far has your acquaintance with Laura Platt gone? She's an admirable girl, I think, and I wish you had seen her. Do any of you girls ever hear from the Carter's? I thought Mrs Carter's letter so cold and unreasonable that I haven't answered it yet.[6] Her friendship is rather tyrannical. I have written to Aurelia some three weeks ago. Are all you "grils" as discontented as ever? I am, and I don't know that I shall ever be otherwise.

Give my dear love to mother and father, and all the rest. Before I mail this letter, I will find out what Joe wants to know of envelopes, but its useless to think of buying them here.

Your affectionate brother
Will.

1. The poem may be "The Royal Portraits," *Harper's Monthly*, December 1865, mentioned among others in Howells' letter to his father, 12 September 1862. He reported to W. C. Howells on 13 June 1862 that it still lacks "those last touches," and on 3 August (MH) in a letter to his mother he enclosed a letter and poems to H. M. Ticknor. The publisher tentatively rejected the poems in his letter to W. C. Howells, 1 October 1862 (MH). The Venetian diary (MH) was used in part in *Venetian Life*.

2. See Howells to W. C. Howells, 7 March 1862, n. 8. On 22 March 1862 (MH), he had simply written his father, "I hope you liked my camp meeting poem, and didn't find it untrue to nature and history." See also Howells to his father, 13 June 1862.

3. "Letter from Europe," Ashtabula *Sentinel*, 14 May 1862, carried the comment, "Extracted from a private letter from Venice dated April 13, 1862." For a description of the revisions in this account of Trieste that later appeared in *Italian Journeys*, see Woodress, *Howells & Italy*, pp. 74–76.

4. The Campo San Bartolomeo is near the east end of the Rialto Bridge.

5. Dorset, a small town about six miles from Jefferson.

6. Howells had written Aurelia, 9 April 1862 (MH), "Mrs. Carter's letter I thought rather cross, and I shall answer it at my perfect leisure." Apparently Mrs. Carter had expressed her displeasure at the lack of Howells' correspondence with her. See also Howells to W. C. Howells, 22 July 1862, n. 2.

13 JUNE 1862, VENICE, TO WILLIAM C. HOWELLS

Venice, June 13, 1862.

Dear father—

I believe I'm now two letters behind-hand—a thing that I haven't suffered to happen before since I left home, where I heartily wish I were to-day. The warm weather coming on has debilitated me somewhat, and I have hints of hypochondria which I don't like. However, now's the time, if ever, to encounter the dragon and overcome it; and as I happen to have made the acquaintance of a good-natured German physician, who speaks English, I think I shall manage to struggle through the hot season, and then I'll feel better again.[1]

My "Louis Lebeau's Conversion" has been here, and after correction has been sent back.[2] The whole line which you had put in was well enough; but each of the other corrections,—and there were three of them—were in violation of the measure. All trouble and delay could have been avoided, by your taking note of the alterations made, and sending me the lines as changed, when you first told me of forwarding the poem to the Atlantic. I wonder that they accepted it as it was—however, the whole thing is right, now. Only, while I have no more faith in your ability to "put the paint of a rose on a poem," my confidence in the severity of Atlantic scrutiny is considerably lessened.[3]

The last two letters which I have received are those of the 13th and 21st May. The last one I answered was that of Joe's. And while we're talking about letters: Did you ever receive one from me, enclosing one to Mrs Smith, at Columbus? I wish that if you failed to receive that letter, you'd drop a line to Mrs S., telling that I wrote to her promptly on receiving her letter, and that I will write again as soon as you can communicate to me that my reply never came to your hands.—The *Gazettes* I didn't receive, though the Sentinels come regularly, and I have got several "Pine & Palms," which are not particularly useful to a retired philanthropist like myself.[4] I suppose Aurelia or Anne sends them; but you can tell the girls that office holding has made me so conservative, I don't care about nigger papers anymore. I'll investigate the postage question more carefully, and if I can send by Bremen so cheaply, it will be a saving of at least $25 in a year.

To-day commences the grand feast of Saint Anthony of Padua, and ever so many people are gone to Padua to witness the ceremonies. On Sunday—the greatest day of the festa—I will go; and then perhaps write you an account of it for the Sentinel—though you *did* butcher that Trieste letter of mine awfully.[5] I learned from that letter (in print,) for the time that Versailles was a sea-port. I always thought it was *Marsailles*.

You seem to have been equally divided on the orthography of Venetia, (the province of which Venice is the capital,) sometimes spelling it with an *e* and sometimes with an *i*. As for *"surprising public stairways"* that's so far from what I wrote, that I can't begin to remember now what I did write.—At Padua on Sunday, they are to bless the cattle; and to celebrate the miracles of Saint Anthony with a great deal of splendor.

As soon as the hot weather abates a little, I'm going to visit the Dalmatian cities of Sara and Ragusi, of which I spoke in my Trieste letter. They were once great seats of commerce and freedom; and a Dalmat with whom I talked the other day at the eating-house told me that they were still very beautiful and interesting cities. All the people of the city, speak Italian—the *contadini* who still dress in the national costume speak Sloavanic. I'm very anxious to go to Athens, and I think I shall do so either this fall, or next spring.[6]

To-day at the Railroad I parted with one of the most affussive and absorbing travelers, whom it has been my misfortune to see here in Venice. He is an old fellow from New York, and partially, also, from San Francisco. He went to California in 1849, where he got gold and the rheumatism—and he's been "doctorin'," now for the last seven years, a great part of which time he has spent in Europe.—He dresses just exactly as he would in the diggings, and looks a great deal shabbier than most beggars here. He was excessively dirty; but he so possessed and insisted upon me that I was obliged to go with him to several places, and finally as he couldn't speak a word of English, I went with him to the depot, where he was excessively outraged at the examination of his baggage, and behaved with scandalous rudeness to the officers, wanting me to tell them constantly that these were his "private things."—If the old wretch had not been nearly blind, I should never have had anything to do with him, but he was in some sort an object of charity. I parted from him with a friendly injunction to "purge and live cleanly like a gentleman,"[7] telling him that he was in Europe and not in California, and he must dress somewhat more decently. Clothes didn't make the man, he said. No, I told him, but they made a great difference in a man, and advised him to try the effect of good ones. He was, I declare, the most outrageous old pork I ever saw. His name was Benj. Richardson.[8]

The war seems to be dragging slowly and bloodily to a conclusion; but I do not understand why there has been a new call for troops—I thought our army was already great enough. But I'm willing to trust old Abe, now, though he's rather disappointing about emancipation. Don't you think it just possible, however, that since he will have to bear the responsibility of freeing the slaves, he ought to have the glory of it, and to be allowed his own time of doing it? In his proclamation annulling that of Hunter, it seems to me that he hints pretty strongly at his own intention to proclaim emancipation, if circumstances should in his opinion, warrant it.[9] I'm not greatly agitated on the subject, perhaps because I've ceased in a great measure to think about it.

I'm much obliged for the portrait of the young man "who has sat for his photograph once before." It seems to me I've seen other photographs of him. I suppose he is the author of the dentist's advertisement in the Sentinel, which for elegance of diction is not surpassed out of the most sonorous papers in the "Rambler." The photograph is good, and Sam looks handsome enough, though one of the boots, on account of the peculiar light on it, shows much larger than the other.[10]

I'm glad that the girls are studying French so diligently. I'm going to take it up myself in a week or two. I've been waiting first to get through with my Italian Ollendorff, before commencing anything else.[11]—The poem doesn't get on very fast, and I don't know when it will be finished. It is really done, except those last touches which it is so hard to give. Joe said something about a poem on *rafting*, that I think I could make, and I begged him and you to tell me whatever you knew of rafts, and that sort of life on the Ohio.

Just as soon as I think my exile has ceased to be profitable here, I shall return home. It long ago ceased to be very cheerful, and if I had the certain prospect of anything to do in Cincinnati or New York, I'd be mighty willing to start home in the spring. As it is I'm going home next summer, on leave of absence, if I can get it; if I can't, I'll go home anyway, on resignation. I sometimes fear I'm losing chances to establish myself in life by remaining away, though business must now be so prostrated in the United States that I couldn't have much chance of doing anything.

I was very sorry to hear that poor grandmother's illness was the cause of unusual pain to her.[12] I suppose it is progressing, and must go on. I wish you would send her my dearest love, and tell her that I do not forget her; but that I remember her great patience and endurance of affliction as one of the most beautiful lessons my life has ever had. I scarcely can think of her without tears.

Tell mother and the girls that the flowers they sent were something "dried up," but none the less precious to me on that account; and say to Annie that it is past the season for flower seeds in Venice, now; but I'll send her some for next year. The flowers are much the same as in America. I haven't seen any seeds at the florists for two months.

I'll send you the Gazetta di Venezia, and Annie some Venetian music.

Has Annie got a school yet? Joe wrote me she had a certificate of her ability to teach six months.

There's nothing more to write at present. Dear love to all.

Affectionately,
Will

    1. The German physician was probably Dr. Günzberg.

    2. H. M. Ticknor had returned "Louis Lebeau's Conversion" to Howells with his letter of 7 May 1862 (MH), but he expressed the hope that "you will not keep him forever, because Maga took a fancy to him...." "Maga," the familiar name of *Blackwood's*, had frequently been used to refer to the *Atlantic*, beginning with Lowell's editorship. See H. E. Scudder, *James Russell Lowell* (Boston: Houghton, Mifflin & Co., 1901), I, 419.

    3. See Howells to Victoria, 26 April 1862, n. 2.

    4. "Pine and Palm" is mentioned in Moncure D. Conway's *Autobiography* (1904) as the title of his first novel.

    5. Howells' letter to his family, 29 June 1862 (MH), partly reprinted in "From Europe," Ashtabula *Sentinel*, 30 July 1862, says that he missed the feast of St. Anthony at Padua. For the "Trieste letter," see Howells to Victoria, 26 April 1862, n. 3.

    6. Howells went to Milan and Como the week before his letter to his father of 22 July 1862. There is no record of his having gone to Zara, Ragusi, or Athens during his Venetian years.

    7. See Shakespeare, *Henry IV, Part I*, V, iv, 168–69.

    8. See H. H. Bancroft, "Pioneer Register and Index," in *History of California* (San Francisco: The History Company, 1886), V, 695. The San Francisco *Bulletin*, 23 October 1884, announced the attachment of Richardson's extensive real estate in that city.

    9. On 9 May 1862 General David Hunter had proclaimed the emancipation of all slaves in his department (including Georgia, Florida, and South Carolina), but Lincoln annulled this action ten days later.

    10. Probably Howells refers to the advertisements for Samuel Howells' dental practice, Ashtabula *Sentinel*, 30 April and 21 May 1862.

    11. Probably Henri G. Ollendorf, *Ollendorf's New Method for...Italian Language* (1859).

    12. Anne Thomas Howells.

22 JULY 1862, VENICE, TO WILLIAM C. HOWELLS

Venice, July 22, 1862.

My dear father—

Of course it wasn't because I didn't as perfectly confide in you, that I told Vic first about my engagement;[1] but she and I were nearer the same size and age; and I knew you'd find it out directly. Your kind letter is a reproach to me, however, and I'm sorry if my seeming want of trust has given you the slightest pain. I don't expect any opposition from any of the family, after you have all seen E. G. M. and you particularly will like her.—She's not violently intellectual, by any means.

She has artistic genius, and a great deal of taste, and she admires my poetry immensely. *I* think she's good looking, and rather suppose she was picked out for me from the beginning of the world.—The girls and mother have got their idea of her from Mrs Carter's descriptions, which were by no means just.[2] She's good as well as smart—and in fine I love her very much, which may remotely account for my intending to marry her. Of course, I understand that if she were an angel with wings, the girls would pluck out the feathers, and declare that they had been put on with tar. As to my asking Vic to keep the matter from you, particularly, that was merely a joking reference to your habit of finding everything out all that *she* wished to keep secret. I quite comprehend your feeling in regard to me, and it is a matter of grief to me that I may not realize all your expectations. Here I shall not, I know; for the climate is decidedly against me. What little vitality I have is kept at so low an ebb; that I can scarcely more than exist, and work of any kind is almost impossible. No one, who has not felt the *scirrocco* can quite appreciate the limberness of a wet rag. In nine months—that is, some time in next April,—you'll see me at home, either on leave of absence, or by resignation. Then, if I can get anything to do in America, I sha'n't come back to Europe.—Following your advice and my own inclination, I've begun to see something of the country, now. I returned from Lake Como and Milan yesterday, after a delightful absence of a week. You'll find a partial record of my trip in my letter to Mrs Carter; but I have yet to tell you about Lake Como.[3] It is of all imaginable things the loveliest. Picture to yourself, a little Lake lying in the lap of mountains, whose snowy heads are above the clouds. The vineyards climb halfway up their sides; the convents crown the lesser acclivities; the fair villages and country-houses nestle upon the water's edge. The faces of the mountains are all seamed and furrowed with torrent courses; and now and then foamy cascade, leaping from a dizzy height, "to fall, and pause, and fall, did seem."[4] The mountain road winds white over the hills; and steals through tunnels, and runs down here and there to greet the water.—The lake itself is dotted with little sail, and gay flags emulate the bright colors of the painted towers upon the shore. Here and there a village is so gray with age that you can hardly make it out from the rocks upon which is built; and occasionally a grim castle or an ancient church looks out from a piny hollow, or beetling cliff.—It is useless: I can't give you the blueness of the water and the sky, the fine rush of the little steamer; the sweetness of the mountain wind. We made the tour of the whole lake—starting at eight in the morning, and returning at seven in the evening; having an interval of three hours, for a ramble over the mountains. I'd mailed something for the Sentinel; but I think of doing the whole thing for the Atlantic, and so I leave you to read it there.—For the first time in Europe, I felt at home when in free Italy. Milan is a glorious city; and bubbles over with the freeest life. *Garibaldi* is everywhere; in all the shop windows and on everybody's lips. People are talking politics all the time; caricatures abound; and in that city of 250,000 there are sixteen daily papers. I had a lot of them which I intended to bring here, and send to you; but I concluded that it wouldn't be prudent to run the risk of their being found in my possession at Peschiara, where the Austrians are ferociously strict and forgot to send them from Milan until too late. But I *will* send you some Italian papers, and Annie some music to-day.—Believe, dear father, that I had no earthly intention of wounding you in whatever I said in that letter to Vic, of which I nearly forget the contents. I don't think any son ever more truly loved and lauded his father than I do mine; and I should be very sorry to give an idea to the contrary. I long to see you, and tell you of all the things I've seen and felt, in Europe; but the months will soon go by that separate us. Dear love to all.

                                                  Affectionately,
                                                  Will.

Mr. Tortorini, who is here at this moment, sends regards

1. Howells' most recent extant letter to Victoria is dated 26 April, but it does not announce the engagement. Probably he had written her at the end of May, since the delivery of letters usually took a month or a little less.

2. Mrs. Carter's disapproval of Elinor may account for the tone of her earlier letter (see Howells to Victoria, 26 April 1862, n. 6). On 3 August (MH) Howells wrote his mother that he had expected to hear from her about his engagement and that he intended to marry next summer.

3. "Minor Italian Travels; II. Como," *Atlantic*, September 1867, later used as one of the chapters in *Italian Journeys*, differs markedly from the description in this letter.

4. See Tennyson, "The Lotos-Eaters," line 9.

22 AUGUST 1862, VENICE, TO WILLIAM C. HOWELLS

                                                  Venice, Aug. 22, 1862.

Dear father—

Your letter of July 31, came yesterday, and also the Sentinel containing extract from my letter to Vic.[1] It was miraculously well printed—only one error of any consequence occurring. If you'll recollect that *Venice* is the name of the city and *Venetia* the name of the province, the error wont occur again. I'll write again for the paper soon, but I don't know exactly when, now.[2] In the meantime I send the sketch for the Atlantic, which I didn't send last time. Will you post it to the address of H. M.

Ticknor, Boston, with an explanatory note?[3] I'm glad that the letters can go by way of Bremen for 15 cents, and I'll pay the postages in a lump afterwards.

I've been dreadfully discouraged about the war. Two other letters which came with yours yesterday—one from Brattleboro', and the other from Columbus—breathed the same desolation that yours did. People seem so utterly disheartened, and that's the worst feature.—We *can't* treat with the South on the basis of our defeats, unless we mean to yield everything. We *must* conquer before we can think of peace. When we have gained two or three battles, I suppose we'd better stop and let the south go. I'm satisfied that even the people of the North care more about slavery than about the Union, and so what's the use of keeping up the bloody farce any longer? Ah my God! If we only had met secession with entire leave to secede when this first began, we should to-day have been a stronger and freer and better people than ever we were before.—I see by last night's paper there's been a fight in Cedar Mountains, Va., and that the rebels retired.[4] I believe none of our reports: the lying has been so persistent and systematic.—The Garibaldian project upon Rome has fallen through. I much doubt if Garibaldi ever meant **anything** but a demonstration.[5] As it was he scared all the tyrants in Europe. If he only lifts his finger, they're frightened. I wish we had some man so brave and true, and noble as he to lead our armies—that is, if we should have any armies by the time he could reach America. But its of no use to talk in this way.

I shall await mother's letter very anxiously, for I suppose she will have something to say on a subject very interesting to me.[6] I'm glad to hear that grandmother bears up so well, and I earnestly hope she may live to see me again.[7]

I rather wonder that no one but you feels sufficient interest in me, to ever write a line. Affection isn't reasonable, you know, and I can't help feeling hurt that neither of the girls nor boys thinks worth while to write to me.

On Monday here, we had a celebration of the emperor's birthday—that is, the Austrian party did. I attended the divine office in the Cathedral with the other consuls, and afterwards called with them upon the Lieutenant Governor.[8] In the evening, there was a gondola procession on the Grand Canal, which was indescribably fine. The gondolas were adorned with thousands of chinese lanterns.

I'm very well, now, except for the scirocco, to-day. That always makes one feel unpleasant. Goodbye for the present. Dear love to all.

Your affectionate son
Will.

1. Since the letter from Howells' father is dated 31 July, he had probably sent "From Europe," Ashtabula *Sentinel*, 30 July 1862, which, however, partly reprinted a letter addressed to the family rather than to Victoria. The piece in the *Sentinel* may also be "Letter from Europe," 14 May 1862, datelined 13 April, of which no holograph is extant. The 30 July article was later revised for "Some Islands of the Lagoons," in *Venetian Life*. For later revision of the 14 May letter, see Howells to Victoria, 26 April 1862, n. 3.

2. Howells did not write other letters for the *Sentinel*, though it frequently reprinted "Letters from Venice" from the Boston *Advertiser*.

3. "A Little German Capital" was apparently rejected by the *Atlantic*. It appeared instead in the *Nation*, 4 January 1866. See Howells to W. C. Howells, 12 September 1862.

4. The Battle of Cedar Mountains, 9 August 1862, was a Union victory, though with heavy losses.

5. In 1862 Giuseppe Garibaldi (1807–1882) tried unsuccessfully to attack Rome in order to wrest it from the Pope.

6. Presumably Howells' engagement to Elinor Mead.

7. See Howells to W. C. Howells, 13 June 1862, n. 12.

8. Howells had mentioned an earlier ceremonial visit to Count Toggenburg in his letter to his father, 22 March 1862 (MH).

28 August 1862, Venice, to William C. Howells

Venice, Aug. 28, 1862.

My dear father—

Your letter about drafts and rafts came last night; but I have only been able to digest that part concerning drafts. And one thing seems decidedly clear to me. If unhappily the lot should fall upon Joe, you must get a substitute, and you shall have every cent I've saved, to help you do so. At the end of September, I could give you $450, I think, which would go a great way toward getting some one to take Joe's place. It will cost me no effort to part with the money, though the loss of it will postpone my coming to see you, indifinitely, and will put off another event which I had hoped was to happen next summer.[1] But there's no use talking; you couldn't do without Joe—you've leant upon him so long. I'm in hopes that the second conscription wont be made, but you can tell best. In regard to Sam, I don't know what to say. I hope if the chance fell upon him, he would be willing to go. If he should be very unwilling, then my offer remains the same for him as for Joe—I could not forgive myself otherwise; though if both should happen to be drafted, the substitute must be got for Joe.—You don't know how wretched and restless your letter has made me. I kept dreaming all night long that Joe was drafted, and I shall not be at peace till all is over.

Don't be too hard upon the government, and don't blame old Abe too much. As I judge it from this distance, there never was a man in a position so fearfully embarrassing before. I'm inclined to be merciful to him. I know that it is from no mistaken clemency to rebels that he refuses to arm the negroes; but from the well-founded fear that it would turn all the border States against us. In view of the separation which I think must now shortly come, it will be well to keep the border States with us. This war wont last much longer—the Union it seems to me is gone forever—we must only fight now until we can treat on a victorious basis.

Don't let mother worry too much—I feel so miserable about her. What a disastrous day it is!

It doesn't seem as if there was anything more to write you now. My health is very good, and I'm only unhappy about you at home.

Of course I can't think about the poem I proposed to write, though it seems to me the subject of rafts is good, and the material you send will be useful.[2] Some day I'll get you to send me some pioneer books—but all is chaos now.

Goodbye. Dear love to all. I send this by way of England that it may reach you quickly.

Your affectionate son
Willie.

1. Since by the end of September Howells would have received only a little more than $875 (seven months' salary as a consul), $450 seems a large sum to have available, especially since he may have been paying off his debts to Dr. Smith, his brother Joe, and Tortorini. The "event" he expected to take place next summer was of course his marriage to Elinor Mead.

2. For the poem on rafts, see Howells to his father, 13 June 1862.

12 SEPTEMBER 1862, VENICE, TO WILLIAM C. HOWELLS

Venice, Sept 12, 1862.

Dear father—

It was a great disappointment to me last night, when, after waiting more than three weeks to hear from you, the mail only brought me a "Sentinel." I can only conclude that you have written to me and that your letter has been lost. Consequently, I am very anxious. The last letter I had from you was that in which you gave me some notes on rafts—it was written, I think, after the first of August, but very shortly after. It left me in a fever concerning the draft, which was shortly to be made, and which I was afraid might take Joe from you. I wrote an answer immediately, which I hope you got.[1]

By the way, I'm afraid that the "Atlantic" may not have received "Louis Lebeau's Conversion," which I returned in June. In the same envelope were a story and a brief copy of verses. The letter was addressed to H. M. Ticknor. Will you please write, and ask if it ever came to hand? I have sent you for transmission to the "Atlantic" successively the following poems: The Mulberries, The Royal Portraits, Sweet Clover, and a prose sketch entitled A Little German Capital.[2] Did you get them all, or any of them?

Being so uneasy as I am, I hardly know what to write to you. It seems that at last our series of defeats has ended, where it first began—at Manassas.[3] So at least the Milan papers stated yesterday. But what a terrible price we paid for victory! A four days' fight, and a loss of 8,000 men! I take it that the hanging of the officers of negro regiments by the rebels is not a fact, inasmuch as I don't know of any negro regiments that could have been engaged in the battle.—I see that the good old days of "alien and sedition" imprisonments have come again in the United States. I suppose that the thing has to be done, but what a terrible necessity it is. Well, the war is impartial in one respect—if it hasn't given liberty to the blacks, it has made no presents of that kind to the whites. I notice that even Wendall Phillips has had to back down from some lofty position taken by him.[4] It is a good thing to have a strong government. I hope it wont cost us the next administration— because I think after the Republicans the Deluge. The Democrats will make capital of all this business of arrests for discouraging enlistments, and it is so contrary to the instincts of our people, that I'm afraid they'll succeed upon that dodge alone. And yet I don't see what else the government is to do.

You seem, according to the Sentinel, to be moving on in the same old way. "Dishus" Wade has made a speech in Wayne; D. Cadwell will be a candidate before the Congressional Convention; W. C. Howells has again a post of barren honor on some Central Committee.[5] But for all this, I fancy things must be greatly changed since I left home. Couldn't you give me some idea of how people actually talk and feel— what they hope and fear? It would be very interesting to me, for I dread this war has wrought many sad changes not apparent on the surface. Upon the newspaper accounts, I place no reliance whatever. The lying has been so shameless and systematic, that it has disgusted me.

I have to report from Venice that my health just now is good enough; and that the least oppressive summer I ever spent in my life, has already ended in a charming autumn. There is no climate so gentle and equable as this, and though the scirrocco is somewhat debilitating, I think the absence of violent transitions from heat to cold is sufficient compensation for all damage suffered from scirrocco.

The other day, there was an old gentleman here from Columbia, Pa., where he was the cashier of the bank. He told me that he knew Jacob and William Dock intimately. His name is Shock. He rather gave me to understand that Wm Bigler might be the next Democratic Candidate for the presidency. This Shock himself is a Republican of strong anti-slavery feelings.[6]

Very few other American travelers have been here this summer. Now, when there used to be more Americans than English here, en route for Rome, there is not one that I know of in the city, while the latter swarm everywhere.

How anxious I am to hear from you, you can understand. Your letters for a long time had been so brief. I hope when the next does come, it will be a long one. I hope you will attend to writing to the "Atlantic." The poem would have been published before this, I think, if they had got it.

If all goes well, I expect to see you in about six months—or next May—which is a long way off, but is something definite to look forward to.—I keep on working and studying, and I think my time is not altogether spent fruitlessly.—But my life is very lonesome here.—If you ever should see Price, or hear from him, will you please ask him if he got a letter from me this summer? I wrote him a very long one, which he never answered. Dear love to all,

Your affectionate son,
Will.

Just as I was directing this letter's envelope, your and the girls' letters came all together with one from Cousin Henry and 2 from Brattleboro. I'm more anxious than ever to hear the fate of all the poems I've sent. *Did* you get "The Mulberries." Why does mother never write. I'm so distressed to hear of her sore foot. Dearest love to her

1. See Howells to his father, 28 August 1862.

2. "The Royal Portraits," *Harper's Monthly*, December 1865; "Sweet Clover," *Harper's Monthly*, February 1866. "The Mulberries" was not published until 4 January 1871 in the *Nation*. See Howells to his father, 22 August 1862, n. 3.

3. The second battle of Manassas, 29–30 August 1862.

4. Wendell Phillips (1811–1884) began his "Letter to the Tribune," 16 August 1862, with the statement: "You misrepresent me when you say that I discourage enlistments in the Union armies...." See *Speeches, Lectures, and Letters* (1864), p. 464.

5. Decius S. Wade (b. 1835), a nephew of Senator B. F. Wade, practiced law in Jefferson and was active in politics; he later served as chief justice of Montana (1871–1877). His Wayne (Ashtabula county) speech was apparently not mentioned in the Ashtabula *Sentinel*. W. C. Howells was cochairman with H. Fassett of the Ashtabula delegation to the Union Congressional Convention (2 September) and also signed the call for the county convention (4 September) with D. W. Cadwell, who was slated as a candidate for U. S. representative at the Congressional Convention. See *Sentinel*, 6 August 1862.

6. Samuel Shock was cashier of the Columbia National Bank. Jacob and William Dock were uncles of Mary D. Howells. See *Years of My Youth*, HE, p. 9. Their

nephew, William Bigler (1814–1880) was governor of Pennsylvania (1852–1855) and U. S. senator (1856–1862).

19 SEPTEMBER 1862, VENICE, TO FREDERICK W. SEWARD

Consulate of the United States,
Venice September 19, 1862.

Sir:[1]

In response to your despatch of August 27, 1862, I beg to state that the office of this Consulate, as I found it kept by Mr Sprenger was near Piazza San Marco, and sufficiently convenient of access as far as locality was concerned. It was up three pairs of stairs, in a small room, not devoted to any other than consular business, unless the fact that Mr. Sprenger slept in it, is to be regarded as a devotion of the place to other purposes. I do not remember for how long a time Mr Sprenger had this room, though I think that it was some five or six months. The rent was seven silver florins a month, and was paid monthly. I do not know the other places in which Mr Sprenger had kept the office; but I do not think that he at any time permitted the transaction of any other than consular business in it.[2]

A list of the articles of consular property received by me from Mr Sprenger was enclosed to the Department at the time of the transfer to me.[3] I subsequently wrote in regard to the safe of the consulate.[4] Mr Sprenger had deposited the books of statutes, and volumes of Commercial Relations, in the care of a banker (Mr Blumenthal, former acting consul,)[5] for the reason, as I understood, that his room was too small to hold them conveniently. I found them in good order. The books of consular record were also in as favorable state as one could expect to find such veteran volumes. The papers belonging to the office, i.e. letters, dispatches, etc., were endorsed according to date of their receipt, and arranged in order of date. The imperfect collection of seals was also in good condition. The same is true of the flags.

I presume it is only the state of the consular property in regard to which you inquire. There was no stationery, very few blank forms, and no seal press—the consular seal being affixed to documents after first blacking it over a candle. I was at once obliged to buy these things.

Trusting that my response to your inquiries will be found satisfactory,

I am, sir,
Your obedient servant,
W D Howells,
Consul at Venice.

Hon. F. W. Seward,
Acting Secretary of State.[6]

1. Frederick William Seward (1830–1915) became assistant secretary of state in charge of the consular service (1861–1869, 1877–1881) when his father became secretary. At times he served as acting secretary.

2. The tone of this passage suggests that the relationship between Sprenger and Howells had become strained since his letter to W. C. Howells of 7 December 1861. This is confirmed by a comment in a letter to Howells from Daniel C. Payne, 9 June 1862 (MH), who was then at the U. S. legation in Madrid: "Old Sprenger behaved like a base beast to you...."

3. Signed autograph document, W. D. Howells and J. J. Sprenger, 24 February 1861 (DNA).

4. On 7 March 1862 (DNA) Howells had written F. W. Seward that he had secured possession of the "iron fire-proof safe," which had remained with Mr. Zaccharia (elsewhere spelled "Zaccaria"), late acting consul.

5. Howells later remembered that the Jewish banker Blumenthal was helpful in cashing drafts. See *Years of My Youth*, HE, p. 230. Blumenthal also served as acting American consul at various times, according to Howells' letter to Hunter, 28 June 1865.

6. For a full record of official endorsements of consular reports and correspondence see Textual Apparatus.

23 SEPTEMBER 1862, VENICE, TO BAYARD TAYLOR

Casa Falier, Venice. Sept. 23, '62

Dear Sir[1]—

Seeing Mr Cameron this morning,[2] and ascertaining certainly that you were secretary of legation at St Petersburg revived in me the desire to write to you, and crave some intelligence of the Stoddards in New York. I suppose that I ought to excuse myself in some way for venturing to do so. Will you suffer me to plead my regard for the people in question? I see Mrs Stoddard's book has come out, and that it is much praised.[3] She promised to send me a copy, but has not done so. Is Mr Stoddard still connected with Vanity Fair? Pray, do you know in what part of America Stedman is? I heard that he was no longer connected with the World, newspaper, and that in the spring he was doing something at Washington.[4]

Of yourself I heard something from my friend Mrs. Dr Smith of Columbus, who wrote me of your being at her house—where, indeed, *I* should very gladly be, at this or any other moment. I saw a rumour that you were to be appointed, but now today first actually learned of your residence at St Petersburgh. Someone ought to be congratulated, and as I can't understand how anyone should want to live in Russia, I congratulate our government.

I hear recently that the health of Mr Hildreth at Trieste, grows worse.[5]

Will you forgive the liberty I have taken, and if you ever come to Venice, come to see me?

Very sincerely
W. D. Howells.

Mr Bayard Taylor

1. Bayard Taylor (1825–1878) was a prolific writer of poems, travel books, and fiction, best known today for his translation of Goethe's *Faust* (1870–1871). Howells first met him in Columbus probably early in 1860, and then again in Quebec where Taylor snubbed him—an action for which he later apologized. See *Literary Friends and Acquaintance*, HE, pp. 9–14. In his reply to this letter, 1 October 1862 (MH), Taylor begins on a note responsive to Howells' reticence: "You ought to be far enough advanced in the freemasonry to literature, to know that one poet needs never excuse himself for writing to another. I should have been very glad to hear directly from you, even were we not known to each other through many mutual friends."

2. Simon Cameron (1799–1889), a Pennsylvania newspaper editor in the 1820s and 1830s, was U. S. senator at various times in the period 1845–1873, and served as secretary of war (1861–1862) and as minister to Russia (January–November 1862). He was a powerful leader of the Pennsylvania Republicans.

3. Elizabeth Drew Barstow Stoddard, *The Morgesons* (1862). See *Literary Friends and Acquaintance*, HE, pp. 77–78.

4. Taylor informed Howells that "since the death of his little boy [in 1861],... he [Stoddard] has not written for *Vanity Fair*" and that "Stedman is clerk in the Attorney General's office, Washington...."

5. Richard Hildreth (1807–1865) was best known for his *History of the United States* (1849–1856). He was U. S. consul at Trieste (1861–1864) and had published one of the first antislavery novels, *The Slave; or, Memoirs of Archy Moore* (1836), republished frequently under other titles. See *Literary Friends and Acquaintance*, pp. 85–86; and Howells' Venetian diary (MH), pp. 49–61.

22 AND 23 OCTOBER 1862, VENICE, TO VICTORIA M. HOWELLS

Venice, Oct. 22, 1862.

My dear Sister—

Your letter, with those of father and Joe, and notes from mother and Annie, got here a few days ago. I was glad to see Annie's dear little face in the fotograf, though her position is that of the utmost constraint and discomfort, apparently. In return I send one of mine, which I got done last Saturday; I should be very glad to have one of you, Vic, and also of Aurelia.

The weather, here, is splendid now, I don't think you can have finer, although you have Indian summer at home. To-day I went to row, as usual, in a gondola, and stopped at the Lido, or sea-shore, where I took a long walk on the beach. Nothing could have been bluer than the sky, except the sea; and nothing so fresh and pure as either, except the air. It was absolute delight to breathe it; and after my long row of two miles, I enjoyed it intensely. The trees are now nearly all bare of leaves; and the birds were holding meetings to decide upon their route southward. But the grass was green, and it was more like spring than fall—so fresh and *young* everything felt.

23d. To-day I got letters from nearly all of you. That from dear mother made me hesitate about a project which I mentioned in my last—that of being married in Europe, here, instead of going home, first. It would be a saving of money certainly, and in that point of view, a good idea, but then it would prevent me from seeing you for so long a time; and you all seem so anxious to have me come home next spring. How gladly I would start to-day! The weather has changed, and I'm very heartsick and homesick. I've written to Elinor to come, but now I think I'll write again, postponing a final decision in regard to the matter. If mother is not quite agreed to this part of the arrangement, I'll change it all, and go home in the spring as I intended. I shall await the replies from home to my last, very anxiously.

In the meantime, there is very little to write, beyond telling you that my health is the same as usual. Father did quite right in holding back that sketch from the "Atlantic" until he had heard whether it was wanted.[1] It would be useless however, to send it to the N. Y. Times from publication, for all city papers are so crowded with war matters. If the *Atlantic* doesn't want it, father can use it in the Sentinel.

Things don't seem quite so desperate, now, in the States; tho' I'm far from sanguine concerning the effect of Lincoln's proclamation.[2] It can't make matters any worse between North and South, and therein consists its chance of doing good. Confidentially speaking I think the only idea worth fighting for is *Peace*! however that may come. It's been pretty clear to my mind, with the news of each successive *"victory"* of ours, that our conquest of the south has been all the other way. Indeed, the news of a great Union triumph rather depresses me than otherwise.

I've lately got a letter from Price, who is editing a paper in Toledo. Aurelia ought to have spoken to him when she met him, by all means. He would have been delighted.

—Dear mother's letter was so kind and good, it made me long to take her about the neck and kiss her—but if I speak so, I must cry. Do you mind the night I left home? How I sat up reading "Christy Johnstone," until the moment before I started?[3] Ah! dear sister, how I long and long to see you all!

I'm glad that you liked my poem of The Mulberries. I had a great deal of heart in that. We pay too much for pride and ambition. I have given home, and peace and almost hope for them; and now I feel that if I died to-day my name would perish to-morrow. And I would hardly care.—So little it comes to, after all, this world.—As I write I seem to find my way back to your heart, my dear sister. Do you forgive me for much unkind forgetfulness and neglect? Write to me always, my dear sister, for you know how much we need to be to each other. And try and write just as you used to talk. My fotograf is for *you*. Dear love to all.

> Your affectionate brother
> Will.

1. Evidently "A Little German Capital."
2. See Howells to Chase, 1 November 1862.
3. In *My Literary Passions* (1895), pp. 195–97, and *Heroines of Fiction* (1901), II, 34–42, Howells comments on Charles Reade's *Christie Johnstone* (1853).

1 NOVEMBER 1862, VENICE, TO SALMON P. CHASE

> Venice, Nov. 1, 1862.

Dear Sir—

I was touched and flattered by your remembrance of me, and truly valued a letter written to me at a time when so many demands must be made upon your time and care. Even in these gloomy days of the Republic, and amid all the toils of office, you could think of one whose chief merit is your friendship; and I, remote and anxious for the country's future, can be proud and grateful for your notice. I think that the best part of life is inalienable—that there is always some corner of our existence, out of which we keep all intruding troubles, and reserve for friendly recollection and for gratitude. At least, would it not be a pity, if it were not so?

The telegraph said the other day that you were dangerously ill. I hope it was in error, or that by this time you are recovered. There are so few clear heads and true hearts, that neither the Republic nor humanity could spare the clearest head and truest heart of all.

What I fear about the President's emancipatory proclamation is that it has come too late.[1] It seems to me that its moral effect upon a jaded, suffering and divided people must be null; that the spirit which would have hailed it a year ago, and given it a vigorous and effective support, is dead. It cannot recall the wasted lives and treasure which it might have spared before. I hope it may be the means of our salvation—but my belief, that is not so easy to control.

I do not think finances have any existence in me as a science, and there is nothing in the system of Austria worth writing to you. I am far better qualified to execute the other commission you gave me. There are many things characteristic of Venice which I could buy. First, photographs of Venetian palaces—the architecture the richest and the photographs the best in Europe. Or, then I might get in the way of jewelry, a chain of the peculiar fabric of Venice. (I send a little one to

Mr Piatt which I think he will oblige me by showing to you.) Or I might pick up a picture for $25 or $30, or get a tolerable copy of a great picture, here. There are of course abundance of trinkets in glass and jewelry, as souvenirs de Venise. I hope you'll let me know, how you prefer the outlay to be made.

Of myself I have little to tell you. I've learned Italian, and I've written some things. But these are not the days for rhymes.

I beg to be remembered to Miss Chase and Miss Nettie.[2]

Very respectfully,
W. D. Howells.

Hon. S. P. Chase.

1. Howells here refers to the Preliminary Emancipation Proclamation of 22 September 1862; the Proclamation itself was made on 1 January 1863.
2. Miss Chase was the elder daughter, Kate Chase (Sprague). Nettie was Kate's half-sister, Janette Ralston Chase (b. 1847).

24 DECEMBER 1862, PARIS, TO LARKIN G. MEAD, SR.

Paris, Hôtel du Louvre, Dec. 24, 1862.[1]

Two young persons, after a great deal of preliminary tribulation, were married to-day at the American legation in the presence of Mr. Dayton, his secretary of legation, and Larkin Mead (who especially desires to have his conduct on the occasion recommended).[2] It was found that a seven days' residence in England was necessary to matrimony, and so, after the most distressing failure to procure a special license, they—that is Elinor and I—pushed on to Paris, where the affair was arranged as already stated, the ceremony performed by Rev. McClintock, and took place at 3 o'clock P.M.[3] After which the happy couple and the adjacent brother went to see some churches and things, all looking remarkably like Elinor. This is the story in brief. To-morrow we leave for Italy at 10 A.M. and expect to be in Venice Saturday night. The writer has a vague impression that he's rather glad he's married and Elinor seems to be satisfied with her husband, although she doesn't consider him at all comparable in excellence or elegance to the table d'hôte dinner to-night at the Louvre. I remember myself to everybody and view myself in the light of an universal brother and son-in-law.

W. D. Howells.

1. As reprinted in *Life in Letters,* I, 62, there is no salutation at the beginning of this letter, but Mildred Howells identifies it as being addressed to Larkin G. Mead, Sr., Elinor's father, a lawyer, who founded Brattleboro's first town library and first bank.

2. William L. Dayton (1807–1864) was U. S. senator from New Jersey (1842–1851) and American minister to France (1861–1864). The secretary of legation at Paris, William S. Pennington (b. 1823), was a son of the former U. S. Senator William Pennington (1796–1862). Larkin G. Mead, Jr., Elinor's brother, had already established a reputation as a sculptor by the time he arrived in Europe. He later became honorary professor of sculpture at the Accademia di Belle Arti in Florence.

3. John McClintock (1814–1870) had charge of the American chapel in Paris during most of the Civil War. In 1867 he became president of Drew Theological Seminary.

22 JANUARY 1863, VENICE, TO JAMES L. GRAHAM, JR.

Venice, Jan. 22, 1863.

My dear Graham[1]—

I shall be able to let you know in about a week whether I can come soon to Florence; and if yes, just what time. Deeply pierced by the thought of that hospitable room standing empty for me—absolutely, as it were, yawning with the weariness of long expectation—I was still not probed into the recollection of having promised to visit you before now. *The early part of February* was fixed as the time of my visit, over a mug of mutual beer, and sealed with a pocketfull of cigarettes,—as Mrs Graham will remember, with the distinctness which is so graceful an attribute of her character (or if she wont, it's no matter.)

In the meantime, old fellow, take the bridal decorations off your room and fancy, and expect to meet two very commonplace married people.

Lark had no business to tell of our tribulations in search of matrimony.[2] I know he spoiled the story—which I alone have the right of telling, for I alone can tell it fully.

I'm rather glad Strodtmann[3] didn't use any of my things, for it goes some way to prove my theory that nobody can do anything for anybody; and I'm sorry I let you write him about me. Of course his publication will go down very soon.

I congratulate you on Stoddard's dedication.[4] It's a thing to be proud of.

Is there an American Dentist in Florence?

—We walk, boat, write and read together—Elinor and I,—and our days would be perfect, if only we met you and Mrs Graham at dinner, and had you at breakfast every morning. Such breakfasts! O!

The Tubbses[5] are still here, but go to Milan the 14th prox., and thence very soon to Florence.

Mrs Howells and I both remember ourselves to you and Mrs Graham.

Yours sincerely,
W. D. Howells.

Will you please write on getting this?

1. James Lorimer Graham, Jr. (1835–1876), was a connoisseur and collector of art and literature and the friend of many artists and writers. He was in Europe in 1862 and 1863 and later U. S. consul general in Italy, living in Florence.

2. See Howells to Larkin G. Mead, Sr., 24 December 1862. "Lark" was Elinor's brother, Larkin G. Mead, Jr.

3. Adolf Strodtmann (1829–1879), a minor German poet, is now best known as the editor of the first complete edition of Heine's works. He edited the literary periodical *Orion* (1863–1864) as well as two anthologies of English and American poetry in German translation.

4. Richard Henry Stoddard dedicated his poem *The King's Bell* (1862) "To James Lorimer Graham, Jr., from his friend, R. H. S."

5. Captain Tubbs, formerly of the East India Company, held joint ownership of a gondola with Howells. See Woodress, *Howells & Italy*, p. 167.

31 JANUARY 1863, VENICE, TO CHARLES HALE

Casa Falier,
Venice, Jan. 31, 1863.

Dear friend[1]—

When Elinor gave me the charming volume of Holmes with which you remembered me—it was in Liverpool, and only a few moments after our meeting—I determined to write you directly we reached Venice. But a month has gone by so indolently, and yet so swiftly, that it has seemed better not to do anything that had no immediate reference to being selfishly happy. Few cares of mine—thoughts, rather, for I have cares no longer—have wandered outside of this house, (which has a surprising capacity for holding happiness); but now and then they have strayed off to you; and sometimes I've felt a vague sort of gratitude to you for your kindly remembrance of me, and a still vaguer shame that I had done nothing to deserve or acknowledge your friendship. Shall I pretend to have felt anything else? Beyond this I have been utterly dead to every noble sentiment of friendship and justice.

Now at last I write. I've posted that letter of yours to Mr Thayer,[2] and shall have occasion to write to him myself in a few days. I also read the account of the trial of Count Johannes, and I think I can find out that matter of the record in the archives of Bologna.[3]

Elinor told me you were curious to know something more of your water-color painting (which I'm glad you like.) I only know that it is a Venetian fine lady of the last century; and that the figure is copied from a painting called "The Dancing Master" by Pietro Longhi,[4] in the Academy here. There is a series of paintings by this master, illustrative of Venetian life in the last age, which have the oddest flavor of Goldoni in them all—and might almost have been painted in illustration of his comedies.[5] I think the copyist has done his work very spiritedly, and I like the out-door isolation of the figure.—Thanks for "Janet's Repentance,"[6] which you left me.

We're very anxious to have you sure that we live in Casa Falier (*not* Valier.) We're very near the iron bridge, and just opposite the Academy. Our house-keeping is the funniest and delightfullest thing in the world. The house was furnished with an absolutely irreproachable servant among other things, and she takes care of us as tenderly and jealously as if we were children.[7] She is a Genius, and has inspirations for breakfast, which are triumphant. The roast potatoes which she achieves are in themselves, miracles of art, and her fried mush beggars description.— I've a boat, and what time we are not engaged with pen and paper, or in bragging over our breakfasts or ourselves, we spend on the lagoons. I've learnt to row gondolier-fashion, and never take anyone with me to help.

I send fotograf of E. and me, and we want yours in return. Mrs Howells puts in a prayer that her friend Miss Kitty Gannett[8] may be acquainted with the great fact that the fotograf has been done, and that one is coming to her. Of course we make the usual pretense that the fotograf does not look nearly so well as we do.

There seems to be very little to say on the subject of the country. I'm afraid something curiously like ruin is impending. Divided politically in the north, everywhere beaten with dreadful slaughter in the field— it's sickening to read the accounts from home, and moves one to wonder if there *is* no divine interest in a good cause, or if we are fatally mistaken after all, and ours is a bad cause. But it only discomforts me to write so of what I cannot help.

We have had no snow at all this winter, and the weather for the past week has been

"Blue, unclouded summer weather,"[9]

We wish you were here. We feel glad enough to gladden the whole world, and I'm sure there's no one to whom either of us would be more pleased to offer the hospitalities of Casa Falier—consisting of good will, roast potatoes and tea,—than to yourself. Mrs Howells sends her regards, and prays you with me to find this letter better deserving an answer than it really is.

Yours cordially,
W D Howells.

Mr Charles Hale.

1. Charles Hale (1831–1882) was an editor of the Boston *Advertiser* (1850–1864), U. S. consul general in Egypt (1864–1870), and later held various public offices. The *Advertiser* printed Howells' "Letters from Venice" in 1863 and 1864 (see Gibson-

Arms, *Bibliography*, pp. 87–89), which later formed the basis for *Venetian Life*. See also *Literary Friends and Acquaintance*, HE, p. 80.

2. Alexander Wheelock Thayer (1817–1897) held a small post in the U. S. legation at Vienna. He prepared a biography of Beethoven and was U. S. consul at Trieste (1859–1882).

3. In a letter to Howells, 17 March 1863 (MH), Hale indicates that this Count Johannes had filed a number of damage suits, including one against Hale. The material in the archives presumably related to the count's claim of nobility. Further references to this matter appear in letters from Hale to Howells, 29 April 1863, 26 May 1863, 29 February 1864 (MH).

4. Venetian painter, 1702–1785.

5. For a discussion of the influence of Carlo Goldoni (1707–1793) on the development of Howells' realism, see Woodress, *Howells & Italy*, pp. 131–37, 139–47.

6. The third of three tales by George Eliot, collected in *Scenes of Clerical Life* (1858).

7. For a description of Giovanna, the serving woman, see *Venetian Life* (1872), pp. 111–24.

8. Kitty Gannett probably lived in Boston, but no further details of her life are known.

9. See Tennyson, "The Lady of Shalott," part 3, stanza 3, line 1.

3 FEBRUARY 1863, VENICE, TO JAMES L. GRAHAM, JR.

Venice, Feb. 3, 1863.

Dear Graham—

I'm sorry we can't go to Florence this spring, and I count not seeing you, there, the sorest part of it. The truth is, we've just got settled, and I've just got to work, and after the journey from America, and the journey to and from England, we don't feel like renewing our travels immediately. We know you're coming here in May, and that we shall then all meet and be merry together—and for Florence, that may be far less regretfully postponed. If I thought we should not see you here—or that your projected eastern tour would in any way interfere with your coming to Venice again, I'd bolt for Florence at once. But as it is—I forgive myself with the most angelic sweetness for everything but making you (however innocently I did it) take that room for us. If you go to the Isles of Greece, may your whole progress be one flattering unction, and may you slip back as smoothly to Venice as—as (something else, you know, supposed to be sentimental and witty about Grease and Oils.)

I've been making toothache a steady thing, now, for nearly three weeks, and am basking at presence in the joyous possession of a swelled face, that bulges considerably beyond the line of beauty. I never did have the gout, but I'd be willing to run a sore race with you on almost any other indisposition you've a mind to name.

Have you heard lately from Bayard Taylor? Is he still in St Petersburgh? When I was in Paris (did I tell you?) I met your friend Brooks, and took a liking to his pleasant genial face at once.[1] I only saw him for a few minutes, at the Consulate.

I was at Pickerings in London, and gave him charge concerning the remembrance of your books.[2] I also left my Ms. with him,[3] and he kindly promised to offer it to McMillan's Magazine for me. Your letters of introduction I had no time to deliver.

How did you "come by" the manuscript of "Cumberland?" Which *is* a magnificent poem.[4]

Hildreth's clerk was here to-day, and told me that Mr Hildreth's health was much improved—though as he said he was writing day and night, I fancy that his health will have to be very persevering in its attempts at ameliriation, or it wont succeed.

If you see Lark,[5] will you please hand him these scraps, which his father enclosed to him from America?

Remember Elinor and me to Mrs Graham, and believe us always cordially yours.

W. D. Howells

Mr Jas. Lorrimer Graham, Jr.

1. Brooks was probably on the staff of the U. S. consulate at Paris.
2. Basil Montagu Pickering was in the publishing and rare book business; his father, William Pickering, was the founder of the Aldine Press.
3. The manuscript was "Disillusion: A Little Venetian Story," as indicated in Howells' letter to Moncure D. Conway, 23 May 1863 (NNC). The complex publication history of this poem is reflected primarily in the correspondence between Howells and Frank E. Foster: on 11 April 1863 (CLSU) Howells promised to make a Christmas book for the publisher; on 13 May 1863 (CLSU) he definitely proposed that Foster publish it with illustrations by Elinor Howells; on 21 August 1863 (MH) Foster acknowledged receipt of Howells' two letters, the design for the cover, and the first part of the poem; on 30 October 1863 (MH) Foster sent Howells the proofs. In a letter to Joseph A. Howells, 16 December 1866 (MH), Howells reported that Hurd & Houghton were to publish "my poem which Foster stereotyped." The work was eventually published as "No Love Lost / a Romance of Travel," *Putnam's*, December 1868, and as a book of the same title by G. P. Putnam & Son, in November 1868. See Woodress, *Howells & Italy*, pp. 87–89.
4. Longfellow, "The Cumberland," *Atlantic*, December 1862.
5. Larkin G. Mead, Jr.

12 AND 20 FEBRUARY 1863, VENICE, TO WILLIAM C. HOWELLS

Venice, Feb. 12, 1863.

Dear father—

Your affectionate children in Venice found your letter of the 14th to-day waiting their return from the Gardens, and pounced upon it with that ardor which the sight of U. S. postage-stamps inspires in the exiled bosom. The Sentinel had come in the morning, and I had dismally made up my mind that the letters by the same steamer were lost. Not only yours came, however, but two others—and we were very glad little people to know that news of our marriage had reached you. Though I can't say that beside the love in your letter there was anything very cheerful there. Upon literary topics you were particularly depressing, and quite made poetry a burden to me. I suppose it will really be better to versify for Elinor—whom I find a most indulgent public,—at present, and put aside all thoughts of celebrity. "The Young Volunteer"[1] I can *not* come—much as I honor that person. "There are souls which must be saved, and there are souls which must not be saved. As for me, I hope to be saved,"[2]—though not by martial poetry.

You might, at the rate good counsel is commonly afforded, have still given me some advice, with the discretionary power usual in such cases. Elinor and I find ourselves fortunate in being so far away from all affectionate criticism, and are quite as absurd and silly as we like to be. Not that we really do very flat things, you know—except that persons naturally seek level surfaces, who ever come out of our exalted state of feeling at all; and there is a pervading softness in our lives which would probably surprise blood-relations. At present the English language experiences a breathless exhaustion in its diminutives, and the name of a bird commonly associated with onion sauce, recurs continually to our utterance. We naturally argue that all this tender exhuberance will pass away with time, as we do not observe elderly or even middle-aged married people to call each other ducks, and then behave like geese. We suppose that there is not honey enough in two small lives, to make all the noons, and that sooner or later the use of beeswax must begin. But as yet there is no lapse from the ideal, and it is hard to understand that the world has not just been made for us to enjoy ourselves in.

Elinor's father said he would send you a Boston paper containing an anticipatory notice of our marriage. I wonder.... The affair... in New England[3] before Elinor left—to our no small disgust; and I learned for the first time what a disagreeable thing a prodigious reputation for poetry like mine might become. I shall never be able to think of dying with the least satisfaction, for fear some donkey will bray my virtues into print before I've ceased to practise them.

Elinor is quite Yankee enough to know what "snug weather" means. At present she's devoting most of her faculties to achieve some idea of the letter R as pronounced by correct speakers of English, and I've been trying to teach her to say *toad*, though I'm ashamed to add she's done nothing better than *to-ed* as yet.

Supposing that she will write news and gossip, I content myself with sending my love to all (grandmother included.)

> Your affectionate son,
> Will

Would you send me a few newspapers—Evening Post, when used . . . , and the State Journal, and Price's paper if you exchange,[4] and the N. Y. World or Times. I'm sorry to hear of all your colds, but when you are all recovered couldn't the girls write a little?

> Feb. 20th.

I found this letter in a perfect state of preservation in my portfolio, and now send it with the explanation that I suppose Elinor has destroyed a letter she had been writing to accompany it. The production was submitted to me, and I pronounced it calculated to relieve you of the impression that I had married a too severely intellectual wife. It had no other merit, and you lose nothing in not getting it—if I except the neat criticism of its artless simplicity of style, with which I endorsed it. The drawing I send is much better than the epistle.

I've got a letter from Piatt in which he acknowledges that of mine about which he was unhappy.

You know the Count of Chambourg,[5] the Bourbon claimant of the French throne, lives in Venice. His majordomo, the Duc de Levis died the other day,[6] and last Friday a most imposing funeral service was performed in the Church of San Stefano near which we live. The poor Duc possessed the canine virtue of fidelity, and gave his life and fortune to the service of a man who pretends as hopefully to a throne as children to the moon. The king, and his sister the (ex) Duchess of Parma, were in attendance. The king is lame; but he has the real Bourbon face as we see it in pictures. He spends most of his time in hunting ducks in the lagoons, and it was in one of these excursions that the dead Duc was made ill.

I have nearly finished the translation I was making,[7] and now I think of taking another book to do from the bookseller here—a book of biographical sketches of Venetian painters.

You're quite right about the *Atlantic*. It's only to be valued as a medium of publication, but as such I can't afford to despise it.

You will read that the Poles are in revolution. They have no prospect of success whatever—which is possibly a pity.—At home, things appear to be progressing in the old way—from bad to worse.—I've had a letter from Comly, whom the war seems to have made an abolitionist. *Does* the proclamation do any good?

The weather here is very beautiful—slightly cool, and very still and clear. It is hard to think of you as being still in mid-winter—meaning snow drifts and "slippin'."

Elinor (who's not very well with a cold) sends her love to all, and I am again

Your affectionate son
Will.

Father couldn't you have that medallion of mine fotografed for me?

1. Probably an early title of "For One of the Killed," *Poems* (1873), p. 133. See *Years of My Youth*, HE, p. 203.
2. See Shakespeare, *Othello*, II, iii, 106–7, 109–11.
3. Deterioration of paper has rendered one line of text mostly unrecoverable.
4. See Howells to Holmes, Jr., 25 November 1860, n. 1.
5. Henri Charles Ferdinand Marie Dieudonné d'Artois (1820–1883), whose sister, the duchess of Parma, was Howells' neighbor in Venice. See *Venetian Life* (1872), p. 119.
6. Howells wrote an obituary for the Duc de Lévis (1794–1863) in "Letters from Venice," *Advertiser*, 27 March 1863.
7. *Venice. Her Art-Treasures and Historical Associations.... Translated from the second German Edition of Adalbert Müller*. See C. and R. Kirk, "Howells' Guidebook to Venice," *American Literature* 33 (1961), 221–24.

15 MARCH 1863, VENICE, TO WILLIAM C. HOWELLS

Venice, March 15, 1863.

Dear Father:

From a primary motive of laziness and further to avoid all future cause of complaint regarding my handwriting, I have adopted Elinor as an amanuensis. As I always have a great deal to say without much disposition to say it, and as Elinor never has anything to say with the greatest possible desire to talk continually, I think you will be perfectly satisfied with the result of our arrangement. You will have no fault to find with the shortness of her letters and you will find the literary merit of the joint composition improved through my furnishing the ideas and their expression. (Elinor is so well pleased with my way of saying things that she is quite willing to write herself down anything I want, and I have continually to regret that the general public which I have an equal desire to entertain and abuse, is not as complaisant). Your letter came this morning. I met the postman with it as I was going out for some medicine of my own prescription for Elinor. (I think it is well to begin taking medicine in the family at once, and as I don't like it myself, Elinor is obliged to carry out the principle). The postman had two letters for me; one from you and the other from Geneva acknowledging the receipt of my draft in payment for a gold watch which I have just bought there, out of the proceeds of the translation so continually dinned into all our correspondents.[1] As I was getting rather impatient to have a letter from you and as the postman gave me the Geneva letter first, under the impression that it was all he had for me, yours came in the nature of an agreeable disappointment; and enlivened our breakfast considerably. Touching the pig-tail—the oars and the paper—I will attend to it directly.[2] I have no idea, however, that the project can be made to work, and you must be careful not to involve me in any business either as principal or agent, forbidden by the terms of my bond, which you remember were very strict against trading. I will however, as I said, make all the preliminary inquiries and report progress.

The usual monotony of our Venetian Sundays was broken today by the event of English service at one of the Hotels. Even my limited experience has known livelier sermons, and I do not think there was ever so stern a conflict between my patriotism and my piety as when I was obliged to pray for Queen Victoria and the English Cabinet generally. The preacher was a mild young divine, overflowing with the milk and water of human kindness, and he is not, I am glad to say, a slated, but only an accidental preacher in these parts. Our customary spiritual fare is served up by a person now temporarily absent. Him I have heard twice, and this other once. The three occasions forming the sum resulting from the best intentions of church-going during the past sixteen months. I do not however feel myself altogether a heathen. Elinor instigated me to buy a volume of sermons which we have found very good, and singularly imbued with the practical spirit of the New Church doctrines. They are by a Rev. F. W. Robertson of Trinity Chapel, Brighton, of whom you may possibly know something.[3] Then we have some other devotional formalities, observed in the occasional spirit. We hope the custom will establish something like regularity, but we have a reluctance to force things. Elinor is a member of the Congregational Church and I am a sinner under conviction, which I am sorry to say does not occur to me so vividly when in perfect health as at other times. I have written to Larkin Mead at Florence, to get me some Swedenborgian works, if any are to be had at the English book-store there. Powers, you know, is a Swedenborgian and Mrs. Mowatt-Ritchie is also living at Florence.[4] I thought you would be interested in this presentation of our religious state, which a bad habit of talking has made me seem to speak more jocularly of than I would have done. As for the rest, we spend most of our time now in reading up the history of art. I had no idea that I could come to feel so great an interest in the matter as I have done. But in Venice the influences of art pervade the whole atmosphere and it is hard not to inhale something of them. The intellectual life of the place is dead. All that remains are the triumphs of past genius, but these are everywhere. So our talk is a jargon, more unintelligible on my part and less so on Elinor's, of Titians and Tintorettos, of paintings and sculptures and mosaics, of schools and of manners, and our reading naturally takes that direction, too. I do not think the time lost, either, that I spend in this way. I do'n't know how it is with others, but some part of every study that I have pursued with honesty, has been of use to me at one time or other; and I do'n't feel my intellectual muscle so fully developed, that I could travel on it just yet without a little more exercise. This is the general view of the usefulness of looking at art a little. A particular purpose is to make some biographical sketches of the Venetian schools, for the book-seller here, who wants me to do it and who only hesitates about the price I want him to pay me for the work.—Besides these books on art I have got one of the most fascinating autobiographies that I ever read. It is that of Goldoni, the Venetian dramatist.[5] While on this subject I may as well tell you that I have revived the notion that I once mentioned to you of fitting myself for something in the nature of a professor of modern languages, in case I should find on my return to America the intellectual life of the country yearning more decidedly for professors of modern languages than for journalists, or even poets.

We went rowing today—Elinor and I—making a tour of part of the Grand Canal which she, like most of the Venetians, has never seen as a whole. The boating has rather given place, of late, to walking, but I find it so pleasant that I think I shall take to it actively again. I have bought Elinor a sketch-book and she proposes to unite sketching with boating. Yesterday she made her first sketch in public,—a fisherman presenting a birdseye view from one of the bridges of "a fisherman mending his coat." The subject was quite unconscious and sat still for a long time, in spite of the eager and applausive multitude scuffling about the elbows of the artist for the best view of her creation. At last the fisherman changed his position, to get his knife, and the artist suspended her labors amid the ill-disguised disgust of the multitude. The crowd, in fact, is the only draw-back on these occasions, and I hope that it will not prove too great a one. But I find that it is quite impossible for a short man like myself to stare starers out of countenance, when he can only bring his eyes to a level with their shirt bosoms, and I must confess that the crowd is a sore trial to my spirit. However, the privileges of a *forista*[6] are almost unlimited in Venice, and if people, bearing any marks of Anglo-Saxon descent, were to swarm up the pillars of the Piazzetta in order to sketch the Ducal Palace from the back of St. Mark's Lion, the eccentricity would be readily forgiven by the Venetians as a perhaps rare, but by no means impossible, form of the *spleen*.

That little poem of mine which you saw in the Commonwealth was first printed in Mr. Conway's "Dial" some two years ago.[7] I have got out of the well sometime since, and have so little prospect of unhappiness before me that I think I shall probably give up seeing the stars by day in the forlorn manner indicated by the poem.

We have dined at home for a long time now, and have consequently translated our housekeeping into English. I hope the girls will be able to understand it better. Mother must consider a letter like this written as much to her as to you, but the girls are only directly addressed when they have found time to write to their exiled relatives in foreign parts.

I suppose that we shall get the papers you sent eventually, but they hav'n't come yet. From motives of disgust as deep as your own I do not say anything about politics either. Elinor and I unite in love to all and I am affectionately

Your son
Will.

I notice, on looking over this letter, that it has a curiously stilted effect—as if I had been posturing for print, rather than writing at ease to you, father. But as I get used to dictating, I can do better perhaps. Write me something of grandmother in every letter, and always give her my love. You might send her that fotograf of Elinor and me.—We take the Venetian Gazette now, and I file it. There is nothing more. I hope you'll find this letter long enough at any rate.

Affectionately,
Will.

1. See Howells to W. C. Howells, 12 and 20 February 1863, n. 7.
2. See Howells to Mary D. Howells, 18 April 1863.
3. Frederick William Robertson, *Sermons Preached at Trinity Chapel, Brighton* (1863).
4. Hiram Powers (1805–1873), an American sculptor, lived in Florence from 1837 until his death. Mrs. Anna Cora Mowatt-Ritchie (1819–1870) was an American author and actress.
5. *Memorie di Carlo Goldoni per l'istoria della sua vita e del suo teatro* (1831), mentioned in "Recent Italian Comedy," *North American Review*, October 1864. In 1877 Howells edited *Memoirs of Carlo Goldoni*, a translation of the original French *Memoires de M. Goldoni* (1787) by John Black, first published in 1828.
6. "Foreigner."
7. "A Poet," Cincinnati *Dial*, June 1860; reprinted in the Boston *Commonwealth*, 14 February 1863. Moncure D. Conway (1832–1907), editor of the *Dial* (1860), edited the *Commonwealth* (1862–1863) with Franklin B. Sanborn. In 1863 he went to England in behalf of "some antislavery folks in Boston to mingle awhile with the people and their leaders here, and reassure them that our cause [in the Civil War] is that of Humanity and Justice." See Conway to Howells, 6 May 1863 (MH).

23 MARCH 1863, VENICE, TO JAMES L. GRAHAM, JR.

Venice, March 23, 1863.

My dear Graham—

Your very welcome little letter came yesterday morning, and relieved me of a fear that I don't mind confessing, now I don't feel it any more. I thought perhaps you were vexed out of all friendship for me by my failure to go to Florence; but as things have turned out, I should be in the most embarrassing predicament if I had gone, for there has been a delay in the payment of my last drafts on the Treasury, and I've barely got money enough to rub through, as it is.

Why can't you come to Venice and spend the summer instead of going to Germany? We want to see you so much. You'll at least take us on your way to Germany? *Do.*

We spent Saturday going about with the Chapins,[1] who left this morning for Vienna. I liked Chapin very much. He's a man with a heart as well as a brain—a somewhat rare combination of merit. He spoke of you in the most cordial manner—doing you a justice which your partial friends here were eager to applaud.

I've finished that translation I was at work on when you were here,[2] and now I talk of making for the bookseller here a little sketchy, biographical handbook of Venetian painters.[3] It will educate me in that branch of study, and I shall make a little money by it.

Just now, I'm writing occasionally at my sketches of Venice.[4]—I hear nothing from any literary body in America, and the little you told me—of Stoddard's illness—was depressing. I wish I could hear the "King's Bell."[5]—Poetically I've done one or two little things, but nothing really worth mentioning since I saw you.

My wife and I spend most of our time in reading up about art. We've got Kugler, and several books of reference, and I'm meditating Vasari.[6]

Let us hear oftener from you wherever you go, and *try* to come to Venice.

We write in love to you and Mrs Graham.

Yours sincerely,
W. D. Howells.

1. Possibly James Henry Chapin (1832–1896), an educator, clergyman, and author of *From Japan to Granada...A Tour Around the World in 1887–8* (1889).
2. See Howells to W. C. Howells, 12 and 20 February 1863, n. 7.
3. If the handbook was written and published, no copy has been discovered. See *Life in Letters*, I, 65.
4. "Letters from Venice."
5. See Howells to Graham, 22 January 1863, n. 4.

6. Franz Theodore Kugler, *Kugler's Handbook of Painting* (1851); Giorgio Vasari, *Lives of the Most Eminent Painters, Sculptors, and Architects* (1850–1855).

24 March 1863, Venice, to Moncure D. Conway

Venice, March 24, 1863.

Dear Mr Conway—

I thought that after I had neglected so long to write to you, you would have had the greatness of soul to overlook my neglect, and write to me. I wonder at you, while I forgive you, and I hope that if these verses (which are offered to the Commonwealth,) are not so good as to act in the nature of coals of fire heaped upon your head, they may still be a retribution in their way.[1]

To tell you the truth, you and Mrs Conway are two people whom we should very much like to see in Venice.[2] The spring is coming on, after the "slow, sweet" fashion of spring in southern lands; the Adriatic is warming up with the view of being bathed in; the sun is bringing out all that is brightest and loveliest in the city, and embroidering the islands and the terrafirma with flowers. Four weeks ago we gathered daisies on the Lido; and now the almond-trees are heavy with bloom and bees. Besides all this we live in the old Palazzo Faliero (where Marino Faliero,[3] according to all the gondoliers, was born,) and we have a piano, and a balcony on the Grand Canal, and the most delightful little breakfasts in Venice. You *will* come, wont you?

The We is not used editorially here. Of course you know that I am married, and to whom. Though I've never heard directly from you, I used to hear a great deal about you in letters from Cincinnati. You have an additional merit in my eyes, because you met Elinor there.

I wish you'd send me the Commonwealth regularly, and let me pay for it in occasional contributions. Please send it by way of Bremen, charging pre-payment of postage in the account against me. (Letter postage is collected on papers not prepaid. That's why.)

When you write, pray tell me of the great battle which you men are fighting unseen amidst the dust and smoke of war. Tell me something to knit me closer to truth of which ease and indolence and office, may have somewhat relaxed the ties.

Many intellectual changes you and I should have to talk over, and perhaps laugh over. It is not Heine, now, but Dante, and perhaps Art more than either. It is to be hoped certainly that something good will come out of it all—ma! ci vuol pazienza.[4]

Did the Commonwealth make any notice of "Louis Lebeau's Conversion," when that great poem appeared?[5] If it did, will you send me copy of the notice?

Elinor unites with me in love to Mrs Conway, and we both send cordial regards to you. Do write soon, wont you?

Yours sincerely,
W. D. Howells.

1. "For the Commonwealth, By the Sea," *Commonwealth*, 1 May 1863.
2. On 6 May 1863 (MH) Conway replied: "I want to see Venice in her glory; notwithstanding I told Emerson the night before I left that I was going to Venice to see Howells & he declared that it was a most unruskinian motive for the visit."
3. Marino Faliero (1279–1355) was a doge of Venice who was executed for treason. See *Venetian Life* (1872), pp. 14, 15, 100–101, 283.
4. Italian for "But you need patience."
5. Conway informed Howells in his answer to this letter that the *Commonwealth* did not receive a copy of the printed poem.

5 April 1863, Venice, to Charles Hale

Venice, April 5, 1863.

My dear friend—

We got your welcome letter yesterday, just as I was meditating the enclosed to the *Advertiser*.[1] I wish (pleasure before business,) you'd send me the Advertiser, and take it out in letters, or scribbling of some sort, if you can find your account that way. Some weeks ago, I sent you a letter by the State Department, which I hope you got.[2]—The name of your artist (while I think of it) is the Nobile, Francesco Barbaro.[3] I saw him the other day making a very fine little copy of a Veronese, in the Academy. Looking again at the original of your picture, I found that Barbaro had so changed and improved it in the copy as almost to make it his own. It is certainly a very graceful and spirited little thing.

Mrs Howells sends you enclosed as you wished, a list of my published "works." I shall be very glad to read your article on Buckle[4]—it was only the night before your letter came that we were thinking and talking about him. The "Atlantic" has not come to me at all this year, for some reason or unreason.

I think nothing could surpass the lovely spring weather that we have. Days of blue and gold embellish nights of moonlight poetry, making the edition of each twenty-four hours perfect.

At present Elinor is not perfectly well, but till a week ago when she became interested in a bad cold, we were all absorbed in art. We have read up pretty thoroughly on Venice, and now we're reading Kugler. His book gave me a relish for mosaics, and I happened on the place described in my letter, just at the right time. Perhaps I exaggerate the beauty of this art, but I can't help wishing that it were introduced and cultivated in America. As we don't paint our churches, (artistically I mean) we could apply mosaic art to profane subjects, and immortalize in smalts, say the Presidents for the Capitol.

Many Americans are in town now, and we see nearly all, and waste ever so much time enjoying ourselves. I am surprised to find so great a number of Americans still abroad, in spite of war and exchange. It was encouraging to see that so calm and sensible an observer of events as yourself took a cheerful view of our affairs, and I took heart from you. Nothing however of late has seemed to me such an unjust and mistaken thing as some Americans furnishing munitions and provisions to the French for the invasion of Mexico, while we are breathing incessant maledictions against England for assisting our rebels. I don't see how we're any better than J. B.[5] as far as that goes.

Larkin Mead who has settled in Florence, set up a little statue called "Echo" about two months ago. Corcoran,[6] the Washington Banker saw it in clay, unfinished, and bought it at once for $500—the artist's price.

I hope that you wont let our correspondence drop. I write a short letter to you personally, because I count this for the paper as first addressed to you. Write soon, and believe both of us your cordial friends.

W. D. Howells.

I saw Maggie Mitchell[7] in Columbus, Ohio, several years ago. She has long been a favorite in the west.

An Englishman, somewhat posted in such things, told me he thought there were no such records at Bologna as Count Johannes claims, but I go shortly to that city on my way to Florence, and will enquire.[8]

Atlantic Poems.[9]

Andenken	January, 1860.
The Poet's Friends	February " .
Pleasure-Pain	April "
Lost Beliefs	same number
Pilot's Story	Sept—1860
The Old Homestead	Jan. 1861.
(Mr. Howell's name for it was The Empty House)	
Bubbles	April "
Louis Lebeau's Conversion	Nov. 1862

Mr. Howells also published a book in Columbus with J. J. Piatt in 1862—called Poems of Two Friends. Others were published in the late Saturday Press, New York, and a few in The Dial, Cincinnati.

1. Hale's letter to Howells is dated 17 March 1863 (MH). Howells' subsequent comments about his interest in mosaics suggest that the enclosure was "The Revival of Mosaic Painting in Venice," *Advertiser*, 2 May 1863.
2. Most likely Howells' letter of 31 January 1863.
3. Howells may be humorously suggesting that the copyist is as illustrious ("Nobile") as his namesake, Candiano Barbaro (1395–1454), a Venetian patriot.
4. "Personal Reminiscences of the Late Henry Thomas Buckle," *Atlantic*, April 1863.
5. John Bull.
6. William W. Corcoran (1798–1888) had begun to build the Corcoran Gallery of Art in 1859. Because of his sympathies for the South he left the United States in 1862 and remained abroad until the end of the Civil War.
7. Margaret Julia Mitchell (1832–1918) was one of the most popular American actresses of the last half of the nineteenth century. Hale had written about her to Howells on 17 March 1863.
8. See Howells to Hale, 31 January 1863, n. 3.
9. In his letter of 17 March, Hale had asked for a complete list of Howells' printed pieces. As Howells indicates in an earlier part of his letter, the list is written in Elinor Howells' hand.

18 APRIL 1863, VENICE, TO MARY D. HOWELLS

Venice, April 18, 1863.

Dear Mother:

Your part of the last family letter was, as it always is, the welcomest and shortest. But it was full of fears about my health which you need not have felt. I never was better, nor so well in my life, and have almost forgotten that I ever was unwell or downhearted. Try and think of me as widening out in every direction,—as having actual dimples in the fatness of my cheeks, and as growing a magnificent double chin.

I want to get through with the business first, and to tell father that the oar project cannot be made to go here: good oars can be bought in Venice for 75 cents apiece, and even if oars were not so cheap, the sort made in Jeff., could not be used, for the Venetian oar is to be pushed, not pulled, and is therefore very heavy in the blade, and very light and slender in the handle. This is no place where ship's oars could be sold to advantage, for there is scarcely any shipping. Such is the report of the growing ship-broker to whom I referred the matter.—I have been half a dozen times (since I last wrote) to the paper-warehouse, but, always found it closed. However, there is little more to be told of paper and prices than what I have written already.[1]—There is one other little matter. I wish father would send me viâ Hamburgh, prepaid, that poem of mine, Bopeep, which I left on a shelf in the library.

When it comes to telling you news of our life, here, I find myself as much at fault as you do when you write from home. Like everything happy, it hasn't much event in it, and we go on from day to day, with nothing to mark them, but letters written or letters received. Between us, I think we get four a week; but never enough come from home. For the past week or two Elinor has been not very well. The warm weather coming on makes her feel the change of climate, and I think the sea-air doesn't perfectly agree with her. We intend trying a change next month, for seven or eight days, and making a jaunt to Florence.—This week we made an excursion to Torcello—five miles away in the lagoon, where four hundred years there was a prosperous city, and where now there are some broken walls, and a few scattered cottages, and vineyards and gardens. We went partly to see the old Cathedral (built A.D. 600), but principally to do our good old Giovanna a pleasure. She is fifty years old, and has never been out of Venice—never "out of these stones," as she says. We took her and her two little children, Beppi and Nina, who fairly went wild to see grass and flowers growing. In all their lives they have never set foot on anything but stone, and they ran riot over the island clutching up weeds and blossoms, and making bouquets, with the pretty instinct of the Italians. Of course the little girl fell into the water, and broke dishes, and of course poor Beppi fell asleep in the bottom of the gondola, coming back, and lost all pleasure of the return trip—for all the world like me, coming back from Cincinnati in the buggy in old Hamilton days.

And that makes me think, sadly enough, of Henry. Does the poor little fellow actually improve, or only in your anxious love? I wish some one would write to me all about it.[2]

We send a fotograf in this letter for grandmother. Elinor would write something, but is really too unwell, and I would make this longer, but I expect a letter every day from home, and then I'll answer that. Elinor with me sends love to all.

Your affectionate son,
Will.

Your speaking of fried ham put me in mind of having it, and now Giovanna gets it up every morning.

1. See Howells to W. C. Howells, 15 March 1863.
2. See Howells to V. M. Howells, 18–24 April 1859, n. 16.

18 MAY 1863, VENICE, TO AURELIA H. HOWELLS

Venice, May 18, 1863.

Dear Aurelia:

As Elinor has set the good example of writing to you, I think I'll follow it for one or two pages. Though E's style is so exhaustive that I feel there is very little to say when she has written.—I want you to give the little fotografs enclosed to father. They're only copies of pictures, he'll see. When I send views—which I'm going to do soon—they shall be stereoscope size.

I was particularly glad to hear from you, knowing how hard it is for you to write letters, and I answer you. Vic's turn next. Annie's bliss deferred to the last.

I suppose you girls remember that pride is sinful, although father *is* prospering so splendidly in business. Do you wear silk dresses when you're scrubbing and white-washing? I suppose Vic has a satin Ironholder, and mother a silver hook for taking off stove covers, and Annie a brocade dish-cloth. But don't forget your relatives, who, though much better than yourselves, are not so successful in a business point of view.— I expect, when I return home, to see our lot all cut up with ditches, and a Pelton[1] in every one of them. I don't know of anything now to prevent father from having several cisterns dug, and devoted to perpetual leakage and repair. However I'm unspeakably glad of the streak of luck.

Aurelia, do you correspond regularly with any of the Carter's? I suppose Mrs C., will hardly write to me again—I neglected her so long.— Tell father I do write occasionally for a paper—The Boston Advertiser— which I have directed to be sent to him whenever it contains anything from me.

Do send us fotografs of all of you, wont you? I have pictures of ever so many people I don't care for, but of my own family only two or three.

I've got neuralgia frightfully, and must stop. Dear love to all.

> Your affectionate brother,
> Will.

1. Probably Howells is referring to a family of plumbers in Jefferson.

1 JUNE 1863, VENICE, TO JOHN B. HOWELLS

> Venice, June 1, 1863.

My dear Johnny—

I believe you've written me several letters and I've never answered one of them yet. So I'll write this time to you, and in token of your sole proprietorship it shall be addressed to you on the outside.

In talking over the family to Elinor and trying to make her understand something about each one, we always have to discuss you. This morning I was telling how I used,—when you were a very much smaller boy than you are, and not so toughened by slinging this heavy world—how I used to pretend I was mad at you, just to see you "put up a lip," which you did very charmingly.—Now, I suppose the only thing that will induce you to put up a lip is some young lady who consents to put up two at the same time.—Johnny, do you go much to dances? And do you schottische? When I was a young man I did both—but it is a long time ago. Are you a dandy, Johnny? I rather think you must be,— and that's much better than to be a sloven.

Johnny, when young men are about seventeen years of age, it sometimes happens to them to pass through a strange experience. They sometimes fall in love, and are pretty nearly always jilted. If you should do the one thing, and endure the other, will you take the word of "a man and a brother," that it's a great good fortune for you? When you are much older, you will understand that the first object of one's affections is fearfully overrated, and is apt to be the most commonplace little creature in the world. I once knew a young man in Jefferson, who was thrown very high and had a very hard fall. It affected his mind for several years, and he thought that most if not all of his feelings were blighted. But he outlived the occurrence, and is now happily married, and extremely glad to have escaped the danger and the lady whom he once courted.—It is before breakfast. After that meal, we will resume in a less didactic strain.

Since breakfast, Elinor and I have been out shopping, and have bought you a couple of ties, which I hope you'll like. They're the latest fashion in Venice for summer. There's another kind worn now, which is passed through a ring in front, instead of being tied, but as I couldn't send you the ring, I don't send you the cravat.

It's almost a month now, since I've heard from home. The two last Bremen steamers brought me papers from father, but no letters. The postman this minute came with three more papers—but no letters. I can't understand it, and it's certainly very provoking. In my last letter home, I sent father some fotografs, which I hope he'll get.

I wish you were here, Johnny, to go swimming in the sea, with me. I haven't been yet, this summer—partly for want of company, but last summer I went three or four times a week. We could hunt, too, in the lagoons, where they shoot ducks with a small cannon mounted in the prow of the boat, and loaded with shot. The hunters also go out, and sit in large casks all night. The ducks come at dawn, and they fire at them through holes pierced in the casks.

Johnny, are you still working in the printing-Office? It's a good place even for a boy who doesn't intend to be a printer; but if I were you I would study some profession in a year or two. What books do you like best, now? You'll have to go through a good deal of stuff, of course, before you form a good taste in literature; but if I were you, I would drop every book, that seemed wicked, no matter how splendid and brilliant you found it. I can't tell you how sick at heart and stomach it made me—the other day, to look over some bad poems of Byron that I admired at sixteen. If such things don't spoil you, they'll make you ashamed and remorseful, some day, and sham and remorse are to be avoided.

About this time, you'll form some friendship, I suppose, that will have more influence upon your life than you can know, at once. A young fellow must have some friend; but you'll do better not to have any than to be taken with one who is a funny chap, and at the same time a blackguard. Later you'll find out that you don't care for the best friend you make now, and that friends are hardly worth making, for all the good they'll do you. If they don't do you harm—that's all. You've got to be your own friend,—not in the selfish sense, but in the highest meaning of the word. If you're not, no one else can help you.

Well, this has turned out a sermon. But I hope it wont bore you—I've been thinking about you a good deal, and how you stand now at the beginning of the years, when father and mother can't do much to form your character, and you come upon yourself. If you can't do all you want to, at present—don't give up trying to do something. There's a way out of everything. I think hopelessness is about as bad as atheism.— I'm talking to own old self, as much as to you.

Tell Vic, I'll write to her next—very soon, I hope, for I expect letters from home, any day. Elinor sends Aurelia a flower she forgot to enclose from Mrs. Mowatt, and love to all. So do I—beginning with mother. Write to me, Johnny.

Affectionately
Your brother,
Will.

13 June 1863, Venice, to Charles Hale

Venice, June 13th, 1863.

My dear friend—

Your letter came to hand last night, and I answer it at once for several reasons—principally because I can't put off answering letters without damage to correspondents.

The Advertisers, four of them, came to hand yesterday, and brought me back my Florentine letter.[1] But in spite of the generous postage you paid on them, and the Atlantic received with them, I was obliged to pay it all over again three times, simply because the journals were *not* marked "viâ Prussian closed mail" and came to me through France. Will you please note this fact, hereafter? For once it is nothing, but for a year?

I was quite sincere when I proposed to write out my subscription to the Advertiser, and do not care now to make any other demand for the letters. They are written at odd hours, and they keep my hand in. But if it is not pleasant for you to receive them on these terms, you can estimate their value by their success and pay that according to your convenience. I assure you, however, that I shall be satisfied with what they cost me—nothing; and that I should be very sorry if your friendship for me induced you to make an expense not justified by the times. Thank you for your thoughtfulness about the initials. But the Dep't only prohibits correspondence on political subjects, and forwarded you my first letter, which I enclosed in a dispatch. Still I do not wish that my initials,—still less any nom de plume—should be appended to the letters.—You are very kind to send me the Atlantic, but I get that as contributor, regularly, now. Why has it broken out in wood-cuts? And so badly? I remember with sadness that something of the kind preceded dissolution in *Putnam's*.—Arthur Hildreth was here, the other day, and reported all well at Trieste, except Mr Hildreth who still suffers from his foot, hurt last fall.[2]—M. D. Conway of Boston is to be here in a little while, and I hope will spend the 4th of July in Venice. He is an old and very cordial friend of mine, and I look forward to his coming with delight. We think of going with him to Como, next month. Few Bostonians have been here this spring, but the average number of Americans from other places.—Elinor has almost finished her copy of John the Baptist, whom, from the impulse of an irresistible irreverence, we call "J. B.", and I'm writing away on some desultory sketches which I call "Life in Venice."[3] The other day I took a sea-bath, and we're looking forward to spending a good deal of time, that way. Beyond this, the programme will not be greatly varied.—Mrs Bethune, widow of Dr Bethune,[4] is spending the summer in Venice—which, by the way, is a far pleasanter place than Florence, to my thinking.—Mrs Howells begs a favor of you—to tell Miss Kitty Gannett that she sent her a Venetian handkerchief by some Americans bound for Boston direct, a few weeks ago, and wrote her at the same time.

I wrote you a letter for the paper June 5th, which I suppose you'll get before this. Mrs Howells sends regards, and I am

Very cordially yours
W. D. Howells.

The Semi-weekly Adv. will suit me exactly.

1. "From Venice to Florence and Back Again," *Advertiser*, 25 May 1863.
2. Arthur Hildreth was the son of Richard Hildreth, whose illness Howells mentions in *Literary Friends and Acquaintance*, HE, pp. 85–86; see also Venetian diary (MH), p. 61.

3. Howells' comments about these sketches suggest that he thought of them as a project quite apart from his letters to the *Advertiser*. Later that year he wanted to discontinue the letters, and he asked Hale to publish these sketches in the *Advertiser*. See Howells to Hale, 25 October 1863 and 2 November 1863. Eventually, material from both the letters and the sketches was used in *Venetian Life*. See Woodress, *Howells & Italy*, pp. 52–53.

4. Mary Williams Bethune was the widow of George Washington Bethune (1805–1862), American clergyman of the Dutch Reformed Church.

18 JUNE 1863, VENICE, TO MARY D. HOWELLS

Venice, June 18, 1863.

Dear Mother—

Though I have just posted a letter to Vic, (on the cover of which I said that I had received yours of May 27,) I must write again, for your letter distressed me very much. I have written pretty regularly every two weeks, and it seems to me far oftener than I have heard from home. If they reach you irregularly, I am very sorry, for I cannot help that, but I certainly send the letters.

And now, mother, in regard to my absence: I know how it grieves you; and why you should feel it peculiarly, for I remember how hard it used to be for me to leave home, and you doubtless remember that, too, and contrast it with my present willingness to be away. But when you think, dear mother, you cannot believe that I love you less, but only that being now a man I judge more clearly of evils and bear them better. I wish we might always be together; but what comfort after the moment should we find in meeting, if with new cares and responsibilities before me, I left my place here to go to America and trust chance to throw something in my way? Be sure that when I can leave with a fair probability of finding suitable work at home, I shall do so, and I am trying gradually to carve myself out a place. You'll try and think of this, wont you, mother?—and that I remember your anxious love all the time? It grieved me deeply to learn the reason of your not writing, but I hope you will find some comfort in the assurance I give you that I only await the proper opportunity to go back to our country. Then, you may feel secure, that whatever may be my plans for the future, a long visit home will be first thing on the list.—I suppose the very fact that you have all the rest of your children about you, makes it all the harder to have one away—and where all are loved equally, I know it is little comfort to think it's *only* one gone. You must not put in any more doubting *evers*, when you write of seeing me, for that makes it rather too hard for me to bear—and besides, there's no doubt about it.

I hope dear old Joe is quite well, by this time. I should think, Sam might help him a good deal in collecting, and the general management of the business.—Johnny will find that I have written him a long and confidential letter, and that I don't deserve to be complained of. I dare say he wont write me half so long a letter in return.—I'm at a loss, tell father, to account for the amazing friendship between the *Telegraph* and *Sentinel*.[1]

This is just a sort of little comforting letter, and doesn't pretend to news. Indeed, as I said everything in my letter to Vic this morning, there couldn't be much to say now. With dear love to all, including grandmother and aunt Anne

Your affectionate son,
Willie.

1. Howells' comment was probably caused by the fact that the Ashtabula *Sentinel*, 27 May 1863, had printed a front-page story on a "Democratic Meeting" which was headed by the following credit: "The following report is copied from the Ashtabula Telegraph, to which paper the notes belong."

22 AUGUST 1863, VENICE, TO MONCURE D. CONWAY

Venice, August 22, 1863.

My dear Conway—

Returning last night from a pilgrimage to the house and tomb of Petrarch at Arquà,[1] we found your valued letter awaiting us, in company with a select circle of newspapers.

I'm greatly beholden to you, but as yet I hardly dare hope that you will enslave me forever by a successful negotiation for the publication of my poems. Yet it seems to me that it would be unreasonable to despair. Indeed I took more encouragement from McMillan's asking for time, than from the few, faint words of praise bestowed by Browning.[2] But as I say, I hold my hopes in check; and I do not begin to thank you yet.

Success to you in all good things—chief of which is to see your wife and children soon. I know that you will not forget to come to Venice, and I rest content. You'll send me all you print in England, wont you? I wish you, honestly, luck with the "Atlantic." I have had some Venetian Sketches[3] on probation in that purgatory for seven months.

I don't think I should have written you so soon as this; but Giovanna, while we were gone, had a "clarin'-up time," and brought to light the correspondence which I make haste to enclose. Have you ever heard from Seward?[4] (You left the enclosed in an open envelope, which I don't send, for postage sake.)[5]

This is written before breakfast, and can't be long, you know. I'll write very soon again.—We enjoyed our visit to Petrarch's house immensely, and have come back to Venice, much improved in body and mind. The weather had changed—it had rained, and was cool, and the little journey was delightful. I think you would have gone wild, with it.

That pipe lies heavy on my soul, and the pieces are so arranged as to torture my sensibilities into an agony of regret.

With Elinor's regards, a brief good-bye.

Yours faithfully,
W. D. Howells

1. "A Pilgrimage to Petrarch's House at Arquà," *Nation*, 30 November 1865; reprinted in *Italian Journeys* (1872), pp. 216-34. See Woodress, *Howells & Italy*, pp. 32-33.

2. Conway had written Howells on 5 and 6 August 1863 (MH), quoting from Robert Browning's letter to Conway, 1 August 1863 (MH): "I had read the Pilot's Story and liked it much: the other verses show similar power and beauty. I wish the author well with all my heart." Conway also promised to see some literary man other than Browning or to go at once to a publisher. This comment suggests that Macmillan & Co. could not have gotten the poems until some time after 6 August, and it is unclear when the publisher made the request for more time, and when Howells was informed of it. In his letter of 11 May 1864 (MH), Conway wrote Howells that he could not find a publisher; he returned the manuscripts and probably also enclosed the letter from Browning. See also Howells to Conway, 18 September 1863.

3. See Howells to Hale, 13 June 1863, n. 3.

4. Howells' inquiry about Seward shows that Conway was still concerned about official reaction to his unauthorized correspondence with James Murray Mason, one of the Confederate commissioners to England—an action that had brought down on Conway's head a storm of both American and foreign criticism. See Conway, *Autobiography* (London: Cassel & Co., 1904), I, 410-34.

5. The enclosure has not been identified.

2 SEPTEMBER 1863, VENICE, TO JOHN B. HOWELLS

Venice Sept. 2, 1863.

My dear Johnny—

I was very glad to hear from Vic that you are to go to school in Cleveland; and while I don't doubt, my dear brother, that you appreciate and will improve the great opportunity offered you, I want to tell you how I envy you—retrospectively.[1] Joe will remember how, when I was seventeen, I longed for a far poorer chance than you now have. I thought in those days that if I could only have a year at Austinburg, it would be the greatest and finest possible thing. Well, I think so, yet— but then father could neither afford to pay my schooling nor to lose my work from the office. Will you recollect this, my dear Johnny, and do a little studying on my account, as well as your own?

At a military school you will naturally have exercise enough. It must be your care, therefore, not to neglect any study. Few persons are hurt by overwork, but a great many by overplay.

I suppose in Cleveland, you'll have some temptations and trials you've never met in Jefferson. Don't be taken with the shallow folly that anything which your conscience tells you is bad, can be brave or fine. You'll find a great many brilliant fellows in this world who are also vicious. You must not believe that it is their vice gives them brilliancy.—And that's about all I think of to say to you, in addition to the advice that father and mother will give you.—My dear brother, I remember you as such a kindhearted, earnest, good boy. I hope I shall find you, when I return, just the same old Johnny, enlarged and improved.—Do you remember what a good cry we had together that night I left home, when I came up stairs and kissed you, in bed?

Johnny, I want you to write to me from your school, and tell me all about it, and who your friends are, and what you study. You owe me one letter now, you know. I wish you would write to Cousin Martha[2] at Hamilton, and tell her that I'm going to answer her letter, soon. Father's fotografs were first-rate,—and looked wonderfully like him.—I will send him some for Griswold,[3] one of these days.—This morning I went out to buy you a pair of white gloves, for occasions, but Elinor told me you military men used a kind of thread gloves, and so I didn't buy the kids. If there is any little thing like that, which I can send you in a letter, tell me.

Elinor would write to Eliza,[4] tell Vic, but I think that as Eliza has been longest in the family, it would be best for her to write first. If Elinor wrote without hearing from Eliza, it would be a kind of patronage, which I don't want her to assume towards Eliza.

Tell little Willie that I'm going to send him a perfect model of a gondola, about a foot long, and that he will get it about the middle of October, I hope. Send my love to grandmother, and give it to all the family.

Your affectionate brother,
Will.

1. John Butler Howells was soon to be enrolled in the Cleveland Institute, apparently at Howells' urging. An undated one-page autograph note (MH) reads: "Suggested to Joe: Why not send Johnny to College, and let one Howells have the stamp of the schools? I remember how I longed to go, and I lost much by not going. You couldn't afford it when I was seventeen. You can now when Johnny is the same age." See *Life in Letters*, I, 72–73, and *Years of My Youth*, HE, pp. 95–97.
2. Cousin Martha was probably a daughter of Henry Charles Howells, of Hamilton.
3. M. W. Griswold was a photographer in Columbus who did work in ambrotype.
4. Eliza Whitmore Howells was the wife of Joseph A. Howells.

18 September 1863, Venice, to Moncure D. and Ellen D. Conway

Venice, Sept. 18, 1863.

Dear Conway—

Your letter of the 13th came to-night, and administered a foreboded settler to several little fluttering hopes.[1] Now that all is over, I have to thank you cordially again for the interest you have taken in me and the trouble you have taken for me. By all means keep the poems, and offer them to Chapman & Hall with whatever friendly support you get, after the season (cuss it!) is over.[2] But by all means, also, however, let not "Saint Christopher" appear in print before December, for the poem, with Elinor's illustration, is to appear in Harper's Magazine of that month[3]—as we learn by a letter from Foster, who tells us that "Disillusion" will be got out about Christmas.

I'm delighted to learn of the engagement to write a review of Browning for the "Westminister."[4] May you have plenty to do of that sort of work! And may you prosper exceedingly every way! I'm not at all disheartened by my unsuccess. Soon or late I know my time *must* come.

> "Fields cannot wither me, nor Trübner stale
> My infinite variety."[5]

Intanto, thanks to you and all friendly friends.

There is a little matter of Cymrian nomenclature about which we wish to trouble you. The name Howells, you know is Welsh, and inasmuch as we expect to have a Christening here, some day, we want a lot of Welsh christian names to choose from. Now, will you apply to some eater of leek among your acquaintances, and get us a lot of Welsh given names, male and female? Do! This is a really a very important matter, and Elinor wants it particularly insisted upon. You *will* attend to it, wont you?—By the way, did you ever get my Soldini facts? I looked up the whole matter, and sent you a full account of it.[6]

I have received the Cmnwlth with "Venice come True" in it.[7] If there were any way of goading to madness the editors and proof-readers of that journal, I'd like to know it, in order to give them a faint idea of what I suffered in finding all my gondolas with asses' *iers* on them.

It is too bad to ask any more services of you. But will you get this twenty-franc note changed into English money, and subscribe its worth in the London Daily News, to be sent postpaid to me in Venice?

Yours faithfully,
W. D. Howells

Dear Mrs Conway—

I must write to both you and your husband this time, Elinor not feeling quite equal to her share of the work. We are so glad you are re-united, even though you must come together in that dreary London. Believe me that our hearts followed you all through a time that seemed so much worse than it has turned out to be, in its burden of trouble.[8] Indeed, Conway did not know how heartily we entered into his feelings and partook of anxieties now so happily past.

Elinor sends you her love, and we both hope that correspondence between Venice and London, may only be terminated by your coming here in the spring. Bring your handsome boys, and let them wash away the London grime in the Grand Canal.—Trusting for both of us to hear soon of your renewed strength and health, I am very sincerely,

W. D. Howells.

My dear sir, you got "awfully mixed up" in your account of Othello as known to the Venetians. It was not a "lady," but a gondolier who told us the story of Othello, as you repeat it, and he did not put its authorship out of the question disdainfully, but regretfully. The tragedy is perfectly familiar to educated Italians—there is an opera founded upon it, and a translation of the play itself has been acted since I have lived in Venice. The conjecture that Shakespeare mistook Il Moro of the family Moro for a Moor, is one of English criticism, not my gondolier's. He believes Il Moro *was* a Moor, as faithfully as Shakspeare did.[9]—I venture to mention this to you, so that if it forms any link of your "Venetian Chain,"[10] you may alter later publication.

I once told you I didn't get enough Cmmnwlths. I do, now—more than enough, three copies of a single number, for what earthly reason I don't know, unless it be to make me stand insufficiently-paid postage. —As I've made an arrangement to get details of American news in Galignani every day,[11] I conclude not to take the Daily News, and so don't enclose money—I went this morning and bought an old picture that laid hold of me the other day, paying eighteen francs for it. I would not sell it again at all; but I would not take less than $75 for it, if I did sell it. I think it is an Antonio Zanchi[12]—both from internal and external evidence. It is a young girl's full face looking archly at you, while her one visible hand toys with a pearl ear-drop. It is old, and the color is mellow as autumn. I wish you could see it.—Don't forget about the Welsh names, please. We saw a charming little new house yesterday (unfurnished) with three rooms and kitchen for $5.00 a month. Thought I'd tell you.[13]

1. Conway's letter of 13 September 1863 (MH) informed Howells that Macmillan had refused publication of his poems and that Trübner & Co. declined even to look at them.

2. Conway had written that because "the London 'Season' " had not yet begun all influential persons (among them Ruskin and Browning) were out of town. He then continued: "Perhaps, if you shd not wish to use these MSS. you had best leave them with me until the Season is over. I doubt much now if I can do anything; but I wd make another trial with Chapman & Hall, Browning's Publishers...." See also Howells to Conway, 26 January 1864, n. 3.

3. "Saint Christopher," *Harper's Monthly*, December 1863.

4. Conway's review of *The Poetical Works of Robert Browning*, 3d ed. (1863), eventually appeared in the *Victoria Magazine*, February 1864.

5. See Shakespeare, *Antony and Cleopatra*, II, ii, 240–41.

6. See *Venetian Life* (1872), p. 160. For a description of Howells' four-page autograph note (NNC) see Reeves, "The Literary Manuscripts of W. D. Howells," *Bulletin of the New York Public Library* 62 (1958), 360.

7. "Venice Come True," *Commonwealth*, 28 August 1863. Conway had informed Howells on 13 September of the appearance of "Venice Come True" in an issue of the *Commonwealth* to which he refers as "the last for Sept." He also pointed out that the editors had substituted "gondoliers" for "gondolas."

8. See Howells to Conway, 22 August 1863, n. 4.

9. The opera was most likely Rossini's *Otello* (1816). See *Venetian Life* (1872), pp. 328–30.

10. Conway's "Venetian Chain" has not been located.

11. *Galignani's Messenger* was published in Paris (1814–1904). In *A Fearful Responsibility and Other Stories* (1881), Howells writes that "Galignani's long columns were filled with the hostile exultation and prophecy of the London press" about the progress of the Civil War (p. 14). See also *The Lady of the Aroostook* (1879), where Mr. Erwin is "reading Galignani's Messenger" at breakfast (p. 249).

12. Venetian painter (1631–1722).

13. On 13 September Conway had asked Howells to find out the monthly rent for "two big & one little room furnished...."

3 OCTOBER 1863, VENICE, TO SALMON P. CHASE

Venice, Oct. 3, 1863.

Dear Sir:

I shall send on Monday, an Alethoscope, with photographs to Mr Humphrey's, and to Mr Cameron.[1] I have not sent any new photographs to you, and shall not send any, this opportunity, because those you have, represent Venice pretty effectually, and Ponti has taken no new ones of interests.[2] But I will be on the lookout, and when he has any new thing, will send it. I am glad you are pleased with the Alethoscope, though I made sure of your pleasure before hand. It is the only thing of the stereoscope kind that does not fatigue almost more than it amuses. I read your letter to the inventor, who was extremely gratified.

As you desired, I have kept you in mind when looking at curious and beautiful things, which were also purchaseable at reasonable prices; and to-day I have seen a painting which I think you would like. It is a Santa Elena, and might be fairly authenticated as a *Padovanino*.³ The price is $36. We both—that is Mrs Howells and myself—admired it almost alone among a great number of other paintings which were shown us by a gentleman, here, whom a passion for pictures has impoverished. I confess myself loath to advise a purchase which you must make so blindly, and I merely say that I should buy this picture myself if I could afford it.—As for me, I can only keep watch of the baser order of the curiosity shops, in the hope that I may find something within my slender means. And the other day I did chance upon an old painting, that I bought for an absurd little price—18 francs. Its real worth I don't know; I merely know that *I* wouldn't sell it at all. We saw it and priced it on a Saturday; all day Sunday we resolutely declared we couldn't afford to buy it; Monday, I rose early, rushed across the city before breakfast, and bought the picture just as the auroral shopkeeper had taken down his shutters. Now it hangs upon our parlor wall—a monument to the expansive virtues of a small income, and a warning to us never to shake the moral fabric by the practice of impossible prudence.

I was so pleased to learn that you expected anything from me again in literature, that I experienced all the sensations of one of those Fourth of July celebrations which have "the eyes of the world upon them."[4] I multiplied your friendly words by the recollections of past kindness and encouragement, and felt very brave and strong in the possession of a good-natured public, eager to welcome a new book from me. Well, the book will appear in New York, about Christmas time, and will try its best to amuse the least worthy of your half hours.[5] It is a poem, about half as long as "Evangeline," and will be illustrated with sketches by my wife. Perhaps, also, you may think to look for Harper's Magazine, when the December number appears.[6] I have been told that it will contain an artistic and literary contribution from this Consulate.

I am writing in the desultory fashion proper to such work, some sketches of Life in Venice, in which I hope really to give an idea of how people live here.[7] Literary travel seldom consents to treat of such small interests as go to form a knowledge of countries, being too generally devoted to experiences of bed bugs, tables d'hote, galleries, and so forth; and I think such a book as I propose to myself would have the merit of novelty. But who can tell what a day or a publisher will bring forth?

—The war had declared itself as such a dreadful and perilous disease, that I was watching what seems to be its cure with more patience than I did before I knew how near to death it could bring us. And yet, when you did not care to conceal that you tho't the truth had been found too gradually—that we had dug round in ditches and small puddles for it, instead of going at once to the bottom of the well where it lies—my heart gave a responsive bound. Events have gone a long way round;—we all know a hand that would have driven them across lots. A melancholy confusion of metaphors, but I think a clear sentiment of admiration and reverence for the ideas which you happen to embody better than anybody else.[8]

Acknowledging your remittance to Mr Meade,[9] I am very

Respectfully yours,
W. D. Howells.

1. On 25 August 1863 (MH) Chase reported to Howells his satisfaction with a stereoscope he had previously requested, and he ordered alethoscopes in behalf of William G. Moorhead and General Simon Cameron. Moorhead was a partner of Jay Cooke & Co. and Humphrey may have been the person to whom the instrument was to be forwarded. In a letter of 8 November 1863 (DLC) to Hiram Barney, collector of the Port of New York, Howells wrote that Cameron's "stereoscopic instrument" together with "16 alethoscopic views, boxing, Consular certificates, etc." cost $55.00.

2. Carlo Ponti was a Venetian photographer and optician.

3. Alessandro Varotari (1590–1650), Italian painter, was often called "il Padovanino."

4. In his letter of 25 August 1863, Chase had written: "We, that is all your friends, are expecting some grand things from your sojourn in Venice. If you do not give us a very charming Book, we shall all be greatly disappointed. You must beat Ruskin."

5. Howells is here referring to "Disillusion."

6. "Saint Christopher," *Harper's Monthly*, December 1863, is illustrated with a sketch by Elinor Howells.

7. See Howells to Hale, 13 June 1863, n. 3.

8. Chase had remarked in his letter of 25 August 1863: "The War moves a little too slowly and costs a great deal to [*sic*] much to suit me.... It took our Head about a year to determine that negroes could be employed as military laborers, and nearly another year that they could [be] enlisted as soldiers. It took a year to find out that McClellan was unfit and unworthy.... Meantime we have piled up a debt of twelve hundred millions of dollars, and are adding to the pile about two millions a day."

9. As directed by Howells, Chase had sent $70 in U. S. notes to L. G. Mead, Sr.

25 OCTOBER 1863, VENICE, TO CHARLES HALE

Venice, Oct. 25, 1863.

Dear friend—

If you have received from the editors of the Atlantic, the mss. I begged you to ask for, I have a proposition to make you concerning the sketches of Venice which you will have found among them.[1] I have continued writing these sketches, and have now a mass of material ready for publication about three times as great as that sent to the Atlantic. This I am going to publish some time next year in book form, but I first wish to publish it in some newspaper. The subject matter is about the same as that of my letters to the Advertiser, which I must now discontinue because it is hard here to find occasions on which to talk dates, and I always feel that the letter-form is a pretence. I would like to publish these sketches in the Advertiser, because they would thereby reach just the public I wish to please, and which I happen to know my letters have pleased. Well, finally, if you think you can afford to pay me five dollars a column for these sketches, you may commence publishing them whenever you like under the title of "Life in Venice," without any introduction or preface, except such as may seem best to you to make. As I have proceeded in writing these sketches, I have grown earnester in style, and solider in matter, without losing sight of my original purpose of making them very readable, and I think they would afford a good and candid view of Italian life and character—esthetically, morally and materially. I hope that in considering this matter, you will do so quite apart from the friendship I trust we shall always have, and purely in a business way. You may consider the Atlantic's rejection of the sketches as against them, and think me wanting in delicacy to offer them to you at second hand. I don't know yet if they *are* rejected; but I should consider their acceptance by the Atlantic a cheap compliment, and their refusal a literary disaster to be easily survived, and not at all disgraceful. I am willing, however, you should attach whatever weight you like to the Atlantic's decision.

If you conclude to take my sketches, care must be exercised with the first two or three, which were written with pale ink and must now be hard to read. Hereafter they will be made plain as print.

Mrs. Howells desires to be remembered, and I, hoping to hear from you soon, am

Yours truly,
W. D. Howells.

Charles Hale, Esqr.

Mr Hicks, late the money editor of the Evening Post (N. Y.), leaves Venice with his wife, to-morrow, for Egypt.[2] We cut out your letters about Egypt and gave to them. They were delighted, and really I think they could take nothing along in the way of tourist literature, which would be half so useful.

Titles of sketches besides those sent to the Atlantic:

>Story of Basio, luganagher;
>My Priest, the Inventor;
>Giovanna and her Friends;
>Expedition to Torcello;

A Venetian Funeral;
The Marionette Theatre;
Gondoliers and their Stories;
Love-Making and Marriage in Venice;
The Mouse that Posted with us to Ferrara;
Our friend the Grand Canal;
Life of the Caffè and Restaurant.

Please send me three copies of my present letter.

1. H. M. Ticknor wrote Howells on 6 October 1863 (MH): "not one of the MSS. you have sent us swims our sea. The Venetian Sketches, we could not make room for—the 'Small German Capital' ["A Little German Capital"] seemed lonely without companions which we could not give—the little story [perhaps "Fast and Firm: A Romance at Marseilles," Ashtabula *Sentinel*, 24 and 31 January 1866] was rather too slight—and the poems were not like those beautiful ones which you have before printed in the Magazine." The rejected poems probably included "Clement," *Galaxy*, 1 June 1866, "The Royal Portraits," and "Sweet Clover." Ticknor sent his letter with the manuscripts to Hale, who wrote Howells on 13 October 1863 (MH) that he was forwarding everything he had received from Ticknor.

2. Hicks has not been further identified. Hale's letters on Egypt had appeared in the Boston *Advertiser*.

2 NOVEMBER 1863, VENICE, TO CHARLES HALE

Venice, November 2d, 1863.

My dear Hale:

I got your letter announcing your great kindness in seeing the Atlantic people for me, and the next day I received Mr H. Ticknor's letter and all my mss. back again.[1]

In your letter you tell me not to discontinue my papers in the Advertiser. Well, before this reaches you, I supposed you will have got my No. VIII,[2] accompanied by a proposition to continue the letters from mss. rejected by the Atlantic. Happily that ms. is now in my possession, and I can use parts of it to better advantage in my communications, than you could have used the whole. So now, I send you letter No. IX in the more comprehensive style I propose to continue the letters.[3] You are perfectly *padrone* to take the letters or not as you like, of course, on the terms I have proposed. It is my wish you should, or I would send no more—but you are to judge of whether they will suit your readers. All I have to say about Venice can be said in twenty letters or *less*, of this one's length, and I can let you have them as often or as seldom as you wish. Comparatively little of the material sent to the Atlantic will be used without re-writing.—If you do not care to take the letters, I beg you to re-enclose me the present letter *viâ Bremen*.

Prepay it, and I will send you a fotograf of some kind for the postage. The material in this letter is almost wholly new.

We hope you will have seen Miss Mead before her departure.[4] Mrs Howells can hardly forgive you for not stopping at Brattleboro'.

Has my publisher in New York ever written to you about my forthcoming poem?[5] I told him to send you advance sheets.

The weather is charming—we have all the doors open and no fire.

Yours truly,
W D Howells.

Chas. Hale, Esq.

1. Howells had received Hale's letter of 13 October 1863 (MH). See Howells to Hale, 25 October 1863, n. 1.
2. "Letter from Venice—VIII," *Advertiser*, 21 November 1863, was the last of the nonliterary newsletters.
3. "Letter from Venice—IX, i, Sentimental Errors about Venice," *Advertiser*, 26 November 1863, was written in the literary, "more comprehensive style." Since its subject does not appear in the list enclosed in Howells' letter to Hale, 25 October 1863, this sketch must have been one of those rejected by the *Atlantic*.
4. Elinor's sister Mary had left for Europe to visit the Howells family in Venice.
5. Follett, Foster & Co. was planning to publish "Disillusion."

14 AND 19 NOVEMBER 1863, VENICE, TO WILLIAM C. HOWELLS

No. 5.
Venice, Nov. 14 '63.

Dear father—

Your letters which you intended to go from New York by the Bremen steamer of the 17th, did not leave till the 24th, and so only reached us day before yesterday. Annie's fotograf has added another beautiful face to our album. I really feel proud of the good looks of my sisters; Annie has also a sweetness of expression better than beauty. Of course I don't want to spoil you at home by flattery—I think fortune is doing her worst in that way at present—but certainly you have all great reason to be satisfied with yourselves.—I read aloud your address before the Lake Co. Agre. Soc., to Elinor, and we both united in the terms of the Telegraph editor's subtle appreciation.[1] "It was a very fine production," for one of your age, and gives great promise. Your eight or nine thousand majority was the largest (wasn't it?) ever given in that Senatorial District.[2] I fancy you seated somewhere near Stanley Matthews old place.[3] You must be sure, father, to send us the plan of the Senate Chamber, when it is published.—I wonder if you couldn't help old Price to a clerkship, this winter? I hope you wont pledge your influence to anybody else, before you know whether he is a candidate.—We want you to tell us which of the girls you take to Columbus with you. Elinor and I are going to write to our friend Laura Platt Mitchell, who will be a warm friend to the girls.

We expect Mary Mead to-morrow. She arrived in England last Tuesday (this being Saturday) and by this time she must be in Milan. How I wish one of my sisters were with her! *Ma pazienza.* I hope to be recompensed for waiting, by seeing *you* here, before I am sucked out of office by the falling tide.—From what you wrote, we think you must have reached New York before Mary Mead left, and I am tempted to keep this letter till I have the latest news from you by her. I would be provoking if you have failed to see her.

I am glad you like my "Advertiser" letters. Don't be afraid that I shall not improve my advantages in Venice. I have a mass of material for a most charming book about this city, which no one could write who had not lived here and studied Venice as I have. The book will be published very soon, if my poem now in press does not prove a dead failure.[4]

Nov. 19.—Mary Mead has not yet come, but I infer from a letter received last night from her mother that you and Vic did not go to New York in time to see her before she sailed.—But I have just got a letter from Johnny which puts everything else out of my mind, for in this letter he says, "I suppose you have heard of Sammie enlisting in the army." He speaks of his being at home on a short furlough, and of his rejoining his regiment at Chattanuga. This is the first I have heard of the matter, and I am greatly troubled about it. I suppose Sammy must have been in the army some time from the way Johnny writes, but none of you have ever told me a word of it. How did he go in? As private, or has he some rank? I do hope that you will tell me everything you can about an event that has come with such a sudden shock. Poor Sam! He puts us all to shame, and I pray God will keep him safe through the war. I enclose a note to be sent to him. This thing is so heavy on my mind that I cannot write anything else.—I have just returned the proofs of my poem to Foster, but I can't tell when the book will come out. Dear love to all. We are both well.

Your aff'te son,
Will.

1. Presumably W. C. Howells' address before the Lake County Agriculture Society was printed in the Ashtabula *Telegraph* together with comments by its editor, James Reed.

2. W. C. Howells' election to the state senate by a plurality of 9,725 votes was reported in the *Sentinel*, 28 October 1863. The election was held on 18 October, and Howells may have received early news, via letter, of his father's victory.

3. Stanley Matthews (1824-1889) served in the Ohio senate (1855-1858) and ultimately became U. S. senator from Ohio (1877-1879) and an associate justice of the U. S. Supreme Court (1881-1889).

4. The "poem now in press" was "Disillusion." Howells' optimism about the early publication of his book on Venice (*Venetian Life*) was probably increased by the encouragement he had received in Frank E. Foster's letter of 21 August 1863 (MH): "Keep on with your Life in Venice[;] it *will* do." There is no evidence, however, that at this time Howells had made any arrangements for book publication.

9 DECEMBER 1863, VENICE, TO JOSEPH A. HOWELLS

Venice, December 9, 1863.

Dear brother Joe—

Your letter of the 11th and father's of the 12th November, both came to hand this morning. It was a very long time since I had heard from home, and the time seemed longer than it really was. I do not find that distance and absence have at all weakened the ties which bind me to you at home, but these long silences strain them. Can't you contrive to write a little more regularly, if not more frequently? You never can understand how anxious we are about letters, but can't you take our word for it, and amongst you, do something to keep the postman from forgetting where we live?

There was a great deal in both the letters received this morning, to set me thinking somewhat sadly. There was, to begin with, the beautiful face of poor little Henry—beautiful, but *so* melancholy. It is not at all changed in expression—the same longing, appealing look, the same painful effect of an effort to remember something beyond recall. Ponti, the fotografer here, has given me one of his alethoscopes, and there is a slide arranged for cartes de visite. We put Henry's into this, and have seen it the size of life. Elinor pronounces it the most perfectly modeled face she ever saw. The lines are pure Greek—the oval contour is exquisite. A sculptor might copy it with fair hope of selling his work as an antique. Indeed, the poor child has a wonderful gift of beauty, and the soul, (poor, dumb thing!) is visible in his face. Surely, there is another world!

The news of dear Sam's going into the army distressed me greatly, not for the danger alone that he must run, but for the tacit confession involved that he had exhausted every other resource; for I think that he could have no love for a soldier's life. God keep him. His character, with so many excellent traits, and with so great helplessness, has always been a puzzle to me. I hope he may live and be wrought into somebody able to grapple with life. There is a sting of remorse at the bottom of my anxiety for him, for I have not always been so patient with him, nor so mindful of him, as I ought to have been. But, indeed, of whom have I ever been thoughtful, but of myself?

Father says his Senatorship has comes to him with the edge taken off by delay. The case is not a new one, as he knows better than you or I. You remember he used to say to us when we wanted a thing very much, "we wouldn't like it if we had it." I once thought this whimsicality, but I am afraid it was wisdom, looked at by the light of the fact that you pretty much cease to want a thing before you get it. Six or seven years ago, you longed to be out of debt, but you say it don't elate you so much, now. Perhaps you are mistaken in your notion that a man needs education to enjoy things. Maybe a man needs education not to desire things.—And yet, there is a great deal for father to be proud of in his success. It is certainly a very distinguished one, and *we* know how nobly it will be employed. I wonder if father finds any great satisfaction in being a true and good man? I was reading a preacher the other day who said good people were no happier in this world than bad. You can buy peace with goodness—not happiness.

The title of my poem is "Disillusion," and it will come out, perhaps not till May, perhaps at Christmas. Look here, how a thing comes about: I wrote to Foster last May that I had this poem, which I had never offered to anybody else, and asked him if he would like to publish it with illustrations by Elinor, for we thought that these would give the book certain éclat. He answered Yes, directly. So poor E. worked all the broiling summer at the illustrations, and made six exquisite ones. These and the Ms. were sent. We waited a month and a half for an answer. No answer. We waited another month. No answer. Then, thinking Foster found it too expensive to engrave the sketches, we wrote him that if such were the case he might issue the book without them. But it appeared that Foster had merely been out west, and had failed to reply on that account. As soon, however as he got this unlucky letter of ours, he answered that he would act on our suggestion, and print the book without illustrations. *Then* we wrote immediately saying the sketches. Meantime although I wrote for proofs in every letter, Foster failed to understand that I wanted them, till it would perhaps make the book too late for Christmas and then sent them. As the matter now stands, he is to print the book with *one* illustration, whenever he can; and as we are sick of the whole business, we don't care when, if ever.

But I am at work now on another poem, greater than any I have yet written. I have put a great deal of heart and real feeling in it, but I've grown doubtful of great success—at least sudden success. I've been chasing celebrity all my life, with only a glimpse of it now and then, and now I shall try to be content, if I can tell some truth and do some good. Since I commenced writing many others have outrun me in popularity, and sometimes I've felt bitter and despondent at what I thought their unmerited good fortune. Strange things happen—what I think best and greatest never sees the light; and I am gradually taught patience if not wisdom. My new poem is called "Ordeals," and it touches the war. It is in four parts: The Mourners, The Comforters, The Comrades, The Victors.[1] I think you at least will like it.

Elinor's sister Mary arrived here Monday of last week—the 30th November. She will probably stay with us a year. We should be so glad to have one of "our" girls here with her. Perhaps you and father may conclude to send Aurelia out in the spring or summer. It would be a great opportunity for her—too great, I think, to be thrown away.

I have written to Piatt and heard from him long since you were in Washington. I do not know any reason why I should write to Cousin Henry particularly.[2] He was pleasant enough to me when I was in New York, but I fear he took out all my gratitude in a certain offensive way of patronizing me. As for Hurd, he of course never wrote to me, which is just as well, for he could write me nothing worth answering, and was never anything but a pretender to my friendship.[3]

I think that if your scheme for advance payments is not a perfectly good one,—and I don't see why it isn't good—you are now in the best possible position to make the experiment. I see that the two other publishers join you—which is a good idea.[4] Are all old scores settled between the Sentinel and the other papers?—all your other schemes have succeeded so well, that I don't question the project of the soldier's scrap-book.[5] I wish you'd send me a copy of it when it is out.

—Dr Günzberg,[6] our physician, was just here, and I showed him Henry's fotograf. He said that at the age of puberty, it was possible that the renewed activity of the brain would absorb a deposit made on it by the scarlet fever. At any rate, his advice was to the effect that Henry's mind should be excited and kept awake by everything he could possibly be taught.

—You say something about Eliza's getting well, but we never were told that she had been sick. I hope there has been nothing serious the matter. I can't tell you how much I should like to see dear little Will. I sent him a gondola ink-stand by a gentleman going home, which I hope he has got before now? He must be a great delight to you, now. I cannot think of any delight so great and pure as that which must come from a little child when his mind is opening, and little body is still bounded by home. But Willie is going to school already, and I suppose he is learning to look beyond you a little, and to be making tremendous friendships with other boys.

I suppose poor grandmother can hardly be alive, yet, and I can hardly lament that she is at last released from her great suffering.[7] It will always be a great regret with me, however, that I could not see her again.

I can't make out why Price has never written to me.[8] I suppose because he's down on his luck, and feels too bad to write anything. I wish father could be instrumental in getting him a clerkship in the legislature.

The weather is wonderfully mild and beautiful. We had our first frost last night, but at noon the sun was as warm as in April.

We had news night before last of Bragg's defeat by Grant.[9] I am very anxious to know if Sam was in the battle, and I hope that you will write me somewhat more fully about his going. Had he any rank? It must be a great trial to mother.

Do somebody at home, try and make a decent return for my letters. Dear love to all, with particular kisses for Willie.

Your affectionate brother,
Will.

I'll see about the binder. I think I can get one.

1. "Ordeals" was never published. See J. K. Reeves, "The Literary Manuscripts of W. D. Howells," *Bulletin of the New York Public Library* 62 (1958), 357.

2. Henry C. Howells, Jr., of New York.

3. Probably William T. Hurd.

4. New procedures and rules for subscription payments, advertisements, and notices were adopted simultaneously by the *Telegraph*, the *Sentinel*, and the *Reporter*. See Ashtabula *Sentinel*, 4 November 1863.

5. The soldier's scrapbook was published by J. A. Howells.

6. See Howells to W. C. Howells, 13 June 1862, n. 1.

7. Anne Thomas Howells died 20 November 1863. See Ashtabula *Sentinel*, 2 December 1863, for her obituary.

8. Howells had made several attempts to get Samuel Price to write him: on 4 June 1863 (MH) he wrote his mother, expressing the wish that his father write to Price; on 14 July 1863 (MH) he wrote to Victoria, enclosing a letter to Price; on 17 September 1863 (*Life in Letters*, I, 76) he mentioned to Annie that Frank E. Foster had written on 21 August 1863 (MH) that Price was living at Perrysberg and not doing very well. The only known letter from Price to Howells, 28 November 1865 (MH), has a Toledo dateline and is addressed to "Dear Willie"; its tone is warm and affectionate.

9. The Confederate general Braxton Bragg (1817–1876) was decisively defeated by U. S. Grant in the battle of Chattanooga, 23–25 November 1863. Howells had been informed by his brother Johnny that Sam's regiment was stationed at Chattanooga. See Howells to W. C. Howells, 14 and 19 November 1863.

17 December 1863, Venice, to William C. and Mary D. Howells

Venice, Dec. 17, 1863.
2 o'clock P.M.

Dear father and mother—

About an hour ago, we were given a little daughter, who is just now trying to do all she can to keep her much-contented mother from falling asleep. She was provisionally and contingently named Winifred Howells, a long time ago, and as yet we have no reason to change the name.

As to Winifred's looks, I have Giovanna's word that she *rassomiglia molto a suo padre*.[1] I have heard a like observation on similar occasions in the English language.

Elinor had not a very hard time, and, indeed, as five Italian women-servants, one German doctor[2] and the same number of American consuls can truly testify—*tutto è andato a meraviglia*.[3]

We all three send our love to all at home in America. Thanking God with a fervent heart,

Affectionately,
Will.

You must write this news to dear Sam in the army. Baby weighs about eight pounds.

1. "Greatly resembles her father."
2. Dr. Günzberg.
3. "Everything has gone wonderfully."

22 December 1863, Venice, to William C. Howells

Venice, Dec. 22, 1863.

Dear father—

Long before you receive this letter you will have got one I wrote last week, viâ Liverpool, informing you of the birth of a granddaughter. Elinor is slowly recovering, and little Winifred seems to like the new world she has entered, very well. She is very pretty, and very hearty, and we are happy in her, beyond expression. I wish that you and dear mother could see her, as she lies in her cradle, with her eyes tightly shut under her fat cheeks, and her little hands pressed to her temples. She has a wet-nurse[1]—a handsome *contadina*—and is the subject of the drollest Venetian baby-talk from the nurse and our Giovanna. This easy tongue she will learn to speak in a year, and she will hardly have English to salute you in, when we bring her home.

—I suppose I have always been old and grave enough, but the new relation put upon me, has made me more thoughtful than ever, and has awakened new desires to be good for the little one's sake, if I cannot for my own. I think I realize the greatness of my trust. I hope that when my child grows old enough to judge me, she may regard me with the love and honor I bear for my father and mother. I ask nothing more. I wish poor grandmother had lived to know of the little one's birth. Perhaps it may be part of her heavenly life to watch over our Winifred, who came into the world so soon after she left it. No purer or gentler spirit could be charged to guide her through life. I will teach her to honor and revere the memory of one who seems to me to have been perfect in Christian patience and love.

I have felt keenly Vic's reproach that I had not written more than once to poor Sam since I have been in Venice. I have been greatly to blame, but now I will try to repair the wrong as far as I can. Immediately on hearing from Johnny that he had enlisted, I wrote him a letter, which you must have seen, and now I enclose another. But I find it hard to forgive you all for not letting me know of Sam's enlistment at once. Instead of that, Johnny mentioned it casually October 31st, when Sam had been in the army a month!—Another thing: Vic is entirely mistaken in thinking she ever mentioned the present I sent her, until now. *You* merely said she had got it, but she never a word. So I felt hurt. I'm not mistaken about this—but it is a little matter—the acknowledgment was not *the* pleasure to me, for the *giving* satisfied me. I merely mentioned that among other matters, to make you write.—I am sorry if I miss answering things. I generally take the letters from home, and go over them word by word, as I write, but *some* things must escape me.

We have not yet seen *Harper* for December, but this morning I got the verses in the Gazette and Sentinel.[2] I am much pleased with your praise of the poem. I am writing a new one,[3] in which the love is love between brothers; and I think there you will find a new phase of thought and a fresh inspiration. The idea is briefly this: One brother being killed in battle, another takes his place because he thinks his brother would have had him do so, and because he cannot endure to think he has died in vain. All the while his trust in what he does is through his trust in his brother, in whom he loves country and truth incarnate. Conway was delighted with the first part of the poem; said it was the best thing I had written.—I have got all my things back from the *Atlantic*,[4] with which I think I have ceased to have favor. But if now and then I can reach their public through the magazine, I shall do so. I have a great contempt for the people who manage it, but I can't do without them altogether, though I have ceased to depend on them soley. I am still kissing hands.—My letters will appear more frequently and regularly now in the Boston Advertiser. I have a contract to write at five dollars a column on these letters for that paper.[5]

I am glad to hear all about your new office, and that you are in it. Do not think for a moment that my interest in anything at home is lessened. Tell dearest mother, that as rapidly as I can, I will shape things for a return home. But that takes time.

I would write more, but I am in torture with elongation of the *uvula*, which has afflicted me now for a whole week.

Dear love to all.

Your affectionate son,
Will.

I'll write again before hearing from you.—What have I done that you should send me the Dayton Journal with such unsparing regularity?—I suppose you will understand now why Elinor has not written of late. She has not been able to do so.—Sometime ago, I asked mother to send the page from a *Harper* containing my poem. If she should have forgotten it, will you enclose it to me? As to my poem in Foster's hands,[6] I don't know, any better than you, when it will be out.—Annie must write me from Cleveland, and tell me how she likes Commercial College life.

1. Woodress identifies the nurse as "Elizabetta Scarbro, the 'Bettina' of *Venetian Life...*" (*Howells & Italy*, p. 34).
2. *Harper's Monthly* contained "Saint Christopher" with Elinor's illustration. The verses were reprinted in the Cincinnati *Gazette,* the Ashtabula *Sentinel,* and *Poems* (1873).
3. The new poem was "Ordeals."
4. See Howells to Hale, 25 October 1863, n. 1.
5. See Howells to Hale, 24 December 1863, n. 1.
6. "Disillusion."

24 DECEMBER 1863, VENICE, TO CHARLES HALE

Venice Dec. 24, '63.

My dear Hale—

Immediately on getting your letter accepting my correspondence,[1] I went to work on the enclosed.[2] In ten days, I hope to send you another, telling you how New Years and Christmas are kept in Venice,[3] and hereafter the letters will reach you regularly once in two weeks. I suggest, would it not be better to print them every other Saturday, so that people who read them may know when to look for them?

I've to repeat my request for two more copies of my letters about the Armenians,[4] who are anxious to file them in the Convent; and I again beg you to charge your proofreader concerning me. Where I spoke of Mr Cooke, in one letter, I was invariably made by the printer to call him *Coake*, and I was therefore prevented from sending him a copy of my letter, as I wished to do.[5] In the last letter I have seen, I am made to call the *pozzi, wells*, in the Ducal Palace, *pazzi* or *madmen*.[6]—I take great pains with the handwriting and the literature of the letters, and it is extremely mortifying to have them misprinted.

We have a little daughter—Winifred Howells—who was born on the 17th December, and who unites with her mother in regards to you.

You say nothing about the little water-color by Zona,[7] which I proposed to buy for you. Would you like it?

In haste,

Very truly yours,
W. D. Howells.

1. Hale wrote Howells on 4 December 1863 (MH) that he acceded to Howells' request of 25 October for payment of $5 per column. However, in recognition of the unfavorable exchange rate for U. S. greenbacks Hale later offered to pay one pound sterling per letter. See Hale to Howells, 9 May 1864 (MH).
2. The enclosed material was printed as "Letter from Venice—XI," *Advertiser*, 18 January 1864.
3. "Letter from Venice—XII," *Advertiser*, 6 February 1864.
4. "Letter from Venice," no. VII and VIII, i, *Advertiser*, 29 September and 21 November 1863, respectively.
5. "Letter from Venice," no. VIII, *Advertiser*, 21 November 1863, dealt with the English painter Edward William Cooke (1811–1880).
6. See Howells to Hale, 2 November 1863, n. 3.
7. Antonio Zona (1813–1892), Italian painter.

26 JANUARY 1864, VENICE, TO MONCURE D. CONWAY

Venice, January 26, 1864.

My dear Conway—

I have heard from Signora Salviati that her husband or her son had seen you in London,[1] and that you had said you send him the book I asked you for—the Signory of Venice by Sir James Howell.[2] If you have not yet bought the book, I beg you wont trouble yourself any further about it. I suppose it is very hard—perhaps impossible to get at.

I am greatly your debtor in all you have done for my poems,[3] and I am very sorry that I should have appeared ill-naturedly impatient about that matter, in the letter I wrote you. I *was* provoked at your long silence, and your apparent neglect of my wishes concerning the book I asked for; but I never doubted that you had done and would do all you could with the Mss., though I have long ago relinquished belief in your success. You have done much more, than I, with even *my* pestilent and unlucky disposition to oblige, would have done for another, and I thank you most sincerely. You have made it possible for me to feel pleasure enough in your own success in London, to almost compensate me for my failure there.—And so let us turn to something else for to write of literature makes my soul sick within me.

Elinor has brought little Winifred in from her nurse's room (it is that in which I had my office last summer, and I have now moved my office up stairs *dai Dolmati*[4] into the room where you slept) and is giving her the first lessons in staring. The child was remarkable at first for a very heavy head of dark hair, which she does not lose, but which is turning lighter. She has very regular features, and blue eyes like her mothers, and of course we think her very pretty, and destined to great beauty. If she is half so good as her mother, she must thank her mother for that half. Already she is beginning to assume her just authority in the house, and to demand a great deal of society. Nothing pleases her so well as to be the centre of the whole household's attention; when she consents to make some absurd attempts at smiling, and leaps up and down in the portable bed which compasses her small existence day and night. But as yet her chief points of character are eating and sleeping, and these are remarkably prominent. I find on turning to the pigmy diary, which her papa presented her on New Years, and which he keeps in her name, that she "is very good, also," and certainly she cries very little. She will be six weeks old day after to-morrow.

We are enjoying Venice very much, this winter. Elinor has a little coffee and cake and cards Saturday evenings, and we see friends that night—principally the Przemysl, who grows more delightful and brilliant the better she is known to us. Then we have Miss Mary Mead with us, E.'s youngest sister; and an American artist, Kellogg of Cincinnati Kelloggs,[5] is spending the winter in Venice, and his wife is very nice person. We go to the opera, and to the theatre, and we walk a good deal on the Malo, now the weather has relented. Ecco tutto vaccontato.[6]

By the way if you ever see Miss Evans, or those who see her perhaps she would care to hear that I, who think myself a knower of Italian character, do homage to her pourtrayal of it in *Romola*, and especially in the personage *Nello*, the barber.[7] Mr Kellogg, en passant, is painting a *Romola* from his own wife, who is very young, very beautiful, and with hair golden as sunlight.

I suppose that before this time you will have received the expected "call," and I hope you will not have to work so hard hereafter, though I know that under any circumstances you wouldn't consent to be *"fumo in aer."*[8]

Do you think you could find a copy of Harper's Magazine for December anywhere in London—perhaps at Trübner's. Our poem and picture of Saint Christopher are in it, and we are very anxious to see them.—*I* can't write you political gossip from Venice, but when there is anything to tell, maybe Mrs. H. may think Mrs. C. interested to know it.

We both join in expression of cordial regard to you and yours.

Ever sincerely yours
W. D. H.

1. Antonio Salviati (1816–1890) was largely responsible for the revival of mosaic art in Venice. Howells described a visit to his factory in "The Revival of Mosaic Painting in Venice," *Advertiser*, 2 May 1863. See also *Venetian Life*, pp. 250–52, and Woodress, *Howells & Italy*, p. 28.
2. James Howell, *S. P. Q. V.: A Survey of the Signorie of Venice* (1651).
3. Conway had written Howells on 10 January 1864 (MH) that Trübner & Co. would publish the poems only if the cost were borne by Howells or by subscription; he further reported that Chapman & Hall were considering the poems for publication. See also Howells to Conway, 22 August 1863 and 18 September 1863.
4. "At the Dalmatians" is a reference to the Dalmatian family who lived at Casa Falier. See *Venetian Life*, pp. 101–3.
5. Miner K. Kellogg (1814–1889), an artist who specialized in Oriental scenes, lived abroad during much of his career. Miss Przemysl later became the Countess Capograssi. See Woodress, *Howells & Italy*, p. 35.
6. "That's all vacant."
7. George Eliot (Mary Ann Evans), *Romola* (1863).
8. In Dante's *Inferno*, Vergil says that he who spends his life without fame leaves such a trace of himself as smoke in air ("fummo in aere," XXIV, 51).

1 February 1864, Venice, to Edmund C. Stedman

Venice February 1, 1864.

My dear Stedman—

Somebody sent me the other day an *Evening Post* containing a notice of your book,[1] and not long after I saw a very ill-natured notice of your connection with a literary journal called *The Round Table*, in the Boston *Commonwealth*.[2] It is contrary to all usage and precept among friends, and yet I read the flattering critique of the *Post* with a great deal more pleasure than the other notice. I wish I could see your book, but at this distance many pleasant things are forbidden me. So I lay aside my hope of reading your idyll at present:—when I do open its pages, it will be with the same zest that I shall tramp through American woods and fields. There is no reason, however, why I should not see the *Round*

Table—except the negligence inseparable from true friendship. You, Stoddard, Winter and Aldrich are the editors, and you are all my friends—at least none of you can hate me for literary success—and so I have never seen a copy of the *Round Table*. I begin to think it is bad in literature to have friendships, and from this time out I shall cultivate the most ardent enmity with everybody. My publisher[3]—or rather the holder of my manuscript in New York—has been, unluckily, my friend, and consequently doesn't write me anything of the time he intends to get out my poem, about which I know rather less than nothing. I heard, indirectly, that its publication had been postponed, and again indirectly, that it is to come out in May. Puo darsi![4] But I know nothing. Could you do me the service—out of the hatred which I hope you will bear me hereafter—to find me some publisher who despises me from every point of view, and get him to take the matter out of Foster's hands?[5] If then I had two or three good malignant critics, I think I need not despair.

—I should like to see your book for two or three reasons—chief of which is to find what has been your poetic growth or change, since we cracked up the Subjective together in our talk at Washington. As to me, I confess freely that I think my once excessive admiration of that principle in poetry was an error—to which conclusion I have come by study of our divine masters the Italian Poets. Perhaps I have been insensibly moulded to this shape by other influences which I could not so readily specify. It may be that becoming acquainted with or rather seeing other arts than poetry—arts essentially objective, like sculpture, painting and architecture—I have come to dislike personality and consciousness, and to hate any work in which I find present anything of the author besides his genius. I don't know absolutely that this result indicates mental improvement; I only say that I have changed. The charm is broken that the subjective German poetry and its kindred English and American schools once had for me. I would not if I could—and I certainly can not—now write such verses as I used to contribute to the Saturday Press. I am conscious that by cultivation of the subjective, I worked out of admiration of Popish materialism, but I believe now that a purer ideal exists in the objective. I mean the objective as Dante, Spenser and Chaucer knew it, and as I find it in Tennyson's *Idylls of the King*. It seems to me that a story is essential to a poem, and that all poetic efforts without a story are beautiful only in the proportion that the frondage on St. Marks, growing and budding in human heads and busts, is beautiful when compared with definite and perfect statues. There is sweetness and beauty in it, but it is incapable of translocation and can give enjoyment only from a certain point, and to a peculiar state of mind.

—You have heard perhaps that I am become a father. The little girl is called Winifred. She is very hearty and strong, and *we* think, of course, remarkably pretty. All her spiritual gifts are yet musica dell' anima,[6] but we have both faith and hope for her, and everybody praises her—to her parents. As to my fatherhood, though it does not take the objective form of getting up nights, and carrying our padroncina,[7] it is nevertheless a constant content to me; and though I am not dead yet (except in a literary sense) I venture to pronounce myself happy.

—You were most kind to write me all the gossip you did,[8] and I wish I could give you back in sort. But you are at the centre, and must be content to be the more blessed of the two. Sometimes I wish that fortune, who snatched me from too-far west had not set me down too-far east, in her violence. But who knows? I suppose if you were as disagreeably frank as I am, you could tell me of drawbacks to the delight of being continually in literary society. It must be stimulating, but I doubt if it is conducive to independent thought. This appeared to me the trouble of Bohemianism—of which I noticed your ill-conditioned critic in the Commonwealth accused you Round Tablers. And yet, how glad I should be to live in New York among you!—If you ever meet James Lorrimer Graham, I hope you'll remember me cordially to him and his wife. He is an excessively good fellow—but he went home without coming back to Venice as he promised.

We have planned some little journeys for the spring which will soon open, and intend to go to Verona, Mantua Parma and Modena. We have already seen Milan and Florence, and I have been at Como.—Do you remember Tennyson's "Daisy"? It is worth all the books of travel—it and the "Marianna in the South"—that ever were written about Italy. Indeed, to understand Tennyson perfectly you must read him under a southern summer's sky.

Mrs. Howells joins me in expression of regard to you and yours. Do let me hear from you.

Very cordially yours,
W. D. Howells.

1. "Mr. Stedman's New Poems," New York *Evening Post*, 12 December 1863, a review of *Alice of Monmouth, an Idyl of the Great War and Other Poems* (1863).
2. The notice has not been identified.
3. Follett, Foster & Co. was delaying the publication of "Disillusion."
4. "It may be so."
5. Stedman had written Howells on 1 October 1863 (MH) about having met Frank E. Foster a few days earlier: "Going with him to his store, I gained...the acquaintance of a right good fellow—and you may be sure that nothing which I said reduced his enthusiastic opinion of your powers and prospects. It is something to have an aesthetic publisher, and I congratulate you, since I think F. F. & Co. will ere long work up into a good position here. They made a mistake in starting at the West."

6. "Music of the soul."

7. "Young mistress."

8. In his letter of 1 October, Stedman had written of his return to New York, after having left his position in the attorney general's office in Washington: "Everyone appears to return with me this Fall. Lorimer Graham & wife, for instance, who tell me of pleasant hours passed with you in Venice, Bayard Taylor, who has just arrived with six Russian frigates. Aldrich is here as usual—he got out a blue & gold vol. [*Out of His Head: A Romance*] last winter. Stoddard & his wife are doing well—Mrs. Stoddard will issue another novel [*Two Men*], and a child, about the same time and ere the winter is over. They speak affectionately of you. Piatt & his Sallie are cosy in a Georgetown cottage."

20 February 1864, Venice, to Harper & Brothers

Venice, February 20, 1864.

Gentlemen:

In connection with a proposition I wish to make, I beg to submit to you the accompanying drawings by my brother-in-law, Mr. Larkin G. Mead, of Florence, whom you probably know as a sculptor, and whom you will recollect as one of the artists for "Harper's Weekly" during McClellan's Peninsular Campaign. Mr. Mead has employed his leisure since his residence in Florence, in making sketches of out-door objects of art, in that city, and has now a collection of some thirty to fifty drawings, executed in the careful and spirited style of these enclosed, and embracing in their range of subject, nearly everything at which persons of artistic taste and feeling would stop to look in the streets of Florence. You will recognize at once the bronze Boar of the fountain in the Mercato Nuovo, and the "Devil" of John of Bologna, which serves as torch-holder on the corner of a palace.[1] The drawings on the sheet marked X have a racier interest to me from the fact that they faithfully represent those pieces of iron-work on and near the Strozzi palace, which we owe to the eccentric and ingenious blacksmith Niccolò Caparra,[2]—one of the historic characters, by the way, introduced into Miss Evans' "Romola." The other drawing is a statue of Michelangelo.—It has been my wish, ever since Mr Mead showed me his sketches in Florence, last spring, to write the text of a work on this Out-Door Beauty of Florence, to which they should serve as illustrations, and to which they would give its best interest; and I have now to suggest the idea of such a work to you. It would not be at all in the nature of a guide-book, and yet I should try to make it the vade mecum of every cultivated person visiting Florence, while I aimed to interest in it persons who had never seen the city, or the art of which it would treat.—I believe some three years' residence in Italy, which have been spent, voluntarily and involuntarily, in study of Italian character, literature and art, would give me peculiar facilities in making the book which I suggest, and which I would try to render interesting with materials drawn from my reading and observation. It would be in some sort biographical of artists whose works were noticed, but I should try not to fatigue anybody with critical disquisition. Anecdotes of the artists, scenes of cotemporary and historic Florentine life in the vicinity of things mentioned, the flavor of an honest, unsentimental liking for the Italian civilization, and above all, a sincere wish not to say more than I knew, and not to say anything at all when I had done with a subject, are elements and purposes with which I should try to make the book.

As to the artistic part of the work, the enclosed drawings and Mr Mead's reputation can speak much better than I.

If the scheme strikes you with favor, can you make me some offer to justify me pecuniarily in carrying it out? The work would require one or two months' residence in Florence, during which time, I must relinquish my salary from the government here, and I must first obtain leave of absence from my post. There is still some work required to complete all Mr Mead's drawings, and he must take time for it from his studio. It is therefore necessary that we should be assured of re-imbursement for actual outlay; and it would be preferable to us, to accept a direct offer to make the book, out and out, for a certain sum. I suppose it would not exceed three hundred pages octavo, small pica, but that would depend upon the interest developed in arranging the material. I do not know if I have given you the idea that while this would be a book "without which no gentleman's library would be complete," it would also "form an elegant ornament to the centre-table," etc.

I enclose my address, and if, as I think quite possible, you should know nothing whatever of me, I venture to refer you to Mr. Guernsey,[3] the editor of your Magazine.

The sketches will be called for, after a time, by a friend in New York.

Hoping to hear from you, I am, gentlemen,

Yours very respectfully,
W. D. Howells.

Messrs. Harper & Brothers.

1. Giovanni da Bologna (1524–1608), also known as Jean Bologne, was a French sculptor who worked mostly in Italy. Howells apparently felt that the torchbearer embodied the artist's conception of the devil. The projected book of sketches by Mead and text by Howells was never published.

2. Caparra worked in Florence around the end of the fifteenth and the beginning of the sixteenth century.

3. Alfred Hudson Guernsey (1818?–1902) was editor of *Harper's Monthly* (1856–1869). During his visit to New York in August 1860 Howells had offered him the poem "Forlorn." See *Literary Friends and Acquaintance*, HE, pp. 75–76.

25 March 1864, Venice, to Samuel D. Howells

Venice, March 25, 1864.

My dear brother Sam—

We got a letter from father to-day, and as I have not written to you for a long time, I shall write to you now exclusively, and father can take my letter as an answer to his. It is always more or less sad to write you, for we never can know how, when or where our words shall reach you—there are as many thousand doubts between us as there are miles. But we hope each time our letter shall find you well, and that it will bring what we have only had from you once as yet—a letter direct, in return.

We reached home last Sunday after a little tour which we had made to cities that once seemed too famous for me ever to see, but of which we speak here as familiarly as they do of Painesville, Cleveland and Toledo at Jefferson. We left Venice Monday morning before last, and reached Verona about half-past one, and passed the afternoon, and part of the next day there. It's one of the most interesting cities in northern Italy, and there's an old Roman amphitheatre there, built in the time of Augustus, which is somewhat more extensive than the circuses at home. It's built of red and white Veronese marble, and all the interior is perfect yet, as well as most of the cells for the wild-beasts, and the Christians and criminals condemned to be devoured by them. I can't give you any idea of the massiveness of this structure, but you can guess its size, when I tell you it was intended to seat 20,000 spectators. It was intended for gladiatorial shows, etc., such as Bulwer describes in "The Last Days of Pompeii."[1] Verona, you know, is the scene of two of Shakespeare's plays: The Two Gentlemen of Verona, and Romeo and Juliet. So they show you the house where the Capulets lived, and the tomb of Juliet. The latter is in an old Convent, and has a striking resemblance to stone horse-trough.—Well, Tuesday we went to Mantua, whither Romeo, you remember, was banished for killing Mercutio, and where the apothecary lived who sold him the poisonous drugs, although

—"Mantua's present law was death
To any he that uttered them."[2]

O Sam! that's a beautiful town! The streets are wide and regular, clean and perfectly paved, and the girls look at you of the first floor windows, and the doors open in the friendliest fashion right upon the sidewalk from the houses, and you don't have to enter dismal courts to get in. Mantua, you know, is the strongest hold of the Austrians in Italy, and of course the Italians would like to have it. But I don't understand how they will ever take it. Besides being very strongly fortified by the Austrians, it is a fastness by nature, which has surrounded it with impassible rivers and equally impassible swamps. The marshes render the air very unhealthy, and there is a vast deal of fever. One of the old Dukes of Mantua built a palace (which we visited) on made ground in the heart of one of these swamps, and where the air was so fatal, that none of the court ever dared pass a night there. They called it the Palazzo del Tè, because it was only used by the Dukes to take lunch and a cup of Tea, in. (At least, so the guardian of the Ducal palace said.)

"If ever you should go to Modena," you would think, no doubt, as we did, of the sweet old poem by Rogers, which we used to read at school, about the young girl who on her wedding-day ran off, to play a trick upon her husband, and hid herself in a chest which closed upon her with a spring-lock, forever. Her husband,

> grown weary of his life,
> Flung it away in battle with the Turks,"[3]

and her father went mad, looking for her in vain. At last—you know the sequel—strangers who inherited him, found her skeleton in the chest when the latter was so old and worm-eaten that it dropped to pieces as they lifted it.—They were making a change of garrison in Modena, and in Parma, too, the days we were there, and so I had a good opportunity of seeing the Italian troops again. They are not so strong-looking as the Austrians, but they are livelier—they look like Americans, in fact, and I think they would fight very well. Everybody in Italy worships Garibaldi— he's much greater than king Victor Emanuel in the latter's own kingdom. Modena is a place is about as large as Cleveland, and it put us in mind of an American town in some respects, though in others it is very old and quaint. Parma pleased us much better, and there we saw the beautiful paintings of Correggio, which we had traveled there to see, principally. The best of these is painted on the interior of a cupola nearly two hundred feet from the ground, and as it is intended to represent the Virgin's ascent into heaven, with all the angels triumphing round her, it is pretty much arms and legs from below.

We came home by way of Milan—taking one moonlight glance at the wondrous cathedral, as we passed through the city. But after all, there is no place so beautiful and delightful as Venice, and we are glad to be at home again. We left the baby in charge of her nurse, and the other servant, and found her grown fat and saucy on our return. She is very forward, and has numbers of amusing tricks, which I'm sure you'd rather see than read of. She's going on four months now, but she's bright enough for six.

Elinor will finish this letter, and give any gossip I've omitted. I hope you'll write to us, and always believe me

> Your affectionate brother,
> Will.

Dear brother Sam.,

Your being in the army makes this war quite a different thing to us and we search the papers carefully to find news of your regiment—though to be sure, we've had to think of you in the hospital a great deal of the time—and I do'n't know which is worse to be sick in a hospital or to be making forced marches.[4] My brother who is in Florence went once with the army six months as "special artist" for Harper,[5] and even that, without his having any military duty to perform, quite used him up. But I've no doubt that after one gets "broken in" the rough life of the camp is a good thing—just as the outdoor air is going to do the baby good when she doesn't take cold from it, as she did on her first essay. We read your description of the tramp from Nashville to Chattanooga to several persons here to give them an idea of what volunteers, young men who had been delicately brought up, were willing to suffer for the cause. Here the young Venetians are pressed into the Austrian Service, to serve for ten years, and fight against their own country. The conscription is being made now in a square through which we have to pass every day and we witness horrid scenes—mothers falling down in fits &c. The other day a young conscript jumped from a high window of the office of the conscription into the canal below—on hearing that he was taken. As they cannot find his body it is supposed that he swam under some building and thence escaped—perhaps out of the city into the kingdom of Italy. I like the new photograph which Vic sent very much. It gives me quite a different idea of you from what that old one did and I see a good deal of resemblance to Will, which of course I like. Hoping to hear of your continued health and success,

> affectionately
> Elinor

1. Bulwer-Lytton, *The Last Days of Pompeii* (1834).
2. Shakespeare, *Romeo and Juliet*, V, i, 66–67.
3. Samuel Rogers, *Italy* (1822–1828), "Ginevra," lines 77, 79.
4. There is no evidence of Sam's hospitalization; but Howells' letter to Sam, 19 May 1864, mentions his return to active duty.
5. Larkin G. Mead's assignment was with *Harper's Weekly*.

7 April 1864, Venice, to Victoria M. Howells

Venice, April 7, 1864.

My dear Vic—

Your letter and dear mother's reached us this morning, and relieved me of anxiety which I was just beginning to feel at not hearing from home for several weeks. There were ever so many pleasant things in your letter, and mother's was extremely welcome to Elinor, for it gave her just those reminiscences of my babyhood for which she has been longing ever since Winifred was born. It gave me the usual charges about coming home soon, which I would *so* willingly obey! Mother must try to forgive my absence, when she remembers that it is no sense separation from her love. I do not intend to apply for re-appointment, and if Lincoln were to be elected again this fall, I sho'd ask for leave of absence to visit the United States, where I would try to remain. Elinor and I both feel that we have got nearly all the good out of Europe that we can, and we are full of busy schemes to justify a return home. My idea now is—though you needn't mention it out of the family, to try to get a place on the Boston *Advertiser*, for which I have been writing a long time. The editor told me in a recent letter[1] that he hoped to see me before the summer was over; but if he does not come to Europe, or write me positively of his coming, I shall ask for the place I want by letter. My wish is to go home next spring,—a year from next month,—and I am shaping all my efforts to that end. Anything more definite than this, I can't say at present, though I should like to name the hour and the day of my departure, and tell you just when to put that bedroom in order.

You said nothing about Aurelia's coming in your letter received this morning, and I was sorry, because I wanted the certainty to decide me whether I should change house this spring or not. If she comes the present house will not be large enough. If Aurelia undertakes this journey she ought not to start with less than $500 in gold; for traveling in Europe is expensive, and I could advance her nothing. We dine at a restaurant, and only breakfast at home, so that Aurelia would have to pay for her dinners. I feel ashamed to make any question of money, but I should be to blame if I did not. It costs my whole salary to live here, and I cannot spend more without borrowing. It is not what I wish to do, but what I can do. Elinor's father re-imburses us for all actual outlays on Mary's account. Of course there are a great many things we can do for the girls, and save them very great expenses without particularly increasing our own, but where it comes to perceptible downright silver florins over and above what we spend now—why the salary can't stand it. You wont misjudge me, I know, but you wont understand how exactly the cost of living can be squared to an income, and leave no margin till you understand how people live in these closely-ground countries of Europe. Nothing, absolutely nothing, can be touched without money. It would grieve me deeply to have you think me close—I know you wont and can't—and I hope Aurelia will come to visit us. It would be of inestimable benefit to her in every way, and I really long so to see her. As soon as we know she has started, we shall move to the Palazzo Giustiniano, where Aurelia will see life in the stately old Venetian style. I think Elinor is writing her full instructions about everything she must bring, etc.—I wish you would send me Sam's letters, I'm so anxious to hear from him. Do you always remember us to him?—Has Joe got out my song?[2] It is a matter of rejoicing both with Elinor and me, to know that he met her sister[3] in N. Y. and that they liked each other. Both Meads and Howellses write of it. I am only sorry that Joe called on the Shepards just as he was to leave the city. You must make up for his loss of time.—You've no notion how hard I work now. I'm very busy with an article on Recent Italian Comedies,[4] and I shall commence a story in verse[5] as soon as that is finished. Not much seems to come of all this labor, but I *must* succeed, sooner or later, though if I think of the delay it sickens me. Happily my health is good, and I *can* work. I shall write half a dozen lectures just before going home, and try to make capital of them. As soon as the "Comedies" are disposed of, I shall write dear mother a long letter. I suppose my poem[6] (Foster pub.) will be out in May. Dearest love to all, beginning with mother. Your affectionate brother,

Will

Of course I speak of Aurelia's coming throughout, with the understanding that she is coming for a year, or till we return home.

1. Charles Hale's letter to Howells is dated 29 February 1864 (MH).
2. *The Battle in the Clouds: Song & Chorus Inscribed to the Army of the Cumberland,* with music by M. Keller, was first published by J. A. Howells & Co. (1864).
3. Mrs. Joanna Mead Shepard.
4. "Recent Italian Comedy," *North American Review*, October 1864.
5. "The Faithful of the Gonzaga," New York *Ledger*, 18 March 1865.
6. "Disillusion."

16 MAY 1864, VENICE, TO TRUEBNER & CO.

Venice, May 16, 1864.

Gentlemen:

My friend, Mr. M. D. Conway, has submitted some poems of mine to you, which he says you like, but of which you are not willing to undertake the publication, unless guaranteed the expenses of printing.

I think it would be of such advantage to me to have my poems brought out in London and by your house, that I would stretch my very narrow means to the utmost, if I could approximate the sum you deem sufficient to warrant you in printing them. I beg therefore to know from you precisely on what terms you would undertake their publication.[1]

I have aesthetical objections to a big book, and in the present case I suppose a small one would be a less costly luxury to me. So I propose to put into the volume, only a part of my verses, and such as I think the best, making a book (duodecimo) of some hundred and fifty pages. You can make your estimate of expense upon some such basis.

Hoping soon to hear from you,

> Very truly yours,
> W. D. Howells.

1. In their reply of 4 June 1864 (MH) the publishers offered to issue 500 copies for £38 16s. and to sell the book for a ten percent commission of the net trade price. Howells did not accept this offer.

16 AND 22 MAY 1864, VENICE, TO MONCURE D. CONWAY

> Venice, May 16, 1864.

My dear Conway—

I want to thank you very cordially and sincerely for all the trouble you have taken for me and my unlucky verses, and to express to you how highly I appreciate the good-will and friendship shown.[1] I could not have been more grateful if you had been more successful, and then I should have been ashamed, remembering that I would not have done so much for you or anybody else. So it's much better as it is. I've written the enclosed letter to Trübner & Co.,[2] which explains itself to you, and I will be glad if you will drop it into the London post, with a line of your own, reminding them of the circumstance of the poems being offered them, etc. In connection with this last sad office, I have merely to say, that if T. & Co. are reasonable, I'll try and do something, for I think it would be of the greatest use to me at home to have my book printed in London. But I have not much idea that we can make a trade.

I was very glad to hear from you at last—but I'm afraid you're working too hard for too little money. I can quite understand your longing to get back to America, for I have myself grown very homesick of late—and I've had none of your care to weigh me down. In fact, we're now living very pleasantly in Venice. We've removed from Casa Falier to Palazzo Giustinian, (next to Ca' Foscari, Grand Canal), and as far as plenty of beautiful airy houseroom goes, are quite happy. Then our baby is grown to be a great delight—she is so pranksome and pretty and good. She would weigh as much, I think, as both her father and mother, and knows, I'm persuaded, a great deal more than either. As soon as we can have a tolerable fotograf of her made, we'll send it you.—For the summer we've no plans. Possibly we may take a short run to Como, but that's problematical, especially, if I have to pay something for publishing my book. We're going to Rome next November. So we'll be at home the whole summer long expecting you. Do come, if you can.—J. J. Piatt writes me that his book "Nests at Washington," has met with rather poor success. He's sent me his book, and I've found it very fine. Some of the verses are exquisite. He's improved greatly, and his wife's poems are beautiful also. His book is published by Walter Low of New York, and is to be found in London at Sampson, Low & Co.'s. I wish you might be able to say a good word for it in some English print. You know what book-notices at home, are. The book's not been justly dealt with.—My own poem is not out yet, and I don't know when it will appear.[3] Foster's treated me very ill about it—I think, though I dare say he thinks differently.—The poem (copperhead) which I read to you in Venice, I continued more patriotically and more or less mystically, and sent it to the *Atlantic*.[4] I expect to hear from it through posterity, long after I've gone to heaven.—At present, I'm just finishing up an article on Recent Italian Comedy, on which I've bestowed a good deal of attention and study. The subject is one of a good deal of interest, and I've treated it in my usually lively manner. It is at present awaiting rejection at the hands of a series of editors to whom I think of sending it.—I liked your review of Browning very much—the only trouble was that you talked to your reader as if he knew as much of Browning as you do.[5] This gave you room, and was in its way, charming and flattering enough, but as I had not read Browning, it provoked me. I should like to read "Sordello," for I know all about Eccelino, Guelphs, and things.[6]—I see your letters in the Commonwealth and the Gazette. It must take a great deal of labor to write them, if I can judge from my own experience in writing for the Boston Advertiser. Then when you get back your pay in England, it can amount to very little. Everybody says that living has grown frightfully dear in America, and that it is hard to get on there, but I'm going back as soon as I can shape things.—From bad in Sherman we seem to be going to worse in Banks.[7] I'm afraid it makes very little difference who is next President. I think it's about time to put our trust in Providence.

I hope, my dear Conway, you wont take the slightest additional trouble with my letter to Trübner, beyond that shamelessly suggested. With renewed thanks, and with many regards from Elinor and self to Mrs Conway,

Yours faithfully,
W. D. Howells.

Write at any moment of leisure—if you have it.

P. S. I have received the rejected poems by post.[8] Thanks.

May 22—Your letter escaped posting, for a day or two, because I thought it idleness to have written to Trübner & Co., and was hesitating about sending. Meantime came the saddest news I ever had. My brother John, who was a lad at school in Cleveland, died April 27th of an epidemic fever now raging in Northern Ohio.[9] He is the first of us whom God has taken back. You can understand better than I can tell you how sore a burden this is.

1. See Howells to Conway, 26 January 1864, n. 3.
2. See Howells to Trübner & Co., 16 May 1864.
3. "Disillusion."
4. This poem has not been identified.
5. See Howells to the Conways, 18 September 1863, n. 4.
6. Eccelino da Romano (1194–1259) was a prominent Ghibelline, mentioned in Dante's *Inferno*, XII, 109–10. The conflict between the Guelphs and the Ghibellines provides the historical background for Browning's *Sordello* (1840).
7. General Nathaniel P. Banks (1816–1894), a former governor of Massachusetts (1858–1861), had failed in his attempt to gain control of western Louisiana; he was censured and relieved of his command in May 1864. The reasons for Howells' comment about General William T. Sherman (1820–1891), who had recently been appointed commander of the entire southwestern region of the United States, are not clear.
8. Conway's letter to Howells, 11 May 1864 (MH), introduced Thomas B. Potter (1817–1898), an English politician sympathetic to the Union cause, by whom Conway returned the manuscripts of Howells' poems.
9. Howells' elegy "John Butler Howells" appeared in the Ashtabula *Sentinel*, 29 June 1864.

19 MAY 1864, VENICE, TO SAMUEL D. HOWELLS

Venice, May 19, 1864.

My dear brother Sam—

I never forget you, but your letter to Joe, which they enclosed me from home, brought you freshly to mind, and makes me remember the promise in my last letter to father, that the next should be written to you.

There has not been a word of news from home concerning the war, for many days in the Venetian paper, and the American papers are so old when they get here, that they can hardly be said to bring news. So I only know of the war by guessing. I don't even know who your general is

—whether you're under Sherman or not—but I do know that my anxious hope is with you wherever you are. Your letter to Joe interested me a great deal, and made me proud of you in more ways than one—for in that letter I saw that you were not only brave, but good and wise. You have learned to think by experiences which tend to make good men better, and I feel that you have acquired wisdom that I shall never find in books, let me study never so hard.

We have been on no journey since I wrote you about our trip to the Ducal Cities, and I have only to write you our little family gossip from Venice. With the exception of an attack of diarrhea which brought me down last week, and a good deal of present nervousness, we are all very well, especially Winifred. She sends you her fotograf (taken about a month ago) and a lock of her long, curling brown hair. She was five months old day before yesterday. Already she begins to monopolize the attention of the whole house, and has a great idea of playing tricks, and making fun. Her great joke at present, is to close her eyes, and coo. This she thinks about the best thing in the world.

We moved the first of this month from Casa Falier, where we had lived so long, to Palazzo Giustinian, one of the finest on the Grand Canal. I send you a view of it. From our balconies (just at the turn of the Canal,) we can see both ways—Rialto Bridge being at the bottom of the distance on the left. Next palace (*palazzo Foscari,*) is at present a barracks for Austrian soldiers. I wish your regiment was quartered there instead of the Croats. It is a shame to use the palace—the stateliest on the Canal—for those barbarians.

Ever so many Americans are in town now—this being the season of northward travel from Rome and Naples to Germany. Nearly all come to see us, but they are seldom interesting, and there is only one now and then whom I should be sorry to have missed.

I am very anxious to get news from the war. We expected long ago to get news of a movement of Grant's, but that army of the Potomac seems to paralyse every general set over it. There has been a prospect of a general row here in Europe over the German and Danish war, but I think the English—who are dreadfully afraid of war, will patch up a kind of peace.

I'll try hereafter to write you a line in every letter home. Elinor sends love, and Winny kisses.

Your affectionate brother,
Will.

20 JUNE 1864, VENICE, TO ANNE T. HOWELLS

Venice, June 20, 1864.

Dear Annie—

Your dear, thoughtful, kind letter came to-day. It was just the sort of letter I longed to read, for it told me all those things concerning our brother which I had pondered over ever since I had the news of his death. I cannot tell you what a mournful pleasure I had in learning all the sad particulars of his illness, though some of these touched me with inexpressible pain. I do not like to think that I have been so long from home that any of you should be different from what I left you. And yet I left Johnny a boy, and he died a man, and many of his traits which you describe are new to me. He is doubly lost to me, therefore, because I have not seen the unfolding of a character which promised so much. When I think of this loss, it seems to great to bear, and yet selfishly speaking, I have gained so much. I have fresh tenure of the world to which he is gone, and if through his dying I have not made friends with death, I am at least no longer so much afraid to die. O my dear sister! I wish I were as fit to die as he was. But I am not, and never was since I was a little child.—I have received all the printed notices of Johnny's death, and have cut them out, and put them away in father's letter to Elinor. It is very pleasant to find how much he was beloved, and what you have told me gratifies me still more. When you see Johnny's friend, young Kellogg,[1] remember me to him, and tell him that I recollect him as one whom I am glad to have had my brother's friend.—It seems to me that our family through this loss has entered into new sympathies and relations with other people. We have always been rather exclusive, but now I think we are in the way to learn how much good there is in people's hearts. I am pleased to think of father and mother and Vic as being so active in offering comfort to the Giddingses. The world has lost a steadfast, faithful man in Giddings' death.[2]

A week or two later, I hope to be able to tell you something definite about my plans for the future. I am to have an interview with Charles Hale on his way to Egypt, when he will be able to tell me what we can do for each other. I expect to see him every day, now. In the meantime, I am quite busy preparing in a literary way against my return. In addition to my book on Venice, I want to get ready several lectures, which I intend to make, on the cities of Lombardy, such as Padua, Verona, Mantua, Modena and Parma. I go every day to the Library of St. Mark to make notes on Mantua. I delight in the work, and consequently though I work pretty hard, it doesn't fatigue me much.[3]

To-night a lot of Elinor's relations came, and brought all sorts of presents for the baby, who is now much the most important member of our family. Her long-expected teeth haven't made their appearance yet; but she's sufficiently delightful without them. You'd be surprised to see what a great thing she is grown in six months. She spends most of her time loafing with her nurse at the house of a serving-woman who does work in our palace, and sometimes goes to sleep there on Augusta's (Ow-goost-a, the Italians say) bed.[4] The Italians all call her *baby* from hearing us; and though she's blue eyes and light hair, she's brown as any of them. Her nurse Bettina has made a pun on her name, Winifredda, as it is Italianized. *Fredda* means *cold* in Italian, and *calda, hot.* So B. says Winifredda will do for a winter name, but in summer she must be called Winicalda. Baby's got a Pagliaccio (clown, in pasteboard) for her first toy, and when it jumps, she yells with delight. We got her a kitten for a little while, but she *wooled* it too savagely, and we sent it home. She's quite like me, and has a trick of frowning and staring that she couldn't well have got from anybody else. She has all the Howells traits, and resembles Johnny in many ways.

As Sam can be quite as useful out of the field as in it, I'm very glad that he is not exposed to the worst dangers of the war. Though it is a hard life at best, and full of perils. I hope his discharge can be managed, or at least that he can come home to you for a while. Give him my love when you write him.

I wish dear mother could write me a line. She knows how precious her letters are to me, and I now especially long to hear from her.

There is nothing particularly new to write you. We are all well, and have commenced taking our sea-baths. Elinor's friends who have come are a great-aunt, recently married, with her husband, her adoptive daughter, and a distant cousin of E.'s. I never saw any of them before.—Your letter was most beautifully written, Annie, and I wish I could make a better return for it than this. Elinor is too much taken up to write anything in this letter, which I want to send at once. She sends her love with mine to all.

Your affectionate brother,
Will.

1. Young Kellogg was probably a son of Abner Kellogg (1812–1878), a lawyer in Jefferson.

2. Joshua R. Giddings died on 27 May 1864 in Montreal, where he had been serving as U. S. consul general since 1861.

3. Howells' studies of these cities eventually bore fruit in "Ducal Mantua," *North American Review*, January 1866; "At Padua," *Atlantic*, July 1867; and *Italian Journeys*.

4. Augusta, the serving woman, has not been further identified.

22 July 1864, Venice, to William C. Howells

Venice, July 22, 1864.

Dear father:

Yours and mother's letters have just reached me, bringing me a lock of poor Johnny's hair, and telling me some things that I desired to know of him. The hurt seems as fresh as ever. I tried to read your letter to Elinor and could not, and I must put by the precious memento of his mortality for some days, till I gather strength to look on it.—I hope anxiously that your next letters will bring me intelligence of Sam's discharge, and of his safe return home with Joe. But I tremble when I think of the dangers that lie in wait for him till he is beyond the rebel lines.—I am sorry to tell you that there is no truth in Conway's report of my forthcoming publication in London. There were some negotiations with Trübner & Co., but we could not come to terms. Before any result could be known, Conway to my great surprise and mortification, put that absurd paragraph in one of his letters.[1] However, I've pretty much ceased caring for things.—As for Foster, he has imposed upon you, as he has often imposed upon me. He has not only treated me with very culpable and stupid neglect, but he wrote me, in answer to my remonstrances, an insulting letter.[2] He has now had the meanness to misrepresent me to you. I shall never write him but upon business, and I think he will not write me. I always treated him with respect, though latterly with coolness. You can judge of his regard and friendship for me by the fact that four months ago, I asked him to return me the illustrations for the book, which he is not going to use, and that he has never to this moment made me a response of any kind. This is of a piece with his whole performance.—I am very glad to hear that the song I wrote for Joe is to be published.[3] I thought it pretty good, and I hope it is well set to music. Don't forget to send it to me. If you want it noticed in the east, you had better send it, with my name marked, to the Commonwealth, and Advertiser, Boston, N. Y. Post, and Springfield Republican.—I have finished my ballad, "The Faithful of the Gonzaga," but I don't think I shall offer it anywhere till I get home. I commenced work to-day, compiling and putting together my book on Venice.[4] There is a great deal more work in it than I supposed.—To-day we have invited to see us, one of the pleasantest young fellows I ever met.—He is a Peruvian, and an attachè of the Peruvian Legation at Torin.[5] I heartily wish you could meet him. He is so earnest and true a Republican, and so full of good principle. He is quite young, but extremely intelligent and well read. I never felt proud of our whole hemisphere till I met him.—I have not received the Sentinel containing my verses on Johnny,[6] but I hope you have not forgotten to send it to me. I have the fotograf of which you speak, and will cause it to be copied, but I think it will be better for Elinor to color a copy when we get home, after your own instructions. As soon as the fotografs are done, I will send them to you.—Cousin Edward[7] has not yet shown himself in Venice, and I am still waiting for Hale, without any intelligence from him.— You must tell dear mother that as yet, I cannot fix the day for our return, and can only reiterate my promise to come soon. As Elinor is very busy, and withal not very well she begs me to send mother her love, and to say that she will soon write to her. She is now so determined to go home, that if I wanted to draw back, I could not.—Baby is fat and flourishing, and has made her first experiment on peaches, which she seems to think even superior to cherries. She takes a romp with me every day on the floor, and considers a ride on my foot the last excess of happiness. She is marvellously beautiful, and makes my heart ache with her dear little goodness.—The weather has at last grown very hot, and I go about in my shirt-sleeves. Thanks to the stone floors and the lofty ceilings, one *can* keep cool in Venice. I think with pity and horror of the poor souls fighting for us in the steaming swamps of Virginia. Good-bye, dear father. Don't believe that I've been cross to Foster or anybody. With love to all,

> Your affectionate son,
> Will.

Elinor wants you to send a copy of the Sentinel containing the verses to her father.

1. Conway must have prematurely announced the publication of Howells' poems— probably in the Cincinnati *Commercial*.
2. Frank E. Foster wrote on 8 March 1864 (MH), replying to Howells' complaint about Foster's failure to send proofs of "Disillusion."
3. *The Battle in the Clouds*.
4. *Venetian Life*.
5. The young Peruvian has not been identified.
6. "John Butler Howells."
7. Cousin Edward (1815–1872) was a son of Henry Charles Howells.

21 AUGUST 1864, VENICE, TO JAMES R. LOWELL

> Venice, August 21, 1864.

My dear Sir—

If you are so frank to praise me, why may I not tell you just as freely how glad and proud I am of your praise?[1] I was particularly delighted to learn that you liked my studies of Venetian life in the Boston Advertiser, because while I wrote those things I pleased myself with thinking that you and another dear friend (as I hope I may call Dr Holmes) would see them and read them. I had never forgotten—how could I?—the cordial and flattering reception you both gave a certain raw youngster who visited you in Boston five years ago[2]—you old ones who *might* have put me off with a little chilly patronage. And so I thought that though you might have forgotten the dinner at Parkers (I can tell you everything you ever said there) you still remembered having in a general way been kind to me, and would be glad to see in what I did evidence that your encouragement was not mistakenly bestowed. I wrote the Venetian studies laboriously enough, adding and altering, re-writing and throwing away as my wont is, and now when I come to put them together for a book, I find my account in all that work, for I shall have to change the printed matter very little. I shall however, add several chapters of new matter—one on Venetian painting (treating chiefly of the pre-Titianic painters,) and several chapters on Venetian national character, as I have developed it from observation, and study of the old Venetian customs. Of course, in my book, I shall have something to say of the political situation here and the attitude of the Venetians since '59—an attitude which has influenced their character for good and evil in many ways, and which I cannot help thinking a kind of historic phenomenon, like the flight of the Crim-Tartars, and other movements arising from the universal impulse of a people. There is a great deal of work in all this—but how light-heartedly I shall do it now! The truth is, I have worked under great discouragement since I've been in Venice. The first year—after writing "Louis Lebeau," I idled away in a kind of homesick despair. Then when I did set to work, my literary luck seemed to go against me. I sent the first of my Venetian sketches to the "Atlantic," and the editors refused them as they refused everything else in prose and verse I sent them—refused them with a perseverance and consistency worthy of a better cause. I think it a weakness to charge failures of this kind upon want of judgment in editors, and so I chiefly blamed myself, and tried to find out the fault and mend it—though I confess I *thought* the Venetian sketches good. I offered them to my friend Hale of the *Advertiser*, thinking it right at the same time to tell him that the "Atlantic" had declined them, and to my surprise they were accepted. During their publication, breaths of applause have reached me—but no such gale as you—God bless you!—have given me. I shall first offer the book to a London publisher (for a first appearance in England will brighten my prospects in America,) and perhaps with your leave I will show your letter. I'm anxious to succeed with this book, for I've got to that point in life where I cannot afford to fail anymore. Besides, I'm going to resign my office and go home, (either at Christmas or next March,) and as I have no prospect of place or employment in the States, I must try to make this book a pecuniary success. I go home in this imprudent way, because at the end of three years, I find myself almost expatriated, and I have seen enough of uncountryed Americans in Europe to disgust me with voluntary exile, and its effects upon character. Moreover, though I have by no means fulfilled all the high objects for which I came hither, I have at least so arranged my line of study that I can continue it at home. But with what unspeakable regret shall I leave Italy! You see, that's the trouble—I am too fond of Italy already, and in a year or two more of lotus-eating, I shouldn't want to go home at all.—But before I quit Venice, I shall prepare notes on some Italian subjects, to write up for you, though you need not be afraid that I shall *rush* anything upon you, and I don't think you are, for in your kind letter there was no holding back with the Weg-like[3] prudence that I have noticed in editors who did not like to cheapen their concessions.—And I have not got Heine out of me yet? I hoped I had. He did me evil both in my heart and my literature, but I trusted that I had overcome him in both. Well,—*pazienza*! I shall try again.—I wish you could see a longish ballad of mine now awaiting refusal at the "Atlantic" office, called The Faithful of the Gonzaga. The subject is from Mantuan history; and I have notes enough on Mantua—travel-notes of a visit paid that dear old city, and notes of researches made afterward in the Library St. Mark—to make you an article on Mantua, if I only could find the title of some recent book to hang the review upon.[4]

Forgive me for writing you so long a letter—but I have wanted to write you ever since I came to Italy, and you have given me no chance till now. My wife desires that I remember her to you very cordially; and I have no doubt our daughter (whom the whole palazzo unites, without distinction of nation, in calling La Bebi,) would join us if she were capable of forming the easiest Venetian compliment. But she isn't—being merely mistress as yet of a little Italian pantomime with the right hand signifying *serva sua*, which the whole north would perish before it could imitate. Remember me to Dr. Holmes, and believe me very gratefully and cordially yours,

W. D. Howells.

I know *now* why you told me to study Dante. What a God's mercy (as the Irish say) it was to me, that I was sent to Italy, instead of to Germany whither I wished to go.

I will be very glad if you will send the "honorarium" to L. G. Mead, Esqr., Brattleboro', Vermont.[5]

James Russell Lowell, Esqr.

 1. Lowell's letter to Howells, 28 July 1864 (MH; printed in Norton, *Lowell Letters*, I, 338) is quoted at length in Howells to W. C. Howells, 25 August 1864.
 2. Howells' visit to Boston took place in 1860, not 1859, as suggested by this erroneous statement.
 3. Silas Wegg is a character in Dickens, *Our Mutual Friend*, the second installment of which had appeared in *Harper's Monthly*, July 1864.
 4. Instead of using the material for a review, Howells eventually published his essay "Ducal Mantua."
 5. The honorarium was for "Recent Italian Comedy."

25 August 1864, Venice, to William C. Howells

Venice, August 25, 1864.

My dear father—

Your letter of July 31 came just now, more than a month after I had last heard from home. You may imagine it was welcome, but the news in it was extremely distressing—Sam's sickness and Joe's possible absence from home—I can't think of anything worse for you. Rest assured that if Joe is taken from you, I will fill his place as well as I can; though I really doubt my competency to carry on a business of any kind, much less a business so extensive as yours seems to have grown. Your wish must be law with me in such a case, and I cannot think of anything more unworthy than my shrinking from a duty of the kind. But I hope you will not let a desire to have me at home with you blind you to my inefficiency in matters of business. I could certainly edit the paper,[1] and carry on that part of the schooner, but I confess that the thought of subscription, advertising and stationery fills me with dismay. I know no reason, however, why I should not try what I am good for in that way, for I have no prospect of any certain place before me.—*See Postscript*, for the *unless*.

Let us now understand each other clearly about the time of my return, and to this end let me copy you a letter which I received the other day from the poet Lowell, now editor of the North American Review, to which I sent an article some months ago, on Recent Italian Comedies. He says:

"Your article is in print, and I was very glad to get it. Pray instruct me to whom I shall pay your *honorarium.*—Write us another article on modern Italian Literature, or anything you like. I don't forget my good opinion of you, and my interest in your genius. Therefore

I may be frank. You have enough in you to do honor to our literature. Keep on cultivating yourself. You know what I thought. You must sweat the Heine out of you as men do mercury. You are as good as Heine—remember that. I have been charmed with your Venetian letters in the Advertiser. They are admirable, and fill a gap. They make the most careful and picturesque *study* I have ever seen on any part of Italy. *They are the thing itself.*"[2]

Now setting aside the complimentary part of this letter—and I don't think the writer could have gone *much* further—this certainly opens up a prospect for me, and gives me standing. If I had only got the letter a year ago! How I could have worked! But that is spilt milk. I hope yet to save something of the precious fluid. So before I go home I shall make notes on all sorts of subjects for articles—I think of a dozen at least—(good deal like the man that shot one coon and cut sticks to stretch 365 coonskins during the coming year, isn't it?) but my great object before I leave Venice is to finish my book on Venice,[3] which is chiefly composed of the Advertiser letters. This I earnestly hope will be done by the end of November, but it may run a little later. I confidently expect to get a publisher in London, as I go home—that will take a week, at least. Then, if it is necessary that I should go out to Jefferson to stay 3 or 4 months, you must allow me time to arrange for publication also in Boston or New York before I go out. I suggest, therefore, that some of you come to meet us at B. or N. Y., on our return; but this can be arranged in another letter. I confess freely that if Joe were not likely to leave you, I should have asked you for leave of continued absence till March, so profitably does it seem to me I could put in the time, here. But I do not think of that now, and shall not, till I hear that it is definitively concluded that Joe remains at home. And you must think of me coming cheerfully and gladly to your assistance. I'm sure I can't lose much in doing my duty as a son. At the same time, I do not conceal from you that I have not yet in three years shaken off my old morbid horror of going back to live in a place where I have been so wretched. If you did not live in J. and my dear Johnny did not lie buried there, I never should enter the town again. It cannot change so much but I shall always hate it.—Of course, long before you get this letter, you will have written me further and more fully about this business.

I am very sorry to hear of dear Sam's continued sickness, but if it will only procure him his discharge, I hope he will be able to stand it. I should think that if his continued sickness should be represented, that the matter might be managed. I was very glad to get his brief note, and I hope that in the next letter from home, he will write me more at length, and announcing his discharge.

The girls have indeed sent me a precious memorial. Alas! who could have dreamed that the clover would be growing over the eternal stillness of what was so much life, one little half year ago! It is hard to bear—I think of it very often. Only Sunday night I walked down to the grassy field that forms the shore of the western lagoon, and saw the sunset on the solemn Alps; and as I walked there, my heart was wrung with the thought that the noble soul I should have loved to tell of all beautiful things I have seen could never commune with mine on earth. A thousand things suggest his memory, and his "loved idea" visits me in all my better moments. It is too much.

Your affectionate son,
Will.

P. S. There is this, father, to be considered on my part, relative to making so long a stay at the west when I first return to the United States. As my pursuits are of literature, and my only usefulness is in that direction, I must seek my fortune at the great literary centres. Few men live by making books, and I must look to some position as editor to assist me in my career. Well, I hope that I should return from a three years' residence in Europe with a certain éclat, but I must profit by this éclat at once. A three months' residence in Ohio would dissipate it all, and I should have about the same standing I held before I came to Europe. This would be not altogether in other men, but great part in myself. I should be dispirited and discouraged. Many subjects that I could write up at once in New York or Boston, and thus open place to me, would pass from my mind, and the struggle for position would be twice as hard.

As to my fitness to conduct your business I greatly doubt it. I think if you could get some one to take hold before Joe leaves (if he does at all,) and learn the ropes it would be better. Our old friend Price would be just the man—he is perfectly able, true and faithful.

I speak of all this plainly, because I think it may not have occurred to you, and that you ought to know what my hopes and purposes are. Do not fear but that I should visit you long enough, or that I grudge you my help at a time you need it. Finally, you know, you have but to look the ground over. If poor Joe must be taken from you, and it appears desirable to you, you have only to say come, and I come.

Will.

A word from me about the baby, of course. At present she is taking a nap on my sister's lap,[4] here in the parlor. When she wakes up she has a warm bath, which she enjoys hugely, splashing the water all about on the stone floor of her bed-room; after her bath she eats some rice for luncheon and then is carried about the neighborhood by her nurse to see her friends. Generally, she comes back from this round of calls rather weary and munching a pear, which she holds herself with both her hands. Then comes another nap, a frolic with her father in the parlor, by gaslight, and then bed and a good sound sleep till morning. This is the way the little thing passes her days, and, as she is never sick and never cries scarcely we conclude she leads rather a happy life altogether. Her mamma is making her four little white aprons now, to wear with her woolen dresses when she visits her grandmother in Ohio next winter

Elinor

1. The Ashtabula *Sentinel*.
2. Howells' quotation from Lowell's letter of 28 July 1864 (MH) differs in some ways from the original. Besides changing some of the punctuation marks, he omitted a sentence, replacing it by a dash after "*honorarium*." It reads: "We don't pay very well, but 'tis better than nothing." He also underscored the last sentence and omitted the concluding part of the letter: "Pray introduce me with my best regards to Mrs Howells, & believe me with real interest your friend / J. R. Lowell / Only think of losing Hawthorne! I cannot stomach it."
3. *Venetian Life*.
4. Mary Mead.

6 OCTOBER 1864, VENICE, TO WILLIAM C. HOWELLS

Venice, October 6, 1864.

Dear father—

Your long, kind letter, enclosing that of Annie, came yesterday, bringing me great relief; for you will have seen before this, how great difficulty I had in making what seemed my duty square with my interest and wish. But now that I have heard Joe is not to go into the army, and that I need not go home so soon, I feel much easier, and shall work much better. It takes me longer to finish my book[1] than I expected, and I have deferred going to Rome till January, hoping when I return thence to continue my journey on toward home, with but a few days' pause at Venice. We shall go from Rome to Naples, and then shall certainly visit Pompeii—indeed, I would rather miss Rome itself than fail to see Pompeii. It is a matter of constant and very great regret with me that Aurelia could not have come out with Cousin Edward, when she would have been here to make this journey with us; and I doubt if it has been wisely judged that she should not come. The new anxiety which her absence would have given, must have done something to divert your sorrowful thoughts at home, while it would have been a great mercy to her, not to speak of the actual benefit of the experience. But all this must come too late to influence you. You give me distressing news of poor

Sam, but I cannot help hoping that the case is not really such as you fear; and I am very glad that he has not to go back to hardships of the service in the field. O, if he only could get a discharge, and come here to Italy for the winter! I am sure that it would do much toward his recovery, and we would be so glad to take care of him and make him happy. If his lungs are affected, the voyage to Europe might be his cure. I cannot make out what difficulties of heart, he should have, unless it be rheumatism. I think in regard to heart-diseases, that plenty of amusement, and of incredulity are the best remedies.—But alas! what can I say to you? The tone of sadness in which you write, distresses me greatly, for I know how you are used to look at the bright side of things, and can guess how gloomy your feelings must be. I hope soon to be with you, and to interest you in other things. Why couldn't you come to England in the spring, and sail back with us?—or better still, to Venice, and make the journey home through Lombardy and Germany in our company? Failing all these projects, can't you at least, tell me something you'd like specially to have from Europe, and give me hints of any little preferences of the others?—I hope that *you* are very, very far from being tempted into any connection with the State Journal.[2] No one but a scoundrel or a humbug could make it pay, and there are a set of men in Columbus who harrass the life out of State Journal editors. That's a mill that grinds you up very fine indeed, and turns you out nothing but shorts, after all.

Tell dear little Annie that we all read and admired her article[3] very much. Mary Mead exclaimed over its beauty, before we told her who wrote it. And I think it was remarkably well written. It did not occur to me till I had read it half through, and glanced several times at the initials, that it was Annie's. She has a gift in that way which ought to be cultivated.

I get (very thankfully) all the papers you send me; and I see the difference in the *Sentinel*. But I don't think you put on either pull or ink enough—the impression is so very faint and pale.—I think it's splendid the way Ashtabula county has cleared herself of the draft. Mr Motley is here,[4] and I was telling him about it last night; and giving him your notion of Lincoln's prospects, with which he was greatly encouraged. I think, indeed, we have all reason to be very hopeful about the war as well as the election. It seems that the corrupt party which so long ruled us to the good of slavery, has fallen hopelessly with slavery. It is a long road, but I think we have found the turning; I am not sanguine, however, about anything, in politics; the more history I read, the more I am persuaded that states have only to be true, through justice, to themselves to endure happily, and the more I doubt the possibility of this truth.

I have now nearly completed my article on Mantua, which I intend to send Mr Lowell for the *North American Review*.[5] By the way, if you see any notices of my paper on "Recent Italian Comedy," in the Review for October, I wish you'd clip them and send them to me.—I shall, of course, try very hard to get a London publisher for my book on Venice, but I'm afraid it will be difficultly done. Conway is no longer in London, and I could scarcely find him useful, if he were.

We're having a touch of very cold weather in Venice, just now, and the breezes blow from all quarters in this old palace. We've swathed Baby in flannels, and put up her little feet in fur shoes. The women move about, and I sit writing with my dressing-gown on over my coat, and a cushion between my feet and the stone floor.

I hope, father, that you'll remember me kindly to all friends in Columbus, especially Smith and Cowen,[6] and so with dear love to all at home,

Affectionately your son,
Will.

1. *Venetian Life*.
2. Apparently W. C. Howells had been offered a position as editor on the staff of the *Ohio State Journal*.
3. "The Jefferson Light Artillery," Ashtabula *Sentinel*, 31 August 1864, signed "A T H."
4. John Lothrop Motley (1814–1877), distinguished historian best known for *The Rise of the Dutch Republic* (1856), served as minister to Austria (1861–1867) and as minister to Great Britain (1869–1870). See *Literary Friends and Acquaintance*, HE, pp. 81–85.
5. "Ducal Mantua."
6. Probably William Henry Smith and Benjamin Sprague Cowen (1793–1869), both former journalists, Ohio political figures, and strong supporters of the Union cause.

14 OCTOBER 1864, VENICE, TO FREDERICK W. SEWARD

Consulate of the United States,
Venice, October 14, 1864.

Sir:

Instead of sending the usual annual report on the commerce of this consular district—which grows every year more and more meagre—I desire to make a sketch of the History of Venetian Commerce from the earliest times to the present, and to offer it to the Department for publication in the Commercial Relations.[1] You are aware, of course, that this work requires time; and unfortunately the Marcian Library, in which I shall find my material, has been closed for a month past. It is now open, however, and I hope to send you my report by the middle of November at the latest, and perhaps much sooner.

I have received twenty volumes (ten of the first, and ten of the second part) of the Diplomatic correspondence for the year 1863,[2] but no instructions concerning the disposition of the nine copies not needed in this consulate. I shall send one copy to Prof. Messadaglia of Padua,[3] and await your instructions as to the rest.

    I am, Sir,
    Your obedient Servant,
    W D Howells,
    Consul.

Hon. F. W. Seward,
Assistant Secretary of State.[4]

1. The report was issued by the Government Printing Office (1865) and later expanded and included in *Venetian Life*, 2d ed. (1867). See Gibson-Arms, *Bibliography*, pp. 18, 20.

2. The secretary of state's annual report (1863) contains Howells' consular report for 1863. See Gibson-Arms, *Bibliography*, p. 18.

3. Professor Angelo Messadaglia of the University of Padua had reviewed "the work on the Hydraulics and Physics of the Mississippi," mentioned in Howells' letter to F. W. Seward, 2 March 1863 (DNA). Early in 1864, Howells forwarded several copies of the review to the State Department.

4. For a full record of official endorsements of consular reports and correspondence see Textual Apparatus.

28 OCTOBER 1864, VENICE, TO MARY D. HOWELLS

    Venice, October 28, 1864.

Dear Mother—

I will enclose a few lines in Elinor's letter, for though I have hardly time to write, I should feel guilty to let a letter go home without my hand in it.

Father speaks of my taking office for four years more. I doubt if I could manage it, and if I could, I wouldn't. When I go home, I want to go home to live, "be it ever so humbly." I am sure it will be better than the proudest life here. I only consent to remain here till spring because I think I see very great advantage in doing so; and as soon as I have notes for half a dozen papers on Italian cities I shall be off for home. Home! How my heart leaps at the thought! O mother, you mustn't think that this separation has not been as hard for me as for you. Many a time I've been so homesick I hardly knew what to do—almost as homesick as in the old childish days when it almost broke my heart to be five or ten miles away from you. (Do you remember how one Sunday morning Joe and I came riding back on the same horse from Dayton to Eureka? It was in the fall, and I can hear the hum of a spinning-wheel now, that sounded out of a log-cabin door. O me—O me! I am so sorry to be no longer a child, though then I had my troubles too!) The world isn't so wide now as it was then, and for three years I have borne to be four thousand miles away from you. Well, patience. It will not be much longer now—but O, my dear mother, we can never meet again in the old way. I am wrong to tell you, but every morning I think of someone lying so lonesomely there under the red autumn leaves,[1] and I reproach myself for each moment's happiness, as if it were forgetfulness of him in a sad captivity.

—I long to show you our little girl, who grows so good and fair. You should see how sunnily her hair is coming out of the darker color she was born with; and how sunnily her little life has issued from my gloomier nature. I hope she will be as much like her mother in character as she is like me in looks. The little thing is weaned now, and sleeps all night long by herself—she has so much *giudizio* (good sense) as the Italians say.

Thank father for his kind interest in the payment of the tax on my salary; but I am obliged to deduct the amount of tax from each quarter's account against the government, and pay it in that way. It is some $25.00 a year.

I'm rushing my book forward,[2] and it's nearly done—there are but three chapters more to copy. I have very great hopes of it, as a book calculated to succeed and to do good.

Dear love to all.

Your affectionate son
Will.

1. Howells' brother John, who died on 27 April 1864.
2. *Venetian Life*.

2 DECEMBER 1864, ROME, TO ANNE T. HOWELLS

Rome, Dec. 2, 1864.

Dear Annie:

Your letter, with father's and Sam's was forwarded to us from Venice, and reached us yesterday. It seemed, as it always does, a long while since I had heard from home; but I suppose that not more than the usual interval between letters had elapsed.

When I think of you at home, it takes me away from the famous places in which my life is passing, and I doubt if I shall talk much about Rome to you. I have thought, since getting your letter, chiefly of poor Vic, and the trouble which has overtaken her, and I long to hear fully how and what it is.[1] Of course, I knew nothing of her engagement, and can imagine no probable person of my acquaintance on whom her choice could have fallen. I am quite powerless, in view of this added sorrow, to say anything to my poor sister, and must wait her letter before I try to offer consolation. Alas! how the shadows have overtaken us! Those that make your gloom so far away, reach their arms across the sea to darken me, and I falter in this wild chase of something that lures me on, and would be glad to sit down and rest in the obscurity a little. Father says he has learnt to look forward very timidly to things in this world; but on the contrary I have little fear, now, knowing how bad the worst is, and I think I have won a kind of faith out of the want of hope.

The other day as we rode along a lonely road within the half-empty walls of Rome, we stopped the coachman to ask him what a certain ancient pyramid was; and when he had told us it was the tomb of Caius Cestius, he added casually, that there was the protestant burial-ground. I knew that Shelley and Keats were buried there, and so we got down to look at their graves. It was the first cemetery I had seen in Europe, that at all reminded me of those at home; and I could not help contrasting the old indifference I used to feel in such places, with my present sense of ownership in their sad beauty. My poor brother seemed to be lying in his sleep under those flowery robes of earth,[2] and I could not tread too softly around the lovely head that the roar of storms would not have stirred upon its pillow. When I came to the grave of Keats, it was with a pang of personal grief that I read how "in the bitterness of his heart," he had asked that it might be written there, "Here lies one whose name was writ on water." The world has long ago written his name in the brass of its useless praise; but how vain and empty is the compensation! As I stood by this saddest spot on earth, it seemed now to be Johnny lying there, and now my own earlier youth, on which "the malice of my enemies" has had power even to death,—my enemies of my own house, my restless ambition, my evil thoughts, my scornful hopes, my sinful deeds. What if the world shall some day wake to applaud what I do? I fear my name will still be writ on water.—I plucked, half ashamed of the sacrilege, three little leaves from the rose bush that grew by Keats' grave, and I send two of them to Vic with my love.[3]

We have already seen many marvellous things in[4]

1. The reference is to the death of Victoria Howells' fiancé, which is mentioned in Elinor Howells' "Venetian Diary" (typescript copy at MH) in the entry for 19 December 1864: "One [letter] is from poor Vic Howells telling of the death of the

young man to whom she was to have been married shortly—the saddest letter I ever read. It is one wail of despair. Benas Anther Northway was his name. He was surgeon in an Ohio regiment and died of fever brought on by overworking in the hospitals. His body arrived instead of a letter announcing his death.... He is buried (at her request) beside Johnny Howells."

2. John Butler Howells died in April.

3. For further descriptions of the visit to the Protestant Cemetery in Rome, see Howells to Lowell, 29 November 1864 (MH) and *Italian Journeys*, pp. 166–68.

4. The balance of this letter has not been recovered.

9 JANUARY 1865, VENICE, TO WILLIAM C. HOWELLS

Venice, January 9, 1865.

Dear father:

I send by the same post with this letter a dispatch to the department of State, asking whether the present consuls will probably be continued in office during the President's ensuing term of four years, or not; and applying for 3 months' leave of absence to visit the United States, if it should be the president's pleasure not to make any change in the consulate at Venice. I have said nothing to urge the granting of this leave, because I could not refer to the sad family changes which chiefly call me home, in an official letter; but I have thought that if Mr Garfield[1] could call upon Mr. Fred. W. Seward, or either of the President's private secretaries,[2] he could perhaps make some statement that would operate in my favor. The more I look at the matter, the less advisable it seems to me to relinquish my office at present, and I am consequently very anxious to get this leave. I hope, therefore, you will write to Mr. Garfield, and beg his friendly interest in the matter. This must be done immediately, and so I send this letter to you at Columbus. You could state to Mr. Garfield the peculiar circumstances which make us anxious to see each other, and I have no doubt he would comply with our request, to make these known to Mr. Seward.

I have not got fairly to work since my return, but hope to begin before long. I finished my book on Venice, and sent to Trübner & Co., in London, about two months' ago.[3] I do not yet know whether it will be accepted or not—indeed, if I could get leave of absence, its fate would be comparatively indifferent to me. Conway, whose help you suggest, could, with the best intentions in the world, be of no use. Tubs stand on their own bottoms in publishing houses.

We have bought Aurelia a very beautiful black veil of Venetian lace, which we shall send in the first letter home. Most of the family presents—Roman pearls and Roman scarfs—got ruined in our upset, in the diligence, coming from Rome.[4] However!

—Don't, father, unless you want to make me perfectly wretched, write me such gloomy letters. You know I, at this distance, must bear the family affliction alone—though Elinor sympathizes deeply,—and your melancholy depresses me beyond measure. When I think of your old cheerfulness and contrast it with your present sadness, it frightens me.

Remember me to all kind friends at Columbus, especially the Mitchells.[5] Love to dear Sam, and to all at home.

Your affectionate son,
Will.

Send the "Nile," this time.[6]

1. James A. Garfield (1831–1881) was the congressman representing the Ohio district containing Jefferson (1863–1880).
2. John Hay and John G. Nicolay.
3. *Venetian Life* was completed in November 1864.
4. See *Italian Journeys*, pp. 190–93.
5. General and Mrs. John Grant Mitchell.
6. On 25 December 1864 (MH) Elinor Howells had given W. C. Howells a detailed report on the mishap that had occurred on their return from Rome. Toward the end of the letter she writes: "All our photographs got wetted, and peeled off the cardboard. One, the famous 'Nile' at the Vatican I slip in, as it will amuse you to see all those babies and the tributary streams I believe."

9 JANUARY 1865, VENICE, TO FREDERICK W. SEWARD

United States Consulate,
Venice, January 9, 1865.

Sir:

I have the honor to ask whether, so far as the knowledge of the Department goes, it is the purpose of the government to continue the present consuls in place during the President's ensuing term of office, or whether they are to be removed, as (according to former usage,) at the incoming of a new administration. I trust that the exceptional nature of our system in respect to tenure of offices in the gift of the President, as well as the obvious importance of some information, on the present point, to a class of public servants remote from the country, and liable to be peculiarly embarrassed by sudden removal, will tend to excuse the irregularity of the inquiry I make; and I feel sure, from the unvarying consideration with which the Department of State has treated applications made to it, that it will respond frankly and kindly to a question not in itself, I believe, wholly improper.

If it should be the pleasure of the President not to make any change in my own case, I would respectfully beg to apply to him for three months' leave of absence to visit the United States, before entering upon a prolonged term of residence abroad.

You will see by my Dispatch No. 17, 1864, that I availed myself of only thirty-four days of the leave of two months' absence before granted me, and I hope that the fact of the former leave will not, consequently, operate against the success of the present application. I can efficiently supply my place by my vice-consul, Mr Mead, during the temporary absence proposed, and the public interests need suffer nothing while I am gone.

I am, Sir,
Your obedient servant,
W. D. Howells,
Consul.

Hon. F. W. Seward,
Assistant Secretary of State.[1]

1. For a full record of official endorsements of consular reports and correspondence see Textual Apparatus. In addition to the usual endorsement the verso of the first page bears the notation "Leave of absence cannot be granted at present," probably in the autograph of F. W. Seward.

28 AND 29 JANUARY 1865, VENICE, TO ANNE T. HOWELLS

Venice, January 28, 1865.

My dear Annie:

I think, as you have allowed yourself and others to drop us broken little hints of a conspiracy of yours—just enough to make me curious and Elinor anxious—you ought to come out and avow the whole plot, with name, place and date. I only know that he is a soldier and that he smokes, which is scarcely enough even for a brother who thinks ten thoughts of the article (whatever it may be) on hand to one thought of young ladies and their lovers.[1]—The only thing of which I'm thoroughly informed is the good heart of my good little sister, and I hope whoever has won that, comes somewhere near being half worthy of its brightness and purity.—It is odd to think of you as so grown-up as this affair shows you must be, and yet I'm old enough to have grown-up sister, since I'm to be twenty-eight the first of March. I don't like it, quite, but it has not been arranged yet for people to grow younger.—Elinor's feeling about the matter is that she has not been fairly treated. She has nothing to say against the young soldier, but he ought to have waited till she found him for you. I tell her there is Aurelia left, but she says, very justly, I'm not sure of that, and turns pensively to Winnifred, who, though certainly a forward child, is not ready to be married for some time. I hope, my dear little girl, we shall be at your wedding, and that the blood-red blossoms of war will all have fallen dead before your orange-buds are gathered.

Edward's letter was enough like him to be very funny.[2] I'm glad he remembers us all so well, and that he has been so kind as to tell you about us. I shall write him as soon as I can get my hand up from a review on "Italian Brigandage," which I've nearly finished.[3]

I send in this letter a pair of black gloves as you requested; and you must take them as a present from me.—In a late letter to Aurelia, Elinor sent her a veil of Venetian lace, which I hope came safely to hand.

None of you have yet had the grace to mention my article in the "North American Review," of which I was very proud.[4] I see it is time for me to go home. You forget me, and take little interest in my hopes and ambition. I doubt if the article has been read in the family at all.—You don't deserve to have me tell you how anxious I am about the fate of my book now in the hands of a London publisher.[5] If it is accepted, I shall feel *made*, in literature. *Ma, ci vuol pazienza!*[6]

Why has Harvey Green never a message to send me? You must remember me cordially to him.

29.—A much-removed cousin of Elinor's has come this morning, full of presents and messages from Brattleboro' and New York, for Bebi and all of us.[7] The girls have just gone up to the Piazza with him, and I'm left at home, writing to you. It's a bright sunny, Sunday morning—such as would make a hen lay hundreds of eggs at home, and cackle her throat dry with exultation. But the sea-gulls, the only domestic fowls in Venice, don't like it half so well as the ghostly white fogs we've been having the whole month.

Baby's just gone out with Bettina, to take the air, and in fact, the cat and I have the whole place to ourselves.—You know how I used to hate cats? I'm grown better natured, and the present Minin and I are friends. She is not happy in the morning till I have played with her; and she takes being made to patty-cake with her fore-paws for the baby's amazement, with great good-humor.

—I am glad poor Vic's visit has done her good. She has so sad a fate, that I shrink from writing to her, lest what I mean for consolation should only wound her.[8] But she knows my love; and I hope she will write to me very soon, in answer to the letter I sent her. Poor, dear, good girl! How I long to see her in her trouble.

Annie, it seems to me that it is the duty of you and Aurelia to make all the sunshine you can in that darkened home, and I hope you try at all times to be bright and gay. Don't let the soldier take your heart altogether away from the circle around the fire at home, but be *cheerfully* ....[9] The family error is to be *sadly* good.

... d love to dear mother and all, ... of it for you, I'm

>Your affectionate brother.
>Will

1. Annie's soldier fiancé has not been identified.
2. Edward Howells, a cousin.
3. "Italian Brigandage," *North American Review*, July 1865.
4. "Recent Italian Comedy."
5. Howells had sent the manuscript of *Venetian Life* to Trübner & Co. in November 1864.
6. Italian for "But you need patience."
7. Elinor's cousin has not been identified; Bebi was Winifred Howells, then thirteen months old.
8. See Howells to Anne Howells, 2 December 1864, n. 1.
9. A tear in the manuscript has made portions of the rest of the letter unrecoverable.

15 FEBRUARY 1865, VENICE, TO JOHN J. PIATT

>Venice, February 15, 1865.

My dear Piatt—

I got your little note in a letter from home to-night, and I answer it at once. I know so little of my future that I hardly understand how to speak of it. I've written to the Department for leave of absence, and if I get that, shall not think of giving up here at once; and if I don't get it, I shall be all taken aback, and won't know what to do. I'm extremely anxious to go home this spring, but am loth to resign, not having any certain prospect before me, and being still able to serve myself here. In regard to yourself: there is certainly no one whom I would rather help to this place; but I am already promised, two deep, to give inquiring friends foreknowledge of my time of resignation. I suppose you understand that the salary at Venice falls to $750 as soon as peace is made. I don't know how it will be about consulates generally. It has been truly said of office-holders, "Few die and none resign", and I have talked with no consul who does not think, or seem to think, the place ought to be made perpetual for him. There is no denying that there are conspicuous advantages in office-holding abroad; and there are certainly a great many draw-backs. Whoever attempts it must have courage, French, and patience, especially in Italy. I should think you would like some German place better, and I may give you a hint about Munich, where the Consul is in very poor health.[1] But I don't know that he is not one of the few, and it won't do to count on his resignation.

The tone of your note was rather gloomy, and I think you had not quite got the funeral out of you. I am not myself so lucky as some men

I know, and am at the throat-cutting level most of the time. If any one, in the fall of 1861 had predicted that I should have advanced no farther than I have by 1865, I would have laughed that prophetic ass to scorn. And yet, here I am.—Did you read my article on "Recent Italian Comedy," in the October number of the "North American Review"? My wife's friends, and my own blood relations, speak of it as a noble production.

You treat me coolly and curtly, my dear old fellow, (as if I had neglected you,) in your little note; and perhaps I have, for I'm conscious of a meanness in me equal to it. But you had long owed me the last letter, you know, and it was hardly fair not to make us some mention of your family.

We are getting on with a tranquil kind of dullness, but have lately made a great cackle over baby's upper teeth, which have come through too far apart. We hope she'll do better, the second time.

The other week there was a grand masked-ball given by a Russian princess, to which Elinor and I were asked; but being too old to go, we sent Elinor's sister with the Russian Consul's wife.[2] Mary went as "Folly", and I should have made verses at seeing her in cap and bells if I had been six years younger—Ma! This is the first masquerade in Venice for a great while—since 1859, and no Italians took part in it.

You know we have been recently to Rome and Naples. The ruins and other things are much better as you suppose them to be, than as you find them. On the whole, I was disappointed with Rome; but so I was with Niagara. Pompei is the only town worth seeing.

Love on our part to you and yours,

W. D. H.

1. Franklin Webster was U. S. consul at Munich.
2. The Russian princess has remained unidentified, but Elinor Howells describes her in her "Venetian Diary" (MH) entry for 10 February 1865 as having "a face uglier than any woman ever possessed—cross eyed and scrofulous—and no brain at all, scarcely, but rich as Croesus." Mary Mead went to the ball with Mr. and Mrs. Baleormini.

19 March 1865, Venice, to Edward E. Hale

Venice, March 19, 1865.

Dear Sir:[1]

I beg to thank you most cordially for all the trouble you have taken with my ballad, and to acknowledge the receipt of the golden residuum of fifty dollars greenbacks, for which you sold the verses.[2]

I hardly expected to have come to Write For It, but know no good reason for not doing so, if It pays me. The terms *Atlantic Monthly* and *New York Ledger*, are, after all, merely conventional, as Martin Van Buren said of East and West, when asked to state directly, just where the sun rose.

My experience of publishers is, that they never send you a copy of anything printed, and I therefore venture to ask this added kindness of you. Please send me two copies by different steamers, and pray command my services here in some way. Perhaps there is some old book you want? I am such a known loafer at book-stalls here, that the *banchetto* people usually bring me any rare thing they get, and perhaps I might chance on something you'd like, if you named it.

At any rate, very many thanks, and believe me

Your obliged servant,
W. D. Howells.

Rev. E. E. Hale.

1. Edward Everett Hale (1822–1909), a Unitarian clergyman, author of short stories, and writer on religious and historical subjects, was the brother of Charles Hale. The extant correspondence between E. E. Hale and Howells from 1865 to 1909, fifty-one letters in all, is located at MH and MNS.

2. A letter from C. Hale & Co., 23 February 1865 (MH), advised Howells that in addition to payment for four "Letters from Venice" the company enclosed "fifty dollars, avails of a poem ["The Faithful of the Gonzaga"] sold to Bonner, by Rev. E. E. Hale." Robert Bonner (1824–1899), the publisher of the New York *Ledger* (1851–1899), became famous for the large sums he paid to authors. According to Charles Hale's letter to Howells, 12 January 1865 (MH), the poem had been provisionally accepted by James T. Fields for publication in the *Atlantic*, but was later returned for lack of space. E. E. Hale then proposed to dispose of it otherwise. See *Literary Friends and Acquaintance*, HE, p. 80.

19 MARCH 1865, VENICE, TO WILLIAM C. HOWELLS

Venice, March 19, 1865.

Dear father—

Elinor has expressed about all that I want to say concerning our uncertainty of movement. I had a dispatch from the State Dep't saying: "Your leave of absence cannot be granted at present, but your application will be filed for future consideration." I shall, of course, with the light you throw on the subject, not press the matter at once, and neither shall I give up here immediately. At the same time, if the Cleveland project should take tangible shape, it would be a very great temptation.[1] I should be more than flattered by such mark of confidence in me as an offer of the kind would be; for I assure you that I am touched deeply by the notion that old friends have not forgotten me. I should like to cast my lot with the west, if I can do so without using myself up; but I know how hard a life is that on a daily paper. If, however, I had a chief editorship, with reasonable assistance, I might hope to do something for literature also; and still not make the end my ex-neighbor, poor Hildreth, has done.[2] I hope you'll write me farther concerning Cleveland. In the meantime tell Smith and Cowen how much I am obliged to them.[3]

The history which I think of making notes for, would be that of the Fall of the Venetian Republic. I would undertake now a history of Venice from the first, but it would be almost a life's work,[4] and I ask myself whether I didn't start as a poet?

By the way, if you should see my ballad in the Ledger (W. D. Howells Writes For It,) or elsewhere, please send it to me. It is called "The Faithful of the Gonzaga." I'm writing a series of letters on our recent journey for the Boston Adv., which I hope you see.[5]

I'm very glad to hear of Sam's double good luck, and you must give him my love, and say he owes me many answers to letters. Poor Vic! I hope she had found some respite from her great trouble. I think of her often, and always with love and pity.

Father, I want you to tell Mr Garfield, how much I am bound for his kindness. I shall try to do such things that my friends wont be ashamed to have helped me.

—Of course, I'm greatly pleased with the notion of having pleased the government in my place. I shall write to Mr. Fred. Seward myself in regard to time of leave, but am very glad you have anticipated me in a very good suggestion.

Your letter has made me very happy in every way.

Dear love to all.

Your affectionate son,
W. D. Howells.*

*Signed my whole name from habit in certifying to invoices. I suppose Joe doesn't know that he always signs his letters to me, "J. A. Howells & Co."

1. According to Elinor Howells ("Venetian Diary," 22 March 1865), J. A. Garfield had "proposed a plan—W. H. Smith and others are getting up a Corporation to buy out Cleveland Leader and will ask Poke [Howells] to be chief editor." On 6 June 1865 Howells wrote his father that he was sorry that the Cleveland project had fallen through.

2. Richard Hildreth, who had worked for the Boston *Atlas* and the New York *Tribune* before becoming U. S. consul at Trieste, resigned his government position because of ill health. He died on 11 July 1865.

3. See Howells to W. C. Howells, 6 October 1864, n. 6.

4. Howells worked on a history of Venice at several intervals in his life but never completed the project.

5. "The Road to Rome and Home Again," *Advertiser*, 18 February, 4 March, 13 April, and 3 May 1865.

27 APRIL 1865, VENICE, TO WILLIAM C. AND MARY D. HOWELLS

Venice, April 27, 1865.

Dear father and mother:

You are thinking today of him who passed one year ago out of the caresses of our helpless love, into the light of the infinite Affection,[1] and in this thought, I join my heart with yours; and if his place be not always near us, he has won from the Divine Compassion leave to be also with us this day, and distance and death are annulled, and we are all together again. As this time has drawn near and nearer, I have thought more of our loss, and now at last I have realized his immortality, and begin to feel how much happier and wiser he has grown through death. He seems to look with his immortal eyes upon our life and all its troubles, with the compassionate and tender regard which men bend upon children's woes: he understands and pities our sorrow, but he does not feel it, being now lifted in his wisdom and goodness above all pain. Does our joy seem as little to him? In the degree that it is unselfish, it must be immortal, and no doubt he and his brother angels share the exultation which we feel that war is ended and that the bonds of slaves are broken. Surely the purest spirit in heaven must rejoice that another obstacle is removed from men's progress toward peace on earth and good will to men; that once in the story of the long struggle, the right has won.—God grant that its defeats are forever ended, and it shall never again vindicate its power by the sword! Some gentle soul that passed in that last fight under the gates of Richmond,[2] has told our beloved the great news: let the light of his purified spirit suffuse our own, and purge them of every dark and revengeful thought that spots their joy!—The other night when the news came to us, it fell upon a heavy heart in me, for a young American, who came here some three weeks ago, and took a room in our house, was lying near to death with typhoid fever.[3] I had just heard the doctors say there was barely hope, when I went into the parlor where they had the dispatch announcing Lee's capitulation. The room was full of Americans, and there was great handshaking among them, and our exultation was all the more cordial because we were in a strange land, and had to make up an America among ourselves. We decorated the room with flags, and hung banners from the balconies; but I scarcely realized it all, till I went back to the sick man's room, and found him quiet, and already better. Now he is decidedly better, and we hope out of danger.

Father's letter of the 4th of April, came accompanied by one from Aurelia, and was preceded a day or day by one from Victoria. I wrote three weeks since to Mr Fred. Seward, urging that my leave of absence should be granted, and I expect a favorable response from him in a little time. In the meanwhile, I beseech you to have patience, and to put some faith in me when I tell you that *I* too suffer from our prolonged separation, and am shaping everything to return to you at the earliest possible moment. So many letters from home urging my return at any cost, almost distract me, and I pray you to have a little more consideration. You do not yourselves want me to embarrass my future, and I think the face of a discontented and unsuccessful man which you might see after the first days of greeting, would be harder for you to bear, than a few weeks more of absence. I have an eye to all chances, and I am doing the best I can. The book I sent to London, with every reason to expect success, failed to be accepted,[4] or I should have been with you now, leave or no leave. As it is, we must all wait till I get the leave, which cannot now be long in coming.—We've got a big box, which we're packing, and we are laying in presents for everybody, though we find some difficulty in reconciling slim purses with portly purposes. You may be sure I shall not forget father's cane and old book, and I'll try to think of something mother would like. Venice was a famous place for printers in the old time, and you can get books almost as old as the art for a very little money. I bought a large volume of universal history, date of 1525, and illustrated with amazing woodcuts for 75 cts.—I'm now reading up all the Italian literature of this century which I can, in order to make some articles on it for the N. American.[5] Of course this keeps me very busy, and what with the sickness in the house leaves me scarcely a moment of my own. The poor baby and I have grown almost strangers, and should be quite so, except for meeting at breakfast and dinner.—Her dearest grandmother may rest assured that she will come soon to claim her tall chair, and will not suffer herself to be cast into the shade by any brown-haired babies. Her favorite places at present are the balconies over the canal, and the terrace where the women wash. She only says a few words (in Italian) as yet, and utterly refuses to walk alone, though she can walk very well. Elinor joins me in dearest love to all.

Your affectionate son
Will.

1. John Butler Howells.
2. The Battle of Richmond, 3 April 1865, in which the army of General Robert E. Lee was defeated, gave the Union forces a decisive victory over the Confederacy.
3. The young American has not been identified.
4. A letter from Trübner & Co., 30 March 1865 (MH), had informed Howells

that the firm could not undertake the publication of *Venetian Life* unless he could assure them of a market of 500 copies in America.

5. Howells' reading eventually led to the writing of "Modern Italian Poets," *North American Review*, October 1866 and April 1867, and to his comments on Italian authors in later articles. One of his Italian friends giving advice in these matters was Eugenio Brunetta, whom Howells later described in "A Young Venetian Friend," *Harper's Monthly*, May 1919, where he is called Biondini. Brunetta wrote Howells on 20 March 1865 (MH): "Instead of reading the Pastor Fido [1590, by Giovanni Battista Guarini], I advise you to read the works of the modern Italian writers.... La Battaglia di Benevento [1827] is estimed (after the Assedio di Firenze [1834]) the best work of [Francesco] Guerrazzi, and his fame as a novelist is based on that novel. I understand yet why you prefer the Isabella Orsini [1845], it is because there the fact (plot) is more concentrated and the author goes straight at the end of it without stopping." See Woodress, *Howells & Italy*, pp. 112–31.

28 APRIL 1865, VENICE, TO WILLIAM C. HOWELLS

Venice, April 28, 1865.

Dear father—

We received intelligence last night of the frightful crimes perpetrated at Washington on the 14th,[1] and feel a grief and dismay which I cannot express. This loss is one which must fall upon every American like a personal calamity. It blackens our future more awfully than the dreadfullest defeat of battle; but thank God, they cannot assassinate a whole Republic: the People is immortal.

This trouble makes me homesick and impatient of return to you; but now, as the generous Assistant Secretary who had taken an interest in my leave of absence is dead,[2] that matter must rest in abeyance, unless you can go to Washington, and urge it forward yourself. If Garfield were there, he could do it, but I believe he is on his way to California and so I ask this favor of you. At a time like this of course I cannot write the Department, to prefer a private request, and in any case, a few minutes' talk with some person of influence at Washington would do more to get me the leave, than many applications in writing. In my letter to poor young Seward, I told him that I wanted the leave soon, because my vice-consul Mead desires to go home in the fall, and you had better mention the same fact. Try to see somebody in the State Dep't, and if you can't, get an interview with Hay, the president's private secretary.

Dear love to all.

Affectionately,
Will.

If you can't go to Washington, write Mr Chase or some one about it,[3] and inform me immediately of what you've done. But I think you can go.

1. Lincoln was mortally wounded on 14 April 1865.

2. On the same day, Secretary of State William H. Seward and his son Frederick W. Seward, the assistant secretary of state, were also attacked and seriously wounded; however, neither of them died, as Howells seems to have believed.

3. Salmon P. Chase had resigned as secretary of treasury in June 1864 and received his appointment to the U. S. Supreme Court in December 1864.

1 MAY 1865, VENICE, TO WILLIAM H. SEWARD

>Consulate of the United States of America,
>Venice, May 1, 1865.

Sir:

I cannot refrain from uttering my share of the national sorrow which every American citizen feels with the poignancy of a personal grief, in view of the untimely loss of the great and good man whom the people had called, after a term of most arduous, devoted and triumphant service, to continue at the head of their affairs, and whom a horrible crime has removed. While deeply lamenting the death of President Lincoln, I desire to express as sincere a rejoicing that the life of the Secretary of State, so atrociously attempted, was spared in the calamitous hour when the country would have been least able to bear his loss, and to utter the earnest hope that the life of the Assistant Secretary, hazarded in his father's defence,[1] may be, ere this, beyond all danger from the injuries received, and preserved to the state of which he has been the valued servant.

I have the honor to be, Sir,

>Your obedient servant,
>W. D. Howells, Consul.

Hon. W. H. Seward,
Secretary of State.[2]

1. See Howells to W. C. Howells, 28 April 1865, n. 2.

2. For a full record of official endorsements of consular reports and correspondence see Textual Apparatus.

8 MAY 1865, VENICE, TO JOHN L. MOTLEY

>Venice, May 8, 1865.

Sir:

I beg to acknowledge your Dispatch communicating your instructions from the Department of State relative to the demonstrations of mourning for our national and individual loss in the death of President Lincoln.

Immediately upon receiving the first telegraphic announcement of this calamity, I caused the arms of this consulate to be draped with black, and put out a flag, also tied with crape, above the arms. I have since received the circular of the Department with instructions to wear crape for six months.

I desire to thank you for the kind terms in which you make known to me the wishes of the Department. I think it was the natural impulse of every American to express mutely the grief for which there was no language, and I am sure that the instructions of the Department of State to its representatives abroad have been everywhere anticipated in this respect.

> I am, sir,
> Your obedient servant,
> W. D. Howells, Consul.

Hon. J. L. Motley
Minister of the United States of America, Vienna.

14 MAY 1865, VENICE, TO JAMES R. LOWELL

> Venice, May 14, 1865.

Dear Sir:

You will think I have Micawber's own passion for writing letters, I'm afraid;[1] but since I promised you an article about Miss Cobbe's *Italics*,[2] and wrote that it was nearly ready to send, I cannot, now that I have given over all idea of sending it, do less than notify you of the fact, in order that you may take anything else you like on that argument. When I had finished my article, I read it to my small public, here, and it was unanimously pronounced to be perhaps the dullest and flimsiest article that ever was written. So, as there was no question whether I could afford to offer you a stupid thing, I tried to give my work some livelier flavor by boiling it down: I wrote it all over again; but original sin was too much for it, and now I've put it away with a monumental mass of similar manuscripts.—The truth was, that there was nothing to do except to say to Miss Cobbe, she was all wrong about Italy; and as that could be said in a word, there was no occasion for an article. Unluckily for me I only found this out after writing the article: it was a bad thing from the beginning—I paid twenty francs for the book, wrote two months about it, embittered myself by saying bitter things of it, and at last found that I had been working to no purpose, except, perhaps, that my work has led me to rather closer study of modern Italian literature than I at first intended to make.

A professor of the university at Padua has lately sent me the enclosed translation, which I have thought Mr. Longfellow might be pleased to see,[3] but to whom I do not send it directly, because I have not his acquaintance. Will you be so kind as to give it to him?

The intelligence of the president's death remains news—a horrible, ceaseless surprise. There seems nothing to say of it.

Yours very sincerely,
W. D. Howells.

J. R. Lowell, Esqr.

1. Wilkins Micawber, a character in Dickens, *David Copperfield* (1850). Howells had written Lowell on 11 February 1865 (MH): "Is there such a thing within your knowledge as a diffident little college in want of a professor of modern European literature—some genial little college where a man's ignorance would not be counted against him? I ask for a modest friend." The letter accompanied the manuscript of "Italian Brigandage."

2. Frances Power Cobbe, *Italics* (1864), was among the books reviewed by Howells in "Modern Italian Poets," *North American Review*, October 1866.

3. The enclosure was most likely an Italian translation of Longfellow's poetry by Angelo Messadaglia. In a printed document with autograph entries, dated 9 April 1867 (MH), the Corporation of Harvard College acknowledged Howells' gift to the college library of "Alcune Poesie di Enrico W. Longfellow Traduzione dall' inglese di Angelo Messadaglia."

6 JUNE 1865, VENICE, TO WILLIAM C. HOWELLS

Consulate of the United States of America...
Venice, June 6, 1865.

Dear father—

Your letter enclosing those of Joe and Piatt reached me this morning. I was in hopes it would have brought me some news concerning my leave, or something to encourage me to go home without it. I'm very sorry that Cleveland project fell through, for I think it would have been the place for me; and I'm quite discouraged about finding any other.[1] I was talking the other night with a N. Y. newspaper man, and he said it was almost impossible to get an editorship in that city. I'm so homesick and tired of Europe that it seems impossible for me stay a day longer, and yet it seems the greatest rashness to return to America on an uncertainty.—I'm glad poor Joe's trip on the river did him good, and hope that he will soon be perfectly restored. How much I wish that he could come to Venice before I leave. It would set him up at once, and he might as well come as not. No doubt that Lake Shore climate is very irritating to the nerves. I never was well there, and here I have scarcely ever been sick. It is the contrary with Elinor, and she has grown very delicate in the Venetian climate.—I'll answer Piatt's letter.—As to Foster's not giving Joe my book,[2] it's a characteristic bestiality. He wrote to me distinctly that he had given up publishing, and on this I instructed Joe to take the poem off his hands. What do you think of a publisher who doesn't know the name of the engraver he gets to work for him? If I can sell my poem, now, to any publisher, I will do so. I also asked Joe to inquire about some articles of mine in the hands of the Editor of *Harper*,[3] but I suppose he forgot it.—Elinor and I went to see Tortorini at last, after three years' invitation. He is mayor of a pretty town, settled about two thousand years ago, called Monselice, and he is a person of immense importance there. His dinners were execrable, and we came away on account of them. You have no idea how badly people can feed till you sit down at an Italian's table. Think of rice soup, boiled beef, fried brain and strawberries with wine on them. Ugh!—It's broiling hot this summer in Venice, but I keep my pen going from morning till night. I'm making a great lot of translations from Italian poets for my articles.[4] How do you like the series of letters about the journey to Rome?[5] I am conscious of greater literary power each day, but success hangs fire yet.—An English authoress was here the other, she went into raptures over my things, poetry and prose, and is to send me a letter to Antony Trolloppe, which she hopes will get me a London publisher for my book on Venice.[6] As for me, I work, and hope for little or nothing, and look at other paper balloons going up.—I rather think that Jefferson Davis had one side of his head shaved, and were put into striped clothing, and set to work for life in a penitentiary, it would be much better for us than if he were hanged. The English put Napoleon out of sight at St Helena, and the world forgot him. If they had put him to death, they would have made a martyr of a great sinner. I wouldn't like to see the farce of Davis' capture in his wife's clothes, taken away by the tragedy of his execution. The only objection to his imprisonment could come from the murderers, horse-thieves and burglars obliged to lock step with him. *They* might reasonably complain.

You say nothing about mother and the girls, and so I infer they are all well. Give them our love, with many kisses from the baby, and take for yourself.

Your affectionate son,
Will.

Love to Joe and his family. Winifred will nurse Mary[7] when she comes to Jefferson. She thinks herself as large as anybody now, and blandly patronizes all her friends.

1. See Howells to W. C. Howells, 19 March 1865, n. 1.
2. "Disillusion."
3. Howells had probably submitted to Alfred H. Guernsey some of his articles on Italian subjects that were published in the *Nation* later in 1865. See Gibson-Arms, *Bibliography*, pp. 89–91.
4. The order in which Howells wrote his articles on Italian topics, published in 1865 and 1866, cannot be determined.
5. "The Road to Rome and Home Again." See Howells to W. C. Howells, 19 March 1865, n. 5.
6. The "English authoress" who helped Howells find a publisher for *Venetian Life* has not been identified.
7. Mary Elizabeth Howells, daughter of Joseph A. and Eliza Whitmore Howells.

21 JUNE 1865, VENICE, TO WILLIAM C. HOWELLS

Venice, June 21, 1865.

Dear father—

Elinor wrote her letter to Aurelia last night when we were still uncertain about leave of absence. To-night, thanks to your great kindness, it has come, and we are getting ready for flight the first day of July.[1] There are a thousand things to do, and little or nothing to say, except to thank you over and over again. I think my luck wonderful in getting the leave at this time, and yours none less so in getting it extended from three to four months. I'm very greatly obliged to Mr Cooke[2] for his services in our behalf, and shall not forget them. It's good to hear of the old friends you mention, and to think of them as still friendly.

Our plan is to stop a week or ten days in London, where I shall still try to make my book go.[3] I have a letter to Anthony Trolloppe, asking his interest in my favor, and I think he will be able to help me to a publisher.[4] My article on "Comedy,"[5] has made me quite a reputation in Italy, amongst the Italian literati, and the English living in Italy. Curious, isn't it?—Poor Italy! shall I ever see her sunny face again?

From London, I shall write you again concerning the day and steamer that shall bring us either to N. Y. or Boston—probably the latter place.

Meantime everything is strange as a dream. Love and kisses all round.

Your affectionate son,
Will.

1. See Howells to W. C. Howells, 28 April 1865.
2. Henry D. Cooke.
3. *Venetian Life*.
4. After Howells' arrival in England, he received a letter from Trollope, dated 13 July 1865 (MH), which reads in part: "I got your letter this morning, having been some days away from home. I hardly know when I may be in town. Could you come to my house on Saturday, or Sunday? We can give you a bed. On Satur-

day Mrs. Trollope will not be at home but I shall be there with a friend—Mrs. Trollope will be home on Sunday...."
5. "Recent Italian Comedy."

28 JUNE 1865, VENICE, TO WILLIAM HUNTER

Venice, June 28, 1865.

Sir:[1]

I beg to express a profound sense of gratitude to the Department of State for the great favor shown in procuring me leave of absence for four months, and to state the confidence I feel that the interests of the Consulate will suffer nothing in the hands of Mr Mead, while I shall be away. The Vice-Consul will enter upon the duties of his office, on Monday, the 3d day of July, and I shall quit Venice the same day.

You will notice in the account to be rendered for miscellaneous expenses, that I have during this quarter, made an unusual outlay for book-binding. I have caused to be bound, not only the pamphlets accumulated during the last year, but all the Dispatches and Official Letters belonging to the Consulate, except those received during the present year. The record thus formed runs from 1850 to the end of 1864: from the time of Mr. Donald G. Mitchell, to the fourth year of my own time.[2] I have carefully arranged all these communications in order of date, and have distributed into separate volumes those of the State Department, Treasury, Venetian Authorities, and the U. S. Legation, Consulates and miscellaneous correspondents. I have also affixed a carefully prepared and full index to each of the four volumes, in order that the Consul hereafter, in cases where a doubt arises which has already been settled, may turn to the old correspondence, without being put to the delay and expense of asking fresh instruction.

Mr. Mitchell seems to have been the only Consul, previous to my own appointment, who preserved all the official communications addressed to him. I found his papers in perfect order, and intelligibly endorsed; Mr. Blumenthal, Acting Consul, at various times, had also done something to arrange the papers, as had Mr. Sprenger, but the latter had evidently lost some dispatches addressed to him, if I may judge from the fact that one letter represents all the correspondence he had with the State Department during a whole year. During my own tenure of office, the communications, circulars and letters, received up to the end of 1864, numbered, from the State Department, forty-eight.

Former consuls seem to have generally acted on the principle that they ought to render service corresponding in quality to their pay in quantity: which was very poor. None but a rich man could maintain this office respectably with the salary of $750.00 formerly attached to it; and the effort of consuls to maintain a decent footing on that pay, must always have resulted in failure, with numberless mortifications calculated to destroy just pride in their charge, and to make them indifferent agents of a government which underpaid them. But I think that the carelessness of consuls has not been altogether to blame for the meagreness of the record afforded by the correspondence preserved. I fear that until the time of Mr. Lincoln's administration, minor consular officers did not receive due attention from our government, and were too seldom made to feel that good conduct would be approved, and bad conduct reprehended. On the contrary, during my own time the Department has invariably responded to all applications with promptness and thoroughness; and the consciousness which I have always felt that what I did would be viewed with a due degree of interest by the government, has been the greatest possible encouragement to me in official capacity.

> I am, Sir,
> Your obedient servant
> W. D. Howells,
> Consul.

Hon. W. Hunter,
Acting Secretary of State.[3]

1. William Hunter (1805–1866), chief clerk of the Department of State (1852–1866), served as acting secretary of state during the incapacity of W. H. Seward and F. W. Seward.
2. Donald Grant Mitchell (1822–1908), pseudonym "Ik Marvel," American author. was U. S. consul at Venice (1853–1854).
3. For a full record of official endorsements of consular reports and correspondence see Textual Apparatus.

10 JULY 1865, LONDON, TO WILLIAM C. HOWELLS

London, July 10, 1865.

Dear father:

You'll see by the date of this letter that I'm on my winding way homeward. And truly so far it has been most decidedly winding. I wish you'd go to the map, and look at our route. We left Venice last Monday—just a week ago—and traveled the first day to Milan, where we passed the first night. Tuesday we ate a fourth of July dinner with the American prostestant minister in Milan,[1] and at eight that night pushed on toward Turin; from Turin we went by rail to the foot of the Alps, which we crossed by night in the diligence; Wednesday night, we cut across a corner of France and reached Geneva. Next day we left at 2 p.m. and went as far as Berne, the Swiss capital, and next morning, we rushed up to Manheim through Baden. Here we ought to have taken the Rhine steamer, but were too tired to get up for it, and so we went by rail to Mainz, the next Rhine city, and took the steamer there. It is at this point that the magnificence of the Rhine scenery begins, and the glory of it ends just before you reach Cologne. The river is well enough and the hills are good, but the scenery is not nearly so fine as that of the Ohio, and is infinitely inferior to the Hudson's. My feeling was consequently one of great disappointment, as I shall explain to you later. The truth is, that Italy and Switzerland are the only countries in Europe comparable to America in natural loveliness. Switzerland is charming, and one feels that atmosphere of freedom which is the best air in the world. I saw only proofs of industry and happiness among the Swiss, who produce a supper of cold chicken and honey of unequaled magnificence.—Well, Saturday night we reached Cologne, and after seeing its famous cathedral, left on Sunday at noon, and this, Monday morning, arrived in London at seven o'clock.

We expect to stay in London till Friday of next week, and on Saturday sail from Liverpool in the "Asia," for Boston. I suppose the passage will be from ten to twelve days. As soon as we arrive, we expect to go to Brattleboro', and when a decent time has been given Elinor to greet her friends, we shall make for the west. Our money is frightfully short, and we must look well to the outgoes in transatlantic travel: otherwise I should run out to you at once, and then go back later to fetch Elinor. I suppose we shall be at least a week in Brattleboro', before starting to Ohio. How I wish Joe or you could meet us at Boston! But I don't ask so great a kindness, feeling that you have done more than enough in getting me leave of absence. So, "if your love do not persuade you, let not my letter."[2]

—We are all unspeakably tired. Poor baby behaved angelically all the long way from Venice, but now lies sleeping as heavily as a little log. As in Venice, she had never seen any horses, she pronounced them all to be *cani* (dogs,) and by a sort of attribution, locomotives, and every moving thing which was not a man came to be *cani* with Baby, who spent half of her time at the windows looking at them. The other quarter she slept, and the fourth quarter she played and cried. She does not seem to have missed her nurse, from whom it almost broke our hearts to part her. And indeed it was too much like parting mother and child, to be anything but cruel. Poor Bettina was not good at saying what she felt, and her grief being all-but dumb, was so much the more touching.—I can scarcely write anything of Venice without tears.

Recollect how long it had been home to me.—But I'm very glad and very anxious about going home, and wish I could banish the days between us. However,

> "The slow, sad hours that bring us all things ill,
> The slow sweet hours that bring us all things good,"[3]

Will soon go back, and God willing, we shall briefly be with you. Dear love and kisses to every one.

Your affectionate son,
Will.

1. The American minister has not been identified.
2. See Shakespeare, *The Merchant of Venice*, III, ii, 323–25.
3. See Tennyson, "Love and Duty," lines 57–58.

19 August 1865, Jefferson, to James R. Lowell

Jefferson, Ashtabula co., Ohio.
August 19, 1865.

Dear Mr. Lowell:

I venture to enclose the accompanying letter for Mr. Fields and to beg that you will give it him, and pray him to answer it at once. You will observe in it, that I have found a publisher in the bosom of my family, and I think it best not to look further.[1] My brother does not, of course, share the generous confidence which *I* feel in the success of my book, but he is certain that five hundred copies can be sold in America.[2]—When it arrives and is ready for publication, I shall unblushingly ask all manner of favors from you in the way of bringing it to notice; but for the present I can think of nothing to trouble you with but the delivery of this letter to Mr. Fields; though I should certainly not object to your saying anything *you* think of to my advantage now.

I called on Dr. Holmes after seeing you, and most cordially shared his great regret that I had not been able to find a publisher in Boston, for my book. Indeed, I don't think I fully appreciated my own disappointment, till I talked with him about it. Now, if you think it doubtful that Mr. Fields will act even the step-fatherly part toward my book that I ask, I am sure that Dr Holmes would unite in pulling the wires of that sensitive organization, and putting it in motion. Perhaps you will wonder that I trouble you with a purely business affair: the truth is, Ticknor & Fields are so used to neglecting me, that I suppose they would hardly receive money from me if they could help it; and I wish to have my letter answered at once.

I hope that you like "Mantua,"[3] but I don't think I shall like you the less if you don't. Though I can't tell. I've known my feelings towards able editors to undergo very curious changes.

Faccia, La prego, i miei complimenti alla di Lei Signora consorte. Mi raccomando a Lei, e spero molto nella sua bontà.—Fra un mese intendo andar a Boston, e recarmi da Lei: non abbia, nè d'aprire questa lettera nella mia presenza, nè di scusarsi d'averla negletta: ecco la mia umile preghiera. Fidandomi di Lei ("di chi mi fido mi guardi Iddio!"), mi pregio di scrivermi,

Suo devotissimo[4]
W. D. Howells.

1. Howells' enclosed letter to James T. Fields, 19 August 1865 (CSmH; printed in *Life in Letters*, I, 96–97), bearing a friendly endorsement by Lowell, announces that Joseph A. Howells has undertaken to publish the American edition of *Venetian Life*, but asks Fields to "act as his agent" and to help in other ways. On 17 October 1865 (MH) Lowell wrote Howells: "I did what I could with F. about the book, but to no end. I expected as much. But see if I don't say a good word for it when it is published! *There* I have my own way."

2. For the terms set by Trübner & Co., see Howells to his parents, 27 April 1865, n. 4.

3. "Ducal Mantua."

4. "Give, I pray you, my regards to your wife. I entrust myself to you, and have great faith in your generosity.—Within a month I intend to go to Boston and come to your home: you don't have to open this letter in my presence or excuse yourself for neglecting it: there is my humble request. Trusting you ('may God protect me against those I trust'), I have the honor to sign myself, Yours faithfully."

5 SEPTEMBER 1865, JEFFERSON, TO DON L. WYMAN

Jefferson, Sept. 5, 1865.

My dear Sir:[1]

The extremely hot weather, much writing to do, and infinite talking, must be my excuse for the ungracious failure to answer long ago the letter from you which my father gave me on my arrival at home. Let me thank you very cordially for the praise you give my verses, and for the opportunity you have afforded me of reading some of your own. There are many felicities of expression, and much poetic feeling in the "Onion and the Dolphin," which the editors of the *Atlantic* must have seen; but on the whole I am not surprised they rejected it, and I think you will one day be amazed that you offered it for publication. There are licenses of diction in it, which no one should permit himself, and the author's knowledge of the Latin sources of many words is too apparent:

it is scarcely worth while to puzzle the English reader, in order to afford the classic scholar a doubtful pleasure.

The "machine poetry" is better than the long poem. In the three stanzas of "Only a Year," a bit of genuine feeling is pathetically expressed—which is to say they are true poetry. If you care to have them printed, and will send them to the editor of the *Saturday Press*, N. York, I think he will accept them.—The *Press* is a journal recently revived: in old days it was the best literary paper in the country. The editor's name is Henry Clapp, Jr.

Am I right in inferring from these verses that you read German? The German poetry is the best of the subjective sort; but I value it less than I once did, and indeed like objective poetry better. There is, however, a wonderful charm in the shadowy expression of some of the German poets. Heine I like best of all, and Uhland next. Of late I have only read Italian poetry, and modern Italian poetry; of the poem by Jane Ingelow,[2] which you mention, I'm ignorant, and I don't know *Bitter-Sweet*,[3] either. In fact, I've met the fate of all expatriated people, and have to learn a great deal about my own country and language, now I've come back to them.

Do you care to know that I think you have the poetic faculty in an uncommon degree? What we westerners all need is culture; many people in the west might have written more poetry if they had written less; there has been abundant impulse towards literature here, but it has not been wisely controled nor well directed. I look to you to do something creditable to us.

The article on Italian literature to which you alluded in your letter was of Recent Italian Comedy only: it was in the October (1864) number of the *North American Review*. I am now working on an article about the modern poets of Italy.[4]

Your letter gave me a great deal of pleasure—even the critical part of it—and I shall be very glad to hear from you.

Very sincerely,
W. D. Howells.

Don. Lloyd Wyman, Esqr.

1. Little is known about Wyman, except that he lived in Cleveland and sometime later in Painesville, Ohio. None of the poems mentioned in this letter have been identified. In a letter to W. C. Howells, 1 May 1870 (MH), Howells expressed his reservations about Wyman's plans to write a biographical article based on information obtained from the Howells family: "I sympathize with his desire to make a readable article, but I wish he were not going to serve me up. However, I don't think you can avoid telling him the main facts of my Christian sufferings; but I wouldn't go into the personal anecdote business, and shouldn't make any disquisition on character.... At least five hundred men whose books I've mangled would be glad of the occasion that Mr. Wyman might thus give them to come back on me."

2. Jean Ingelow (1820–1897) was an English poet and novelist.
3. Josiah Gilbert Holland, *Bitter-Sweet: A Poem in Dramatic Form* (1858).
4. "Modern Italian Poets."

14 SEPTEMBER 1865, NEW YORK, TO ELINOR M. HOWELLS

New York, Sept. 14, 1865.

Dearest Sweety—

I walked down to the *Round Table* office, this morning, and found that my engagement had taken wings overnight and flown away. The publishers could only say that for the present they couldn't give me the place: that they must wait, and see how their paper succeeded. In the meantime they begged me to write for it, and they would pay me by the column; and gave me the book (one on Dante) which they proposed to have me review.[1] On inquiry, I find it is thought doubtful whether the R. T. will succeed, and as I don't care to go down with it, perhaps it's as well that my *engagement* was so brief.—I shall look round for another engagement, here.

As some slight compensation for this disappointment, I may tell you that I met our friend Hurd on the street, to-day, went with him while he lunched, and proposed my book on Venice, to him.[2] He figured the matter over, and accepted: didn't want to see the manuscript: knew it was good. I am sure father and Joe will be glad of this, for it relieves them of a slight risk which, I confess, I was always loath to put them to; and I have acted on father's advice in trying for a publisher here.—Hurd has given me a letter to Trübner & Co., and will forward the manuscript for me. I go to take tea with him to-morrow night. He made very cordial inquiries about you, and wants to look at *Disillusion*, with your illustrations. He gave me a manuscript to read and decide on, his reader being out of town.—It *looks* much as if I could get as much writing to do here, as I wanted; still I shall look for a place.

Question is: Shall I go to Washington, or not? I wish you would give me your opinion about this.

I've seen Henry Howells this afternoon, and found him extremely cordial. He wanted me to come to him at once, but I shall stay here a while yet. I like Gus's father exceedingly.[3]

I'm rather disappointed in not hearing from home to-day, but suppose letters will come moping along before a great while.

I don't know when to tell *you* to *come*. Perhaps to-morrow will decide something.

To-night I'm going to dine with Graham. I think he can be made useful to Larkin.[4] He inquired very particularly about him, and about you.

A. D. S. intends to return in about two weeks. I'm very comfortable, here, and enjoy things exceedingly.

Write me full, long letters. Be good to father and mother, and all.[5] My love to them. Poor baby! How I'd like to see her!

I hope you're well, my dear, and so good-bye.

Husband,
W. D. H.

1. "Dante as Philosopher, Patriot, and Poet," *Round Table*, 30 September 1865, is Howells' review of Vincenzo Botta's *Dante*.

2. Howells had met Melanchthon M. Hurd while crossing the Atlantic in July 1865. He was a partner in Hurd & Houghton, publisher of the American edition of *Venetian Life*. See *Literary Friends and Acquaintance*, HE, p. 89.

3. Augustus Dennis Shepard (1835–1913) had married Joanna Mead, sister of Elinor Howells. His father was Fitch Shepard (1802–1881), founder of the National Bank Note Company, a firm in which Augustus served before and after its merger with the American Bank Note Company in 1879.

4. James L. Graham, because of his reputation as an art connoisseur and his wide circle of friends in New York, might have been instrumental in the award of the commission for a Lincoln monument to Larkin G. Mead, Jr. See Howells' second letter to Elinor Howells, 19 September 1865, n. 2.

5. Elinor's family. W. C. Howells did not visit Brattleboro until late September or early October 1865.

15 SEPTEMBER 1865, NEW YORK, TO ELINOR M. HOWELLS

New York, September 15, 1865.

Sweetest:

I can only write you a short letter to-day, because I've been working on a review for the *Round Table*,[1] and must soon go down to take tea with Hurd. I left him *Disillusion* and proposed to him that he should publish that with the Pilot's Story, Louis Lebeau, and Clement, all in one volume, to be called Rhythmic Ballads.[2] He told me to leave the poems and he would see. I couldn't guess from his manner what he means to do.

Last night at Graham's I met Morphy, the famous chess-player:[3] he's a nice, quiet little man, just like me; and I told him I was glad to find him so good-looking, for Dr Holmes had said I looked like him. He made a pun or two, and kept quiet for the most part.—R. H. Stoddard was there, and the secretary of the Century Club, who gave me an invitation to drop in at the Club. I also have a card for the Atheneum. Mrs Graham wants us to come visit her, and I told her I would, as I always do. She offered us the whole third story, but I said we couldn't possibly use it all.

To-morrow I'm to go to the Custom House and try to get our goods through.

Henry[4] was very much pleased with the bronze and cameos.

Dearest love to all. Kisses for poor B.[5]

Yours
W. D. H.

I've no letter from you yet.

1. See Howells to Elinor Howells, 14 September 1865, n. 1.
2. Hurd & Houghton did not publish the proposed volume.
3. Paul Charles Morphy (1837–1884) was a champion chess player in the 1850s.
4. Henry C. Howells, Jr.
5. Howells' abbreviation for "poor Baby," that is, Winifred Howells. The adjective is evidently inspired by the fact that the child was suffering from whooping cough.

19 SEPTEMBER 1865, NEW YORK, TO ELINOR M. HOWELLS

New York, Sept. 19, 1865.

Dear Elinor:

I write this letter at the Colonel's office,[1] and at his desk, for he isn't in, just now. He returned to New York yesterday, and is not going out of town again.

The *Round Table* has taken *The Royal Portraits* for $20, and this morning I sold *Sweet Clover* to Harper's Mag. for $10. Harper's use neither *Petrarch*[2] nor *The Mulberries*, but I think I can work the former into *The Round T.*

Yesterday I saw John Swinton, and he thinks it not impossible that I should get a place on the Times. At any rate he will see Raymond about it next week.[3] Whether to go Washington, or not, in the interim, I don't know. It's dangerous and it's expensive: perhaps it would effect something, perhaps nothing. It is said Chief-Justice Chase is in town, and I shall try to see him.

This morning I received a letter from your father, who said John Mitchell told him that if the Columbus people could not buy the State Journal, they were going to start another paper, and offer me the charge of it.

I shall write to Secretary Smith concerning the matter.[4] It is well to keep a lookout in all directions.

My darling, you don't know how much I miss you, and our blessed little baby. I go to bed sick for you every night, and wake up forlorn in the morning: I think of you at all hours in the day. It's very good and patient of you to stay where you are; but you know I'm hurrying up everything I can to bring us together again.

Your father tells me to take time, here; that I'll have found a place long before they shall get tired of you and B.[5] at Brattleboro'.

Stoddard admires greatly my Italian translations of poetry. Everybody regards me here as having *scholarship*.

Swinton has asked me to write for the *Times*, and I could get work enough here to support myself very finely this winter. Love to all.

Dearest love, your love.
W. D. H.

1. Elliott Fitch Shepard (1833–1893), brother of Augustus D. Shepard, had been a colonel of volunteers in the Civil War. By profession a lawyer, he was founder of the New York Bar Association (1876) and publisher of the New York *Mail and Express* (1888–1893), and in 1868 married Margaret Louisa Vanderbilt, granddaughter of Cornelius Vanderbilt.
2. "A Pilgrimage to Petrarch's House at Arquà."
3. Henry J. Raymond (1820–1869), the editor of the New York *Times*.
4. William Henry Smith.
5. "B." was baby Winifred.

19 SEPTEMBER 1865, NEW YORK, TO ELINOR M. HOWELLS

Wednesday
New York, Sept. 19, 1865.

Sweetest D.

I should think you'd hate my letters, which you have to read, and which you always find empty. I'm lingering in New York now till next week, because Swinton thinks I may possibly get something to do on the Times, and I'm loath to leave any stone unturned. It's sickening business, however, it must be confessed, and as the empty days go by, I hardly know how to stand it.

This afternoon I called on Mr. Chase, who happened to be in town, and who said he thought I should have no trouble in getting another post, if I wished to affect an exchange.[1] He spoke in the highest terms of Mr. Fred. Seward's kindness and goodnature; so I think I shall certainly run down to Washington next Tuesday.

No letter has come from you to-day, and none came yesterday, and I'm doubly desolate. Why don't you write every day? When does father or Joe think of coming east?

I called again to-day at the Times office to see Swinton on Lark's account, but he wasn't there. I hope I can do something for L. in Washington.[2]

I think Hurd & Houghton will bring out my book of Rhythmic Ballads.³ Hurd seemed well-affected towards the enterprise to-day. To-morrow I shall try to nail him. The Round T. seems also inclined to take the Petrarch sketch.⁴

My dearest one, good-bye. Dear love to all, with kisses for our little girl. Think how much I love you both.

W. D. H.

1. According to his letter of 28 June 1865 to William Hunter, Howells had received permission for a four-months' leave of absence from his consulship, beginning on 3 July 1865. Consequently he had until 3 November 1865 to return to Venice, to arrange for an exchange of consular posts, or to find a different means of livelihood. He submitted his resignation in a letter to F. W. Seward, 13 October 1865 (DNA).

2. Evidently Howells was attempting to help Larkin G. Mead, Jr., obtain the commission for a monument to Abraham Lincoln. Mead was given the commission, and the monument was dedicated at Oak Ridge, near Springfield, Illinois, on 15 October 1874. In a letter to Howells of 3 August 1865 (MH), John Hay had acknowledged the receipt of photographs of Mead's design, and he enclosed a letter to Governor Richard J. Oglesby, head of the Springfield Monument Association.

3. See Howells to Elinor Howells, 15 September 1865, n. 2.

4. "A Pilgrimage to Petrarch's House at Arquà."

23 September 1865, New York, to Elinor M. Howells

79, 27th street,
Sept. 23d, 1865.

My dear good sweet wife—

I've been so busy and so good-humored since I arrived in N. Y., that I didn't know I'd had time to be gloomy, or to write gloomy letters. I've certainly no cause to be discouraged with what I've done: listen! I've sold The Royal Portraits and Sweet Clover *both* to Harper's Magazine, for $30.00
I've done work on the Round T., for   20.00
I've sold two articles to the Daily Times[1]   20.00
                                                                    $70.00

which I think is pretty good for ten days. I've got Hurd & Houghton to take my book, on Venice, and they will bring out my book of Rhythmic Ballads in the Spring, if there happens no unforeseen contingency to prevent it.² Everybody's very good and kind, and stretches out a cordial helping hand. On Tuesday Swinton and the managing editor of the Times³ are both going to make a grand rush on Mr Raymond to get me a place on the paper: to contribute three columns for $30.00 a week. If I *could* get such a place! I hardly dare think of it. Why I could average $50 a week the year round. I tell I don't leave a stone unturned, nor a wire unpulled. To-day I called on the editor of *The Nation*.⁴ He had read my articles in the North American Review,[5] and liked them: besides Mr. Chas. Norton had spoken of me to him. So he's asked me to contribute for him, and says he's no doubt he'll take a great deal of me.

There's no doubt of my being able to support myself here this winter.

If I get my engagement on the Times (Iddio lo voglia!)[6] I'll run up to kiss you at Brattleboro' next week.

I've written a letter to Annie to-day, which you may possibly see before leaving Jefferson.

I'll have the box sent right on to Brattleboro'.—My articles in the Times are Spanish Italian Amity (to-day, Saturday) and *The Jenkins of Tragedy* (tomorrow). I shall carry them another for Monday.[7] If I don't go up to Brat. next week I'll send yound the Round T. with articles marked.[8]

Yours sweetly, sweetly,
W. D. H.

I've seen Swinton about Larkin, who is in good hands.—Saw Williams, of the Post—go to lunch with him Monday.[9]

    1. Payment from the *Round Table* was probably for "Dante as Philosopher, Patriot, and Poet"; the two articles for the New York *Times* were "Spanish-Italian Amity" and "The Jenkins of Tragedy," *Times*, 23 and 24 September 1865, respectively.
    2. See Howells to Elinor Howells, 15 September 1865, n. 2.
    3. Since the *Times* had no formal editorial structure in 1865, the identity of the managing editor is uncertain. One possibility is George Jones (1811–1891), who founded the paper together with Henry J. Raymond and was its business manager (1856–1869).
    4. Edwin Lawrence Godkin (1831–1902) was editor of the *Nation* (1865–1881). Howells' reminiscence and evaluation of Godkin are most fully given in "A Great New York Journalist," *North American Review*, 3 May 1907.
    5. "Recent Italian Comedy" and "Italian Brigandage."
    6. Italian for "God grant it!"
    7. There appears to be no item by Howells in the *Times* for Monday, 25 September 1865; however, "Courtesy in Cars," *Times*, 27 September 1865, may be by him.
    8. No item in the *Round Table*, 30 September 1865, other than the Dante review has been identified as being by Howells.
    9. Both Walter F. Williams, a former war correspondent, and William F. Williams, a music and drama editor, were at this time associated with the New York *Evening Post*. See Allen Nevins, *The Evening Post: A Century of Journalism* (New York: Boni and Liveright, 1922; rpt. 1968), pp. 318, 421, 425–26.

18 OCTOBER 1865, NEW YORK, TO ELINOR M. HOWELLS

441 West 47th street,
October 18, 1865.

Dearest but untrustful darling—

Of course, I'm going to the Shepards', to see Mr Fuller; and you needn't be afraid of my disgracing you in *any way*. If you're half as good in Brattleboro as I am here, it's all you need ask.—As to the consulate, I cannot recommend Mr. Fuller after having recommended Mr. Piatt, without committing an absurdity.[1] I'm sorry, but the matter can't be helped now.

I've just received a charming and characteristic letter from Lowell, acknowledging the lobster, which he's given the place of honor in his study.[2] He expresses regret at not having seen me, and says: "I tried to find you in Boston, but in vain. I had hoped to have you and Mrs. Howells make us a little visit. But that shall come, one of these days." Then he desires to be remembered to you. He accepts, "Mantua,"[3] but doesn't know just when he shall use it, though he hopes to use it soon. He expresses his old confidence in me, but gives me much grave, good advice.[4] Is it not great to have such a friend? How much I honor and love that man! It would cut me to the heart, I think, if ever I lost his esteem.

I have written two short articles for the Times,[5] to-day, but otherwise have made light of things. I shall not be worth while till you are with me. I think I shall bring you down here to look about you a little, when I return from visiting Brattleboro', the next time. When shall you have the Mitchells to see you?[6] Better make it soon.

Glad to hear that the poor B is better.[7] Thanks for her dear little face. But with what a reproachful pathos Bettina looks out of the picture at the perfidious Signor, who goes back to Venice no more! Alas and alas!

Be a good sweet Piggy, and don't write short doubting letters.

Yours ever,
Will.

---

1. There is no record of Howells' recommendation for J. J. Piatt. Fuller has not been identified.
2. Howells had presented Lowell with a bronze lobster that concealed an ink pot and a sand box.
3. "Ducal Mantua."
4. Lowell's letter to Howells, 17 October 1865 (MH), written two days after Howells had submitted his resignation from his consular position, reads in part: "I wish you every success in your new career, & fling my old shoe after you for luck. I tremble for you, though—for I think a life of mere letters an unhappy one. But don't let it drag you down. Keep your ideal alive in your soul, a thing sacred & apart from all your drudgery & yet ennobling even that. Do not write in a hurry, for one thing *well* done is worth more in 'the end to a man's reputation' & therefore also to his pocket, than a thousand pretty-wells or even very-wells. Never write anything personal. People are small, but principles are great & enlarge by their Contact. But you will say my sermon is an impertinence. You do not go to my church. Very well. At any rate, I take a real interest in you, for I believe you have in you the chance to make something really fine. But you must study. After all, the really big fellows have known *ever* so much! I saw a little thing of yours the other day in the 'Saturday Press' ["Consolation," 17 October 1865] & I fear you have not yet washed yourself clear of sentimentalism into sentiment. The one seems to me the lees of

the other, which, in the first ferment of thought or feeling, pervade the whole & roil it. The real wine cannot be drawn off clear & fragrant till the emotion has had time to settle. Read Lessing & Göthe as a tonic. You see I respect you, for I speak frankly & treat you as a friend."

5. Only one article has been found to be probably by Howells: "Marriage Among the Italian Priesthood," New York *Times*, 19 October 1865. However, in the *Times* of the same date as this letter there appears Howells' "The Discomforts of New York and Their Remedies."

6. General and Mrs. John G. Mitchell.

7. Winifred Howells.

27 OCTOBER 1865, NEW YORK, TO ELINOR M. HOWELLS

441 West 47th street,
Friday, October 27, 1865.

Dearest girl—

Your letter hasn't come yet, to-day, though it is nearly four o'clock, but you've been so lovely in all the letters of the week, that I can forgive you, if I do not hear from you at all to-day.

We had a very charming dinner at Graham's yesterday, and I liked the company so well that I was loth to leave it and go to the theatre. Booth[1] has one of the most beautiful faces I ever saw: it is so finely cut, so sensitive and full of character. He is not much of a talker, but very simple and unaffected in what he has to say. It was a cruel wrong to his gentleness, and yet I had to think all the time when with him of his brother. Up in Graham's library, there were two plaster casts of hands lying on a shelf: one extended, and the other closed into a fist. Booth asked Graham, "Whose hand is that Lorry?" "Tennysons." "No, I mean the other one, the one shut." It was an inexpressible affliction to me when Graham had to answer, "Lincoln's." Booth did not speak a word of comment.[2]

The play at Wallack's was a new one, The Needful, but it was extremely stupid. If you're not down here by next week I'll send you the *Nation* containing my criticism on it.[3] To-day when I carried it to him, Mr. Godkin said, "How would you like to write exclusively for the *Nation*, and what will you take to do it?" I said fifty dollars a week, and he answered that he wanted time to think the matter over, and would let me know soon. I should prefer this sort of connection with the paper, but I don't care a great deal, for I foresee that if these journals live they will take my articles at my own prices. One thing I'm to do for the *Nation* at a fixed price however: give it a page each week of philosophized foreign gossip for $15, which is $5 more than usually paid. Both the N. and the Round T. are glad to get everything I can give them. Don't set your heart on my getting a regular engagement, or of course I shall not. "Just let things go on."

I *hope* you are coming down here next week. When I think of seeing you possibly on Monday, I'm almost crazy. Soon it's getting to be near a month since we were together. I left Brattleboro' the first of October. I only wish you were going to bring poor B.[4] along with you. Do you think she's really getting the better of her whooping-cough? Do you allow her to go up to Charley's yet?[5]—I've moved up into the rooms that we shall occupy if you come to board here. They're very cunning and pretty, and I think you'll like them.—I don't think you need be in any doubt on account of father's feelings toward you: he was only a little less in love with you than I. You may be sure, also, that he enjoyed his visit very well, and that he talks about it a great deal at home. But I think he can never be quite happy anywhere but at home.—*I* think it's rather hard on your mother, too, to be obliged to come down here on that interesting occasion.[6] But if she didn't she'd be still more wretched. When Llewellyn is born she need not come.[7] (Burn this!) Ma!—I must write a little on an article before leisure, and so, sweet love, with kisses for B.

Good-bye;
Your Hub.

1. Edwin T. Booth (1833–1893), the actor and brother of John Wilkes Booth (1838–1865), the assassin of President Lincoln.
2. For a slightly different version of the dinner at James L. Graham's, see *Literary Friends and Acquaintance*, HE, p. 93.
3. "The Drama, the New Play at Wallack's," *Nation*, 2 November 1865, a review of H. T. Craven's *The Needful*.
4. Winifred Howells.
5. Charles L. Mead (1833–1899) was Elinor's oldest brother.
6. The "interesting occasion" was the anticipated birth of Elinor Shepard, daughter of Joanna Mead Shepard. Howells reported to his father on 17 December 1865 (MH) that the child was born on 11 December.
7. This comment suggests the possibility that Elinor Howells was also expecting a child at this time, "Llewellyn" being Howells' name for the unborn child. However, their second child, John, was not born until 1868.

6 NOVEMBER 1865, NEW YORK, TO JAMES R. LOWELL

441 West 47th street,
New York., November 6, 1865.

Dear Sir:

I see you have conspired with my own conceit to spoil me,[1] and I confess that I am sometimes afraid you will get the better of me. I think no young cub of literature, while remotely conscious of not being at all licked into shape, was ever so near persuaded of a perfection of culture, as I was for a whole half hour after reading your last letter; and though I have since doubted whether I might not be touched here and there with improvement, I suspect that if my reveries could be turned inside out, they would be found full of secret self compliment as well as secret misgiving. Nevertheless, I have a great safeguard against the danger of praise, for though I am conceited, I am also despondent, and no elation lasts long with me. I found an antidote to your letter in the fact that I'm leading just the life here least calculated to contribute to literary refinement: I write for three or four periodicals, and am tempted to form new engagements. My salvation will be a place on *The Nation*, which I'm diligently striving for, and which, if won, will give me time for breathing: for study, and the repair of wasted tissue generally.

I hope you don't count me among the enemies of man who misconceive the purpose and value of the "Bigelow Papers"?[2] Out in Ohio and out in Venice we did not need to have morals driven like nails into our skulls, in order to be impressed with the gravity of a purpose that came to us laughing. I loved the parson always, but I never found Hosea other than a gentleman of unerring principles and highest sentiment—but you *know* all this much better that I can say it, and I half suspect you of laying a trap to catch me in a doubt concerning what is really refined and really vulgar in literature.

I'm going to send you a *Round Table*, this week, with a criticism of mine on Walt Whitman's new book,[3] which I hope you'll like: it's jerky and awkward, and maddeningly imperfect, and yet I think it contains here and there an idea; and at any rate it is a dash away from the style of New York reviews, of which the principle is to pinch lines out of books and examine and discuss them—as if one should try to judge a tapestry picture by a sample of the fabric.

I was not (alas!) present at the Fiesta di Dante,[4] and I should not know how to collect material for the kind of article you want, within any reasonable time. But I've been thinking that the poet Dall'Ongaro,[5] who knows the *Review*, and would be proud to write for it, could make a very charming paper, and one of great value.[6] If you like I will write, and ask him to do it, or if you prefer to write him directly, I will send you his address. Of course his article would be in Italian, and you would be at the trouble of having it translated. He could, however, be so instructed as to make a paper of suitable length and tenor, in which there would be compensation for the absence of American "standpoint," in the superior accuracy of information.

I am delighted to hear that you think of coming to New York, and count upon seeing you with a warmth of expectation which I am aware is absurd in one not of the emotional nations.

Very sincerely yours
W. D. Howells.

1. In his letter to Howells, 2 November 1865 (MH; printed in Norton, *Lowell Letters*, I, 350–52), Lowell praised both "A Day in Pompeii," *Nation*, 5 October 1865, and "A Visit to the Cimbri," *Nation*, 19 October 1865. He also commented at length on what he considered to be the major threats to American literature—"lawlessness & want of scholarly refinement" and "democracy misunderstood." The refinement so evident in Howells' writing, Lowell continued, was the necessary "prophylactic" for this dangerous situation.

2. In the same letter, Lowell's comments on "refinement" in literature contain the following remark: "Perhaps you will be inclined to send back a stone at the glass house of the 'Biglow Papers'—but 'twas for this very reason that I made a balance for Hosea in the pedantic parson."

3. "Drum Taps," *Round Table*, 11 November 1865.

4. Lowell had asked Howells to write an article on the Dante Festival for the *North American Review*.

5. Francesco Dall'Ongaro (1808–1873) was most noted for his political poetry. A letter to Howells from Mrs. Frances M. Jackson, dated Florence, 27 March 1865 (MH), advised him of Dall'Ongaro's pleasure in "Recent Italian Comedy." She also sent Howells the Italian poet's works and a note from him to Howells. Two letters from Dall'Ongaro to Howells are extant (MH).

6. Lowell did not follow Howells' suggestion.

17 NOVEMBER 1865, NEW YORK, TO ELINOR M. HOWELLS

441 West 47th St.,
November 17, 1865.

Dearest—

I've been disappointed, to-day, in not hearing from you, but I'm unwilling you should wait till Monday for a letter, and so I write now, without hearing from you. I'd send you some money, but there's always a risk of losing it in the mail, and I think you'd better borrow of your father. Say you ask for $20, for I'm afraid if you borrow only a little, he wont let me pay it back. I suppose you desposited the $100 you carried to B.[1] with you.

To-day Mr. Godkin engaged me to write for the *Nation* on a salary of $40 a week.[2] This leaves me free to write for all other papers except the Round T.; and does not include articles on Italian subjects, and poems, which will be paid for extra. Are you happy?

Trübner & Co., announce the publication of my book on Venice,[3] on their publishers' circular.

I can't write much, for I feel the *fagging* influence of the close, damp weather, and besides I'm unutterably desolate without you. When I think of the long weeks that are still to pass before we live together, I'm almost in despair, and get heartsick.

> With kisses for baby,
> Your true lover,
> W. D. H.

You needn't speak of my engagement outside your family.

1. Brattleboro.
2. For Howells' pleasant memories of his work on the *Nation*, see *Literary Friends and Acquaintance*, HE, p. 92.
3. *Venetian Life*.

22 DECEMBER 1865, NEW YORK, TO ELINOR M. HOWELLS

> 441 W. 47th str.,
> N. Y. Dec. 22, 1865.

Duck—

I must scribble you only a very hasty line, to keep you over Sunday. I've not time to say much, and there isn't much to say.—Your mother answers in regard to the balmoral, that she will look, but that she thinks it will not be well to buy anything now, for the holydays have made all sorts of goods so dear. After New Years there will be a fall in prices.

Last night I dined at Mr. Godkin's with Mr. Chas. Norton, of the North American Review, and had a magnificent talk with him about Italy, which he knows very well.[1] "Mantua" comes out in the N. American for January.[2] Mr. Norton is greatly pleased with it, and says he doesn't understand how I contrived to get at so much information on the subject. He also complimented the Thanksgiving verses.[3]

Of late, Ducky, I've become very homesick for Italy. Let's go back, as soon as we get money enough!

I'm counting the days till your coming. Your mother says it will be two weeks from Tuesday.

Good-bye, till next week, when I will write again.

Love to B.[4]

> W. D. H.

1. This was Howells' first meeting with Charles Eliot Norton (1827–1908), who was coeditor with Lowell of the *North American Review* (1864–1868) and had helped to found the *Nation* in 1865. Howells' fullest account of his long friendship with Norton appears in "Charles Eliot Norton: A Reminiscence," *North American Review*, December 1913.
2. "Ducal Mantua."
3. "Thanksgiving," in "Minor Topics," *Nation*, 7 December 1865.
4. Winifred Howells.

24 DECEMBER 1865, NEW YORK, TO WILLIAM C. HOWELLS

441 W. 47th st.
N. Y. Dec. 24, 1865.

Dear father—

I hope that dear Vic is quite well by this time, and I wish I could be there to see that she is. Give her my love, and tell her how tenderly I am concerned about her. I do not much believe in the power of anniversaries to conjure up old associations, but last night (which was properly Christmas eve,) as I walked down Broadway, I remembered all the Christmases of my childhood. There was a very happy one which fell in the year we lived at Columbus; and Vic will remember it by poor Johnny's drollery (he was scarcely more than a baby, then,) as we sat before the fire in the morning.—Father, you must tell the other girls that Elinor feels slighted by their not writing to her. She is afraid that she has offended them in some way.—Tell Joe, please, to take the $3 he owes me, (if he has not already sent it,) and buy Willie the nicest pair of skates he can get for that money in Jefferson, and let them be a New Years' gift from his uncle.—I am glad that you are getting the Nation, and I have spoken to have you put down on the exchange list of the Saturday Press, so you will receive that paper hereafter.—Young Mr. Coggeshall[1] picked up the Sentinel last night, and said it was one of the best country papers he had ever seen. I, too, think it excellent.—I will try to write to Dr. Smith and the Carters, but I assure you that from constant writing, my right-hand thumb is swollen to almost twice its natural size, and is very uncomfortable. It seems as if my work never ended, and then as to letters it is terrible.

I was invited to meet at Mr. Godkin's, for dinner, Mr. Charles Norton *de facto* editor of the North American Review, (though Mr. Lowell is nominally in charge,) and enjoyed his acquaintance thoroughly. He is very bright, and was full of compliments to me. My article on Mantua is to be in the January number;[2] and I think there will always be a warm corner for me in the review. Mr. Norton praised particularly the little poem in my Thanksgiving article. Indeed, I now feel that my literary fortune rests with myself, and that if I have a mind to do good things, they will always be recognized and appreciated. I want now to do some sketches of New York life, just in the spirit I should write of Italian life. Mr. Godkin said to me yesterday (as you have often said,) ("I think you have a remarkable talent for description."—The London publishers advertise my book on Venice[3] in the *Atheneum* as one of the works to be published "shortly," but I can't tell how soon that will be.—I called last Sunday at Charley Howells', but did not find him at home.

Henry Sr.,[4] told me the other day that Charley had received a splendid offer for his invention of the hair-pin.—I'm very glad of what you tell me about Mr. Garfield, and I hope you will remember me when you write, to him.—I received letters from Sam and Emma,[5] the other day, but have not answered them yet.—Mrs. Shepard and her baby continue to do remarkably well. I believe I told you that the little one is called after Elinor.—Mrs. Mead returns to Brattleboro' on Tuesday, and Elinor will come down two weeks from that day.—You may imagine I am impatient to have my own with me at last, and I don't wish ever to be parted from them for a day again.

Georgy[6] always sends love to you. With dear love to all,

Your affectionate son
Will.

1. Henry Coggeshall, probably the son of William T. Coggeshall. In later letters to his father, 29 November 1868 (MH) and 15 January 1872 (MH), Howells mentions both a visit by the younger Coggeshall and his marriage.
2. "Ducal Mantua."
3. *Venetian Life.*
4. Henry C. Howells, Sr., an uncle of W. D. Howells, was the father of Charles and Henry C. Howells, Jr.
5. Mr. and Mrs. Samuel Dean Howells.
6. Mrs. Henry C. Howells, Jr.

27 December 1865, New York, to Charles E. Norton

441 W. 47th street
New York, Dec. 27, 1865.

My dear Sir:

I shall best thank you for your beautiful little gift, by reading the book,[1] which came to my hand to-day. I am all the more desirous now to know something of Clough's poetry, since your memoir has interested me in his life. His seems a very pathetic fate to me: to die before the world had acknowledged the genius, which had been so cordially recognized by the gifted few. I hope to find that in his work which shall make me believe that fame will yet be his.

I send you my ballad (which I mentioned, when you were here,) about the Faithful of the Gonzaga, and by a superhuman effort refrain from sending the other poem (one in hexameters,) of which I spoke to you.[2] You will understand the greatness of my self-denial when I tell you that I think it will be long before you will see the poem published.

I am waiting anxiously to have a look at Mantua in print,[3] and in the meantime I have glanced inertly at my article on the late Italian poets.[4] If I could only "skip" Manzoni![5]

Pray make my compliments to Mrs. Norton, and believe me

> Very truly and gratefully yours,
> W. D. Howells.

C. E. Norton, Esqr.

1. The American edition of Arthur Hugh Clough's *Poems* (1862) contains a memoir of Clough by Norton.
2. "Disillusion."
3. "Ducal Mantua."
4. "Modern Italian Poets."
5. Alessandro Manzoni (1785–1873) was best known for his poem on the death of Napoleon, "Il Cinque maggio" (1821) and his novel *I Promessi sposi* (1825–1827). See Woodress, *Howells & Italy*, pp. 126–28.

III

The Early Atlantic *Years*

1 8 6 6 – 1 8 7 2

Introduction

HOWELLS returned to America after nearly four years in Europe determined to make his way in literature, even if such a goal involved a detour into journalism. Most of his younger literary acquaintances were in New York, and he thought that his best chances for making a start were there. For a time he sold articles to the New York *Times*, the *Round Table*, and the *Nation*, whose editor, E. L. Godkin, soon offered him a full-time position. This brief connection was amicably terminated when Howells accepted James T. Fields' offer of an assistant editorship with the *Atlantic*, starting on 1 March 1866, his twenty-ninth birthday.

Howells' responsibilities consisted of reading manuscripts, corresponding with authors, reading proof, and writing book reviews and notices. For this he was to receive fifty dollars per week plus additional pay for any contributions to the body of the magazine. By the end of the second year Ticknor and Fields, the magazine's publishers, raised Howells' salary, promised to reduce his proofreading burden, and expressed their hope that he would increase his literary contributions to the *Atlantic*. Encouraging as this development was, Howells found little time for the kind of writing he wanted to do. Between March and December 1868, for example, he published only two pieces, other than reviews, in the *Atlantic*—an article on Ulysses S. Grant and a story, "Tonelli's Marriage." He felt, with some justice, that he "worked almost ceaselessly," earning "just enough money to live on."

Although Howells gradually shifted some of the burden of book-reviewing to Thomas Wentworth Higginson and other contributors, his responsibilities continued to grow. During the absence of James T. Fields in the spring and summer of 1869 Howells had charge of the entire editorial operation, and his lengthy reports to Fields suggest the complexity of his task. For full measure, the publication of Harriet Beecher Stowe's attack on Byron precipitated a public reaction that rocked the acting editor's chair. Nonetheless, in 1869 and 1870 Howells found the time to contribute to the *Atlantic* a series of descriptions of people and scenes around Cambridge, which he later reworked for *Suburban Sketches*.

During these early years on the *Atlantic*, Howells also mined the materials he had accumulated in Italy. He published *Venetian Life*, *Italian Journeys*, and his poetic romance written in Venice, *No Love Lost*.

His reputation as an expert on modern Italian literature, based largely on his articles in the *North American Review* between 1864 and 1867, brought him an offer of a professorship at Union College. He declined it, but then succumbed to pressure from President Charles W. Eliot and James Russell Lowell to present a series of lectures at Harvard in the spring of 1870 and again the following year. Howells recognized, however, that he was not a gifted lecturer and that writing was his proper calling. He began treating American materials in the tone and manner that had proven successful in his books on Italy, and, using a simple travel narrative to order his observations of places, people, and manners, he wrote his first extended fiction in *Their Wedding Journey*. It was serialized in the *Atlantic*, beginning in July 1871, the month in which Howells succeeded Fields as editor.

Howells' genius for forming new friendships and maintaining old ones did not desert him even under the heavy burden of editing a magazine and establishing himself as a novelist. He corresponded with authors he had met in New York, such as E. C. Stedman, R. H. Stoddard, and Bayard Taylor. He kept up his connection with Charles Eliot Norton, developed his acquaintance with James Russell Lowell into a lasting friendship, and became better acquainted with Thomas Bailey Aldrich, who had recently moved to Boston. The mutually stimulating friendship of Howells and the younger Henry James dates from this period and is recorded in letters to his family and friends. Howells enthusiastically reported their walks and literary talks and announced each new story James submitted to the *Atlantic* as better than any he had yet done. Howells and his wife entertained and in a manner sponsored the Bret Hartes early in 1871 when the "westerner" made his triumphal journey to the literary worlds of Boston and New York. From his office at the *Atlantic* he corresponded with New England's established men of letters—Emerson, Holmes, and Longfellow—and with the younger contributors, for whom he had advice and encouragement. Among the latter were Sarah Orne Jewett, John Hay, Ralph Keeler, Hjalmar Hjorth Boyesen, Clarence King, and Samuel Clemens. Through this correspondence Howells learned the art of rejecting a piece of writing without impairing a personal friendship.

The ties with his family remained strong, and the weekly letters "home" to Jefferson recorded, with personal anecdotes, all aspects of his early Cambridge years. Besides the advancement of his career and his literary associations, he reported the moves from house to house, the births of John Mead in 1868 and Mildred in 1872, and the progress of all three children. Howells responded to the news he read in his father's Ashtabula *Sentinel* and sent tender, teasing, and cautionary messages to his brothers and sisters. The death of his mother in 1868 elicited a series of touching but rather morbid letters to his father, and in the winter of 1871–1872, while he and Elinor were pursuing a course of theological reading which they finally abandoned as "a little too exciting," he shared his theological speculations with his father. As Howells entered his thirty-sixth year his period of apprenticeship was ending, and his letters reflect the growing independence and self-confidence that gradual recognition as a man of letters had brought him.

J. K. R.

14 JANUARY 1866, NEW YORK, TO JAMES T. FIELDS

New York, January 14, 1866.

My dear Sir:

My engagement on The Nation is as permanent as anything in newspaper life, I suppose, but it is one that can be terminated at any moment either by the editor or myself.[1] The question is whether I can be of sufficient use to justify you in offering me something better than I now have in the way of place and pay. My income is about fifty-five dollars a week, and is nearly all from *The Nation*, for which I write reviews, and articles on such subjects as I like.

I should be glad to have you write, saying whether you could pay me the salary named, and stating more distinctly the duties you wish me to perform. I can then make an explicit answer.

I am gratified to have been first thought of for the vacancy on The Atlantic, and I beg to thank you for offering me the place.

Very truly yours
W. D. Howells.

J. T. Fields, Esqr.

1. Fields had written Howells on 11 January 1866 (MH): "I wished to ask you when I called at 'The Nation' office, as a vacancy was about to occur on 'The Atlantic' staff, if you cared to consider this situation (in connection with some other matters here) as one you would like to fill.... Perhaps you are permanently engaged at 'The Nation' bureau, and dont wish a Boston or Cambridge life; and it may be your present emolument is larger than I could offer you for the place to be filled in our establishment. Proof-reading for the A. M., correspondence, and reading Mss. belong to the situation. If you care to come East let me know, and tell me what salary will content you. I think I could promise you a not unpleasant lot hereabouts." (The A.l.s. at MH bears the dateline "Boston: Jan. 11. 1865.")

28 January 1866, New York, to William C. Howells

New York, Jan. 28, 1866.

Dear father:

I didn't write last Sunday, as usual, because I wanted to know something about the type, first; but on Wednesday I wrote enclosing proofs of the type, some letters of the type, and statement of price and quantity.[1] I dare say you will be suited with it.

As regards my going to Boston, nothing is decided, yet. Mr. Osgood,[2] of the firm of Ticknor and Fields was here last Sunday, and offered me the associate editorship at $40 a week. He said Mr Fields was going to Europe, in about a year, and that then the Atlantic would be left in my charge, and it was doubtful if F. would ever want to resume the charge of it. I made answer in general terms that I thought the pay too little, and that I wanted a positive assurance from Mr. Fields to the effect that when he left the *Atlantic*, it should be given to me, and not to any other. Mr. Osgood said he had no doubt I could make some such terms: that F. was very anxious to have me, and that he would write at once; but I have not yet heard from him. I suppose I shall hear in a day or two.

Cousin Henry[3] reached home Friday night, after an extremely rough passage. He was only in England, and did not go on the continent at all. He and his wife always send love to you.

Baby is perfectly recovered from her croup, and is in excellent health. She learns new tricks every day, and is a constant delight. Yesterday we took her to visit her aunt Joanna,[4] and she walked several squares, but I had to carry her at times, and she's a prodigious load. Just now her nurse Tilly (Slowboy,) is dressing her for a little promenade. I've put on her rubbers amid her lamentations of "O poor baby! poor baby!" I've to read Mamma Goosy to her every day after dinner, and I know every syllable in the blessed volume by heart.—Grandpapa Mead is coming down to New York to-morrow.

Elinor has gone to church with the Howellses, but will write a line when she comes back. Dear love to all.

                                               Your affectionate son,
                                               Will.

"Tilly Slowboy," as we call her, is a little German girl who lives in the neighborhood and comes in to take care of Baby, when we both, want to go out. Her real name is Matilda Hecker I believe. Baby's greatest achievement in talking is saying "tum in rags, tum in tags, tum in **velvet gown**". She is in splendid health again, and has cut three of her eye-teeth since she came to New York. Mr. Russell,[5] state agent of Ohio, called the other evening. He advises Will to go to Boston. I think it is very strange Will does not hear from Mr. Fields. He should have heard by Thursday. Until this matter is decided I cannot settle down to do anything, so I hope it will be determined soon whether we are to go or not.

Then we will write again

Love to all
Elinor

1. Howells' father had asked his son to buy some nonpareil font, and Howells, in his letter to his father of 7 January 1866 (MH), agreed to do so the following day. See also Howells to W. C. Howells, 8 February 1866.

2. James Ripley Osgood (1836–1892) was with Ticknor & Fields, first on the staff and later as a partner (1858–1868). Except for the time he worked for Harper & Brothers (1885–1890), he was a member of several publishing companies bearing his name. The Osgood-Howells correspondence, 195 letters in all (1861–1891), is located at MH. See *Literary Friends and Acquaintance*, HE, pp. 104–5.

3. Henry C. Howells, Jr.

4. Mrs. Joanna Mead Shepard.

5. Addison Peale Russell.

6 FEBRUARY 1866, NEW YORK, TO JAMES T. FIELDS

New York, Feb. 6, 1866.

My dear Sir:

I write to accept the place you have offered me,[1] and to say that I shall be ready to assume its duties on the 1st of March. These duties I understand to be: examination of mss. offered to the "Atlantic," correspondence with contributors, reading proof of the magazine after its revisal by the printers, and writing the critical notices of books; for which I am to receive fifty dollars a week, while anything I may contribute to the body of the magazine shall be paid for on such terms as we may agree upon.—If you will be kind enough, in your reply, to recapitulate these conditions, I suppose your letter will form all the agreement there need be between us.[2]

—Monday's ride home was given in equal halves to hard thinking and hard freezing, and I found myself quite resolved and rigid on my arrival in New York.

Pray present my regards to Mrs. Fields, and say to her that my first leisure shall be given to copying Dall'Ongaro's *Stornelli* (my translations,) and that I will then send them to her.[3]

Hoping to hear from you,

I am very truly yours,
W. D. Howells.

J. T. Fields, Esqr

1. In his letter of 29 January 1866 (MH), Fields had asked Howells to come to Boston to "talk over the matter" and to "see if your residence hereabouts can be managed." Howells went to Boston on 1 February and returned on 4 February.

2. A letter from Ticknor & Fields to Howells, 8 February 1866 (MH), gives in slightly greater detail the duties and conditions here stated by Howells.

3. Perhaps some of the translations Howells had made were among those later printed in his reviews of Francesco Dall'Ongaro's *Stornelli italiani; Fantasie drammatiche e liriche*; and *Poesie, North American Review*, January 1868. Annie Adams Fields (1834–1915), a poet in her own right, was famous for her literary *soirées*.

8 FEBRUARY 1866, NEW YORK, TO WILLIAM C. HOWELLS

New York, Feb. 8, 1866.

Dear father—

I've just finished up the type-business,[1] by paying for it to-day, and I enclose herewith the receipt of the Bible Society, and that of the Erie R. R., by which the type was shipped to you. I send you also the address of the superintendant of the B. S., who wishes me to tell you that he will be glad to supply you with any *sorts* he may have, and that you must write to him for them before applying elsewhere. I've been told by the printer of the Nation that the type was a bargain at 40 cents a pound. You will find the balance of money due you from the check for $100, enclosed in this letter.

I went on to Boston last Thursday, and concluded, on looking over the ground to accept Fields' offer. He gives me $2,500 a year for work that will not occupy my whole time, and my chances of succeeding him will fairer than anybody's else. But I do not care for the succession, much, my object in life being to write books, and not to edit magazines.[2] —The place at Boston will be permanent, and that will be its advantage over any thing in New York. I shall be the assistant editor of the Atlantic. I've written, since my return, to accept the place, and I suppose the affair is now concluded. I suppose we shall go on to Boston to live about the 20th of this month. The editor of the Nation[3] says that if I can find time to write the "Minor Topics," he will give me $20 a week for that alone. It seems as though my turn had come at last.

Tell Aurelia that neither of us has forgotten about her visit, and that if she doesn't make it in New York, she shall in New York.—We are all quite well, and Baby is beaming and blooming. She seems to be growing tall, and she learns to talk with amazing rapidity. We unite in dear love to all.

Your affectionate son,
Will.

I find that I cannot make change, and so do not send your balance.—There were no $2 in the letter in which you said you enclosed them.

1. See Howells to W. C. Howells, 28 January 1866, n. 1.
2. See, however, Howells' comment on the succession to the editorship in his letter to W. C. Howells, 28 January 1866.
3. E. L. Godkin.

20 FEBRUARY 1866, BOSTON, TO EDMUND C. STEDMAN

16 Beacon street,
Boston, February 20, 1866.

My dear Stedman:

I reached Boston yesterday evening, and have merrily spent the day in search of lodgings at Cambridge, with nothing at all for result. However, we shall see, to-morrow, and to-morrow, and to-morrow.[1]—And Shakespeare (it is Shakespeare?) brings one to Booth. Mr. Fields doesn't like the notion of the long minion note, and suggests that you add the note to the article,[2] in the body-type of the magazine. I think that so far as his own feeling is concerned, he does not care to have much biographical notice of Booth, though he thinks with you that B's wishes should be consulted. He spoke of the article on Keene (which you, also, mentioned to me,) as the sort of thing he would like to have done.[3]—I am not regularly in harness, yet; but Mr. F., knowing I would write to you, begged me to mention this matter to you.

Mr. Norton of the N. A. R.[4] helped me to-day about house-hunting, and was extremely kind. We spoke of you, and your proposed article, and I said as little to your prejudice as I could with any degree of honesty. On the street, we met Mr. Longfellow, whom I saw for the first time: such a looking poet as I should like to be (and couldn't, if I lived a thousand years) at his age: white locks, white beard, and autumnal bloom. At T. & F.'s I had a little chat with Aldrich, who is immensely contented with Boston.[5]

So far, my impression has been very pleasant, except that there seems little hope of finding shelter—and though we're visiting delightfully, one's friends cannot last forever.[6]

Remember me to the Taylors, Stoddards, Grahams, and both of us to all the Stedmans.[7]

Yours ever,
W. D. Howells.

1. Shakespeare, *Macbeth*, V, v, 19.
2. "Edwin Booth," *Atlantic*, May 1866.

3. No article by Stedman on either Edmund Kean (1787–1833), the famous English actor, or Laura Keene (1820–1873), whose company was performing at Ford's Theatre on the night of Lincoln's assassination, has been located.

4. C. E. Norton, editor of the *North American Review*.

5. Thomas Bailey Aldrich (1836–1907), formerly a member of the New York literary circle, had moved to Boston late in 1865 to become editor of *Every Saturday*, published by Ticknor & Fields. In 1881 he succeeded Howells as editor of the *Atlantic*. The Aldrich-Howells correspondence, covering the years 1878–1906, is located at MH. See *Literary Friends and Acquaintance*, HE, pp. 103–5.

6. The Howellses were staying in the home of the ophthalmologist Dr. Henry Clay Angell (1829–1911). Dr. Angell had established medical practice in Boston about 1856, and Howells met him in Venice. After leaving the Angells, Howells took an apartment for a short time on Bulfinch Street in Boston and then, with some financial assistance from Elinor's father, purchased a house at 41 Sacramento Street in Cambridge.

7. In a letter incompletely dated "Feb. 1866" (MH), Stedman expressed the sentiments of the New York literary circle obout Howells' departure: "we miss you already. While you resided here you gained a knowledge of the *perturbations* which obtain in our 'literary circle,' but all it's [*sic*] segments unite when your name is mentioned—for in the the [*sic*] mourning over your loss we are all agreed...."

24 May 1866, Boston, to Benjamin S. Parker

...The Atlantic Monthly,...
Boston, May 24th, 1866.

My dear Sir:[1]

I will serve you very willingly in any way I can, and shall be ready whenever you make definite application.—Any book house will undertake the publication of your poems, if you pay the expense; but otherwise I think you will find it hard to get a publisher. The best house in New York is that of Hurd and Houghton; in Boston, Ticknor and Fields. It is well to consider a little about printing a book of poetry—it hardly ever pays. You will do better to try to make a magazine reputation first. And my own experience in regard to the reception which the mss. of unknown authors receive from editors is that they are fairly and attentively considered everywhere. I know this to be the case in the *Atlantic* office, and the office of The Nation, N. Y. The Galaxy is a young N. Y. magazine to which you could also send with anticipation of proper attention.

Hoping that I have satisfactorily answered your questions, and that I may in some way be useful to you,

I am very sincerely yours,
W. D. Howells.

Benj. S. Parker, Esq.

1. Parker has not been identified, but this letter is a good example of Howells' response to inquiries by fledgling authors.

25 MAY 1866, CAMBRIDGE, TO CHARLES E. NORTON

Cambridge, May 25th *1866*.

Dear Mr. Norton:

We are safely housed here in Cottage Quiet,[1] and have commenced the long-deferred process of feeling at home, and of growing old. There is a fine sense of landed proprietorship about the present experiment which is as novel as it is agreeable, and which pleases me almost as much as the security and peace in which we live. I make the most of the sensation, for it is about the only one in the neighborhood. After the life which we have hitherto led in cities, this is singularly free from tumult. Everything is so tranquil about us that I find the agitation of a cow in the pasture across the street very stimulating, and am quite satisfied with it. This morning, however a large dog appeared at the corner of the fence. Presently two men walked up Oxford street, and I was greatly excited. A few minutes later a man drove by in a trotting-buggy: this appeared incredible.

Everything goes wonderfully well. The house is snugly furnished, but for a trifle of window-curtains, which we are not likely to need, since there is no probability that the sun will shine this summer. (The enterprise of the vegetation is very astonishing to me: in an atmosphere as cool and dark as that of a cellar, the grape-vines are already set with clusters; the trees are full of young pears, and the currant-bushes are bowed down with their detestable fruit.) Our girl Katy was born in the house of the gridiron under the sign of the spider: she is so good a cook; and all things about us are prosperously in keeping. We exclaim constantly over our happiness, which I am tempted to challenge as being of ghostly and unsubstantial event.

I meant to be at Mr. Longfellow's Wednesday evening, for the purpose not only of enjoying myself, but of reporting the affair to you. We inadvertently let Katy go into Boston, however, and then Elinor was afraid to stay alone in the house, and so I failed of my wish. But another time I shall not wrong myself, and I shall try to write you after next Wednesday.[2]

Mrs. Norton's very kind note came after we had engaged to take milk of an adjacent Irishman. Elinor begs me to thank her for mentioning Bernard, and for her trouble taken on our account with the tradesfolk.—Will you oblige me with the address of Mr. W. S. Bullard?[3] I do not remember whether, according to the receipt I gave you, the interest is to be paid quarterly or monthly, and should be glad to know.

Mrs. Howells wishes to be cordially remembered with me to all of you.

Very sincerely,
W. D. Howells.

Charles Eliot Norton, Esqr.

1. See Howells to E. C. Stedman, 20 February 1866, n. 6.
2. Howells' comment here and in later letters to Norton, 8 June and 14–15 June 1866, contradicts his later assertion that he first attended meetings of the Dante Club at Longfellow's in October 1866. See *Literary Friends and Acquaintance,* HE, p. 154.
3. William S. Bullard, Norton's brother-in-law, was a partner in the Boston firm of Bullard and Lee, East India merchants. He loaned Howells most of the money necessary for the purchase of the house at 41 Sacramento Street, Cambridge, which Norton had found and for which he endorsed a second mortgage.

27 MAY 1866, CAMBRIDGE, TO EDMUND C. STEDMAN

Cambridge, May 27th, 1866.

My dear Stedman:

Your letter after lying on my desk for two weeks—every day reproaching me with my neglect of it—is nowhere to be found, now that I wish to answer it. I should have written at once to you, but the appearance of "Spoken at Sea" in The Galaxy, relieved me of duty in the matter, and left writing a pleasure. I liked that poem, and I wish we had printed it instead of The Mountain; but I did not know that either of the poems were in Mr Fields' possession until both were in print.—I have lately seen two or three of your things that pleased me: Anonyma, for one, was artistically and effectively done.[1] I was amused to find it pitched into for immorality, for I thought it conveyed the gravest moral.

Piatt has written to me, refuting my criticism in the Atlantic.[2] I suppose such things are hard to bear, and he makes his defence in a manly way, but still he does not convince me. I have not replied to him yet; and my conscience is sore about a delightful and very friendly letter which Mrs. Stoddard wrote me just before she left New York.[3] I think if I knew how to spell the name of her sea-side post-office, I should venture to implore her forgiveness anyhow. Remember me to Stoddard.—Taylor has written me a charming note of praise for my review of "Kennett,"[4] and I'm greatly pleased to have pleased him.

Perhaps you will have noticed by the head of this letter that we have removed to Cambridge. In fact I've bought a house here, by the help of the best of friends,[5] and have settled down to the pursuit of happiness. If ever you turn your feet towards Boston, remember that you put up at this house—both you and Mrs Stedman. Isn't this on the way to Lake George? We expect to be here all summer—unless Mrs. Howells should go to Brattleboro' for a few weeks—and I shall take my vacation in the fall, when I intend to go to Ohio. I think I shall take New York *en route*, though I confess that I have not your curiosity to observe a pestilence.

You said something in your letter about future contributions to the *Atlantic*. Need you be told that all the prejudices here are in your favor?

—I thought I should write an article for every number of the magazine, but so far, what with furnishing our house, and anxiously prospecting in many ways, I have only furnished one short paper.[6]

—I'm very glad to hear of your improved health, and I hope you wont throw away any advantages you have gained in this way, upon newspaper work.

—Is Stoddard still on The Nation? What a pity you and he couldn't get the Round Table into your hands?

—Mrs Howells sends love to your wife, and I wish also to be remembered to her, and to those handsome boys.[7] Winifred has passed the last three weeks at Brattleboro', but we expect her to-morrow.

Very truly yours,
W. D. Howells.

Mr. E. C. Stedman.

1. Stedman's poems were published as follows: "Spoken at Sea," *Galaxy*, 15 May 1866; "The Mountain," *Atlantic*, June 1866; "Anonyma," *Round Table*, 14 April 1866.

2. Review of J. J. Piatt, *Poems in Sunshine and Firelight*, *Atlantic*, May 1866. Stedman's letter to Howells, 5 May 1866 (MH), to which Howells is here replying, commented on Piatt's reaction to the *Atlantic* review and his feelings about Howells: "He seemed to feel badly at hearing little from *you*. I wrote him, shewing how driven a practical writer, earning his living by his pen, always is, & hinting that in his dreamy literary life at The Treasury he could hardly understand it & assured him you & all of us remember him in inverse proportion to the length of our letters. Just then, *The Atlantic*, with a notice of his book, came in, & I triumphantly appended a P. S., ascribing it to your friendship &c. He writes me that Prof. Lowell did it, & seems to think you don't care much for him .... Write him when you can, & write soothingly." Whitelaw Reid (b. 1837), formerly a journalist writing for the Cincinnati *Gazette* and as of 1872 editor of the New York *Tribune*, wrote Howells on 7 June 1866 (MH), giving further details about Piatt's attitude toward Howells: "Did I tell you that Piatt seemed very much exercised about your review? Comly has reproduced it in the O. S. Journal, attributing it, with many soft phrases, deprecatory of its severity, to James Russell Lowell. In the most innocent way in the world, I mentioned to Piatt that you had inquired after him, & had casually spoken of having reviewed his volume in the Atlantic. He seemed greatly surprised, came to see me the next day about it, & professed special astonishment that *you* shouldn't be able to understand him, or that, being unable, you should say so."

3. Mrs. Elizabeth D. B. Stoddard, in her letter of 25 March 1866 (MH), had invited Howells and his family to her big house at Mattapoisett, Massachusetts.

4. Review of Bayard Taylor, *The Story of Kennett*, *Atlantic*, June 1866.

5. See Howells to Norton, 25 May 1866, n. 3.

6. "Question of Monuments," *Atlantic*, May 1866.

7. Arthur and Frederick Stedman.

8 JUNE 1866, CAMBRIDGE, TO CHARLES E. NORTON

Cambridge, June 8, 1866.

Dear Mr Norton:

I get all my letters and papers through Ticknor and Fields, and I did not think to inquire at the Cambridge postoffice till your note had been there several days. In the meantime I was very much embittered against you, and forgot all the kindnesses you had ever done me, in the thought of the sole neglect,—which after all, you had not been guilty of. I shall be very glad to write the notice of which you speak:[1] shall I, after writing it, send it to you, or give it directly to the printers, and let you do what you like with it in the proofs? Do not forget that you have promised me a place in the October number for my article on Italian poetry.[2] I am working on it now and shall have it ready. I fancy it will be livelier than you would think the subject could allow: I have in the first place the character of Vincenzo Monti,[3] one of the greatest rogues and swindlers that ever existed in life or letters.

I was at Mr. Longfellow's this week and last. There was a full session last week, but of the memorabilia I can recall only two or three things—per esempio: Lowell's asking Mr Longfellow, out of his regret that the suppers were coming to an end, whether there was not an Indian epic in an hundred thousand lines which he was going to translate next. The talk was not at all general, each supperer chatting with his next neighbor, until we came to the subject of lonely walks home by night when Lowell told of a man's jumping over a fence, and alighting directly in front of him, whereupon he tried "to look as if he had always been in the habit of having men jump down in front of him as he was walking home at night."—This week Dr Holmes was present, and he and Mr. Appleton[4] talked spiritualism somewhat. The latter told of going to Frascati's gaming-place in Paris when he was young. "But it was horribly dull, and I shouldn't have had any comment if it had not been for Sam Ward's[5] borrowing a guinea of me." Mr. Dana[6] was also present, and told traveller's stories—mighty well, too.—The cantos were wonderfully translated—perhaps Mr. Longfellow sends you a proof? Week before this we had the 31st canto, and the translation from

"Senza risponder gli occhi su levai,"

to

"Poi si tornò all'eterna fontana"[7]

was incomparably good.—Mr. Lowell has Cranch the painter staying with him,[8] and last Saturday I was invited to meet him at dinner. Mr

Forceythe Willson[9] was also invited, and I made his acquaintance.—I set the trap of my poem[10] for Mr. Fields, and temptingly baited it with your praise and Mr. Lowell's, but Mr Fields after nibbling cautiously about it, refused to go in. I must say that the affair was managed beautifully on both sides, and I hardly know which to admire more: myself or Fields. I'm so well satisfied with my own skill in the matter that I can scarcely persuade myself that I failed of success.—Last night Mrs. Howells and I took tea at Professor Child's,[11] greatly enjoying ourselves.

The deed for the house has come from Florida, and though there is an informality in it—or rather in the acknowledgment of it before the Notary, who failed to date the acknowledgment, I am advised by my lawyer, to take it. To-day, I expect to pay over the money. The deed will be recorded, sent to Florida for fresh acknowledgment, and then recorded again.

Mrs. Howells joins in expression of cordial regard for you all. Baby also wishes to be remembered.

Very sincerely yours,
W. D. Howells.

C. E. Norton, Esq.

1. See Howells to Norton, 14–15 June 1866, n. 1.
2. "Modern Italian Poets."
3. Vincenzo Monti (1754–1828) was an Italian poet and dramatist.
4. Thomas Gold Appleton (1812–1884), author and patron of the arts, was Longfellow's brother-in-law.
5. Samuel Ward (1814–1884), entrepreneur, gourmet, and occasional poet, was a close friend of Longfellow's.
6. Richard Henry Dana, Jr. (1815–1882), author of *Two Years Before the Mast* (1840), was the husband of Longfellow's niece.
7. From "Without reply I lifted up mine eyes" to "Then unto the eternal fountain turned." See *The Divine Comedy of Dante Alighieri*, translated by H. W. Longfellow, *Paradiso*, XXXI, 70, 93.
8. Christopher Pearse Cranch (1813–1892) was a painter, critic, and poet.
9. Howells later remembered that he met Forceythe Willson (1837–1867), a poet, at Longfellow's rather than Lowell's. See *Literary Friends and Acquaintance*, HE, pp. 234–35.
10. Perhaps the poem was "Forlorn," although Howells later remembered that it had been offered to the *Atlantic* before his departure for Venice. See *Literary Friends and Acquaintance*, HE, p. 75.
11. Francis James Child (1825–1896), on the faculty at Harvard (1851–1896), was one of Howells' closest friends in Cambridge. See *Literary Friends and Acquaintance*, HE, pp. 211–15.

14 AND 15 JUNE 1866, CAMBRIDGE, TO CHARLES E. NORTON

Cambridge, June 14, 1866.

Dear Mr. Norton:

I've written you a notice of "Fifteen Days" which I hope will find all the favor with you that it fails to find with me.[1] There was more than the natural difficulty in the case, for I had already written a notice of the book for The Atlantic, and I had some trouble in effacing a family resemblance between the two criticisms, and even now I think their sisterhood might be detected. I hope you will be quite pitiless to the younger if you do not like her looks in print.

Last night we had the last canto of the Paradiso, and a most famous season at table afterwards. We had Mr. Green[2] again, and Mr Forceythe Willson, and Dr. Holmes stayed till half-past eleven. The talk was desultory and delightful, and the supperers sat till two o'clock this morning. Mr. Lowell said so many good things one on top of the other, that I became a mere palimpsest in the attempt to store them all way, and the record must be deciphered with more patience than I have at present.—I try to think at what a great event I have assisted; but even the sense of that escapes me. Yet I feel that Longfellow's Dante is the first book of really translated poetry, to which all former versions are but transformations more or less Bottomnal.[3] I think of my wretched übersetzungen from the moderns and take a private dose of humiliation and despair.—By the way, I am amused at the part I have borne in all these sessions. At Venice, the first year, I was so utterly worthless that I used to regard writing a letter or reading a comedy, or transcribing a dispatch, as something extraordinarily noble and virtuous. So also at Mr. Longfellow's, by dint of long sitting silent with Dante in my hand and of never opening my head at table except to put something into it, I came at last to regard giving the reading in my edition, as a very great personal merit, and helping the cheese at supper as something that could not have been without me.

"Venetian Life" has appeared in London, and has been much more civilly received than I could have hoped. The Review, Examiner, and Atheneum[4] have all noticed it. Possibly as there is now some political interest felt in Venice the English edition may sell. The book will be published here in about two weeks, and then I will send you a copy. You and Mr. Lowell have both kindly offered to notice it in The N. American—could you not divide your forces, so as to take possession of The Nation also?[5] By dint of cancelling and reprinting *eighty* of the worst pages of the book, it will be brought out here almost free of errors—but the correction absorbs all the profit I should have received from it.[6] Though I don't care for this. Very few things are worth as much as they cost, I find, and books are an ungrateful generation. I do not complain of literature in general, for the little I've produced has won me your acquaintance, and I'm disposed to think your friendship a compensation for all I have suffered in the cause of letters—if it *is* a cause, and if I *have* suffered, which I doubt, seeing so many reasons why I should consider myself a man blest beyond his deserts. But this blessed book (in the sense of Ah! libro maledetto![7]) has caused me much more woe than I should like to sing, and I think hereafter I will stick to publication in such periodicals as will admit me.—The notices in the Atlantic for July will be all-but idiotic,—excepting Mr. James's review of Ecce Homo—and I wrote three of them.[8]

Very sincerely yours
W. D. H.

Later.

June 15. Dear Mr. Norton:

I've thought of the notice of "Fifteen Days" rather more seriously than I wrote last night, and it seems best to send you the book after all. Mr. Bigelow[9] says he can get in a notice any time within a week; and I do not feel at all right about the one I've made. "Fifteen Days" is a very earnest book, and I fear that the author, whose motive I honor so highly, would be justly mortified if ever it came to her knowledge that the same person had written both the Atlantic and the N. A. notice. I should not like it myself, were I in her place.—Of course I was very stupid not to have thought of this when you first asked me to write the notice, but then I thought only of doing you a pleasure, and it was only last night, when Elinor put the case ad hominemly that I saw the absurdity of it. I hope you'll forgive my awkwardness in all this. I send my notice herewith, hoping it may facilitate you as notes to your reading of the book.

W. D. H.

I send a copy of Fifteen Days by this mail.

1. In spite of the misgivings expressed in the 15 June part of this letter, it seems certain that Howells wrote reviews of Mary Lowell Putnam's *Fifteen Days: An Extract from Edward Colvil's Journal* for both the *North American Review*, October 1866, and the *Atlantic*, July 1866.

2. George Washington Greene (1811–1883) was an author and old friend of Longfellow's. See *Literary Friends and Acquaintance*, HE, p. 163.

3. An allusion to Nick Bottom, in Shakespeare's *A Midsummer Night's Dream*.

4. Reviews of *Venetian Life* appeared in the *London Review of Politics, Society, Literature, Art, and Science*, 26 May 1866; the London *Examiner*, 26 May 1866; the London *Athenaeum*, 2 June 1866; and the London *Review*, July 1866.

5. Norton did review *Venetian Life* in the *Nation*, 6 September 1866. Lowell's review appeared in the *North American Review*, October 1866.

6. Howells' indignation over Trübner & Co.'s failure to submit proof to him and the poor printing of the book is expressed in two letters to M. M. Hurd, 19 February (the first of two of this date) and 22 February 1866 (MH). Howells suggested that Hurd not accept the sheets for the five hundred copies of the American edition, that the poorly printed English sheets be destroyed, and that an order to Trübner & Co. for one thousand instead of five hundred copies for the American edition be made conditional upon destruction of all sheets printed. Howells also expressed his willingness to relinquish all claims on Trübner & Co. for compensation if the firm would reprint the book with his corrections; but none of his proposals was accepted.

7. Italian for "Ah! cursed book."

8. Henry James, Sr., reviewed J. R. Seeley, *Ecce Homo*. Howells later remembered the older James (1811–1882) as "one of the vividest personalities in my recollection." See *Literary Friends and Acquaintance*, HE, pp. 223–26. The two reviews by Howells in the July *Atlantic* are of J. L. Porter, *The Giant Cities of Bashan; and Syria's Holy Places* and of G. P. Fisher, *Life of Benjamin Silliman*.

9. Marshall Train Bigelow (1822–1902) was part owner of the University Press, which printed both the *Atlantic* and the *North American Review* for Ticknor & Fields.

17 JUNE 1866, CAMBRIDGE, TO VICTORIA M. HOWELLS

Cambridge, June 17, 1866.

Dear Sister:

It is a long time since I wrote to you but not since I thought of you, and you must try to let my long thoughts count for long letters. I write from six to eight letters a day—letters which I have no interest in writing, too—besides reviews and articles; and I am either making or reading manuscript all the time.

Dear Vic, I wish you could step into our quiet little home this pleasant Sunday morning, and be out of the old circle of your cares a while. We grow more and more in love with our house every day, and as the summer advances, it grows prettier and friendlier. The two pines on either side of the gate have put on a vivider green than they wore all winter long, and within a day or two the sweet-briar over our door has all burst into blossom. As to blackberries and grapes and pears, it's wonderful to see how they flourish.—Baby has the range of everything, and she's out doors from breakfast time till dark—Elinor and I taking her for a long walk the last thing. There's a small boy next door, who is her partner in the mud-pastry line; and except for the unhappiness that comes from over-enjoyment, I think she is perfectly contented in "papa's house."

For papa himself he suffers also a little from the same trouble that afflicts baby. My book has been noticed in the London Atheneum more favorably than unfavorably—it was my fear that it would be cut up, there—and all the English critics have treated it very kindly.[1]—The other night at Mr. Longfellow's, Mr. Lowell declared to the whole company, "It is the best book ever written about Italy." But that was only what he had said before in his letters to me.—We've had the last of the Dante readings. On Wednesday night Mr. Longfellow finished the final canto, and we honored the close by sitting at supper till two o'clock in the morning.

I'm thinking now about commencing a romance[2]—the scene of it to be laid in Italy, or Venice, rather—but I have ever so much work begun which I must finish first.—I do no more writing for The Atlantic than I can help—that is, I merely write the critical notices,—and try to reserve myself for more extended efforts. But my regular day's work on the magazine is by no means a light task, and it is hard for me to find time for other writing.

I hope you are well, dear Vic, and that Henry does not grow more troublesome. When I consider your task and mine, you may be sure that I do not think mine the heavier or nobler.

—I'm thinking constantly of my visit home in the fall, and of the pleasure of bringing mother back with me. You must not let her get the notion that she cannot come. Dear love to all. Elinor is at church, or she would join me in this message. Tell Aurelia that I miss her ever so much.

Your aff'te brother
Will.

1. See Howells to Norton, 14–15 June 1866, n. 4.
2. Mildred Howells identifies the romance as *A Foregone Conclusion*. See *Life in Letters*, I, 111.

19 JUNE 1866, CAMBRIDGE, TO MARY D. HOWELLS

Dear Mother[1]—
I was delighted with your criticism, for it showed a deeper interest in my literary success than I had before thought you felt. But I laughed at it all the same, for it was quite mistaken. I have from five to seven pages in every number of the Atlantic, for I write nearly all the literary notices. I know that we have flat stories in occasionally, but as to supplying their place with something of my own, why I've nothing written, and poetry will *not* be pumped nor will such prose as I choose to publish over my name. I'm not less ambitious for myself than you are, but I'm very busy with my regular work, and I find that I get fame quite as fast as I know what to do with it.—Here you on one hand are urging me forward, while Mrs. Mead on the other is holding me back. That poor old lady suffers terribly from the publicity into which her distinguished son[2] and son-in-law have brought her, and longs for a little seclusion.—When I go to

Ohio, I'll tell you all about my doings and duties here, and I've no doubt you'll be perfectly satisfied.

Tell father I'll try to see his engine-men to-morrow. In the meantime, I'm very sorry for him, and hope he wont let himself be made sick by his machine, or even the loss of its whole value. Dear love to all.

Your affectionate son
Will.

1. This letter bears no date. The date assigned is inferred from the contents of the final paragraph and a letter from Howells to his father, dated 20 June 1866 (MH), in which he says: "I called at Butterfield and Haven's this morning, and was told that they had already written you about the engine."

2. Larkin G. Mead, Jr., had found public recognition as a sculptor. See Howells to Elinor M. Howells, 19 September 1865 (second letter of that date), n. 2.

23 JUNE 1866, CAMBRIDGE, TO CHARLES E. NORTON

Cambridge, June 23d, 1866.

Dear friend:

Elinor said on hearing of your new happiness: "Well, there can't be too many Nortons in this world," which expresses all I could more elaborately say in congratulation.[1] I believe we sympathize perfectly with you and the little one's mother, for though Baby frequently reminds us of erring humanity, there is so much also of angelic beauty in her spirit, that we feel awed to think how great a treasure has been given into our keeping. Yes, I think we have much to learn of children, for they can still remember something of the primal innocence of the race, while we poor grown people have only a dreary recollection of apples and fig-leaves and exile.—For my part I am often ashamed when I come to correct Baby for her pretty faults, reflecting how much better she could correct me, if she would give her mind to it.—Da mi daga un baso alla piccinina, as they say in Venice,[2] and tell Mrs. Norton how cordially glad we are for her as a mother and a convalescent.—Alas! you will never see our baby in her glory! Yesterday we had her hair cut, and she has come out of the barber's hands as unpoetical as Mr. Casby.[3] From being more or less seraphic in appearance, she is now strongly suggestive of the spring-fishes, and has a slight dash of Fenia in her general effect.[4]

Since I wrote you, Mr. Lowell has called upon us, and we have also had the honor of a call from Mr. Longfellow, with whom came Mr. Greene. So we feel more than ever of Cambridge. Although I am not sure that I should like to be buried at Mt. Auburn, I am almost willing to spend my days here, and I continually rise superior to a wish that haunts me when the Atlantic proof is particularly bad—to disappear by night, and come up somewhere west of the Mississippi with a false name— though my own is concealment enough, for the present. The impulse of wandering does not die out at once, and we occasionally go into the room appropriated to our trunks, and view them with much the same feeling that I suppose the first dwellers in cities used to regard their folded tents.

Class-day came and went with its dust and clamor, on Friday. We were on the grounds to see—or rather imagine, for we had little chance to see—the dance round the elm, and the strife for the wreath. It was very funny, and amused me more than even the doleful moaning of the Glee-Club which supposed itself to be singing, in the evening.—We had tea and talk—both very pleasantly flavored—at the Misses Ashburners'.[5]

With regards of Mrs. Howells and myself to all of you,

Very sincerely yours,
W. D. Howells.

Chas. Eliot Norton, Esqre.

1. Elizabeth Gaskell Norton, the third child of the Nortons, had recently been born.
2. Venetian dialect for "Give a kiss for me to the tiny little one."
3. Christopher Casby is a character in Dickens, *Little Dorrit* (1857).
4. "Fenians" was the name of an association of Irish nationalists and revolutionaries in New York and Ireland, founded in 1858.
5. Grace (1814–1893) and Anne Ashburner (1807–1894) were maternal aunts of Mrs. Susan Sedgwick Norton (1838–1872), C. E. Norton's wife.

8 JULY 1866, CAMBRIDGE, TO JAMES M. COMLY

Cambridge, July 8, 1866.

My dear Comly:

I have received the papers you sent me, and agree with you in some of your strictures on The Atlantic, though I think "George Dedlow" an ingenious and well-written paper, and Longfellow's Dante sonnet exceedingly fine.[1] As far as I am concerned in making up the magazine, I usually say my say in the critical notices, and exercise a jealous care in regard to such contributions as come first into my hands. For the rest, I remember that Dr. Smith once said to me, when I was about to die of one of my fatal disorders, "You mustn't expect an entire physical change in twenty-four hours."

Don't think I sent you the London Review's notice of my book in order to "bone" a notice out of you.[2] I merely hoped that you would like to read an English criticism of me, which was rather friendly than otherwise. I have seen generally the flattering allusions the Journal has made to me, and I may confess that they have given me great pleasure, because I valued both your friendship and your judgment.—Venetian Life is ready to publish here, and it now depends upon Messrs. Hurd & Houghton when it shall appear. I will send you an advance copy.

About the middle of September I'm going to my father's in Jefferson, and then I expect to visit Columbus, if only for a day or two. Last year, in the uncertainty I felt about the future, I had no heart to go anywhere, but since prospects have brightened, I find myself homesick for the west, and particularly for Columbus.—I see the Journal frequently, and think it lively. After "cruel Barbara" and the immense Coggeshall,[3] you must be an astonisher to old subscribers. It seems to me that your news-column is the best in the country, and I like your literary criticisms, and am glad the Journal is first in that department in the west.

Mrs. Howells joins me regards to Mrs. Lizzie.[4] Remember us kindly to all the Doctor's family, and believe me

Yours,
W. D. H.

1. In the *Atlantic*, July 1866, appeared Longfellow's "On Translating the Divina Commedia: Second Sonnet" and S. Weir Mitchell's "The Case of George Dedlow."
2. A review of *Venetian Life* appeared in the Columbus *Morning Journal* (formerly the *Ohio State Journal*), 8 July 1866.
3. "Cruel Barbara" was Dr. Isaac J. Allen who, with F. W. Hurtt, took control of the *Ohio State Journal* in 1861. William T. Coggeshall edited the paper in 1865.
4. Comly's wife, Elizabeth Smith Comly, was the daughter of Dr. Samuel M. Smith.

13 AUGUST 1866, CAMBRIDGE, TO MELANCHTHON M. HURD

Cambridge, August 13, 1866.

My dear Mr. Hurd:

I received the package of books on Wednesday, and your letter concerning the day of publication at the same time. The latter I answered at once, accepting your suggestion of the 24th ult.[1] Of course I shall not give away any of the copies I have, without stating when the book is to appear.

I suppose you have the list of papers which we made out together as best deserving copies of this great work. I shall send it to Mr. Lowell, who says he will notice it in the next *N. American Review*, and to Mr. Norton, who, I think, will review it in the *Nation*, though of course I cannot state my expectation to him. I will give a copy to Rev. W. R. Alger for the *Christian Examiner*, and to Mr. Justin Winsor, here, for the *Round Table*. I will also hand a copy to the *Advertiser* folks.[2] All the gentlemen named have themselves offered to notice the book, or I should not place it in their hands for review. In fact, I'm willing—so far as I'm concerned—that the book, should appear as friendlessly here as in England, where I have reason to be pleased with its reception. Do you wish to make use of the English notices in advertising? Let me suggest that the notice of the *Westminster Review*, for July—about half a page in the *Current Literature*[3]—puts in a nutshell all of British opinion you need use.—First and last, the book has received a good deal of praise, but I assure you that no applause has gratified me more than your own, for I think you have always been rather skeptical concerning it.[4] Mr. Fields is equally pleased with it—and if publishers really know as much as they pretend about public taste, the favorable opinion of two publishers should give us some hopes of success with "the general reader." As to a second edition, of which you spoke, that is a matter quite in your own hands, and I suppose you can determine about it very shortly after publishing this edition. I shall not begin correcting a copy till you know, for I'm fearfully busy.—I wish you to send an advance copy to my friend, Col. J. M. Comly, of the *State Journal*, Columbus, Ohio, so that he will have it as soon as the Eastern papers; and I don't think it would be a wise economy to stint the press of copies anywhere.—Please send the book, for me, as soon as published, to Bayard Taylor, Stedman, Stoddard, and J. Lorrimer Graham, Jr., N. Y.

Mrs. Howells joins me in sending regards to all your family.

Very sincerely yours,
W. D. Howells.

To what bookseller in Boston will you send the book?

1. Since Howells is here referring not to a previous letter by Hurd but to Hurd's suggestion that *Venetian Life* come out on 24 August 1866, the original transcriber of the letter (the holograph has not been located) probably erred in writing "ult." rather than "inst." It is, of course, possible that the error is Howells'.

2. The following reviews of *Venetian Life* have been identified: Lowell's in the *North American Review*, October 1866; Norton's in the *Nation*, 6 September 1866; and Winsor's in the *Round Table*, 8 September 1866. William Rounseville Alger (1822–1905) was a Unitarian clergyman and author. Justin Winsor (1831–1897) was an author and librarian at the Boston Public Library (1868–1877) and at Harvard University (1877–1897).

3. A brief notice appeared in "Current Literature," *Westminster Review*, July 1866.

4. Hurd had written Howells on 5 July 1866 (MH): "I took a copy of your Venetian Life with me which I had bound for the occasion and am now reading it. I cannot refrain from expressing my delight at its freshness, originality and humor. I am constantly coming across quiet bits of humor which are really refreshing and I believe that you have the materials (in portfolio and brain) for a first class novel or poem. I think that the book will take well and if so we must have it stereotyped and corrections or alterations should be considered at once. It seems to me it ought to remain a classic as surely as Geo[.] S. Hillard's Italy [*Six Months in Italy* (1853)] but perhaps I am too enthusiastic after a first reading."

3 SEPTEMBER 1866, BOSTON, TO EDMUND C. STEDMAN

...*The Atlantic Monthly,*...
Boston, Sept. 3, 1866.

My dear Stedman:

I write rather to thank you for your review[1] than to answer your letter. The notice was extremely kind and good: the character of the book was fairly presented, and some exceptions to the style and manner were well taken—especially that constant recurrence of "I think" and "it seems to me," etc. I ought to say in defense of this and of the typographical errors which you must have observed, that I had no chance to revise in proofs, at all. The book was hideously misprinted, averaging one error to every page. On the remonstrance of Mr. Hurd, Trübner caused 24 cancel pages to be printed in England, and after the arrival of the sheets here, I had 56 more printed at a cost which bids fair to devour all the profits I should have from the work. Of glory, I think I shall have something. So far the book has met nothing but praise—especially from the London press by which it has been most cordially noticed.

Concerning the R. Table review:[2] Mr. Winsor asked me for the book nearly two months ago; and I did not have you in mind except as one of the friends whose private good opinion was very dear to me. I felt that if I sent you the sheets much in advance of publication, I might seem to be asking public notice of you, and I didn't like to do it.

Bayard Taylor has written me a letter—full of that sweetness which belongs to him and you,[3] and which makes my own temper seem to me a very sour and ungenerous one.

—I told Hurd to send Lorrimer Graham a copy of V. L., and I suppose he has done so, though I have not heard from Graham.

Mrs. Stoddard wrote me from Mattipoisett, the other day, in reply to a letter I sent her.[4] She seems to be getting on with her novel—of which I confess I have much hope—and to be very well and contented.—Please to remember me to Stoddard when you see him.

Mrs. Elinor sends love to Mrs. Laura, and I am

Your obliged and faithful
W. D. Howells.

You'll believe that I'm sorry to hear of any trouble of yours. I hope it is not your health?

1. Stedman's review of *Venetian Life* has not been identified.
2. For the *Round Table* review, see Howells to Hurd, 13 August 1866, n. 2.
3. Taylor's letter to Howells, 26 August 1866 (MH), gives a detailed response to *Venetian Life*. It reads in part: "When I consider how much more you might have made out of Venice, I wonder at your *Enthaltsamkeit* ('abstinence' don't

exactly express my meaning)—but I am sure the book is the better for it. I am rejoiced to find so little architectural and historical, and, although I don't quite accept your remarks on Art, I think you are right in not saying more. You have thus given us a book which is fresh in every chapter, which is new after all that has been written on the subject,—and which, *I* think, is a permanent contribution to our literature. The style is exquisite, and I don't know any young writer in the country who has selected a better basis upon which to build. It is remarkably *plastic*: the refining processes are never seen: it becomes grave without the slightest heaviness or dullness, and runs, as if spontaneously, in to light and sparkle. A prose style without humor is like unleavened bread, but your loaf is aerated through and through." In a letter to Howells of 25 August 1866 (MH), Longfellow also expressed his liking for the book: "I have read it with true delight, and not without some pangs of regret, for it makes me feel how much I missed seeing in Venice, and how little I really saw of what I did see, by being there at the wrong season. Clearly I must do it all over again. [¶] Your book is full of light and color, and that insight into life, without which a book is not a book, but a volume only. I heartily congratulate you on your success."

4. Howells had written Elizabeth Stoddard on 28 August 1866 (NN) about the favorable response by the English critics to the English edition of *Venetian Life*. In her reply of 31 August 1866 (MH), she wrote: "My good opinion of you is sustained then, by your critics! I know no writer standing a better chance than yourself. Your qualities of hard intellect, hard character, and a certain patient tact ought to butt down the American Public, and they will." She also informed Howells that she was working on a new novel, to be called *Temple House* (1867).

12 SEPTEMBER 1866, CAMBRIDGE, TO MELANCHTHON M. HURD

Cambridge, September 12, 1866.

My dear Hurd:

I have considered the proposition you make me relative to the copyright on such part of an edition of Venetian Life as you may sell to Messrs. Trübner and Co., and I do not think I can accept it. I should be very glad to have a second edition of the book published and should be pleased to have you do it, provided you pay me ten per cent of the retail price of all copies printed. The volume has received more cordial commendation from the English press than any American book since Hawthorne's last[1]—every literary journal of London having favorably noticed it; and in this country its reception has been equally encouraging. I do not know enough of the book business to say how much weight these facts should have in my favor, but you tell me that you have only a few copies of the book left unsold. It seems to me, therefore, that I ought not to treat with you for a second edition on the same terms which were offered me by Trübner & Co., when both the book and myself were perfectly friendless.[2]

Of course I cannot judge whether it will or will not pay you to stereotype the book; but I think that if another edition is to be printed, it should be announced at once, and without waiting to hear from Trübner & Co. If you can sell them a number of copies, it would be fortunate, but in the meantime while you write to them, and wait for their answer, you suffer the present success to cool and the impression of it to fade out of the public mind. I think the book will be a standard, but for the sake of its future sale, we should try now to make it as widely known as possible.

I wish, then, that you would write to me whether you will announce a second edition. It is important to me to know this, and I suppose you can let me know soon, for you need not judge so doubtfully of the matter as you need if the book were unknown.

I start for Ohio on Monday, and shall be absent three or four weeks, but as I wish an early reply to this, I give you the following address "W D Howells, Care of J. A. Howells & Co., Jefferson, Ashtabula co., Ohio."

Mrs. Howells sends regards—in which I join—to Mrs Hurd and yourself.

Yours very truly
W. D. Howells.

P. S. If you wish to write me before I leave for Ohio, a letter written Friday afternoon would reach me on Sunday, if addressed to me here *in Cambridge.*

1. *Our Old Home* (1863).
2. In his reply to Howells, 13 September 1866 (MH), Hurd wrote: "I think from the tone of your letter that you must have misunderstood the import of mine, in regard particularly to the proposed sale to Trubner. I would not of course offer you less than 10 per cent upon all copies sold (not on all printed as you suggest, the percentage being paid on all sold, in all contracts which we have made with authors) the proposition in regard to Trubner being that you should accept 5% on the sheets *sold him only* and only in order that we might offer him an edition of 500 copies at the same price that he in turn had offered to us. I do not believe in reducing the profits of authors and do not want you to suffer in this case, you should know however that if we ask a higher price Mess. Trubner & C may decline purchasing altogether and you may not receive any of the *supposed* profit on the sale. We have about fifty copies of Venetian Life on hand and there are some copies in the hands of booksellers. Until the edition is exhausted entirely, it would not be prudent to announce a second edition[.] I should be glad to stereotype a new set of plates and think the sale will warrant it but I cannot speak for my partner Mr Houghton[.] If you are willing that we should do so, receiving a copyright of ten per cent upon the retail price of all copies sold and will prepare copy for the press I think there will be no obstacle in the way for the immediate issue of the second edition."

15 September 1866, Boston, to Edwin P. Whipple

...*The Atlantic Monthly*,...
Boston, Sept. 15th, *1866*.

My dear Mr. Whipple:[1]

I had seen the notice of Venetian Life which you kindly enclosed me,[2] and had attributed a criticism at once hearty and delicate in its praise, to you. Allow me to thank you most cordially for it, and for the expressions of kindness in your note.

I am preparing the book for a second edition, which Messrs. Hurd and Houghton will publish as soon as it can be printed. I think I am very fortunate in having the first edition all sold before my step-grandmother, the Advertiser, told people that my accounts of Venetian society were quite untrustworthy.[3]

Very gratefully yours
W. D. Howells.

1. Edwin Percy Whipple (1819–1886) was a well-known Boston lecturer and author of books on literary subjects. See *Literary Friends and Acquaintance*, HE, pp. 109–10.

2. In a letter to Howells, 10 September 1866 (MH), Whipple had enclosed his review of *Venetian Life*, Boston *Transcript*, 13 August 1866.

3. The review in the Boston *Advertiser* has not been identified; Howells here refers to the newspaper as his "step-grandmother" because much of the material in *Venetian Life* had first appeared in it as "Letters from Venice."

15 October 1866, Boston, to James T. Fields

...*The Atlantic Monthly*,...
Boston, October 15, *1866*.

Dear Mr. Fields:

I send back our cosmopolite's scenes of foreign life.[1] I have seldom looked at anything more slangy, silly and vapid, and I think we could not possibly "find room for them." My examination of the Ms. has been very careful, and my judgement is decidedly against it.

—At the risk of being disagreeable I must say that I do not like our reverend friend's notice of Whipple's book,[2] which to my thinking is the best and strongest book you've published for a long time; whereas the review is diffuse and ineffectual. Are you hopelessly in for it?

Have you answered Stedman, accepting his poem,[3] or shall I write him?

—I am suffering frightfully with influenza; but by keeping in the house I can keep at work. Please send me Bayard Taylor's poem,[4] and whatever new books have been received for review.

Yours
W. D. H.

1. J. W. Palmer, "My Heathen at Home," *Atlantic*, December 1866. See James C. Austin, ed., *Fields of the Atlantic Monthly: Letters to an Editor, 1861–1870* (San Marino, Cal.: The Huntington Library, 1953), p. 147.

2. The reviewer of E. P. Whipple's *Character and Characteristic Men*, *Atlantic*, December 1866, has not been identified.

3. "Pan in Wall Street," *Atlantic*, January 1867.

4. Howells wrote the review of Bayard Taylor's *The Picture of St. John*, *Atlantic*, January 1867.

20 NOVEMBER 1866, CAMBRIDGE, TO THOMAS W. HIGGINSON

Cambridge, Nov. 20, 1866.

My dear Sir:

Your letter about my poem gave me so much pleasure that I should hardly dispute your criticisms even if I disagreed with them.[1] Mr. Lowell, who went over it with me after it was printed, made almost exactly the same objections to it which you have offered, and I am afraid you are both right. I don't know, however, that I could have mended the poem if I had received your strictures before its publication. It was written more than six years ago, and as my atoms have almost entirely changed since then, I count the author of it dead, and myself his not very capable literary executor, who has scarcely a right to meddle with his work. I had merely to raise money on the verses, and apply the proceeds to the relief of his suffering family.—Indeed, I am very happy that it has in any manner pleased you, and I thank you sincerely for the frank and cordial way in which you have expressed your opinion of the poem.

We had the pleasure of seeing your sister[2] twice during her recent visit to Cambridge. I liked her exceedingly, and could almost wish to make a protestant of her. She gave me the hope, which you renew, of your personal acquaintance. We live in a very high-perched little wooden house, the fifth from North Avenue on the north side of Sacramento street.

Mrs Howells sends remembrances, and I am

Very sincerely yours,
W. D. Howells.

Colonel T. W. Higginson.

1. Higginson had written Howells on 11 November 1866 (MH), giving a favorable but detailed criticism of Howells' poem "Forlorn."

2. Louisa Higginson (1816–1875) was considered an accomplished poet; for a period of her life she was a Roman Catholic.

5 DECEMBER 1866, BOSTON, TO EDMUND C. STEDMAN

... The Atlantic Monthly.
Boston, Dec. 5th, *1866.*

My dear Stedman:

I cannot write letters any more, but I can still in some sort answer them. Yours always give me delight: partly because I like to hear from you and partly because I like to be over-praised.[1] I think it does me good to be taken for what I ought to be, and I am sure I thank you for thinking better of me than I deserve.

The proof of "Pan in Wall Street" was duly sent you, and we waited two weeks for its return. Thereafter I read the proof very carefully myself, comparing it line by line with the original, and I hope you will find it free from errors. At any rate, it is now sixty thousand Atlantics too late to help it, for it goes into our January number.

The small but enthusiastic admirers of Walt Whitman could not make him a poet, if they wrote all the newspapers and magazines in the world full about him.[2] He is poetical as the other elements are, and just as satisfactory to read as earth, water, air and fire. I am tired, I confess, of the whole Whitman business.

Though you do cut us off from the hope of a visit, I am glad that you do not quite forbid us to expect seeing you. We never did quite have any talk *out,* and I think that the future owes us a chance at one another. Talking of talks: young Henry James and I had a famous one last evening, two or three hours long, in which we settled the true principles of literary art. He is a very earnest fellow, and I think extremely gifted—gifted enough to do better than any one has yet done toward making us a real American novel. We have in reserve from him a story for the Atlantic, which I'm sure you'll like.[3]

With Mrs. Howells's love to Mrs. Stedman, and our joint regards to both of you, and a kiss for Stoddard.

Yours truly
W. D. Howells.

1. In his letter of 2 December 1866 (MH), Stedman expressed his admiration for Howells' "Modern Italian Poets," *North American Review,* October 1866: "It gave me just the information which I needed, & I honestly confess that your prose style is to me a recurring wonder *&* content.... Every success of a true artist is a new hope & encouragement to his *bretheren* [sic] *of the blood.*"

2. In the same letter Stedman commented on recent reviews of the 1867 edition of *Leaves of Grass,* and then gave his own opinion of Whitman's poetry: "Well, I find *heaps* of melody & imagination in Whitman's poems, & have always said that he had enough stuff in him to set up a dozen small singers. But—breadth & liberality being his strong points, it argues a curious *bigotry* in him & his friends that they denounce all established rhythm as piano-jingle & .. & .. They fail to see that the

ways in which other great poets have chosen to express themselves, are just as much *outgrowths of nature* as the way most natural to Walt & them. Now I am liberal enough to comprehend *all* excellencies—those of their sort & of ours—& they wd be greater if they could do the same."

3. Henry James, "Poor Richard," *Atlantic*, June–August 1867. See Leon Edel, *Henry James: The Untried Years* (Philadelphia: Lippincott, 1953), pp. 269–70.

31 DECEMBER 1866, CAMBRIDGE, TO WILLIAM C. HOWELLS

Cambridge, Dec. 31st, 1866.

Dear father:

Unless I make that elk-horn the subject of a special letter, I am afraid I shall never think to ask you for it.—Wont you send it to me by express as soon as you get this,—letting the expense follow it, of course? Elinor and I can never be happy till we see that it *wont* do for a hat-rack. At present we think it would serve admirably for something of the kind, of which we are in great need.

To-day we are getting the snow-storm that overtook you some days ago. It is as well that the year should go out in this gloomy way as any—but what a pity it should go out at all! The artificial division of time into hours, weeks and years is horrible. I wish we counted by days, for we don't miss them—but when a year expires, it is a kind of heartbreak for every one (past twenty-five. If I live 1867 shall make me thirty! Pazienza!—It looks rather well, when written—1867; but I prefer '57 or '47; though the world is better than in either of those years, and I daresay the negroes and the Venetians are very glad it is '67 instead.—John Brown made me a very pleasant call, the other day, and promised to give my love to you all on his way home. He is such a great-hearted man as it does one good to come near. I was glad to hear that he was about to publish a new life of his father.[1]

The meetings at Mr. Longfellow's on Wednesday nights have begun again—for a last revision of Dante. I am invited for the course, and am as usual "the youngest gentleman in company."

I begin to see my way through the hard work a little; though that is a thing never finished on earth, I believe. My new book of Italian sketches[2] —those in The Nation, etcetera,—will probably go to the printers this fortnight coming; and I think I shall delay the poem[3] awhile. I shall have two articles in the April North American—one on Italian poets, and one on Longfellow. I have a brief sketch—*Forza Maggiore*—in the February Atlantic.[4]

We are all well, and looking eagerly for Annie. Let her come as soon as possible. Love to all.

Your affectionate son,
Will.

1. John Brown, Jr., never published a life of his famous father, who was executed in 1859.
2. *Italian Journeys.*
3. "Disillusion."
4. "Modern Italian Poets" and "Henry Wadsworth Longfellow," *North American Review*, April 1867; "Forza Maggiore," *Atlantic*, February 1867.

4 JANUARY 1867, BOSTON, TO JAMES T. FIELDS

... *The Atlantic Monthly*, ...
Boston, January 4th, *1866*.[1]

Dear Mr. Fields:

Mr. James has given me the manuscript of a story about which he has already spoken to you,[2] and I find it entirely acceptable.

If you haven't made up the March number entirely yet, wouldn't it be well to get this story into it? I send you the manuscript in order that you may look at it if you like. The title is of course to be changed.

W. D. H.

1. Since Howells began to work for the *Atlantic* in March 1866, the earliest possible date for this letter is 1867.
2. Henry James, "My Friend Bingham," *Atlantic*, March 1867.

10 FEBRUARY 1867, CAMBRIDGE, TO WILLIAM C. HOWELLS

Cambridge, February 10, 1867.

Dear father:

I am very glad to hear that you have been invited to write for the N. Church Magazine, and I hope that you will do so, for I don't think there's any danger of your falling below their standard, and I believe there are many chances that you will astonish their readers by unwonted force and liveliness. So far the New Churchmen I've met here are not—with the exception of Judge Parsons[1]—very forcible people: James being, as you know, Swedenborgian, but decidedly *not* New Church.[2] The night of my lecture, a good many of the "brethren" came up on the platform to speak with me, and the elders among them all remembered my name as the same with that of the editor of the "Retina",[3] which they had taken in former years. Last week Judge Parsons and all his family called upon us: the Judge wanted to know if my father was Doctor Howells,[4] whose name was so prominent in the proceedings of the last Ohio Convention. He's a very jolly old gentleman, and takes the greatest delight in my book[5]—which is very much to his credit. He and James are of course Antipodes: James would call him a "Spiritual Jew" and heaven knows what he would call James. Yet I think you would like both these men and I hope that some day you will meet them. I would send you James's book, but I've not yet finished it myself, and it would be rather ungracious—since he gave me it—to lend it unread.

I'm writing in rather a sprightly way, to-day, for last night I had my ideas jogged by a fall so terrible that if you had seen it you would have felt yourself fully avenged for the abuse I gave you for smashing your foot. I was at Mr. Norton's taking supper with the Dante Club, and coming away slipped from the terrace in front of the house, and struck on my back upon the ice. I was stunned for a while, and was with difficulty kept from fainting; but nothing was broken, and to-day I have only a stiffness to remind me of my accident.

Annie is getting on nicely here, and seems to be enjoying her visit. Elinor and I both think her very talented, and we are encouraging her to write a story for The Young Folks.[6]—Hurd and Houghton are going to publish a new book of travel-sketches for me in September, entitled The Road to Rome and The Way back to Venice.[7] The new edition of Venetian Life is now ready, and will be published immediately, I suppose.—I've been very busy of late on my "Italian Poets"— second article,— which appears in the April North American, together with another article of mine on Mr. Longfellow.[8] I have another brief sketch of travel—A Glimpse of Genoa—in the March Atlantic. In fact I'm amazed at the amount of work I manage to put through.—Our snow has all gone at last, and today it is clear and windy weather. Tell mother the next letter shall be to her. With love to all,

> Your affectionate son,
> Will.

1. Theophilus Parsons (1797–1882) was Dane Professor of Law at Harvard (1847–1882); he also wrote on Swedenborgianism. In 1873 Howells became Parsons' neighbor on Concord Avenue, Cambridge.

2. In his letter of 23 December 1866 (MH), Howells had reported to his father that Henry James, Sr., had given him his latest book, *Substance and Shadow; or Morality and Religion in Relation to Life* (1863).

3. W. C. Howells had edited the short-lived journal, *The Retina* (1843–1844), a paper supporting the New Jerusalem Church. See Cady, *Howells*, I, 16–22.

4. Perhaps Dr. Henry C. Howells, of Hamilton, or W. C. Howells himself.

5. *Venetian Life*.

6. *Our Young Folks* was published by Ticknor & Fields (1865–1873), and was edited by Lucy Larcom (1826–1893), a poet and author.

7. *Italian Journeys*.

8. "Modern Italian Poets" and "Henry Wadsworth Longfellow."

16 FEBRUARY 1867, CAMBRIDGE, TO DON L. WYMAN

Cambridge, February 16, 1867.

My dear Mr. Wyman:

I have both your letters, and should have answered the first some time ago, but for the fact that must make me very brief at the present time: ever so much work. I enclose the advertising-cover of a Spanish book with some works marked which I thought you might like to read. As to Italian, I do not think of a more charming book than *I Promessi Sposi*, of Manzoni, which you can get in Cleveland. *Marco Visconti*, of Tommaso Grossi, is also delightful; and any of the comedies of Goldoni (except those in the Venetian dialect) would please you. These books can be got of Chas Lockwood and Son, and Westermann & Co., N. Y. There is a very admirable and brief history of Spanish Literature by Bouterwek, which must be for sale in Cleveland. In New-York I dare say you could get Cesare Cantù's Storia della Letteratura Italiana.[1]

Of the verses which you send me, I think you may profitably write a very great many. It is good practice, and Heine from whom they are principally studied is one of the greatest masters of poetic art. But till you feel quite sure that you have not imitated him you ought not to publish. I am quite frank with you, and I wish I had not been tardily frank with myself. If ever I collected a volume of my verses I should declare in a preface that such and such things of mine were echoes of Heine and Tennyson. Nobody will deny that you have real poetic feeling. Be just to yourself before you are generous. Do those poems express the life you have lived or have known? No other sort of poem is worth reading—though I think you may write unrealities to learn ease and aptness of diction.

It was a great pleasure to hear from you, and I hope you will write me again.[2] I would send you my fotograf, but I have none. In the meantime wont you let me have yours, trusting me to return you favor when I have a likeness taken?

Yours very cordially
W. D. Howells.

1. Howells had reviewed *Della letteratura italiana* by Cesare Cantù in "Modern Italian Poets," *North American Review*, October 1866. The history of Spanish literature he recommended to Wyman was probably *Historia de la literatura española escrita en aleman por F. Bouterwek, traducia al castellano y adicionada por D. José Gomez de la Cortina y D. Nicolas Hugalde y Mollinedo*, published originally in 1829, rather than the original German or one of the English translations.

2. On 7 April 1867 (MH) Howells wrote his father: "I have lately had two long letters from Don Lloyd Wyman, who is a man of undoubted talent, and who tells me of a great amount of study that he is doing this winter. Couldn't you make such a man useful in the Sentinel office?—Though I don't know how, either."

10 MARCH 1867, CAMBRIDGE, TO MONCURE D. CONWAY

Cambridge, March 10, 1867.

My dear Conway:
Peccavi!

I send you the "Pilot's Story" and "Louis Lebeau's Conversion." I do not know what other poems you want of mine, but on the whole I think those printed in the Atlantic are the best I have done. I have not time to copy them, but you can find them in the numbers for January (*Andenken*), February (*The Poet's Friends,*) April (*Pleasure-Pain and Lost Beliefs*) 1860; in February (*The Old Homestead*, which I called and will have called *The Empty House*) in April (*The Bubbles*) 1861.

To be quite frank, I would not have chosen to appear poetically before English criticism in a volume of younger American poets, and I only help you to anything of mine because I remember with affectionate gratitude the friendship and kindness you showed me in past days when I needed both more than I do now.[1] I have very small respect for the younger American poets, and for myself as one of their number, but I think I might some day stand upon my own dactyls, & that it will not advantage me much to be shown in poetic long-clothes to people who already know something of my prose. If you should speak of me, in connection with my verses, I wish you to make known how sensible I am of my obligation to Heine in my lyrical attempts. In the rhythmic poems— The Pilot's Story and Louis Lebeau—I think I achieved something like originality of manner,—of matter certainly. Do not say (as you did to Browning)[2] that The P. S. is founded upon an actual incident. It is not, and would not have half its artistic value if it were.

I was very greatly pleased with your review of Venetian Life in the Forthnightly,[3] and but for your telling me that it was printed in a less cordial spirit than it was written, I should not have known that you could have given me greater praise. Indeed all the English notices took me by surprise with their cordiality. Do you know the Pall-Mall Gazette people well enough to ask from me who wrote the review of my book in their journal?[4] I should like to know, for that notice was particularly good.—I thank *you,* my dear Conway, very heartily for the interest you took in the book's success and the things you did to help it.

My life here is one of excessively hard work, but is very pleasant in all its relations. The climate agrees with all of us—though the winter is simply infamous—and generally we "keep our health," though just now Elinor is not very well. When she gets better we intend to see more than we have done of Mrs. Conway's cousin[5] who called upon us, but whom Elinor missed in returning the call.—Another day I will write you a long letter of friendship. This is merely a business note, scribbled in the monthly paroxysm attending the closing up of the magazine.

With our best love to Mrs. Conway, believe me

Yours ever
W. D. H.

1. Conway accepted some of Howells' poems for publication in the Cincinnati *Dial* and the Boston *Commonwealth*; he had also tried to find an English publisher for a volume of Howells' poetry. Conway's anthology of younger American poets was apparently never published.
2. See Howells to Conway, 22 August 1863, n. 2.
3. The generally favorable review appeared in the *Fortnightly Review*, 15 August 1866.
4. The review has not been located.
5. The cousin has not been identified.

13 APRIL 1867, BOSTON, TO JAMES M. COMLY

...*The Atlantic Monthly*,...
Boston, April 13th, *1867*.

My dear Comly:

I see by my father's paper that you are being talked of for governor of Ohio, and I cannot help writing to tell you with what pleasure I view the possibility of your nomination, and with what delight I should celebrate your election.[1] If the Atlantic Monthly can help you in any way, command it!

I understand that it is not much to be governor of a State, but it is a great deal to have deserved the highest honor the people can confer.

In the meantime, however, what shall I do with Judge Warden's mortal manuscript?[2]

Father tells me in a recent letter that you have gone to housekeeping. I am glad of this, for it doubles life—cares and all. Give my regards to all your family and family's family.

Yours always
W. D. Howells.

If you are elected, and I could get into State's Prison for some slight offence I should be almost willing to try it for the pleasure of being pardoned out by you. How would plagiarism answer?

1. "The Next Governor," an unsigned editorial, Ashtabula *Sentinel*, 10 April 1867.
2. Robert Bruce Warden (1824–1888), lawyer and judge, wrote many books, although none appeared between his campaign life of Stephen A. Douglas (1860) and his life of Salmon P. Chase (1874). In a letter to Comly, 23 December 1866 (OHi), Howells expressed his "full sympathy with the idea of the book," but could not recommend it to Ticknor & Fields.

28 April 1867, Cambridge, to William C. Howells

Cambridge, April 28, 1867.

Dear father:

After getting that last letter from you, Annie and I debated whether the family, in a certain event, had better go to live in Columbus,—so you see we take your nomination for governor very seriously. I was amused at the paragraph in the Sentinel,[1] for I thought I saw through all its jocosity a willingness "to be induced." Well, there have been worse governors of Ohio than the one proposed—some scores of them, in fact. I shall try not to be proud—because it's sinful—till you are elected, and then I will give a loose to my vanity. The only thing I object to in your nomination is that it might prevent you from coming to see us this summer, with mother, and we count upon your visit.

I suppose Annie will have written to you about her trip to Brattleboro'. I thought it well for her to go, and she seems to have enjoyed it thoroughly. We were there three days, and in favorable weather. We left Elinor in pretty good health—though still very weak, and we expect her home to-morrow afternoon.

Your last letter but one—that in reply to mine about Annie[2]—was good enough to convince me on all contested points. It certainly made me ashamed of the poor, careless letters I write you. But letter-writing seems to be among the lost arts with me, and I shall leave particular charges to my biographer not to make free use of my correspondence.

Annie and I were out to tea last night, and when we got home we found a box in the entry with two splendid hams of smoked venison in it. Will Dean[3] had sent it from Minnesota.—We have just returned from a long walk, and must get ready soon to go to the Fields's, where we are to spend the evening. On Friday we took tea at the Nortons'. So you see Annie does not lose a moment of her time.

Hurd, my publisher sent me a check for $200—copyright on 2d edition of Venetian Life, and next Wednesday I hope to pay $500 on my house. I did not expect to do this for a year yet.—Annie will write to-morrow. Love to all. Winny is well.

Your affectionate son
Will.

1. An editorial in the Ashtabula *Sentinel*, 24 April 1867, quotes and comments on a suggestion in the Ashtabula *Telegraph* that W. C. Howells be nominated for governor.

2. In his letter of 7 April 1867 (MH), Howells had praised Annie's common sense and manners; he also commented on her talents and shortcomings as a writer.

3. William B. Dean was Howells' cousin in St. Paul. See *Life in Letters*, II, 338.

4 JUNE 1867, CAMBRIDGE, TO JAMES T. FIELDS

Cambridge, June 4, 1867.

Dear Mr. Fields:

I have your list of articles for August, and grieve to see that you have left no place for "Little Italian Travels" by W. D. Howells, author of a campaign life of Lincoln. The same writer was to furnish us a review of "May-Day" as a body article.[1] Please to let me know your mind about these things, for Mr. Howells, next to Mr Hazewell[2] is the most difficult gent to suit on our list.[3]

I will have Mr. Bigelow estimate the articles named by you, and we shall know within 50 pp of how much they make.

Isn't old Thackeray beyond expression?[4]

W. D. H.

1. Howells' "Minor Italian Travels" and his review of Emerson's *May-Day and Other Pieces*, *Atlantic*, September 1867.
2. Charles Creighton Hazewell (1814–1883), a frequent contributor to the *Atlantic* between 1857 and 1868, was considered an authority on biographical and historical subjects.
3. In his reply of 12 June 1867 (MH), Fields informed Howells that Charles Sumner insisted on getting his article, "Prophetic Voices about America," into the August issue of the *Atlantic*, and then continued: "We must consult about those articles by the author of The Campaign Life of Lincoln for he is a man for us to look well after." The Sumner article did not appear until September 1867.
4. Howells is referring to Thackeray's *Early and Late Papers, Hitherto Uncollected*; a review (not by Howells) of it appeared in the *Atlantic*, August 1867.

30 JUNE 1867, CAMBRIDGE, TO MARY D. HOWELLS

Cambridge June 30, 1867.

Dear Mother:

The peacock came yesterday just as the last course was put on the table; and we all ran down with our mouths full of hot pudding, and welcomed him. Fifteen minutes later we wished him to Jefferson or Jericho. For, we first tried to habitude him to the place by tying him with one leg to a tree, and letting him have the range of a pretty long tether. Words cannot tell the trouble we had in effecting this apparently simple matter. Elinor had first to sew a piece of buckskin about P's leg, then the string had to be hunted out of drawers, and then the knots untied from it, and then all the pieces put together. I was expected to do everything. P. thrashed about with his wings and kicked. Winny cried, Elinor danced up and down with fury at my awkwardness and suggested every impossible way of doing things quicker; our nigs continually came and went upon torrents of excitement. When P. was let loose he ran out to the end his tether, extended his tied leg behind him in a manner that threatened to break it, and alternately flopped himself tired and reposed upon his breast. Winny cried more, we all got madder and madder, and at last I cut the string and carried P. into the cellar, where he now remains. All yesterday he refused food and water; but this morning he has both eaten and drunken. He waked us at dawn by a wild shriek which seemed to come from under our bed and made Elinor think I was beating Winnie to death. I've now bought an immense crockery crate, in which we are going to pen P. for a while. After that we shall try the experiment of letting him out, and heaven knows where he'll go to.—We are very grateful to you for sending him, but I don't conceal that he is as yet a blessing in disguise which might be easily mistaken for a calamity. If you have any thoughts of giving us Charles, the horse, please consider our unprepared state. The peacock at present occupies the cellar, and we should have no place for a horse unless we gave him Annie's bedroom; and I have an idea that he would expect—having always been treated as one of the family—to eat at the first table, and be introduced to company.

How good it is of father and Joe to give us the sewing-machine! Elinor has declared that we mustn't accept it on their generous terms, but she shows no signs of returning it, and I suspect we shall keep it after all. She's prouder of it than of anything else we've got. Annie and Joe will conceive the unmeasured joy with which she flourished it over Mrs. Aldrich who called a few days since. Mrs. A. said *she* preferred a Wheeler and Wilson.

We looked for political news from Ohio with a great deal of anxiety, and we "accepted the situation" with a resignation worthy of our southern brethren. Galloway is in a contemptible position, I think.[1] I send part of a letter from Mr. Follett,[2] which father will like to see. The Sentinel's endorsement of the nomination is enthusiastic.[3] Well, I would rather be such a man as father than twenty lieutenant-governors.

We're glad to hear that you don't think of giving up, your visit to us, mother. You know you could stop a night in Buffalo and another night in Albany; and that way the journey could be made less fatiguing. You ought to come early in September, so as to get the fine weather in Cambridge. Elinor says not to leave off deciding so long that you'll have to give up as you did last on account of trouble about dress. She joins me in rejoicing that we are to see you. Love to all, with special thanks from Winnie to Willie for the Peacock. We enjoyed the joke "To the Humane."

Your affectionate son,
Will.

I hope Annie has written to Mr. Longfellow.

1. Samuel Galloway (1811–1872), a Columbus lawyer, was defeated in his attempt to obtain the Republican nomination for governor; but he accepted the nomination for lieutenant governor, thus dashing the hopes of W. C. Howells, who had run second to Galloway in early balloting at the 1867 State Convention.
2. Oran Follett, formerly of Follett, Foster & Co.
3. In "The State Convention," Ashtabula *Sentinel*, 26 June 1867, W. C. Howells expressed his support for the entire Republican ticket.

31 JULY 1867, CAMBRIDGE, TO CHARLES E. NORTON

Cambridge, July 31, 1867.

Dear Mr. Norton:

We have heard of the birth of your son,[1] and Mrs. Howells and I join in congratulations upon the event. I hope that Mrs. Norton is doing well, and that the little one is born with all the health of Ashfield in it. Please to give our most cordial regards to both.

Here in Cambridge there is little news to write you. Our small family has been much excited by a visit made last Friday to the Agassizs[2] at Nahant, where we spent a day of notable enjoyment. It was so long since we had left home before that we fancied ourselves gone a great while, and I looked to find my table heaped with postal accumulations. But there was nothing but the usual quantity and quality of work awaiting me. The next day I was invited to the Saturday Club dinner, where the attendance was rather sparse—Mr. Emerson being the only poet besides Mr. Read,[3] (T. B.) of Cincinnati, and Dr. Holmes. The talk was chiefly by Mr. Sumner, who said among other things that he never met a well-educated man from the west.[4] This appeared very felicitous, and endeared him to both the western men present, who, however, had previously known themselves to be ignorant. There was rather an early break-up. Mr. Lowell, I believe, was in Plymouth, and of course Mr. Longfellow did not come up from Nahant. Speaking of him, I must tell you that I liked very much your review of Dante in the North American.[5] I thought I recognized also your neat hand in the arrangement of Dryden on Swinburne.[6] At any rate, and whoever did it, it was exceedingly fortunate. How good the whole number was in fact—that is, Mr. Lowell's article and Mr. Godkin's![7] My book[8] is hurrying now so much that I shall not be able to count myself—as I had hoped to do— among the contributors to the October number. I am aware that this will shut me out from any continuation of the Italian Poets;[9] but I think you have had enough of them, already. I have been writing a notice of "May Day,"[10] in which I leave what I think its defects to the justice that rules the world. This is a slow method, but a safe one—for the critic. With Jean Ingelow I have not dealt so patiently.[11] I could understand her absurdities, and I treated them according to knowledge. But it is a very different thing with a poet so many heads above one as Emerson.

Mrs. Howells's family have offered us their house for a month in Brattleboro', and it is possible that we may pass August there, though we have not yet decided.—Larkin Mead's foreman from Florence,[12] has been with us for several weeks, and tells us that we could live imperially upon seven francs a day in Sienna. O, to go there, and write historical sketches forever! No proofs any more! No notices!—Remember us, pray, to all your family.

Very sincerely yours
W. D. Howells.

1. The Nortons' second son, Rupert, was born 27 July 1867.
2. Jean Louis Rodolphe Agassiz (1807–1873) was professor of natural history at Harvard (1848–1873). His second wife, Elizabeth Cabot Cary Agassiz (1822–1907), was the first president of Radcliffe College (1894–1902), of which she was a cofounder.
3. Thomas Buchanan Read (1822–1872) was a painter and occasionally a sculptor, but he was best known as a poet.
4. Howells later recalled Charles Sumner as "not a very gracious person." *Literary Friends and Acquaintance*, HE, p. 120.
5. Norton's review of Longfellow's translation of *The Divine Comedy*, *North American Review*, July 1867.
6. The critical notice in the *North American Review*, July 1867, of A. C. Swinburne's *A Song of Italy* consists only of a lengthy quotation from Dryden's dedication to his translation of the *Aeneid*, in which Dryden belittles certain poets as poets only for young men.
7. "Rousseau and the Sentimentalists" and "The Labor Crisis," respectively.
8. *Italian Journeys*, published in early December 1867.
9. Two installments of "Modern Italian Poets" had already appeared.
10. See Howells to Fields, 4 June 1867, n. 1.
11. Howells' review of Ingelow's *A Story of Doom, and Other Poems*, *Atlantic*, September 1867.
12. The younger Mead's foreman has not been identified.

10 August 1867, Cambridge, to Charles E. Norton

Cambridge, August 10, 1867.

Dear Mr. Norton:

This has been so busy a week with me, that I have just now found time to answer your letter. We are going to Brattleboro' next week, and I have of course, had to fight my way to this possibility through myriads of infuriate manuscripts. Besides, the magazine went to press, this week, and as usual cost me unspeakable anguish at the last moment. I am not yet so far removed from the event but that I still regard my book-notices as so many elements of Ruin.[1]

I think we shall remain at Brattleboro' a month, but not longer. Our purpose is leisure and nature, but I should not be surprised if the fact proved to be literature and society. And I suppose the change of air will be the great advantage, after all.

A certain matter troubles me. I have seen no criticism of the Paradiso in the Nation; and I have begun to wonder whether you and Mr. Godkin are not depending upon me for it. My understanding was that I was to write only the second criticism, and so I have made no preparation for the third. It is now late to write it in sequence, but if it is desirable, I suppose that I can, while in Brattleboro' write something on the Paradiso independently of what has gone before, and regarding it in some special lights. As yet I have not had time even to read the poem.[2]

Mr. Lowell came to see us yesterday.—You know he has been at Plymouth, camping-out with Mr. John Holmes and professor Gurney;[3] and he claims to have greatly enjoyed himself.—I see the Jameses rather frequently. They are all in town. Harry James has written us another story, which I think admirable; but I do not feel sure of the public any longer, since the Nation could not see the merit of Poor Richard.[4] It appeared to me that there was remarkable strength in the last scenes of that story; and I cannot doubt that James has every element of success in fiction. But I suspect that he must in a very great degree create his audience. In the meantime I rather despise existing readers.—I walked through the beautiful woods about your house, near nightfall a few days since, and though the sarcastic mosquito there hummed about my ears, I must say that I have seldom seen anything so lovely as that lookout from the trees west of the avenue towards the old mansion. The local colors were all so finely indicated in the light that also gave softness to all the outlines of the trees, dropping their branches so low that they almost touched the sloping ground. I doubt if you have anything half so fine at Ashfield.—All day long here on Sacramento street, we remain

> "Close-latticed to the brooding heat,
> And silent in our dusty vines."[5]

At two o'clock, John[6] appears with the express bag from Ticknor and Fields, and an excitement like a breath of the simoom, breaks over us. Then we lapse back again into merely negative existence. During the interval immediately following dinner, we read Campbell's Life of Petrarch[7]—a book to the unsparing wisdom, of which the proverbs of Solomon are as the babblings of folly. With our united regards to you all,

Very truly yours.
W. D. Howells.

1. In the preceding letter to Norton, Howells had already expressed his concern over his review of Emerson's *May-Day and Other Pieces*.

2. Howells did not supply a criticism beyond his "Mr. Longfellow's Translation of the Divine Comedy," *Nation*, 20 June 1867.

3. Howells later remembered John Holmes (1812–1899), the younger brother of Oliver Wendell Holmes, in *Literary Friends and Acquaintance*, HE, pp. 235–37. Ephraim Whitman Gurney (1829–1886) was at this time an assistant professor of philosophy at Harvard; in 1868 he replaced Norton as coeditor of the *Nation*.

4. Henry James, "The Romance of Certain Old Clothes," *Atlantic*, February 1868. The first two installments of "Poor Richard" were reviewed unfavorably in the *Nation*, 30 May and 27 June 1867; and the third installment was dismissed by the *Nation*, 1 August 1867, as containing "Nothing new or striking." James was just as complimentary in his comments about Howells' work as Howells is here in respect to James. He had written Howells on 10 May 1867 (MH), expressing his reaction to several parts of *Italian Journeys* that had appeared in the *Nation* and the *Atlantic*: "They are utterly charming, & a 100 times the most graceful, witty and poetical things yet written in this land.... I like the real laxity of your lightness & the real feeling of your soberness; and I admire the delicacy of your touch always & everywhere.—The worst of it is that it is almost *too* sympathetic. You intimate, you suggest so many of the refinements of the reality, that the reader's soul is racked by this superfluous enjoyment."

5. See Tennyson, "Marianna in the South," lines 3–4.

6. John apparently was a messenger boy for the publishing firm.

7. Thomas Campbell, *The Life of Petrarch* (1841).

17 AUGUST 1867, BRATTLEBORO, TO EDMUND C. STEDMAN

...*The Atlantic Monthly*,...
Boston, August 17, *186* .

My dear Stedman:

You will see by the postmark of my envelope that I only officially date from Boston, but really write from Brattleboro' Vt., whither I'm come for a change of air. It's not a relief in any other way, for I bring all my Atlantic work with me. Here I've received your letter and noted its contents, and I have begun to write you about it, without knowing in the least what I ought to say. It seems hard that a man who plays a silver-voiced pipe should refrain from a certain air because another performs it on a steam-calliope;[1] and yet I can see a certain propriety in what you urge against yourself. I wish your poem were in season for our September number, but as it isn't—well, if it were mine, I would withhold it from present publication. This is not the first peace harvest, and next year we shall have another, and this poem of yours will always be in time—with its proper date—for a volume. There! I've got the murder out at last, and here you have your poem again.

Once, in Venice, I found a subject which promised to cure me of mortality, and I wrote thirty undying stanzas upon it. Then I went out for a walk—stopped, as my fashion was, at the first book-stall, picked up the first book, and found my story all told in it, and given to the world three years before the date of my birth. I am still mortal. But you, old fellow, will not suffer as much as I did though you have lost far finer work. Let me tell you how exquisite I think your idealization of the Grass is, and how full of delicate beauty I find many of your lines; and let me ask you, finally, not to accept my judgment in this case. I send back your poem, because I wish to deal sincerely with you, but I am not sure that I deal wisely with you, and I'd desire you to forward the verses to Mr. Fields all the same as if I'd never seen them.[2] They will be in time any time before the 25th of August, unless he has filled out the number since Wednesday.

I suppose all your family is with you in Milford, and Mrs. Howells joins me expression of regard for you all. My father-and-mother-in-law are boarding, this summer, and have lent us their pleasant old house for a month. So we've shut up our house at Cambridge, and have brought our household gods up here.

As to the treadmill, I would willingly help own one with you, for I feel the need of some income besides that I receive from my pen; but I do not see the hour of acquisition yet. Treadmills are much more costly to start and keep going than they used to be, and there are several running already. However, it is not a thing to despair of.

Hoping that I have not acted stupidly,

Yours cordially
W. D. Howells.

1. Since Stedman's poem was "The Feast of Harvest," *Atlantic*, November 1867 (identified by Mildred Howells, *Life in Letters*, I, 118), Howells is most likely comparing it here to Whitman's "A Carol of Harvest for 1867," *Galaxy*, September 1867 (later changed to "The Return of the Heroes"), which had probably already appeared by the date of this letter.

2. The appearance of Stedman's poem in a later issue of the *Atlantic* indicates that he must have accepted Howells' advice.

26 SEPTEMBER 1867, CAMBRIDGE, TO ANNE T. HOWELLS

Cambridge, Sept. 26th, 1867.

Dear Annie:

I've read your story, and admire its pretty fancy and invention; but it is not near so good as the first, because you have left the solid ground which you knew for regions in which you could only guess your way. You wrote successfully of wild life in a cabin, because we had all led such a life; but you've not been at sea, and I think that the fairies died some years before you were born.[1] You may be sure that the imagination can deal best with what is of most familiar experience. I want you to celebrate incidents of our western life, no matter how rude or how thinly disguised, and then you cannot fail. Have patience and courage, for a great prize is within your reach. I wish that I could have you near me to advise you; but after all you are good enough critic yourself.— Now, if you wish to take the risk, I will offer your story to Ticknor, but I'd hate to have it refused, and would much rather you tried something else. I imagine your eyelids getting a little red at this plain talk, but you know that it comes from the best, though the bluntest, of brothers.

We are eagerly awaiting the coming of father and mother, and shall next week get the stoves in so that they can be comfortable. We've got new paper for the dining-room, and expect to have it put on to-morrow. It is to have ornamental corners and be bordered at top and bottom.

We are only tolerably well. Elinor is still weak, and I am suffering from having had a tooth pulled. Crump[2] is in perfect health, however, and on Monday starts to a Kindergarten school on North avenue. Elinor and she join me in love to all.

Your affectionate brother,
Will.

1. Neither the story of "wild life in a cabin" nor the sea story has been identified, though the latter may be "Jaunty," mentioned in Howells' letters to his family in Jefferson, 6 March and 22 November 1868. The first published story in *Our Young Folks* by Annie is "Frightened Eyes," May 1868; it may have been submitted to Ticknor by Howells.

2. Winifred Howells.

25 NOVEMBER 1867, CAMBRIDGE, TO MARY D. HOWELLS

Cambridge, Nov. 25, 1867.

Dear Mother:

It was very pleasant to hear from you, though you had to tell us of some sickness of your own, and of poor Henry's growing worse. All I can do is to say that I sympathize most deeply with you in the trouble. Perhaps that medicine may begin after while to affect him favorably. In the meantime, I know how much you must all suffer on account of him. It must have come particularly hard upon you who had been away, and had not seen him gradually growing worse.

Mother, it's a great thing to us to think you enjoyed your visit so much, and it made Elinor and me both happy to have you express your enjoyment. We certainly tried to do all we could to make you welcome, and I assure you our family was very sad and lonesome after you left.

The evening after your departure was indescribably dismal. It was such a great favor of you to undertake the long journey, but we fully appreciated it.

How did Vic like her book?[1] None of you say; and I am only left to hope that it pleased her. My new book[2] is now ready, and I'll send you a copy early in the week. Annie must have Dr. Dio Lewis's work on Light Gymnastics[3]—I'll look for it, and send it the next time I'm in Boston. It's used in all the Kindergarten.

Joe sent us a short note from New York, which was but a small compensation for our not seeing him. Had Willy really kept a journal of his proceedings here? It ought to be a most valuable record; but he must not give it up even after getting home.

Poor Crumpy is suffering from those terrible sores that broke out on her face last year with the coming of cold weather. She's very good, but a little dispirited. We've not taken her away from school yet, but must do so if the trouble gets worse.

Night before last, I took supper at Mr. Longfellow's with Charles Dickens. You must tell Goodrich[4] that he was everything in manner that his books would make you wish him to be. I had quite a little chat with him, and sat next but one to him at table. His face is very flexble, and he is very genial and easy in talk. Lowell, Darley the artist, Mr. Sam Longfellow,[5] Fields, and Prof. Greene were the other guests; and we sat till midnight. It was a lovely time. But it was hard at the moment to remember that this man so near me was so great and had done so much to please and better the world.—Everybody here is wild about the readings, and the tickets of the second course will be sold at Auction. We have tickets for the whole first course.

With love to all,

Your affectionate son,
Will.

1. Most likely a volume of *English and Scottish Ballads*, ed. F. J. Child, 8 vols. (1857–1859, 1864). See *Life in Letters*, I, 123.

2. *Italian Journeys*.

3. *The New Gymnastics for Men, Women, and Children* (1862).

4. William Goodrich (b. 1818?), a native of England, is listed in the 1860 Jefferson census as a painter. He was the Dickens-worshiping "misanthropical Englishman" mentioned by Howells in *Years of My Youth*, HE, p. 91, and in *My Literary Passions*, pp. 94–96, 101–4.

5. Felix Octavius Darley (1822–1888) was primarily an illustrator of books who became famous for his illustrations of James Fenimore Cooper's novels. Samuel Longfellow (1819–1892), brother of the poet, was a Unitarian clergyman, biographer of his brother, and poet in his own right.

8 DECEMBER 1867, CAMBRIDGE, TO VICTORIA M. HOWELLS

Cambridge, Dec. 8, 1867.

Dear Vic—

You never saw an anthracite coal-fire, did you? It's jolly, malignant looking heat—a sort of merry devil; and makes the room very warm, without asking to be sawed or split or even allowed the poor boon of making everything black about it. I've just got my little open stove up, and full of blue blazing anthracite, and looking (after writing my date,) at its now familiar glow, I couldn't help being struck with the fact that you'd probably never seen it burning. We drift sadly apart in this world, and store away new associations and customs; but I suppose it will be arranged hereafter that all these shall drop away, in the process of our becoming as little children.

I'm glad you liked the ballad book.[1] It's very carefully and sympathetically edited; and I sent it to you in remembrance of the fondness you used to have for those old things. I never forget how much we liked some books in common, as well as hated some people together.

I've heard Dickens twice since I last wrote: the first time he read The Christmas Carol and the trial from Pickwick; the second time Paul Dombey and the trial again. It was the perfection of acting, and as the parts were all well played, it was better than any theatre I ever saw. It was rather sad, however, for an American who had naturalized Dickens's characters to find that after all they were English. But there was some compensation in the fact that abstractly, my conceptions of his characters were for the most part exactly the same as the author's. Toots was a little different, Sam Weller was not quite so sharp as I would have made him. Tony Weller was prodigious, and Mr. Winkle enough to kill. When I thought how much Goodrich would have enjoyed the Christmas Carol I felt guilty to be there in his place.—The whole audience rose with a shout when Dickens entered; but after that he held them almost quiet. It's been a great excitement.

Meantime I've had a little excitement of my own. My new book's out, and I've seen some half dozen notices, all very favorable.[2] I sent mother a copy, which I hope she's got by this time.

You can tell Henry that Winny's pim*pells* are pretty nearly gone. I've had an awful cold for some days past, but otherwise we're all well.

—Winny's come in, and says to tell granma that's she's making a little bead basket at the Kindergarten, which she'll bring out to Ohio to the little girl (Mary)[3] when she comes.

We've just got a letter from Will Dean, who wants to engage Dickens to read at St. Paul; but I think he'll hardly succeed.

As we had tickets to the whole course of readings, we invited Elinor's father and mother to go each one night with one of us, and they've been with us the past week. In fact Mrs. Mead is still here, and will probably remain a week longer. They are both very sorry they could not get here to see the senior Howellses.

Give our love to all, and believe me

Ever your affectionate brother
Will.

1. See Howells to Mary D. Howells, 25 November 1867, n. 1.
2. *Italian Journeys*. Howells wrote his cousin William B. Dean on 9 December 1867 (MnHi): "I don't know how it's selling, yet, but so far all the notices are favorable. Of course I don't expect the luck of Venetian Life over again." Oliver Wendell Holmes praised the new book in his letter to Howells of 23 November 1867 (MH): "I thank you, not merely for myself, but in the name of everybody who loves the pleasantness of travel-incidents and the most interesting of travel-lights framed in English so lucid and so sweet, with just the opal-gleam of humor as you look at a sentence here and there in the light for it,—that we hardly knew how to match it without calling up one of the dead Maestri.—I am not sure that in the mere matter of style I enjoy anybody so much as yourself since Hawthorne—and I do not mean to place yours beneath his in excellence."
3. Mary Elizabeth Howells, daughter of Joseph A. Howells.

15 DECEMBER 1867, CAMBRIDGE, TO ANNE T. HOWELLS

Cambridge, Dec. 15, 1867.
Dear Annie:

Don't let Elinor fool you with her nonesense about the Higginsons; but I think it would be graceful in you to write to Annie H.,[1] and repeat what we said, namely: that she must stop at Jefferson if she goes out to Antioch next spring. It seems to me you'd all enjoy a visit from her greatly.

I suggested to Elinor what she has written with regard to Laura Mitchell; and I don't think Columbus would be at all a good point to begin. Besides, I'm afraid you're not ready to begin anywhere yet. You can hardly have made thorough acquaintance with your manual yet, and there are gymnastics and dancing to be learned besides. There is a school to train teachers for Kindergarten in Boston and at Oswego, New-York, where the course of instruction occupies a year, so that, studying alone, you see that you have a good deal of work before you. Dio Lewis's book is out of print; I'll send you the new edition as soon as it is published.[2] Now it seems to me, Annie, that if you are in earnest about this matter, you had better begin for the sake of practice (after you've thoroughly studied your manual) in Jefferson. Take half a dozen children between five and eight years old and teach them for nothing—it will pay you in the end. A Kindergartnerinn's trade is not to be learnt, any more than Rome was built, in a day. I want to impress patience, patience, patience on you—it's the only power in the world, and success is its slave.

In the meantime what are you doing with your pen? Is the Lame Turkey's Tragedy written, yet? I want to offer that to the Riverside Magazine where it would probably be printed at once.[3]

Crump and all of us are delighted with the fotograf of beautiful little Mary. What a funny small English woman she is—and how very pretty! We are quite proud of her. I'm delighted to hear that Joe is fixing his house so nicely, for I know he'll take great comfort in it—I think father may well be permitted the use even of such a word as récherché in speaking of the parlor, which must be a charming room.

With "New Arcady Mills"[4] I'm getting on slowly but satisfactorily. There are about five chapters written, and the whole story is pretty clear in my mind. Tell father I think (with him) that the Cimbrian *Dandern* and *Borandern* are undoubtedly corruptions and contractions of Die andern and Wir andern—Thy-others and We-others;[5] just like the Italian Noi-altri and Voi-altri.

We've got a little negro boy—say a *page*[6]—through the Freedman's Bureau, to help about the house. He's ten years old, and about a yard square; but bright and very helpful. Winny adores him—tucks her chair close to his, and manifests none of our "natural antipathy" to the black race.

We're all pretty well: I've got over my cold; though the weather hasn't by any means got over *its* cold. We have snow about a foot deep, and it has been very hard to keep warm the past week.

Give our love to all.

Your affectionate brother
Will.

1. Anna Higginson (1809–1892) was a sister of Thomas Wentworth Higginson.
2. See Howells to Mary D. Howells, 25 November 1867, n. 3.
3. It did not appear in the *Riverside Magazine for Young People*, a magazine published by Hurd & Houghton and edited by Horace E. Scudder (1867–1870).
4. The work was to be laid aside, worked on at intervals, and finally published as *New Leaf Mills*. Howells had written his father on 3 November 1867 (MH) that he had finished the first chapter of "New-Arcady Mills" and would send it to W. C. Howells for comments.
5. See *Italian Journeys*, pp. 241–42.
6. The young Negro has not been identified.

15 December 1867, Cambridge, to Melanchthon M. Hurd

Cambridge, Dec. 15, 1867.

My dear Hurd:

I've no idea of offering my books hereafter to any one but you. I'm at work on the novel when I can get a moment, but it's slow business, and may turn out a failure.[1] I'm very much obliged for the hint about Putnam.[2] Should you have any objections to his publishing my Venetian poem before you book it?[3] And do you think he'd like to? It would make nine pages of his magazine. I would not take less than $125. for it.

Mr. Norton will have a notice in the *N. A. Review* of Hassaurek's admirable book if you send it to him immediately.[4]

How does *I. Js.* sell?[5] I'm sorry to have disappointed the *Post*; but these things can't always be helped. *Per contra*, Mr. Hillard (of *Six Months in Italy*)[6] writes me the following letter, which I send you for your private pleasure and perusal. It's a proof of a vast expanse of cheek in me to send it at all; but I'm particularly proud of it because it was not provoked by a presentation copy; besides, I show it in strict confidence to you. Please return it.

"I still think" (as you always say when you're particularly stubborn) that you'd better have sent early copies to the English journals whether the book was for sale in England or not.

Your truly,
W. D. Howells.

1. Since Howells was at this time mining his Italian materials, the novel was probably *A Foregone Conclusion*.

2. George Palmer Putnam (1814–1872) established *Putnam's Monthly Magazine* (1852) and founded the publishing house of G. P. Putnam (1848).

3. The Venetian poem was the ill-fated "Disillusion." Replying to a letter from Howells of 19 December (which has not been found), Hurd wrote on 30 December 1867 (MH) : "You have written two most excellent works, the critics have praised them, your friends have read and admired them, the public has bought them. What more could you ask?...But will you injure this enviable reputation in the least by publishing a work which is not equal to the other two already published?"

4. F. Hassaurek, *Four Years Among Spanish Americans*, was published by Hurd & Houghton in 1867, and Howells reviewed it in the *Atlantic*, February 1868.

5. *Italian Journeys*.

6. George Stillman Hillard (1808–1879), Boston lawyer, politician, and journalist, was the author of *Six Months in Italy* (1853), which Hurd considered a "classic." See Howells to Hurd, 13 August 1866, n. 4. Hillard's letter containing his favorable comments about *Italian Journeys*, which Howells forwarded to Hurd, has not been located.

6 March 1868, Cambridge, to William C. Howells Family

Cambridge, March 6, 1868.

Dear father, mother, and girls—

All things have conspired to celebrate my last birth-day with a brilliancy known to few fourths of July. As for you at home, I hardly know which to thank most or first: mother for the watch-rack, father for his beautiful letter, or the girls for their superb present of a fruit-knife. If the knife were far sharper than it is, it could not cut our love in two; but still it cuts me and Elinor (who's as proud of it as I am) to the heart with a sense of our undesert.—or undessert? What have I done to merit such kind remembrance from all of you? I look back over the past year, and unanswered questions and neglected letters rise before me answering, Nothing! And I own they're right, but cling to the fruit-knife all the same; and I shall not give up the watch-case either, which is in a taste that just suits my odd fancy, and which so fascinates Winny that she can think of no greater pleasure than to be allowed to look at it beyond breaking distance. You may be sure that the candy had its attractions, too—in fact we've all done justice to Henry's present. Father need not be discouraged when he thinks of the generous family about him. I thank him for his letter, and will try to make it prophetic if it isn't exactly historic concerning the things I've done. Life has opened fairly for me, and the years promise me new chances. I have an increase of salary ($1000) from the 1st of March, and I'm assured that the proof-reading will be made less and less burdensome to me, because they all feel, as Mr. Clark[1] told me, that my value to the Atlantic is in my writing. Isn't this pleasant? My salary is put up to $3500 but this pays also for articles.

We've got back to our perch on Sacramento street, and have all but settled down to peace and quietness. Elinor has a new broom in the kitchen, and we are having a furnace put in, and everything comfortable. It's pretty hard to bear: for as Elinor says you can get along with discomfort or unhappiness because you're sure of it, while bliss is appalling from its insecurity. The fact that we're all very well just now increases our trepidation. If there were not a foot of snow on the ground, and our rain-pipes hadn't frozen up, I don't know what we should do.

I enclose a note from Ticknor of the Young Folks, which will explain itself to Annie. I hope the sweet will help her to swallow the bitter. In fact, the rejection of "Jaunty" has nothing to do with its merit, and she must try again. I'll offer it to the Riverside, though I don't think it would stand so good a chance as something longer and older.[2]—Yesterday I dined with Dickens at the Fields's. He was charmingly simple and unaffected, and I had a good deal of talk with him as I sat next him.

One of the principal topics of discussion at table would have interested Joe: How far all the manuscript that Dickens has produced would reach if strung out line after line. Fields guessed 100000 miles, Dickens 1200, Mrs. Field 1000. But by actual calculation it would only reach 40 miles.

—I don't feel that is an answer to father's letter—in fact it is merely a general acknowledgment, and I must reserve a better reply. Elinor joins me in love to all, and Crumpy sends a drawing of our new clock as seen with the pendulum (or *tick,* as she calls it) in motion.

Yours affectionately,
Will.

Has it ever rained in that southern tier of towns since you and I were there, father? It seemed to have forgotten how.

1. John Spencer Clark (b. 1836) was a member of the firm of Ticknor & Fields. He had written to Howells on 5 February 1868 (MH): "You will understand therefore that for the current year, commencing (I think March 1st) we are to pay you $3500.—and in return you are to give us your services as editor of the Atlantic as heretofore; and at the same time contribute as much to the body of articles of the magazine as your time will permit."

2. For earlier comments on Annie's attempts to find a publisher, see Howells to Anne Howells, 26 September 1867, n. 1, and 15 December 1867, n. 3.

26 April 1868, Cambridge, to James M. Comly

Cambridge, April 26, 1868.

My dear Comly:

I got a Journal,[1] the other day from some one, containing a sprightly and clever review of Dixon's Spiritual Wives[2]—who are no doubt better than Dixon himself—and as I suppose you wrote the review, I will hazard thanking you for the paper. I take so great a pride in the attention you pay to literature, that I felt it almost a personal compliment when the man who opens the Atlantic exchanges said the Columbus Journal had the best book notices published in the West.

I blame myself that I do not hear how you are prospering, and what you are thinking and hoping, for I believe you were the last to write long ago. As for my own life here, it is taking pretty much its own course, and finding hard work in the way, but here and there a comfortable eddy, and a sunny stretch of level. If I don't rejoice, I at least don't grumble.

Our great sensation here has ceased with the sailing of Dickens. I dare say you'll have read of the parting scenes at New York. I saw the great man twice in society—once at Mr Longfellow's, and once at Fields's.

He was amiable and unassuming enough, and was very far from saying anything half so good as Lowell said about him—that he was a Lion fit to lie down with Charles Lamb.—Europe is making a great demand upon our literati this summer: Mr. Longfellow is going abroad, and Mr. Norton of the N. A. Review takes his family.

I hope you and Mrs. Libby and the children (I don't trust my imperfect mathematics in speaking of them,) are well as we at this writing, when the problem seems to be, what shall we do to squander our immense stock of health? I myself have a quarrel after dinner regularly with my waistband. Sometimes I think I'm getting fat; but this is only in moments of great unhappiness.

Mrs. Howells joins me in regards to your own and Dr Smith's family.

Yours
W. D. Howells.

1. The Columbus *Morning Journal,* of which Comly was editor.
2. William H. Dixon, *Spiritual Wives* (1868).

7 JULY 1868, BOSTON, TO JAMES M. COMLY

... The Atlantic Monthly, ...
Boston, July 7, *1868*

My dear Comly:

I have a very obliging note from your book-keeper placing at my disposal some files of the State Journal.[1] As I know this very great favor is done me by you, I wish to thank you for it most cordially. I don't know why I accept it, except that I've long outgrown the idea that I must take only what I deserve.—I forget whether Mr. Cooke's administration began in 1859 or 1858, but if it began in '59, I shall be very glad of both the files offered me, namely, from July to December '59, and from Jan. to Dec. '61. Otherwise, there is no reason why I should deprive you of the former. If the latter is not bound, I need not trouble you for the entire file. I only want it up to the end of August, when Cruel Barbara Allen displaced poor Price and me, though I should be glad of the copies containing two letters I sent from Europe.—On second thought, I believe we *did* begin in 1858. But still I am not certain—I am getting to be an old man, and forget easily.

—In our hot days, here, last week, I couldn't help thinking of Columbus, and how the dear old place must smoke. "Dust, how dost thou?"— T. Ferguson.[2] The author here quoted obliged me, one of the hottest nights of my life by occupying Fullerton's ex-bed, in my room at the

College.[3] In compliment to its having no sheets or pillow-cases on, he went into it naked, and all night chaunted a lay of hapless love, getting up and lying down as his spirits rose or fell. You imagine the scene. The incident took place shortly after his rejection by Miss Sinks.[4]—what happy years—what happy years! I never shall see their like again. I shall always think Columbus the gayest, most brilliant capital in the world. Where were there ever better fellows, more charming girls? The other day, an exceedingly pleasant Ohio man, Mr. Horton of Pomeroy,[5] who had graduated here, and is still lingering about these classic and cankerwormy shades, asked me how I thought the women I used to meet in Columbus society compared in culture and agreeableness with those of Cambridge. (We two are always at this sort of thing, getting little puffs out of each other for our native State.) In answer, I gave him such an account of Columbus and its social advantages, that in the end I had to caution him not to go there, for I had heard that it was very much changed.—Still, I think he may visit the city sometime, for he's going to practice law in Cincinnati; and I shall arrange for you to know each other. He's jolly and good.

With regards to all,

> Yours affectionately
> W. D. Howells.

Write now and then a line to say how your Mother is.

1. The files are from the *Ohio State Journal,* and the persons mentioned in this paragraph were all associated with it: Henry D. Cooke, Dr. Isaac J. ("Cruel Barbara") Allen, and Samuel D. Price. In a letter to Comly, 9 August 1868 (OHi), Howells acknowledged receipt of the files and added: "I've been looking over my performances somewhat, and on the whole I rather wonder that I wasn't drummed out of Columbus for them. Their innocent wickedness dismays my experience, and is the greatest evidence of youth in the writer."
2. See Howells to Victoria Howells, 16–22 May, 1859, n. 7.
3. See Howells to Victoria Howells, 26 December 1858, n. 1.
4. "Miss Olive Sinks" is listed in the 1862 Columbus directory as boarding at 168 East Broad.
5. Edwin Johnston Horton (1838–1897) graduated from Harvard in 1860. Until 1886 he served as an officer of salt and coal companies in Pomeroy, Ohio, then moved to New York.

13 JULY 1868, CAMBRIDGE, TO MARY D. HOWELLS

> Cambridge, July 13, 1868.

Dear Mother:

It is a long time both since I've written to you and since I've heard from you, but I've no doubt that I've been in your mind a great deal, as you have been in mine. Yesterday when I had time to write, I couldn't for the terrible heat, which made any sort of exertion impossible. The mercury stood at a hundred degrees in my room, during the day, and after night-fall, the air grew almost suffocating. Poor Elinor suffered a great deal, but on the whole bore it better than I expected; and about day break an east wind rose that greatly relieved the oppression. We hope the worst is over.

I trust it hasn't been quite so bad with you. The summer puts me in mind of that awful year of drouth which to me is now shrouded in what I must almost call the blackness of insanity. Now, however, I have not a shadow of hypochondria upon me. But I must always be a different man from that I could have been but for that dreadful year.—Do you remember how we used all to get up at night, and go out on the porch, and pant there? And the long days in which we desired the rain that did not come for weeks and weeks!—how vividly they return to me.

Annie's letter came a few days ago, and delighted us as her letters always do, for they are literature, and perfectly charming. Is it really a plan for her and Joe to go to the Bermudas? To the Azores would be much better; but any voyage has its attractions to you poor land-locked folk.—Elinor will try to answer Annie though it's hard work for her to write.—Joe's letters in the Sentinel are capital.[1] I've read them all with the greatest interest, and though I dare say a prejudiced public might not agree with me, I find them quite as entertaining as Venetian Life. Don't you, mother?—Joe wants me to point out their faults. Please tell him that in literature, if not in morals, we correct our faults by increasing the number of our virtues. So I don't say anything of errors, but recommend him to write as often as he can in the vein in which he described the clam-bake. That was admirable. And let him always remember that he can't tell things too minutely, or carefully. No fact alone has any importance, but a fact particularly stated must interest. But I'll write to him. Tell him he mustn't fail to make a letter about the Cushing-place, which we went to see together.[2]—There is very little family news. Elinor has one of her six-year teeth drawn the other day. It had never come out, but had retreated to the roof of her mouth. She stood it very well.—Winny seems to flourish like a weed on the hot weather. She looks very much like you, especially when she has her hair knotted up behind, and she's as dark as all the Deans and Howellses put together. She gave me a violet to carry to you, yesterday, and I'm sorry I haven't it to put in this letter. I send her love instead with her papa's and mamma's to you for all.

Your affectionate son,
Will.

1. Joseph A. Howells' letters written for the Ashtabula *Sentinel* described a trip to New England earlier that summer. They are signed "J. A. H." and appeared on the following dates: 3 June, 10 June, 24 June, 1 July (the clambake), 9 July, and 16 July 1868.

2. No letter on the "Cushing-place" has been located.

15 AUGUST 1868, CAMBRIDGE, TO JAMES R. LOWELL

Cambridge, August 15, 1868.

Dear Mr. Lowell:

Thanks to the powerful interest created by your declaration of principle, we had a son born yesterday afternoon about five o'clock[1]—an immense boy with an hexameter voice, and a highly poetical disposition to use it. His mother is very well, and his father, giving himself a half-holiday, ventures to apprize you of a fact that *may* appear less important at Elmwood than it does on Sacramento street.

Yours very truly
W. D. Howells.

1. In his letter of 27 July 1868 (MH), Lowell had written: "I hope Mrs. Howells is getting on famously. Give her my kindest sympathies & hopes, & tell her I vote for a boy." The son was, of course, John Mead Howells.

29 AUGUST 1868, CAMBRIDGE, TO CHARLES E. NORTON

Cambridge, August 29, 1868.

My dear Mr. Norton:

If I were not such a mere intellectual ruin, I would frame or feign some excuse for not having written to you before now; but as it is, I should bungle the best lying intention, and I wont attempt anything in exculpation. I am wracked by too great good fortune—I am dashed to pieces on the Happy Isles. The event into which our whole life and world had so long resolved themselves, has taken place with such blissful result that it has seemed scarcely worth while for the past two weeks to do anything but idly exult. You must know before this—one continent could not contain the news—that we have a boy,[1] born on the 14th of August, who came into this republic with as little disturbance as ever attended a citizen's advent, and whom I can't help introducing to you in this political character because of the remarkable and amusing resemblance he bears to Wm. H. Seward. The nurse and his mother find beauty in these looks, but I content myself with saying that he is a fine, *healthy* boy, insisting rather more upon the latter than the former qualification. His weight, including what I should call an unjust allowance of blanket in the case of alien offspring, was ten pounds, and I am told that "he hasn't gone back any," and if I may judge from his habit of "repairing his wasted time," I don't think he's likely to go back any. This may appear to you as all very weak and trivial in a letter; but I began by representing myself as an intellectual ruin; and I can assure you that I think nothing and say nothing wiser to any one. I think my state is partially attributable to too much female society; and what becomes of literary men in Paynim lands, where wives, nurses, and grandmothers are indefinitely multiplied in households, I couldn't in my enfeebled condition guess. I have caught quite a professional tone from the nurse, which I suppress with some difficulty here. Let me add only that Mrs. Howells has recovered without so much as a headache, and it is our reasonable hope that her health may at last be firmly reestablished. She asks me to send her love to our dear Mrs. Norton, and to each and all of you.

You will imagine that I have little to tell you of the world outside our hedge. Mr. Lowell I have seen oftener since you left than during the whole time I've been in Cambridge. The truth is I am about the only literary thing still extant here, and he comes to my house, and takes me walking with him—each time, I can see, with the vague hope that he wont bore himself, which I behold gradually give way to a settled despair as our walk draws to a close, and he finds that I have nothing in me.[2] If the fact were not so ghastly, I think I should almost enjoy it; but it is too horrible. I look at it in quite an impersonal light, and sympathize with his disappointment as if it were my own, though I've long got done expecting any entertainment from myself.—I've passed several times through your grounds of late, and found them charming. I think they are in greater beauty now than at any other time of year; and the loneliness of the house sympathizes with the first faint sentiment of autumn in the woods. What a curious little pang it gave to go, the other day, and ring your door-bell! I was there with Mead,[3] who is at home on a few weeks visit with his wife, and whom I wanted to have see your Tintoretto. He was greatly charmed with that and with Stillman's[4] picture, and I moped gloomily about the rooms which have pepper enough in them to make your worst enemy weep you. This pilgrimage, and journeys into Boston, have made up the variety of my life, and I have so little courage to attempt anything grander that I gave up with a shudder an excursion down the harbor which I had meditated. It seems incredible to hear of all that you are doing, and the varied enjoyments that you are undergoing, and I am glad that you & every one bear it so well.—I have seen Sedgwick and Miss Dora[5] since their return from Canada, and have enjoyed over again, in their talk, my elder travel in that province. Godkin has written two very delightful and thoughtful papers on some characteristics of society there;[6] and generally the Nation continues admirable. To-day I've read an amusing review, on the whole, of Italian Journeys, in the London Saturday Review of Aug. 15. To you and me who know me, and what manner of person I am, is it not delightful to read of me as a skeptical "citizen of the world"? I am not all that the Review could wish, it seems—but who is? It appeared to me that the book was rather happily misconceived by the critic; but he was just enough in some strictures.[7] —I write entirely of myself this time because I know of nothing else just now; and I hope you will be as personal. Pray give my best respects to your mother, and remember me most heartily to all your party, who are more in my thoughts than they are even in numbers.

Yours ever,
W. D. Howells

1. John Mead Howells.
2. A warm and friendly attitude towards Howells is expressed in Lowell's letter of 5 July 1868 (MH; reprinted in M. A. DeWolfe Howe, ed., *New Letters of James Russell Lowell* [New York: Harper & Brothers, 1932], pp. 128–30). Lowell thanked Howells for having saved him from inadvertently committing plagiarism in his poem, "The Footpath," *Atlantic*, August 1868. See *Literary Friends and Acquaintance*, HE, pp. 189–90.
3. Larkin G. Mead, Jr.
4. William J. Stillman (1828–1901), an artist, who was U. S. consul at Rome (1861–1865).
5. Arthur G. Sedgwick (1844–1915), a Boston lawyer and assistant editor of the *Nation* (1872–1884), and his sister Theodora. They were Norton's brother- and sister-in-law.
6. "French Canada," *Nation*, 13 and 20 August 1868.
7. The reviewer called Howells "an easy-going citizen of the world who knows when to be suggestively vivacious and when to fall into a sympathetic half slumber" but regretted his "lapses from the light into the funny style."

30 AUGUST 1868, CAMBRIDGE, TO WINIFRED HOWELLS

Cambridge August 30, 1868.

Dearest Crumpy True:

I promised to write to you when you got to Brattleboro', and here is the first letter. I hope that you had a pleasant journey, and found grandpa waiting for you at the station. Poor Pipe[1] felt very sad after parting with you; and you may tell your gran'ma, with his love, that he wouldn't have let any body but her take you away.—Mamma and the little boy are both well to-day, Mamma taking dinner with Mrs. Hyde[2] and me at the table.—You know that loose horse which has been in our street? Well, and you know papa took the gates off their hinges so they wouldn't bang and disturb mamma? Well, this morning the horse walked in, and commenced eating the grass on our embankment, and when Pipe tried to drive him out he turned round, and plunged into the morning-glory bower, and broke it all down, and killed nearly all the vines. Perhaps some will live. Wasn't it awful?—I send you a bit of heliotrope out of our garden.

I hope my dear little maid is behaving very prettily, and lovingly with every one, not showing any crossness or selfishness. I know you must be having a nice time, and I'm sure you'll have a pleasant visit. But you must make your visit pleasant to others, and that you can do only by treating them kindly and gently.

Papa will write to you often, and you must keep his letters to read for yourself when you're a young lady.[3] Give our love to Grandma and Grandpa and aunt Marietta and Mary,[4] and take some for yourself with a kiss from little baby brother.

Your affectionate father.

P. S. White Owl's Feather won't have so much to do, will he, now the morning-glories are gone.

1. "Pipe" was most likely one of Winifred's names for her father. She had been sent to visit her maternal grandparents after the birth of John Mead Howells.
2. Probably John's nurse.
3. There is another letter to "Dear Crumpy," 2 September 1868 (MH).
4. Aunt Marietta was the Italian wife of Larkin G. Mead, Jr. Aunt Mary was Elinor Howells' sister, Mary Noyes Mead.

4 OCTOBER 1868, CAMBRIDGE, TO WILLIAM C. HOWELLS

Cambridge, October 4, 1868.

Dear father:

We were delighted to get your long letter to Elinor a day or two since; and I will try to make some return for it in news at least. As to Sam's marriage, I can't say that we were greatly surprised: still it is rather sudden, considering that he has only been baptized four months and divorced three. I remember *Mr.* but not *Mrs.* Deming, and I don't locate the bride very satisfactorily by your explanation.[1]—You'll be a good deal pleased, I dare say, and considerably amused to hear that I have been offered a *professorship*. Yesterday, a gentleman called upon me, who had come all the way from Schenectady, New York, with authority from the trustees of Union College, to ask me to become professor of Rhetoric in their institution. You know it is a very old and respectable college. They had all read my books and articles, and they had decided that I was the man for them if they could get me. It was immensely flattering, but, with many thanks, I declined—seeing my way clearer here. I told the ambassador that I wasn't the graduate of even a common school: that didn't make any difference; I was afraid of young men: I'd get over that; I didn't know anything about Rhetoric: having read I. Js. and V. L.[2] he didn't believe that. So I was obliged to fall back upon selfish objections, and I urged these so forcibly that he saw my mind was made up; but we made friends over some claret, and he left me saying that if the college had sent him to no purpose, he was still very glad he had come. A gratifying thing about it was that all the college magnates here gave me the "most flattering testimonials" when he asked them about me. Would you—or Joe—like to be professor of Rhetoric in Union College? Perhaps as Sam is beginning a new race, with the bridegroom's strength, he'd like to turn his hand to professing.

I'll send you sheets of Gnadenhütten[3] as soon as it's all in type. We were obliged, on account of its length to postpone it till the December number; but I can let you see it in a week or two: I think it pretty good, and the Rev. Edmund de Schweinitz of Bethlehem[4] pronounces it excellent.

My poem will be out in the December Putnam. As it's the only thing of mine that Elinor's entirely liked, I tell her I'm afraid it will fail. It's called "No Love Lost," and will be issued very handsomely as a Christmas book.[5]

Winny came home last Tuesday night, and so we're all together again, and very happy on that account. Crump adores her little brother, and hangs about him all the time. We see how pretty she is after being separated from her a little while, and she's angelic goodness itself.

I'm very, very sorry to hear that mother's been so poorly. I did want to see her this fall, but I've been so driven that I could not get the time. I don't understand that she's been seriously, though very uncomfortably, sick. If I did, I'd come to her at whatever risk. I hope that you have good medical treatment for her: I doubt about the Jefferson doctors generally.

Elinor says if you'll commute the apples you propose to send, to such a cheese as you brought with you last fall, we'll be very glad to get them. Really, it seems scarcely worth while to trouble you to send fruit such a long way, especially as we are not great fruit eaters. But we are very grateful for your offer, and shall thank you kindly for the cheese when it arrives.

We had a charming call from Annie Bates[6] the other day, who spoke of you all with great affection, and her visit generally with delight.

Dear love to mother, and all the rest, in which we all join.

Your affectionate son,
Will.

1. The maiden name of Sam's second wife was apparently Florence Brown; that she also had been married before is indicated in Howells' letter to his father and sisters, 10 January 1869 (MH).

2. *Italian Journeys* and *Venetian Life.*

3. "Gnadenhütten," a historical paper on a Moravian settlement in Ohio, *Atlantic,* January 1869. According to Howells' letter to his father, 26 January 1868 (MH), W. C. Howells had suggested the subject matter.

4. Edmund de Schweinitz was a Moravian minister in Bethlehem, Pennsylvania, according to Howells' letter to Victoria M. Howells, 8 November 1868 (MH).

5. See Howells to Graham, 3 February 1863, n. 3.

6. Annie Bates has not been identified.

20 OCTOBER 1868, JEFFERSON, TO JAMES M. COMLY

Jefferson, October 20, 1868.

My dear Comly:

I ought before this to have written you from Cambridge, but for two months before I left home every instant seemed taken up, and my wrist was sore with constant writing. I was not well, either, and was in a continual excitement. We had a son born on the 14th of August, and you know how many anxieties precede and follow an event of this kind. After they were all past, and I was looking forward to a month of comparative rest, with a visit here about Thanksgiving day, I got an alarming letter from father, which determined me to come to Ohio as soon as possible. The same night, a dispatch arrived saying that mother was very sick, and telling me to take the first train. I did so, waiting seven weary hours for it, and arrived here at 7½ Saturday 10th, when my poor mother had already been five hours dead. I am incapable of telling you anything of that time, or of writing intelligibly about the event. Partly, perhaps, because my grief was too violent to be opposed, the first sorrow exhausted itself, and left me more calm and cheerful than I could have dared to hope. I don't think any of us wholly realize the fact of mother's loss; but at the same time I am sure that something of which I have taken no account in happier moments, is present here, consoling and supporting us. No mother was ever more dearly loved by her children. Even with me, who had been separated from the rest by ten years' absence from home, the thoughts of her were always fresh and clear; and her praise of what I did was always the sweetest in the world. It appears very strange now that she could pass out of this atmosphere of love almost without raising a fear of her death till she was gone. She had been ailing all summer with a disorder that was known to be weakening, but was equally thought chronic and of no immediate danger. No one here was troubled about her state; she herself was not uneasy; and when I got letters speaking of her sickness, they always conveyed the assurance that she was better. Thursday night, the 8th, she was seized with some kind of sharp attack, which must have been paralysis, and was insensible till her death.—Please accept, my dear Comly, the thanks of all for the sympathy you have tendered us, and forgive me if I have written you at too great length on this sad subject. Every one has lost a mother or has one to lose.

—It was my intention, when I came to Ohio, this fall, to visit Columbus, but all my plans are broken up, and I am going home to work as soon as I can. I shall be here till Thursday, and then I must leave this poor home to form itself anew over the awful void that has been made in it. I scarcely dare think of my father's loss, so incomparably greater than ours, great as ours is; and I cannot be too thankful that in his firm and distinct religious belief, he has so strong a support.

All send regards to you and yours, and to the Doctor[1] and his family.

Yours faithfully
W. D. Howells.

1. Dr. S. M. Smith.

31 OCTOBER 1868, CAMBRIDGE, TO WILLIAM C. HOWELLS

Cambridge, Oct. 31, 1868.

Dear father:

The week since Wednesday has gone pretty much like the days preceding, except that we now have Charles Mead[1] and his family with us, and our quiet is somewhat interrupted. I am also fallen upon times of unhappy leisure; I have finished my Gnadenhütten paper, and have not yet decided what next I shall attempt, though it is probable that I shall look somewhat at the Gallipolis history. I have been reading the manuscript sent me by Mr. Horton of Pomeroy, and find it a full, though very awkward and unliterary statement of the history of the French colony.[2] Much will depend upon the success of Gnadenhütten: if that is generally liked, I shall feel encouraged to go on in the same direction.

I send you a letter from Hinton, which is most kind and feeling, and which I thought you would like to see.—It seemed to me that Harvey,[3] in his paper, spoke of mother with beautiful simplicity and affection. I was greatly touched by his reference to her.—Since I wrote you last, I have seen Mr. James,[4] and had a long talk with him. He was very sympathetic, and his strong faith was very comforting. He related a story out of Swedenborg's diary[5] which I had never heard before, but which I daresay is familiar to you. It was that of the man hanged at Stockholm, who expected the rope to break, and who came into the spiritual world believing that this had happened, and who would not be persuaded of the fact. It was to me a singularly vivid and realizing picture of the *transition* from one world to the other, which it is so hard to imagine. I have read a great part of those extracts from Swedenborg, but have found their fragmentary form unsatisfactory, and have now borrowed the new translation of Divine Love and Wisdom. Still I care as yet less about the *doctrines* than the *facts* of the other life: I long to have the spiritual world described over and over again and ever so minutely. So before going far with this work I shall probably read Heaven and Hell.[6]

—a change has taken place in the firm of Ticknor and Fields, Mr. Ticknor having gone out. The change doesn't affect me at all. The new firm is to be called Fields, Osgood & Co. Mr. Ticknor is going to Europe. The change is quite amicable, I believe.

—I have seen very few people since I returned and have hardly any news, outside of our own family, to write you. Elinor is slowly gaining strength, and the boy[7] is exceedingly well. He is a good natured little fellow, always ready to laugh and crow; and he takes—as a favor—any amount of rough handling from Winny. Though her roughness is only a kind of quick gentleness. I was reading her "Footsteps of Angels"[8] tonight, and explained it as the return of those that had died. She wasn't quite satisfied. She said, "Gran'ma was in heaven and didn't want to come back; and if she died she would n't, because heaven was much more beautiful than this."—Perhaps we are too proud of her when compared with other children. Certainly, besides Charles Mead's boy[9] she appears everything that is gentle and wise. The dear little soul is now filled with hopes of Christmas. Tell Aurelia that the poem[10] she gave me has been read ragged already. Winny knew the piece before, but having it in a little book by itself seems to give it a new zest. Every night after dinner I have to come down the parlor chimney "with a bound"—the idea being represented by rattling on the screen and then jumping out into the middle of the floor. Then I am Winifred Howells, and lie asleep on the sofa while she brings me a Christmas Tree.

I enclose Father Thorpe's[11] kind letters, and that of Laura Platt[12] which Elinor read with much gratification. Here is also a letter from Mrs. Horace Mann about Kindergarten, which I thought might interest Annie.

Elinor will write another letter to be posted to-morrow. In the meantime we all send love.

Your affectionate son,
Will.

Mrs. Platt's letter has been mislaid: Elinor will send it in hers.

1. Elinor Howells' brother.
2. Edwin J. Horton's piece on Gallipolis, Ohio, a French settlement on the Ohio River, did not appear in the *Atlantic*. For Howells' project on Gallipolis, see his letter to W. C. Howells, 7 February 1869, n. 10.
3. Harvey Green.
4. Henry James, Sr.
5. *The Spiritual Diary of Emanuel Swedenborg*.
6. Swedenborg's *Heaven and Hell* was first published in an English translation in London, 1778. The first American edition appeared in 1812, and by the end of the nineteenth century there were at least six translations and more than seventy-five imprints.
7. John Mead Howells.
8. Longfellow's poem.
9. Albert Mead.
10. Clement C. Moore, "A Visit from St. Nicholas."
11. Father Thorpe has not been identified.
12. Although Elinor's cousin was married to John G. Mitchell, Howells used her maiden name; the "Mrs. Platt" in the postscript is therefore Mrs. Mitchell.

13 NOVEMBER 1868, CAMBRIDGE, TO JAMES R. LOWELL

Cambridge, November 13, 1868.

Dear Mr. Lowell:

This morning I read more than half way through your Atlantic paper[1] before I reached Boston, where I had to give up the sheets to J. T. F.[2] The unread half may be altogether unworthy, but it would have to be worse than T-ck-rm-n[3] to make any one think ill of the whole article. I think it is perfectly charming,—so light, so smiling, and so keen.— This is no effect of your ale, but the awkward expression of a most honest delight in your article, which is surely one of the happiest things yet done by a man whose only fault is that he has never made a failure.— But that you said you'd like to know my poor little opinion, how should I dare to offer these wretched praises?[4]

Very sincerely yours,
W. D. Howells.

1. "On a Certain Condescension in Foreigners," *Atlantic*, January 1869.
2. James T. Fields.
3. Henry D. Tuckerman was an *Atlantic* contributor.
4. Lowell's high regard for Howells' critical judgment is indicated in his letter to Howells of 31 October 1868 (MH; partly reprinted in M. A. DeWolfe Howe, *New Letters of James Russell Lowell* [New York: Harper & Brothers, 1932], pp. 130–31): "Do you sit for ever so long thrusting up a meditative underlip & biting the end of your pen, while you contrive how you shall make clever sentences seem to drop by accident? You are going to beat us all in prose. If you do as much in verse, I shall withdraw from my limited partnership with the Muse...."

22 November 1868, Cambridge, to Aurelia H. Howells

Cambridge, Nov. 22, 1868.

Dear Aurelia:

I've just come from the postoffice with your letter, which I went to get after church. Winny and I went to the Episcopal church, where I was with Joe last Sunday, and where I like to go because of the beautiful service and its associations, and because the unprofitable sermon is sure to be shorter than I can find it elsewhere. Winny got very tired, and "I don't see how you could have acted worse," said I, when we were got out. "Why papa I could have acted worse than *that*." "I can't think of anything worse." "Well, *I* can think of screaming, or of running out of church." Isn't she a jade?

—You can imagine how happy I was in having Joe here if it was only for a few days. His presence was a sad comfort of a kind that I hardly know how to analyze. We did not talk much of mother, but we felt that both thought of her, and to be near each other, and do that was a consolation. Besides he had just come from all of you, and though he could tell me little that I did not already know, still it seemed to unite us more closely. I understand, and realized all the time how you must miss him and yet I begged him to stay longer. It was his own good heart that took him home so soon.—I hope Henry found the drum of figs suitable, and that he has enjoyed playing on it. Tell him he must let you all have at least one turn. I'm very glad he continues so good a boy. He must give my love, with a large apple to Charley, and to Annie Maggie and Johnny Stephen.[1]

—It is a pleasure to find you all so well contented with the name we've given our little boy.[2] We had a letter this morning from the Meads expressing their satisfaction. The dear baby seems to thrive under it, and I think it is ominous of all good things for him.—Joe will have told you of our change of nurse. The new arrangement works even better than the old, and we had thought that perfection. Of course, it hasn't been perfectly smooth. The nurse boards out her little boy two years old, and Wednesday night, she was sent for on account of his sickness; but he got better at once, and she came back Thursday morning. She seems a good, kind-hearted creature, and is already very fond of the baby.

—I'm glad to hear that you still think of employing your mind in criticism, and the first book I get that seems of the right sort for you to manage, I'll send you for notice in the Atlantic, though of course I don't promise acceptance beforehand. About "What Answer," do you mean that the Nation's criticism changed your opinion, or that it took just the ground you meant to occupy?³—Annie—and all of you ought to be very proud of her success. I hope she won't rest so long after "Jaunty" as she did after "Frightened Eyes."⁴

I've got a new study-chair, Aurelia, and Elinor has lent me your tidy, and you can't imagine what a bright and cheerful effect it gives to my neutral-tinted little workshop. It seems, with the scarlet geranium, to furnish the whole room.—At one side of the bookcase, where it will not catch unsympathizing eyes, but where I can easily see it, is the little case Ive had made for the few poor relics I have of what was mother. The pot of ivy is on a bracket underneath, and the plant is already beginning to caress the memorial frame with its tiny, soft green leaflets. "So near, and yet so far!" I know all that sadness, dear girl, of which you tell me. I think oftener of you, even, than I do of mother, for the pain of parting is all with us here. Where she is, how short the time must seem till we shall all have each other again!

—There is news from England that Mr. Norton has been very sick, and is by no means well, yet, even if he is entirely out of danger. The family will spend the winter in London instead of France as they had intended. About our neighbors generally there is no news. Mr. Lowell brought me his new volume of poems yesterday.⁵ What do you think of the New England Tragedies?⁶ I found it pretty hard work to get at praiseworthy points in them, but I dare say that after the first disappointment was over, one would like them better.

Give father and the rest my dearest love. I'll write to each as I can.— I don't understand where Sam is keeping house.

Your affectionate brother,
Will.

1. Charley was a horse; Annie Maggie and Johnny Stephen may have been other animals or dolls belonging to Howells' mentally retarded brother Henry.
2. John Mead Howells.
3. No review of Anna E. Dickinson's *What Answer?* (1868) has been located in the *Nation*. Howells reviewed it in the *Atlantic*, January 1869.
4. See Howells to Anne Howells, 26 September 1867, n. 1.
5. *Under the Willows and Other Poems* was reviewed by Howells in the *Atlantic*, February 1869.
6. Longfellow's *The New England Tragedies* (1868) was reviewed by Howells in the *Atlantic*, January 1869.

24 NOVEMBER 1868, CAMBRIDGE, TO BAYARD TAYLOR

Cambridge, Nov. 24, 1868.

My dear Taylor:

I was very glad to have your visit prolonged by letter, though I haven't seemed in haste to say so. It was like your good-nature and delicacy to apologize for a possible faux pas, but let me assure you that none was made as far as Mr. Dennett of The Nation is concerned.[1] He is not even my acquaintance: I never saw him. My regard for him is based entirely upon the fact that has found good some things that I intended to be so; and apart from this perfectly natural feeling, I do respect him as a man of great critical ability and performance. I do not always agree with him—he may cut up my new poem in the next Nation,[2] and then I'm sure I shall not agree with him—and I know that he is a man of strong intellectual antipathies, but I believe him to be sincere, and I see that he is nearly always able to give his reasons. I would have said something like this the other day, but I thought it would come with a bad grace from me whom he has always praised, before Aldrich for whom he has never a good word, and Mr. Fields whom he very evidently dislikes. Moreover, I am a bungler at defence of any kind, and I prefer to let time do justice in most cases.

Have you seen Lowell's new volume[3] yet? It is full of wonderfully good things, and is such a book as it dismays me to think of criticising. I agree with you of course as his being the greatest of American critics, and I am ready to go a step beyond and include those of England. In fact I think English criticism the poorest stuff possible. The tone of it is always bad, and in its sudden friendliness for American authors it is sickening. You see I am disposed to rail a little. It is because I am dissatisfied with what I have been doing lately.[4] I hope that my Thanksgiving Dinner will at least restore my self-esteem. Mrs. Howells joins me in warm regards to you and Mrs. Taylor.

Yours very sincerely,
W. D. Howells.

1. John R. Dennett (1837–1874) was the literary critic of the *Nation*. He was noted for the severity of his criticism.

2. *No Love Lost: a Romance of Travel* was reviewed in the *Nation*, 26 November 1868. The reviewer enjoyed the scenes of Venice and the humor, and forgave such "little matters" as weakness of "plot and passion."

3. *Under the Willows and Other Poems*.

4. Howells' doubts about his most recent work, "Gnadenhütten," were expressed in letters to his father at this time. On 29 November 1868 (MH) he wrote: "It is long, and I am afraid will be thought dull...." And again on 13 December 1868 (MH): "The truth is, the subject got possession of me, rather than I of the subject, and so the matter was not well mastered. However, it is a novel bit of history, and I think it will interest people by its facts if not by its treatment."

20 DECEMBER 1868, BOSTON, TO WILLIAM C. HOWELLS

13 Boylston Place,
Boston, Dec. 20, 1868.

Dear father:
I hope you will not think my Wednesday letters omitted by intention. I have been billious all week, and unfit to write, and I've had to write— to the exclusion of everything else—a notice of Lowell's new book of poems.[1] It seemed to go contrarily from the start, and cost me ever so much labor; but when it was done, Fields liked it, and so I rest quiet if not content. When I reflect upon this life which I have desired to live, and now live, I do not think it is by any means an easy one. I work almost ceaselessly, and never stop except from exhaustion; I am full of cares and anxieties, and I gain just enough money to live on. In literature it costs just as much to make a failure as a success, and while praise loses its charm after while, blame seems to remain as keen-edged as ever. But I do not complain: I'm quite satisfied to contemplate the anomaly—which is no anomaly either, but a perfectly natural thing.— All this is somehow to excuse me for not writing, when I do not feel myself to be quite excusable. I *could* sit down and write you a few lines often, and I'm ashamed that I don't. I only ask you to judge my case by your own.

The week has passed without much event. Elinor writes from Brattleboro' that she is gaining in health, and we are all very well here. Johnny is a very good-natured and pleasant baby; he is ready to smile at any time, and has a fashion of lying on his back and crowing that is very pleasant to hear. Since Joe was here, he has had no sickness, and that last was only from a change of milk.

I began this letter just after breakfast, but finding myself a little too nervous to finish it, then, I went out for a walk, and wandered way down through Dock Square and North Street, till I came to Ferry Street, which is the locality of the poor Italians. Scarcely any other nationality is represented there, and nearly all the organ-grinders whom the summer sends forth, quarter in Ferry Street. As I was passing through it, I was hailed by a little boy, who remembered me from last June, and with whom I had now a little chat. He told me his whole family were going back to Genoa very shortly. The boy's mother was an invalid, and could not bear our climate; and it seemed that the father, who was an organ grinder in summer, and a coal-heaver in winter, had gathered money enough to go home. I confess that as the snow fell thickly around us, I half-envied them their prospect. The winter is very trying to me, and we have six months of it here—not more than you have at home, but somehow more trying.—Dear father, I know where this snow fell as well as in Boston streets, and there is no aspect of the day that does recall that solemn place to my mind.[2] If the impression of our loss is less constantly with me than at first, its recurrences, it seems to me are even more painful, and I have somehow lost the power to idealize or spiritualize the fact. Believe me I do not forget you or those at home. In whatever enjoyment I have, I feel as if I committed a wrong against you; but I know you do not think so. When we meet in the spring, we shall have many things to talk of that cannot be written. I long to see you.

Are you making any sort of preparation for Christmas? We shall hang up Winny's stockings, and in the evening she is to go to a Christmas party at the Fields's, entirely for children. I am to take her about half-past seven, and then retire until nine o'clock, when I may appear again to fetch her away. So the world repeats itself. It isn't such a great while since you gave me a birth-day party in honor of my being seven years old.

—Johnny shows himself of quite a different character from Winny. He is much more pensive, and while he is perfectly good-natured, he is more easily offended. His is no dry crying either, but accompanied with tears of the largest size.

—As I try to keep you posted about my literature, I must tell you that my poem[3] seems not to be liked by the public generally, though Lowell, Harry James, and others whose opinion I value praise it highly. Gnadenhütten seems not to be a success—at least it attracts no attention, and I'm afraid that I've made it too long. Now I have in view some sketches, or biographies from Venetian history,[4] and I am at present writing a little paper on "Doorstep Acquaintance,"[5] in which I tell of certain organ grinders and beggars who visited us from time to time on Sacramento Street.[6] There were some odd characters amongst them.

—I don't know whether I've told you yet that Mr. Norton has been very sick in England. At one time his life was in danger, but now he is much better.

—Winny is waiting for her evening's talk with me, and I must close. Love to all. Tell Henry to remember me to the Cossmuddy.

Your affectionate son,
Will.

1. *Under the Willows and Other Poems.*
2. Howells is here alluding to his mother's grave. Clearly the intended meaning would be expressed by inserting "not" before "recall."
3. *No Love Lost.*
4. These were apparently never written.
5. *Atlantic*, April 1869.
6. Howells' Cambridge residence.

17 January 1869, Boston, to William C. Howells

13 Boylston Place,
Boston, January 17, 1869.

Dear father:

Having written notes to both Joe and Sam today, I find myself with less than usual to say to the rest. I was made very sad the other day by your letter, for I perceived that at last you had begun to feel our loss in its reality. That "waiting for something" that can never happen as long as we live—how hard it is!—Every night, almost, I dream of mother, and she appears in such characteristic ways,—as for instance we all being in a place together where there was some person of distinction whose attention she wished to draw to me, she said to him, "My son," and then when he simply bowed, and went on talking with another, she wore such a grieved and hurt expression that it woke me out of my sleep. At another time it seemed to me we were at home, and I was paying less regard than she thought I should to one of the family, and she insisted with her tender jealousy on my noticing that one, whom she praised. At other times, I see her with something of the awful beauty her dear dead face wore—well, what use?

—The winter that is no winter is passing pretty rapidly, and I am getting through with the usual amount of laborious nothing. I tell you at the first moment of a fact which you must consider confidential, and not mention out of the family nor in any way that it may become public. Fields will probably sail for Europe in April, and I shall be left in charge of the magazine.[1] I can't tell yet whether this will detain me here during May, or not, or how it will affect our proposed visit. I may have to come earlier or later, or I may be able to get off at the time proposed. It depends upon the shape in which he leaves the work. I will write again about the matter as soon as I know something definite. In the meantime, Fields may possibly be prevented altogether from going.—I have thought somewhat of going to Washington during the inauguration.[2] F. O. & Co.[3] would be willing to pay my expenses if I went, and I could write something taking for the magazine, I suppose, but I'm doubtful about going.—I've just finished a little paper called "Threshold Acquaintance,"[4] which is a sketch of some organ-grinding and other Italians I've met in this country, as well as other vagabonds.— The lecture of which Elinor speaks was of course by old James, and embodied the Swedenborgian idea of women.[5] I liked it extremely; but there were only a dozen or two to hear it. I suppose it will be printed, and then I'll send you a copy.—I haven't seen Lowell since I came to

Boston. Of Norton, who has been very sick in England, we now hear the best news.

With love to all your affectionate son

Will.

1. Although Howells was "in charge" during the absence of J. T. Fields, he did not assume the editorship of the *Atlantic* until July 1870.
2. Ulysses S. Grant was inaugurated on 4 March 1869.
3. Fields, Osgood & Co., publishers of the *Atlantic*.
4. "Doorstep Acquaintance."
5. The lecture by Henry James, Sr., may have been the basis of his articles, "The Woman Thou Gavest with Me," *Atlantic*, January 1870, and "Is Marriage Holy?" *Atlantic*, March 1870.

24 JANUARY 1869, BOSTON, TO WILLIAM C. HOWELLS

13 Boylston Place,
Boston. January 24, 1869.

Dear father:

Elinor and I have just returned from Dr. Huntington's church,[1] where we heard that gentleman preach. It was he who left the Unitarians some years ago, and created considerable excitement thereby in the ecclesiastical world. He is an able man and is soon to be made bishop of New York. His church here has been one of the most fashionable, and has tended a little toward Ritualism; but his sermon was rather practical and straightforward, and without being sentimental or elaborate was the best literature I've yet heard from the pulpit. He preached on the necessity of arguing the perfection of creation from the fact of divine goodness, and on the impossibility of solving the problem of evil by the intellect alone.—Yesterday I got a very pleasant little note from Mr. Bonner[2] in acknowledgment of a copy of the Atlantic which I had sent him.—I hope that by this time, father, your back is very much better, and that Henry has recovered from his chicken-pox. Are you having, I wonder, the marvellous weather that we have here? To-day it is mild as April, and this softness and the brine in the air make me think continually of Venice.

Larkin Mead, when here, vaguely sketched the idea of a stone to commemorate dear mother, which I like for its simplicity and beauty.[3] You will see from the sketch, which I enclose that it represents a Gothic window: all the ornamentation within the outer line to be sunken in, and the tablet within the pillars to be yet deeper. He thinks it could be advantageously executed in Italy, all save the inscription which had best be put on here, and he has promised to attend to the matter at an early day, and report to me cost, etc. Of course this sketch would be subject to great modification.—Mead left us on Friday, and will sail very soon.

I have commenced another article for the Atlantic, this time on Going to the Theatre.[4] It is to be of a general character, but I am going to see if I can't do something to laugh down the present vileness of the stage. You can have no idea without seeing it, of the licence of the theatre—which comes as most of the world's wickedness does now from the existence of the French empire. Never before Napoleon III was there one man who was the means of such great and widespread evil.—I don't know when I shall get at my paper on Gallipolis.[5] There are some books on the subject in the Congressional Library which I'd like to see, but I can't quite make up my mind to go to Washington. The paper, when done, will probably be for the North American. We are quite well, all of us this winter. Winny had a little return of the eruption which has troubled her for two winters past, but that is now over with. Brotherkin frets scarcely at all with his teething. We think two teeth are nearly through. He is really a model boy—very sunny tempered, and ready to laugh at the smallest joke. He thinks Winny the wittiest and wisest of human beings, grins and gurgles when she dances to him, and stares open mouthed when she sings. I long to have you all see him.—Tell Aurelia that I took dinner yesterday at the Angells', and found Mrs. Farwell very much better.[6] I do not know if they ever expect her to leave her room, but a very remarkable improvement has taken place in her.—You must take good care of yourself father, and guard against cold and falls. Give my love to Henry and tell him to give the chicken-pox to Stoackel's[7] hens.—All join in love to all.

Your affectionate son,
Will.

1. Frederick D. Huntington (1819–1904), rector of the Emmanuel parish in Boston, was soon to become Protestant Episcopal bishop of central New York.
2. Probably a friend of Howells' father, though possibly Robert Bonner (1824–1899), publisher of the New York *Ledger*.
3. Enclosed with the letter is a sketch of the proposed monument. Along the side of the sketch Howells wrote "Height 6 feet."
4. "The New Taste in Theatricals," *Atlantic*, May 1869.
5. See Howells to W. C. Howells, 7 February 1869, n. 10.
6. Dr. and Mrs. Henry C. Angell. Mrs. Farwell was probably Mrs. Angell's mother.
7. Stoackel was apparently a Jefferson neighbor, as is indicated in Howells' letter to his father, 2 May 1869.

31 January 1869, Boston, to William C. Howells

13 Boylston Place,
Boston, January 31, 1869.

Dear father:

I have just come from hearing Mr. John Weiss preach before the Parker congregation or what is left of it,[1] and I am greatly pleased with him. His discourse was about habit, and how we judged men by the fatalistic mark which habit put on them, but how God judged them by the recuperative and regenerating forces always at work in them. We made, he said, no allowance for these forces in estimating character, and therefore could not conceive of a bad man's redemption, and he contended that the idea of the perdition of a single soul was in the last degree illogical and atheistic. I wish you would tell me in which of Swedenborg's works to find the doctrine of vastation. Mrs. Carter once told me something about it.

Since I wrote you last, very little has happened to vary our lives. Brotherkin has not waited for Henry to give him the chicken-pox but has come out with a large display on his own account. It must be that the eruption which we noticed on Winny two weeks ago was the same disease, and that Johnny took it from her. We can hardly say that he is sick, for he has scarcely any fever, and does not fret much. In fact, the pustules seem to be drying up to-day.—Isn't there something very strange and one-sided in the malignant power of disease to communicate itself, while health makes no impression from one upon another? Evil in the moral world appears similarly gifted, and good similarly powerless. But perhaps we see only one half of the operation.

—I send you a letter from Mr. Norton which I received some days ago,[2] and which contains a message for you, and Annie. Here is also a balance of money for Joe from a draft which he sent by me to Ticknor and Fields.

—It is very horrible news you write in the latter part of your letter, especially of that which happened near you. What ever became of Haynes the murderer of Sutliff? Was that a relative of his I read of in the Sentinel as concerned in a late stabbing affray?[3] Perhaps they are rather a man-slaughtering family.

I have been reading with the greatest interest and pleasure your reminiscences of early life in Ohio based on that old State Register.[4] I think the last number is particularly good. All the matter was instructive to me, and I was touched by the disposition you now have to recur to the past. Don't you think, father, it would be a good think to write out in some full and connected form your recollections of an epoch now so wholly past? You would find amusement in it, and it would be material to which a philosophic historian would some day turn with gratitude. You could do it so intelligently that it would be quite different from the stuff in the pioneer collections, and I hope you will think over my suggestion.—That was very curious about Alexander Campbell's reception of you,[5] and very neatly done. How came such a man to spring up in that part of Virginia? However, remarkable things have always come out of Nazareth.

I have not yet spoken with Mr. Fields a second time about his going to Europe or the time of it, but I think the spring weather will have a good deal to do with the time of our visit. I don't know yet but the fact of Mr. Fields's absence will shorten my stay somewhat, but if it does, we must contrive to have you return the visit very soon afterwards. However, everything is uncertain about it, except my desire to see you all.

Annie wrote me some time ago that she had something in hand for the Young Folks.[6] Is she still at work on it? I think she will always be able to get things in there without trouble. Miss Larcom is now the editor.

I hope your back is quite well by this time.—Tell Henry that one of the deer in the common has broken his horn off—fighting, I guess, with the other stag. He looks silly enough in his stump of antlers, and the other has to be kept in another pen.

All join in love to all of you.

Your affectionate son,
Will.

1. Weiss (1818–1879) was the Unitarian minister in Watertown, Massachusetts (1843–1870), and a contributor to the *Atlantic*. Theodore Parker (1810–1860), the transcendentalist, had been the minister of a new Congregational Society of Boston.

2. C. E. Norton had written Howells on 10 January 1869 (MH), asking him to convey his deep sympathy to W. C. Howells on the occasion of Mary Dean Howells' death.

3. The "horrible news" was probably a murder reported by W. C. Howells in the Ashtabula *Sentinel*, 28 January 1869. The "late stabbing affray" was reported in the *Sentinel*, 21 January 1869; it concerned a feud involving Elisha and Daniel Haines, William Swinton, and John Johnson, in Denmark, Ohio.

4. W. C. Howells' weekly series of papers, "Ohio Fifty Years Ago," appeared in the *Sentinel* from 14 January through 18 March 1869. Based on the *Ohio Register* for 1819, the papers dealt with the principal Ohio towns, the chartered banks, potteries, transportation, and the mails.

5. Campbell (1788–1866), a minister, author, and a member of the Virginia Constitutional Convention, was the founder of the Disciples of Christ, popularly known as the Campbellites. In "Ohio Fifty Years Ago," *Sentinel*, 21 January 1869, W. C. Howells recalled that when Campbell received him in 1828 the "distinguished theologian" offered him a drink of whiskey.

6. For Annie's writings in *Our Young Folks*, see Howells to Anne Howells, 26 September 1867, n. 1.

7 FEBRUARY 1869, BOSTON, TO WILLIAM C. HOWELLS

Boston, February 7, 1869.

Dear father:

This morning I thought I should go to hear father Taylor, the preacher at the Sailors' Bethel, who has been effective with sea-faring men for many years.[1] I was disappointed, however, when I got there, for a younger man preached in his stead, and father Taylor did nothing but sit behind the pulpit, and incite the junior brother by Amens, "That's true!" "Bless the Lord!" and the like pious flatteries—nodding and winking confirmation at the congregation between whiles, and finally giving the benediction. It was a curious sermon, the matter much better than the manner. There were numbers of unmistakeable shipscaptains there with some second mates and common sailors; but the preacher without felicity of language was not plainly awkward, but clothed himself in so much dictionary that he must have worried and puzzled them a good deal. He talked about the impossibility of attaining revealed religion by help of the reason and really had something to say. The congregation was much smaller than I had expected to see, but it was very attentive after an example set by father Taylor. The house within was a very plain, old fashioned affair, heated by two long-piped stoves and adorned with a picture, over the pulpit, of a ship in a storm, which gave it a curious papistical effect. The singing was by the choir only. Evidently, the politeness of the age was penetrating even here.

I see you still continue your reminiscences. You may count upon at least one reader as long as you do so, for I am greatly interested in them. You are writing a good deal just now, it seems to me, and to good purpose. I've been particularly pleased with your articles,—and I am glad to have you touch up such a stupid and selfish interest as that of the woolgrowers, who have succeeded in oppressing us all without profit to themselves.[2]—

Johnny has quite got over his chicken-pox, and is now well in every way, but his mother has been suffering with a bad cold in the head. It's a severe influenza; in fact, and prevails here a great deal. Winny keeps well, and so do I.—Elinor is going to-morrow to a painter who is to give her some critical instruction in drawing. I think of writing out the first year of Winny's life, so as to make a child's book about Venice, and Elinor is to illustrate it.[3]

Tell Annie that prof. Child's book[4] *was* published, as far as the professor was concerned, but the public didn't do its part. It's a beautiful collection and I'll get a copy and send it to her.—I wish you'd remind Joe to answer me at once about employing the printer I wrote to him about. The man has been since to see me, and is naturally anxious to know what the decision is. I am very glad to hear that there is such a good prospect of Joe's getting the postoffice. It will be a great convenience to have in the family.—Now that the bear is done for,[5] I hardly know what to write of for Henry's amusement. Perhaps he'll care to hear that Winny, who doesn't like oysters, said "O, I'm quite fortunate!" when she found a crab—or maybe that's a joke for you. Johnny shall practise daily with a popgun as soon as he is able to hold one. I think such a hunting-party as Henry proposes would be delightful, and perfectly successful. Johnny would have to take a cow along, however, to get milk for luncheon, as he lunches about every hour. The cow might be useful also in hooking bumble-bees, and butter-flies; and Charley[6] could come with us to fetch home the grasshoppers.

I'm dragging on with my theatrical article,[7] though I "don't seem" to find it as good as I intended to make it. Tell Joe I sketch the play of the Three Fast Men[8] in it.—I'm almost discouraged in my attempts to write anything of an historical nature here—the material in the libraries is so very scant. Will you please look at The American Pioneer,[9] and tell me if there is much in it about Gallipolis? I want to do that if I possibly can for The North American Review.[10]—I wish some of you would answer me as to what you think of the design for the monument which I sent you some weeks ago.[11] I am left to infer that it does not please you, but I should like to know what each one thinks of it.—We all send dearest love.

Your affectionate son
Will.

I have Willy's[12] letter and will answer it before long.
Monday. I have Joe's letter about the printer.

1. Edward Thompson Taylor (1793–1871) was chaplain of the Methodist Seamen's Bethel in Boston (1830–1871). He was considered one of the great preachers of his day.

2. Howells is probably referring to "Ohio Fifty Years Ago," Ashtabula *Sentinel*, 4 February 1869, which had subdivisions on farm implements, milling, and home manufactures.

3. This project was apparently never carried out.

4. *Poems of Religious Sorrow, Comfort, Counsel, and Aspiration* (1863), ed. F. J. Child.

5. Howells had written his father and sisters on 10 January 1869 (MH) that the bear on the Boston Common had been killed for some unknown reason.

6. See Howells to Aurelia Howells, 22 November 1868, n. 1.

7. "The New Taste in Theatricals."

8. *The Three Fast Men, and the Female Robinson Crusoes*, by W. B. English, produced as early as 1858.

9. The *American Pioneer* was probably the short-lived monthly magazine published in Cincinnati (1842–1843), edited by John S. Williams.

10. If Howells ever wrote the article on Gallipolis, it was apparently never pub-

lished. The subject matter had been suggested by his father, as is indicated in Howells' letter to W. C. Howells, 26 January 1869 (MH).
  11. See Howells to W. C. Howells, 24 January 1869.
  12. William Dean Howells II.

21 MARCH 1869, CAMBRIDGE, TO THOMAS B. ALDRICH

Cambridge, March 21, 1869.

My dear Aldrich:

Here is a chance to help a forlorn and shipwrecked brother along the sands of time, either by copying entire into your admirable journal[1] (did Fields say anything to you about a little suggestion of mine that it should be turned into an album for the publication of original verse?) or by making a note. The man is an acquaintance, and not an active enemy, of mine. That's all.

Yours,
W. D. H.

I read your Bad Boy's Fourth of July adventures last, and was made to laugh beyond reason by them. It is the best part yet given—this installment. And I *did* like the other parts,[2] which wasn't the case with M-lb-ne.[3]

  1. Aldrich was editor of *Every Saturday* (1865–1874), a magazine published by Fields, Osgood & Co.
  2. Aldrich's *The Story of a Bad Boy* appeared serially in *Our Young Folks*. Howells reviewed the book in the *Atlantic*, January 1870.
  3. T. W. Higginson, *Malbone: An Oldport Romance* appeared serially in the *Atlantic*, January–June 1869.

28 MARCH 1869, CAMBRIDGE, TO WILLIAM C. HOWELLS

Cambridge March 28, 1869.

Dear father:

This is Easter Sunday, and very much the same sort of mild, dreamy Easter that we used to have in southern Ohio. I remember one, at Eureka, when we boys went out and gathered the long, new grass to color eggs. We couldn't do that here to-day, yet a few tender blades of grass have begun to show themselves on the bank south of our house; and there were yesterday plenty of robins and bluebirds about. It was a lovely spring day—I wonder if you had the like?—with the bluest sky, and a soft wind—a heavenly day, such as I imagine must be very common in another world with happy souls. I read proof in the morning, and then went into Boston, and found the city looking incredibly gay after its winter's gloom. The streets *ran* with feet and wheels like so many thawed out rivers with waters.

I hope, after you've delivered it as often as you intend, you'll print the lecture on Camp Meetings as one of the series of Fifty Years Ago papers in the Sentinel.[1] I should like very much to read it. I don't think you're wrong about preachers, but I make great excuse for them. Their calling becomes business, just as journalism or any other intellectual occupation does, and they must very often transact their business in a jaded, mechanical way.—There seems something essentially wrong or obsolete about the present conduct of public worship, but how to remedy it, I'm not master to say. What do you think of the Autobiography of a Shaker in the Atlantic?[2] I have been interested in it from the fact that I knew nothing about the Shakers before I read it. The second paper, which appears in May, develops their peculiarities still further, and contains some curious things about Swedenborg, whom (the author says) Mother Ann[3] called her John the Baptist.—By the way, why should you not send me the MSS. of your lectures after you have delivered them. I should like very much to see them.—We do not now feel any more dread of scarlet fever: it is not in the neighborhood, and the land is drying up, so we don't fear it on account of the damp. I hope Aurelia got the letter I wrote her last Sunday. I have little to add now in the way of family news. Johnny has been out several times to take air, and thrives finely. Winny has been somewhat billious, but is getting over it. Elinor does not gain strength rapidly, but she is better than she has been since her miscarriage.

What you tell me of Henry's allusions to mother is sadly interesting. It is very, very strange, and his becoming so good and gentle at this time does seem like a special mercy of God.—I too have my seasons of great melancholy for our loss. I have the photograph you gave me framed and standing on the mantel of my study here, and I look on that dear face the last thing every night. It often seems sad and longing in its expression, and again cheerful and calm. It is my own mood reflected of course—some more interior mood, for the expression is not always or generally that of my surface-thought, and I cannot believe at times that I authorize it. I think this picture a good likeness of mother, after all. It is she as I remember her—much the dear, anxious loving face she wore that day when she thought I was going to have some trouble with Mr. Fields. But what a little thing our greatest trouble must seem to her now—how brief! how unimportant!

—I met the other day some people at whose house Home the famous spiritualist[4] stays when he comes to Boston. They say he is a perfectly *negative* character, which, you know, is James's[5] view of Swedenborg. He is himself afraid and weary of his spirits—must always have some one to sleep in his room at night.

Dear love to all. I'm glad to hear the girls are better. Tell Joe not to forget me. I wish he'd write now and then. Love to Sam and family.

Your affectionate son
Will.

1. Without giving the name of the lecturer, the Ashtabula *Sentinel* announced the lecture for 21 March. It did not appear in "Ohio Fifty Years Ago," but was published as "Camp-Meetings in the West Fifty Years Ago," *Lippincott's Magazine*, August 1872.
2. F. W. Evans, "Autobiography of a Shaker," *Atlantic*, April–May 1869.
3. Mother Ann Lee (1736–1784), founder of the American Shakers.
4. Daniel D. Home (1833–1886).
5. Henry James, Sr.

5 April 1869, Cambridge, to James A. Garfield

Cambridge, April 5, 1869.

Dear Mr. Garfield:

I have heard that Mr. Lowell, the poet, is spoken of in connection with a foreign mission,—Spain, Rome or Switzerland,—and entirely upon my own motion I venture to write you, and try to interest you in the matter. What manner of man Lowell has always been in politics and literature you know as well as I do, and you will easily conceive that he is such a man as would do the country the greatest honor in any public position abroad. I suppose that if anything stands in the way of his appointment it is the fact that Mr. Motley must have a first-class mission[1] and that Massachusetts ought not to have so many diplomatic appointments. But the truth is Mr. Lowell belongs to the whole country; and I have thought that a word from a prominent western congressman, like yourself, addressed to the right quarter, would have a just influence in his favor. Could you affect the President through Mr. Cox[2] as well as directly?— You see I treat the matter very frankly, knowing that you will act entirely according your own judgment, and hoping that you will not think me too bold or importunate. I suppose that Judge Hoar[3] is Mr. Lowell's best friend at court.

Yours very truly
W. D. Howells.

Hon J. A. Garfield.

1. J. L. Motley had been appointed minister to Great Britain soon after Grant's election in 1868.

2. Jacob D. Cox (1828–1900) was secretary of the interior (1869–1870) under President Grant.

3. Ebenezer R. Hoar (1816–1895), a Boston judge, was U. S. attorney general (1869–1870) and a member of Congress (1873–1875).

CA. 15 APRIL 1869, CAMBRIDGE, TO AZARIAH SMITH

Welch, Bigelow, & Co., . . .
Cambridge, 1869.

Dear Mr. Smith:[1]

In advertising the May number, and in your lists of authors sent to editors, please *do not* give the name of the author of "The New Taste in Theatricals."[2]

Yours
W. D. Howells.

1. Azariah Smith was in charge of public relations and advertising at Fields, Osgood & Co.
2. See Howells to W. C. Howells, 2 May 1869.

16 APRIL 1869, CAMBRIDGE, TO JOSEPH A. HOWELLS

Cambridge April 16, 1869

Dear Joe:

Am I really in debt to you a letter? I should deny it, if I did not believe myself capable of anything in the neglected-letter line. Only the other day I took up those pages of a sketch that you sent me and asked Elinor if I had ever told you how much they pleased me. She was so sure I had not that wild horses couldn't have torn me from the conviction that I had. (Such is female influence.) But now you tell me I haven't, I must give it up.—I did like the sketch very much, and I don't see why you shouldn't go on with it. I wish you would for my pleasure at least, and I re-enclose the pages that you may resume it when the humor takes you. It is odd to me that we got little or no harm out of that Hamilton life which was moral death to so many of our mates.[1] It is more surprising still that we were not drowned, crushed, shot or gored to death every summer of our lives; but here we are, middle-aged men, and the fathers of boys ourselves. On the whole, I shouldn't care to have my boy go through the same experiences; yet they are very delightful to look back upon. I wonder if in another world we shall look upon our life here in the same soft, regretful way? How do we appear now to mother?—It all comes to this at last, whatever I begin to talk or think of.

I'm very glad father and Aurelia think of coming here, and am sorry only for the cause. I think the journey will be greatly to Aurelia's advantage, and you may be sure I will do everything I can to make it so.

—This has been our first real spring day—mildly warm and sunny, bringing out all the hens and gardeners in the neighborhood to dig up the ground. Elinor and I have taken a long walk; Winny has made a whole day of it at play, and Johnny has been in a perfect whirl of delight. Apparently, he did not think this climate to which he has been born capable of such fine weather, and he has shown great astonishment as well as pleasure. You know that sometimes children take sudden starts forward, like grass after a spring rain. So has he to-day.

Elinor and I have been reading a lovely book—a translation of Auerbach's *Edelweiss*, published by Roberts Brothers,[2] which you must get. You'll be enchanted with it.

Winny will attempt the picture you desire at the first opportunity. In the meantime she sends her love to you and her cousins.

Thank you for the scrap from Harvey's paper.[3] It was very pleasant of him to mention my article, which hasn't been too successful. Please give him my love when you write him.

With our united love to all at home, and to yours and Sam's families,

Your affectionate brother
Will.

How does the movement to get you out of the P. O. prosper?

1. The Howells family lived in Hamilton, Ohio, from 1840 to 1849. Howells later wrote about these years in *A Boy's Town*.
2. Berthold Auerbach, *Edelweiss* (1869), translated by Edith Frothingham.
3. Harvey Green, editor of the Medina *Gazette*, had evidently mentioned "Gnadenhütten."

18 April 1869, Cambridge, to William C. Howells

Sacramento St.,
Cambridge, April 18, '69.

Dear father—

Another of these monotonous weeks has made an end of itself, and I am writing you another of my monotonous letters. I long to see you again that we may find each other, or rather make sure of each other. This division by six months and six hundred miles tends so much to cast us in doubt one as to another, for very little after all can be said on paper.—You ought never to reproach yourself for writing me even sadly of our bereavement, for I understand all that is between the melancholy lines—the loving faith and hope. I think it is your letters in which you happen to say nothing of dear mother that make me gloomy; for I cannot help thinking, "Poor father has forced himself to write in this way." I have the shadow of the beloved face where I can look upon it whenever I lift my eyes from my work; and I wish that my work were always such as could please her now where she is. But neither this nor my life is so,—I feel it with shame and despair. It seems the worse for me not to be all I can be, because I feel so deeply the idleness of the worldly success I most strive for. It is as if the Preacher were always whispering in my ear, "Vanity, vanity, all is vanity." And yet I go on from day to day, living the same worldly, sensuous life, doing things that appear to me absolutely wrong, and saying things that I wonder at when said.

—There is little to tell you about the family that is new. The children are both very well, and are enjoying the fine spring weather beyond description. Winny goes to the groves near by, and gathers moss "with roots on" to make a garden; Johnny rides out in his little carriage, and shouts at every thing that pleases him. Day before yesterday was a most lovely day, and he seemed to rejoice in it like a bird. He was not still a minute, but crowed and kicked from a very early hour in the morning till a very late one at night. I long to have you see him, for I'm sure the sight will do your heart good.—I wonder sometimes what people do between the time when their children are grown up and the time when their grandchildren begin to come. The softness of a little cheek against mine, the warmth of a little bald head on my shoulder—it seems to me I couldn't do without these things. I was talking to Lowell, the other day, about the delight of children, and I told him that there was nothing in the world so flattering to me—no, not even a notice by him in the North American—as the cry of protest that Johnny sends after me when I leave the room he is in. Upon which L. said he would study my sorest point, and give me a prod there in the next number.

We have had a British lion with American eagle principles here this week, namely Goldwin Smith, who has left an Oxford professorship to take one in Cornell University.[1] It is an inexplicable piece of heroism; but Smith is a very uncommon Englishman. He was our firm friend, you know, throughout the war, and he is great believer in our high destiny.—Still I doubt if he finds Ithaca so fair as Homer paints it.—Do you remember Daily, our printer, who came from Ithaca?[2] I can't quite dissociate the Cornell University from doubtful jewelry, possibly because Daily sold me a ring that turned out not to be pure gold. By the way, what became of Daily?—I hope you'll soon find time to resume your "Recollections," which I miss very much in the Sentinel.[3]—General Grant seems to be making some pretty wild appointments, don't you think?

He seems to have been taken with a mania to surprise and startle people, and he has succeeded so far, though not in the way he intended.—Mr. Fields sails on the 28th, and the Atlantic will then be left solely to me.[4] He has succeeded only partially in arranging the numbers for his absence, and I shall have it to do, though chiefly with material that was selected a long time since—partly by him, partly by me.

You've got both Elinor's letter and mine, saying how glad we should be to have Aurelia and you come here. So with our love to all I am

Your affectionate son
Will.

1. Goldwin Smith (1823–1910), an outspoken advocate of the Union cause during the Civil War, was professor of modern history at Oxford (1858–1866) and professor of English literature and constitutional history at Cornell (1868–1871) until he moved to Toronto.
2. Daily has not been further identified.
3. "Ohio Fifty Years Ago."
4. See Howells to W. C. Howells, 17 January, 1869, n. 1.

2 MAY 1869, CAMBRIDGE, TO WILLIAM C. HOWELLS

Cambridge, May 2, 1869.

Dear father:

Spring seems to have turned her back on us with the first days of this old humbug of a month. We have a cold, northeast storm raging, and the weather is well-nigh as unpleasant as it can be even in New England. But even this is better than the delusive weather that tempts the vegetation out too soon: as yet there is not a blossom on the trees, and nothing has been nipped, probably, but a few unwise hopes.—Since I wrote you last we have changed our cook, the long list of our experiences being finally illuminated with the episode of an insane serving-woman. Our Bridget, whom we liked so much, had always a habit of talking to herself, and cursing various people, to us unknown, and the habit had lately grown upon her so much that it became very embarrassing. Her thoughts seemed to be running all the time on killing, and the other day, Elinor was shocked to hear her say, "I'll kill Winny," and "I'll stick Mrs. Cabot (a former mistress) with a carving-knife." She was always very fond of Winny, and would break out with "God bless me from Winny!" as if she feared to do the child some harm. I felt that we could not tell what moment such a person would become violent, and that we had no right to take any risks, and so I sent her away, saying that I thought she was not quite right in her mind, and advising her to go to a doctor. She said that the Winny she spoke of was not our little girl, but the mother of the Fenians,[1] and complained that she had enemies who pressed her head between their hands.—She is now staying with the keeper of an Intelligence Office in Boston, who has promised me to have the City Physician see her, with a view to sending her to the hospital or the asylum. I'm going to look further to the matter myself.—We have another girl, now, and a prospect of quiet for a little while.

The other morning, I had such a vivid and strange dream about mother that I must try to tell you of it. I thought that her spirit appeared to us all in some place where we were together, wearing a dress like that in which she was clothed for the last time, as if for our recognition. She spoke with some of us—with Sissy,[2] I believe; but I only saw her as she moved across a garden-space like that between our house and Stoackel's. I was not afraid, but I was filled with an unspeakable awe. In a little while she vanished; but afterwards came again, as if on another day, looking much as in the first apparition. A third time she appeared, but now like a woman young as Elinor, and in beautiful robes of gay colors, that changed themselves from one lovely color to another as she walked away from us on a path through a meadow,—like the blossom of some flower perpetually renewed and varied. As I understood this at the time, the apparition was interpreted to mean that she had already regained something of youth in the other world. She had appeared to us first in a guise in which we should not fail to know her; then again to convince us that it was she; then as I have said. She appeared to us the first time to dispel any doubt we might have of the immortality of the soul (all these were the explanations which seemed to be given me in my dream,) and afterwards to show us that she was blessed and happy. After the third apparition it was made known to us that she would appear once more, to give as it were, the seal to this testimony; we were assembled in some beautiful chapel with many other people who doubted, and asked father where he expected to see her, and he answering "There!" in such a spot, I awoke. There was a strain of grotesqueness, or rather a mere touch of it; but mainly the dream was very beautiful, and I cannot impart to you the tender awe and hope that possessed me in my sleep.

—I'm glad that the paper on the theatres[3] met with your approval; it has been the sensation of the magazine, and has been variously taken by the newspapers to mean approval of the plays, and unjust censure of Boston, and ridicule of the burlesques, and defence of people for going to them. Of course I merely meant to describe the badness of the stage as nearly as I could, and so let the moral enforce itself. I felt that it would do no good for me to preach about it. The Nation gave me very high praise, but utterly mistook the drift of the article.[4]—Have you fixed any time in your own mind for your visit? I'm chiefly anxious that you should not come till the weather is fairly settled, for your own sakes. For ours, you could not come too soon.—I'm greatly encouraged by what you tell me of Henry's tendency to dandyism. It seems to me an excellent sign. Has he had any more of those fits? The Richardson boy next door here[5] has not had one for more than a year, and may fairly be considered cured by Bromide.

All send love to you all.

> Your affectionate son
> Will.

J. J. Piatt is spending two or three days with us.[6]

—Tuesday.[7] I've kept back this letter, doubting whether to send it; because I feared you would think I attached an undue importance to the dream I tell you of. Happily, we need not go to dreams for our assurance of immortality or dear mother's peace, and I know you will not think I believe this or value it otherwise than as a beautiful vision of sleep.

1. See Howells to Norton, 23 June 1866, n. 4.
2. Victoria Howells.
3. "The New Taste in Theatricals."
4. In "The Magazine for May," *Nation*, 29 April 1869, the writer guesses at Howells' authorship, praises the humor and style, but disagrees with Howells' theory of why people attend such performances.
5. The Richardson family has not been identified.
6. This comment and Howells' letter to Piatt of 2 April 1867 (OKentU) indicate that the tensions between the friends (see Howells to Stedman, 27 May 1866, n. 2) had abated. In his April 1867 letter Howells wrote: "Do you ever try your hand at prose, now-a-days, except in reviewing? I used to admire the imaginative things you did for the Louisville Journal. It seems to me that out of the experiences of your Washington life you could make us some charming prose-papers. There must be a great deal of odd character among the dusty office-holders of every sort, which you could utilize. [¶] I heartily wish you could come up to Cambridge about this time. I want very much to see you, and to have you for once under my roof."
7. 4 May 1869.

4 MAY 1869, BOSTON, TO BAYARD TAYLOR

> ...*The Atlantic Monthly*.
> Boston, May 4, *1869*.

My dear Taylor:

We are dreadfully "short on" for poetry, and I should like particularly to have yours, but I'm afraid your letter-writer does not mean what he says, and is not so sectarian as we wish to be in the Atlantic.[1] We have to be much more carful than the unrighteous; and then, the poem *is* long.—I think I'm doing as Mr. Fields would to return it, but I wish to heaven he had it to do![2] There is the grossest absurdity in a chap like me sitting in judgment upon you; but I should be an even more unworthy chap than I am if I failed to be candid, and did not say I think the moral gets the poetry under in this piece.—The worst is out, and so God bless us all, I say.

Yours very truly,
W. D. Howells.

I hope you will like my notice of your By-Ways half as well as I liked your book.[3]

1. Howells' comments refer to Taylor's poem "Shekh Ahnaf's Letter from Baghdad." By "sectarian" he apparently meant "orthodox," since Ahnaf is a strict Moslem from Tangier who expresses his shock about the corrupt faith he finds at Baghdad.
2. Howells was temporarily in charge of the *Atlantic* while J. T. Fields was in Europe. Taylor wrote in his reply to Howells of 10 May 1869 (MH): "If you knew that I will take *anything* from a friend, you would n't feel the slightest delicacy about judging anything of mine. If you were not perfectly frank, you would be unjust to me, as well as to yourself.... There is more moral in the poem, as you say, than poetry.... I should like to write a poem for—or, rather, *publish one in*—the Atlantic, now and then; but Fields poured a bucket of ice-water over my head last winter, and I am shy of repeated drenchings."
3. Howells reviewed Taylor's *By-Ways of Europe* in the *Atlantic*, June 1869.

16 JUNE 1869, CAMBRIDGE[?], TO JAMES R. LOWELL

Dear Mr. Lowell:[1]

We have an article on the Isles of Shoals by Mrs. Thaxter, who has written indistinctly the name of one of the islands. Can you possibly tell me if it is Lo*n*doner's, or Lo*u*doner's, or either of these without the apostrophe?[2]

—You ought really to go to the Peace Jubilee. It is not only a big, but a grand thing,—as you shall learn further in the August Atlantic.[3] I am going every day, though I don't expect to hear anything towards the last.—Somebody said in the crowd yesterday, that the ceremonies were to begin with prayer by a hundred ministers. I got in too late for this; but it is all true about the hundred anvils.[4]

Yours ever
W. D. Howells.

Wednesday morning.

1. Although Mildred Howells dates this letter 1872 (*Life in Letters*, I, 170), Lowell's reply is dated 16 June 1869 (MH), and in 1869 June 16 fell on a Wednesday. Mrs. Thaxter's series of articles, "Among the Isles of Shoals," mentioned in the first sentence, began to appear in the *Atlantic*, August 1869.
2. In his reply Lowell informed Howells that the correct spelling is "Londoner's." Lowell took this opportunity to praise Howells for one of his book reviews in the

Atlantic: "I always had great expectations of you—but I am beginning to believe in you for good. You are the only one that hasn't cheated me by your blossom. I like your flavor now, as once I did your perfume. You young fellows are dreadfully irreverent—but don't you laugh—I take a kind of credit to myself in being the first to find you out. I am proud of you."

3. Howells, "Jubilee Days," *Atlantic*, August 1869.

4. Howells refers to an extravagant performance of Verdi's "The Anvil Chorus" with one hundred firemen beating the rhythm on anvils. See C. W. Kimball, "P. S. Gilmore's Impossible Dream," *Yankee* 33 (1969), 84–87, 160–63.

26 June, 18 and 24 July 1869, Cambridge, to Henry James

Cambridge, June 26, 1869.

My dear James:

I had it in my heart to answer you as soon as I'd read your letter; but I hadn't it in my power; and so your missive has lain upon my table to reproach me, and I've endured torments from it. You see that although you had used me very ill in not writing me sooner, my resentment was all melted away by the air of homesickness in your letter, and for a day I really flattered myself that there was some reason why you should be so fond of me. But that is past now, and the Light Man himself could not address you more coldly than this husband and father.[1] I don't know but I've got a touch of that diarist's style; I confess the idea of him fascinated me. He's one of your best worst ones; and I'm sorry we hadn't him for the Atlantic; though it is good policy for you to send something to the Galaxy now and then. I'll enclose some scraps of print, by which you'll see that Gabriele de Bergerac[2] is thought well of by those whose good opinion ought not to be of any consequence, but is. It really promises to make a greater impression than anything else you've done in the Atlantic.

I suppose I was right to carry your letter to your brother, and that he was wrong to show it at once to the rest of your family. Wherever the error is, it is now too late to repair it. Here we enjoyed it all; and Mrs. Howells hunted up the April Atlantic and read Door Step Acquaintance over again.[3] Just at present, however, we are thinking of things that make even my literature seem unimportant. Mrs. Howells's father has lain very sick for the last three weeks, and it is very uncertain yet whether he will recover. From day to day he was not expected to live; she has been with him for nearly two weeks, at Brattleboro', whence she now writes me that there is a little change in him for the better. Add to these anxieties the horrible tumult of this Jubilee business, and the largely increased editorial business, and you have some thing like an excuse for my not answering you at once. I will enclose what I've written about the Jubilee,[4] which will tell a long story in itself, and help to say also what I've been doing.—The summer has passed very quietly in Cambridge, and as like twenty other summers as possible. Thanks to a slow, but uninterrupted spring, and a good deal of wet weather since the foliage started, we are a thought leafier than usual; and you may guess how pleasant it is in that little grove over the way from us, and in fact in every part of the common-place old town—which like some plain girls has a charm quite independent of beauty. Even in Cambridge, I enter quite into the spirit of your home sickness, and feel the fascination which you miss. The town has very few positive advantages; but it is a prodigious satisfaction to "feel that meeting any" acquaintance upon the street, you are well-nigh sure of meeting some person who is not common or mean in his mind, but is full of appreciation and liberality. This appears to me the character of the whole population. I should think there was less intellectual vulgarity here—the worst sort, by the way—than any where else in the world. And yet it's a hard place to live in, expensive, inconvenient, and at times quite desolate. My own stay here seems often drawing to a close for these reasons, and yet I should be exceedingly unhappy any where else, I'm afraid. At any rate, I don't think we shall remain much longer in this neighborhood. All Ireland seems to be poured out upon it, and there is such a clamor of Irish children about us all day, that I suspect my "exquisite English," as I've seen it called in the newspapers, will yet be written with a brogue.—

July 18.—You see I am not a ready writer—of letters at least. Till now, I've not seen the hour when I could sit down with a clean conscience to finish this—or if it at any time my conscience was clean my head was empty. Since I began to write—three weeks ago—Mr. Mead has died, and I have been to Brattleboro' to see laid in the ground all that was left of the kind, cheerful, simple old man. He was one who felt so friendly toward the whole world that he imagined it a good one, and led the very happiest life here. He was—

> —"So full of summer warmth, so glad,
> So healthy, sound, and clear and whole,
> His memory scarce can make me sad."[5]

But after all it has been a depressing experience, and my wife has felt it deeply. We have now Mrs. Mead with us, and are trying what we can to keep up the illusion of mere absence to her.—For a man who never intended to recognize death as among the possibilities, except in an abstract and general sort of way, I have within a year, seen enough of it to convince me of an error in my theory of life. It can never again seem the alien far-off thing it once did; and yet acquaintance with it, has robbed it of something of its terrors. Shall I say it has been at once realized and unsubstantialized? I had always thought to find death in the dead; but they are "but as pictures"; I feel the operation of a principle which seemed improbable, formerly but I am not frightened at its effect as I had always thought to be. I don't mean, of course, that I don't fear to die—God knows I do—but in other times, the mere imagination of death was enough to fill me with unspeakable anguish.—I had hardly got back from my father-in-law's funeral, when our baby's nurse was called away to her little son, in Charlestown, who after a day's sickness died. Mrs. Howells was still at Brattleboro', and you may guess my troubles in taking care of our boy in the nurse's absence. It was sad enough, but even more absurd than sad;—a bachelor and childless man can never understand it all. I walked the floor nearly the whole night, in flowing robes of white, and threshed my brains to contrive diversions for the little ruffian whom nothing could persuade to drop asleep; and next day, to please the poor soul who had lost the whole world she lived for, in her son, I went to see him. It was a wonderful contrast to the scene, I had just witnessed at Brattleboro', where ages of Puritanism had strengthened and restrained the mourners from every display of their grief. The little one lay there on a kind of couch, with candles and vases of flowers about him— an awful, beautiful vision, hallowing and honoring the shabby room, as the most triumphal aspect of life could not have done, and presently the mother cast herself upon him, and bewailed him with a wild heart-rending poetry of anguish. I could not bear it; I broke down, and cried as heartily as she did.—Well, you've had enough of all this, which has lately occupied me to the exclusion of nearly every thing else; and which I hope you'll forgive my writing about; it had to be this or nothing.

I saw your family shortly before they left for Pomfret, and I've since had a little note from your father saying that they were well and most contented with their place. I miss them a good deal—not because I saw them very often, but because it was a pleasure to be able to see them when time favored.—Nearly every one is out of town, in Europe, or in the country,—Lowell alone of the "few immortal names," is left. He called at my house, yesterday, and I walked down town with him in the windy, sunny forenoon—down Oxford street; and I wish I could picture you here the beauty of those willows, which line the deserted railway track, as the breeze took them and tossed up the white of their leaves. What a lovely bit of wildness it is, along there!—though there's provokingly little of it, and it's as hollow and false as a stage-scene,—absolutely nothing but a few willows, with a growth of lady's-slipper hiding empty tomato cans and other rubbish about their roots.—I'm not sure that the August Atlantic will reach you, and so I shall tear out the installment of Gabrielle and Jubilee Days and send them in this letter. Your story is universally praised, and is accounted the best thing you've done. There seems at last to be a general waking-up to your merits; but when you've a fame as great as Hawthorne's, you wont forget who was the first, warmest and truest of your admirers, will you?—I'm writing now and have nearly finished something I call a "Pedestrian Tour,"[6] and which is nothing but an impudent attempt to interest people in a stroll I take from Sacramento street up through the Brickyards and the Irish village of Dublin near by, and so down through North Avenue. If the public will stand this, I shall consider my fortune made; and shall go on to write out a paper on "Pleasure Excursions"[7] to different places in and near Boston. The Nation hasn't pronounced yet upon Jubilee Days—should it be adverse perhaps I sha'n't feel encouraged to go on. Horrible, is n't it, to have only one critic for 40,000,000 of people?—I don't know whether you'll have heard of the honor conferred on me by the new President of Harvard;[8] but at any rate I'll do myself the pleasure to tell you of it. He's asked me to deliver one set of lectures in a course to post-graduates; and accordingly I'm to lecture along with Lowell, Child and Whitney. Ci pensi! Of course I take modern Italian literature, not knowing anything else, and feeling secure in the general ignorance concerning that.—Now for an honor the new President of the United States did Winny at the Jubilee. He kissed her!—She was very anxious to see him, for reasons of her own, and I led her near the sofa, where he sat, and told her to ask a certain friendly-looking old gentleman who sat near Grant to show her the President. He did more: he led her up to Grant, "And the Presentdent," says Winny, "he took me in his arms, and said I was a nice little girl, and kissed me; and then the Presentdent's son kissed me, and laughed at me; and so I ran away." She was very proud for a day or two, and proposed to "save" the cheek Grant kissed as long as she lived; but really only kept it sacred for a half-day.— She sends her best love to you, and the enclosed tin-type, which she had taken on the Jubilee grounds about an hour after being kissed. It's uncommonly precious, on that account.—The boy is not able to express the friendship he feels for you, but I make bold to send his regards. He grows strong and troublesome, which is all we could wish, I suppose.

July 24. Waiting the receipt of your address from your father, I add a few more lines to this letter, which seems not to grow better with age.—We have lately amused ourselves with the simple joys of a trip down the harbor to Nantasket beach, where we had adventures dear to timid souls—such as getting softly aground in the mud off the pier. The trip was voted a great success, and we mean to take many another like it. Yesterday I got a very tame horse and drove my womenkind over to Lexington—a lovely road, full of that safe wildness which pleases me. In Lexington we added a final charm to the excursion by enquiring the price of board at the hotel, and making ourselves believe for a moment, that we'd go out and spend some weeks there. It was with a kind of dismay that I learnt the pleasure was quite within my means.—You'll have heard from other sources, no doubt, before this letter reaches you, that your brother Wilkie[9] and Arthur Sedgwick have rowed in open boats from Boston to Mt Desert.—I've read the last proof of your Gabrielle, and it's really magnificent—as Mrs. Howells, a very difficult critic, declares. Aren't you going to send us anything about your travels? Do.

Well, good-bye. Write, if youve the heart after reading this—Europe has no such gift as a letter from you to bestow. Mrs. Howells sends her regards, and I am

Ever yours
W. D. Howells.

P. S. Give my best love to the Nortons when you see them. I suppose I must send you this stupidissima letter. And I'm alarmed to find that I've lost the scraps about your story that I intended to send—except one that I enclose.

Give our best love to the Nortons. Mislike me not for my letter, but believe me ever affectionately yours

W. D. H.

I mail an August by this post.

1. Henry James, "A Light Man," *Galaxy*, July 1869, is the story of a young man in New York who tries to inherit a fortune; it is written in diary form.

2. Henry James, "Gabrielle de Bergerac," *Atlantic*, July–September 1869.

3. Apparently James praised Howells' recent publication, joining in the general acclaim with which it was received. In response to an earlier letter by Howells, 4 February 1869 (MH; *Life in Letters*, I, 153–54), M. M. Hurd wrote on 19 April 1869 (MH): "You have hit the true vein I think in selecting subjects for a new volume and if all your sketches are equal to 'Door Step Acquaintences' [sic] you will make a hit." Hurd's suggestions in this letter eventually led to the publication of *Suburban Sketches*. J. R. Lowell, in his letter to Howells of 12 May 1869 (MH), conveyed an appreciative comment about the sketch from "Miss [Grace?] Norton" and added that he shared her view.

4. "Jubilee Days."

5. Tennyson, "The Miller's Daughter," lines 14–16.

6. "A Pedestrian Tour," *Atlantic*, November 1869.

7. Mildred Howells is probably correct in saying that this became "A Day's Pleasure," but the change in title was made before publication in the *Atlantic*, July–September 1870, and not, as she says, before it was reprinted in *Suburban Sketches*. See *Life in Letters*, I, 140.

8. See Howells to Elinor Howells, 28 June 1869, n. 3.

9. Garth Wilkinson James.

28 JUNE 1869, CAMBRIDGE, TO ELINOR M. HOWELLS

Cambridge June 28, 1869.

Dear Elinor:

Of course you must stay as long as seems desirable for your father;[1] but I've already written you something of this kind. All I ask is that you shall have a due regard for yourself, and not overdo. I suspect that your strength is nothing but nerve, and I beg you to keep the fact of your own poor health in mind, as far as you can consistently with present duty. This is a very trying time for all of us, and I fully share the anxieties of it. We get on very well here, and you need not be troubled about home affairs.

Father and Aurelia got back from Salem this evening, and they will probably start for Ohio next Monday, if not sooner.

I'll go in to see Charles[2] to-morrow, though I doubt if I'll have time to dine with him. Here are $5—I don't know how much you want, and only guess that having arrived in New Britain with $15, you are not quite destitute yet. I can send you more if need be. Let me know at once how much you want.

Last evening Mr. Lowell came on the part of President Eliot to urge me to a second decision about the lectureship;[3] I ran in to see Osgood about some possible future partial freedom from proof-reading, and he promised that they would give me time to prepare those lectures *any way*; so I came home, and wrote a letter to Mr. Eliot *declining* the office again on general principles. This morning Mr. Eliot not having received my letter, came personally to urge me, and I "took it for a sign," and accepted! So I'm a professor in spite of myself. I told him what a superficial fellow I was, and warned him of his risk, but it made no difference.

Winny said nothing worth while to-day, but Johnny *fans* himself with a palm leaf fan, and puts his feet on the table when he sits at meal. And is altogether the "wickedest man in" Cambridge, which makes his papa the happiest, of course.—I hope Charley's news of your father will be more encouraging.

Your
W. D. H.

1. Elinor had gone to Brattleboro to be with her father during his last illness.
2. Probably Charles L. Mead, Elinor's brother.
3. Charles W. Eliot (1834–1926), president of Harvard (1869–1909), had written Howells on 9 June 1869 (MH): "Suppose that the following gentlemen would join to give a course of lessons (three a week) through the whole year on modern literature, viz. yourself, Profs [J. R.] Lowell, [F. J.] Child & [Elbridge J.] Cutler of Cambridge, [Ferdinand] Bocher of Boston & [William D.] Whitney of Yale...."

On 14 June 1869 (MH) Eliot wrote again, requesting Howells to talk to Child and Lowell "about that post-graduate course," and informing him "that formal lectures are not at all desired, but rather talks, readings with comment,... conversations." Howells declined the offer, but Eliot, in his letter of 16 June 1869 (MH), urged reconsideration. Howells gave his first lecture on "New Italian Literature" on 16 May 1870. The following year he accepted reappointment and lectured on "Modern Italian Poetry and Comedy."

24 AUGUST 1869, CAMBRIDGE, TO JAMES T. FIELDS

Cambridge, Aug. 24, 1869.

Dear Mr. Fields:

My resolution to keep a diary concerning the editorial business, and send it to you regularly twice a month was altogether too bright, too beautiful to last. Yet while it endured, you will own it must have had its fascinations—such a propriety in it—so amusing to me, so satisfactory to you. Well, we will check the unavailing tear: the business, though unrecorded has been promptly done, and we are already arrived at the time when we begin to look for the return of Autumn and of you. I am glad you liked the August number so well: I put in the things you directed and filled out according to my own judgment, from the mass of material, that seems to grow like the liver of Prometheus the more it is preyed upon. The September is equally good, though Mrs. Stowe's sensation[1] of course benumbs the public to everything else in it. So far her story has been received with howls of rejection from almost every side where a critical dog is kept. The Tribune, and one or two western papers alone accept it as truth; but I think the tide will turn, especially, if its publication in England elicits anything like confirmation there.—As to stories, you know the Foe in the Household[2] ends in December. Mr. Hale[3] brought in a curious thing, a week or two ago called The Brick Moon, which will run from October till December inclusive; and besides this, I've taken five or six short things, of 10 or 12 pp each; but the accepted Mss. have mainly been sketches and essays— a capital essay by Sheldon,[4] among the rest. I've taken one poem, "by and with the advice and consent of" Mr. Lowell, and another upon my own judgment from Bayard Taylor.[5] It's extremely fine, I think (An August Pastoral) and I get it into the October. And then—shut your eyes and open your mouth!—Lowell has written for your pet January number, a glorious poem of 12 pages.[6] He read it to me yesterday, and I thought it magnificent—an opalescent beauty with every sort of intellectual light and color in it, and full of all dreamy tendernesses, too. It's ready now; and think of my denying myself the triumph of putting it in at once and waiting for you to get the glory later. Think, and blush, for having put off those two lectures of Henry Giles[7] on me and my numbers! It's some comfort to remember that I've told everybody you made up the magazines before you left.—I've begun Dr. Jarvis's papers on the Increase of Life[8] in the October; Clarke closes with Mahomet in November (a very successful and honorable set of papers);[9] Shaler ends his Earthquakes in Dec.;[10] Mrs. Thaxter, though her first paper was greatly praised, has not followed it up;[11] Goldwin Smith has sent nothing; (and small loss to us as things have fallen out,) I haven't got to Prof. Wilder's things yet[12]—we had so much other science. Mrs. Agassiz has two charming papers on dredging in the Gulf, (Oct. and Nov.);[13] Mr. King has not yet sent any of his sporting articles.[14]—I followed up the "Recent Travels" in the Sept. with a similar article on "A Poetical Lot,"[15] and I'm glad that the first struck you favorably. I wont repeat what Lowell said of the second because pride is sinful. My notion was to vary the monotony of the notices by a sort of paper that would give me more elbow-room. In Nov. and Dec. I'll have notices,[16] and in Nov., also, a study of some parts of Cambridge, called "A Pedestrian Tour."—I've had such a streak of good luck in volunteer contributions, that I don't lament your bad luck in England so much as I otherwise should. You wont perhaps value the suggestion any more because I offer it unasked; but I don't think it pays at all to take English stuff unless it's first chop: Minor Shows of London[17] and Mrs. Lynton's paper[18] are *not* first chop, and I hope you'll fail in the attempt to get anything more of like quality.—The Morris sonnets are very pretty,[19] and the other little poem[20] will go into the October.—I enclose a list of the articles accepted, that may possibly be interesting or useful to you, and also the Contents of the November number as it has gone to the printers.[21]

I believe I haven't got into difficulty with any one, made you enemies or changed the general policy of the magazine; so there will be no occasion to repeat the scene which took place on the return of the chief editor of the San Diego Herald.—Concerning this last sentence Mr. Kirk would have written on the margin: "A *scene* cannot *take place*," which reminds me that he is no longer reading proof at the University Press.[22] I lament him for some reasons, but I believe on general principles that we're proof-read too much.—The Parton articles[23] are interesting, but have on the whole been received with something more than the usual misgiving. I suppose that they are more popular than otherwise. Shaler's papers have been a very fair success; and Clarke's have been liked nearly everywhere. The Foe in the Household has lost ground a little, I think; Harry James's story[24] is a great gain upon all that he's done before, in the popular estimation.—Dr. Holmes is a firm believer in Mrs. Stowe's article: Mr. Lowell if no longer a doubter of it, still a disliker. It seems to be pretty generally allowed it was awkwardly done.

I see this, but I think the story is true and ought to have been told. People say Mrs. Stowe should have given names, dates and places in full. You saw that she made one mistake, stating the Byrons lived two years together instead of 13 months. We'd the greatest difficulty with her in getting to read her proof at all. Kirk and I both read it carefully, and sent it to her; *and she wouldn't return the proof!* but sent a copy which Dr Holmes had gone over. I then read it again, and enclosed it to Dr. Holmes, who accepted all my corrections;[25] but this was done hastily, with the printers at my back, and with a view to have everything, as nearly as possible, just as Mrs. Stowe had written it. She had misquoted wherever she could, nearly—the (last) conversation as she gave it between Byron and Fletcher was all wrong.

Mrs. Howells joins me in cordial regards to you and Mrs. Fields. I know you must be enjoying yourselves, and I hope you feel easy about the "Atlantic" here. Our family has been uncommonly well; but Mrs. Howells has lost her father: the kind old man died July 5.—There is nothing new in Cambridge. So adieu!

W. D. Howells.

1. Harriet Beecher Stowe, "The True Story of Lady Byron's Life," *Atlantic*, September 1869. All publication dates mentioned in subsequent notes to this letter refer to issues of the *Atlantic*.
2. Caroline Chesebro', "The Foe in the Household," March–December 1869.
3. Edward Everett Hale.
4. Frederick S. Sheldon, "The Dead Level," December 1869.
5. Taylor, "An August Pastoral," October 1869, and "In My Vineyard," December 1869.
6. "The Cathedral." For Fields' policy on the January issue, see Howells to Holmes, 31 August 1869.
7. Only "The Egotist in Life," October 1869, was published.
8. Edward Jarvis, "The Increase of Human Life," October–December 1869.
9. James Freeman Clarke's series on religions of the East appeared in March, May, June, August, and September 1869; it concluded with "Mohammed, and His Place in Universal History," November 1869.
10. Nathaniel S. Shaler's series on earthquakes appeared in June, August, October, November 1869, and March 1870.
11. Celia Thaxter, "Among the Isles of Shoals," August 1869, January, February, and May 1870.
12. Burt Green Wilder, a Cornell scientist, wrote pieces for the issues of March, April, and July 1870.
13. Elizabeth Cary Agassiz, "A Dredging Excursion in the Gulf Stream," October–November 1869.
14. Probably Clarence King, "Mountaineering in the Sierra Nevada," May–August 1871.
15. Howells' "Recent Travels" (a review of travel books) and "A Poetical Lot" (a review of books of poetry), August and September 1869, respectively.
16. In November 1869 Howells reviewed a number of historical books. In December 1869 he reviewed a book on Swedenborg by Henry James, Sr.; a volume of stories by H. E. Scudder; a book of ballads by Whittier; and *The Innocents Abroad* by Mark Twain.

17. Pierce Egan, "The Minor Theatres of London," March 1870.

18. Ethel Lynn Linton, "The Channel Islands" and "Let Us Be Cheerful," May and June 1870, respectively.

19. William Morris, "Rhyme Slayeth Shame" and "May Grown A-Cold," February and May 1870, respectively. None appeared in November 1869, as scheduled in Howells' enclosure.

20. J. T. Fields, "At Rydal," October 1869.

21. Howells enclosed a list of fourteen items he accepted during Fields' absence. One of them is listed as "Mr. Bruce. (Story.) A. C. Eliot." "Alice Eliot" was the pseudonym for Sarah Orne Jewett; the story was her first to appear in the *Atlantic*, December 1869. Howells also enclosed "Contents of the Atlantic for November."

22. Kirk has not been further identified.

23. Three articles by James Parton on Washington politics, September, November, and December 1869.

24. "Gabrielle de Bergerac."

25. The difficulties Howells had with the Stowe article and its author are indicated in Holmes' letter to Howells, which is dated "Friday morning," but was most likely written on either 23 or 30 July 1869 (MH): "I have made red crosses X [in red pencil] where I wished you to reëxamine your comment or correction. I must leave the proof to your discretion now, accepting as you will see most of your changes—perhaps feeling more doubt about altering the last sentence than you do, as this will naturally draw Mrs Stowe's attention to all other acts of aggression. But I must leave the matter to you as Editor."

31 AUGUST 1869, BOSTON, TO OLIVER W. HOLMES

. . . Fields, Osgood & Co. . . .
Boston, August 31, 1869.

My dear Sir:

You know it is Mr. Fields's custom to open the magazine year with a January number of the greatest possible brilliancy, inviting to his table of contents those great names whose united presence on the single occasion almost allows us to be dull all the rest of the year. I think this an excellent custom, and I suppose that in begging you to give us something for the New Year's number I'm only anticipating a request from Mr. Fields himself. We have already a poem from Mr. Lowell,[1] and—I hope to be able to add in writing to Mr. Emerson upon this same business[2]—an essay, or whatever, from Dr. Holmes. If you can oblige us with anything, we should like it before the end of October.[3]

Yours very truly,
W. D. Howells.

1. "The Cathedral."

2. Emerson did not contribute to the *Atlantic*, January 1870, although Howells had solicited a contribution in his letter of 31 August 1869 (MH).

3. Holmes contributed a sonnet, "Nearing the Snow-Line," apparently after first having rejected Howells' invitation. In his letter of 30 October 1869 (DLC), Howells thanked Holmes for the sonnet and for "reconsidering your purpose of not writing

at all." Perhaps Holmes was still piqued about Howells' refusal to publish a review of Charles W. Upham's *Salem Witchcraft and Cotton Mather* (1869), which Holmes had suggested probably because Upham was his brother-in-law. Holmes' displeasure is suggested in his letter to Howells of 28 May 1869 (MH). Howells' unpublished review is at CtY.

5 SEPTEMBER 1869, BOSTON, TO WILLIAM C. HOWELLS

. . . Fields, Osgood & Co. . . .
Boston, Sept. 5, 1869.

Dear father:

I don't, of course, know how to account for my addressing Sam with so much stateliness, unless the "Dear Sir" happened to be on the old sheet of editorial paper which I used, and I forgot to alter it. I'm surprised he should have cared about it, or should have put you to the least trouble to explain it. Joe often signs his letters to me "Yours respt'ly, J. A. Howells & Co." but I never think it necessary to ask what he means by it: there are some things that explain themselves.

I got back Friday from a little visit to Newport, where I went for a few days' rest, and for material to be used in a contemplated article to be called "Pleasure Excursions."[1] I don't think I succeeded exactly in either object, and yet I was a good deal entertained with the extraordinary spectacle of the fashionable life there. For example, every one drives on the Avenue from four to six o'clock, when you see all kinds of splendor and ennui paraded back and forth in every sort of vehicle, from the little pony phaeton, driven by a young lady with her footman behind, to the immense, towering family carriage with the four servants in front and behind, and the poor rich people in every attitude of discontent within. If you reflect that these martyrs thus show themselves on the Avenue daily for four months, and that they have otherwise nothing to fill up their entirely worthless lives but a continual round of dressing, dancing and gobbling costly liquids and solids, you can't help pitying them; and I don't think I ever saw anything more phantasmal or saddening than that endless procession. I'm sorry Aurelia and you didn't stop at Newport. You would have beheld there an absolute novelty such as is to be seen nowhere else in America. Mrs. Field,[2] of Philadelphia, made a sort of little noonday party, to which some of the most resplendent of the martyrs were asked to meet me in my quality of author, and I found them quite what you would suppose, for the most part, but all simple-mannered and friendly enough. I dreaded the ordeal, but I believe I passed through it safely enough.—The girls will be interested to know that one lady I met was the wife of Peterson who publishes the wonderful magazine[3]—

a very agreeable person, and disposed to make me many flattering speeches. In fact everybody was most kind and goodnatured, and several delightful.—I feel rather silly at having told you of all this, and I'm sure you'll say I might have filled up my letter with something better. But there's very little family news. Johnny is walking everywhere, and teething pretty much all over his jaws. He keeps very well, as the rest of us do.—I'm just going to settle down to work on my University Lectures,[4] which have gained me an amount of anticipative celebrity that alarms me. With love to all,

Your affectionate son
Will

James has given me a copy of his new book on Swedenborg,[5] which he says I'm to send to you when I've read it.

1. "A Day's Pleasure."
2. The wife of John W. Field, a friend of Howells and Dr. S. Weir Mitchell.
3. Charles Jacobs Peterson (1819–1887), publisher of *Peterson's Magazine*.
4. See Howells to Elinor Howells, 28 June 1869, n. 3.
5. Henry James, Sr., *The Secret of Swedenborg*; it was reviewed by Howells in the *Atlantic*, December 1869.

5 SEPTEMBER 1869, BOSTON, TO THOMAS W. HIGGINSON

... *Fields, Osgood & Co.* ...
Boston, Sept. 5th, *1869*.

My dear Sir:

I don't see how I can use either of these immortal productions in a mere fleeting magazine of the hour, like The Atlantic; and I dare say you wont be the most surprised man in Newport to get them back. At the same time "we thank you for the opportunity," etc.

Yours very truly
W. D. Howells.

Col. T. W. Higginson.

22 SEPTEMBER 1869, CAMBRIDGE, TO WILLIAM C. HOWELLS

Cambridge, September 22, 1869.

Dear father:

For fear I should forget it, as I have done several times already, I'll say here at the beginning that I never saw Mrs. Stowe's article till it was in type.[1] I think, however, I should have taken it if it had been left to me, for I don't at all agree with those who condemn her. Always supposing that she has producible evidence in support of her story, I don't see why it shouldn't have been told. The world needed to know just how base, filthy and mean Byron was, in order that all glamour should be forever removed from his literature, and the taint of it should be communicated only to those who love sensual things, and no more pure young souls should suffer from him through their sympathy with the supposed generous and noble traits in his character. The need of this was so great, that even if Mrs. Stowe had had no authority to tell the story I should almost be ready to applaud her for doing it. Generally I don't like her or her way of doing things— she did this particular thing wretchedly,—but I don't condemn her for having done it. I believe I'm only one of three or four in America who don't. If it should turn out that she cannot confirm her statements, then it'll be a different affair. But the editor of MacMillan's Magazine in London[2] telegraphs that there is evidence to support them.

I send you a circular to show how our co-operative housekeeping progresses. In the meantime we're perfectly suited with our meals from Porter's tavern, and find the system to work as well here as in Venice. The only thing that troubles us is how to get rid of the superfluous provisions.

Please remember me to the Garfields when you write them. You must have found their visit a great pleasure. I hope you had the governor home, too. You know he's a sort of relation by marriage.[3]— Gen'l Mitchell of Columbus was here until yesterday. He has brought his little girl, who is deaf and dumb, to the school in Northampton where they teach vocal speech to mutes.—Our little ones are very well. Winny has begun going to a school which is kept by a young lady at Prof. Child's.[4] She expresses herself delighted with it. Johnny is bright and very bad indeed. Indeed, I'm afraid that we'll have all the trouble with him which we didn't have with Winny. He's very wilful and passionate, and domineers over every one who will stand it. We shall try to take him in time.—But I won't say more, for you must be almost babied to death at home just now and wont want to hear of our babies. I'm sorry Eliza has such a bad time, but rejoice that her children and Florence's boy are doing well. With love to all

Your affectionate son
Will.

1. The Ashtabula *Sentinel*, 23 September 1869, contained an item, "The Byron Scandal," which concerned itself with H. B. Stowe's controversial article, "The True Story of Lady Byron's Life."

2. George Grove (1820–1900), primarily a writer on music, was editor of *Macmillan's Magazine* (1868–1883).
3. Rutherford B. Hayes (1822–1893), at this time governor of Ohio (1868–1872), was a cousin of Elinor Howells.
4. The Miss Olmstead mentioned in Howells to Norton, 7 and 21 November 1869.

24 SEPTEMBER 1869, CAMBRIDGE, TO JAMES R. LOWELL

Cambridge, Sept. 24, 1869.

My dear Mr. Lowell:

My wife says it is not the custom to tell a gentleman that he does not know how to choose his guests; but I feel pretty sure you've mistaken your man in asking me.[1] You know me for a sluggish person in all companies, and a specially dull one at dinner, and of such corpulence that I can't even serve for a skeleton at a feast. How could you, then, have so little care for those choice spirits and old friends you ask me to meet? The pig and I will be the only people of this generation at table, and I without his excuse for taking up the room of my seniors. But I'm coming, and your good-nature be upon your own head.

Ever yours
W. D. Howells.

1. Lowell had written Howells on 22 September 1869 (MH), profusely praising "A Pedestrian Tour" and inviting him to a roast pig dinner with "J. H." (probably Oliver Wendell Holmes' brother John), Charles W. Story (a lawyer), and G. M. Lane (a classics professor).

2 OCTOBER 1869, BOSTON, TO RALPH WALDO EMERSON

... *The Atlantic Monthly.*
Boston, October 2, *1869.*

My dear Sir:

I beg to return you the poem of Miss Lazarus,[1] of which I think I see the merits, but which I am not able to like well enough to accept for the Atlantic. It is so very plain an imitation in manner of some of the Greekish poems of Tennyson, and all the Greekish poems of Wm. Morris, that it is for that reason alone undesirable; besides though it is prolix, the old bones of fable are too thinly clothed on with new life.

I hope that you will find it possible to give us something of your own for our January number.[2] I for one—if such a thing could be— would be most glad to read in print one of those lectures which we all had so much pleasure in hearing a year ago. I venture to suggest the use of something already done, because Mr. Osgood said you were so much occupied with your University course that you feared you could not find time to write for us.³ However, even something new would be welcome.

I am sorry to have kept Miss Lazarus's manuscript so long: it takes a mood as well as a certain amount of time to read a poetical contribution fairly, and the two can't always be commanded at once.

Very respectfully yours
W. D. Howells.

Mr. Emerson.

1. Emma Lazarus (1849–1887) had submitted "Admetus," which became the title of her first collection, *Admetus and Other Poems* (1871).
2. See Howells to Holmes, 31 August 1869, n. 2.
3. Emerson was preparing a course of lectures on philosophy, which he gave at Harvard in 1870.

16 OCTOBER 1869, CAMBRIDGE, TO JAMES R. LOWELL

Cambridge, October 16, 1869.

Dear Mr. Lowell:

Before the chill of the theme penetrates through the charm you cast about it and cools me off, I must write to you of the pleasure I've taken in your Good Word for Winter.¹ I'm no Winterist, as you know; but your art made me feel almost a tenderness for the old rogue. The essay seemed to me in manner and spirit as good as your very best talk, and for my part I don't think there can be anything better than that. "It's just as Lowell talks!" said the for-once-agreeing critics of this family; and one of them—who is an editor—thought what a sin it was you would not make up your mind to write something like it for every month's Atlantic. As I read I almost smelt the familiar fume of your pipe, and I'm half ready to swear that I saw you put a log on your fire, turn round (you turn round *rounder* than any body else) and stand with your back to the blaze, your hands on your hips, and your eye taking a book on an upper shelf for a land-mark to infinity. Few can praise this precious personal charm in the essay, but all must be conscious of its beauty. I thought the character of the seasons in the beginning of the article exquisitely sketched,—especially the Lamartinish, Heinesque sentimentality of Autumn,—and I marvelled throughout at your luck in making your own thoughts and your quotations of one piece. Mrs. H. considered you particularly delightful in your liberties with W. W.² and I don't say no: only, where were you not particularly delightful? The whole was so good, that I don't think even my admiration—which I'm sensible grows a little hystericky when I try to express it—can make it appear otherwise to the author himself. With all my heart

Yours truly
W. D. Howells.

P. S. The "young Vermont sculptor" (you know?) is Mrs. Howells's brother Larkin Mead. The statue was made on the last night of the year, and he called it, poetically enough, The Recording Angel.[3]

Take all this, padron mio caro, if it seem the touch of irreverence, for that of affection.

1. "A Good Word for Winter," *The Atlantic Almanac for 1870*.
2. Lowell felt that it was impossible to look at nature without having Wordsworth's conception of it interfere with one's own perceptions.
3. Lowell wrote of a "young Vermont sculptor" who had made a snow sculpture. See *Life in Letters*, I, 151, and "The Snow Angel," *Yankee* 20 (1956), 36–38.

19 OCTOBER 1869, BOSTON, TO EDWARD E. HALE

... The Atlantic Monthly.
Boston, October 19, 1869.

Dear Mr. Hale:

Having mislaid your note, I don't know if I can answer exactly the questions in it; but if you've the sequel to the Brick Moon[1] ready, pray let me have it *at once* for the January Atlantic.

—As regard the proof-reading, "I'm very glad you liked it." But I didn't do any of it except that in pencil, though I had—I can't help taking a little of the glory—a supervisory eye over it all. The truth is, we're trying to reach a height to which proof-reading has never soared yet, and to let alone as much as possible, all authors who can by a stretch of charity be supposed to have an idea and a style, and to omit all bothering suggestions, such as, where Smith occurs, insinuating that Jones is more grammatical or better English. Your admired proof-reader is a Mr Müller—a printer, and a nice fellow, who was gratified to hear of your liking. I don't cede to him in enjoying your humor, or the general tone of your story. When those people went up in your B. M. I was ready to shed tears.

Yours truly
W. D. Howells.

1. "The Brick Moon," *Atlantic*, October–December 1869; and its sequel, "Life in the Brick Moon," *Atlantic*, February 1870. They were said to be "From the Papers of Captain Frederic Ingham," Hale's pseudonym.

28 OCTOBER 1869, BOSTON, TO JAMES R. OSGOOD

... *The Atlantic Monthly*.
Boston, October 28, *1869*.

My dear Osgood—

I've read Shirley Dare's article[1] with the greatest delight, but of course it wont do for us. With what a kind of bad-girl cleverness it's done, and at what wicked Parisian possibilities does it not hint! The idea is a sensation of the grossest, and ten to one it's no truer than the Galaxy paper.[2] Yet the woman has skill.—Prythee, was she so very, *very* handsome, then? And why see a proprietor instead of an editor? I know you told her we were all wedded.—Poor old Bohemian business, think of stirring up that again, and in a female form!—You needn't enclose this note to Miss Dare.

Yours,
An Imperialist.

P. S I'll send back the Ms. to-morrow. Tell her it's too sensational for us; or if that wont do after the Byron business, say that we don't want to seem to enter into a direct competition or controversy with another magazine.

1. The article was probably one of several pieces written in the controversy that began with the publication of H. B. Stowe's "The True Story of Lady Byron's Life." Shirley Dare has not been identified.
2. "The Countess Guiccioli" was anonymously published in *Galaxy*, October 1869. It is the story of Byron's last great love and may also be by Shirley Dare.

7 AND 21 NOVEMBER 1869, CAMBRIDGE, TO CHARLES E. NORTON

Cambridge, November 7, 1869.

My dear Mr. Norton—

After my long neglect of your last, I can only hope that a letter from me will be welcomed in a general way as a letter from America, and that you will be affected by it about as much as by a newspaper. I have no right to ask you to regard it more favorably than you would, say, the Cambridge Chronicle, and I don't. My great desire is that it shall find you well and happy. You are a great deal in my mind, and

I get news of you from friends whom I ask in a shame-faced way about you. Not that I've seen many people lately. My lotus-eating days haven't come yet, and it seems to me that the weeks have decreased as much in length as the dollars in value since I began to need them, and that we have a sort of paper currency in time as well as money. If I can get to see Mr Lowell two or three times a month, it's as much as I can expect, and when I scourge myself out for a call elsewhere, I am dismayed with the fear of not finding people at home, and so losing everything. The other Sunday I went to see Sedgwick, and being told that he was out, felt like a ruined man. You see, I've not only the Atlantic work to do with more writing than ever before, but I'm engaged to deliver one of the University sets of lectures,[1] the study for which goads me early out of bed in the morning, goes with me in all my horse-car journeys, and snatches all the scattered moments I used to give to society and dreams. There was a blessed rumor this fall before the lectures began that they were to be given up, and Professor Child and I went to the President's room with the gayety of boys, determined, however, to affect a decent regret. Alas! we came away in a different mood. The President was in intolerably good-spirits; there had been no thought of giving up the lectures. I suggested then a Round Robin of resignation by all the lecturers, but this was thought not the thing; then I trusted to a failure on Mr. Lowell's part, but though he says he's afraid it will give him a brain-fever, he's pushing through with the most odious heroism, and I see no hope for me but to go to Texas. In the meantime it's a perfect day-mare with me. The subject's cold in my mind, and as I try to breathe a little life into the embers, the ashes fly up and choke me. Well, patience. Three thousand years hence very few people will care about my failure or the toil that achieved it.— In my family we get on pretty well. The children are both hearty and good, and seem bent upon childhood's mission of eventually growing out of itself. The boy, whom we call John, inclines to be mischievous, but is good-humored and tractable enough, though registers have fascinations in connection with buttons and pins that he cannot resist. Winny goes to a school kept by a Miss Olmstead at Professor Child's, and is delighted with it. Mrs. Howells does not grow stronger, though I believe she is as well as when you were here. Her ill-health is our one great draw-back, for it is hard for her to bear and for me to see. I'm myself so fortunate as to be nearly always well, and that's everything: when I think of it, life seems easy, and I don't dare to think of being sick. Our Sacramento street has lately become much less desirable than it was: Irish have moved in, and I think it would be the part of prudence to sell the house if I could find a good purchaser. I'm afraid it will depreciate on my hands. I've paid Mr. Bullard a thousand dollars, as perhaps you know, and next year I hope to make other payments, even if I don't sell. The last twelve months I could do nothing. In any case hereafter I shall of course first regard his interests.

Nov. 21. This letter has grown two Sundays older without, I'm afraid, having grown proportionally wiser. I saw a letter of Harry James's, in which he spoke of the great pleasure and advantage he'd had in a ramble with you through Pisa, and now I learnt from Sedgwick, to-day, that you're all got to Florence, and have taken a villa there. The reality is at once better than my envy can paint it, and different, so I needn't fatigue you by exclaiming over the fact that you're where you are. I used to think *that* Italy was made for me, but I don't any more: I've grown modester. Still, I could not hear, without a pang, the other day, that a lady of Newport had written home from Venice, "One thing, Howells is all wrong about Venice—never saw it, in fact." Try not to find me out, more than you can help, dear friends, and if you don't see things as I did, pray believe there has been a great change. At present, I don't aspire above writing some sketches of things about Cambridge, and I go over the ground a dozen times to see if I've told fibs. Some time that Newport pythoness will be writing home "Howells never saw Harvard Square." But at least, thank heaven, I'm believed in above Porter's Station. I've been told in so many words by an inhabitant, "That Pedestrian Tour of your'n created the most intense excitement that ever was known in North Cambridge. All the neighbors took it into Wood'ard [who kept the second-hand store][2] and one of 'em told him, 'Wood'ard, you let that man have anything he wants out of your store for nothing. A puff from so distinguished a pen in such a place is worth a hundred dollars to you!"[3] There's a glory; and consequently the other day, I had great ado to get out of the shop without being loaded with presents.—I wonder how you'll rank the great poem Lowell has just written.[4] It's thought here on Sacramento street to be the grandest thing he's done. It's inexpressibly delightful to me, and seems somehow with its tenderness and humor and sublimity to touch every appreciative chord in me. To think of his several times doubting its value, when he had got it done! One day he was really low in spirit about a thing that if the world lets die, it had better own to having a memory for nothing but trifles.—The Fieldses have got back, and have brought with them an original portrait of Pope[5]—a pathetic and sensitive face that gives one a kinder and better feeling towards the poor little immortal wasp than one could otherwise have had.— We're all glad and proud here in Cambridge that Dennett is coming among us; but I'm sorry for The Nation if, as I fear will happen, he can't do as much there in future as he has done. The paper keeps up wonderfully in quality.—You'd be surprised to find how many changes have taken place in Cambridge,—the outward looks of it. New buildings have transformed whole neighborhoods, especially in our quarter of the town, where there used to be many vacant spaces. As for Cambridge socially, I hardly know anything of it, and with the winter's work on my lectures before me, I don't expect to extend this knowledge. We see the Palfreys[6] now and then; the Jameses at rarer intervals (Mr. James's book is something of a success,)[7] and on Thanksgiving we dined at the Childs.—Mrs. Howells wishes with me to be most cordially remembered to each of you. I hope that your health is quite firm again, and that you are all enjoying life.—This letter is an odiously egotistical affair, with a complaining tone in places that's as false to my real humor as it is disgusting. Pray perceive instead of it a note of the greatest gayety and content. Mrs. Howells is much better than when I commenced writing, and the children are heavenly delights—though I say it. Don't forget—if you think I deserve any answer—that we shall like to hear about your little ones; and do have me always in your charitable thoughts if you never write.

Ever sincerely yours
W. D. Howells.

1. See Howells to Elinor Howells, 28 June 1869, n. 3.
2. Howells' brackets.
3. See *Suburban Sketches*, pp. 77–86.
4. "The Cathedral." Howells' review in the New York *Tribune*, 16 December 1869, praises the poem extravagantly; but later Howells thought that it was "not of his best." See *Literary Friends and Acquaintance*, HE, pp. 188–89.
5. See William K. Wimsatt, *The Portraits of Alexander Pope* (New Haven: Yale University Press, 1965), pp. 203–4.
6. John Gorham Palfrey (1796–1881) was a Unitarian minister, professor of sacred literature, editor of the *North American Review* (1835–1843), and a politician and historian.
7. Henry James, Sr., *The Secret of Swedenborg*.

1 DECEMBER 1869, CAMBRIDGE, TO JAMES R. LOWELL

Cambridge, December 1, 1869.

My dear Mr. Lowell—

I've just been reading The Cathedral over again, and I wish I'd some least touch of your own happiness that I might tell you how greatly it has delighted me. It's given me more pleasure, and of a nobler kind than I—having past a certain age—ever believed any poem would give me. I think it beyond all compare the grandest and completest thing yet written in our younger half of the world; and—you may say it's my ignorance if you will—I don't know of any poem of the time that equals it in grasp of the very innermost life and meaning of the time. It would perfectly satisfy me if it did not fill me with unrest, making me at once exult and bewail myself. It's as many-sided as a play of Shakespeare;—I mean more than this, but I don't know to say it, though I almost feel as if I might profitably sell myself for the phrase that *would* say all.

One thing, however, shall never be made a reproach to me: that I lived near and in the friendship of one of the few true poets of the world, and had not the wit to know it, or the grace or courage to tell him I knew it.

Ever his
W. D. Howells.

24 December 1869, Boston, to Thomas W. Higginson

... *The Atlantic Monthly.*
Boston, Dec. 24, *1869*

My dear Colonel—

I think your question about the principle on which we notice books is a fair one, and I'll answer it. The thing is almost wholly in my own hands, and I try not to let any really important American book go unmentioned. Then I seek such books as something interesting can be written about; and then as I do nearly all the noticing myself, I choose books that I can write intelligently and justly of. If you'll look over the magazine for a year, you'll find the facts of American book-making pretty well reflected in it. You needn't be told that sometimes we have to speak of books not worth mentioning, but I do this as little as possible. I don't by any means think our arrangement a perfect one; but I keep an eye on our neighbors, and I think it less defective than any other. This year we shall try to improve. Most of my criticisms will be cast in the form of general articles, and I'll have the noticing done by other hands. But there are limits to all improvement, and I'm hedged in by a suspicion that people don't read book-notices. I myself fly the critical small print at the ends of magazines as a device of the Enemy of souls.—In this respect, however, I think The Atlantic less mortal than other periodicals, and generally I believe it the best magazine in the world, though I don't deny that some numbers are enough to make one shed tears.—Pray thank Mrs. Higginson from my heart, that she's found it in hers to be pleased with the Horse-Car business.[1] Not to be rude, I must refrain from saying how modestly 'tis esteemed by the author. The fact is it was literally thrown together at the last moment, and made to take the place of another paper, which I withdrew when it was ready to print. What I chiefly ache over in the H. C. is the point you touched—it's shapelessness. Still, there were tolerable bits in it, I thought, and I'm inexpressibly glad of Mrs. Higginson's praise. You couldn't value *that* more than I do.—We'll take the Fuller notice, of course, and I hope you'll find it possible to do the Hedge for March.[2] Can't you?

—I couldn't help the Single Women—they would out. And to tell the truth I'm a little in love with 'em, though I dare say you're right.

Yours, with warm regards to Mrs. H.,
W. D. Howells.

1. "By Horse-Car to Boston," *Atlantic*, January 1870.
2. Higginson's review of *Memoir and Writings of Margaret Fuller Ossoli*, *Atlantic*, February 1870; the review of Frederick Henry Hedge's *The Primeval World of Hebrew Tradition*, *Atlantic*, March 1870, is anonymous.

26 DECEMBER 1869, BOSTON, TO WILLIAM C. HOWELLS

... *The Atlantic Monthly.*
Boston, Dec. 26, *1869.*

Dear father:

We had rather a merry Christmas here yesterday, and we are thankful to have brought both the children through it well. Happily they're neither of them very fond of candy, and so their stomachs were easily managed.—We had trimmed the living-room with wreaths and garlands of ground-pine, and after Winny was abed, we brought up her doll's house, which had been in hiding in the room adjoining the kitchen. It's a very cunning little house of black walnut, some three feet high, with chimneys, two windows in each end, and a great door opening nearly the whole front. We had it painted inside,—the house having been bought at a great bargain at our second hand store here Porter's. Elinor put Winny's doll's furniture in it, and then arranged Winny's other presents with Johnny's and the rest on a table,—fruits and nuts and candies on another table. Then we filled a pair of stockings for each of the little ones, and by that time I'd thought of so many Christmases at home that my heart was aching; and anniversaries in this way are always painful to me. I thought what scanty feasts and presents used to make us happy, and then looked sadly round on Winny's splendor and abundance, and felt that the world was somehow going the wrong way. But I hope that my son will be writing, Dec. 26, 1899, to his father with the love I now feel for you, and then I sha'n't care much how the world has gone.—Last night we all went with Winny to see a most magnificent Christmas tree at the Ashburners';[1] and it was certainly a wonderful sight, trimmed with glass balls, gilt and silver nuts, and every sort of present, blazing candles, and threads of tinsel shining like frost over all.—As to other news (I've been writing this to be read to Henry, partly,) there isn't much. I'm worrying away at the usual things, which have a trick of always requiring to be done over again as soon as they're finished. The college lectures[2] wont, however; for I shall never get myself into that scrape again.—I shall probably get my Atlantic papers ready for publication some time in the spring, though maybe not before July.[3] They'll have to be worked over considerably before they're used in book form, and in the meantime I'm bothered for a name.—I send you sheets of a book[4] which may interest you, and I return herewith Mrs. Garfield's letter to Vic.[5] I hope Sissy is getting ready for her visit. We're counting on it. With love from all

> Your affectionate son
> Will.

1. Anne and Grace Ashburner had come from England to live in Cambridge in 1860.
2. See Howells to Elinor Howells, 28 June 1869, n. 3.
3. *Suburban Sketches* was published 19 December 1870, although the title page gives 1871 as the year of publication.
4. F. H. Hedge, *The Primeval World of Hebrew Tradition*.
5. Victoria Howells had been invited to visit the Garfields in Washington, and a visit to Cambridge was to be included in the trip.

2 January and 6 March 1870, Cambridge, to Henry James

> Cambridge, January 2, 1870.

My dear James:

I may as well *start* a letter to you, and trust fortune for the opportunity of finishing it. I'm not only very busy, but my wrist has somehow got out of order, so that it's a pain for me to write. The doctor encourages me to think that it's lead-poisoning from the pipe that goes from the pump to the well in our kitchen, but this flattering belief I can't indulge. However, it's certainly stiff in writing—the wrist is—and it takes the opportunity of resting to ache a great deal. So you see I have some reason for neglecting you. I wanted to write the moment I got your last letter, for I felt that that was the only way to get another just like it; but I couldn't. All I could do was to ask your news from time to time of your family, and I hope they've mentioned my infirmity to you. I'm not to blame if they haven't, for according to my wont, I've complained about it to everybody. And aproposito of your family, I saw them last night when I went to fetch Mary Mead, who had been dining with them. I don't know whether your sister is really so much better than she used to be, but she looks so, and I've found a very great resemblance to you in her—a fact you've both reason to be proud of. Your father was well, and your mother, as you'll doubtless know from them long before this reaches you. I don't go to any other house, except Lowell's with so much content; though I miss you, my dear fellow, horribly. There's a slouch hat of yours (that you used sometimes to wear when you came to our house in bad weather) that I see now and then on the hall table, and that suggests you in such a way as to give me an intolerable longing for you. I suppose that if the truth were known, I like you enormously; and of course I'm flattered when you pretend to care for me. So please be thanked for asking us to remain in Cambridge, on your account. I really think we shouldn't want to go away if we could, though in looking about for another house, we talk Boston a great deal.—In this sentimental strain I interrupted myself to go down to the post-office, where I got an Italian fotograf Mr. Norton had sent me—a charming picture of an ox-cart loaded with oak boughs and two peasants atop. I had a letter from Miss Grace[1] day before yesterday.—Where you are now, or whether you will see the Nortons or not before you get this, I haven't the smallest notion. I think I could write a little more comfortably if I knew in what land this missive would hit you. Would it might be at Sorrento. To have it read on the terraces overlooking the gulf would almost give me a sniff of the orange-trees, and a glimpse of Capri. Do look up my Antonino Occhio d'Argento, if you would have a good boatman and a thorough rascal while you're at Sorrento. And kiss the pretty muletress that beats your donkey up to the palace of Timberio (as they call Tiberius) at Capri, and dances the Tarantella for you at the inn there.[2] But that it was a sin not proper for a married man, and that my wife and sister-in-law were by, myself had kissed the maid (if I may call her so). I write this to give you an idea of what a mocking and profligate character I am at heart; but really the girl was pretty, and I'm sorry I can't remember her name. On the whole I think Capri the quaintest experience of Italian travel, Pompeii being the strangest. As to the latter place, I let you and the Norton's go there of my free-will, but for other people I envy 'em enough to kill 'em.—I suppose it's in pity of me who think longingly of the places you look on (with bored thoughts sometimes) that we're having such an Italian winter in Cambridge. It's now the 2d of January; a mild October rain is falling, and we've had only one fall of snow and scarce any cold weather. The frost's all out of the ground as in late April. It's really extraordinary, and fills one with old-wife dreads of sickness which must follow such uncommon clemency of the heavens. You imagine of course the gayety of Sacramento street under this sopper of a rain.

Now, you think I've been keeping you from literature long enough. Well, there isn't so much to tell about literature as one at your distance would believe. A new magazine has been started, under the editorship of the Rev. E. E. Hale, by Hurd and Houghton, called Old and New, which has not been enviably good. But it has a chance to grow much better, which isn't the case with the A. M.[3] unless you will write for it. And by the way, why don't you? As the matter goes you're in great danger of having your private letters stolen and published. "What we want," says Mr. Fields, with perfect truth, "is short, *cheerful* stories." And our experience of you is quite in that way of fiction. In all seriousness (as people say who think they've been ironical or playful), I wish you could send us something. Any sketch of what you see or do, would be welcome—I'd almost print an art criticism for you.—Our latest literary event is Lowell's new poem The Cathedral, which I like better than anything I've read for a very long time. I wonder if you get the Atlantic, and if you've seen the poem yet? I doubt if you'd like it as much as I do—your father doesn't. The little paper which your father gave us for January on Woman[4] has been much liked, and I'm instigating him to write more for the magazine.—The N. A. Review is to be cut down to two hundred pages hereafter. Every Saturday is published with very handsome illustrations, now. Generally the literary world is dull, and is I suspect awaiting the appearance of my volume of Atlantic sketches which is to be published in the spring.[5] I sent you one of these sketches (Pedestrian Tour) before it appeared in the November number. Since, I have done By Horse-Car to Boston; and I have in type A Romance of Real Life[6] which records a droll and curious experience of mine. In some ways these things seem rather small business to me; but I fell naturally into doing them; I persuaded myself (too fondly, perhaps) that they're a new kind of study of our life, and I have an impression that they're to lead me to some higher sort of performance. They're not easy to do, but cost me a great deal of work. They seem to be pretty well liked, and I'm told are looked for by readers.—So sweet is it to talk of oneself!—I could go on in this strain for hours and hours.

March 6.

You see how long it takes me to finish a letter. I hope you don't despise me more than half as much as I loathe myself; but I should be glad if you felt something more than the pity I have for your poor unworthy friend. I'm celebrating the presence of your mother in our house by resuming this letter to you. She has come to call, with a perseverance worthy of a better cause, through all the mud and melting snow that shut out Sacramento street from the rest of the world, and she tells me of your being again in England, and of your great homesickness for Italy. Well, I partly understand that; but I think Italy has gone harder with you than she did with me. I find that I'm even ceasing be jealous of other people for loving her, and boasting of her favors. It was n't perhaps a true passion I had for her after all.

A great many things have happened since I began to write this letter. I've been sick a bed for the first time in ten years,—not seriously sick, but very tediously and painfully; and our little boy was dangerously attacked with bronchitis. But all's well now, and these woes are part of the whole incredible past. They originally interrupted my letter to you, however.—Several nights I couldn't sleep, and read till morning. Without this tremendous occasion, I suppose I never should have looked into Erckmann-Chatrian's books;[7] but John Fiske[8] happened to bring me some of them, and I read them with such rapture, that I fire away about them to everybody that lets me talk to him. I think they're amazingly good, and I marvel at the partnership that produced them. I think I never read a more *pleasing* book than *L'Ami Fritz*—unless it's Björnson's Fishermaiden,[9] though that's lovely in such a very different way. What a wonderful atmosphere of springtime in L'Ami F.! The impulse to go and find a cherry-tree in blossom, and to make love to some blonde person was hardly to be resisted even by an enthusiast lying on his back in bed with an abcess on his bowels. As for Björnson, his little romances so enchanted me that I must needs write upon them, and if you've so much patience, you can read my mind in the April Atlantic.—The Romance of Real Life has made all the impression it merited; but I could not help being amused with one adverse criticism in view of the fact that the whole thing was a record of actual experience. The critic praised the style, but said very justly "Mr. Howells has no invention."—Now you are settled, not to say soaking up that water-cure, why couldn't you do something for us in the way of stories, or anything else you've a mind to write? Mr. Fields spoke of the matter only the other day, and I promised to stir you up. So please consider yourself appealed to in the most moving terms by an editor in great suffering.

Mrs. Howells lends me her powerful hand in finishing this letter,[10] for my own hand is still somewhat lame. I do not know that I have so much gossip to tell you about Cambridge as you get from your own family. In fact the winter has been very quiet as far as my own family is concerned. We have seen scarcely anybody but the doctor, who came twice a day for a month—and though we like him very well as a man we dont consider that in seeing him so often we have exactly been in society. After living within a gunshot of Mr. John Fiske for several years

I am beginning to get somewhat acquainted with him, and take as kindly to him as anyone can I suppose who has no idea what positive philosophy is. He has almost a fashion of coming to see us lately, and I find him a very simple-hearted fellow. We have also given each other dinners, and I suppose that in case of a wedding or a funeral we might depend upon each other for the common civilities of life—though this is venturing to say a good deal for Cambridge you will no doubt consider. When we went to the Fiske's we expected to meet Mr. Dennett, but he failed to appear, and I have seen him only once since he came to live amongst us, and that was when I called upon him, immediately after his arrival. He sustains his character of recluse with great rigor, and indeed has lately lost a sister. Mr. Gurney,[11] however, told me the other day that he came often to dine with him. He still writes for the Nation, and it would be a great loss to everybody if he ceased to do so. I am really sorry not to be able to make his acquaintance. Our great excitement at present is Fechter[12]—and I am wholly his—as far as Hamlet goes. I have not seen him in any other character. I wonder if you have seen him in Europe and how you like him. To my thinking he is almost a perfect actor— almost as good as Joe Jefferson[13] with his realistic and untheatrical ways. I was not only interested in his Hamlet, but thrilled and transported by it. I have never seen Booth[14] yet, whose friends of course rage against Fechter.

I believe there is little or nothing to tell you about literature. I think we grow more poverty-stricken in that direction every day. Editorially I have a pretty good survey of the whole field, and the prospect is a discouraging one. The signs of growth are very small and feeble, while there are some striking instances of dwindling. There is no sort of freshness in the things that are sent us at least. One of the new Spring books is a collection of Mr. Bret. Harte's stories from the Overland,[15] which are very good indeed so far as they go—but he has eked out the book with some old and inferior writings of his. Miss Phelps has produced a novel, Hedged In, that is written in her most gasping and shuddering style, and discomforts me exceedingly, though I dare say Miss Phelps likes it, and it is pretty sure to sell twenty thousand.[16] Mrs. Prescott Spofford[17] is exclusively engaged on Frank Leslie,[18] and all the magazines and newspapers continue to grind out the usual amount of fiction and poetry. The latest of the Magazines, Old and New, is a sort of diluted Putnam, if you can imagine it, and one must be a very good Unitarian or a very bad critic to like it. I see this letter is getting to be fearfully cynical, and I seek in vain for a cheerful topic with which to close it up. I will substitute something that is to us, at least, very exciting. I told you in the January number of this letter that we were looking about for a new house. I have now to tell you that we are still looking without an immediate prospect of finding any. For a while our dream was to live near Porter's Station so that we might get easily to and from Boston by the steam-cars, but now we rave of a house near the Square so that we may enjoy Cambridge society, Mrs. Howells having got very much better and having some faint aspirations in that direction. Our project is to have Mrs Mead and Mary[19] come and live with us, and we shall take a larger house than we otherwise should. We have even thought of building—but not in our lucid intervals, and taking into consideration our peculiarities it would not be at all amazing if the whole thing were abandoned. At any rate you need not expect to find us living in a North Avenue palace when you come back. But come back nevertheless. I miss you more and more, and now, when the weather begins to open and the streets all about to reek with the thaw I have a wild longing to take a walk with you, as I used to do in other days.

Mrs. Howells relinquishes the pen that I may assure in my own feeble hand how delighted I am that you're to return next fall. Let me beseech you to use me better than I deserve, and to write very soon. I am joined by my whole family in love to you, and I am

affectionately yours
W. D. Howells.

Winny sends a kiss. "But tell him I think I wont marry him. He'll be an old man by the time I'm grown up."

This is a great lot of stuff hardly better than nothing.

1. Grace Norton (1834–1926) was C. E. Norton's sister.
2. See *Italian Journeys* (1872), pp. 117, 120, 123–24, 131, 133.
3. *Atlantic Monthly*.
4. "The Woman Thou Gavest with Me."
5. See Howells to W. C. Howells, 26 December 1869, n. 3.
6. *Atlantic*, March 1870.
7. This joint name was used by Emile Erckmann and Alexandre Chatrian, coauthors of a popular series of historical novels. *L'Ami Fritz* (1864) is not part of that series, but was similarly successful.
8. John Fiske (1842–1901), philosopher and historian, was soon to become known as an articulate advocate of Darwinian and Spencerian evolutionary theories.
9. Bjornstjerne Bjornson, *The Fisher-Maiden* (1868), *Arne* (1858), and *A Happy Boy* (1860), were reviewed by Howells in the *Atlantic*, April 1870.
10. The rest of the letter is in Elinor Howells' hand except for the last paragraph, signature, and postscript.
11. In 1868 E. W. Gurney replaced Norton as Lowell's associate in editing the *North American Review*.
12. Charles A. Fechter (1824–1879), a well-known European actor, visited the United States (1869–1870) and in 1872 returned to stay.
13. Joseph Jefferson (1829–1905) was an American actor, who became famous for his part in Dion Boucicault's dramatization of *Rip Van Winkle*.
14. Edwin Booth.
15. *The Luck of Roaring Camp and Other Sketches*. Harte was editor of the *Overland Monthly* in San Francisco (1868–1870).

16. Elizabeth Stuart Phelps (1844–1911) was the author of many popular novels; her most famous one is *The Gates Ajar* (1868). She later married Herbert Dickinson Ward (1861–1932).

17. Harriet Prescott Spofford (1835–1921) was a prolific writer of fiction.

18. *Frank Leslie's Illustrated Newspaper* (1855–1922) was founded by Frank Leslie (1821–1880), the publisher, who had come from England in 1848.

19. Elinor's mother and sister.

17 MARCH 1870, BOSTON, TO THOMAS W. HIGGINSON

...The Atlantic Monthly.
Boston, March 17 *1870*

Dear Colonel—

On the contrary, I'm very glad to get it.[1]—Have you any objection to our saying, upon those mysterious slips in which we reveal authorship to the editors that among the reviewers is T. W. H.?

Yours truly
W. D. Howells.

Pray give my regards to Mrs. Higginson, and tell her that I read your note very easily—especially the P. S. Sanscrit itself could*n't* keep me out of a compliment.—I *knew* Mrs. Higginson wouldn't like "Hedged In." I'm curious to see what you've said of it.—I think there may very well be novels of purpose—and sermons. But neither ought to be read on week-days.

1. Probably a review of Elizabeth Stuart Phelps, *Hedged In*. Howells had written Higginson on 10 March 1870 (NN) to inquire whether he could write a favorable notice of this novel for the May issue of the *Atlantic*. The anonymous review appeared in June.

2 MAY 1870, BOSTON, TO THOMAS W. HIGGINSON

...the Atlantic Monthly,...
Boston, May 2, *1870*

My dear Colonel—

Your essay[1] is lovely—but how could you write it, never having so much as seen my boy yet? He's something to eat up—something between peach and olive, with such a smooth, solid surface. Well, children *are* nice—one's own, especially.

—You'll see by the proof that I've stared at your saying *cartoon* where you do. You're *padrone*[2] to say it, of course, but I don't think it's the word, and our refined friend Worcester[3] agrees with me.

Yours truly
W. D. Howells.

Col. Higginson.

    1. "A Shadow," *Atlantic*, July 1870, is about children and childhood.
    2. *Padrone* means "master." Although Howells indicated that Higginson was free to choose his own diction, the word "cartoon" does not appear in the published essay.
    3. Joseph E. Worcester, *Comprehensive Pronouncing and Explanatory Dictionary of the English Language* (first ed., 1830).

22 MAY 1870, CAMBRIDGE, TO JAMES R. LOWELL

Cambridge, May 22, 1870

My dear Mr. Lowell—

I sent, as you suggested, and I desired, the ticket to Mrs Lowell's sister,[1] and I've secured thereby a most patient listener to the lectures on New Italian Literature,[2] which are now making such a stir on Sacramento street. The theatrical people say that a "paper house" is always very cold and inapplausive as compared with a "pay house," but so far, my free tickets have brought me greater glory than the subscriptions have. The base-ball club yesterday seduced all the male students away from my class, but the gentlemen who come in on my passes were there, to a martyr. I have bribed the Cerberean darkey by the way, and now any body comes that likes. The College Steward himself should not be shut out. I've an audience of twenty, and the quality is even more distinguished than the quantity. Up to the close of yesterday's the lectures had not been received with yells of derision—Mr. Child, for example, did not hiss, once, nor Mr. Longfellow ask to have the lecturer put out—and so I'm emboldened to ask if I couldn't, quite unexpectedly to myself, be invited to give the things at Cornell next year. I really think they're not so dull as they might be, nor so absolutely void of instruction; but if you don't care to suggest the matter to Mr. White,[3] by all means, don't. If you do, I shall await the result in modest ignorance of the whole affair.

—I imagine you sighing for Cambridge, in spite of Ithaca the fair; and to tell you the truth, the town is just now looking her prettiest. She seems to be dreaming of the days when she was wholly orchard, and she's all decked in apple blossoms, look what way you will, and orioles, listen when you will.

I don't think there's much news, worthy to be so called.—Harry James is come back from Europe, and Dennett has called upon me. (He went also to see you.) These are the greatest events of life for me, unless the fact that my boy learns a new word every day, is greater.

Yours always
W. D. Howells.

1. Frances Dunlap Lowell's sister has not been identified.
2. See Howells to Elinor Howells, 28 June 1869, n. 3. The first lecture was given on 16 May 1870.
3. Andrew D. White (1832–1918), president of Cornell (1867–1885). Lowell replied on 30 May 1870 (MH): "He would be delighted to have you come—if they can afford it. If not next year, I think they will manage the year after. But if I don't go next spring—I told Mr White he must have you."

30 OCTOBER 1870, CAMBRIDGE, TO WILLIAM C. HOWELLS

Cambridge Oct. 30 *1870*.

Dear father:

Your last letter makes us very sad about you, and we shall be anxious till we hear again. I hope that you will be able in some way to get perfect rest for a time. It seems to be the thing you most need, for I think you have had an uncommonly trying year, what with the hot long summer, the many visits, Joe's poor health, and the labors you have added to your ordinary work by this business of lecturing. That branch at least, I would give up, if I were you, for a good while to come, especially when it calls you away from home.

Since I wrote last, I have given two of my lectures in the Lowell Institute.[1] At the first I was considerably unnerved, and read too rapidly; but last night, I had the severe critical testimony of Elinor in my favor, as well as that of Mr. Lowell, who was kind enough to come in to the lecture, and who declared himself interested and contented with the performance. My audience is about two hundred and fifty, which is much larger than the usual audience: in fact, many courses are delivered to twenty-five or thirty people.—Perhaps the girls will care to know that I appear in evening dress, and Elinor at least thinks I'm very "pretty-looking." In spite of all these encouragements, however, I doubt if I should like lecturing as a profession, and I'm exceedingly glad that I withdrew from the field as a popular-lecturer.[2]

We've got our Hannah back again. She was so sorry to have left us that she refused all other places, and became sick about it. Mrs. Lowell saw her at the Intelligence Office and Hannah opened her heart, and told her that she wouldn't go to anybody but Mrs. Howells. So, as we didn't like our new cook we sent word to Hannah to come back, and here she is. I think the whole affair is a great praise to Elinor.—The things have arrived from Ohio, in good condition, but the charges are dreadful—$15.75— which will make the things cost $3 or $4 more than they would have cost here. But it's well to have made the experiment, and I thank you and Joe very much for your trouble. I hope soon to hear that you are much better. All send love.

Your affectionate son
Will.

I sent a draft for $35 last Sunday. Elinor has got Vic's letter.

1. The invitation "to deliver a course of twelve lectures on modern Italian poetry at the Lowell Institute next winter" was extended to Howells in a letter from John Amory Lowell, 5 June 1870 (MH). The series had the title "Italian Poets of Our Century," and Howells gave the first two lectures on 26 and 29 October 1870.

2. On 11 September 1870 (MH) Howells had written his father: "As for my... lecture on Venice which I proposed to deliver before lyceums this winter, I think I shall give it up; for the Lowell Institute Lectures will take all the time I can give; and I doubt if I should be successful as a popular lecturer."

27 November 1870, BOSTON, TO WILLIAM C. HOWELLS

...the Atlantic Monthly,...
Boston, Nov. 27, 1870.

Dear father:

Thinking this morning that I had not heard from you during the week, I was troubled till I recollected that you were to write your Sunday letter on Wednesday hereafter. I suppose you have been to Pittsburg, and have got Aurelia back, and that you are once again all at home.

We had the usual Thanksgiving, here, and the time since I last wrote has passed off in eventless prosperity. I suppose you have got—that, is Vic has got—Elinor's letter which last Sunday supplied the place of mine. I had been exceedingly busy, and so let myself off.—Yesterday Elinor found the enclosed fotograf in Boston, and she sends it to Vic with Jane Mould's compliments.[1] Perhaps Vic will remember the face as that of a theatrical friend.

I have now given ten of my Lowell lectures,[2] and only two more remain to be given. I shall be *so* glad when they are done. I have had small audiences, for the lectures were not at all popular in character, and few were interested in the subject. Mr. Lowell tells me that I shall probably be asked to deliver them at the Cornell University, but I think I shall decline, if that is the case. The fact is, the conviction has been growing upon me that I am a writer, and nothing else, and that I shall be wiser and happier if hereafter I attempt nothing outside of my proper sphere.— I am now going to push forward my American travel-sketches[3] as fast as I can. Do you think I might make a tolerably accurate description of Jefferson, without giving offense? I don't know that I shall want to do so, but I may.

Since I wrote two weeks ago, John J. Piatt has paid us a little visit. He was a shade or two less gloomy than usual, and went away almost happy, for I had managed to sell a long poem of his wife's, and had procured the publication of her volume[4] by Fields, Osgood & Co.

Mary Mead leaves us in about a week, for New Jersey, where she is to pass the winter with Mrs. Shepard.[5]

The children are both very well. Booah[6] shows no symptoms of taking the mumps. He is fearfully mischievous, and spanking is only a momentary relief. He wants the reputation of a good boy, however, and I touch his ambition by tales of my own goodness when a deenty (little) booah. In these legends I am obliged to appear as a youthful saint, who never touched his papa's pens, nor kicked at his door when he was writing, nor slapped his Winny, nor sauced his gamma. *You* might tell a different story. But the effect is good on Booah. All send love.

Your affectionate son
Will.

1. Jane Mould has not been identified.
2. See Howells to W. C. Howells, 30 October 1870, n. 1.
3. *Their Wedding Journey* (1872) was serialized in the *Atlantic*, July–December 1871.
4. Sarah M. B. Piatt, *A Woman's Poems* (1871). The "long poem" has not been located in any magazine; it may be the title poem of *A Voyage to the Fortunate Isles* (1874).
5. Joanna Mead Shepard.
6. John Mead Howells.

11 DECEMBER 1870, BOSTON, TO WILLIAM C. HOWELLS

...the Atlantic Monthly,...
Boston, Dec. 11, 1870.

Dear father:

I suppose you can't expect much news of so short a week as this has been, and at this moment I can hardly think of a thing. I have spent it in pretty steady work, rejoicing at intervals that my lectures are over,[1] and planning new troubles for myself. At last, I have fairly launched upon the story of our last summer's travels, which I'm giving the form of fiction so far as the characters are concerned.[2] If I succeed in this—and I believe I shall—I see clear before me a path in literature which no one else has trod, and which I believe I can make most distinctly and entirely my own. I am going to take my people to Niagara, and then down the St Lawrence, and so back to Boston. If I do this, I shall leave Jefferson out, though originally I meant to sketch it in the course of the narrative. I should find some difficulty in treating it agreeably with the rest of the plan, and it is material that will keep very well.—By the way, is Annie going to do anything more about her travels? She ought to.

I'm gratified that you like Flitting[3] so well. It forms the last chapter in my book of Suburban Sketches, which is to be published next Saturday. The volume has been delayed somewhat on account of an accident to the mill where the paper was making for it. I believe Hurd expects a good sale, but in order to reserve for myself an "agreeable disappointment," I never hope for anything. In fact the sketches strike me as somewhat too local in character.[4]

J. J. Piatt has been here, and has exploited everybody in the Commercial.[5] I warned him to be very cautious, but I don't see how he could have done worse in some things. As he stayed at my house, what he says of me is in particularly bad taste, and gives me the air of having boasted to him of my "close intimacy", as he calls it, with Lowell. I'm afraid if it comes to the eyes of people here, Piatt had better keep away from Cambridge hereafter. I wonder at his want of tact.

—I hope Elinor told in her last letter something about Booah's progress. He talks all the time now, and forms long sentences with great correctness. His day begins at 5 a.m. when he makes mine begin too by sitting up in his crib and repeating till I wake: "Booah git in beeg bed." After that we all take a nap together, and about half past seven he piles out to be dressed. Then he pays a visit to Hannah and gets a *googhee* (cookey) and presently has breakfast. If there are *gaks* (cakes), he has to have *deenty wans* (tiny ones) and he is very careful that no favor is shown to Winny. After breakfast, he's often bundled up for a play out doors,—he plays alone, Winny being at school. At eleven he takes a nap, and spends the rest of the day in miscellaneous mischief. He pays me a visit and kicks on my door till I let him in. Then he says, *Papa gigenoh-bup*, which from first meaning a train of cars and a boat (reminiscences of last summer's travel) has come successively to mean the pen with which they are depicted, and the act of writing. I put him out by violence and persuasion, and he says "*good-bah!*" and trots off. Between him and literature I am as happy as anybody I know. With love from all to all,

Your affectionate son
Will.

1. See Howells to W. C. Howells, 30 October 1870, n. 1.
2. *Their Wedding Journey.*
3. *Atlantic,* December 1870.
4. One of the earliest favorable responses to *Suburban Sketches* came from John Hay, who at this time was on the staff of the New York *Tribune.* He wrote Howells on 29 December 1870 (MH): "Where the demon did you find that impossibly happy way of saying everything? It is a thing that the rest of us blunder on, once in a while, but you never miss.... You see the critics all notice this, and not knowing what else to say they say Hawthorne and Irving &c."
5. The Cincinnati *Commercial.*

23 DECEMBER 1870, CAMBRIDGE, TO HENRY W. LONGFELLOW

Cambridge, Dec. 23, 1870.

Dear Mr Longfellow:

I think I might boldly defy even your kindness to do better for Faust than I have done,[1] and if Taylor is not content with me, why he will prove himself as hard to please as—any other poet. My bitterest disappointment with the translation came from finding it so very far from literal. When I have my review in proof,[2] with your leave I will show it you, and then I should like to compare a few passages of the English and German with you.

It seemed to me after I came home from you the other night that I had never passed so charming an evening.

Very truly yours
W. D. Howells.

1. Longfellow had written Howells on 21 December 1870 (MH), expressing his admiration for "the address and dexterity with which" Bayard Taylor had translated Goethe's *Faust.*
2. Howells reviewed Taylor's *Faust* in the *Atlantic,* February 1871, commenting on the translation's "very remarkable degree of literalness, though not...so great literalness as we could have desired." In a letter to W. A. Speck, 29 August 1918 (CtY), he wrote that Taylor's *Faust,* "especially the first part, is the most wonderful piece of translation that I know."

7 JANUARY 1871, BOSTON, TO THOMAS W. HIGGINSON

...*the Atlantic Monthly,*...
Boston, Jan. *7, 1871.*

Dear Col. Higginson:

Yes, I shall be very glad to have you notice H. H.[1] whom I was a little puzzled how to dispose of. Do Aubrey[2] when you like—but I remind you that life is short, and *he* may not live to read your praises.

I had a letter from Harte about a month ago,³ and answered it with an invitation to my house, when he should come east, but I've not heard from him since, and have no idea when he's coming except that it's sometime this winter. As soon as I learn anything, I'll let you know.

Thanks that you like S. S. I couldn't keep the drowned girl out. Besides she was no worse than Zenobia—was Zenobia, in fact, on Putnam street, Cambridge.⁴

Mrs. Howells joins me in hearty reciprocation of your good wishes, and over and above in a Happy New Year to Mrs. Higginson.

Yours truly
W. D. Howells

P. S. Pray give Waring⁵ my regards, and tell him I'm a decenter sort of fellow than I seem, in spite of neglecting his kindnesses. I'm to write him shortly.

1. Higginson reviewed Helen Hunt's *Verses* in the *Atlantic*, March 1871.

2. Presumably Aubrey de Vere (1814–1902), the Irish poet; but no review of any of his books appeared in the *Atlantic* at this time.

3. The most recent extant letter from Bret Harte to Howells is dated 5 November 1870 (MH; printed in *Life in Letters*, I, 158), and reads in part: "I expect still to see you this winter. Until then I shall read you—for it might be that a closer and more intimate knowledge of your methods might spoil your work for me. Do you really go through 'a day's pleasuring' grimly, with the intention of *ex post facto* reflections? These and many other impertinent questions I shall ask you, O, most excellent writer of excellent English!"

4. The drowned girl appears in "Scene," the only one of *Suburban Sketches* which was not first printed in the *Atlantic*. Zenobia is a character in Hawthorne's *The Blithedale Romance* (1852).

5. George E. Waring, Jr. (1833–1898), an agricultural and drainage engineer, lived in Newport, Rhode Island (1867–1877), and occasionally wrote for the *Atlantic*.

22 JANUARY 1871, BOSTON, TO WILLIAM C. HOWELLS

...*the Atlantic Monthly*,...
Boston, January 22, *1871*.

Dear father:

I'm glad to hear what you tell me of your health, and I hope Joe will prevail with you to make me that visit. You can't come too soon for us.— By the way you needn't feel the least troubled about Bret Harte on my account. I have the most solemn and repeated pledges from Osgood as to my relations to the magazine when Mr. Fields retires;¹ and if my position here should cease to be satisfactory, I can easily better myself. I should never suffer myself to enter rivalry with any one; but at any rate Harte's and my own lives are so divergent that we should not come into competition. He will be engaged probably as a salaried contributor to the Atlantic, but I shall be editor. This at least is Mr. Osgood's promise. I don't care to have the matter spoken of.

What a wonderfully good fotograf is that of Aurelia! and how very handsome she looks. Talent I knew we had in the family, but beauty!—well, I will try not to be too proud of her, especially as I know she is too wise and good a girl to be vain. But tell her that Elinor and I both delight in it, as a picture of herself, and as the portrait of a beautiful young lady. It has an honorable place on the parlor mantel near the fotograf of a lovely old gentleman.—I heard from the *Independent* people a day or two ago; the publisher[2] wanted me to come on and talk matters over with him. This I respectfully declined to do, saying that if he had any offer to make me, the business could be transacted by letter, thus delicately hinting that I was not seeking anything from him. Perhaps, it will never come to an offer: it would have to be a very heavy offer that would tempt me away from Boston.—I suppose before this you'll have seen a strained and super-subtle notice of my book in The Nation.[3] It does me more than justice, and less; and I'm afraid that some who cannot take it all in will think me a saturnine scoffer. However, you can't write your own criticisms, more's the pity. I believe the book is doing very well, but I've not had any report of sales yet.—Both the children and their parents are in excellent health. They unite in love to you all. Thanks to Aurelia for her letter. It'll be answered another time.—I hope the velvet reached Annie in good state. It was $4.50 a yard; 3½ yards.

Your affectionate son
Will.

1. Howells succeeded James T. Fields as editor of the *Atlantic* on 1 July 1871.

2. Henry C. Bowen was the publisher of the New York *Independent*. On 8 February 1871 (MH) Howells wrote his father: "I have finally declined going to the N. Y. Independent. In fact, the matter rather fizzled out, for I gave them no hopes that I would come, whatever offer they made, and I never thought of changing. But the effect here was very good."

3. "Howells's Suburban Sketches," *Nation*, 19 January 1871, was probably written by J. R. Dennett.

1 MARCH 1871, BOSTON, TO THOMAS W. HIGGINSON

...*the Atlantic Monthly*,...
Boston, March 1, 1871

My dear Colonel Higginson:

I don't know what to do about the Bundy business;[1] but my impression is that the public has got all it can possibly stand of the Bowles and Field controversy.[2] I return your enclosures.

Bret Harte and his family are with us,[3] and we like them extremely. His wife is a most admirable woman, and he is all, and more than, you would expect from the best of his literature. He goes back to New York on Saturday. He sends regards to you.

Very sincerely
W. D. Howells.

P. S. Glancing again at Mr. Wingal's[4] note, I see that he wants us notice Mr. Bundy's (what a name!) pamphlet. Very well, if it seems worth while. But *I* don't know whether we're a nation.

1. Jonas Mills Bundy, editor of the New York *Evening Mail*, was the author of the pamphlet *Are We a Nation?*, a reissue of *State Rights* (1860), which apparently had some bearing on his vigorous campaign against the Tweed Ring in 1871.
2. Samuel Bowles, editor of the Springfield *Republican*, had attacked David Dudley Field, consul for Fisk, Gould, and Tweed, for rigging a meeting of stockholders of the Erie Railroad.
3. Harte had written Howells on 24 January 1871 (MH): "I've just accepted an invitation from Mr. Fields to meet you and other distinguished folk at the Saturday Club on the 25th. prox." In the same letter Harte mentioned an article written by Howells, "Mr. Francis Bret Harte," *Every Saturday*, 14 January 1871, commenting: "You have my thanks for the prose sketch in wh. you handled with your usual delicacy a very commonplace history. I was both amused and gratified at your gentlemanly doubts of certain newspaper reporters' facts—or rather their statement of facts—and the kindly way that you gave me the benefit of those doubts. You are a good fellow and I doubt not I shall like you."
4. Howells probably meant Charles F. Wingate, New York correspondent for the Springfield *Republican*, who in 1874 contributed articles to the *North American Review* on the "History of the Tweed Ring."

5 MARCH 1871, BOSTON, TO WILLIAM C. HOWELLS

...*the Atlantic Monthly*,...
Boston, March 5, 1871.

Dear father:

Our friends[1] went yesterday morning, and we have subsided again into our usual quiet. It has been a very pleasant visit to us—one of the pleasantest that we've ever had made us, but of course we're glad to be alone now, for we were all fairly worn out by the social part of it. Besides our party, the Hartes were entertained somewhere every night. I dined with him at Longfellow's, Agassiz's and Fields's, trying to beg off each time, but urged by him to go. It seems rather absurd for a host to be following his guest about in this way, but it is the custom, and in spite of the enormous fatigue, I enjoyed it. Harte is quite unspoiled by his great popularity—which he values at its true worth—and is a thoroughly charming good-hearted fellow. He reminded me in some things—tones of voice and laughter—of Joe, and I kept wishing that Joe and he knew each other. Perhaps they will, some day, especially if Joe comes east this summer, for it is likely that the Hartes and ourselves will seek some refuge together by the seaside. Till now, Elinor and I have met no young couple so congenial. It came out one day at dinner that we were all of the same age—all born in '37. Harte will probably live in New York, though he may be engaged to write exclusively for Osgood & Co. Next winter he thinks of lecturing; though none of his plans are matured yet.—We are all pretty well; but Mrs. Mead[2] is in bed with a bad cold, and Johnny has a cough to-day from a cold he took yesterday. Neither case is at all serious. Elinor is tired out, of course, though buoyed up by the triumph of her party, which is generally allowed to be one of the most brilliant ever given in Cambridge. I wish the girls could have been here. I haven't had a moment yet to look at your memoir,[3] but I'm going to give the afternoon to it. I'm quite eager and curious about it.

Love from all to all.—I hope Sam will succeed in Ashtabula.

Your affectionate son
Will.[4]

1. Bret Harte and his wife. See *Life in Letters*, I, 160–61, for Elinor's description of the visit.
2. Elinor's mother.
3. Howells commented to his father about the material on 12 March 1871 (MH), suggesting that he write more fully about his childhood, describe in detail the characters of his (Howells') grandparents, and give descriptions of "as many characteristic people as you can."
4. Enclosed with the letter is a clipping from the Boston *Advertiser* announcing the arrival of the Hartes to visit the Howellses.

11 MARCH 1871, BOSTON, TO SARAH ORNE JEWETT

Boston March 11, 1871[1]

Dear Madam;

By all means make a sketch of your story[2] if you don't feel secure of your powers of invention. But in doing this pray remember that you will have to develop character very fully—much more fully than you have done in the piece as it stands.[3] Perhaps also it would be well to curtail some of the preliminary passages. Give ample accounts of the old house, the sea faring and lighthouse people as you propose. I return you the manuscript by this post for your revision.[4] When you come next to Boston, pray let me know, and I will try to call upon you. Or if you have not time to send me your address, and in your leisure feel compassion enough for a busy man to waive ceremony will you come out to Cambridge to see me? I live in Berkeley St one door from Phillips Place (Garden St car) and my name is that of your obedient servant

W. D. Howells—

Miss Jewett,

    1. The letter and signature are not in Howells' hand.
    2. "The Shore House," *Atlantic*, September 1873.
    3. The author of a letter in the same hand, signed "The Editors," and dated 5 March 1871 (MH), pointed out that the story lacked in "picturesque and romantic" incident, and that "the descriptive character of the paper altogether overbalances the narrative"; finally Miss Jewett was advised to "expand the facts to dramatic proportions."
    4. For Miss Jewett's reaction to Howells' comments, see *Sarah Orne Jewett Letters*, ed. Richard Cary (Waterville, Me.: Colby College Press, 1956), p. 29.

1 APRIL 1871, BOSTON, TO JAMES R. OSGOOD

...*the Atlantic Monthly*,...
Boston, March 32d *1871*.

My dear Osgood:

I send you some sheets[1] of *Their Wedding Journey*, from which you can perhaps judge whether it is capable of illustration, though this is the least picturesque part of it.[2] Hereafter follow descriptions of New York, especially the hottest day of last summer there, the Night Boat on the Hudson; the RR. from Albany to Niagara with a night's pause at Rochester; Niagara—very full; the steamboat ride down the St. Lawrence; Montreal, Quebec, etc., etc. Of course fresh characters and incidents are introduced throughout.

I should be glad to know what you think of the thing as literature. I vacillate between a pyramidal pride in it, and a colossal loathing of it. The first number will have two and half pages more than are yet set.

Very truly yours
W. D. Howells.

1. Proofs for most of the first installment, *Atlantic,* July 1871.
2. The illustrations for the first edition were furnished by Augustus Hoppin (1828–1896), well known as a book illustrator.

21 APRIL 1871, BOSTON, TO WILL M. CARLETON

...the Atlantic Monthly,...
Boston, April 21, 1871.

My dear Sir[1]—

I am very glad to have heard from you, though I cannot reply, as I should like to do, by accepting your poem.[2] However, I shall be able, in declining it, to tell you why I liked "Betsey and I are out" so much, and so pave the way, I hope, to our future relations as editor and contributor. That ballad seemed to me extremely good because it took a theme of this common, modern, actual life of ours, and treated it with warm poetic feeling, and perfect artistic self-restraint. In the poem I send, back, I find the same good realistic tendency, but not the restraint. If you'll forgive the phrase, it "slops over" in several places, and it's feeble in others, whereas "Betsey" was thoroughly strong. I've made bold to mark such passages as I most disliked; but I do not like the poem at all. Do me the favor to read it and "Betsey" over again together, and I think my meaning will be plain to you.

What I want you to do for us,—and yourself, too,—is to take some subject of the life about you, and treat it as you did in the better poem. I should avoid the war because it has been overdone. Some romance of country-life—or town life—something native, natural, racy—we want this; and I believe you can give it. Hoping to hear from you again,

Yours very sincerely
W. D. Howells.

Mr. Carleton.

1. Will Carleton (1845–1912) was best known for his popular poetry dealing with domestic and farm life.
2. Carleton had submitted his poem with his letter to Howells of 17 April 1871 (MH); it deals with the decoration of soldiers' graves and is probably "Cover Them Over." None of Carleton's poetry was published in the *Atlantic.*

3 MAY 1871, BOSTON, TO EDMUND C. STEDMAN

...*the Atlantic Monthly,*...
Boston, May 3, *1871.*

My dear Stedman—

I have read your article[1] with all the interest you could have desired for it, and if I do not now write to accept it, it is merely because I wish to refer to Mr Osgood the question you suggest about such a paper on Tennyson in a magazine of his publishers. I myself see no reason why Mr. Osgood should object, but he as a publisher may feel differently. I don't think your paper at all derogatory to T's *genius,* tho' it does assail his *originality*—a non-essential which people are always confounding with an essential, like the former. Many of the resemblances you point out are truly startling; but you dilute the effect a little in some others where the *mood* is imitative rather than the *thought.* I think whenever this is the case, you ought to make the distinction. At times your word *adaptation* struck me as too strong.

I value highly the scholarship and faculty which give us such an article as yours, and I hope—with very little doubt—that I shall be able to write you of its acceptance when Mr. Osgood gets back from New York.

I expect to be in New York myself for a few days week after next, and then we shall have a talk.[2]

1. "Tennyson and Theocritus," *Atlantic,* November 1871.
2. The complimentary close and signature have been cut from the manuscript.

4 MAY 1871, BOSTON, TO THOMAS W. HIGGINSON

...*the Atlantic Monthly,*...
Boston, May 4, *1871.*

My dear Sir—

Of course we take "On an Old Latin Text-book,"[1] which, without being one of your best essays has yet things in it that touch me nearly. That saying that memory flatters like hope, and others of kindred quality do please me mightily. I don't fear for literature, and I don't know if I quite like its enemies to be treated with respect,—but that's your affair.

Yours very sincerely
W. D. Howells.

Colonel Higginson.

1. *Atlantic,* October 1871.

7 MAY 1871, CAMBRIDGE, TO WILLIAM C. HOWELLS

Cambridge, May 7, 1871.

Dear father—

I have decided that I don't want to go to Ohio later than June, this year, and so, if you can bring about your affairs, and start on the trip about the 1st, I should be very glad.[1] I can't give more than two weeks to the whole affair and I could not spend more than a day in Jefferson before starting. I hope you'll have all arrangements made so that there need be no delay after I get there. You see that as I'm to take charge of the magazine on the first of July, it's important to me to be here at least a fortnight before that time. Please keep this in mind, and let me know if you'll be prepared to start by June 1st. Of course you know it's with difficulty I get off at all, and I must be very exact about everything.

Your account of Parker Pillsbury's performances and your own share in rebutting him, greatly interested us.[2] Mrs Mead's old friend Mrs. Williston[3] is here visiting her. I read your letter aloud to them, and they both gloried in it. I think, however, that till you are fairly on your legs again, you had better not fight any more wind-mills of that sort. Tisn't worth while. A people that give up their church for a man to attack religion in, seem to me almost irreclaimable.

I've been amused at the very cold shoulder you turn Cadwell, in praising him as a candidate for governor. Has he any chance? Would Wade really accept the candidacy?[4] He wrote like a man who thought he might be persuaded.

—I was unable to write my letter this morning because I was out breakfasting at Sedgwick's with Godkin of the Nation. He's a most relishing, substantial and solid man—a bit of meat in a world of thin soup. We had a long, and very entertaining talk about political and social topics, and we came to the conclusion that most of our troubles resulted from treating all kinds of enormous rascality as a good joke— from our want of seriousness, and from the doubt that seems to paralyze all thoughtful men as to own fitness to rule. He thinks that the N. Y. City Ring,[5] will be able to control the State at the next Presidential election, and will soon establish itself in Washington at the head of national affairs.

I don't understand what you say about the chapter of Wedding Journey I sent you, not getting the people out of Boston. I carried them as far as to the Battery in New York.[6]

We are all well, and all join in love to you. Remember us particularly to Henry, and tell him Brother Will wants to see him.

Your affectionate son
Will.

1. Howells and his father traveled to the Ohio River by horse and buggy and by train; near Steubenville they visited the father's boyhood home. Howells described the journey in two letters to Elinor Howells, 4–5 June 1871 (MH) and 7 June 1871 (MH); and in a letter to his father, 25 June 1871 (MH), he reminisced about some of the people and places they had seen together.

2. Parker Pillsbury (1809–1898), an antislavery and women's rights reformer, was also active as an opponent of religious faith, especially Christianity. His Jefferson lecture on 23 April 1871 prompted W. C. Howells to present a defense of religious faith on 30 April, which was printed in the Ashtabula *Sentinel*, 22 June 1871.

3. Possibly Mrs. Samuel Williston, wife of a wealthy Massachusetts businessman, legislator, and philanthropist. Mrs. Mead was Elinor Howells' mother.

4. The *Sentinel*, 11 May 1871, printed a statement by Darius W. Cadwell, expressing his decision not to run for the Republican gubernatorial nomination. Benjamin F. Wade had been U. S. senator from Ohio until 1869.

5. The political machine of William M. ("Boss") Tweed (1823–1878).

6. Howells had sent his father proof sheets of the first chapter of *Their Wedding Journey*.

3 JUNE 1871, JEFFERSON, TO ELINOR M. HOWELLS

Jefferson, June 3, 1871.

Dear Elinor:

This morning I am feeling pretty well for the first time since I left home. I got here at half past eight yesterday morning,—just 24 hours from Boston,—and fr'm the heat & loss of sleep ws in an awful state. Fell into a deadly doze just before dinner, and woke up scarcely able to locate or identify myself. I tho't I ws going crazy, though I knew pretty well what I ws about, too. It ws just as it ws in Venice after the *pesca*.[1] I had been very billious since Tuesday but some seidlitz powders & a good night's rest have brought me almost round again, tho' my nerves are still somewhat in a quiver.—I found the family well; and it is now arranged that father and I shall start this afternoon or to-morrow morning, and go straight south to Steubenville, where we'll leave the buggy, and make the rest of the journey by rail. That's the present plan, tho' we may change it. Send anything to Joe, here, that you wish me to get. Now I'll try to tell you about my journey hither.[2]

Annie is going to kindly lend me a hand.[3] My first companion was a very pleasant young fellow going to Millford, who thought I was on a very long journey. We talked about the French war, and he said he hadn't cared anything about the war, since the Prussians had stopped.

Next came a farmer, with whom I talked canker worms. The landscape looked very dry and thirsty all through western Massachusetts. It was very pretty, where it was cultivated, but struck me as being very uninteresting and shabby where it was wild, until you get to the Berkshire Hills. At Framingham, there came in a young mother, with her baby, going to Sacramento, Cal. where her husband had gone for his health. She was to be a week on the road, and thinking what she had before her, and how little I had myself to bear, I hung my head in shame— for about a second. She was rather pale and slender, but seemed strong; and she was the only one who appeared not to realize the horrors of her prospects. The baby was good and "wrestled with my finger." Perhaps you'll understand what sort of woman she was, by the fact that she had short hair, not perfectly clean teeth, and a great over gown of linen. She was very frank, as every body is travelling, and everybody seemed to feel authorized to ask her where she was going; but she was very nice and sensible.

The next man who came into my seat was the travelling partner of a shoe and leather house. He was very kind to this lady, and at Albany, "Here" he said to me, "We must carry her things for her." And so we did, and there were a big lot of them, and a mighty heavy carpet sack, fell to my share. I saw the lady no more. The man stopped at Albany for he said he didn't make "long drives" any more. He had often told his partners, that he did all the dirty work of the firm anyway. He hated travelling, because it kept him away from his family so much, saw them about once a month. He lived in Charlestown near the monument.

You must know that the half past eight train, which I was at great trouble to get, turned out to be the fast train. It brought us to Albany by three o'clock. To Rochester by ten, and Buffalo by midnight. We had supper at Utica, good, but not so good, as dinner last year. At Springfield, where we stopped only ten minutes, we had really the most beastial luncheon I ever saw. From Albany I took a drawing-room car, which we must always take hereafter, its so very much more comfortable. For the sake of "Their Wedding Journey" I noticed the Mohawk Valley landscape again, and found that I had got it all right. River low and full of glittering, ripples, canal beyond, and apparently stationery canal-boats (young fellow who talked to me said "Life on board of one of them would be pleasant, to a stirring ambitious young man", and agreed with me, that if any one of those boats started fair, our train would beat it.) In the background, gentle hills, farmed to the tops, with red barns and houses; This young man was one of the most good-hearted, kindly sociable creatures I ever saw, and we became fast friends before we reached Syracuse. I enclose his card, which you must keep. Noble darkies, came around successively with claret punches, ice-creams and bananas. He treated to the creams, I to the bananas, and he finally to parting punches. It is perfectly astounding how confidential people become in travelling. This young man—he had such gay, beautiful, brown twinkling eyes—told me all about a sunstroke he had, had nine years ago, and a brain fever that lasted him from August, to the first of this year. He told me all about the Seward family.[4] Everybody liked the old man, and called on him every time he came home. But his son and namesake, had no talent at all, could not write a straightforward business letter, and did not use good language. When we got to Oneida, he told me all about the Community, of which I pretended total ignorance, with my customary shrinking from publicity on that subject.[5] He said the men were very sensible, and the women plain & modest looking,—but the children all seemed dull and stupid.—He was ever so much amused with a foreigner at Utica, who spent so much time asking how long we were going to stop that he had no chance to eat his supper. Believed that if *he* only had five minutes, he could always eat *his* money's worth.—Had a vest cut very low to show his breastpin and guard, and kept flipping the ashes and cinders off his shirt: said a white shirt didn't last long, travelling.

I was more than ever impressed with the picturesqueness of the stations at night; and I must try to get something about them into Their Wedding Journey. At Buffalo, where I was half dead with want of sleep, it was very queer. And there I found two very odd coupples in the cars. One couple were undoubtedly on the wedding journey. The bride very young, short, fat and fair, closely buttoned up in a sort of huzzar jacket, wearing a lowcrowned straw hat. In less time than I can tell it, she at a sandwitch as big as my two hands, at half past twelve at night. And then, after a good deal of playful scuffling with her husband, she composed herself to sleep, on one seat, and he on the other. He took off his shoes, and slept with his feet much closer to her face than I should have thought comfortable. The other pair were a woman and her sick husband in a heavy overcoat, whom she was taking West, for his health,— very uselessly, as it seemed to me, when I heard him cough. They had their baby along. At Erie, there came on, a long lank man, with his mother, his wife, two boys and a baby, and walked twice through the car without getting a seat. I and the man nearest me straightened up and made places for them. And then the man gratefully told us how he was born, in Vermont, and had tended a circular saw ever since he came of age, till this spring, when he went to Iowa, bought a farm, planted potatoes, went back to V. and took his family to visit his Sister in Pennsylvania, and had a seven weeks rheumatic fever there. He expected to reach his place in Iowa by the end of the week; and he was wondering how his potatoes would look. His wife went to sleep with her baby at her breast, and toppled against his mother—It was funny to see how everybody tried to make out that he was from a large place. I was quite ashamed to get out at so small a station as Ashtabula.—I rode over to Jefferson with a general fire-insurance agent— a very nice man from Tiffin, O., who said he used to take the Atlantic; but he was never at home, hardly, and his wife, being a woman, preferred Peterson and Godey,[6] where she could get the fashions. He told me a good deal that was very interesting about his business. He described a visit he had made to Providence, and the swearing, drinking and eating people he found there. He treated me with a great deal of respect—a sort of tenderness, almost gallantry—as a literary man.

—Well, now kiss Buah from top to toe—keep the little drops from running down, and make him very happy. Hug Winny for her most loving papa, and give my love to your mother.—Your crayon of mother is an immense success. They all like it and admire it extremely, every one. Father is especially contented with it, and each of them, in his or her kind. Annie will write you the general sense of it to-morrow.—Winny's fotograf is the common delight. It's even more beautiful than ever, as I see it here.—Of course I've told them all the family news. They all send love.

It's not very hot today. Annie will write you tomorrow whether we go to-day or not.

—I see you all as you stood on the step, for good by.

Yours evermore,
W. D. H.

1. "Pesca" means "fishing," but there is no other evidence that Howells went fishing during his years in Venice.

2. This letter contains many notes for the railroading chapters of *Their Wedding Journey*, on which Howells was then working. Several of the characters, incidents, and descriptions appeared in the manuscript but were later canceled; others survived the process of pruning and revision. See the introduction to *Their Wedding Journey*, HE, pp. xvi–xviii, for other materials used in the text; see also pp. 53–54, 58–59, and 60 for passages where Howells incorporated some of the observations recorded in this letter.

3. The next few paragraphs are in Annie's hand. For details on several autograph changes in this letter, see Textual Apparatus.

4. William H. Seward and his son, William H. Seward, Jr., a banker, lived at Auburn, New York.

5. Elinor Howells' mother was the sister of John Humphrey Noyes (1811–1886), the founder of the Oneida Community (1848).

6. *Peterson's Magazine* and *Godey's Lady's Book*.

2 July 1871, Boston, to John S. Hart

...*the Atlantic Monthly*,...
Boston, *July 2, 1871*.

Dear Sir:[1]

I have your obliging note of the 27th, and I will now try to give you the information you ask.

I was born at Martin's Ferry, Belmont co., Ohio, on the 1st of March 1837, of Welsh parentage on my father's side and Pennsylvania-German on my mother's. I learned the printing-business in my father's offices at Hamilton and Dayton, Ohio, and worked pretty steadily "at case," from my twelfth to my nineteenth year. Then I became legislative correspondent of the Cincinnati Gazette from Columbus, and two years later, news-editor of the Ohio State Journal. In 1861 I was appointed Consul at Venice, where I remained till July 1865, when I returned to America, resigning my office in October of the same year. I was engaged for a few months on The Nation, at New York, and on March 1st, 1866 came at Mr. Fields's invitation to be his assistant editor on the Atlantic.* I succeeded him yesterday as chief-editor. I live in Cambridge.

You will have noticed that I have to lament an almost entire want of schooling. However, my father had ardent literary tastes, and an excellent library, and I studied and read as I could, and repaired to some extent a loss which can never be wholly repaired. I learned with little or no help Spanish and German, a trifle of Latin and a soupçon of Greek. Italian was a necessity and a pleasure at Venice, and a little French one knows naturally.

Perhaps I have troubled you with more facts than you care for. You can suppress them at pleasure. I enclose a list of my books.[2]

Very truly yours
W. D. Howells.

Mr. Hart.

Poems of Two Friends. [J. J. Piatt and W. D. Howells.][3] Columbus: Follett, Foster and Company. 1860.
Life of Abraham Lincoln. By W. D. Howells. [In "Lives and Speeches of Abraham Lincoln and Hannibal Hamlin."] Columbus, O.: Follett, Foster and Co. 1860.
Venetian Life. By W D Howells. London: Trubner & Co. New York: Hurd and Houghton.—1866.
Italian Journeys. By W. D. Howells. New York Hurd and Houghton. 1867.

No Love Lost: A Romance of Travel. [hexameters.] By W. D. Howells. New York: G. P. Putnam & Son 1869.

Suburban Sketches. By W. D. Howells. N. Y.: Hurd and Houghton. 1870.

*I had written for The Atlantic as early as 1860, in which year the magazine printed six poems for me.

1. John Seely Hart (1810–1877), educator and Princeton professor of rhetoric and English, was founder of the *Sunday-School Times* (1859–1871).

2. In a letter to Hart of 10 July 1871 (NIC), returning Hart's biographical sketch of him, Howells sent some notices of his books with the following comment: "Venitian [sic] Life was, I belive [sic], favorably reviewed in all the leading English literary journals, and Italian Journeys met a flattering reception there. On the other hand Suburban Sketches was snubbed by the Saturday Review; and the only acknowledgment No Love Lost got was a bodily theft by the 'Broadway' magazine."

3. All brackets in this list are Howells'.

12 AUGUST 1871, BOSTON, TO JAMES A. GARFIELD

...*"The Atlantic Monthly,"*...
Boston, Aug. 12, 1871.

My dear Gen. Garfield—

My sister Annie has some notion of going to Washington this winter as a correspondent;[1] and I venture to trouble you with two or three inquiries. Of course Annie would impress every one who made her acquaintance as a person of refinement—as a lady, in fact;—but I have been troubled with the fear that there is something about the position of correspondent at Washington that attaches a certain disrespect, or disfavor, to the person, especially the woman, filling it. Am I right or not? Annie need not write much of politics, and need have little acquaintance in that direction; but she would probably have to say a good deal, of social life and the superficial aspects of Washington. Would it be agreeable or feasible for a young lady to be at the capital in such a capacity? Are there private boarding-houses where she could live somewhat under the protection of the family, and could she go into society and about the capital alone? I confess I have my doubts about all these matters, and I beg you to write me frankly what you think of her project. I know you to be our friend, and that you will give us good advice.—I could get Annie correspondence for Every Saturday and other papers at good pay; but this is the smallest part of the difficult, as it seems to me.

Pray regard my application to you as confidential.

Yours truly
W. D. Howells

1. Howells had written to Annie on 16 July 1871 (MH): "I spoke hurriedly to Mr. [John Spencer] Clark about the Washington correspondence. He has not engaged any one yet for next winter, and he has promised to keep you in mind. I'll see him again about the matter, which I dare say can be arranged." Among Clark's responsibilities at J. R. Osgood & Co. was the publication of *Every Saturday*.

23 SEPTEMBER 1871, BOSTON, TO RALPH KEELER

...*"The Atlantic Monthly,"* ...
Boston, Sept. 23, 1871.

You wretch![1]

Why did you send me that wine? I shall drink confusion to you in every drop of it. Wasn't it enough that I had already shamefully used you, but you must go and heap bottles of champagne upon my head? Keeler, if you don't make the house pay for that wine, I never *will* forgive you. But I know you've charged it already:

> "*Figaro.*—Due righe di biglietto!
> *Rosina.*—Un biglietto? Eccolo quà!"[2]

Well, wine is wine. I console, I reconcile myself. Some day, you shall hear me say, with tears in my eyes, when I've a quart of it under my waistcoat, "My dear fellow, you oughtn't to have done it!" adding, with the sincerity (in vino veritas) of a symposium aux champignons, "You know you couldn't afford it!"

The flesh was weak, as you've seen, about answering your former letters; but let me assure you of the spirit's willingness. You'll imagine that with my added editorial labors, and my unusual quantity of matter in the magazine, I keep my lame wrist written down to the quick; and you can conceive how that alone might be at fault. I've followed your course pretty diligently in Every Saturday, and I consequently know much more than the truth about you. It seems to me you've managed your material excellently, and I enjoy it all. That description of an explosion on a Mississippi boat was very nicely and lightly done; and I think you're constantly increasing your power to see the interesting things and to reproduce them. I feel more and more persuaded that we have only to study American life with the naked eye in order to find it infinitely various and entertaining. The trouble has always been that we have looked at it through somebody else's confounded literary telescope. I find it hard work myself to trust my eyes, and I catch myself feeling for the telescope, but I hope to do without it, altogether, by and by. I'm very glad you're pleased with Their W. J.[3] Do you know, sometimes *I'm* pleased with it. Just now, I'm writing out the last chapter.

We have spent three delightful weeks in Canada, this summer—chiefly at Quebec, which I'm to write up—a la mode Keeler—for Every Saturday.[4] W. L. Sheppard, of Virginia, was with me to make the pictures. By the way, I think Ward's[5] things are splendid.

Aldrich and all the rest are well. He and I often speak of you, and long, —not without resignation—for your return. When you come back, we will sympote upon the best that Winter Place affords.[6]

Booah remembers you perfectly well, and picks out the fotograf of "big Man Keeler," with the unerring certainty of a learned pig going for the Knave of Spades.

—I haven't tried the wine yet—in fact it's still in Boston—but I know I'll like it, if for nothing but from a foolish fondness for the giver.

Yours sincerely
W. D. Howells.

1. Ralph Keeler (1840–1873) was a bohemian journalist and author, on whom Howells partly based the character of Bartley Hubbard in *A Modern Instance* (1882). For Howells' account of Keeler, see *Literary Friends and Acquaintance*, HE, pp. 231–34.

2. In Rossini's *The Barber of Seville,* act 1: *Figaro*: Two lines of a letter! *Rosina*: A letter? Here it is!

3. *Their Wedding Journey.*

4. Howells' article has not been located, but much of the Quebec material was used in *A Chance Acquaintance* (1873), illustrated by William Ludlow Sheppard (d. 1912), who was also known as a sculptor. On 23 November 1871 Elinor wrote to Howells' sister Annie: "Will's account of Quebec which he wrote for E. S., and Shepard's illustrations, are on the firm's hands, and they don't know what to do with them." See Ellen Ballou, *The Building of the House* (Boston: Houghton Mifflin, 1970), p. 177. See also Howells to W. C. Howells, 12 November 1871, n. 2.

5. Probably J. Q. A. Ward.

6. Howells is probably referring to a predecessor of the Locke-Ober Cafe, which was established on Winter Place in 1875. "Sympote" appears to be Howells' own coinage for "drink together."

5 OCTOBER 1871, BOSTON, TO ANNE T. HOWELLS

..."The Atlantic Monthly,"...
Boston, Oct. 5, 1871.

Dear Annie:

I send back your manuscript,[1] which is *not* declined, but which I agree with Mr. Clark[2] needs working over. Except for a brief notice of the fisheries you have all the needful material here. Now what you ought to do is this: write a letter one half as long as the present; refer first to Put-in-Bay as the chief western watering-place, and then in a very few words give its historical interest as the scene of Perry's Victory;[3] state briefly where it lies with relation to the great cities of the west, and then expand upon the character and appearance of the visitors, having already told how they come—for a day, a week, etc. Bring in here your sketch of social life, the scene in the ball-room etc., but make it more general and less personal. After this, speak of your visit in a very casual way, *and keep your own personality carefully in the background*; tell of the grape-culture (put in all that about the Spaniard and what else you've written on the subject,) and the fisheries, and allude to John Brown, Jr.,[4] very slightly, in describing the scenery, which you should describe only where you can make it intelligible to the reader, and always if possible in relation to the social life of the place.

I hope you will set about all this at once. You have not lost ground by your first attempt, except so far as it indicated that you did not know what was wanted. Mr. Clark, like myself, was satisfied with your literature. If you will send a bill of your expenses, he will re-imburse you for them at once, and pay you for the letter when you send that. Of course he ought to pay only your individual expenses.

Now in regard to Washington:[5] I am not willing you should undertake work for which you have not *proved* yourself fitted, however much confidence I have in your ability. So I think you had better act as soon as possible on a suggestion of Mr. Clark's. Go to W. and write two or three letters describing the aspect of things during adjournment, and just before Congress meets. Hinton[6] can give you advice about material, etc.; but write from your own fresh impressions and then send me the result. You'll be paid for these letters at the rate I named before; and you wont lose money by the experiment. If you make a hit your future is sure. *Make notes of every thing*, and write your first letter at the end of three days.—As soon as I learn that you're going, I'll write you fuller suggestions.—Don't be discouraged: you have a chance offered to one young writer in a hundred, and a prize worth working very hard for. Love to all.

Your affectionate brother
Will

The MS. in another envelope.

1. "A Visit to Put-in-Bay Island," *Every Saturday*, XI, 582.
2. John Spencer Clark.
3. Commodore Oliver Hazard Perry in the battle of Lake Erie during the War of 1812.
4. The Ashtabula *Sentinel*, 29 August 1872, refers to John Brown, Jr., who was visiting in Jefferson, as being "of Put-in-Bay."
5. See Howells to Garfield, 12 August 1871, n. 1.
6. Richard J. Hinton was at this time working as a journalist in Washington.

22 October 1871, Boston, to James M. Comly

...*"The Atlantic Monthly,"*...
Boston, Oct. 22, 1871.

My dear Comly:

I send you the pictures of my girl and boy, and tardily thank you for those of your children, which I got long ago. My wife and I thought they were all the nicest kind of little people—though I confess to a jealous preference for the old boy holding the youngest, if Mrs. Libbie[1] will forgive me. These fellows of a new generation are well enough, but the best of the run were born sometime in the thirtys or fortys. I think there's a strong family likeness between all your children, and Elinor says they all are cunning and beauties. Nevertheless I cling to the preference I've hinted. When I send you my own picture presently, I sha'n't be satisfied with a less expression from you in return. I wish we had your wife's fotograf.

—We have come home to another quiet winter in Cambridge, after a summer's vacation in Canada. We spent nearly the whole time in dear old Quebec, and though it wasn't a long time, it was so full of charming and memorable things that it seems to have stretched over months instead of weeks. Next to going to Europe, it's the most desirable of all journeys.— Which reminds me to say that I put the last touches to Their Wedding Journey a few days ago. It's to be concluded in December, and then it's to be published in book-form with abundant illustrations by Hoppin.[2]— I found a pleasure in writing the thing, though I groaned over it, too, which I miss now; and I am casting about for the frame-work of some new serial.[3] There's nothing like having railroads and steamboats transact your plot for you, but I can't write two W. Js.—We've a famous programme for next year's Atlantic, including a posthumous story by Hawthorne,[4] which I think equal in many respects to the "Scarlet Letter."—My wife joins me in love to all of you and the doctor.[5]

Yours ever
W. D. Howells.

1. Elizabeth Smith **Comly**.
2. See Howells to Osgood, 1 April 1871, n. 2.
3. Howells was beginning to think of the form and material he would use in *A Chance Acquaintance* (1873). See also Howells to W. C. Howells, 3 December 1871, n. 3.
4. "Septimius Felton," *Atlantic*, January–August 1872.
5. Dr. S. M. Smith, Mrs. Comly's father.

22 OCTOBER 1871, BOSTON, TO WILLIAM C. HOWELLS

..."*The Atlantic Monthly,*"...
Boston, Oct. 22, 1871.

Dear father:

I have been greatly pained, since I got your last letter that I should have wounded you by the careless expression I used to Annie,[1] and I hope that you will set it down to anything but intention. All that I know of propriety and delicacy in money matters I got from mother and you, and I meant no reflection upon you. During the past week I have three times met a man who intensely interested me: Robert Dale Owen. He has been staying at our next door neighbor's. He's a very simple, unassuming, lovable old man, with a faith in the other world that is singularly refreshing and re-assuring. He told us that his first spiritual communications took place at the house of the Russian ambassador whilst he was American Minister to Naples—certainly the last city and place in the world where you would look for the presence of spirits.—He has a book in press, and soon to be published, which I think you'll like to read.[2] I'll try to send you a copy.—I knew you'd like John Woolman's journal[3]—I've seldom enjoyed any book so much.—I'm delighted to hear how well Henry is getting on. You must tell him that I'm very proud of the figures he made and that Annie sent me. Perhaps he'll make all the letters some day, and send them for Booah to learn his letters from.— I gave Annie's letter to Clark; it's now in very good shape; and I've no doubt he'll find it all right. Perhaps it wont be published till spring, the season being now so late; but she will be paid whenever she sends her account. I hope she feels in good spirits about going to Washington.[4] I'll send her full instructions as to the kind of letters desired, and she will be able to write them, I know. All of us join in love to you all.

Your affectionate son
Will.

I send back Annies Chatauqua letter, which is beautifully written, but which from the very local character of the subject, I couldn't sell anywhere.

1. In his letter to Annie, 5 October 1871, Howells had given her advice on some financial matters.

2. Owen (1801–1877) published *The Debatable Land Between this World and the Next* in 1872.

3. *Journal of the Life, Gospel Labours, and Christian Experiences of...John Woolman* (1774–1775). Howells probably read the edition published by J. R. Osgood & Co. (1871), edited and with an introduction by J. G. Whittier.

4. See Howells to Anne Howells, 5 October 1871.

8 November 1871, Boston, to James R. Osgood

...*"The Atlantic Monthly,"*...
Boston, Nov. 8, 1871.

My dear Osgood:

I do not know Mr. Julian Hawthorne's address, so I ask you to send him this proof. These 9½ pp. take 31 pp. of the printed copy you gave me, and if there are but 296 pp. in all, you see that the story will only run thro' 10 mos.[1] Pray ask Mr. Hawthorne to return the pf. as quickly as ever he can. I've of course made no corrections, tho' there are some sentences containing 2 or 3 relative pronouns that he will perhaps mend.

In the Editorial Dep't I think we'd better, in justice to the author, mention it as a work that did not receive his last touches, and prepare the reader for the change of plot. This is but fair, and will pique rather than blunt curiosity.[2]

Your truly
W. D. Howells.

1. At the time of her death in 1871, Sophia Hawthorne was preparing a version of Nathaniel Hawthorne's unfinished romance *Septimius Felton; or The Elixir of Life* from the several drafts her husband had left. (See Edward H. Davidson, *Hawthorne's Last Phase* [New Haven: Yale University Press, 1949], for a full description.) This edition was completed by their daughter Una, and was published by Osgood & Co. on 25 July 1872, after serialization in the *Atlantic*. Julian Hawthorne was presumably handling the arrangements. The "9½ pp." were proof for the first installment; the "31 pp. of the printed copy" were probably page proof for the book. The book when published contained only 229 pages instead of 296.

2. The department of "Recent Literature," *Atlantic*, January 1872, included the following: "A posthumous work by Hawthorne must come before the world just as he left it; and the sympathetic reader will not enjoy this the less because of slight defects which the last touches of that exquisite hand would have repaired. Nor do we think he will be wholly discontented when he comes (as it is right to warn him he presently will come) to the change of plot which places some of the subordinate persons in new relations to each other, but does not disturb the unity of the prime idea or the evolution of the hero's character."

12 November 1871, Boston, to William C. Howells

...*Fields, Osgood & Co.*....
Boston, Nov. 12 1871.

Dear father—

I didn't recollect failing to write you, though it is quite likely that in writing to the girls I may have missed my customary letter to you. I have not heard from Annie, by the way, in reply to Mr. Godkin's letter.[1] I should like to make him some sort of answer as possible.—Every Saturday reverts to its old shape and eclectic character on the 1st of January.[2] It was too good an illustrated paper to pay where people don't know the difference between good pictures and bad.—There is very little family news. We are all "kite" well, as Booah says, and are expecting Mrs Mead[3] next week or a little later. She's "putting up" on the way at Wallingford Community.—Elinor and I are reading aloud Beecher's Life of Christ.[4] Poor B. gets into some curious difficulties in his explanations, but I don't think it a waste of time to read him, for it all helps me to realize Christ as a fact of history. So far, all my reading and thinking incline me to the Unitarian belief that Christ was an inspired, divinely commissioned Man, and not deity. But my mind isn't clear upon this point. By far the greater number of Christ's own expressions are of this tendency, I think. It seems to me also that the Testament is full of interpolations and modifications by the superstitious and prejudiced narrators. But again I'm not sure.—You don't speak of Vic's health in your letter, and I hopefully infer that she's very much better, or well. I wouldn't neglecting seeing some good Doctor about her, however she may be.—We've had a light fall of snow this week. With love to all,

Your affectionate son
Will.

1. E. L. Godkin, editor of the *Nation*, had written Howells on 1 November 1871 (CSmH): "You are as good a judge as I am, whether your sister can send us what we want from Washington, if you think she can, I should be very willing to have her try the experiment.... Really good woman's letters from Washington would be very valuable."

2. For a while, *Every Saturday* was published with illustrations, but in January 1872 it reverted to its original unillustrated format.

3. Elinor Howells' mother.

4. Henry Ward Beecher, *Life of Jesus the Christ; Earlier Scenes* (1871).

19 NOVEMBER 1871, BOSTON, TO WILLIAM C. HOWELLS

..."The Atlantic Monthly,"...
Boston, Nov. 19, 1871.

Dear father:

I believe I appreciate your feeling of isolation, and I have often sympathized with you when you did not know it. I earnestly wish that we could be more together, but for the present I don't know how to contrive it. I did hope for a long visit from you this winter, but the new trouble that has befallen the family makes it seem very difficult, for the poor girls must be entirely dependent upon your society.[1]—It seems a great pity about Annie, and yet it may be for the best. It would have been hard to write such letters as the Nation wants, and the pay is not enough to justify her in attempting the enterprise.[2] All may be different by another winter. In the meantime, I hope she will not lose courage about literature, but will try to do some sort of writing at home. If she will make studies or sketches of the life about you, I will engage to sell them for her. I think that an account of Jefferson, politically, socially and religiously she could write in a very admirable way, and could attract notice by it.—Wont you now resume your reminiscences, father?[3] I certainly hope you will. What a lovely evening that was when we went up Will's Creek! And what lovely country! I had no idea that Ohio was anywhere so beautiful; and I don't wonder now that you have always remembered it so fondly.—Robert Dale Owen has sent me the sheets of his new book,[4] which I'll let you have as soon as I've done with them. I've scarcely looked into them yet, but from a glance I imagine them full of astonishment—perhaps conviction. Underneath all my literary activity there is a strong current of spiritual thought—or trouble, and I shall yet end a violent believer or disbeliever. I don't see how I can keep this middle course.—My new book is to be illustrated by Hoppin.[5] I send some of the sketches, thinking they may amuse the girls. With love of all to all

> Your affectionate son
> Will.

1. The nature of the family trouble is unclear, although in a letter to his father, 5 November 1871 (MH), Howells mentioned the death of Howard Howells, the son of Henry C. Howells.
2. See Howells to W. C. Howells, 12 November 1871, n. 1.
3. The last installment of "Ohio Fifty Years Ago" had appeared in the Ashtabula *Sentinel*, 18 March 1869.
4. *The Debatable Land Between this World and the Next*.
5. See Howells to Osgood, 1 April 1871, n. 2.

26 NOVEMBER 1871, BOSTON, TO HJALMAR H. BOYESEN

..."*The Atlantic Monthly*,"...
Boston, *Nov. 26, 1871.*

My dear Mr. Boysen:[1]

It was a great pleasure—greater than you will believe after my shabby behaviour toward you—to get your letter, and of course I *meant* to answer it at once. But I am no longer the luxurious idler you knew last summer,—and so the fragments of my good intention now form part of the Nicholson pavement (laid in the local pitch—down below.—I'm sorry that your poem[2] should have been crowded out from month to month, but I couldn't help it. I devoutly hope to reach it by February, and expect soon to send you a proof. The notice I must send back, for I don't see now how I can find place for it. But we're going, hereafter, to notice French and German literature, and I wish you could send me from time to time a brief notice of some new Scandinavian book. I shall be very glad to see your story when it is ready.[3]—I don't know where to begin on literary news. I dare say you've seen the Atlantic's announcements for '72. The first installment of Dr. Holmes's series[4] on the table before me, and it's delightful. The posthumous romance by Hawthorne[5] is as good in places as The Scarlet Letter. Altogether, I'm extremely proud of our prospectus.

Booah and I have missed you a great deal, and I hope we shall have the pleasure of welcoming you back to Berkeley st. next summer. We had some nice times, didn't we?—What of the three typical Norse-Americans you were going to write a story about? Don't *start* too many things. I remember you had at least a dozen immortal works on hand when you were here.—Give my regards to Mr. Sewall,[6] whose friendship I envy you, and keep a good heart about literature. With one intellectual and sympathetic friend, you have all the stimulus that any literary man can get anywhere. Besides, the air of my native State is favorable to authors. I didn't merit the privilege of breathing it, and conscientiously came away.

Affectionately
W. D. Howells.

1. Hjalmar Hjorth Boyesen (1848–1895), misspelled in the salutation, came to the United States from Norway in 1869, and became a professor of German at Urbana University, Urbana, Ohio, and later at Cornell and Columbia; he was also a journalist, poet, and author of fiction.
2. "A Norse Stev," *Atlantic*, February 1872.
3. The story has not been identified.
4. "The Poet at the Breakfast-Table," *Atlantic*, January–December 1872.
5. "Septimius Felton."
6. Francis Sewall of Urbana University.

3 DECEMBER 1871, BOSTON, TO WILLIAM C. HOWELLS

..."*The Atlantic Monthly,*"...
Boston, Dec. 3, 1871.

Dear father—

Before this reaches you, I hope you'll have got back the deed which you sent me.—With it I enclosed a letter from Whitelaw Reid.[1] I think that if Annie does not go to Washington this winter, she can easily get engagements for next year; though I'm not sure but she'd better consider the matter again for the present time. If she did no more than pay her expenses, it would be richly worth while, with a view to her future establishment. I've not yet answered Reid's very kind letter, for I wait first to hear from you, whether you think it's worth while for me to make any arrangements with him.—I'm glad that you're so well pleased with the close of my story.[2] I had some qualms about the scene with the burlesquers, thinking it might appear coarse; but it doesn't seem to have struck you unpleasantly. Did you really laugh? I couldn't tell, after it was done whether it was flat or funny. The other night I was at Mr. Longfellow's for supper, and he praised the passage about the nun giving the rose—"a beautiful poem," he called it, saying that he had never read anything finer in its way. I've just begun a new story, of which Miss Ellison is the heroine.[3] I think the idea of it is good; and as soon as I get on a little further, so as to be sure I'm going to finish the story, I'll tell you about it. "Their W. J." will be out in book form Tuesday of next week.[4]—I think your article on the Women's Rights trollops is very good.[5] What an abomination they are!—I don't know whether Fiske's theory is right or wrong, but I think his articles very interesting. I have never known any one at once so deeply read and so clear. Perhaps you'll be amused to know that he's going to dedicate to me the book he makes out of these papers.[6]—I shall try to take up Swedenborg before long. But I own that I shall approach him with great distrust.

We have almost as little news as you. We are all well, and Elinor's health seems on a firmer basis than it has been for a long time. Her mother is not well; has a deeply seated cough.—By the way, I wish you'd say on a separate slip in your answer to this letter, so that Elinor need not know I've asked you, whether you've ever got her portrait of mother framed.[7] I think she feels it strange that you never say what you've done with it. I suppose you have little idea how much labor she bestowed upon it. I hope you'll be perfectly frank with me, and if you no longer like the picture, say so. I should be most glad to have it; though I should rather you'd have it, if you like it. But you're never saying what you've done with it, has made me afraid it doesn't please you. I write without the least soreness, and you must answer in the same way.—The editor of Lippincott's magazine writes me that he hoped to publish your paper last summer, and that he expects to reach it very soon.[8] With love to all,

Your affectionate son,
Will.

1. Reid's letter concerned the possible employment of Annie as Washington correspondent for the New York *Tribune*. On 10 December 1871 (DLC) Howells wrote Reid that family problems would prevent Annie from accepting the Washington position. See Howells to W. C. Howells, 19 November 1871, n. 1.

2. *Their Wedding Journey.*

3. *A Chance Acquaintance.* Referring to *Their Wedding Journey*, in which Kitty Ellison first appears, Howells wrote to his father on 9 April 1871 (MH) to tell Annie, who was his model for Kitty, "that she shall see all I have to say about the young lady in light muslin before I print it. I now have a notion of sketching that young lady's adventures throughout. I'm sure that if I could paint her character as it is, it would make the fortune of my story." Annie herself had written the story of her impulsive trip from Niagara to Quebec shortly before her brother and his wife traveled there in 1870. It was published as "Notes of a Quick Trip," Ashtabula *Sentinel*, 1, 8, 15, 22 September; 6, 13, 20 October; and 3 November 1870. Annie also wrote a story based on this experience; it had the title "A Tour in a Basket," but never seems to have been published. On 16 July 1871 (MH) Howells wrote to Annie: "In order not to interfere with you, I take out the hand-basket; but I leave in the young lady."

4. *Their Wedding Journey* was not published on 12 December, as Howells expected at this time. On 24 December 1871 (MH; printed in *Life in Lettters*, I, 163) Howells wrote his father that publication had been delayed until 19 December 1871.

5. The Ashtabula *Sentinel*, 30 November 1871, carried an editorial on "Mrs. Woodhull and Her Set," which attacked her lecture on the "social and legal relations of marriage and intercourse" as reported in the New York *Tribune*, 21 November. Other pieces on women appeared in the *Sentinel*: "Women and Politics," 26 October; "The Woman Question," 2 November; and an editorial, "Dress of Women, Etc.," 16 November.

6. Fiske's *Myth and Mythmakers* (1872) incorporated two *Atlantic* articles: "Light and Darkness" (December 1871) and "Myths of the Barbaric World" (January 1872). The book was dedicated "To my dear friend, William D. Howells, in remembrance of pleasant autumn evenings spent among werewolves and trolls and nixies...."

7. See Howells to Elinor Howells, 3 June 1871.

8. "Camp-Meetings in the West Fifty Years Ago," *Lippincott's Magazine,* August 1872. John Foster Kirk (1824–1904) was editor of *Lippincott's Magazine* (1870–1886).

30 December 1871, BOSTON, TO ROBERT CARTER

..."The Atlantic Monthly,"...
Boston, Dec. 30, *1871*.

My dear Sir:[1]

I am exceedingly gratified by the terms in which you ask me to write of Mr. Lowell; but I really cannot do it. I know he would readily forgive any blunder of mine in such a notice, but it is too delicate a task for me to undertake, and I should not so easily forgive myself if I went wrong. A mysterious Providence preserved me when I was a newspaper man on a first visit East from ever saying a word personally of literary men, and I cannot now fly in the face of that beneficence.

Gratefully and reluctantly,
W. D. Howells.

Mr. Carter.

1. Very probably Robert Carter (1819–1879), who edited *Appleton's Journal* (1870–1873). He had been Lowell's partner on the short-lived *Pioneer*, and Lowell had called him his "kindest and best friend."

31 December 1871, Boston, to Bayard Taylor

..."*The Atlantic Monthly*,"...
Boston, Dec. 31, *1871*.

My dear Taylor:

I feel doubtful still about the Longfellow and the Holmes travesties—especially the Longfellow, and I really think you had better try him again.[1] Neither of those you have made are so successful as others, and they ought to be of the best. Why not try something in the way of hexameters for him? Or a ballad of German or Norse flavor, or a moralized lyric?—On looking again at the Sewing-Machine,[2] I think perhaps that had better stand.—But I send back the Enclosure of the Swine,[3] for you to place something else there. This, I *know* would give offence.—The first Aldrich parody[4] is better than the last you sent: has more of Aldrich in it, and isn't about *eating*—which so many of the imitations are.—If you please, I'd rather you'd omit me altogether. I'm too vague a poetical quality in the public mind—if indeed I'm thought of as a poet at all—for parody; and besides I feel doubtful about the propriety of any mention of me in the magazine.[5]

I suppose you know that the whole fact of authorship is out. It came from New York to the Advertiser, and must have been leaked by some of your friends there. I wish for fun's sake the secret could have been kept a little longer.

On the whole I haven't been able to like The Accolade.[6] It seems to me that the vagueness of a dream still hangs about it, and that the reader would be puzzled by it.

Mrs. Howells joins me in regards to both of you.

Very sincerely yours,
W. D. Howells.

1. In Taylor's "Diversions of the Echo Club," *Atlantic*, January–July 1872, members of a fictitious club carry on a dialogue during which they read parodies of well-known poets. On Longfellow, see "Nauvoo," *Atlantic*, May 1872. In a letter of 1 January 1872 (NIC), Howells returned Taylor's proof and said: "The Whittier ["The Ballad of Hiram Hover," *Atlantic*, March 1872] has a roughness of feeling which no other has, and I hope you'll soften it. He may stand it, but it will shock the reader. I see nothing to blame in the Holmes ["The Psycho-Physical Muse," *Atlantic*, April 1872] but the passages I've marked."
2. "The Sewing-Machine," a Longfellow parody, *Atlantic*, May 1872.
3. "The Lay of the Macaroni," a Swinburne parody, *Atlantic*, February 1872.
4. "Palabras Grandiosas," *Atlantic*, March 1872.
5. After Howells is mentioned in the dialogue, a title, "Prevarication," appears, but the poem is omitted, with a note saying that the editors have broken their rule against changing an author's manuscript.
6. Probably a separate poem by Taylor. It was not printed in the *Atlantic*.

3 January 1872, Boston, to James R. Osgood

...*"The Atlantic Monthly,"* ...
Boston, January 3, *1872*.

My dear Osgood—

I have thought seriously over the whole subject of illustrations for my three books, and I can't believe that the popularity of Italian Journeys or Venetian Life would be promoted by them. If V. L. were fully illustrated by a sympathetic artist, thoroughly acquainted with Venice, it might succeed in an *édition de luxe*, with a luxurious price; but simply to have the pictures done as a job, or to use views from fotografs would injure it with its public, and not procure it another. The same is true of I. J. With Suburban Sketches the case is different, for it has still to find its public, and a dozen character pieces by Hoppin might be of great service. Or they might not—for you know his pictures in T. W. J. which I think so good are only half liked.[1]

Now I can add a chapter to each of the books:
V. L.—A year in a Venetian Palace, 35 pp.
I. J.—Ducal Mantua, 75 pp.
S. S.—New Taste in Theatricals. 20 pp.[2]
and I think if this fact were advertised it would sufficiently draw attention to them anew. The books have never, to my thinking, been thoroughly advertised, nor has anything like a full use been made of the notices they received at home or in England. Every London literary journal fully and favorably reviewed the Italian books—not to speak of American papers.

In fine, I think you'd make a certain outlay for pictures with a doubtful chance of profits. That's of course your affair; but as author of books—while I wouldn't interfere with your business projects—my instincts are against illustrations.

Yours truly
W. D. Howells.

1. Osgood published "new and enlarged" editions of *Venetian Life, Italian Journeys*, and *Suburban Sketches* in 1872. Only the last of these was illustrated, with drawings by Augustus Hoppin, who had also done the illustrations for *Their Wedding Journey*.

2. "A Year in a Venetian Palace" originally appeared in the *Atlantic*, January 1871, and was added to the 1872 edition of *Venetian Life* as "Our Last Year in Venice." "Ducal Mantua" was first published in the *North American Review*, January 1866, and retained its title when reprinted in *Italian Journeys*. "New Taste in Theatricals," *Atlantic*, May 1869, was added to *Suburban Sketches* as "Some Lessons from the School of Morals."

28 January 1872, Boston, to William C. Howells

...*"The Atlantic Monthly,"* ...
Boston, Jan. *28, 1872.*

Dear father:

I hope you've got back safely, and have had a good time. I'm quite curious to know about your visit to Medina. All goes on with us here much in the old way; but for the past week we've suspended our theological readings.[1] The fact is the subject had grown a little too exciting, and I should willingly never resume it if I did not think it a duty to do so. In Swedenborg I'm disappointed because I find that he makes a certain belief the condition of entering the kingdom of heaven. I always tho't that it was a good life he insisted upon, and I inferred from such religious training as you gave me that it made no difference what I believed about the trinity, or the divinity of Christ, if only I did right from a love of doing right. Now it appears to me from the Testament that Christ was a man directly, instead of indirectly, begotten by a divine father; and for this persuasion, which I owe to the reason given me of God, Swedenborg tells me I shall pass my eternal life in an insane asylum. This is hard, and I can't help revolting from it. I am not such a fool as to think that I can do the highest good from myself, or that I am anything in myself; but I don't see why I cannot be humble and true and charitable, without believing that Christ was God. I am greatly disappointed, and somewhat distressed in this matter. At times I'm half-minded never to read another word of theology; but to cling blindly to the moral teachings of the gospels. I should like extremely to talk with you.—I have no news that I can think of. I got Vic's very kind letter, and shall answer it soon. Elinor contritely acknowledges her neglect of Vic's letter of last June, and will write, while she bumptiously wonders why Annie doesn't write to her. We are all well, and send love.

Your affectionate son,
Will.

1. On 15 January 1872 (MH) Howells had written his father that Elinor and he were reading Theophilus Parsons, *Deus-Homo* (1867), and that he had bought Swedenborg's *Heaven and Hell* and Chauncey Giles, *Lectures on the Nature of the Spirit; and of Man as a Spiritual Being* (1868).

16 FEBRUARY 1872, BOSTON, TO THOMAS W. HIGGINSON

...*"The Atlantic Monthly,"*...
Boston, Feb. 16, 1872.

My dear Colonel:

In obedience to your last note I send back your notice of H. H.[1] I am sorry that you could not write what you felt like printing, but I think the principle on which you've acted is the true one. I wouldn't desire an enemy to write of my book; but I shouldn't want a personal friend to do so, either. Nevertheless, (let me guiltily own,) I asked *you* to write of Mrs. Hunt because I knew you were her friend, and I wanted a more cordial review of her book than I knew how to get otherwise. So base are sometimes the motives of editors.

Yours truly,
W. D. Howells.

1. The notice was of Helen Hunt's *Bits of Travel* (1872). In a letter of 15 February 1872 (MH), Higginson asked to withdraw his critique for a variety of reasons: "I don't like it, to begin with; & hate to mix friendship with criticism; then I never like to criticize a book of European travel, not having been there; nor can one who has enjoyed letters in MS. quite speak for those who read in print."

25 FEBRUARY 1872, BOSTON, TO WILLIAM C. HOWELLS

...*"The Atlantic Monthly,"*...
Boston, Feb. 25, 1872.

Dear father:

Each past week seems very empty as I sit down to write of it on Sunday, and I don't know an emptier one of late than this just ended.— I'm discontented with it because I have failed to do any work worth mentioning. Socially, however, it was not so bad. On Wednesday, Elinor and I lunched at our next door neighbor's (Mr. Browne)[1] with Robert Dale Owen and Mr. Tom Appleton—Longfellow's brother-in-law, a rich old worldling, who has never done anything but eat good dinners and say witty things, and who is the most ardent spiritualist in Boston. Of course the talk was of spiritualism, and I was surprised to find how very little that was astonishing either of these people had to say. I can't say that I doubted their experiences, but merely that they seemed unimportant and inconsequent. Still I think Mr. Owen a most charming old man, with a real light of peace and as of spiritual converse in his face. Appleton remarked this while Owen was absent, and said that the same expression was to be seen in portraits of Swedenborg.—By the way, what did you think of James's notice of Owen's book in The Atlantic?[2] I believe that he pressed too far the idea of an impersonal immortality—which practically is no immortality at all. I suppose that I understand Swedenborg very dimly, but if I do understand him, it seems to me that man's state hereafter, whether in bale or bliss, is one of less dignity than on earth—that there is less play for his powers, and that the very union of his will and intellect, deprives him of individual consciousness, and cripples him.—There are a thousand points I'd like to talk with you upon.

Thursday, I dined with Lowell—that being his 54th birthday, and of course we had a most lovely time. No one else but Aldrich and Mr John Holmes (a brother of the Doctor) was there. Aldrich and I had clubbed our resources, and presented Lowell with a drinking-flask to carry to Europe with him—which was a very successful present. He goes in June, and I wish you'd be here before that time, for I want him to dine with you here.—There are *particular reasons*, which you'll know in time, why the fall wont do for your visit.[3] If you'll come in the middle of May you'll find settled weather, and I shall be more at leisure than any other time.—We are all well, now, Elinor having greatly improved. Fred Mead,[4] who sails this week for Europe, is here visiting his mother. I'm very sorry to hear of poor Uncle Jesse's calamity.[5] With love from all to all.

Your affectionate son
Will.

1. Browne has not been identified.
2. Henry James, Sr., "Spiritualism New and Old," *Atlantic*, March 1872, reviewed *The Debatable Land Between this World and the Next*.
3. Elinor Howells was expecting the birth of her third child. Mildred Howells was born on 26 September 1872.
4. Elinor Howells' brother.
5. Jesse Dean, of Rochester, Pennsylvania, a steamboat captain on the Ohio River, died on 28 February 1872, at age 51. See Howells to Joseph A. Howells, 10 April 1857, n. 3.

19 MARCH 1872, BOSTON, TO HJALMAR H. BOYESEN

..."*The Atlantic Monthly*,"...
Boston, March 19, *1872*.

My dear Boyesen:

Your notice of Jonas Lie's book was put in type for April, but had to be postponed till May.[1] The little story[2] you have sent is very prettily written, but as it now is seems to lie between adult and juvenile literature and not fairly to belong to either. I suggest that you introduce a love-passage of decided tone and color. It might be easily done, and then the young ladies would not be disappointed. Might not a lover share the father's search and heartbreak?

I'm glad to hear that Gunnar Henjum[3] is finished, and I shall be eager to see how you have ended it. The time before I shall see you is now so short, I hope, that I'll not ask you to send me the MS., especially as I should not be able to find room for it, if accepted, before next year.

I also look forward to your coming here with the greatest pleasure, for I have a selfish desire to talk over many literary concerns with you. (Pray ask Mr. Sewall,[4] with all respect, whether the little authorial flatteries we find so pleasant here, will be permitted us in any elevated sphere hereafter? *No, don't*—either.) I'm writing a story—a real story, this time, with a plot,[5] and I want you to see it.—How is it with our pretty friend the Huldre?[6] Does she still perplex you with—it seems dreadful to write it—that tail of hers? You owe it to yourself to make a triumphant poem about her, yet—tail and all.

I have very little news. Mrs. Howells has been spending a fortnight in N. Jersey, with Winny, and Bua and I are alone.—*Do* see Mrs Carter,[7] if you can. There's no woman in Cambridge or Boston half so bright.— You ought to read somebody who writes English, not that antic satyr Carlyle.[8]

Yours cordially,
W. D. H.

Osgood is selling the fifth thousand of Their Wedding Journey.

1. Boyesen's review of Jonas Lie, *Den Fremsyute* (1871). *Atlantic*, May 1872.
2. The story has not been identified and was apparently not published in the *Atlantic*.
3. "Gunnar," *Atlantic*, July–December 1873.
4. Francis Sewall.
5. *A Chance Acquaintance*. Howells had written to his sisters, 21 January 1872 (MH): "I've begun another story, which rather drags, but which I hope will improve as it gets on. It's to use up the Quebec material that we got last summer."
6. A note to chapter 2 of "Gunnar," *Atlantic*, July 1873, explains that "The Hulder is a kind of personification of the forest;...a maiden of wonderful beauty,...[with] a long cow's-tail attached to her beautiful frame. This is the grief of her life. She is always longing for the society of mortals, often ensnares young men by her beauty, but again and again the tail interferes by betraying her real nature. She is the protecting genius of the cattle."
7. On 4 February 1872 (ViU) Howells had sent Boyesen a letter of introduction to Mrs. Francis Carter, of Columbus.
8. Howells continued to give Boyesen advice about his writing. On 6 September 1872 (ViU) Howells wrote: "Don't, my dear friend, give up your place for another year yet, at any rate. Indeed you're less prepared with English than you should be for a rough and tumble fight with literature. Recollect that so far you've had a

crutch, to say the least. Perfect yourself, get more reputation, and then go it if you must. But I doubt if you can put yourself, for years, on so good a base as you now hold."

8 April 1872, Boston, to William C. Howells

...*"The Atlantic Monthly,"* ...
Boston, April 8, 1872.

My dear father:

(I began mechanically to write *My dear Sir*; which accounts for the stiffness of this address.) There has been so little in the events of this last week to distinguish it from the one that went before that I suppose five hundred years from now they wont be able to tell themselves apart. I have been writing as usual on my story[1] which steadily grows in quantity at any rate, though what it will turn out in quality, I'm doubtful at times. I know that there's good material in the plot, if I only have the wit to dig it out. My great trouble is to keep it from degenerating into anything like caricature, on one hand, and from something too seriously heavy on the other.—For other mental occupation I have my ordinary sub-conscious speculations about matters spiritual, though I'm convinced that I'm a very terrestrial-minded person, and have little prospect of eternal health if it depends upon a desire for heavenly knowledge or science. At best, I'm able only to check myself in some gross selfishness when I happen to think of it, and to give my thoughts a twitch upwards when I find them getting too much bemired. As for a fixed belief I have none whatever—nothing but a general hope.

We have all been somewhat excited here by the marriage of Mabel Lowell[2] which took place on Wednesday in the episcopal chapel, and was a very pretty spectacle. The Aldriches came home to lunch with us, and we had a merry time. Lowell gave his daughter away, and though such things are in the course of nature, I couldn't help thinking it sad.—Tell Henry that Bua has got what he calls a *bullocipee*—a three wheeled one—which he's very proud of, and shows some faculty for managing. He got it last night, and dreamed a horrid dream that it fell to pieces. He rose very early to see.

All of us are well, and send love to all. *What about your visit?*

Your affectionate son
Will.

Tell Annie the Madam Schwartz novels are not worth reading.[3]

1. *A Chance Acquaintance.*
2. J. R. Lowell's daughter married Edward Burnett.
3. Translations of three Swedish novels by Marie Sophie Schwartz were published in 1871: *The Wife of a Vain Man, Birth and Education,* and *Gold and Name.*

16 APRIL 1872, BOSTON, TO WHITELAW REID

Boston, April 16, 1872.

My dear Reid:

I am the guilty party that made a mess of the advance-sheet-Atlantic-N. Y.-correspondent business for May by giving to a writer for The Evening Post what he ought not to have had before the Tribune writer. I did not know about Mr. Osgood's arrangements, and the correspondent came to my house, and I gave him the sheets.

Let the wrath of Achilles afflict not Osgood nor the Atlantic, but the erring undersigned.[1] Peccavi![2]

I hope you are very well? Do you never come to Boston?

Yours ever,
W. D. Howells.

1. In his reply of 17 April 1872 (MH), Reid, who succeeded to the editorship of the New York *Tribune* upon the death of Horace Greeley on 29 November 1872, wrote Howells: "Your sins had been set in one order before me a day or two before yours of the 16th. came, and I had written the most ferocious of epistles. [¶] What a splendid success you are making! As I said to Mrs. Moulton, in the ferocious epistle aforesaid, I have allowed more space to notices of *The Atlantic* in advance than my own theories of good journalism would warrant, mainly because it seems to me of all things desirable that so excellent and splendid an attempt at making the best magazine in the world, should be heartily sustained. I do hope that the cash corresponds with the excellence." Ellen Louise Chandler Moulton (1835–1908) wrote verse and juvenile stories; her Boston salon was frequented by artists and writers, and she was the literary correspondent for the *Tribune.*
2. "I have sinned!"

20 APRIL 1872, BOSTON, TO ANNE T. HOWELLS

..."The Atlantic Monthly,"...
Boston, April 20, *1872*.

Dear Annie:

I like your letter about the post-office[1] ever so much: it's written with the *shaping hand* throughout, and it's done without violence or smartness, two points in which women are apt to sin in writing. But—there isn't enough of it. You must add to it your account of the Swedes, and all the other incident you can scrape up in relation to the subject. Then

I feel pretty sure I can dispose of it honorably and profitably for you. *Describe closely and realistically, keep the tone low,* and *let the reader do all the laughing.*[2] Success lies so near your hand, that you can scarcely help grasping it. I shall be infinitely more proud of your triumphs than ever I was of my own.—I do hope that you're coming on with father. I think I could do you good just now by criticisms which I can't write. We're counting on seeing you and father both here early in May; I'm going to N. Y. a week from Monday for a few days, and then I shall be all ready for you. I think we can make your visit a very pleasant one.

All of us are very well. I'm so glad that the spring's come at last, and I hope you'll bid adieu to all ailments in all the three families. Elinor joins me in love.

Your affectionate brother,
Will.

1. Annie planned a series of "Letters from a Country Post Office," but they seem not to have been published.

2. In an undated letter to Anne Howells, probably written about 1 September 1872 (MH), just before Annie went to Chicago to work on the *Inter-Ocean,* Howells wrote: "Choose whatever subject you will; but treat it simply and directly, and try never to get on a high young-lady-*falsetto,* in your tone."

7 May 1872, Boston, to Aurelia H. Howells

..."The Atlantic Monthly,"...
Boston, May 7, 1872.

Dear Aurelia:

I hope you are still improving, and that this letter will find you well enough to sit up if not go out doors. I wish you were here to see how lovely the spring looks in Cambridge—it's never been so fine, so gradual, so like the Spring of poetry. Getting home from New York, I found it about ten days later than the spring there, and I dare say we're somewhat behind Jefferson, too, unless the lake ice has kept you back.—My visit in New York was a wonderful round of dinners and breakfasts. I was there five days, and never once dined alone. Osgood, whose guest I was, took me to the Union League Club, where they have some rooms at the disposal of members and their friends, and here I got a glimpse of just such club-life as you read of in Thackeray. The place is a palace, and the men are so comfortable there, that I don't wonder they're in no hurry to marry and set up less splendidly for themselves.—Osgood gave a dinner for me at Delmonico's, at which among other people were Joseph Harper of Harper & Bros., John Hay, Bret Harte, Chas. Dudley Warner, J. W. De Forest, and the sculptor Quincy Ward.[1] The dinner was of course very elegant, and we had lots of fun, giggling and making giggle; but I think the drollest thing that happened was Harper's getting Ward all mixed up with Artemus Ward, Mark Twain and Josh Billings,[2] and complimenting him elaborately on his books! Warner is a very nice fellow, but looks like a Western Reserve Yank. I had breakfasted that morning at Elliott Shepard's, and lunched with Stedman; the next night I dined at Shepard's with some of his Vanderbilt connection—his brother and sister in law,[3] whom I found very agreeable, and the simplest, most unassuming people I almost ever met. Next day I had to go out to Scotch Plains to see Mrs Mead, who is quite feeble, and so I missed a lunch which Mr. Harper wanted to give me. In the afternoon, I went down with Henry Howells[4] to his place on Long Island and spent the night. It's lonely, but one of the most beautiful places in a wild way I ever saw, and the sail to and fro on the East River is delicious. Henry has not changed his spots *much*, but Georgie was very sweet, and I was glad to have gone. I got back in time for a breakfast with John Hay at the Knickerbocker Club—one of the most aristocratic,—where I met a new company of artists, literary men and *dillettanti*—including Harte[5] and Ward again. It was if possible a little finer affair than the dinner, and it fitly crowned the visit.—I made some calls on ladies with Harte, and I saw lots of people of all kinds. This is merely an outline of the business—to write it in full would take "volumes." I enjoyed myself, but I like Boston best and Cambridge best of all. New York is large and jolly, but it's too much of a good thing.—We are all well, and hoping soon to see father. With love to all, and wishes for your health,

Your affectionate brother
Will

1. Of the guests at the dinner given by Howells' employer, J. R. Osgood, all but the following have been previously identified: Joseph W. Harper (1801–1896), at that time head of the literary department at Harper & Brothers, in 1885 persuaded Howells to write the "Editor's Study" for *Harper's Monthly*. Charles Dudley Warner (1829–1900), editor of the Hartford *Courant* since 1861, essayist, travel writer, and novelist, was coauthor with Samuel L. Clemens of *The Gilded Age* (1873). John William De Forest (1826–1906) was a significant figure in American realism; his *Miss Ravenel's Conversion from Secession to Loyalty* (1867) was enthusiastically reviewed by Howells in the *Atlantic*, July 1867.

2. Josh Billings was the pseudonym used by Henry Wheeler Shaw (1818–1885), the author of many humorous dialect stories and of the very successful *Josh Billings' Farmers' Allminax* (1869–1880); his performances on the lecture platform made him a popular entertainer.

3. Mildred Howells' editorial note in *Life in Letters* identifies the Shepard with whom Howells dined as Augustus D. Shepard, Elliott's brother. However, since

Augustus and his wife (Elinor Howells' sister) lived in or near Scotch Plains, New Jersey, where Howells went to see his mother-in-law the next day, the dinner was probably at Elliott Shepard's. Consequently, the "brother and sister in law" were probably the brother (or brother-in-law) and sister of Elliott's wife, rather than Augustus and his wife. It was Elliott, not Augustus, who was connected with the Vanderbilts. See the earlier of Howells' letters to Elinor, 19 September 1865, n. 1.

4. Henry C. Howells, Jr.; Georgie, mentioned below, was his wife.

5. In a letter to Howells of 30 March 1872 (MH), Bret Harte apologized for criticizing a correction Howells had made in the text of one of Harte's poems ("Concepcion de Arguello," *Atlantic*, May 1872) and, in an effort to smooth ruffled feathers, continued: "I have a painful picture of you pathetically leaving me in a moral elevator on your way to the fifth story with your arms full of manuscripts and sorrows, dropping them on the head of your crushed contributor below. I know the trials of a young honest editor too well perhaps to entirely believe in them. But you shall occupy a heroic niche in my imagination along with my other heroes, an you will, or you shall meet me on the ground floor when I go to Boston. I *do* wish you could come to New York, if only for a day and a dinner with [Whitelaw] Reid, [John] Hay and myself."

25 MAY 1872, BOSTON, TO LUCY LARCOM

..."The Atlantic Monthly,"...
Boston, May 25, *1872*.

My dear Miss Larcom:

You take rejection so sweetly that I've scarcely the heart to accept anything of yours. But I do like Phoebe,[1] and I'm going to keep her.

Yours very truly
W. D. Howells.

1. "Phebe," *Atlantic*, October 1872.

31 JULY 1872, BOSTON, TO FRANKLIN B. SANBORN

..."The Atlantic Monthly,"...
Boston, July 31, *1872*.

My dear Mr. Sanborn:[1]

I enclose an article from the Chicago Journal in order to "shew your eyes and grieve your heart" by the printed proof that the supposed Politician of The Atlantic is supposed to have modeled himself upon the editor of The Nation.[2] Beyond the pain that it enables me give a contributor of course I don't care for the article.

I sent you a proof of your two first sections to the care of Mr. Morton,[3] which I hope you'll get. The last section, which came yesterday, is in great part a repetition of the second. I shall try to get a proof of this to you; but we cast the final form on Saturday, and I'm not certain that you can see it unless you could run down here (Cambridge) on Friday *morning*. Failing your revision I will put the two sections together so that they shall not repeat or contradict one another.

Your style and manner of treating politics are quite what I desire, but I'm not sure that you sufficiently separate the Atlantic and the Republican in writing. It seems to me useless to speculate in the magazine about results or chances. We must look at the phases that escape the newspaper eye; deal with motives and character; philosophize the situation; create if possible the tone of contemporaneous history. I believe that this has not yet been done, and that it ought to be done.—If you like, you can give your whole space to one topic, if only you will write something decidedly noticeable and useful on that topic—something no journalist would think of doing.

I should like to talk with you about this matter, for I know that you can do what we want. If you come to Cambridge, Friday, pray call on me at 3 Berkeley St. In writing, send my letters directly to Cambridge (not Osgood's care) and I shall then get them 24 hours earlier.

Yours truly
W. D. Howells.

1. Franklin B. Sanborn (1831–1917), a Massachusetts reformer and secretary of the American Social Science Association, had been an editor of the Boston *Commonwealth* (1863–1867), and became editor of the Springfield *Republican* in 1868.
2. In a letter of 11 June 1872 (OOxM), Howells had invited Sanborn to take charge of the "Politics" department of the *Atlantic*; but by the end of August, political differences caused a separation. See Howells to Sanborn, 25 August 1872, and Howells to James, 28 October 1872, n. 6.
3. Morton has not been identified.

25 August 1872, Cambridge, to Franklin B. Sanborn

Cmbdge, Aug. 25, '72.

Dear Mr. Sanborn:

We seem fated never to meet, and I couldn't arrange by letter for any modification of your attitude towards political affairs,—even if you had been willing to modify it, and so, as I did not agree with you in your view of the Canvass;[1] did not believe in any deep tendency towards union on the question of conciliation, but did believe that the Greeley party as it now stands is mainly the old Democratic party, I thought it best to act upon your suggestion that I should ask some one else to do our political writing.[2] It is possible that if we could have seen each other we might have agreed upon some policy which you could have conscientiously pursued; but I respected you too much to ask you to write to order, and I had no alternative but to apply to some one who held opinions like my own.

I thank you for the consideration with which your letter left me free to act, and sincerely trust that the Atlantic may keep you as a contributor if not as a politician.

Yours truly
W. D. Howells.

1. In the presidential campaign of 1872 Ulysses S. Grant ran for a second term against Horace Greeley.
2. See Howells to Sanborn, 31 July 1872, n. 2.

8 SEPTEMBER 1872, CAMBRIDGE, TO JOSEPH A. HOWELLS

Cambridge, Sept. 8, '72.

Dear Joe:

I don't believe it'll be known before the Judgment who's a failure or who's a success; and I suppose a great many people will be astonished at that time at the estimate put upon different earthly careers. In the meanwhile, if you persuaded me that you were not what it is best to be, you would destroy one of my ideals, and prevent me forever from bragging of "my brother Joe," as I like to do when there's any question of goodness and self-sacrifice.

All goes on well with us, here, and I hope soon to write you of the birth of our son Gwyneth Howells ap William ap William ap Joseph ap Thomas. If it should be a girl we will try to think of a fitting name; but it is not *expected* to be a girl.[1]

What a frightful accident that on the Sound, was![2] It seems almost incredible. But weren't the officers on your boat almost as careless and ignorant of danger as those on the Metis?—I thought the cases very much alike.—It's a very hot day again after weather so cool that we've had to have fires.

Give our love to Captain Cope[3] when you write. We both enjoyed seeing you and him; and Bua's talk is often of "Uncle Joe and the capting." Love from all of us to all your family.

Your aff'te brother
Will.

1. Mildred Howells was born on 26 September 1872.
2. The Ashtabula *Sentinel*, 2 September 1872, reported that the steamer *Metis* had been struck in a fog on Long Island Sound by an unknown schooner, causing

the loss of thirty to seventy lives. In the same issue of the paper there is an editorial by J. A. Howells, "The Metis Disaster."

3. A friend of Joe's, with whom he had recently visited the Howells family in Cambridge. Howells' letter to his father of 27 October 1872 (MH) suggests that Cope had until recently been the owner of the Belmont county, Ohio, *Chronicle*.

22 SEPTEMBER 1872, BOSTON, TO WILLIAM C. HOWELLS

... "*The Atlantic Monthly*," ...
Boston, Sept. 22, *1872.*

Dear father:

I have still no grandchild to announce to you, but I really hope the news wont be much longer deferred, for we're all very tired of waiting.[1] Meantime we have been struggling about names. If a boy we have decided to call him

Owain Rhys Howells,

the middle name being the Welsh spelling of Rees, your grandmother's name, and the first being the same as Owen, a common Welsh christian name. If it's a girl—poor thing—I incline strongly to another family name—Eve. She was a relative—"true, a distant one," as Mark Twain said at the tomb of Adam, but indisputable, all the same, and the name is very soft and beautiful, to my thinking. At present Elinor abhors it so much that there is a reasonable hope that she will violently like it at last.

The carpenters are getting on very rapidly with the framing of our house,[2] and have put together, just back of the foundation, the whole ground floor. It looks very large, and very compact, and altogether satisfactory. The bricklayers go to work to-morrow, and I suppose the underpinning will be ready in a few days.

I'm very hard at work, all the time, on my story,[3] which I've re-written in great part and made much more ship-shape. It's been a most absorbing task, and of course I have my doubts whether it's at all worth while, and then my buoyant beliefs that it is the very worth-whilest thing in the world.

Robert Dale Owen came in last night and read me the first chapter of his autobiography, which he's been writing for The Atlantic.[4] Of course it was very interesting, and I think it will be an attractive feature.—Politics are dull here, just now; but Greeley seems to have been generally given up.—Dyer[5] calls about once a week, and always speaks of you.—I dined the other evening with Mr. Longfellow, who has got back for the winter. Love to all from all.

Your aff'te son
Will.

1. Mildred Howells was born 26 September 1872.

2. Howells wrote to Mrs. Larkin G. Mead, Sr., on 25 August 1872 (MH) that he "bought on very good terms a lot from Prof. Parsons, not very far from here, on Concord Avenue.... There are beautiful pines and maples on it, and all that we have to do, to render it habitable, is to put a house there. So we've caused the cellar to be dug, and we hope that by this time next year the house will exist." The address of the new home was 37 Concord Avenue, Cambridge.

3. *A Chance Acquaintance.*

4. "A Chapter of Autobiography," *Atlantic,* January 1873.

5. Louis Dyer (1851–1908), a distinguished classicist, graduated from Harvard in 1874. He later received degrees at Balliol (Oxford) and from 1890 made his home in Oxford, where Howells saw him during visits to England.

20 OCTOBER 1872, BOSTON, TO JAMES R. OSGOOD

..."*The Atlantic Monthly,*"...
Boston, Oct. 20, *1872.*

Dear Osgood:

Both I and the author of that unlucky slip about Tyndall[1] regret it extremely, as I told you. It's one of those things that escape the best intention—I *never* call names myself, and do not mean that it shall ever be done in The *Atlantic,* and yet that phrase got in.

As for Mr. Higginson, since he chooses to ignore my connection with the magazine, I particularly request that you will not make a word of explanation from me to him. This is not the first time that he has assumed this manner towards me.[2] What I have said is simply for your own satisfaction.

The poem I declined once before.

Yours ever,
W. D. H.

1. William James reviewed John Morley's *Voltaire, Atlantic,* November 1872. Comparing Morley's personality and intellect with those of Mill, Spencer, Huxley, and others, James wrote: "Mr. Tyndall has emotion enough, but, besides being such a coxcomb, he is of too light weight intellectually." John Tyndall (1820–1893) was a physicist and natural philosopher.

2. The occasional strains in the relationship between Howells and T. W. Higginson are apparent in Higginson's letter to Howells, 30 September 1871 (MH): "I would not on any account have you print anything of mine which you only thought 'well enough', so I have arranged for it elsewhere—with a regret which you can hardly understand, as you have not, like me, written for but one literary magazine for thirteen years & felt identified with it." In the remaining part of the letter Higginson expresses his doubt whether he will contribute to the January issue of the *Atlantic,* and concludes with the remark: "I shall...in future count on a merely business relation with the Atlantic, & try to make the additional feeling of freedom (as to writing elsewhere) atone to me for the lost *esprit de corps.*"

24 OCTOBER 1872, BOSTON, TO EDMUND C. STEDMAN

...*"The Atlantic Monthly,"* ...
Boston, Oct. 24, *1872.*

My dear Stedman:

I am not one of the infallible editors, and when my judgments are adverse to the performance of men whom I greatly respect, I'm very doubtful of my judgments. But I am afraid that neither your first paper nor your Landor[1] will do for us. You discuss Landor so entirely from the reader's presupposed acquaintance with him that you will not possess even The Atlantic's comparatively cultivated public with your notion of that eminently unknown author. Your essay is solely for literary men, and for mighty well-read literary men at that. When you come to speak of the Brownings, of Tennyson, Hood, Proctor,[2] Swinburne, Morris, Rossetti, etc., you will not have the same ignorance to contend with; but I think that even in their case you ought to support with as many illustrative passages as possible the points you make.

The first paper I should object to on the general ground that you have yourself suggested, and also because I do not see its necessity in the magazine, though it would properly introduce the other essays in a book. I can't publish the papers as a series under one head, and with the fatally recurrent numbers I, II, III, etc., on the title page: we are destroyed by too many serials. Each article must appear independently.

I propose, therefore, that you shall begin with the Brownings, and follow with the more recent poets. If you can do this, you can begin as late as June, if you like, though I'd like you to begin earlier.—I'm just about to announce your papers in the prospectus for 1873, please *telegraph* me whether I shall do so or not.[3]

Yours truly,
W. D. Howells.

1. Apparently Stedman had written two articles; one is unidentified, the other, on the English writer Walter Savage Landor (1775–1864), was later collected in *Victorian Poets* (1875).

2. Either Thomas Hood (1799–1845) or his son Tom Hood (1835–1874); Bryan Waller Procter (1787–1874) wrote under the pseudonym "Barry Cornwall."

3. Stedman's articles were not published in the *Atlantic*. See Howells to Stedman, 6 November 1872.

28 October 1872, Boston, to Henry James

> ..."*The Atlantic Monthly*,"...
> *Boston*, Oct. 28, *1872*.

My dear James:

I asked them to send you the check some time ago, so that by now I hope you have it. The story I'm going to print in February.[1] Your "Guest's Confession"[2] has on the whole been received with more favor than anything else you've printed in the Atlantic; and though I don't give up my early favorites, I see many reasons why G's. C. should be generally liked. Mrs. Howells, who is not a "genial critic"—of her husband's writings, at any rate—praises it very highly; says your people both speak and act from motives of their own; and the different scenes are intense, and the whole plot new and good. Whereupon I enviously point out that somehow the end does not come with a click, and that there's a certain obscurity in Mrs. Beck's fate, so that your brother and I disputed as to whom she marries. I think you don't make your young man generous enough to merit that good girl. Nevertheless I admire the story greatly.—The first chapter of my own story[3] is in proof, and it seems not altogether loathsome. Perry,[4] who is of a cool temperament, and of a vast experience in novel-reading, has been so good as to read the whole thing in MS., and has had the face to pretend that he likes it.—By the way, that excellent young man is to have charge of the N. A. Review for the present, at any rate, my machinations having succeeded. He has taken rooms in Boston, and has set to work. I think it's just the work for him.—I dare say your family have written you of our happiness, at the prospect of which I hinted. We have a little daughter, now a month old, whom we call Mildred. She bids fair to be the prettiest of the children, and for the time being is all that ought to be expected of a young lady of her age. My wife is very well, indeed, and we are so blest that some sort of retribution must be in store for us.—Cambridge goes forward at the accustomed pace, with some slight symptoms of a social awakening. I was at a small affair at the Ashburner's,[5] the other night, and met the habitual friends. Sedgwick is back again, and is to resume his work on the Atlantic,[6] and is otherwise going to take out letters-of-marque for a privateering cruise on the high seas of political literature.—Prof. Child is "comfortably sick" with a low fever which threatens to keep him indoors for a couple of months.— I've just come in from a long walk up North Avenue, in which I missed you abominably. It's been a very cool, sunny, sparkling day, and the clear evening seemed to demand you by a strength of association that shewed me how long you and I had been friends. We have known each other for about six years, and in the meantime I am thirty five years old. In the spring my new pantaloons measured 32 inches in the waist; those that just came home measure 34. So we go. A man booked for obesity must not sentimentalize about a long standing friendship. Otherwise I should rejoice in ours. But I should like to hear from you. We all send love.

Yours ever
W. D. Howells.

1. "The Madonna of the Future," *Atlantic*, March 1873.
2. *Atlantic*, October–November 1872.
3. *A Chance Acquaintance*.
4. Thomas Sergeant Perry (1845–1928) was on the staff of the *North American Review* (1872–1877). Howells had written to James on 1 September 1872 (MH; printed in *Life in Letters*, I, 171–73): "I have seen something more than usual of Perry, lately; and I'm working hard to get him the sub-editorship of the N. A. Review." See Virginia Harlow, *Thomas Sergeant Perry: A Biography* (Durham, N. C.: Duke University Press, 1950), pp. 36–37.
5. Anne and Grace Ashburner.
6. Arthur G. Sedgwick had started the "Politics" department in the *Atlantic*, January 1872. See Howells to Sanborn, 31 July 1872 and 25 August 1872.

3 NOVEMBER 1872, BOSTON, TO S. WEIR MITCHELL

... *"The Atlantic Monthly,"* ...
Boston, Nov. 3, *1872*.

My dear Doctor Mitchell:[1]

I accept "Miss Helen"[2]—as I think we had better call the story—with pleasure, though I don't think it's so good as some of your psycho-physiological things, at which, by the way, I wish you would try your hand again for us. I am always so glad to have your writing in the magazine that I wish I might have your *name* also.[3]

I find at last something to soften my disappointment—which I thought nothing could assuage—at not seeing you last summer, if Mr. Field had been reporting me as worth knowing. I'm a little worse than nobody at all to meet: one of those men whom it would be well to take at their own estimate and believe the dullest and slowest possible acquaintance; though I wont allow that I'm a bad hand at friendship, and it would certainly have given me the greatest pleasure to see you. I called three times at the Parker House, and once I waited at home all day when you said you were coming to Cambridge; but the luck was against me. I am heartily obliged by your kind invitation, and I can't think of any one thing I'd rather do than accept it; but I dont see my way clear to Philadelphia this winter. Still it isn't an impossible thing. In the meantime I rejoice in your good will, and am,

Very cordially yours
W. D. Howells.

1. Silas Weir Mitchell (1829–1914) was a prominent Philadelphia physician, an authority on physiology, toxicology, and nervous diseases; he was also well known as an author of short stories and novels. For his later association with the Howells family, through his treatment of Winifred Howells, see Cady, *Howells*, II, 97–98, and Lynn, *Howells*, pp. 297–98.

2. *Atlantic*, August 1873. Mitchell had written Howells on 26 October 1872 (PU): "...I sent you a little Newport story—which may or may not please you.—I only desire to add, in the latter case, that you may return it without fear of annoying me—& I say this because honestly speaking it is a bizarre sort of story and may not suit you. [¶]...Field—without an s—says you are very worth knowing & he is as good a judge of men in the social point of view as I am acquainted with. Do—if you are to be here at all this winter—let me know before hand & come to dine quietly with me—who will then cease to consider you a mere myth—" John W. Field, of Philadelphia, was a mutual friend.

3. The story is signed "W. M."

6 NOVEMBER 1872, BOSTON, TO EDMUND C. STEDMAN

...*The Atlantic Monthly*,...
Boston, Nov. 6, *1872.*

My dear Stedman:

It may be that you are right about Landor, but I'd rather you'd begin with something else. After we've tried several of the other papers, I'd like to see the Landor again *entire*.[1] Why not begin with the paper on Swinburne, Morris, etc., and then revert to the older poets? But if you prefer, I'm perfectly willing to commence with Mrs. Browning.

—I used to think extracts a confession of weakness in a critic, but I believe now that they're necessary to possess the reader of the subject.

—It's shabby to send your poem back after begging you to write it. But it's so far from being you at your best, that I'd rather not print it in the January number, and the temporary character of it unfits it for any other.[2] Pray forgive me for putting you to this trouble.

Yours ever
W. D. Howells.

1. See Howells to Stedman, 24 October 1872.
2. The poem has not been identified.

13 NOVEMBER 1872, BOSTON, TO CHARLES W. STODDARD

...*The Atlantic Monthly*,...
Boston, Nov. 13, *1872.*

My dear Mr. Stoddard:[1]

Have you really been on the stage? Then I have a suggestion to make, namely: that you write me half a dozen papers of six pages each, giving in the mood and spirit (as nearly as you can catch them again) of your Prodigal,[2] the record of your theatrical experiences. Of coarse-hand, low-down reminiscences of the stage, we have had enough: you are the man to give us the pathetic humor and the quaint poetry of the life. And don't forget to tell of the audiences. I hoped to get something of this sort out of our mutual acquaintance Keeler,[3] but it wasn't his fault that I couldn't—nor mine, either. Your Tahiti paper was the very *bouquet* of vagabond romance—it was infinitely the best thing of the kind that I ever read.

Now think of this, and write me what points of stage-life you would treat,—what facts,—what shape you would give them. I should want the papers separable—not a series.[4] Write me your idea fully. If we "make affairs," the pay shall correspond to the worth of the papers.

I thank you heartily for all the kindness of your letter.

Yours very sincerely
W. D. Howells.

1. Charles Warren Stoddard (1843–1909) was an actor, poet, and journalist, who worked for the San Francisco *Chronicle* (1873–1878) and traveled extensively throughout the world.

2. "A Prodigal in Tahiti," *Atlantic*, November 1872. Howells had learned about Stoddard's acting career through a comment in Stoddard's letter to Howells, 5 November 1872 (MH), expressing gratitude for Howells' "most encouraging letter." It then continues: "...I would sooner have this commendation from you than from any author I am acquainted with, for your proze [sic] to me is a marvel that never fails to fill me with fresh admiration though it generally ends in my despair."

3. Ralph Keeler was for a while connected with the "Floating Palace," a steamboat fitted up for theatrical performances.

4. The following pieces were published in the *Atlantic* during 1874: "A Prodigal in Buskins" (July); "Over the Foot-lights" (August); "Behind the Scenes" (November).

16 NOVEMBER 1872, BOSTON, TO HJALMAR H. BOYESEN

... *The Atlantic Monthly*, ...
Boston, Nov. 16, *1872*.

My dear Boyesen:

This notice is so far inferior to that you printed in The Nation[1] that I shall not be able to use it. I'm sorry that you did not remember that the Atlantic had the first claim upon you for a criticism of the grammar—which, by the way, has come to hand.

We were all a good deal dismayed by the fire, at first; but we are taking courage again. The ruins are most impressive sight.[2]

Yours ever,
W. D. Howells.

1. Review of *A Norwegian-Danish Grammar and Reader*, by the Reverend C. J. P. Peterson, *Nation*, 7 November 1872.

2. The extensive fire that destroyed much of the business district of Boston occurred during the night of 9–10 November 1872. As he wrote his father on 17 November 1872 (MH), Howells was in Newport, Rhode Island, and returned to Boston on 11 November. He described the effects of the fire in "Among the Ruins," *Atlantic*, January 1873.

7 DECEMBER 1872, BOSTON, TO HJALMAR H. BOYESEN

... The Atlantic Monthly, ...
Boston, Dec. 7, *1872.*

My dear Boyesen:

I think with Mr. and Mrs. Sewall[1] that this is the best poem you've ever written, though it is at the same time such an imperfect one that I cannot use it as it stands. There are very beautiful passages in it, and more beautiful lines than in any poem of yours that I know; but it ends weakly as to the telling of the final incident, and too vaguely, while there are bits of literary conventionality in it that contrast drolly with your own naturalness. You'll see what I mean by looking at the places underscored. Two stanzas, crossed out, simply overloaded the poem which was already staggering under its load of imagery. I think you need greatly to study brevity and simplicity of style. One must n't overdress. It's hard to say just what I mean on paper. If I had you here I could tell you in two minutes how to make this poem acceptable.

I expect to begin Gunnar in July; I don't see at all how you could read the proof in Norway; but as you have had to leave the matter to me heretofore, even after reading your proof, I think you needn't be troubled for the future.

Pray tell Mr. Sewall that I've had it in mind ever since his letter came, to have the Atlantic continued to the U. U.,[2] and I shall yet do so. Give him my regards.

How many weeks yet have you at Urbana? Where do you spend Christmas?—I envy you your dreamed of visit to Norway next summer. I've had such an Italian fever lately it's driven me almost crazy. Good by. All send regards.

**Yours ever
W. D. Howells.**

On the whole, I've concluded to have your poem set up and to see it in print before I decide. So I don't send it back, but will shortly send a proof.[3]

1. Francis Sewall.
2. Urbana University.
3. In a letter to Boyesen of 11 December 1872 (ViU), Howells finally rejected the poem, which has not been identified.

26 DECEMBER 1872, CAMBRIDGE, TO JAMES L. GRAHAM, JR.

Cambridge, Dec. 26, 1872.

My dear Graham:

I thank you with all my heart for the copy of Howell's Signory of Venice,[1] which has reached me by your brother's[2] favor in time to help make this one of the happiest Christmases I have ever seen.

Ten years ago we talked of this book, which I am now so proud and glad to owe to your friendship, in your parlor at the poor dear old Hotel Vittoria in Venice, and afterwards I tried in vain to find it in London. Some people forget, some remember; you remember with a grace which I wish my gratitude could wear. The book is precious to me in itself; I own that I like to be reminded by it that a man of my name wrote of Venice two hundred and fifty years ago; but I shall always value the book first because you gave it me.

My wife joins me in cordial regards to Mrs. Graham and yourself, whom we should like so much to see. Every now and then Italy presents itself in colors of alluring possibility, and we all but pack our trunks for the voyage. In fact I have a little literary scheme which I hope will one day take me there again; but when, heaven knows.[3] My place here is very snug; I am building a house; we have three children; and though the snow lies a foot deep, outdoors, still we linger and hesitate, and shall at least not sail to-day.

When we do, we shall come to salute you in the Orsini Palace.

Yours ever,
W. D. Howells.

P. S. Aldrich and his family went in with us to a Christmas party at the Fieldses. The A's. are living in Cambridge in Lowell's house.

1. James Howell, *S. P. Q. V. A Survey of the Signorie of Venice*.
2. Howells had written to R. M. C. Graham on 21 December 1872 (PSt): "There is no book I would rather have..., and I am more pleased than I can tell you that your brother should give it me. It is just ten Christmases ago since I met him in Venice, and we talked of this book together."
3. See Howells to W. C. Howells, 19 March 1865, n. 4.

29 DECEMBER 1872, BOSTON, TO HJALMAR H. BOYESEN

...*The Atlantic Monthly*,...
Boston, Dec. 29, *1872*.

My dear Boyesen:

I was glad to get your second and cheerfuller letter[1] for though the first seemed evidently a *mood* letter, still it made me feel sorry for you, and afraid that if you went back to Norway, we should never see you here again. I hope you *will* go back on a visit, and that you'll find all imaginable pleasure in it; but I think you fairly belong to us now. Your English grows more un-Norwegian in every letter, and I think you are irrevocably committed to a literary career in America. You have met with generous recognition, and you have an audience not mean in taste or numbers which I'm sure will rapidly increase. *Pray send me all the poems you write*. It needn't hurt you to have them returned, and it may help you to have them accepted.—The B. of Torrisdell goes into Feb'y, and The Mountain-taken Maid into April;[2] Gunnar will begin in July as I told you.—I rejoice with you in the triumph you feel in that chapter of The Midnight Sun.[3] Nothing that tongue or print can say is half so sweet as that consciousness of having done something well. That is literature's true reward. All the rest is but measurable disappointment, or utter bitterness of spirit. But that alone is more than enough; it's a joy almost divine, and is as unselfish as love.—I'm glad you like A Chance Acq.[4] I don't expect much favor for it—sometimes I think it may quite fail. Still, I believe it was worth doing. Love to Mr. Sewall.[5]

Ever affectionately yours
W. D. Howells.

1. Boyesen had written Howells on 21 December 1872 (MH), expressing satisfaction with his own current literary accomplishments.
2. "The Bride of Torrisdell," *Atlantic*, February 1873. "The Mountain-Taken Maid" did not appear in the *Atlantic*; Howells apparently preferred "St. Olaf's Fountain," *Atlantic*, April 1873.
3. In his letter of 21 December 1872, Boyesen mentioned having "just completed a chapter of my 'Legend of the Midnight Sun,' which appears to me at this moment simply magnificent." This seems to have been the working title for a book published under another title.
4. In the same letter, Boyesen expressed his liking for *A Chance Acquaintance*, which began to appear in the *Atlantic*, January 1873: "Kitty Ellison & the scenery of the Lawrence fairly transported me—to Cambridge & to your study, where you read those charming chapters to me. I know no higher praise to bestow. I was delighted to see, that the N. Y. Ev. Mail [of 21 December 1872] so fully agrees with me, thinking the picturesque effects 'absolute perfection.'" Howells had also received lavish praise from James Parton (1822–1891), the popular biographer. He wrote Howells on 17 December 1872 (MH) that the first chapter of *A Chance Acquaintance* "has all the finish and fulness of meaning which made the Wedding

Journal [*Their Wedding Journey*] so satisfying, and there is much in it that promises well for the future—veins never yet worked.... [¶] You have begun quietly and promisingly.... [¶] The utter freedom from all false, intense effects will please the more because we are cloyed with them in Reade and Dickens. But don't be more quiet than nature requires. Tremendous things really do happen."

5. Francis Sewall.

31 DECEMBER 1872, BOSTON, TO JAMES A. GARFIELD

...The Atlantic Monthly,...
Boston, Dec. 31, 1872.

My dear General:

Mr Parkman the historian has been speaking to me of a literary enterprise in which he thought the government might possibly interest itself. We neither of us know *how* this could be done, but we vaguely imagined, through the appropriations for the Congressional Library, or something of that sort. Pierre Margry, Custodian of the Archives of the Ministry of Marine and Colonies, in France, proposes to publish six volumes of documents relating to the discovery of the Mississippi, the great Lakes, the Rocky Mts., etc., including the original journals, dispatches, letters and memoirs of the early French explorers and discoverers of the West. None of these documents have heretofore been printed though Mr. Parkman had access to them in the preparation of the his life of La Salle,[1] and they form a most valuable mass of material, particularly serviceable to the history of the West. Unhappily Pierre Margry wants to sell to some American purchaser 500 copies of each vol. for 12 frs. a copy, or about $7000 in all. It is not an unreasonable price, but it is an outlay which no publisher would make, for there is no money in the enterprise.

There you have the project, and I confess that having put it on paper, it does not look hopeful. Mr. Parkman has written to Mr. Librarian Spofford,[2] but will you not also kindly interest yourself in the matter, and tell me if anything can be done?[3]

I hope that Mrs. Garfield and all your family are well. Pray remember me to her, and tell her that my wife and I do not yet despair of seeing you both under our roof in Cambridge.

Yours very sincerely
W. D. Howells.

1. Francis Parkman, *The Discovery of the Great West* (1869); Howells reviewed the book in the *Atlantic*, January 1870.
2. Ainsworth R. Spofford (1825–1908) was Librarian of Congress (1864–1897).
3. In his reply of 3 January 1873 (MHi), Garfield wrote: "I took the liberty of reading your letter to the Com^e on Appropriations. They were much interested in it and are disposed to do whatever they can to secure these documents."

TEXTUAL APPARATUS

Introduction

THE letters selected for inclusion in these volumes of Howells correspondence are printed in clear text in the form reproducing as nearly as possible their finished state. The record of the alterations which took place during composition and which are evidenced on the pages of the manuscripts is presented in the textual apparatus which follows, in combination with the record of editorial emendations. The letters have been editorially corrected only in specific details and only when the original texts would make no conceivable sense to the reader. Thus Howells' few eccentricities of spelling and punctuation and his occasional mistakes and oversights have generally been retained. However, inadvertent repetitions of letters, syllables, or words—usually a result of moving the pen from the end of one line to the beginning of the next—have been emended and recorded in the apparatus. In cases where the actual manuscripts are not available and transcriptions or printed versions of letters have served as the basis for printing here, errors in those materials have also been retained, since the actual source of the error—Howells, the transcriber, or the printer—cannot be identified.

Except where extraordinary conditions have made it impossible, the following procedures have been followed step-by-step in the preparation for publication of the text of each letter, whether the extant form of it is the original document or an unpublished or published transcription. First a clean, typed transcription of the final form of the extant material is prepared from a facsimile of it. Then duplicate copies of this prepared transcription are read and corrected against the facsimile by the editor of the volume and by one of the editors of the letters series. At the same time drafts of the apparatus material are prepared, recording all cancellations, insertions, revisions, and illegible words or letters in the text, as well as possible compounds, end-line hyphenated, which must be resolved as hyphenated or unhyphenated forms. These drafts of the apparatus also include questions about proper interpretation of textual details. The corrected and edited transcriptions and accompanying apparatus are conflated at the Howells Center and any discrepancies identified and corrected. At this stage transcriptions and textual apparatus are completely reread against the facsimile of the original. The resultant material is next checked by a different editor against the original holograph, copy, or printing; he verifies all details, answers insofar as possible all remaining questions, and indicates matter in the original which has not been reproduced in the working facsimile. This completes the process of preparing printer's copy.

At this point the texts of the letters—though not the corresponding apparatus—are set in type. The typeset texts are proofread once against the facsimiles of the original documents and once more against the prepared printer's copy; necessary corrections are made in both typeset texts and apparatus, and the apparatus is keyed to the line numbering of the typeset texts. After correction by the printer of the typeset text and the setting in type of the textual apparatus, these materials are proofread in full once more against the printer's copy, and the apparatus is proofread again separately. At every point at which revises are returned by the printer they are verified against the marked proofs.

This procedure—involving as many different people as possible from among the editors of the volumes, the series, and the Howells Edition staff—has been adopted to guarantee that the printed texts are as accurate as the combined energy and attention of a group of trained and experienced editors can make them. It will, we hope, warrant our statement that the errors, oversights, and possibly unidiomatic readings of the texts are those of the original documents and not of the editors. Further, since even the detailed textual record presented in this apparatus cannot fully indicate the physical condition of the letters, the editorial materials prepared during the assembly of these volumes are all being preserved, and can be consulted by anyone who wishes to see them—at the Howells Center at Indiana University as long as it is in operation for preparation of texts for "A Selected Edition of W. D. Howells" and in a suitable public depository thereafter.

The editorial considerations and procedures outlined above underlie the actual presentation of the letters printed in these volumes. Each letter is introduced by an editorial heading identifying the date and place of composition and the name of the correspondent to whom it is directed. The date and location identified in this heading may be different from those provided by the letter itself, since the content of the letter or other pertinent evidence can indicate that those details are inaccurate. When such cases arise, they are discussed in appropriate footnotes.

The translation of the ranges of handwritten and typewritten material and printed stationery into the stricter confines of the printed page obviously demands the adoption of certain formal and stylistic conventions. Regardless of their arrangement or placement on the original page, inside addresses are presented in one or more lines above the single line containing the place of origin and date provided in the letter. This format is followed regardless of the placement of the dateline at the beginning or at the end of a letter. When handwritten or printed letterheads provide more elaborate information than basic identification of place of origin and date, the additional information is omitted and its absence signaled by the appropriate placement of ellipses. The use of capitals or a combination of capitals and small capitals in printed letterhead forms has been reduced here to capitals and lowercase letters. In the printing of letters and datelines in the present text, italic type is used to indicate matter which occurs in the original as part of printed stationery, and roman to indicate portions supplied by Howells himself. The distinction between print and handwritten or typed portions of heading information can be significant in that a printed letterhead in particular does not necessarily indicate that the letter itself was written in that place. If Howells supplied location information different from that of a printed letterhead, the printed letterhead is considered simply a mark on the paper and has been ignored in the presentation of the text.

The beginning of the body of the letter after the salutation has been consistently set off by a paragraph even if Howells continued on the same line or used any other unconventional spacing. Similarly, the positions of the complimentary close (e.g., "Yours ever") and the signature in relation to the body of the letter have been standardized without regard to Howells' widely varying usage. The relative spacing of the indentations of paragraphs has been normalized to conform to the typography of these volumes; this principle has been applied also to unindented paragraph breaks which occur in the originals. The interruptive or appositive dash within sentences and the transitional dash between sentences (the latter almost the equivalent in sense of the paragraph break) have been set in standard typographical form, and relative length not indicated. The long *s* of Howells' youthful hand has been set consistently in the ordinary typographical form. Underlined words have been set in italics without regard to the position or relative length of the underlining; when the form of the underlining indicates, however, that Howells clearly intended to emphasize only part of a word (e.g., *every*one), then only that part has been italicized.

When texts are derived from machine-printed rather than handwritten telegrams, the full capitalization used there has been reduced to capitals and lowercase letters, with an appropriate note in the textual apparatus. The same procedure has been followed for letters typed on typewriters using only capital letters. Where texts are derived from copies of now-missing letters rather than from manuscripts, any typographical peculiarities of those forms—indentation, employment of capitals and small capitals in proper names, and so on—have been altered to conform to the format of the present edition. But only this strictly typographical alteration has been enforced: the errors in spelling and punctuation and the revisions and cancellations within these materials have all been considered textually significant and a potentially accurate record of the originals upon which they are based.

Postscripts which follow upon the signatures in the original letters are placed in this same position in the printed text, but marginal notes and postscripts placed eccentrically are printed where they seem to belong within or after the body of the letter, and their original locations indicated by editorial notes in the apparatus to the letter. The presence or absence of page and leaf numbering or the location of such numbering on the original pages has not been recorded.

In the preparation of the texts and apparatus, those marks, and those marks alone, in the text of the letter which could be interpreted as slips of the pen have been ignored. All other marks, including wiped-out words or letters, erased material, incomplete words either canceled or uncanceled, and random letters have been recorded. Illegible words or letters are identified in the apparatus by the abbreviation *"illeg."*

The presentation of this information in the apparatus demands the use of certain symbols and abbreviations to conserve space. The record for each letter is introduced by the same editorial heading that introduces the item in the text proper. Then follows a note on the number of pages (i.e., sides of individual sheets or of segments of sheets created by folding which have been written on). Next is provided an abbreviated indication of the kind of text and the presence or absence of authorial signature (A.l. = Autograph letter; A.l.s. = Autograph letter signed; T.l. = Typescript letter; T.l.s. = Typescript letter signed; A.n. = Autograph note; A.n.s. = Autograph note signed; T.n. = Typescript note; T.n.s = Typescript note signed). If the authorial text is of a kind not represented by these eight abbreviations, it is described fully (e.g., "Mostly in autograph of Elinor M. Howells"; "Telegraph form written in Howells' hand"; "Typed telegram"). If the text is based on a transcribed copy, that fact is noted together with information about the source of the transcription, if known; if the transcription is a published text, the author, title, and other bibliographical information are provided —in the cases of both published and unpublished transcriptions the number of pages of text is ignored as textually irrelevant. This information is followed in turn by the standard abbreviation for the library in which the original document or extant transcription is located,[1] or by the short-form designation for a private collection.

Following this heading appears the record of the internal revisions and cancellations in the letter document and any emendations made by the editors. All such revisions, even in typed letters, may be assumed to be by Howells, unless otherwise noted in the apparatus. Each entry in this record begins with the citation of the number or numbers of the lines in the text of the printed letter in which the cited material occurs. This numbering is based on the count of full or partial lines of type, and begins with the first line of the document, whether that be inside address, date, or salutation; it does not include the formal editorial heading which precedes each letter.

Sentences, phrases, words, or parts of words inserted into the running text of the document are indicated in the record by placement within vertical arrows, ellipses being used to abbreviate passages of four or more words. Thus:

↑evade↓   with↑out↓   ↑directly ... exchange.↓

No distinction is made between words inserted above the line and those inserted below it or manuscript revisions fitted into typescript lines, and the color of ink or the medium (pencil, pen, typewriter) used for corrections or additions is not described. The presence or absence of a caret or other conventional symbol for the insertion of the material is not recorded. When a word has been written over some other word or part of a word, that fact is indicated by the use of the abbreviation "*w.o.*" (for "written over") following the final reading and preceding the original. Thus:

parties *w.o.* party   people *w.o.* ple

Words canceled in the original are indicated by placement in pointed brackets in the context of citation of sufficient words from the text of the letter (either before or after the canceled words or phrase) as printed in this edition to identify its location. Thus:

went ⟨to⟩   ⟨we went⟩ I walked

An italic question mark within brackets following a word indicates a degree of uncertainty about the interpretation provided. The combinations of these various symbols and abbreviations should be self-explanatory: e.g., ↑⟨this⟩↓ indicates that the interlined word "this" has been canceled.

All editorial revisions are signaled in the apparatus by a left-opening bracket (]); preceding it appears the reading of the text as printed in this edition, and following it the reading of the original. When the editorial revision involves only the emendation of punctuation, each curved dash (∼) following the bracket stands for a word preceding the bracket. When it has been necessary to supply words, letters, or marks of punctuation missing in the original not because of oversight or error in composition but because of the present physical condition of the

---

1. The system of abbreviations used in this edition is that described in *Symbols of American Libraries*, 10th ed. (Washington: Library of Congress, 1969).

document—badly faded ink, deteriorated or torn paper, blots, or waterspots—the reconstructed portions are signaled by being placed between vertical lines. Thus:

af|te|r |the| commit|tee| met

Virgules (slashes) are used to indicate the end of a line of writing in the original document. All other editorial comments, including description of the placement of postscripts and marginal notes or the presence in a document of notes or comments in another hand believed to be contemporary with the composition or receipt of the letter, as well as information about specific textual details not covered by the basic system of symbols and abbreviations outlined here, are provided in italic type within brackets.

In addition to the textual record which follows, this edition of letters contains a section headed "Word-Division," consisting of two separate lists: one, List A, indicates the resolution of possible compounds occurring as end-line hyphenations in the original documents, and the other, List B, the form to be given to possible compounds which occur at the end of the line in the present text. A description of the keying system employed in these lists and the process by which editorial decisions about the resolution of such end-lines were reached are provided in the headnote to that section.

C. K. L.
D. J. N.

Textual Record

25 July 1852, Ashtabula, to William C. French. 3 pp. A.l.s. MH.

3 ↑can↓   11 ↑token↓   11 the *w.o.* that   11 ↑edition↓   12 has] his
13 go⟨t⟩   14 lake.] ~   15 ↑walk↓   19 ⟨floating⟩ ↑knocking↓
25 light-⟨night⟩ house   26 light⟨ing⟩ house, ⟨co⟩   28 harbor⟨s⟩
30 appropriate ⟨a⟩ ↑the↓   33 ↑these↓   34 ↑up,↓   37 gulches and ⟨and⟩
38 filling *w.o.* falling   41 — *w.o.* of   45 hills ⟨of⟩   47 hills, ⟨a⟩
51 ⟨not⟩ ↑been↓

10 April 1857, Cincinnati, to Joseph A. Howells. 2 pp. A.l.s. OFH.

7 ⟨about⟩ upon   8 fatherhood *w.o. illeg.*   9 you|r| 9 ⟨tha⟩ dont
12 is ⟨being⟩   17 use ⟨my⟩   24 ⟨So far⟩ ↑every↓   28 ⟨I⟩ they
[*below signature, on second page, in another hand*: W D Howells]

20 April 1857, Cincinnati, to Victoria M. Howells. 2 pp. A.l.s. MH.

12 does.] ~,   17 ↑for me↓
29 Don't . . . envelopes] [*written above dateline, on first page*]

9 and 11 September 1857, Jefferson, to Dune Dean. 8 pp. A.l.s. MH.

1 ⟨June⟩ ↑Sept.↓   8 ↑gone↓   13 which I] which I which I
22 beat *w.o.* bear   27 given ↑you↓   28 out↑side↓
35 satisfaction] satisfac/faction   43 ⟨up⟩ down   45 ↑whom↓
46 ⟨equally⟩ ↑that much↓   49 that one] that I one   49 ⟨truth⟩ true
52 As *w.o.* So   53 one happy *w.o.* a happy   56 ⟨bring⟩ fill
58 ⟨immediate⟩ circle   58 whom *w.o.* which   60 ↑no↓
76 battle ⟨that⟩   89 been *w.o. illeg.*   91 ⟨have⟩ find   94 ⟨genu⟩ state
95 about ↑her↓   104 ⟨have been to⟩ attended   108 ↑at↓   112 ↑am↓
114 assures ⟨of⟩

27 October 1857, Jefferson, to Victoria M. Howells. 4 pp. A.l.s. MH.

3 excuse ⟨that excuse⟩   4 while *w.o.* ag
7 nothing has] nothing has / has   8 ↑not↓   13 ↑me↓
16 ⟨the⟩ Columbus   20 ⟨feroc⟩ sodden   21 ⟨time⟩ day

422   *TEXTUAL APPARATUS*

22 ⟨death⟩ ↑sickness↓   22 starvation] starva/vation   28 ↑of↓ all
37 ↑up↓   37–38 unpleasant⟨n⟩   41 ↑us↓   42 lilies *w.o.* lilles
45 life. ⟨Fa⟩   47 ⟨feared⟩ ↑looked up to↓   58 to⟨o⟩   60 dicide *w.o.* dis
61 ↑to↓ all

30 November 1857, Jefferson, to Harvey and Jane Green. 3 pp. A.l.s. MH.

12 ⟨which⟩ ↑and↓ on   13 hint *w.o. illeg.*   15 spent the] spent tha⟨t⟩
18 a fever *w.o.* of fever   21 an⟨y⟩   25 towards ⟨any⟩   41 ⟨whis⟩ tea
47 wonder *w.o.* wont   51 story] [*possibly* stony]
66 community] commity   68 ↑be↓   74 but you *w.o.* but I
83 ⟨*illeg.*⟩ despair   86 out↑side↓

21 September 1858, Jefferson, to Gamaliel Bailey. 2 pp. A.l.s. MH.

4 a copy *w.o.* some   15 afloat ⟨by⟩

9 October 1858, Jefferson, to Martin D. Potter. 2 pp. A.l.s. MH.

10 come *w.o.* g   15 answer] an/   18 ↑not↓   19 I *w.o.* w

26 December 1858, Columbus, to Victoria M. Howells. 4 pp. A.l. MH.

13 ⟨This⟩ In   18 can] can / can   18 appears *w.o.* is
37 Address *w.o.* address   39 have] [*MS ends here*]

2 January 1859, Columbus, to Victoria M. Howells. 4 pp. A.l.s. MH.

12 be *w.o.* do   21 have *w.o. illeg.*   22 the translation *w.o.* that
translation   25 ↑editor↓ [*insertion in Mildred Howells' hand*]
27 can⟨not⟩   28 heaven! ⟨the⟩   28 them] theme   29 O *w.o.* I
29 how ⟨I⟩   29 this ⟨little⟩   38 made *fifty-one w.o. illeg. fifty-one*
40 if ↑I↓   40 ↑him↓   44 Love *w.o.* Y

23 January 1859, Columbus, to Victoria M. Howells. 4 pp. A.l.s. MH.

[*Embossed ornament and the word* Extra *in upper left corner, first page*]
12 I was] I / I was   20 made *w.o.* make   31 other ⟨of⟩
34 keep ⟨fo actly⟩   43 week.] ~,

15 February 1859, Columbus, to Victoria M. and John B. Howells. 4 pp. A.l.s. MH.

10 more ⟨are⟩   14 ↑is↓   19 has *w.o.* have   33 ⟨I⟩ economise
34 have ⟨not⟩   36 salary. ⟨before long.⟩   42 ⟨wont⟩ ↑afraid↓
44 ⟨with⟩ at   47 ↑a↓   55–56 ⟨away⟩ ↑a week↓   56 think⟨*illeg.*⟩

TEXTUAL RECORD 423

4 March 1859, Columbus, to John J. Piatt. Location of MS unknown. *Life in Letters,* I, 22–24.

13 March 1859, Columbus, to Victoria M. Howells. 4 pp. A.l.s. MH.

    18 and *w.o.* as   25 come *w.o.* be   27 speaking, ⟨speaking⟩
35 party ⟨of⟩   41 She *w.o. illeg.*   42 last ⟨pla⟩   57 ⟨my⟩ "Lazarillo
58 sent ⟨h⟩

18–24 April 1859, Columbus, to Victoria M. Howells. 4 pp. A.l. MH.

    27 ↑him↓   33 To-day ⟨wall⟩   34 ⟨peace⟩ peace   43 |this|
45 walking *w.o.* watking   46 romantic ⟨romanti⟩   57 Affinities.] ~
58 Sun|d|ay   62 hear ⟨moth⟩ [*in margin on fourth page appear three words in another hand; only the first,* Sanguinaric, *is legible*]

25 April and 1 May 1859, Columbus, to Victoria M. Howells. 6 pp. A.l.s. MH.

    16 this, *w.o.* ,   29 did *w.o.* h   30 ↑bad↓   35 |dia|ry
51 Joe *w.o.* Joes   52 delightful *w.o.* delighted   56 be *w.o.* a
57 ↑her↓   59 ⟨and⟩ but   68 that ⟨S⟩   71 ↑away,↓   74 ⟨eff⟩ attempt

16–22 May 1859, Columbus, to Victoria M. Howells. Location of MS unknown. Typed transcription at MH.

    23 ↑, in the↓ [*inserted by hand*]
32 [*blank space after* you *and in copy-text*]   35 looks] lokks
67 ⟨hearing⟩ having   72–73 |the prisoners|

24 May 1859, Columbus, to Mary D. Howells. 3 pp. A.l.s. MH.

    5 |for| Vic   7 |It| 7 to⟨o⟩   10 |I| saw   19 the *w.o.* then
21 ⟨Ne⟩ I

14 August 1859, Columbus, to Joseph A. Howells. 2 pp. A.l.s. MH.

    3 swiftly *w.o. illeg.*   6 sweep *w.o.* sweet   10 place *w.o.* places
10 ↑mind↓   11 ↑comes,↓   14 Tears *w.o. illeg.*   24 quarrels; ⟨but⟩
29 had *w.o.* has   34 anxiety *w.o.* anxiou   40 uncle's ⟨fath⟩

10 September 1859, Columbus, to John J. Piatt. Location of MS unknown. Handwritten copy at NjR.

424   *TEXTUAL APPARATUS*

[*Below dateline, presumably copied from Piatt's hand*: (sent to me at Louisville, Ky. J.J.P.) *Embossed in upper left corner, first page*: A. T. Valentine & Co. Extra] The following list of internal revisions is based on the transcriber's attempt to copy all details of Howells' MS.

    4 ↑not↓   5 one⟨'s soul⟩   12 |up the| 15 "Klosterheim"] "∼""

19 September 1859, Columbus, to John J. Piatt. 4 pp. A.l.s. NjR.

[*In upper left corner, first page, in Piatt's hand*: Sent to me at Louisville, Ky J.J.P.]

    5 süß⟨e⟩te   5–6 *der...Dichtern*] [*written in Sütterlin script*] 7 ⟨that⟩ when   8 was *w.o.* is   28 — *w.o.* ?   31 and will] [*pencilled in left margin, in another hand*: N.B.]   31 ⟨poets⟩ ↑poems↓ 31 ⟨like⟩ feel   41 suppose ⟨I⟩   44 speech⟨.⟩ ↑and↓ 44 every *w.o.* Every

22 September 1859, Columbus, to John J. Piatt. Location of MS unknown. Typed transcription by W. M. Gibson (InU) and by C. and R. Kirk (NjR). Variants in transcriptions as follows:

Gibson (copy-text)	*Kirk*
3 laying	saying
4 Barkis-ean	Barkis-ian
4 (willin'ness)	(willin'ness,)
5 are reasons	are many reasons
10 verses	verse
23 languid	lanquid
33 draught[?]	drought
34 *overset*	overset
35 Romantische	Romantesche
36 exquisitely	exquisitly
38 "already".	"already"!
43 Howells	Howells.

5 October 1859, Columbus, to John J. Piatt. 2 pp. A.l.s. NjR.

[*In upper left corner, first page, in Piatt's hand*: Sent to me at Louisville Ky J.J.P.]

    3 you⟨r⟩   18 ↑them↓   19 just⟨ice⟩   27 Silence *w.o.* silence 28 room.⟨"⟩   33 here *w.o.* hea   38 is min|e.| 39 eff|ec|tually 48 ↑inquiry↓   53–54 [*pencilled in paragraph space and in left margin, in another hand*: NB]   54 publish, *w.o.* publisher   61 Nacht⟨.⟩"?

TEXTUAL RECORD   425

26 October 1859, Columbus, to William C. Howells. 2 pp. A.l.s. MH.

 14 month. *w.o.* months 15 ⟨sort⟩ *so* ⟨h⟩ 16 ↑not↓ 18 her ⟨at⟩

6 November 1859, Columbus, to William C. Howells. 2 pp. A.l.s. MH.

 11 while ⟨th⟩ 13 desire *w.o.* ask 15 desire *w.o.* be 23 ↑times↓

13 November 1859, Columbus, to Anne T. and Aurelia H. Howells. 2 pp. A.l.s. MH.

 5 are ⟨are⟩ 10 Insurrection⟨"⟩ 22 our ⟨le⟩ 23 ↑dem↓
24 him in *w.o.* him *illeg.* 28 preparing *w.o.* prepared 34 you⟨?⟩
37 from your] from your your 37 loving *w.o. illeg.*

31 January 1860, Columbus, to William H. Smith. 2 pp. A.l.s. OHi.

 26 Yours *w.o.* Iours

7 February 1860, Columbus, to William H. Smith. 1 p. A.l.s. OHi.

 5 Mr *w.o.* mr 6 ⟨tribunal⟩ ↑authorities↓ 10 ↑have↓ 22 Glenn.] ~

27 February 1860, Columbus, to Gail Hamilton. 1 p. A.l.s. MSaE.

 5 ↑as↓ I 7 |I s|hould 9 peculiar *w.o. illeg.*
10 referred *w.o.* referres 13 book *w.o.* books 16 manner ⟨which⟩
21 W. D|. H|owel|ls|.

1 April 1860, Columbus, to Artemas T. Fullerton. 2 pp. A.l.s. NN.

 14 of recent book] [*Howells either omitted the indefinite article after of or it is obliterated by fold in paper*] 15 sized *w.o.* zized 15 Muigs']
[*partial obliteration of first letter results in uncertain reading*]
16 the world *w.o.* wor world 17 |i|f 18 |t|o

21 April 1860, Columbus, to William C. Howells Family. 3 pp. A.l.s. MH.

 11 not ⟨f⟩ 15 there] ther 18 over ⟨a⟩ ↑the↓ 22 ⟨p⟩ autograph
27 ⟨but⟩ and 27 literary *w.o. illeg.* 33 Joe *w.o. illeg.*

29 April 1860, Columbus, to Joseph A. Howells. 4 pp. A.l.s. MH.

 16 off ⟨of⟩ 18 ↑much↓ 19 is⟨t⟩ 24 ↑the↓
24 future *w.o.* Futures 33 delicious *w.o.* lelicious

3 August 1860, Boston, to William C. Howells Family. Last of several pages. A.l.s. MH.

22 August 1860, Jefferson, to James T. Fields. 3 pp. A.l.s. CSmH.

    10 ↑me↓   28 ⟨and,⟩ and   31 me to *w.o.* t to

27 August 1860, Columbus, to Editors, Cincinnati *Gazette*. 1 p. A.l.s. OCoO.

    3 ⟨that⟩ if

31 August 1860, Columbus, to James R. Lowell. 4 pp. A.l.s. MH.

    5 look *w.o.* lok   21 accompanies ⟨whi⟩   25 ↑all↓   34 are *w.o.* is a 35 ↑it↓   40 mischievous. ⟨as insincere praise.⟩   42 shall *w.o.* should [*at bottom of last page, in another hand*: 31 Aug. 1860.]

1 September 1860, Columbus, to Oliver W. Holmes, Jr. 4 pp. A.l.s. MH.

    6 cacography *w.o.* cacographical   7 apologize *w.o.* apologise 18 fact] [*ink smear results in questionable reading*]   27 ↑an↓ 29 the catholic] the ⟨windows of⟩ the catholic   37 ⟨and⟩ ↑or↓ 42 ⟨holy⟩ saints   43 a⟨n⟩   45 anguished *w.o.* and   48 ↑on↓ 52 be *w.o.* me

12 September 1860, Columbus, to Anne T. Howells. 3 pp. A.l.s. MH.

    3 have *w.o.* having   8 ↑be↓   24 of the *w.o.* of of 26 for you *w.o.* y you   30–31 You ... visit] [*on verso of first page*]

14 November 1860, Columbus, to Oliver W. Holmes, Jr. 4 pp. A.l.s. MH.

    10 on *w.o.* b   19 always *w.o.* of   20 ↑just↓ 25 half-earnest *w.o.* halff earnest   41 Das *w.o.* Die 44 ⟨ich bin⟩ ↑bin ich↓   48 sind *w.o.* ist   49 die *w.o.* eine

25 November 1860, Columbus, to Oliver W. Holmes, Jr. 7 pp. A.l.s. MH.

    16 ↑an↓ anachronism⟨s⟩   21 am ⟨*illeg.*⟩   23 ⟨relation⟩ romance 28 if ↑it↓   41 wholly *w.o.* wll   43 young ⟨Sch⟩   46 ↑so↓ 56 piercing] piecing   56–57 the thorn *w.o.* a thorn   60 ↑week.↓

14 December 1860, Columbus, to James R. Lowell. 4 pp. A.l.s. MH.

    9 there↑fore↓   19 incredulous).] ~)   31 ↑wanton and↓

TEXTUAL RECORD 427

24 December 1860, Columbus, to James R. Lowell. 2 pp. A.l.s. MH.

6 January 1861, Columbus, to Oliver W. Holmes, Jr. 4 pp. A.l.s. MH.

   3 much ⟨from⟩   11 Thank you⟨r⟩   15 Common *w.o.* common
19 ⟨in⟩ which   22 pictured *w.o. illeg.*   23 parties *w.o.* party
24 while *w.o.* wi   25 had a *w.o.* have   34 ↑author↓
36 amazed *w.o.* at   40 two- *w.o. illeg.*

17 January 1861, Columbus, to James R. Lowell. 4 pp. A.l.s. MH.

[*In margin of first page, in another hand*: 17 Jan. '61.]
   5 with⟨out⟩   8 sorry *w.o.* sorrow   13 as ⟨ju⟩   17 ↑all↓
21 intropection *w.o.* inat   22 ↑however,↓   23 ↑own↓   34 ⟨the⟩ its
37 ⟨and⟩ among   37 ↑them from↓

24 February 1861, Columbus, to Oliver W. Holmes, Jr. 8 pp. A.l.s. MH.

   17 some ⟨blu⟩   18 taste,] taste, ⟨*illeg.*⟩,   18 ↑by the editors↓
24 *young* ↑and↓   31 think *w.o.* hinted   36 years] years / years
36 girl *w.o.* cam   37 ⟨our⟩ ↑my father's↓ office. ⟨at⟩   48 with ↑the↓
54–55 ↑have↓ graced   57 ↑or positive↓   59 a- *w.o.* m   61 ↑her↓ husband
62 understand⟨*illeg.*⟩   64 ill *w.o.* in   68 ⟨that⟩ one

13 March 1861, Columbus, to John G. Nicolay. 2 pp. A.l.s. DLC.

   4 Bavaria *w.o.* Bararia   5 ⟨the⟩ our   20 Mr . . . Nicolay.] [*at bottom of first page*]

24 March 1861, Columbus, to Victoria M. Howells. 7 pp. A.l.s. MH.

   7 ⟨can't⟩ ↑can↓   11 if ⟨a⟩   16 ↑me↓
18–19 ⟨have may⟩ ↑may have ever↓   21 ↑tried↓   23 poor *w.o.* l
24 achieve *w.o. illeg.*   26 ⟨base⟩ ↑base"↓ ⟨as ev⟩   33 that *w.o.* the
33 lure⟨s⟩   41 spring.] ~   45 your] you   54 well. ⟨She⟩

21 April 1861, Columbus, to Victoria M. Howells. 2 pp. A.l.s. MH.

   14 ↑them↓   14 but *w.o.* and   15 ↑I↓   21 ↑more↓

22 May 1861, Columbus, to Oliver W. Holmes, Jr. 2 pp. A.l.s. MH.

   9 contemplate⟨s⟩

26 May 1861, Columbus, to Mary D. Howells. 2 pp. A.l.s. MH.

6 ↑should↓   6 seeing him. *w.o.* seeing.   7 when *w.o.* him
8 has *w.o.* had   18 Besides⟨,⟩   18 service, ⟨would⟩

24 June 1861, Columbus, to John G. Nicolay. 2 pp. A.l.s. **DLC**.

5 ↑to go↓   7 be *w.o.* ba   8 me *w.o.* b   13 rather ⟨have⟩
17 give ↑you↓   22 ⟨Munich⟩ ↑place↓   23 me.] [*Howells cancelled the upper part of a question mark, letting the period stand*]
29 don't *w.o.* do not   32 Mr . . . Nicolay.] [*at bottom of first page*]

4 August 1861, Columbus, to John J. Piatt. Location of MS unknown. Typed transcription by C. and R. Kirk. NjR.

25 enough in] [*transcriber notes that a gap appears between these words*]

7 September 1861, Washington, to William C. Howells, 2 pp. A.l.s. MH.

[*Embossed in upper left corner on first page is a female figure*]
5 and arrived] and / and arrived
19–20 Disappointed *w.o.* disappointed   21 make *w.o.* a
22 war.] [*the period is written over a comma*]   23 home *w.o. illeg.*

28 September 1861, Jefferson, to Mrs. Samuel M. Smith. 5 pp. A.l.s. OHi.

9 ↑directly . . . exchange.↓   17 imagined *w.o.* imaged
28 Their *w.o.* This   33 Fanny *w.o.* fanny   37 declared, ↑⟨*illeg.*⟩↓
44 ⟨cru⟩ curious   47 ⟨l⟩ very   51 re—turned] [re *and* turned *are connected by a long curved line*]   52 ⟨and⟩ today   53 and I *w.o.* an I
56 Miss *w.o.* Mrs   56 you *w.o.* yow   61 ↑if↓

6 October 1861, Jefferson, to Oliver W. Holmes, Jr. 2 pp. A.l.s. OOxM.

8 ↑improve↓   9 shall not] shall

28 October 1861, Jefferson, to William H. Seward. 1 p. A.l.s. DNA.

[*The following State Department endorsements appear on the MS. in upper left corner on first page*:
      Recd   7. Octr.   *Above dateline*: Mr Abbott.
      Ansd 18   "   *Below dateline*: Venice]

31 October 1861, New York, to William C. and Mary D. Howells. 2 pp. A.l.s. MH.

TEXTUAL RECORD 429

9 don't *w.o.* di 11 this *w.o.* This 29 Charlie *w.o.* Charles
35 ↑you↓ 35 ⟨in⟩ care 36–38 I suppose...passports.] [*above date-line on first page*]

6 November 1861, New York, to Mary D. Howells. 3 pp. A.l.s. MH.

11 do *w.o.* to 17 livelihood *w.o.* s 20 She *w.o. illeg.* 34 that⟨'s⟩
38 ↑not↓ 38 him *w.o.* S 49 ⟨dirty⟩ dear

24 November 1861, London, to William C. Howells Family. 4 pp. A.l.s. MH.

16 ↑were↓ 18 reach ⟨to reach⟩ 18 pocket ⟨at⟩ 25 ⟨and⟩ ↑are↓
29 features *w.o. illeg.* 31 had *w.o.* have 35 things *w.o. illeg.*
36 it *w.o.* its 36 ↑as↓ often 37 ⟨landscape⟩ scene 41 ⟨hill⟩ mansions
42 village⟨s⟩ 49 ↑had↓ 50 ↑men↓ 53 to⟨o⟩ 70 a⟨n⟩ sensation
71 Houses *w.o. illeg.* 89 believe ↑it↓

7 December 1861, Venice, to William C. Howells Family. 4 pp. A.l.s. MH.

17 ⟨aft⟩ evening 20 ↑by↓ 22 ⟨where⟩ where 36 ↑I↓ made
41–42 confiding *w.o.* confident 42 creature⟨,⟩ 47 four *w.o.* Four
50 ↑a↓ 61 ⟨here⟩ ↑Vienna↓ 66 Grand Canal *w.o.* grand canal
75 ↑able↓ 78 can⟨not⟩ 83 war *w.o.* wh 95 ⟨Write⟩ Write

19 December 1861, Venice, to Anne T. Howells. 2 pp. A.l.s. MH.

10 G *w.o.* J 16 of all] of of all 18 ↑am↓ 18 ↑them↓
31 ⟨with⟩ into 32 ⟨and⟩ always 35 this *w.o.* these
36 ⟨beautiful⟩ grace 39 charming] charing 46 Everywhere] Evywhere
47 ↑once↓ 49 brooding *w.o. illeg.* 51 ⟨that⟩ ↑what perils threaten↓

18 and 21 January 1862, Venice, to Victoria M. Howells. 8 pp. A.l.s. MH.

6 you wrote.] ↑~ ~↓ 14 ↑N. Y.↓ Times 15 toke*n w.o.* tog
30 by *w.o.* my 42 and *w.o.* but 44 but *w.o. illeg.* 44 ↑though↓
47 have ⟨b⟩ 52 interesting↑, and↓ suffering ↑family↓
52 justification|.| 53 either *w.o. illeg.* 54 said *w.o. illeg.*
58 the *w.o.* m 64 base *w.o. illeg.* [*uncertain reading*]
70 today *w.o. illeg.* 73 ↑a↓ mass 73 bronze *w.o.* bromze
74 court.] ~ 75 ⟨shovle⟩ shoveling 77 ⟨weather⟩ winter
86 poem— *w.o.* poem of 86 a love-story] a a love-story
87 Conversion *w.o.* conversion 87 Conversion."] ~," 87 the *w.o.* it
87 ↑poem↓ 99 her] he|r| *w.o. illeg.* 104 ⟨and⟩ or

108 Saturday *w.o.* T   115 slightly *w.o. illeg.*
117 hard- *w.o. illeg.* [*uncertain reading*]   123 ↑have↓
125 heard] head

27 January 1862, Venice, to John J. Piatt. Location of MS unknown. *The Hesperian Tree*, ed. John J. Piatt (Columbus: S. F. Harriman, 1903), pp. 425-29.

7 March 1862, Venice, to William C. Howells. 5 pp. A.l.s. MH.

7 ↑not↓   7 anything *w.o. illeg.*   18 ↑day↓   28 ↑good↓   29 live⟨d⟩
33 ↑⟨with lodging⟩↓   33 ↑florins↓   34 ⟨hu⟩ you   40 ↑which↓
41 kind ↑of↓   51 ↑with ... lodge↓   58 who⟨se⟩ ↑is↓
84 they *w.o.* there   88 than *w.o.* that

26 April 1862, Venice, to Victoria M. Howells. 8 pp. A.l.s. MH.

9 money *w.o.* monies   13 earnestly ⟨and,⟩   33 things *w.o. illeg.*
36 here] her   41 ↑something↓   45 his *w.o.* him   51 ⟨number⟩ weight
70 medium of] medium of medium of   74 think ⟨I⟩   85 ↑here,↓
87 ⟨the unr⟩ ↑our↓   92 can ⟨f⟩   91 ideas.—] [*dash is more than half a line long*]   99 has *w.o. illeg.*   107 ↑will↓   107 Joe ⟨what⟩

13 June 1862, Venice, to William C. Howells. 6 pp. A.l.s. MH.

13 ⟨with⟩ ↑were↓   19 on *w.o.* of   24 ↑you↓   43 that's ⟨som⟩
52 city, ⟨wh⟩   54 either] eeither   70 ⟨live⟩ "purge and ⟨lively⟩
71 telling ⟨th⟩   72 dress ⟨dress⟩   73 ⟨don⟩ told   88 photograph⟨"⟩
96 The *w.o.* This   101 Ohio *w.o.* ohio   121 seeds *w.o. illeg.*
122 Venezia *w.o.* Venizia   123 ⟨any been to sc⟩ ↑Annie↓

22 July 1862, Venice, to William C. Howells. 7 pp. A.l.s. MH.

3 ↑as↓   10 ↑deal↓   20 ↑all↓   34 Lake *w.o. illeg.*
37 ⟨cheeks⟩ ↑faces↓   38 ⟨here⟩ ↑now and then↓   46 ⟨can⟩ can't
55 ↑on↓   60-61 ↑and ... late.↓   65 ↑more↓   67 ↑but↓
71 Mr. ... regards] [*on verso of fifth page*]

22 August 1862, Venice, to William C. Howells. 4 pp. A.l.s. MH.

5 ↑error↓   11 a *w.o.* 1   22 ↑had↓   31 and ⟨true and⟩ true
38 ↑wonder↓   40 ↑while↓

28 August 1862, Venice, to William C. Howells. 4 pp. A.l.s. MH.

26 ↑us.↓   26 view *w.o. illeg.*

12 September 1862, Venice, to William C. Howells. 8 pp. A.l.s. MH.

12 received ⟨"Lebeau⟩   17 ⟨Th⟩ Sweet   19 ⟨*illeg.*⟩ or   36 ↑our↓   39 according⟨ly⟩   47 ⟨It⟩ Upon   51 ↑ended↓   61 ⟨fall.⟩ summer   62 route *w.o.* Route   79–81 Just... Brattleboro.] [*in margin and at top of first page*]   81 I'm... all the] [*in margin of second page*]   82 poems.... does mo-] [*in margin of fifth page*] 82–83 -ther.... her] [*in margin and at top of sixth page*]

19 September 1862, Venice, to Frederick W. Seward. 4 pp. A.l.s. DNA.

[*The following State Department endorsements and comments appear on the MS*: *at top of first page*:   Recd Oct. 11   Mr Abbt
                                                          An   ″   14   Mr Cox
at bottom of last page, in Howells' hand: U. S. Consulate. / Venice, Sept. 19, 1862 / W. D. Howells, Consul. / Dispatch No. 13. / No enclosures. / Received, / Referring to office rented / by Mr Sprenger, etc.]
   5 ↑I found it↓   6 Piazza] [*the following words, in another hand, appear in margin*: Locality of the office as kept by Mr Sprenger]
8–9 the... it] [*underlined in pencil, but probably not by Howells*]
9 regarded] regard/ded   12 seven silver florins] [*underlined in pencil, as above*]   18 safe] [*the following words, in another hand, appear in margin*: Condition of consular property.]   22 to⟨o⟩ hold

23 September 1862, Venice, to Bayard Taylor. 2 pp. A.l.s. CLSU.

4 ↑me↓   9 ⟨my⟩ Mr   10 ↑know↓

22 and 23 October 1862, Venice, to Victoria M. Howells. 6 pp. A.l.s. MH.

16 ⟨w⟩ were   50 the *w.o.* this   53 ⟨*illeg.*⟩ ↑see↓   56 given *w.o.* gav   60 unkind] [*crossed out in pencil, presumably not by Howells*]

1 November 1862, Venice, to Salmon P. Chase. 4 pp. A.l.s. PHi.

[*At top of first page, in another hand*: Wm D Howells *and beneath dateline*: Nov 1 1862]
   3 ↑truly↓   7 remote *w.o.* an   29 ↑Or,↓   29 then *w.o.* Then   34 hope *w.o.* beg   35 ⟨shou⟩ ↑you↓   36 I've learned *w.o.* I'm learned

24 December 1862, Paris, to Larkin G. Mead, Sr. Location of MS unknown. *Life in Letters*, I, 62.

432　　　　　　*TEXTUAL APPARATUS*

22 January 1863, Venice, to James L. Graham, Jr. 4 pp. A.l.s. PSt.

　　6 were *w.o.* was　　17 telling *w.o. illeg.*　　25 ⟨boat⟩ boat

31 January 1863, Venice, to Charles Hale. 7 pp. A.l.s. MNS.

[*In upper left corner, first page, in another hand*: Recd Mch 6.]
　　12 ↑felt↓　　25 is *w.o.* are　　25 series *w.o.* serious　　40 ↑in↓
　　40 on *w.o. illeg.*　　48 There⟨'s⟩　　54 help.] ~　　58 ↑here.↓
　　59 ↑to whom↓

3 February 1863, Venice, to James L. Graham, Jr. 4 pp. A.l.s. PSt.

　　4 ↑there,↓　　9 ↑less↓　　21 but] but / but　　21 I'd *w.o.* I'm
　　22 ↑other↓　　29 Magazine *w.o.* magazine

12 and 20 February 1863, Venice, to William C. Howells. 4 pp. A.l.s. MH.

　　3 ↑of the 14th↓　　6 and ⟨h⟩　　15 there ↑are↓　　18 still ⟨have⟩
19 |s|ome　　36 I wonder.... The affair...] [*one line partly obliterated*]　　50 W|ill|　　51–52 |Would| yo|u sen|d me a few ne|wspa|pers— |E|vening Post, |whe|n used |...|, |a|nd　　51–56 Would.... portfol-] [*in margin and across dateline, salutation, and beginning of text, first page*]　　56–69 -io, and.... live.] [*across second page*]　　69–83 The poor.... of suc-] [*across fourth page*]　　70 virt|ue|　　71 ↑as hopefully↓
72 ↑(ex)↓　　73 b|ut|　　75 t|he| dead　　77 translatio|n|
79 painters.] ~　　80 *Atlanti|c.|*　　81 pu|b|lication
83–94 -cess whatever.... me?] [*across third page; at top of page, in Howells' hand*: (from page 4.)]　　83 |h|ome

15 March 1863, Venice, to William C. Howells. 10 pp. A.l.s. (Mostly in autograph of Elinor M. Howells.) MH.

　　1 Venice] [*begin Elinor Howells' hand*]　　10 ↑improved↓
14 complaisant).] ~)　　26 considerably.] ~　　38 ↑a↓
41–42 ⟨of⟩ ↑resulting from↓　　46 F. W. ⟨F⟩　　51 |con|viction
71 mor|e|　　88 — *w.o.* ⟨of⟩　　93 ⟨br⟩ changed　　110 We] [*in margin, presumably in Howells' hand*: ¶]　　120 Will.] [*in Elinor Howells' hand, followed by Howells' own signature*]　　121–29 I.... Will.] [*in Howells' hand*]

23 March 1863, Venice, to James L. Graham, Jr. 4 pp. A.l.s. PSt.

　　8 delay *w.o.* a　　20 Venetian *w.o.* venetian　　24 illness *w.o. illeg.*

24 March 1863, Venice, to Moncure D. Conway. 4 pp. A.l.s. NNC.

TEXTUAL RECORD

433

5 April 1863, Venice, to Charles Hale. 5 pp. A.l.s. (with 1 p. enclosure in Elinor Howells' hand) MNS.

    25 ↑time↓   25 time.] ~   33 events ⟨of⟩   34 yourself took⟨s⟩
40 called ⟨the⟩   47–51 I .... enquire.] [*across fifth page*]
52–64 Atlantic .... Cincinnati.] [*in Elinor Howells' hand*]

18 April 1863, Venice, to Mary D. Howells. 3 pp. A.l.s. MH.

    3 letter⟨,⟩   13 pulled *w.o. illeg.*   16 matter.] ~   18 ↑be↓
19 ↑have↓   19 written *w.o.* wrote   23 ↑you do↓   24 we *w.o. illeg.*
26 For] Four   30 This *w.o.* La   45 ⟨to⟩ days   47 ↑fellow↓
47 ↑only↓

18 May 1863, Venice, to Aurelia H. Howells. 2 pp. A.l.s. MH.

    10 |letter|s   17 ⟨and⟩ ↑are↓   18 ret|urn| 19 th|em| 21 g|l|ad
22 Aurelia *w.o.* V   24 ↑a↓   28 two *w.o.* one

1 June 1863, Venice, to John B. Howells. 8 pp. A.l.s. MH.

    17 Johnny] [*in margin, presumably in Howells' hand*: ¶]
21 that⟨'s⟩   21 for ⟨her⟩   26 and ⟨t⟩   48 Office *w.o.* bu
54 found *w.o. illeg.*   62 ↑you↓ don't   66 word⟨s⟩
74–80 Tell .... Will.] [*in margin and across dateline, first page*]

13 June 1863, Venice, to Charles Hale. 4 pp. A.l.s. MNS.

    34 ⟨f⟩ spring   44 handkerchief⟨s⟩   50 [*a pointing hand appears at the beginning of this line*]

18 June 1863, Venice, to Mary D. Howells. 4 pp. A.l.s. MH.

    11 doubtless⟨ly⟩   17 America ⟨with⟩   21 mother?⟨,⟩—   24 ↑back↓
28 it all *w.o.* it *illeg.*   28 ↑where↓   37 ↑write↓

22 August 1863, Venice, to Moncure D. Conway. 3 pp. A.l.s. NNC.

    4 Petrarch ⟨of⟩   4 awaiting ⟨for⟩   13 good] good / good
14 ↑will↓   16 ↑the↓

2 September 1863, Venice, to John B. Howells. 4 pp. A.l.s. MH.

    13 enough⟨t⟩   18 conscience *w.o.* conscious   20 ↑not↓
29 write *w.o.* writte   33 gloves, ⟨and⟩

18 September 1863, Venice, to Moncure D. and Ellen D. Conway. 6 pp. A.l.s. NNC.

25 a very] a very / a very   32 asses' ⟨ea⟩   43 |i|n
47 terminated] terminat/ted   48–50 them.... strength] [*in left margin, first page*]   50–51 and... Howells.] [*in right margin, first page*]
52–55 My.... regretfully.] [*in left margin and at top of second page*]
55–61 The.... your] [*in right margin, second page, and in left margin and at top of third page*]   56 ↑educated↓   58 ⟨Ot⟩ Shakespeare
61–62 "Venetian... publication.] [*in right margin, third page*]
62 ma|y alter later pu|blication.   75 ⟨names⟩ names

3 October 1863, Venice, to Salmon P. Chase. 6 pp. A.l.s. PHi.

3 pho-/ *w.o. illeg.*   10 than *w.o.* that   13 were *w.o.* I
20 ↑picture↓   22 within *w.o.* without   26 ↑it↓   33 ↑so↓
37 brave ↑and↓   47 ↑to treat of↓   48 countries *w.o.* country
56 ⟨it⟩ we

25 October 1863, Venice, to Charles Hale. 4 pp. A.l.s. (with 1 p. enclosure) MNS.

9 ⟨them⟩ ↑it↓   11 ⟨t⟩here   12 letter↑-form↓   22 ↑they↓
24 ⟨trust *w.o.* have⟩ trust   30 ↑however,↓   33 ↑ink↓   45 Titles] [*a pointing hand appears in margin at this point*]   55 ↑Our friend↓
55 the *w.o.* The   57 Please] [*another pointing hand here*]

2 November 1863, Venice, to Charles Hale. 2 pp. A.l.s. MNS.

12 ↑more comprehensive↓   12 continue *w.o. illeg.*   15 ↑to↓
16 ⟨about⟩ twenty   17 ↑or *less,*↓   17 ↑one's↓   18 ↑as↓ seldom
23 Mead⟨e⟩

14 and 19 November 1863, Venice, to William C. Howells. 4 pp. A.l.s. MH.

5 ⟨when⟩ and   12–13 the ⟨the⟩ Telegraph   19 ↑a↓   22 ⟨y⟩our
29 reache|d| 33 ↑my↓   35 had not lived] had lived   36 ⟨sud⟩ soon
43 f⟨o⟩urlough   53–56 when.... Will.] [*in margin and across salutation, first page*]

9 December 1863, Venice, to Joseph A. Howells. 4 pp. A.l.s. MH.

5 seemed *w.o. illeg.*   19 size *w.o.* same   54 thought *w.o.* think
65 ⟨f⟩ wrote   71 ↑at↓   78 ↑their↓   92 ⟨f⟩ which
112 got before *w.o. illeg.*   114 his *w.o.* he   123 write *w.o. illeg.*

TEXTUAL RECORD 435

17 December 1863, Venice, to William C. and Mary D. Howells. 2 pp. A.l.s. MH.

22 December 1863, Venice, to William C. Howells. 4 pp. A.l.s. MH.

    6 hearty *w.o.* hap   21 may *w.o. illeg.*   21 ↑her↓   23 or *w.o.* n
35 ↑said↓   37 ⟨no⟩ ↑not the↓   40 ⟨bu⟩ as   47 another *w.o.* a other
72 mother *w.o.* me

24 December 1863, Venice, to Charles Hale. 3 pp. A.l.s. MNS.

    5 Years *w.o. illeg.*

26 January 1864, Venice, to Moncure D. Conway. 4 pp. A.l.s. NN.

    10 that *w.o. illeg.*   14 ↑with even↓   17 enough ⟨to⟩
22 *Dolmati*] Dol/*mati*   28 half *w.o. illeg.*   28 ↑assume↓
30 when *w.o.* When   32 ↑portable↓   46 ↑her↓   46 perhaps *w.o.* her
53 and ⟨will⟩   54 ⟨suppose⟩ ↑know that↓

1 February 1864, Venice, to Edmund C. Stedman. Location of MS unknown. Typed transcription. NNC.

    9 forbidden] forbodden   23 Puo darsi] [*copyist typed* Puo dorse; *someone crossed this out and wrote in margin*: Pui dorse. *The editorial emendation is based on the assumption that Howells used the correct Italian phrase*]   47 Dante,] ~.   48 Spenser and Chaucer] Spencer and Chancer   59 anima] [*in place of this word the copyist left a blank space, and someone wrote in margin* avnonire, *which is probably an incorrect reading*]   76 excessively] excesively

20 February 1864, Venice, to Harper & Brothers. 4 pp. A.l.s. MH.

    24 now ⟨come⟩   27 ↑who↓   30 ⟨a⟩ study   30 ↑literature↓
31 book ↑which↓   31 and ↑which↓   34 but *w.o.* and   34 try *w.o.* n
44 justify ⟨f⟩   44 require ⟨some⟩   47 required ⟨of⟩   48 ⟨ha⟩ take
50 ⟨o⟩for   54 that ⟨it⟩   55 ↑library↓   59 Magazine *w.o.* magazine
64 Messrs. . . . Brothers] [*at bottom of first page*]

25 March 1864, Venice, to Samuel D. Howells. 4 pp. A.l.s. (2½ pp. by Howells; 1½ pp. by Elinor M. Howells) MH.

    3 and *w.o.* as   13 ↑they do↓   49 ⟨Ever⟩ "If   50 old ⟨R⟩
51 ran ⟨to⟩   55 ↑it↓   58 the *w.o.* it   58 ↑latter↓   64 than *w.o.* that
68 had traveled *w.o.* were traveling,   68 ↑there↓   70 two *w.o.* one

436   TEXTUAL APPARATUS

75 and⟨,⟩ we   75 ↑are↓   76 We ⟨had⟩   85 Dear] [*begin Elinor Howells' hand*]   102 &c.] ~
103–4 ↑of the ⟨of⟩ office of the conscription↓
109–12 I . . . . Elinor] [*across salutation on first page*]   109 like.] ~

7 April 1864, Venice, to Victoria M. Howells. 4 pp. A.l.s. MH.

14 got *w.o.* good   29 traveling in] traveling in / in   30 could ⟨not⟩
35 ⟨f⟩ us   35 ↑actual↓   38 ⟨perce⟩ perceptible   39 ⟨Wh⟩ You
45 ↑us.↓   62 dis/↑posed↓   66–67 Of . . . home.] [*across writing on fourth page*]

16 May 1864, Venice, to Trübner & Co. 1 p. Autograph draft signed. MH.

4 ↑you↓ are   8 ⟨the⟩ deem   13 ↑So↓   13 propose ⟨therefore⟩

16 and 22 May 1864, Venice, to Moncure D. Conway. 2 pp. A.l.s. NNC.

10 ↑it↓   11 reminding ↑them↓   53 ↑from↓   68 ↑rejected↓
69–75 May . . . . is.] [*over dateline and salutation on first page*]
72 ⟨S⟩ school   74 than *w.o.* that

19 May 1864, Venice, to Samuel D. Howells. 3 pp. A.l.s. MH.

12 me *w.o.* my   27 where ⟨h⟩

20 June 1864, Venice, to Anne T. Howells. 2 pp. A.l.s. MH.

6 sad⟨ness⟩   10 ⟨w⟩his   27 ↑as↓

22 July 1864, Venice, to William C. Howells. 4 pp. A.l.s. MH.

7 mortality ⟨before⟩   22 ↑with↓   26 ⟨p⟩ whole   30 ↑and↓
35 ⟨meet⟩ ↑see↓   42 but *w.o.* and   49 only ⟨ret⟩   52 ⟨go⟩ ↑draw↓

21 August 1864, Venice, to James R. Lowell. 4 pp. A.l.s. MH.

6 ↑those↓   21 pre-Titianic *w.o.* pretitianic
28 the universal *w.o.* an universal   35 they ⟨have⟩   57 ↑line of↓
64 have noticed] have / have noticed   78 no⟨-⟩/doubt   82 ↑hand↓
83 could ⟨co⟩   86 I] [*a pointing hand appears immediately before this word*]   86 ↑you↓   91 James . . . Esqr.] [*at bottom of first page*]

25 August 1864, Venice, to William C. Howells. 6 pp. A.l.s. (**with note** by Elinor M. Howells) MH.

TEXTUAL RECORD 437

12 let ⟨my⟩   17 See] [*a pointing hand appears immediately before this word*]   29 thought.] ~   41 good ⟨li⟩   42 it? *w.o.* it,   49 ⟨and⟩ ↑or↓   49 ↑before ... out.↓   50 ↑be↓   52 ↑have↓   60 lie *w.o.* liv   68 the *w.o.* his   72 ↑what was↓   77 ↑I have seen↓   84 ↑is↓   96 ↑if↓ you   96 ↑get↓   99 speak⟨s⟩   106 A word] [*begin Elinor Howells' hand*]   110–11 ↑to ... friends.↓ ⟨and,⟩   111 Generally *w.o.* generally   112 weary *w.o.* r   116 ↑scarcely↓

6 October 1864, Venice, to William C. Howells. 4 pp. A.l.s. MH.

10 ↑toward↓   12 than *w.o.* that   14 when ⟨should⟩   21 the *w.o.* he   32 gloomy ⟨fee⟩   36 ↑at least,↓   40 pay *w.o.* may   57 ⟨were⟩ ↑has↓   58 long ⟨l⟩   58 turning *w.o.* turned   58 ⟨but⟩ I   59 ↑however,↓   59 politics; ⟨and⟩   60 ↑through justice,↓   73 with *w.o.* in   73 ↑on↓

14 October 1864, Venice, to Frederick W. Seward. 1 p. A.l.s. DNA.

[*The following State Department endorsements appear in the upper left corner, first page*:
                    Recd Nov 1.
                    Ans   "   4
on verso, in Howells' hand: United States Consulate, / Venice, October 14, 1864. / W D Howells, Consul. / Dispatch No. 15. / Concerning / Annual Report on Commerce / and duplicate volumes of / Diplomatic Correspondence. / Received Nov 1]

28 October 1864, Venice, to Mary D. Howells. 2 pp. A.l.s. MH.

4 ↑should↓   7 could,⟨n't⟩   16 Sunday ⟨I⟩   18 ↑a↓   26 moment's ⟨*illeg.*⟩   28 you⟨r⟩

2 December 1864, Rome, to Anne T. Howells, 2 pp. A.l. (fragment) MH.

13 choice *w.o. illeg.*   18 obscurity ⟨at⟩   23 ↑half-↓   33 would *w.o.* could   34 the *w.o.* a   37 ago⟨n⟩   38 useless *w.o.* endless   45 little ⟨rose⟩   45 ↑rose↓   47 ↑many↓   47 in] [*MS ends here*]

9 January 1865, Venice, to William C. Howells. 2 pp. A.l.s. MH.

5 four *w.o.* of   8 ↑of↓   24 ↑get↓   29 ⟨lettler⟩ letter   29 ↑family↓

9 January 1865, Venice, to Frederick W. Seward. 2 pp. A.l.s. DNA.

[*The following State Department endorsements appear in upper left corner, first page*:

438 TEXTUAL APPARATUS

        Recd Feb 6.
        ack   " 10
in upper right corner, first page: +Mr. Jones
in right margin, at head of first paragraph: Asking information concerning continuance in office.
in right margin, at head of second paragraph: Conditionally asking renewed leave of absence.]

28 and 29 January 1865, Venice, to Anne T. Howells. 3 pp. A.l.s. MH.

  12 odd ⟨enough⟩   17 ⟨you⟩ she   18 her⟨e⟩   20 ⟨but⟩ ↑is↓
26 ⟨tell⟩ ↑write↓   26 from ⟨an⟩   44 ⟨one⟩ ↑would↓   51 ↑till↓
52 she⟨s⟩   54 good.] ~   56 ↑only wound↓   62 |cir|cle
63 *cheerfully* ....] [*here and in next line portions of text are missing because of torn paper*]

15 February 1865, Venice, to John J. Piatt. Location of MS unknown. Typed transcriptions by F. C. Marston and W. M. Gibson. InU. Variants in transcriptions as follows:

	Marston (copy-text)	*Gibson*
1	February	Feb.
1	1865.	1865
2	My dear Piatt—	[*no salutation*]
3	to-night	tonight
12	resignation.	resignation,
15	resign",	resign,"
29	I am.—	I am.
38	on [*word supplied by transcriber*]	on
50	Pompei	Pompeii
51	you	your

19 March 1865, Venice, to Edward E. Hale. 2 pp. A.l.s. MNS.

[*On verso of second page*: Rev. E. E. Hale, / Boston. / Favored by Charles Hale & Co.]
  6 ↑have come to↓   6 ↑no↓   19 Your] X Your
21 Rev. E. E. Hale] [*at bottom of first page*]

19 March 1865, Venice, to William C. Howells. 4 pp. A.l.s. MH.

  10 ⟨the⟩ ↑an↓   11 assure ⟨th⟩   12 ↑me.↓   14 ↑how↓
19 would *w.o.* is   20 undertake ⟨*illeg.*⟩   20 ⟨Venetian⟩ Venice
25 ⟨hid⟩ series   31 ⟨I⟩ how

27 April 1865, Venice, to William C. and Mary D. Howells. 3 pp. A.l.s. MH.

 4 Affection *w.o.* affection 5 ⟨thought⟩ ↑heart↓ 5 his *w.o.* he
6 ⟨too⟩ has 6 ⟨the⟩ leave 6 ↑also↓ 11 look⟨s⟩
12 ⟨sad⟩ compassionate 16 he ⟨fe⟩ 17 and that *w.o.* and the
19 ⟨good⟩ peace ⟨and⟩ 21 has ⟨been⟩ 22 ⟨decide its⟩ vindicate
29 ⟨T⟩ typhoid ↑fever.↓ 29 say⟨s⟩ 30 dispatch ⟨of⟩ 32 ↑all↓
33 ⟨a⟩ ↑an↓ 34 America *w.o. illeg.* 37 ⟨well⟩ ↑better↓ 39 ↑was↓
44 the *w.o. illeg.* 47 You⟨r⟩ 48–49 ↑which . . . greeting,↓
59 get *w.o.* b

28 April 1865, Venice, to William C. Howells. 2 pp. A.l.s. MH.

 6 awfully *w.o.* dreadfully 10 but *w.o.* and

1 May 1865, Venice, to William H. Seward. 1 p. A.l.s. DNA.

[*The following State Department endorsements appear on the MS*: *in left margin*: Nos. 6 and 7 also recd. *center top*: No. 8 *upper right corner*:
     Recd. May 14.
     ack " 20
on verso, in Howells' hand: United States Consulate / Venice, May 1, 1865. / W. D. Howells, Consul. / Dispatch No. 8. / Received *above that, in another hand*: M. Jones]

 4 cannot *w.o. illeg.* 12 able⟨r⟩

8 May 1865, Venice, to John L. Motley. 1 p. Author's autograph copy. DNA.

14 May 1865, Venice, to James R. Lowell. 2 pp. A.l.s. MH.

 6 ↑over↓ 7 in *w.o. illeg.* 16 word *w.o.* way 16 ⟨*illeg.*⟩ occasion
19 embittered ⟨*illeg.*⟩

6 June 1865, Venice, to William C. Howells. 4 pp. A.l.s. MH.

 1 [*Letterhead embossed*] 12 ⟨↑it↓⟩ yet ↑it↓ 22 off his] of his
31 people ⟨col⟩ 41 look ⟨th⟩ 42 think] thank 46 have ⟨hi⟩
48 ⟨exect⟩ execution 50 obliged ⟨at⟩ 57 Joe *w.o.* Jos

21 June 1865, Venice, to William C. Howells. 2 pp. A.l.s. MH.

 1 1865 *w.o.* 1861 12 to *w.o.* s 14 ⟨fath⟩ favor

440   *TEXTUAL APPARATUS*

28 June 1865, Venice, to William Hunter. 3 pp. A.l.s. **DNA**.

[*The following State Department endorsements appear on the first page of the MS*: *upper left corner*: Read with much interest and action approved. *center top*: No. 10 *upper right corner*:
Recd. July 24
ack   "   "
on verso, in Howells' hand: United States Consulate / Venice, June 28, 1865. / W. D. Howells, Consul / Dispatch No. 10 / Thanks for leave of absence; bind/ing and putting in order offi/cial letters. / Received,]

 21 Consul ⟨may⟩ 27 ⟨*illeg.*⟩ various 30 ↑judge↓ 35 ↑they↓ 40 ⟨j discharge⟩ destroy 45 receive⟨d⟩ 50 ⟨some⟩ ↑a due↓

10 July 1865, London, to William C. Howells. 4 pp. A.l.s. **MH**.

 10 cut⟨s⟩ 18 well] will 19 ↑of↓ 27 ⟨night⟩ noon 35 go ⟨t⟩ 45 thing⟨s⟩ 46 who *w.o.* whi 56 things ⟨good, *illeg.*⟩ 58 be *w.o.* s

19 August 1865, Jefferson, to James R. Lowell. 3 pp. A.l.s. **MH**.

 13 ↑with↓

5 September 1865, Jefferson, to Don L. Wyman. 3 pp. A.l.s. **CLSU**.

 5 ↑you↓ 6 ↑and↓ 34 ⟨and⟩ many 47 Don. . . . Esqr.] [*at bottom of first page*]

14 September 1865, New York, to Elinor M. Howells. 3 pp. A.l.s. **MH**.

 2 Sweet|y| 11 ↑well↓ 28 and *w.o. illeg.* 30 ⟨look⟩ ↑like↓ 32 letters ⟨to⟩ 32 while|.| 38 two *w.o.* one 38 ⟨months⟩ weeks 41 her⟨e⟩

15 September 1865, New York, to Elinor M. Howells. 2 pp. A.l.s. **MH**.

 11 man⟨*illeg.*⟩

19 September 1865, New York, to Elinor M. Howells. 2 pp. A.l.s. **MH**.

 25 ↑are↓

19 September 1865, New York, to Elinor M. Howells. 2 pp. A.l.s. **MH**.

23 September 1865, New York, to Elinor M. Howells. 2 pp. Al.s. **MH**.

 12 got *w.o.* good 13 ↑on Venice,↓ 21 The *w.o.* the 32 I⟨t⟩ shall

TEXTUAL RECORD 441

18 October 1865, New York, to Elinor M. Howells. 3 pp. A.l.s. MH.

 16 ↑it,↓ 24 ↑from↓

27 October 1865, New York, to Elinor M. Howells. 4 pp. A.l.s. MH.

 6 do *w.o.* did 17 ⟨A⟩ answer 23 ↑you↓ 26 ⟨let⟩ live 28 ↑a↓ page 41 ↑toward↓ 46 ↑occasion↓ 46 occasion.] ~
46 Llewellyn *w.o.* Llleyellyn 48 an article] an an article

6 November 1865, New York, to James R. Lowell. 4 pp. A.l.s. MH.

 5 ↑sometimes↓ 7 ↑ever↓ 13 no] [*added in margin*]
23 ↑the gravity of↓

17 November 1865, New York, to Elinor M. Howells. 2 pp. A.l.s. MH.

 12 ↑all↓ 13 include ⟨papers⟩

22 December 1865, New York, to Elinor M. Howells. 2 pp. A.l.s. MH.

 17 ⟨retur⟩ coming

24 December 1865, New York, to William C. Howells. 4 pp. A.l.s. MH.

 17 ↑glad↓ 22 ↑you↓ 30 ↑will↓ 31 ⟨He⟩ ↑Mr. Norton↓
31 the little *w.o.* m little 49 ⟨again,⟩ ↑at last,↓ 51 love ⟨tol⟩

27 December 1865, New York, to Charles E. Norton. 2 pp. A.l.s. MH.

 5 desirous *w.o.* desire 6 ⟨for⟩ since

14 January 1866, New York, to James T. Fields. 2 pp. Autograph draft signed. MH.

 8 reviews *w.o.* receiews 12 answer. ⟨My ambition would be to hold on The Atlantic the position of editor, subject, of course, to your advice and instruction.⟩

28 January 1866, New York, to William C. Howells. 6 pp. A.l.s. (in part by Elinor M. Howells) MH.

 3 wanted ⟨first⟩ 23 constant ⟨day⟩ 28 I've ↑to↓
31 gone *w.o. illeg.* 35 "Tilly] [*begin Elinor Howells' hand*]
38 tum *w.o.* some 38 tum *w.o.* some 38 tum *w.o.* s 40 ↑state↓
42–44 not . . . . soon] [*across dateline and salutation, first page*]
44–48 whether . . . . Elinor] [*across third page*]

6 February 1866, New York, to James T. Fields. 2 pp. A.l.s. MH.

8 February 1866, New York, to William C. Howells. 4 pp. A.l.s. MH.

6 ⟨ad⟩ superintendant   19 since⟨,⟩   23 though⟨t⟩

20 February 1866, Boston, to Edmund C. Stedman. 2 pp. A.l.s. CLSU.

4 have ⟨merri⟩   5 with ⟨at⟩   27 ↑me↓

24 May 1866, Boston, to Benjamin S. Parker. 2 pp. A.l.s. InU.

15 ↑also↓

25 May 1866, Cambridge, to Charles E. Norton. 3 pp. A.l.s. MH.

7 live⟨d⟩   7 of the *w.o.* of this   29 let ⟨Elinor⟩   29 Boston, ⟨als⟩
31 ↑you↓

27 May 1866, Cambridge, to Edmund C. Stedman. 4 pp. A.l.s. NNC.

19 Stoddard *w.o.* Stodford   24 ↑down↓   24 happiness. ⟨Ev⟩
25 feet *w.o.* fac   32 are ↑⟨all⟩↓   35 paper.] ∼, ⟨as yet⟩.

8 June 1866, Cambridge, to Charles E. Norton. 4 pp. A.l.s. MH.

4 ↑not↓   7 ↑of↓ the   12 ↑on↓   13 ↑you↓   14 rogues ⟨and rogues⟩
28 ⟨place⟩ Paris   40 baited *w.o. illeg.*   49–50 ↑by my lawyer,↓

14 and 15 June 1866, Cambridge, to Charles E. Norton. 6 pp. A.l.s. MH.

6 had ⟨I⟩   7 their *w.o.* this   10 a ⟨I⟩
20–21 übersetzungen *w.o. illeg.*   24 ↑to↓   29 at ⟨table⟩   36 ↑it↓
46 which *w.o. illeg.*   50 ↑me↓   60 I've ⟨h⟩

17 June 1866, Cambridge, to Victoria M. Howells. 4 pp. A.l.s. MH.

12 than *w.o.* that   13 door *w.o. illeg.*   25 ever⟨y⟩

19 June 1866, Cambridge, to Mary D. Howells. 2 pp. A.l.s. MH.

5 in ⟨nu⟩

23 June 1866, Cambridge, to Charles E. Norton. 4 pp. A.l.s. MH.

5 ⟨*illeg.*⟩ ↑believe↓   11 have *w.o.* can   11 ⟨recoll⟩ only
12 when *w.o. illeg.*   19 less ⟨sep⟩   20 fishes *w.o. illeg.*
23 ⟨*illeg.*⟩ Greene   25 rise ⟨to⟩   26 ↑me↓   31 ⟨*illeg.*⟩ first
31 cities *w.o.* city   36 ↑more↓

TEXTUAL RECORD 443

8 July 1866, Cambridge, to James M. Comly. 4 pp. A.l.s. OHi.

    6 magazine] mag/zine   9 ↑to↓ me   10 an *w.o.* a   10 ↑entire↓
10 physical *w.o.* physiological   17 ⟨both⟩ because   17 ↑both↓

13 August 1866, Cambridge, to Melanchthon M. Hurd. Location of MS unknown. *Life in Letters*, I, 113–14.

3 September 1866, Boston, to Edmund C. Stedman. 4 pp. A.l.s. NNC.

    4 ↑your↓ review   21 ↑public↓

12 September 1866, Cambridge, to Melanchthon M. Hurd. 4 pp. A.l.s. MH.

    4 such ⟨a⟩   4 ↑of Venetian Life↓   5 Messrs. *w.o.* Messr.
7 of the *w.o.* on the   12 much ⟨effect⟩   15 ↑not↓   18 ↑not↓
22 ⟨suff⟩ wait   29 of the *w.o.* of a   33 ⟨Ashtabula⟩ Ashtabula

15 September 1866, Boston, to Edwin P. Whipple. 2 pp. A.l.s. CtY.

15 October 1866, Boston, to James T. Fields, 2 pp. A.l.s. CSmH.

    4 seldom *w.o. illeg.*

20 November 1866, Cambridge, to Thomas W. Higginson. 2 pp. A.l.s. CLSU.

    8 ↑had↓

5 December 1866, Boston, to Edmund C. Stedman. 3 pp. A.l.s. NN.

    25 ↑do↓

31 December 1866, Cambridge, to William C. Howells. 3 pp. A.l.s. MH.

    4 it ⟨for⟩ to

4 January 1867, Boston, to James T. Fields. 1 p. A.l.s. CSmH.

10 February 1867, Cambridge, to William C. Howells. 4 pp. A.l.s. MH.

    15 whose *w.o.* whom   20 ↑men↓   23 to↑-↓day   24 ↑you↓ would
25 the *w.o.* I   25 smashing *w.o. illeg.*   26 ⟨with⟩ ↑taking supper with↓
28 ↑upon the ice.↓   28 ice.] ∼..   31 Annie ⟨was⟩

16 February 1867, Cambridge, to Don L. Wyman. 3 pp. A.l.s. **CSmH**.

11 ⟨In⟩ There *w.o.* there   18 ought ↑not↓   19 ↑with↓   20 my⟨s⟩
29 ↑me↓ have

10 March 1867, Cambridge, to Moncure D. Conway. 3 pp. A.l.s. **NNC**.

6 done. ⟨with the exception of those⟩   18 ↑poetic↓   20 wish ⟨you to say something to the foregoing effect, saving of course my poor opinion of my contemporaries, and⟩ ↑you↓   40 ↑day↓   42 ↑monthly↓

13 April 1867, Boston, to James M. Comly. 2 pp. A.l.s. **OHi**.

18 are *w.o.* w

28 April 1867, Cambridge, to William C. Howells. 4 pp. A.l.s. **MH**.

3 you, ⟨and⟩   9 I shall try] I shall I try   14 Brattleboro'.] ∼,
26 Fields's *w.o.* Fieldses

4 June 1867, Cambridge, to James T. Fields. 1 p. A.l.s. **CSmH**.

3 ⟨Ju⟩ August

30 June 1867, Cambridge, to Mary D. Howells. 4 pp. A.l.s. **MH**.

1 Cambridge ⟨July⟩   6 ⟨wh⟩ tying   11 ↑do↓
15 ⟨exceeding⟩ excitement   16 leg ⟨and⟩   21 both ⟨*illeg.*⟩
27 yet ⟨only⟩   33 ⟨the⟩ company   37 anything ⟨of⟩   37 ↑got↓
38 ↑joy↓   42 resignation ⟨of⟩   47 giving ⟨us⟩
51–52 ↑leave ... account of↓   58 I ... Longfellow.] [*above dateline, first page*]

31 July 1867, Cambridge, to Charles E. Norton. 4 pp. A.l.s. **MH**.

26 ⟨Howells⟩ Lowell's   31 ↑what I think↓   33 ↑not↓
37 possible *w.o.* possibly   43–44 Very ... Howells.] [*across salutation, first page*]

10 August 1867, Cambridge, to Charles E. Norton. 4 pp. A.l.s. **MH**.

3 me *w.o. illeg.*   12 ↑air↓   17 ⟨been⟩ ↑made↓   32 a *w.o. illeg.*
33 ↑there↓   34 that lookout *w.o. illeg.* lookout   43 ⟨breathes⟩ ↑breaks↓

17 August 1867, Brattleboro, to Edmund C. Stedman. 3 pp. A.l.s. **NNC**.

11 ↑steam-↓   25 ↑how↓   27 ↑am↓   37 ↑one↓

TEXTUAL RECORD 445

26 September 1867, Cambridge, to Anne T. Howells. 2 pp. A.l.s. MH.

    5 ⟨at⟩ ↑in↓   5 ↑your way.↓   23 had *w.o.* hav

25 November 1867, Cambridge, to Mary D. Howells. 4 pp. A.l.s. MH.

    10 ↑thing↓   34 artist⟨s⟩

8 December 1867, Cambridge, to Victoria M. Howells. 4 pp. A.l.s. MH.

    7 looking ⟨up⟩   18 ⟨the⟩ Pickwick⟨s⟩   24 ↑for . . . part↓
31 had *w.o.* have   34 ↑can↓   39 ⟨little⟩ letter

15 December 1867, Cambridge, to Anne T. Howells. 3 pp. A.l.s. MH.

    14 course *w.o.* crurse   36 ↑⟨with him⟩↓

15 December 1867, Cambridge, to Melanchthon M. Hurd. Location of MS unknown. *Life in Letters*, I, 125.

    9 Hassaurek's] Hassanek's

6 March 1868, Cambridge, to William C. Howells Family. 4 pp. A.l.s. MH.

    9–10 done ⟨but⟩ to ⟨des⟩   10 back⟨,⟩   17 present *w.o.* presence
19 ⟨We⟩ I   22 ↑($1000)↓   23 ⟨"⟩because   24 feel,⟨"⟩   24 ⟨was⟩ ↑is↓
25–26 ↑My . . . articles.↓ [*in right margin*]   27 got⟨*illeg.*⟩
43 ⟨would⟩ ↑all↓   44 after ⟨long⟩

26 April 1868, Cambridge, to James M. Comly. 4 pp. A.l.s. OHi.

    3 ↑day↓   7 it *w.o.* is   13 a *w.o.* an   26 shall ⟨I⟩   26 do *w.o. illeg.*

7 July 1868, Boston, to James M. Comly. 4 pp. A.l.s. OHi.

    7 ↑know↓   30 ⟨let⟩ lingering   38 ⟨pl⟩ practice
43 Write . . . is.] [*above letterhead, first page*]

13 July 1868, Cambridge, to Mary D. Howells. 4 pp. A.l.s. MH.

[*In upper left corner, first page, in another hand*: Very interesting criticism]
    6 whi|ch| 15 shadow *w.o. illeg.*   32 ↑him↓   40 ↑hair↓
41 Howells⟨'⟩es

15 August 1868, Cambridge, to James R. Lowell. 1 p. A.l.s. MH.

29 August 1868, Cambridge, to Charles E. Norton. 4 pp. A.l.s. MH.

7 ⟨world⟩ life   8 ⟨its-⟩/ themselves   12 disturbance ⟨with⟩ as ⟨little⟩
40 ⟨I⟩ our   44 ⟨down⟩ ↑done↓   67 world"? ⟨illeg.⟩   72 me] me / me
73–75 are even.... Howells] [*above salutation, first page*]

30 August 1868, Cambridge, to Winifred Howells. 2 pp. A.l.s. MH.

11 the⟨y⟩

4 October 1868, Cambridge, to William C. Howells. 4 pp. A.l.s. MH.

7 don't *w.o. illeg.*   20 ↑back↓   23 ↑still↓   27 ↑new↓
46 medical] medical medical   56 ⟨all⟩ and

20 October 1868, Jefferson, to James M. Comly. 3 pp. A.l.s. OHi.

14 five *w.o. illeg.*   17 itself, ⟨at⟩   38 ↑home↓   43 in ⟨illeg.⟩
43 ⟨bef⟩ belief   44 ↑and yours,↓

31 October 1868, Cambridge, to William C. Howells. 3 pp. A.l.s. MH.

17 ⟨would⟩ ↑was↓   30 ⟨I⟩ ever   34 ↑change↓   35 to be *w.o.* to to
45 ↑if↓   64 Mrs.... hers.] [*a closing parenthesis encloses the two-line postscript*]

13 November 1868, Cambridge, to James R. Lowell. 1 p. A.l.s. MH.

22 November 1868, Cambridge, to Aurelia H. Howells. 2 pp. A.l.s. MH.

19 miss ↑him↓   21 ↑he↓ must   25 ⟨glad⟩ pleasure
33 Thursday *w.o.* Wed   37 ⟨l⟩ criticism   37 ↑book↓   42 ⟨your⟩ her
56 has *w.o.* is   62 ↑the↓

24 November 1868, Cambridge, to Bayard Taylor. 2 pp. A.l.s. NIC.

20 December 1868, Boston, to William C. Howells. 4 pp. A.l.s. MH.

9 have ⟨alw⟩   10 ⟨always have,⟩ now   25 ⟨real⟩ sickness
31 summer⟨s⟩   54 isn't *w.o. illeg.*   59 size⟨d⟩

17 January 1869, Boston, to William C. Howells. 4 pp. A.l.s. MH.

14 time *w.o. illeg.*   22 ⟨a⟩way   23 left *w.o. illeg.*   34 sketch⟨es⟩

TEXTUAL RECORD 447

24 January 1869, Boston, to William C. Howells. 4 pp. A.l.s. (with 1 p. enclosure) MH.

    7 ↑man↓   25 ↑and... deeper.↓   26 ⟨exect⟩ executed   27 an⟨y⟩
37 there ⟨wo⟩   43 ⟨it⟩ is

31 January 1869, Boston, to William C. Howells. 4 pp. A.l.s. **MH**.

    6 men ⟨ju⟩   7 ↑on↓   10 bad⟨s⟩   11 l⟨e⟩ast   12 ↑me↓
28 ↑a balance↓   41 now] no   42 ⟨*illeg.*⟩ turn   61 ↑the↓ deer

7 February 1869, Boston, to William C. Howells. 4 pp. A.l.s. **MH**.

    12 preacher ⟨were⟩   14 dictionary *w.o.* dictionaries   27 ↑you↓
32 influenza *w.o.* influence   62 sent *w.o.* send
68 Monday.... printer.] [*above salutation, first page*]

21 March 1869, Cambridge, to Thomas B. Aldrich. 1 p. A.l.s. **MH**.

    7 ↑an↓ acquaintance   11 Bad *w.o.* bad

28 March 1869, Cambridge, to William C. Howells. 5 pp. A.l.s. **MH**.

    14 ⟨ice⟩ waters   20 ↑they↓   21 ⟨ab⟩ obsolete
29 delivered *w.o.* lilivered   30 ⟨k⟩now   42 ⟨let⟩ look
45 always ⟨*illeg.*⟩   55 ↑one↓

5 April 1869, Cambridge, to James A. Garfield. 2 pp. A.l.s. **DLC**.

    12 ↑thought↓   15 ↑you↓   16 ↑will↓

Ca. 15 April 1869, Cambridge, to Azariah Smith. 1 p. A.l.s. **NjP**.

16 April 1869, Cambridge, to Joseph A. Howells. 3 pp. A.l.s. **MH**.

    7 ↑me↓   14 ↑not↓   28 Apparently, ⟨the⟩   28 climate *w.o. illeg.*

18 April 1869, Cambridge, to William C. Howells. 4 pp. A.l.s. **MH**.

    1–2 Sacramento... April] [*in Elinor Howells' hand*]   8 ↑as↓
10 ⟨y⟩ our   16 ⟨be⟩ please   28 Day *w.o.* day   30 crowed *w.o.* crown
35 ⟨wart⟩ warmth   35 bald *w.o. illeg.*   41 ⟨sorest⟩ ↑sorest↓
42 ⟨feelings⟩ ↑principles↓   52 Recollections *w.o.* recollections

2 May 1869, Cambridge, to William C. Howells. 4 pp. A.l.s. MH.

7 ↑out↓   9 ↑our↓   35 but] but / but   40 ↑away...meadow,↓
44 which] which / which   44 convince *w.o.* conf   47 ↑which...be↓
50 ⟨wh⟩ we   60 the badness *w.o.* their badness
75–80 —Tuesday.... sleep.] [*partly above complimentary close and partly to right of signature, fourth page*]

4 May 1869, Boston, to Bayard Taylor. 1 p. A.l.s. NIC.

16 June 1869, Cambridge [?], to James R. Lowell. 1 p. A.l.s. MH.

4 or Lou*d*oner's *w.o.* — Loudoner's

26 June, 18 and 24 July 1869, Cambridge, to Henry James. 13 pp. A.l.s. MH.

16 ↑ought↓   23 ⟨now⟩ ↑at present,↓   23 present,] ~,,   24 ↑seem↓
28 ↑now↓   35 ↑deal↓   37 ↑is↓   38 ⟨a⟩ ↑some↓   43 well-nigh ⟨*illeg.*⟩
44 ⟨and⟩ but   46 ↑here↓   56 ⟨not⟩ now   76 formerly *w.o. illeg.*
78 ⟨the⟩ times   80 ⟨friend⟩ funeral   89 ⟨last⟩ scene
91 ⟨against⟩ ↑from↓   93 ↑and honoring↓   98 ↑nearly↓   101 ↑since↓
103 ⟨must⟩ ↑miss↓   103 because I] because I I   113 ⟨with⟩ ↑a growth of↓
113 ⟨and⟩ ↑hiding↓   121 "Pedestrian] [*lower case marked by Howells for capitalization*]   128 ↑adverse↓   132 deliver *w.o. illeg.*
135 ↑feeling↓   140 near⟨, to⟩   141 Presentdent," ⟨sh⟩
142 said *w.o.* says   159 In ⟨the⟩   162 learnt *w.o.* ler
168 Europe *w.o.* is   173 see⟨m⟩   174 |let|ter   175 |lost|
175 scraps ⟨that⟩   175 |I in|tended

28 June 1869, Cambridge, to Elinor M. Howells. 4 pp. A.l.s. MH.

6 but ⟨not⟩   9 ↑not↓ [*inserted in another hand*]
23 morning] moning   28 ⟨fans⟩ *fans*   30 man ⟨liv⟩

24 August 1869, Cambridge, to James T. Fields. 4 pp. A.l.s. CSmH.

16 every *w.o. illeg.*   21 ⟨return⟩ ↑run↓   31 ⟨tendernesses⟩ tendernesses
32–33 ⟨*illeg.*,⟩ ↑at once↓   33 glory *w.o.* glorious   36 begun *w.o.* been
41 ↑us↓   49 ↑also,↓   51 ↑good↓   79 Byron⟨'⟩s   81 proof⟨s⟩
87 ↑⟨last⟩↓   90 yourselves *w.o.* yourself

31 August 1869, Boston, to Oliver W. Holmes. 1 p. A.l.s. DLC.

13 oblige⟨,⟩

TEXTUAL RECORD 449

5 September 1869, Boston, to William C. Howells. 4 pp. A.l.s. MH.

19 with ⟨with⟩   20 ↑the↓ poor   25 solids, ⟨and⟩   28 as ⟨it⟩
30 ⟨resp⟩ martyrs   31 ↑them↓   32 part⟨y⟩   38 ⟨*illeg.*⟩ delightful
44 me|.| 47–48 James . . . it.] [*across salutation, first page*]

5 September 1869, Boston, to Thomas W. Higginson. 1 p. A.l.s. NjR.

[*At bottom of page, in Higginson's hand*: In answer to some poems, I had been requested to forward him. T. W. H.]

22 September 1869, Cambridge, to William C. Howells. 4 pp. A.l.s. MH.

8 ⟨needn't⟩ ↑needed↓   15 ↑story↓   21 them *w.o.* it   34 ⟨a⟩ expresses
35 all ⟨already⟩   40 ↑babies.↓

24 September 1869, Cambridge, to James R. Lowell. 2 pp. A.l.s. MH.

8 ↑and old friends↓

2 October 1869, Boston, to Ralph Waldo Emerson. 3 pp. A.l.s. MH.

6 It is so] It so

16 October 1869, Cambridge, to James R. Lowell. 3 pp. A.l.s. MH.

22 Mrs. *w.o. illeg.*   22–23 liberties *w.o.* liberty
33–34 Take . . . affection.] [*across part of second page*]

19 October 1869, Boston, to Edward E. Hale. 2 pp. A.l.s. MNS.

8 ↑that↓   9 The⟨y⟩   10 soared ⟨to⟩   11 ↑let↓

28 October 1869, Boston, to James R. Osgood. 1 p. A.l.s. MH.

4 ↑read↓   4 Shirley⟨'⟩   5 With] with   8 Yet *w.o. illeg.*   8 ↑she↓
10 wedded *w.o.* ma   15 ↑her↓   15–18 P. S . . . . magazine.] [*in margin and across beginnings of lines of letter text*]

7 and 21 November 1869, Cambridge, to Charles E. Norton. 4 pp. A.l.s. MH.

9 of ⟨fr⟩   61 fatigue ↑you↓   63 ⟨l⟩ more   63 hear⟨*illeg.*⟩
72 ⟨*illeg.*⟩ so   74 Cambridge.⟨"⟩   75 ↑–hand↓
82 inexpressibly *w.o.* inexpressible   85 One⟨s⟩   87 Fields⟨'⟩es
93 much ⟨as⟩   106 ⟨read⟩ ↑perceive↓

1 December 1869, Cambridge, to James R. Lowell. 2 pp. A.l.s. MH.

3 The *w.o.* the

24 December 1869, Boston, to Thomas W. Higginson. 4 pp. A.l.s. NN.

15 other⟨s⟩   16 ↑done↓   19 ⟨*illeg.*⟩ device   24 heart ⟨for me⟩
25 saying ⟨I⟩ ↑how↓   30 inexpressibly *w.o.* inexpressible

26 December 1869, Boston, to William C. Howells. 4 pp. A.l.s. MH.

12 inside, ⟨th and⟩—the ⟨whole⟩   27 ↑tinsel↓

2 January and 6 March 1870, Cambridge, to Henry James. 22 pp. A.l.s. (partly in autograph of Elinor M. Howells) MH.

5 ↑of↓   6 ↑think↓   7 ↑in our kitchen,↓   38 read ⟨under⟩
43 inn ⟨up⟩   70 ↑been↓   84 ↑have↓ done   85 Life⟨,⟩
86 things *w.o. illeg.*   89 they're to⟨o⟩   89 lead *w.o. illeg.*
93 March 6 *w.o.* March 1   95 but *w.o.* and   97 the *w.o.* a
100 shut⟨s⟩   104 of her *w.o.* ⟨for of⟩ her   107 a ⟨a⟩bed   109 ↑now,↓
115 talk ⟨about⟩   115 him *w.o.* them   120 ↑love↓   123 me *w.o.* o
127 ⟨The⟩ The   130 a⟨n⟩   134 Mrs. Howells] [*begin Elinor Howells' hand*]   198 as ⟨we⟩   199 Mrs. Howells] [*resume W. D. Howells' hand*]   202 ↑my↓   205–7 Winny....nothing.] [*above salutation, first page*]

17 March 1870, Boston, to Thomas W. Higginson. 2 pp. A.l.s. NN.

10 ↑especially the P. S.↓

2 May 1870, Boston, to Thomas W. Higginson. 2 pp. A.l.s. NN.

22 May 1870, Cambridge, to James R. Lowell. 7 pp. A.l.s. MH.

11 Cerberean *w.o. illeg.*   24 ↑truth, the↓   25 wholly *w.o.* all
30 These *w.o.* This

30 October 1870, Cambridge, to William C. Howells. 4 pp. A.l.s. MH.

18 to⟨o⟩ twenty-five   24 it⟨s⟩   29 ⟨Of⟩ Ohio
32–36 you are....letter.] [*across salutation and letterhead, first page*]

27 November 1870, Boston, to William C. Howells. 4 pp. A.l.s. MH.

15 lectures *w.o.* let   20 been] been / been   23 ⟨go⟩ going
29 poem *w.o. illeg.*   37 ⟨*illeg.*⟩ saint

TEXTUAL RECORD 451

11 December 1870, Boston, to William C. Howells. 4 pp. A.l.s. MH.

7 launched] lauched   21 a] a / a   27 ↑in some things.↓
38 ⟨pres⟩ breakfast   46 ↑him↓

23 December 1870, Cambridge, to Henry W. Longfellow. 1 p. A.l.s. PHi.

4 me *w.o.* it

7 January 1871, Boston, to Thomas W. Higginson. 2 pp. A.l.s. NN.

6 not ⟨not⟩

22 January 1871, Boston, to William C. Howells. 4 pp. A.l.s. MH.

11 lives] [*possibly* lines]   24 be *w.o. illeg.*   25 hinting *w.o.* hinted
31 can't ⟨yo⟩   32 well] will   35 ↑good↓

1 March 1871, Boston, to Thomas W. Higginson. 2 pp. A.l.s. NN.

7 ⟨wit⟩ we   13 Mr. *w.o. illeg.*   15 worth ⟨worth⟩   [*at bottom of first page, below signature, in Howells' hand*: (over)]

5 March 1871, Boston, to William C. Howells. 4 pp. A.l.s. MH.

[*A newspaper clipping, with the following text, is pasted over part of the letterhead*: Mr. F. Bret Harte arrived in this city about eleven o'clock Saturday forenoon, and went immediately to the residence of Mr. W. D. Howells in Cambridge. Mr. Harte is accompanied by his family, consisting of his wife and two children. *Immediately below appears the word* Advertiser *in an unknown hand.*]

9 ⟨beg to⟩ beg   10 ⟨him⟩ It   11 ⟨*illeg.*⟩ custom   13 and ⟨*illeg.*⟩ is
21 he *w.o. illeg.*   26 ↑the triumph of↓

11 March 1871, Boston, to Sarah Orne Jewett. 2 pp. Letter and signature in an unknown hand. MH.

3 ⟨sure⟩ ↑secure↓

1 April 1871, Boston, to James R. Osgood. 2 pp. A.l.s. CtY.

13 ⟨coll⟩ colossal   14 ⟨*illeg.*⟩ set

21 April 1871, Boston, to Will M. Carleton. 3 pp. A.l.s. NRU.

4 ↑have↓

3 May 1871, Boston, to Edmund C. Stedman. 2 pp. A.l. NNC.

5 ⟨k⟩now   15 ↑me↓   19 in ⟨a⟩ New   20 talk.] [*complimentary close and signature excised*]

4 May 1871, Boston, to Thomas W. Higginson. 1 p. A.l.s. NN.

8 ⟨essay⟩ enemies

7 May 1871, Cambridge, to William C. Howells. 4 pp. A.l.s. MH.

24 ⟨made⟩ ↑might↓   25 out ⟨B⟩   27 ↑man↓   30 ↑joke↓
33 ⟨contl⟩ control

3 June 1871, Jefferson, to Elinor M. Howells. 12 pp. A.l.s. (partly in autographs of Anne T. and William C. Howells) MH.

6 ⟨utterly⟩ ↑scarcely↓ ⟨un⟩able   9 had *w.o.* have   11 well *w.o.* will
13 ⟨*illeg.*⟩ and go   17 Annie] [*begin A. T. Howells' hand*]
31 prospects.] ~,   34 She...travelling,] [*in W. D. Howells' hand*]
34 and everybody] [*resume A. T. Howells' hand*]   38 house.] ~,
39 her⟨e⟩ things   49 To *w.o.* to   64 ⟨The⟩ Noble *w.o.* noble [*W. D. Howells' correction*]   70 family.] ~,   73 did *w.o.* could
77 looking, *w.o.* looking— [*W. D. Howells' correction*]
77 —He was] [*resume W. D. Howells' hand*]   78 amused⟨,⟩
78 foreigner] foreign-/   84 I was] [*begin W. C. Howells' hand*]
84 of the] of/of the   85 Their *w.o.* their   86 Wedding *w.o.* wedding
89 closely *w.o.* Closely   91 she ↑at↓ [*in W. D. Howells' hand*]
92 ↑she↓ [*in W. D. Howells' hand*]   95 pair⟨, who⟩   96 husband⟨,⟩
98 there *w.o. illeg.*   98 lank⟨,⟩   101 told ⟨h⟩
104 potatoes, ⟨to⟩ ↑went...took↓ [*in W. D. Howells' hand*]
107 look.⟨'⟩   107–8 His wife...mother] [*in margin; insertion marked by asterisks; W. D. Howells' hand resumes here*]   114 ↑could↓
125 even *w.o.* every   126 the⟨se⟩   129 not.] ~   130 ⟨boy⟩ by

2 July 1871, Boston, to John S. Hart. 3 pp. A.l.s. (with 1 p. enclosure) NIC.

5 ↑the↓   11 ⟨a few⟩ ↑two↓   12 later,⟨—⟩
15–16 on March *w.o.* in March   19 have ⟨had⟩ to
23 ⟨a⟩ Latin *w.o.* latin   32 ⟨Follett⟩ Follett   36 Co.⟨,⟩
38 ↑New York↓   44–45 I had...for me.] [*on verso of first page*]

12 August 1871, Boston, to James A. Garfield. 3 pp. A.l.s. DLC.

11 ↑need↓ not   17 ↑and...capital↓   21 papers at] ~.~

TEXTUAL RECORD 453

23 September 1871, Boston, to Ralph Keeler. 4 pp. A.l.s. CLSU.

9 bigl↑i↓etto   21 Every *w.o.* every   28 The⟨y⟩   35 which ⟨were⟩

5 October 1871, Boston, to Anne T. Howells. 4 pp. A.l.s. MH.

22 ↑except↓   29 as *w.o.* at   29 ⟨on⟩ soon   39 ⟨hard⟩ hard
43 The . . . envelope.] [*above salutation, first page, and preceded by pointing hand*]

22 October 1871, Boston, to James M. Comly. 4 pp. A.l.s. OHi.

12 send *w.o.* sent   21 It's ⟨all⟩   24 ↑am↓

22 October 1871, Boston, to William C. Howells. 4 pp. A.l.s. MH.

26 and ⟨if⟩ she   30–32 I send . . . anywhere.] [*across letterhead, first page*]

8 November 1871, Boston, to James R. Osgood. 2 pp. A.l.s. Gordon N. Ray, New York.

9 containing] contain/taining

12 November 1871, Boston, to William C. Howells. 4 pp. A.l.s. MH.

7 ↑some↓

19 November 1871, Boston, to William C. Howells. 4 pp. A.l.s. MH.

20 Creek! *w.o.* Creek?

26 November 1871, Boston, to Hjalmar H. Boyesen. 4 pp. A.l.s. ViU.

14 a *w.o.* as   19 ⟨excellent⟩ ↑extremely↓

3 December 1871, Boston, to William C. Howells. 4 pp. A.l.s. MH.

6 easily ⟨*illeg.*⟩

30 December 1871, Boston, to Robert Carter. 1 p. A.l.s. NN.

8 ↑me↓   8–9 ↑on . . . East↓

31 December 1871, Boston, to Bayard Taylor. 3 pp. A.l.s. NIC.

4 ⟨styles⟩ still

3 January 1872, Boston, to James R. Osgood. 3 pp. A.l.s. CaQMM.

 8 simply *w.o.* symply 9 ↑or . . . fotografs↓ 17 Mantua *w.o. illeg.*

28 January 1872, Boston, to William C. Howells. 4 pp. A.l.s. MH.

 7 fact⟨s⟩ 16 owe *w.o.* own 16 to ⟨my⟩ ↑the↓
21 ⟨charable⟩ charitable 23 ⟨to⟩ never 27 June,] ~„
27 ↑will . . . she↓

16 February 1872, Boston, to Thomas W. Higginson. 2 pp. A.l.s. NN.

25 February 1872, Boston, to William C. Howells. 4 pp. A.l.s. MH.

 6 because ⟨it⟩ 18 ↑seen↓ 24 that there *w.o.* than there
25 will ↑and↓ 29 time.⟨,⟩ 31 ⟨*illeg.*⟩ resources 37 ↑all↓

19 March 1872, Boston, to Hjalmar H. Boyesen. 4 pp. A.l.s. ViU.

 20 ↑*No don't*—either.↓ 23 ⟨*illeg.*⟩ make 24 ↑poem↓

8 April 1872, Boston, to William C. Howells. 4 pp. A.l.s. MH.

 6 ↑last↓

16 April 1872, Boston, to Whitelaw Reid. 2 pp. A.l.s. DLC.

 5 to *w.o.* h

20 April 1872, Boston, to Anne T. Howells. 3 pp. A.l.s. MH.

7 May 1872, Boston, to Aurelia H. Howells. 4 pp. A.l.s. MH.

 15 so *w.o. illeg.* 19 ↑the sculptor↓ 26 dined ⟨with⟩
34 delicious.] ~

25 May 1872, Boston, to Lucy Larcom. 1 p. A.l.s. NjP.

31 July 1872, Boston, to Franklin B. Sanborn. 4 pp. A.l.s. NjR.

 5 by *w.o.* the 5 proof *w.o. illeg.* 12 ↑of↓ this
21 contemporaneous *w.o.* contemporary

25 August 1872, Cambridge, to Franklin B. Sanborn. 4 pp. A.l.s. MCo.

 6 ↑the↓ Canvass 12 ↑conscientiously↓

8 September 1872, Cambridge, to Joseph A. Howells. 4 pp. A.l.s. OFH.

12 ↑name↓

22 September 1872, Boston, to William C. Howells. 4 pp. A.l.s. MH.

15 ↑hope↓   20 bricklayer⟨'⟩s

20 October 1872, Boston, to James R. Osgood. 2 pp. A.l.s. MH.

24 October 1872, Boston, to Edmund C. Stedman. 4 pp. A.l.s. NNC.

11 literary *w.o.* literat   18 properly *w.o.* probably   25 like ↑you↓
26 ⟨l⟩ announce

28 October 1872, Boston, to Henry James. 4 pp. A.l.s. MH.

11 and ⟨that⟩ the   12 ↑and↓ good   32 other ⟨day⟩   32 ↑met↓
38 been *w.o. illeg.*   45–48 from .... Howells.] [*across salutation, first page*]

3 November 1872, Boston, to S. Weir Mitchell. 3 pp. A.l.s. PU.

3 Doctor *w.o.* Sir

6 November 1872, Boston, to Edmund C. Stedman. 2 pp. A.l.s. NNC.

10 ↑now↓

13 November 1872, Boston, to Charles W. Stoddard. 3 pp. A.l.s. CSmH.

15 what ⟨shape and⟩   18 worth *w.o. illeg.*

16 November 1872, Boston, to Hjalmar H. Boyesen. 1 p. A.l.s. ViU.

7 December 1872, Boston, to Hjalmar H. Boyesen. 3 pp. A.l.s. ViU.

7 ↑in↓   10 naturalness *w.o.* naturally   17 ↑had↓
18 needn't *w.o.* needed

26 December 1872, Cambridge, to James L. Graham, Jr. 4 pp. A.l.s. NNCenC.

3 ↑you↓   4 reached me] reached

29 December 1872, Boston, to Hjalmar H. Boyesen. 4 pp. A.l.s. ViU.

4 ↑letter↓   18 ↑done↓   19 rest *w.o. illeg.*

31 December 1872, Boston, to James A. Garfield. 4 pp. A.l.s. **DLC**.

5 |he| 5 |pos|sibly   6 |nei|ther   7 Cong|res|sional
9 |Ministry| 11 origi|nal| 12 |mem|oirs   13 |documents|
22 Librar|ian| 23 inter|est| 23 ↑yourself↓

Word-Division

In the two lists below, entries are keyed to the line numbers of the letter texts; the line-count includes all lines of type of a letter proper, beginning at the internal address or dateline. List A records compounds and possible compounds hyphenated at the end of the line in the authorial document or extant transcription used as copy-text for the present edition, and indicates how these end-line hyphenated forms have been resolved. If the compounds occur in consistent form elsewhere in the authorial document or in other such materials of the same general period in time, including literary manuscripts, then resolution was made on that basis; if these other occurrences are inconsistent, resolution was based on the form in closest proximity in time to the possible compound in question. If neither of these resources was sufficient, then resolution was based on the evidence of published texts of Howells' works or on the prevalent usage of the period. List B is a guide to transcription of compounds or possible compounds hyphenated at the end of the line in the present text: compounds recorded in this list should be transcribed as given; words divided at the end of the line and not listed should be transcribed as one word.

LIST A

25 July 1852, to W. C. French	41	mountain-growth
9 and 11 September 1857, to D. Dean	7–8	*frater-meus*
9 and 11 September 1857, to D. Dean	44	-be-sufficiently-
9 and 11 September 1857, to D. Dean	66	beefsteak
2 January 1859, to V. M. Howells	19	Odd-Fellow's
23 January 1859, to V. M. Howells	10	homesickness
23 January 1859, to V. M. Howells	24	after-appearance
18–24 April 1859, to V. M. Howells	30	common-sensible
18–24 April 1859, to V. M. Howells	46	midnight
6 November 1859, to W. C. Howells	6	antislavery
13 November 1859, to A. T. and A. H. Howells	14	proslavery
1 September 1860, to O. W. Holmes, Jr.	32	thorn-crowned

12 September 1860, to A. T. Howells	31	thanksgiving
14 November 1860, to O. W. Holmes, Jr.	3–4	pen-and-
25 November 1860, to O. W. Holmes, Jr.	6	post-office
25 November 1860, to O. W. Holmes, Jr.	7–8	mutton-chop
24 December 1860, to J. R. Lowell	4	meadow-stream
6 January 1861, to O. W. Holmes, Jr.	40	two-ahead
17 January 1861, to J. R. Lowell	14	-before-dropping-
24 March 1861, to V. M. Howells	14–15	village-life
24 March 1861, to V. M. Howells	37	Bowling-green
7 September 1861, to W. C. Howells	3–4	office-seeking
31 October 1861, to W. C. and M. D. Howells	8	whole-hearted
31 October 1861, to W. C. and M. D. Howells	38	passports
7 December 1861, to W. C. Howells Family	63	half-inch
7 December 1861, to W. C. Howells Family	97	prepaid
18 and 21 January 1862, to V. M. Howells	59	hackmen
27 January 1862, to J. J. Piatt	39	easy-going
27 January 1862, to J. J. Piatt	125	half-dollar's
13 June 1862, to W. C. Howells	40	sea-port
15 March 1863, to W. C. Howells	87	sketch-book
15 March 1863, to W. C. Howells	95	draw-back
18 September 1863, to M. D. and E. D. Conway	30	proof-readers
25 October 1863, to C. Hale	41	to-morrow
9 December 1863, to J. A. Howells	11	postman
24 December 1863 to C. Hale	16	handwriting
26 January 1864, to M. D. Conway	9	ill-naturedly
26 January 1864, to M. D. Conway	37	to-morrow
2 December 1864, to A. T. Howells	15	overtaken
28–29 January 1865, to A. T. Howells	22	orange-buds
28–29 January 1865, to A. T. Howells	45	sea-gulls
28–29 January 1865, to A. T. Howells	52	patty-cake
24 December 1865, to W. C. Howells	23	right-hand
25 May 1866, to C. E. Norton	14	trotting-buggy
27 May 1866, to E. C. Stedman	43	to-morrow
17 June 1866, to V. M. Howells	13	sweet-briar
19 June 1866, to M. D. Howells	14	-in-law
23 June 1866, to C. E. Norton	11–12	fig-leaves
5 December 1866, to E. C. Stedman	6	over-praised
31 July 1867, to C. E. Norton	38	foreman

WORD-DIVISION

13 July 1868, to M. D. Howells	8	night-fall
20 December 1868, to W. C. Howells	66	Doorstep
7 February 1869, to W. C. Howells	49	hunting-party
28 March 1869, to W. C. Howells	8	bluebirds
28 June 1869, to E. M. Howells	13	to-morrow
24 August 1869, to J. T. Fields	39	Earthquakes
28 October 1869, to J. R. Osgood	5	bad-girl
7 and 21 November 1869, to C. E. Norton	31	brain-fever
1 December 1869, to J. R. Lowell	10	innermost
1 December 1869, to J. R. Lowell	12	many-sided
2 January and 6 March 1870, to H. James	31	post-office
2 January and 6 March 1870, to H. James	145	simple-hearted
2 January and 6 March 1870, to H. James	165	poverty-stricken
22 January 1871, to W. C. Howells	28	super-subtle
5 March 1871, to W. C. Howells	24	to-day
21 April 1871, to W. M. Carleton	10	self-restraint
21 April 1871, to W. M. Carleton	20	country-life
8 April 1872, to W. C. Howells	15	terrestrial-minded
16 April 1872, to W. Reid	3	advance-sheet-

LIST B

9 and 11 September 1857, to D. Dean	7–8	*frater-meus*
14 August 1859, to J. A. Howells	19–20	-hopper-eaten
1 September 1860, to O. W. Holmes, Jr.	32–33	bas-relief
14 November 1860, to O. W. Holmes, Jr.	3–4	pen-and-
25 November 1860, to O. W. Holmes, Jr.	7–8	mutton-chop
17 January 1861, to J. R. Lowell	13–14	just-before-
24 February 1861, to O. W. Holmes, Jr.	52–53	thin-skinned
24 March 1861, to V. M. Howells	14–15	village-life
7 September 1861, to W. C. Howells	3–4	office-seeking
27 January, 1862, to J. J. Piatt	24–25	phrase-books
7 March 1862, to W. C. Howells	60–61	country-life
12 September 1862, to W. C. Howells	59–60	anti-slavery
18 May 1863, to A. H. Howells	14–15	Iron-holder
17 December 1863, to W. C. and M. D. Howells	12–13	women-servants
25 August 1864, to W. C. Howells	113–14	gas-light

2 December 1864, to A. T. Howells	26–27	burial-ground
19 September 1865, to E. M. Howells (2nd letter)	22–23	To-morrow
28 January 1866, to W. C. Howells	39–40	eye-teeth
19 June 1866, to M. D. Howells	13–14	son-in-
23 June 1866, to C. E. Norton	11–12	fig-leaves
23 June 1866, to C. E. Norton	19–20	spring-fishes
10 August 1867, to C. E. Norton	8–9	book-notices
6 March 1868, to W. C. Howells Family	12–13	fruit-knife
6 March 1868, to W. C. Howells Family	22–23	proof-reading
7 July 1868, to J. M. Comly	30–31	canker-wormy
15 August 1868, to J. R. Lowell	6–7	half-holiday
29 August 1868, to C. E. Norton	31–32	re-established
20 December 1868, to W. C. Howells	52–53	half-past
24 January 1869, to W. C. Howells	53–54	chicken-pox
19 October 1869, to E. E. Hale	14–15	proof-reader
24 December 1869, to T. W. Higginson	10–11	book-making
2 January 1870, to H. James	117–18	Fisher-maiden
3 June 1871, to E. M. Howells	64–65	ice-creams
5 October 1871, to A. T. Howells	15–16	grape-culture
28 January 1872, to W. C. Howells	22–23	half-minded
19 March 1872, to H. H. Boyesen	7–8	love-passage
16 April 1872, to W. Reid	3–4	-Atlantic-N. Y.-
3 November 1872, to S. W. Mitchell	5–6	psycho-physiological
13 November 1872, to C. W. Stoddard	7–8	low-down

FAMILY GENEALOGIES

The Howells Family

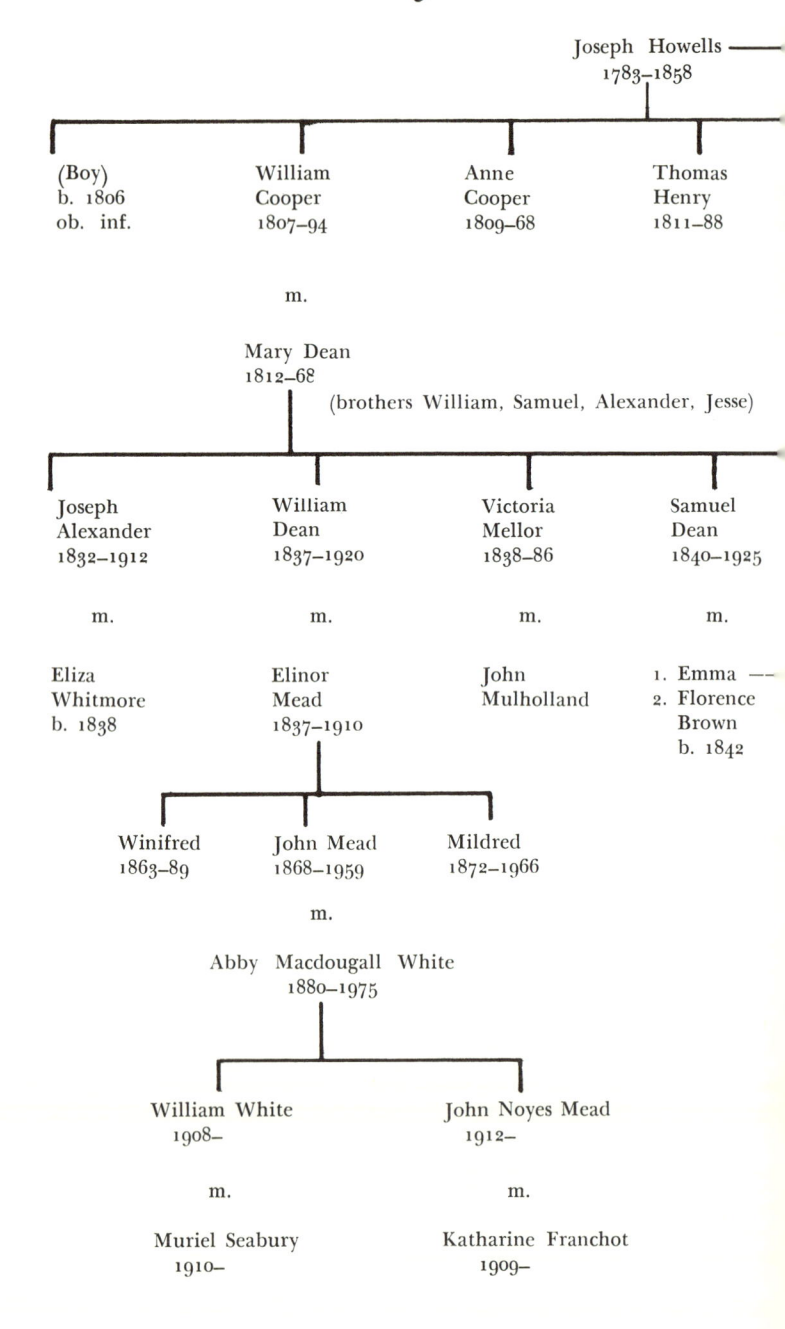

Joseph Howells
1783–1858

(Boy)	William	Anne	Thomas
b. 1806	Cooper	Cooper	Henry
ob. inf.	1807–94	1809–68	1811–88

m.

Mary Dean
1812–68

(brothers William, Samuel, Alexander, Jesse)

Joseph	William	Victoria	Samuel
Alexander	Dean	Mellor	Dean
1832–1912	1837–1920	1838–86	1840–1925

m. m. m. m.

Eliza	Elinor	John	1. Emma
Whitmore	Mead	Mulholland	2. Florence
b. 1838	1837–1910		Brown
			b. 1842

Winifred	John Mead	Mildred
1863–89	1868–1959	1872–1966

m.

Abby Macdougall White
1880–1975

William White	John Noyes Mead
1908–	1912–

m. m.

Muriel Seabury   Katharine Franchot
1910–   1909–

───── Ann　Thomas
　　　　1782–1863

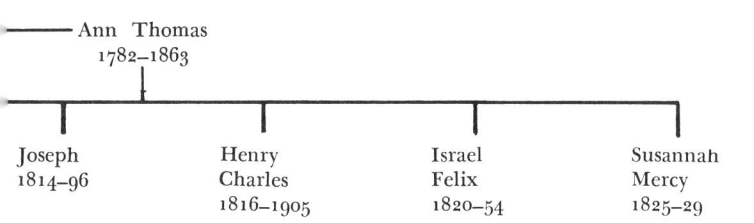

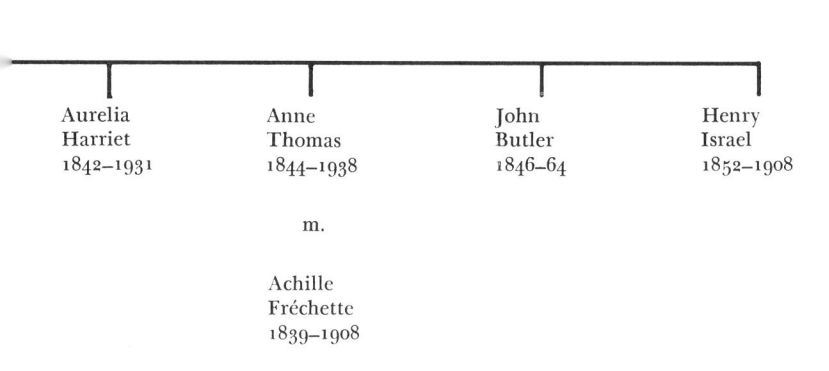

Joseph　　　Henry　　　　Israel　　　Susannah
1814–96　　Charles　　　Felix　　　Mercy
　　　　　 1816–1905　　1820–54　　1825–29

Aurelia　　　Anne　　　　John　　　　Henry
Harriet　　　Thomas　　　Butler　　　Israel
1842–1931　　1844–1938　　1846–64　　1852–1908

　　　　　　　m.

　　　　　　Achille
　　　　　　Fréchette
　　　　　　1839–1908

463

The Mead Family

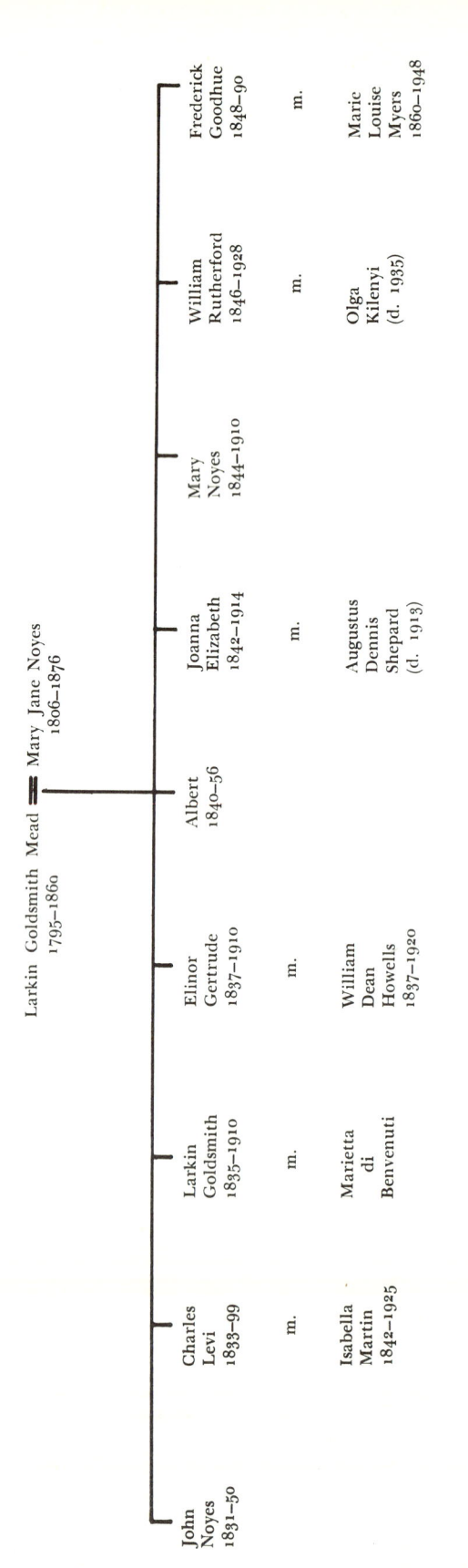

Larkin Goldsmith Mead = Mary Jane Noyes
1795–1869   1806–1876

John Noyes 1831–50	Charles Levi 1833–99	Larkin Goldsmith 1835–1910	Elinor Gertrude 1837–1910	Albert 1840–56	Joanna Elizabeth 1842–1914	Mary Noyes 1844–1910	William Rutherford 1846–1928	Frederick Goodhue 1848–90
	m.	m.	m.		m.		m.	m.
	Isabella Martin 1842–1925	Marietta di Benvenuti	William Dean Howells 1837–1920		Augustus Dennis Shepard (d. 1913)		Olga Kilenyi (d. 1935)	Marie Louise Myers 1860–1948

Biographical Notices

BENVENUTI, MARIETTA DI. See Larkin Goldsmith Mead, Jr.

BROWN, FLORENCE. See Samuel Dean Howells.

DEAN, MARY, wife of William Cooper Howells and William Dean Howells' mother. She was living in Wheeling, [West] Virginia, when she married in 1831. Evidence suggests her early disappointment in her husband's quixotic career and a strong desire to give her children the financial stability that she began to achieve after the move to Jefferson, Ohio, in 1853.

DEAN, WILLIAM (and brothers Samuel, Alexander, and Jesse). Steamboat captains and owners. Much admired by Howells, the Dean uncles were evidently men of substance.

EMMA ―――――. See Samuel Dean Howells.

FRÉCHETTE, ACHILLE. See Anne Thomas Howells Fréchette.

FRÉCHETTE, ANNE THOMAS HOWELLS, sister of Howells. In 1877 she married Antoine Léonard Achille Fréchette, a Canadian journalist and official translator at Parliament. With Howells' constant interest, she published fiction and essays. She had one son (Howells Fréchette) and one daughter (Marie Marguerite Fréchette).

HOWELLS, ANN COOPER, sister of William Cooper Howells. She did not marry and lived with her parents until their deaths.

HOWELLS, ANN THOMAS. See Joseph Howells.

HOWELLS, AURELIA HARRIET, sister of Howells. She did not marry and largely devoted her adult life to the care of her father and her retarded brother Henry.

HOWELLS, HENRY CHARLES, brother of William Cooper Howells. A dentist in Hamilton, Ohio, he had at least one son ("cousin Henry," who later lived in New York) and three daughters.

HOWELLS, HENRY ISRAEL, youngest brother of Howells. An accident in early childhood left him mentally incompetent and sometimes violent.

HOWELLS, ISRAEL FELIX, brother of William Cooper Howells. A druggist in Dayton, Ohio, he married and had probably four children.

HOWELLS, JOHN BUTLER, brother of Howells. He died while attending school in Cleveland, when his brother was in Venice.

HOWELLS, JOHN MEAD, son of Howells. He achieved distinction as an architect. In 1907 he married Abby Macdougall White, by whom he had two sons, William White Howells and John Noyes Mead Howells.

HOWELLS, JOSEPH, father of William Cooper Howells. He came to Boston from Wales in 1808, attempted to set up woolen mills, eventually moved to Hamilton, Ohio, where he ran a drugstore until his death. In England he married Ann Thomas, the orphaned daughter of a schoolmaster, also Welsh. After her husband's death she lived briefly in Jefferson and then near Bowling Green, Ohio.

HOWELLS, JOSEPH, JR., brother of William Cooper Howells. A physician in Hamilton, Ohio, he married but apparently had no children.

HOWELLS, JOSEPH ALEXANDER, older brother of Howells. Journalist and politician, he succeeded his father as editor of the Ashtabula *Sentinel*. In 1856 he married Eliza Whitmore, by whom he had two sons and three daughters (William Dean II, Mary Elizabeth, Beatrice Rebecca, Bernice, and Joseph Alexander, Jr.).

HOWELLS, MILDRED, younger daughter of Howells. A poet and artist, she mostly devoted herself to the collection of her father's archives after his death.

HOWELLS, SAMUEL DEAN, brother of Howells. His varied and lacklustre career included dentistry and an appointment in the government printing office in Washington. He married Emma ―――― about 1866, was divorced in 1868, and in the same year married Florence Brown. He had one son and four daughters.

HOWELLS, SUSANNAH MERCY, sister of William Cooper Howells. She died in early childhood.

HOWELLS, THOMAS HENRY, brother of William Cooper Howells. Reputed to be the wealthiest of the brothers, he may have been married but apparently had no children.

HOWELLS, VICTORIA MELLOR, the favorite sister of Howells. In 1883 she married John Mulholland, who deserted her. She died of malaria three years later.

HOWELLS, WILLIAM COOPER, father of Howells. Printer and politician, he established himself as editor of the Ashtabula *Sentinel* and as a wellknown figure in the Ohio Republican party. He served as U. S. consul in Quebec and Toronto, briefly turned to farming in Virginia, and was a lifelong ardent Swedenborgian.

HOWELLS, WINIFRED, daughter of Howells. Of unusual artistic talent, she suffered both physically and psychically in the last ten years of her life.

KILENYI, OLGA. See William Rutherford Mead.

MARTIN, ISABELLA. See Charles Levi Mead.

MEAD, ALBERT, son of Larkin Goldsmith Mead, Sr.

MEAD, CHARLES LEVI, son of Larkin Goldsmith Mead, Sr. He married Isabella Martin, by whom he had four children.

MEAD, ELINOR GERTRUDE, daughter of Larkin Goldsmith Mead, Sr., and wife of Howells, whom she married in 1862. A native of Brattleboro, Vermont, she was related to several wellknown New England men, including John Humphrey Noyes and Rutherford B. Hayes. She was of frail health during most of her married life, took an interest in painting and drawing, and acted as a privately influential critic of her husband's work.

MEAD, FREDERICK GOODHUE, son of Larkin Goldsmith Mead, Sr. He married Marie Louise Myers, by whom he had a son and two daughters.

MEAD, JOANNA ELIZABETH, daughter of Larkin Goldsmith Mead, Sr. She married Augustus Dennis Shepard, for many years an officer of the American Banknote Company of New York. They had six children.

MEAD, JOHN NOYES, son of Larkin Goldsmith Mead, Sr.

MEAD, LARKIN GOLDSMITH, SR., father-in-law of Howells. A lawyer, he founded the first bank and the first town library in Brattleboro, Vermont.

MEAD, LARKIN GOLDSMITH, JR., son of the senior Mead. A sculptor who lived most of his adult life in Italy, he married Marietta di Benvenuti, of Venice, in 1866. They had no children.

MEAD, MARY NOYES, daughter of Larkin Goldsmith Mead, Sr. Unmarried, she frequently visited the Howellses.

MEAD, WILLIAM RUTHERFORD, son of Larkin Goldsmith Mead, Sr. A partner in the wellknown architectural firm of McKim, Mead & White, he married Olga Kilenyi in 1884. They had no children.

MULHOLLAND, JOHN. See Victoria Mellor Howells.

MYERS, MARY LOUISE. See Frederick Goodhue Mead.

NOYES, MARY JANE, wife of Larkin Goldsmith Mead, Sr. Married about 1829, she was the sister of John Humphrey Noyes, the founder of the Oneida community.

SHEPARD, AUGUSTUS DENNIS. See Joanna Elizabeth Mead.

WHITE, ABBY MACDOUGALL. See John Mead Howells.

WHITMORE, ELIZA. See Joseph Alexander Howells.

List of Howells' Correspondents

The following alphabetical list of Howells' correspondents provides page references for (1) letters written by Howells TO others and (2) letters FROM others addressed to Howells. Page numbers in italic type indicate letters appearing in full or as fully as the source permits; page numbers in roman type indicate letters cited in footnotes, with "cited" used broadly to mean quotation from a letter, description of part of its contents, or mention of it whether printed in this edition or not. The few cited letters *about* Howells, e.g., from Lowell to Hawthorne, appear not in this list but in the main index.

Aldrich, Thomas B., TO *318*
Atlantic, Editors of, FROM 42, 43

Babb, Edmund B., FROM 8
Bailey, Gamaliel, TO *18*
Barney, Hiram, TO 162
Boyesen, Hjalmar H., TO *384–85*, *392–93*, *393–94*, *407*, *408*, 409, *410*; FROM 410
Brunetta, Eugenio, FROM 215

Carlton, Will M., TO *368*; FROM 368
Carter, Isabella E. (Mrs. F.), TO *393*
Carter, Robert, TO *387*
Chase, Salmon P., TO *131–32*, *160–62*; FROM 162
Cincinnati *Gazette*, Editors of, TO *59*
Clark, John S., FROM 293
Comly, James M., TO 82, *263–64*, 277, 277, *293–94*, *294–95*, 295, *302–3*, *380*
Conway, Ellen D. (Mrs. M. D.), TO 109, *159*
Conway, Moncure D., TO 109, 136, *145–46*, *155–56*, 156, *158–59*, 160, *174–76*, 176, *186–88*, 188, *276–77*, 277; FROM 143, 146, 156, 158, 160, 176, 188
Cooke, Henry D., FROM 82

Dall'Ongaro, Francesco, FROM 237
Dean, Dune, TO *10–12*, 35
Dean, William B., TO 289
Dodge, Mary A., TO *52–53*, 82

Eliot, Charles W., FROM 333, 334
Emerson, Ralph W., TO 337, *341–42*

Fields, James T., TO *58–59*, 225, *247*, *249*, *269*, *273*, *279*, *282*, *334–36*; FROM 247, 250, 279
Foster, Frank E., TO 136, 137; FROM 136, 137, 167, 170, 192, 193
French, William C., TO *6–7*
Friends, sixteen, FROM 70
Fullerton, Artemas T., TO *53–54*

Garfield, James A., TO *320*, *376*, 379, *411*; FROM 411
Godkin, Edwin L., FROM 383
Graham, James L., Jr., TO 133, *136–37*, *144*, 144, 302, *409*
Graham, R. M. C., TO 409
Green, Harvey, TO *15–17*
Green, Jane (Mrs. H.), TO *15–17*

Hale, C. & Co., FROM 211
Hale, Charles, TO *134–35*, *146–47*, 148, *152–53*, 154, 156, 162, *162–64*, *164–65*, 165, 173, *173–74*, 174; FROM 136, 148, 164, 165, 174, 184, 185, 211
Hale, Edward E., TO *210–11*, 343
Hamilton, Gail. See Dodge, Mary A.
Harper & Brothers, TO *179–80*
Hart, John S., TO *375–76*
Harte, Bret, FROM 363, 365, 398
Harvard College, document FROM 218
Hay, John, FROM 81, 231, 362
Higginson, Thomas W., TO 270, 339, *348–49*, 356, 356, *356–57*, *362–63*, 365, 369, 391; FROM 270, 391, 402
Hillard, George S., FROM 291
Holmes, Oliver W., TO 337, *337–38*; FROM 289, 337, 338

469

Holmes, Oliver W., Jr., TO 61–62, 64–65, 65, 65–67, 67, 69, 69–70, 72–74, 78–79, 85–86, 140, 336; FROM 74
Howells, Anne T., TO 10, 29, 39, 49–50, 63, 100–102, 170, 190–91, 203–4, 207–9, 209, 285–86, 289–90, 293, 307, 315, 377, 378–79, 381, 387, 393, 395–96, 396
Howells, Aurelia H., TO 10, 29, 39, 49–50, 115, 149–50, 306–7, 317, 393, 396–97
Howells, Elinor M., TO 227–28, 228, 228–29, 229–30, 230–31, 231, 231–32, 232, 232–33, 234–35, 237–38, 238, 262, 338, 339, 347, 350, 358, 371–74, 371, 387
Howells, John B., TO 24, 24–25, 150–52, 156–57
Howells, Joseph A., TO 8, 15, 18, 39–40, 56–57, 137, 157, 167–70, 321–22, 392, 400
Howells, Mary D., TO 35, 38–39, 77, 79, 79, 80, 82, 87–88, 88–89, 109, 112, 115, 121, 148–49, 154–55, 170, 171, 202–3, 213–14, 225, 261–62, 279–81, 286–87, 289, 290, 295–96
Howells, Samuel D., TO 181–83, 183, 188–89
Howells, Theodora, TO 90
Howells, Victoria M., TO 8, 9, 10, 13–14, 19–20, 21–22, 22–23, 24, 24–25, 28–29, 30–32, 32, 33–35, 35, 35–37, 37, 48, 75–77, 77–78, 88, 90, 102–5, 109, 113–15, 115, 116, 117, 119, 121, 123, 129–31, 149, 170, 184–85, 260–61, 288–89, 295, 302, 393
Howells, William C., TO 47–48, 48, 48–49, 49, 50, 80, 82–83, 87–88, 89, 102, 109, 109–12, 112, 115, 116–19, 119–21, 121–22, 123, 123–24, 124, 124–26, 126, 137–40, 140–43, 143, 144, 149, 165–66, 170, 171, 171–73, 192–93, 196–99, 199–201, 205–6, 211–12, 212, 213–14, 215, 216, 218–19, 220, 220, 222–24, 225, 226, 235, 239–40, 240, 248–49, 249, 250–51, 251, 262, 272, 273–74, 274, 275, 278, 278, 290, 300–301, 302, 303–5, 305, 308, 309–10, 311–12, 312–13, 313, 314–15, 316–17, 318, 318–19, 321, 322–24, 324, 324–26, 338–39, 339–40, 349–50, 355, 358–59, 359, 359–60, 360, 360–61, 362, 363–64, 364, 365–66, 366, 370–71, 371, 378, 380, 381, 382–83, 383–84, 384, 385–86, 386, 387, 390, 390, 391–92, 394, 401, 401, 408, 409
Howells, William C., family, TO 54–55, 57, 95–97, 97–99, 100, 109, 116, 119, 123, 286, 292–93, 302, 317
Howells, Winifred, TO 299–300, 300
Hunter, William, TO 128, 221–22

Hurd, Melanchthon M., TO 260, 264–65, 266, 267–68, 291, 291, 332; FROM 265, 268, 291, 332

Jackson, Mrs. Frances M., FROM 237
James, Henry, Jr., TO 399; FROM 284
James, Henry, Sr., TO 328–32, 350–55, 404–5, 405
Jewett, Sarah O., TO 366–67, 367

Keeler, Ralph, TO 377–78

Larcom, Lucy, TO 398
Longfellow, Henry W., TO 362; FROM 267, 362
Lowell, James R., TO 60–61, 67–68, 69, 69, 71, 193–96, 205, 217–18, 218, 224, 235–37, 297, 305, 327, 341, 342–43, 347–48, 357–58; FROM 58, 61, 68, 72, 196–97, 199, 225, 233–34, 237, 297, 299, 305, 327–28, 332, 341, 358
Lowell, John A., FROM 359

Masson, David, FROM 67
Mead, Larkin G., Sr., TO 132, 134
Mead, Mary J. N. (Mrs. L. G., Sr.), TO 402
Mitchell, S. Weir, TO 405; FROM 406
Motley, John L., TO 216–17; FROM 106

Nicolay, John G., TO 74–75, 80–81, 81
Norton, Charles E., TO 240–41, 253–54, 255, 256–57, 257, 258–59, 261, 262–63, 281–82, 282–83, 297–99, 326, 341, 344–47; FROM 314, 315

Osgood, James R., TO 344, 367, 380, 382, 384, 389, 402

Parker, Benjamin S., TO 252
Parton, James, FROM 410–11
Payne, Daniel C., FROM 128
Piatt, John J., TO 26–27, 40–41, 42–43, 43–44, 45, 45–46, 53, 81–82, 83, 105, 106–9, 209–10, 326; FROM 82, 109
Potter, Martin D., TO 19
Price, Samuel, FROM 170

Reid, Whitelaw, TO 386, 395; FROM 255, 395

Sanborn, Franklin B., TO 398–99, 399, 399–400, 400, 405
Seward, Frederick W., TO 127, 127, 128, 201–2, 202, 206–7, 231
Seward, William H., TO 85, 86, 87, 216
Smith, Azariah, TO 321

Smith, Ellen, TO 30
Smith, Dr. Samuel M., TO 85; FROM 85
Smith, Mrs. Samuel M., TO *83–85*
Smith, William H., TO 8, *51*, 52
Speck, W. A., TO 362
State, Department of, FROM 127, 128
Stedman, Edmund C., TO 78, *176–78*, *251*, 254, *254–55*, *266*, *271*, *284–85*, 326, *369*, *403*, 403, *406*; FROM 78, 178, 179, 252, 255, 271
Stoddard, Charles W., TO *406–7*; FROM 407
Stoddard, Elizabeth (Mrs. R. H.), TO 267; FROM 254, 255, 267

Taylor, Bayard, TO 105, *128*, *307–8*, *326–27*, *388*, 388; FROM 129, 266–67, 327
Ticknor and Fields, TO 69; FROM 250
Ticknor, H. M., TO 115; FROM 119, 164
Treasury, Department of, TO 102
Trollope, Anthony, FROM 220–21
Trübner & Co., TO 185–86, 188; FROM 186, 214–15

Whipple, Edwin P., TO 269; FROM 269
Winter, William, FROM 55
Wyman, Don L., TO 225–26, 275

Index

This index records all names of persons, organizations, monuments, ships, hotels, public buildings, and titles of magazines and books (the last recorded under the names of their authors, if known). It excludes the names of relatives of Howells' correspondents when they are mentioned for the primary purpose of sending love or minor information; the titles, journals, or publishers of post-1920 criticism and scholarship; and geographical names and government divisions. Some topics are listed as independent entries, but most can be found under Howells' name, where information is divided into two major lists: WORKS and TOPICS. The TOPICS section is further subdivided.

Within entries, the general order of information is: brief and/or general references; citation of correspondence other than that with Howells (e.g., Lincoln to Theodore Canisius); works by that person, including reviews and presumably unpublished work; and descriptive modifications, arranged in ascending page order. Finally, the frequent occurrence of some dozen entries has required the use of "passim" (e.g., "*Atlantic*, WDH as assistant editor and contributor, 191, 245–375 passim").

Italic numbers designate pages on which significant biographical information is given. An asterisk preceding an entry indicates that a full record of correspondence between Howells and the person or institution so marked is provided in the separate "List of Howells' Correspondents," pages 469–71, where the headnote explains its arrangement.

Abbott, George J., *87*
About, Edmund, *King of the Mountains* (reviewed by WDH), 70
Abraham and Isaac, 16
Accademia di Belle Arti, Florence, 133
Accademia di Belle Arti, Venice, 134, 146
Achilles, 395
Adam, 401
Agassiz, Elizabeth C. (Mrs. J. L. R.), 281, *282*; "A Dredging Excursion...," 335, 336
Agassiz, Jean L. R., 281, *282*, 366
Agricultural Society, Lake County, Ohio, 165, 166
Aldine Press, 137
*Aldrich, Thomas B., 177, 246, 378, 409; *Ballad of Babie Bell and Other Poems* (reviewed by WDH), 43; *Out of His Head*, 179; *The Story of a Bad Boy* (reviewed by WDH), 318; chats with WDH, 251, 252; and J. R. Dennett, 308; and B. Taylor, 308; dines with Lowell, 392; lunches with WDHs, 394

Aldrich, Mrs. Thomas B., 280, 409
Alger, William R., review(?) of *Venetian Life*, 264, 265
Allen, Isaac J., 80, 264, 294, 295
Allen, W. R., *13*
American Bank Note Co., 228
American Pioneer, 317
American Social Science Association, 399
Amphitheatre, Roman, Verona, 181
Andrews, John W., 28, *30*
Angell, Dr. and Mrs. Henry C., 251, 252, 313
Annie Maggie (animal or toy), 306, 307
Anthony, Miss, 30–31, 32, 34, 36
Anthony, St., feast at Padua, 116, 117, 119
Appleton, Thomas G., 256, 257, 391
Appleton's Journal, 387
Armenian Convent, Venice, 174
Arms, George. *See* Gibson-Arms.
Asia (ship), 223
Ashburner, Anne, 263, 350, 404, 405
Ashburner, Grace, 263, 350, 404, 405

INDEX

Ashtabula(?) *Reporter*, 170
Ashtabula *Sentinel*, articles and developments of interest to WDH, 3–401 passim; publishes WDH European letters, 85–123 passim
Ashtabula *Telegraph*, 6, 7, 29, 30, 31, 32, 170; and Abel Krum, 40; and W. C. Howells, 155, 165, 166, 278
Associated Press, Western and New York, 51
Aston, Isaac C., 21
Athenaeum (London), 239; reviews *Venetian Life*, 258, 259, 260
Athenaeum Club, New York, 228
"Athenaeum lectures," Columbus, 68
Atlantic, publishes WDH's poems, 4, 41–139 passim, 147, 153, 275, 375; WDH on November 1857 issue, 17, 18; WDH plans to send poem, 22; publishes Piatt poem, 26, 27; WDH proposes story, 58, 59; WDH asks for assistant editorship, 59; WDH reviews November 1860 issue, 64, 65; C. Hale essay published, 146, 148; Venetian sketches and other MSS by WDH rejected, 155, 162–63, 164, 172, 187, 194, 195; WDH as assistant editor and contributor, 191, 245–375 passim; payments compared, 211; rejects D. L. Wyman's poems, 225; WDH as editor and contributor, 246, 275–411 passim
*Atlantic, Editors of.
The Atlantic Almanac for *1870*, publishes WDH's "Bopeep," 67; publishes Lowell essay, 343
Augusta, 191
Augustus, Caesar, 181
Austin, James C., 270
Auerbach, Berthold, *Edelweiss* (trans. E. Frothingham), 322

*Babb, Edmund B., *8*, 20, 21, 49
*Bailey, Gamaliel, *18*, 53
Baleormini, Mr. and Mrs., 210
Baleormini, Mrs., 104, 105
Baldwin, Clara, 33, 35
Baldwin, Margaret H. (Mrs. W. J.), 33, 35
Baldwin, William J., 33, *35*
Balliol College, 402
Ballou, Ellen, 378
Baltimore and Ohio Railroad, 57
Bancroft, H. H., 119
Banks, Nathaniel P., 187, *188*
Barbaro, Candiano, 146, *148*
Barbaro, Francesco, 146, 148

Baring-Gould, W. S. and C., 63
Barnes, Frank, 7
*Barney, Hiram.
Barrozzi, Signor, 105, 106
Bates, Annie, 301
Bascom, W. T., 75
Beecher, Henry W., *Life of Jesus the Christ*, 383
Beethoven, Ludwig van, 136
Bellini, Vincenzo, *I Puritani* (opera), 105
Belmont County, Ohio, *Chronicle*, 401
Benedict, George A., 20, *21*
Benjamin, 46, 47
Beppi, 149
Bernard, 253
Bethune, George W., 153, *154*
Bethune, Mary W. (Mrs. G. W.), 153
Bettina, 191, 208, 223, 233
Bible, 383, 390
Bible Society, New York, 250
Bigelow, John, 58, *59*
Bigelow, Marshall T., 259, *260*, 279
Bigler, William, 126, *127*
Billings, Josh (pseud.). See Shaw, Henry W.
Bishop, H. R., "My Boat Is on the Shore" ("To Thomas Moore," comp.), 33, 35
Bjornson, Bjornstjerne, 355; *Arne*, 355; *A Happy Boy*, 355; *The Fisher-Maiden* (reviewed by WDH), 383
Black, John, *Memoires de M. Goldoni*, 143
Blackwood's, 14, 15, 119
Bloss, Clara, 10, 16
Bloss, Jim, 9, 10
Blum, Robert, 50
Blumenthal, Mr., 127, 128, 221
Bocher, Ferdinand, 333
Börne, Karl L., 10, 11, *13*
Bologna, Giovanni da, statue by, Florence, 179, *180*
Bonner, Robert, 211, 312, *313*
Booth, Edwin T., 354, 355; at J. L. Graham's, 234, 235; article on by Stedman, 251
Booth, John W., 234, 235
Boston *Advertiser*, 366, 388; publishes "Letters from Venice," 85, 94, 123, 135–219 passim; publishes C. Hale letters, 164; reviews *Venetian Life*, 264, 269
Boston *Atlas*, 212
Boston *Commonwealth*, 159, 192, 277, 399; publishes WDH's "A Poet," 143;

INDEX 475

"By the Sea," 145, 146; "Venice Come True," 158, 160; notices *Round Table*, 176, 178; publishes Conway letters, 187
Boston *Continental Monthly*, 108, 109
Boston *Courier*, 46
Boston fire of 1872, 407, 408
Boston Public Library, 265
Boston *Transcript*, reviews *Venetian Life*, 269
Botta, Vincenzo, *Dante* (reviewed by WDH), 228
Boucicault, Dion, *Rip Van Winkle* (play), 355
Bouterwek, F., *Historia de la literatura española*, 275
*Boyesen, Hjalmar H., "The Bride of Torresdale," 410; "Gunnar," 393, 408, 410; "Legend of the Midnight Sun" (working title), 410; "The Mountain-Taken Maid," 410; "A Norse Stev," 384–85; poem set in print but rejected by WDH, 408, 409; review of Jonas Lie's book, 392, 393; review of C. S. P. Peterson's book, 407, 408; "St. Olaf's Fountain," 410; encouraged by WDH, 246, 385, 410; rejections by WDH, 385, 392–93, 407; visits WDH, 393
Bowen, Henry C., 364
Bowles, Samuel, 365
Bragg, Braxton, 170
Bridge of Sighs, 108
Bridget, dismissed for madness, 324–25
Broadway (London), 376
Brooks, Mr., 136, *137*
Brown, Florence. *See* Howells, Florence B.
Brown, Harrison B., 87, *88*, 97
Brown, John, 83, 272, 273; WDH's attitude, 48–49, 54–55; WDH's comment to sisters, 50
Brown, John, Jr., 48, 272, 273, 379
Brown, Thomas, 9, *10*
Browne, Charles F., 99, *100*, 397; "Sayings," 100
Browne, Mr., 391–92
Browne, S. E., 75
Browning, Elizabeth B., 403, 406
Browning, Robert, 160, 276, 403; letter to Conway cited endorsing WDH's poetry, 155, 156; *Sordello*, 187, 188; reviewed by Conway, 158, 160
*Brunetta, Eugenio, 93, 215
Bryant, William C., 59
Buckingham Palace, 96
Buckle, Thomas, 146, 148
Bullard and Lee, 254

Bullard, William S., 253, *254*, 345–46
Bulwer-Lytton, Edward G. E., 66; *The Last Days of Pompeii*, 181, 183; *Pelham, or The Adventures of a Gentleman*, 41; *What Will He Do with It?* 14, 15
Bundy, James M., *Are We a Nation?* 365; *State Rights*, 365
Burnett, Mabel L. (Mrs. E.), 394
Butterfield and Haven, 262
Byron, George G., 152, 245, 334, 336, 340, 344; "My Boat Is on the Shore" ("To Thomas Moore"), 33, 35

Cabot, Mrs., 324
Cadwell, Darius W., *18*, 21, 22, 125, 126, 370, 371
Cadwell, Mrs. Darius W., 16, 18, 23
Cadwell, Clara G., *18*
Cady, Edwin H., 3, 5, 32, 49, 52, 85, 274, 406
Cambridge *Chronicle*, 344
Cameron, Simon, 128, *129*, 160, 162
Campanile, Venice, 101, 108
Campbell, Alexander, *315*
Campbell, Thomas, *The Life of Petrarch*, 283, 284
Canisius, Theodore, 98, *100*; letter from Lincoln cited, 100
Cantù, Cesare, *Storia della letteratura italiana* (reviewed by WDH), 275
Caparra, Niccolò, 179
Capograssi, Countess. *See* Przemysl, Miss.
*Carlton, Will M., "Betsey and I Are Out," *368*; "Cover Them Over" (rejected by WDH), 368
Carlyle, Thomas, *The French Revolution*, 64, 65, 393
Carrington, H. B., 75
Carter, Annie, 24, 31, 32, 33, 63
Carter, Francis, *24*, 32
Carter, Francis, family, 63, 115, 150, 239
*Carter, Isabella E. (Mrs. F.), 4, 23–28 passim, 31–34 passim, 76, 99, 100, 103, 105, 150; visits Urbana, 55; sends WDH cold letter, 115; on Elinor M. Howells, 120, 121; on vastation, 314
*Carter, Robert, *387*
Cary, Richard, 367
Capitol, U.S., Washington, 147
Catholic Orphan's Home, Columbus, 37
Cedar Mountains, Battle of, 122, 123
Century Army and Navy Chronicle, 46
Century Club, New York, 228
Cervantes, *Don Quixote*, 68, 69

Cestius, Caius, Tomb of, 204
Chambourg, Count of, 139
Chapin, James H., *From Japan to Granada...*, *144*
Chapman & Hall, 158, 160, 176
Charley (W. C. Howells' horse), 280, 306, 307, 317
Chase, Janette R., *132*
Chase, Katherine. See Sprague, Katherine C. (Mrs. W.).
*Chase, Salmon P., 20, 109, 215, 216, 277; WDH calls on, 22, 229, 230; lends WDH book, 26, 27; gives party for J. R. Giddings, 31, 32; advocate of WDH, 81
Chatrian, Alexandre. See Erckmann-Chatrian.
Chattanooga, Battle of, 170
Chesebro', Caroline, "The Foe in the Household," 334, 335, 336
Chicago *Inter-Ocean*, 396
Chicago *Journal*, 398
Child, Francis J., 257, 340, 357, 404; *English and Scottish Ballads* (ed.), 287, 288; *Poems of Religious Sorrow...* (ed.), 316, 317; lectures with WDH, 331, 333, 334, 345
Child, Mr. and Mrs. Francis J., 347
Chispa (early pseud. of WDH), 19
Chaucer, Geoffrey, 177
Christ, Jesus, 62, 390
Christian Examiner, possibly reviews *Venetian Life*, 264
Christianity, 371. See also WDH: Religion.
Cincinnati *Commercial*, 112; WDH applies as correspondent, 19; publishes Conway letters, 192, 193; Piatt articles, 361, 362
Cincinnati *Dial*, publishes WDH's "A Poet," 143; and other poems, 147, 277
Cincinnati *Gazette*, 112, 116; WDH as city editor, 3, 8, 9; as correspondent, 3, 16, 17, 19, 375; and S. R. Reed, 24, 55; and E. B. Babb, 49; and *Poems of Two Friends*, 51, 52; publishes WDH's "Glimpses of Summer Travel," 57, 62; reprints WDH's "Saint Christopher," 172, 173; publishes Conway's letters, 187; and Reid, 255
*Cincinnati *Gazette*, Editors of.
City of Glasgow (ship), 89, 90
Civita Vecchia, consulship, 87, 88
Clapp, Henry, 82, 226; review of *Poems of Two Friends*, 51, 52
Clapp, Otis, 32

*Clark, John S., 292, *293*; and Anne T. Howells, 377, 378, 379, 381
Clarke, James F., "Mohammed...," 335, 336
Clemens, Samuel L., 246, 397, 401; *The Gilded Age* (with Warner), 397; *The Innocents Abroad* (reviewed by WDH), 335, 336
Cleveland *Herald*, 21
Cleveland Institute, 156, 157
Cleveland *Leader*, 211, 212
Cleveland *Plain Dealer*, 100
Clinton Bank, Columbus, 25
Clough, Arthur H., *Poems*, 240, 241
Cobbe, Frances P., *Italics* (reviewed by WDH), 217, 218
Coggeshall, Henry, 239, 240
Coggeshall, William T., 20, 22, 68, 75, 240, 264; "Pay as You Go: A Story for the New Year," 21; *Poets and Poetry of the West* (ed.), *21*, 43, 53; Lowell asked to review, 60, 61
Cologne Cathedral, 223
Coleridge, Samuel T., "A Day-Dream," 28, 29
Columbia National Bank, Pennsylvania, 126
Columbia University, 385
Columbus *Morning Journal*, 265; reviews *Venetian Life*, 263, 264; reviews W. H. Dixon's book, 293
Columbus Review of Medicine and Surgery, 85
Commercial College, Cleveland, 173
Commercial Relations of the United States..., 127
Congregational Church, 141
Colvil, Edward, *Fifteen Days* (reviewed by WDH), 256, 258, 259
*Comly, James M., 255, 265, *293*; review of W. H. Dixon's book, 293; early friendship, 4, *32*, 36, 37, 38, 55; goes to New Orleans, 30, 31; becomes abolitionist, 139; as possible governor, 277
Constant, Wilhelm (early pseud. of WDH), 18
*Conway, Ellen D. (Mrs. M. D.).
*Conway, Moncure D., *143*, 153, 172, 201, 205; letter from R. Browning cited, 155, 156; *Autobiography*, 119, 156; letter announcing WDH's unpublished poems, 192, 193; letters to Boston *Commonwealth* and Cincinnati *Gazette*, 187; review of *The Poetical Works of Robert Browning*, 158, 160, 187; review of *Venetian Life*, 276;

"Venetian Chain," 159, 160; as WDH's literary agent, 94, 185
Cooke, Edward W., 174
*Cooke, Henry D., 32, 47, 111, 220, 294, 295; owes WDH money, 48, 78, 79
Cooke, Mrs. Henry D., 30, 32
Cooke, Jay, 32
Cooke, Jay, & Co., 162
Cooper, James F., 287
Cope, Captain, 400, 401
Corcoran Gallery of Art, Washington, 148
Corcoran, William W., 147, *148*
Cornell University, 323, 336, 385; possible WDH lectures, 257, 358, 359
Cornwall, Barry (pseud.). See Procter, Bryan W.
Corregio, 182
Corwin, Thomas, 47, *48*, 49
Courrier des Etats-Unis, 27
Cowen, Benjamin S., *201*, 212
Cowen, B. R., 75
Cox, Jacob D., 75, 320, *321*
Coyle, William, 18
Cranch, Christopher P., 256, 257
Craven, H. T., *The Needful* (reviewed by WDH), 234, 235
Crawford, L. M. J. M., "Kathleen Marvourneen," 33, 35
Croesus, 98, 210
Croissant, Philip, 31, 32
La Crónica, 27
Crouch, F. W. M., "Kathleen Marvourneen" (comp.), 33, 35
Cutler, Elbridge J., 333

Daily, Mr., 323, 324
*Dall'Ongaro, Francesco, 236, 237; *Poesie* (reviewed by WDH), 249, 250; *Stornelli italiani* (reviewed by WDH), 249, 250
Dalmatian family, 175, 176
Dana, Richard H., Jr., 256, 257; *Two Years Before the Mast*, 257
Danieli, Hotel, Venice, 99, 100
Danish-German War, 189
Dante Alighieri, 177, 263; *The Divine Comedy*, 62, 176, 188, 256, 257, 258, 281, 283, 284; WDH's pleasure in, 145, 195
Dante Club, 254, 256, 258, 261, 272; at Norton's, 274
Dante, Fiesta di, 236, 237
Dare, Shirley, "The Countess Guiccioli," 341
d'Argento, Antonino D., 351

Darley, Felix O., *287*
d'Artois, Henri C. F. M. D. *See* Chambourg, Count of.
Darwin, Charles, 355
Dayton *Journal*, 173
Dayton, William L., 132, *133*
Davidson, Edward H., 382
Davis, Jefferson, 219
Davis, Mrs. Sarah M. H., *The Life and Times of Sir Philip Sidney* (noticed by WDH), 26, 27
Day, Selden, 79, *80*
*Dean, Dune, *13*, 33, 63
Dean, Jesse, 392
Dean, Samuel, 13
Dean, William, and brothers, 8, 9
*Dean, William B., 278, 288
De Forest, John W., *Miss Ravenel's Conversion* (reviewed by WDH), *397*
Delmonico's, New York, 396–97
Dennison, W., 75
de Nerly, Mr., 105, 109
Dennett, John R., *308*, 346, 354, 358; "Howells' Suburban Sketches," 364
DeQuincey, Thomas, *Klosterheim*, 41
Deshler, Ann E. S. (Mrs. W. G.), 25
Deshler, Betsey G. (Mrs. D. W.), 25
Deshler, David W., 25
Deshler National Bank, Columbus, 25
Deshler, William G., 25
Deshler family, 24
Dickens, Charles, 33, 35, 288; "The Christmas Carol," 288; *David Copperfield*, 43, 97, 217, 218; *Dombey and Son*, 288; *Little Dorrit*, 262, 263; *Martin Chuzzlewit*, 50; *Our Mutual Friend*, 195, 196; *Pickwick Papers*, 96, 97, 288; presence in England, 95; meets WDH, 287, 292–93, 293–94; contrasted with WDH, 411
Dickinson, Anna E., *What Answer?* (reviewed by WDH), 306, 307
Disciples of Christ (church), 315
Dixon, William H., *Spiritual Wives* (reviewed by J. M. Comly), 293, 294
Dock, Jacob, 125–*126*
Dock, William, *126*
*Dodge, Mary A., 81, 82; review of *Poems of Two Friends*, 53
Doge's Palace, Venice, 104
Douglas, Stephen A., 277
Drew Theological Seminary, 133
Dryden, John, "Dedication," *Aeneid* (trans.), 281, 282
Ducal Palace, Venice, 142, 174
Durer, Albert. *See* Dürer, Albrecht.

Dürer, Albrecht, 64, 65, 66
Dutch Reformed Church, 154
Dyer, Louis, 401, *402*

East India Co., 134
Ecclesiastes, 323
Edel, Leon, 272
Egan, Pearce, "The Minor Theatres of London," 335, 337
Eldridge, Charles W., 87, *88*, 100
Elena, St., 161
*Eliot, Charles W., 246, 331, *333-34*, 345
Eliot, George, *Adam Bede*, 41; "Janet's Repentance," *Scenes of Clerical Life*, 135, 136; *Romola*, 175, 179
*Emerson, Ralph W., 55; "Illusions," 17, 18; *May-Day and Other Pieces* (reviewed by WDH), 279, 281, 282, 284; meetings with WDH, 4, 246, 281; talks with Conway on WDH, 146; lecture requested, 341-42
Emmanuel parish, Boston, 312, 313
English, W. B., *The Three Fast Men*, 317
Ensign, Josiah D., 16, *17*
Ensign, Kate A. J. (Mrs. J. D.), 13, *15*, 26, 29
Episcopal chapel, Cambridge, 394
Episcopalianism, 7. See also WDH: Religion.
Erckmann-Chatrian, *L'Ami Fritz*, 353, 355
Erckmann, Emile. See Erckmann-Chatrian.
Erie Railroad, 250, 365
Essays and Reviews, 67
Esther Institute, Columbus, 29, 30
Euripides, German trans. by C. T. Gravenhorst, 110; *Medea*, 112
Evans, F. W., "The Autobiography of a Shaker," 319, 320
Eve, 401
Every Saturday, 383; ed. by T. B. Aldrich, 252, 318, 352; publishes WDH's "Mr. Francis Bret Harte," 365; and Anne T. Howells, 375, 376; publishes Anne T. Howells' article, 378, 379; publishes R. Keeler's reminiscences, 377, 378
Examiner (London), reviews *Venetian Life*, 258, 259

Faed, James, 73, 74
Faed, Thomas, 73, 74
Falier, Casa, Venice, 135-89 passim
Faliero, Marino, 145, *146*
Farwell, Mrs., 313

Fassett, Henry, 6, 7, 126
Fechter, Charles A., 354, *355*
Ferguson, Thomas, 36, 37, *38*, 294
Field, David D., 265
Field, John W., *339*, 406
Field, Mrs. John W., 338, *339*
Fields, Annie A. (Mrs. J. T.), 249, 250, 293
*Fields, James T., 71, 86, 305, 318, 319, 405; "At Rydal," 335, 337; as *Atlantic* editor and WDH, 59, 84, 211, 245, 248, 249, 326, 327, 352, 375; and WDH's *Venetian Life* and writings, 224, 225, 257, 265, 309; European trip, 245, 311, 312, 315, 324; and Stedman's contributions, 251, 254, 285; and Dickens, 287, 292, 293; and J. R. Dennett, 308; and James, Sr., 353; retirement as editor, 363, 364; and Harte, 365, 366
Fields, Mr. and Mrs. James T., 278, 310, 346, 409
Fields, Osgood & Co., 304, 311, 312, 321, 360
Fisher, G. P., *Life of Benjamin Silliman* (reviewed by WDH), 259, 260
Fisk, James, 365
Fiske, John, "Light and Darkness," 386, 387; *Myth and Myth-Makers* (dedicated to WDH), 386, 387; "Myths of the Barbaric World," 386, 387; becomes friend of WDH, 353, 354, 355
Fletcher, William, 336
Follett, Foster & Co., and WDH, 37-75 passim, 88, 165, 177, 178, 281. See also Foster, Frank E.
Follett, Oran, 32, 280, 281
Ford's Theatre, Washington, 252
Fortnightly Review, reviews *Venetian Life*, 276, 277
Foscari, Palazzo, Venice, 187, 189
*Foster, Frank E., early association, 30, 32, 42-47 passim; *No Love Lost* negotiations, 94, 158-87 passim; Stedman comment, 178; denounced by WDH, 192, 193, 219. See also Follett, Foster & Co.
Frascati's gaming-place, Paris, 256
Franco-Prussian War, 371
Frank Leslie's Illustrated Newspaper, 354, 356
Franklin Bank, Columbus, 35
Franz Joseph I of Austria, 105, 106, 122
Fréchette, Anne T. (Mrs. A.), 40. See also Howells, Anne T.
Fréchette, Marie M., 40
*French, William C., 7

French, Mansfield, 87, *88*, 108
Freyer, E. L., 54, 55
*Friends, sixteen.
Frost, Robert, 35
Frothingham, Edith, 322
Fuller, Mr., 232, 233
*Fullerton, Artemas T., "The Birthmark," 20; "By the Dead," 20; "Two Years After," 20; early friendship, 4, 22, 25, 37, 294

Galignani's Messenger, 108, 109, 159, 160
Galloway, Samuel, 280, *281*
Gangewar, A. M., 108, *109*
Gannett, Kitty, 135, 136, 153
*Garfield, James A., 215, 240; letter to Lincoln cited, 74, 75; supports WDH consular appointment, 74, 75, 205, 206, 212
Garfield, Mrs. J. A., 350
Garibaldi, Giuseppe, 121, 122, 123, 182
Garrison, Wendell P., review of J. G. Holland's novel, 70
Gazetta di Venezia, 111, 118, 143
Galaxy, 252; publishes WDH's "Clement," 164; Stedman poem, 254, 255; Whitman poem, 285; James story, 328, 332; "The Countess Guiccioli," 344
Genesis, 47
Georgius (W. C. Howells' pet or servant), 50, 51
"German Columbus Republican," 31, 32
Ghibellines, 188
Gibson-Arms, 21, 22, 54, 55, 59, 62, 78, 85, 135–36, 202, 220
Gibson, William M. See Gibson-Arms.
Giddings, Joseph A., 87
Giddings, Joshua R., 3, *17*; at S. P. Chase party, 31, 32; speech on John Brown, 48, 49; death, 190, 191
Giddings, Joshua R., family, 16
Giddings, Laura Ann, 16, 17
Giddings, Lura Maria, 16, 17
Giles, Chauncey, *Lectures on the Nature of the Spirit*, 390
Giles, Henry, "The Egotist in Life," 335, 336
G-ll-tt, Ell-n, 16, 17
Gilman, James R., 109
Gilmore, P. S., 328
Giovanna, 135, 136, 155, 171; excursion with WDHs, 149
Giustiniani, Palazzo, Venice, 185, 186–87, 189
Glenn, Joseph, 52, 59

Godey's Lady's Book, 17, 18, 374
*Godkin, Edwin L., 398; "French Canada," 298–99; "The Labor Crisis," 281, 282; first acquaintance with WDH, 231, *232*, 237, 238, 239; employment of WDH, 245; on "Minor Topics," 250, 251; later associations, 283, 370, 382, 383
Goethe, Johann W. von, 30, 62, 234; *Elective Affinities (Die Wahlverwandtschaften)*, 31, 32, 33, 34; *Faust*, 64–65, 129, 362
Golden Book of the Republic (of Venice), 105, 106
Golden Cross Hotel, London, 95, 97
Goldoni, Carlo, 93, 134, 136, 275; *Memorie de Carlo Goldoni...*, 142, 143
Goldsmith, Oliver, *The Vicar of Wakefield*, 29, 30
Gomez, José, *Historia de la literatura española* (trans.), 275
Goodale House, Columbus, 9, 10, 13
Goodrich, William, *287*, 288
Gould, G. M., 78
Gould, Jay, 365
Graham, James, 26
Graham, Miss, 23, 25, 26
*Graham, James L., Jr., *134*, 265, 266; returns to New York, 178, 179; entertains WDH, 227, 228, 234, 235; gift of book, 409
Graham, Mrs. James L., Jr., 133, *137*, 144, 178, 179, 228, 409
Graham, James L., Jr., family, 251
*Graham, R. M. C.
Grant, Frederick D., 331
Grant, Ulysses S., 170, 189, 311, 312, 320, 323–24, 400; WDH writes "The Next President," 245; Grant kisses Winifred, 331
Gravenhorst, C. T., *Griechisches Theater*, 110, 112
Great Eastern (ship), 84, 85
"The Greek Soldier," 55, 56
*Green, Harvey, 208; notice of WDH's "Gnadenhütten," 322; obituary on Mary D. Howells, 303, 305; early friendship and marriage, 4, 9, 10, 14
*Green, Jane (Mrs. H.).
Greene, George W., 258, *259*, 262, 287
Greene, J. H. See Green, Harvey.
Greene, Miss, 25
Greenwood, Grace (pseud.). See Lippincott, Sarah Jane (Clarke).
Greeley, Horace, 395, 399, 400, 401

Griswold, M. W., 157
Grossi, Tommaso, *Marco Visconti*, 275
Grove, George, 340, *341*
Guarini, Giovanni B., *Pastor Fido*, 215
Guelphs, 187, 188
Guernsey, Alfred H., *180*, 219, 220
Gurney, Ephraim W., 283, *284*, 354, 355
Guerrazi, Francesco, *Assedio di Firenze*, 215; *La Battaglia di Benevento*, 215; *Isabella Orsini*, 215
Guiccioli, Countess, 344
Günzberg, Dr., 116, 119, 169, 171

Haines, Daniel, 315
Haines, Elisha, 315
*Hale, C., & Co.
*Hale, Charles, *135*, 194, 211; letters on Egypt, 163, 164; "Personal Reminiscenses of the Late Thomas Buckle," 146, 148; visits in Venice, 184, 190, 193
*Hale, Edward E., 211; "The Brick Moon," 334, 336, 343, 344; "Life in the Brick Moon," 343, 344; *Old and New* (ed.), 352, 354
*Hamilton, Gail (pseud.). See Dodge, Mary A.
Hamilton, Sir William, *Lectures on Logic* (noticed by WDH), 66, 67; *Lectures on Metaphysics*, 67, 71, 72
Hamilton *Journal-Daily News*, 30
Hannah, 358, 359, 361
Hannay, James, "Douglas Jerrold," 17, 18
Harlow, Virginia, 405
*Harper & Brothers, 249, 397
Harper, Joseph W., *397*
Harper's Ferry, raid on, 48, 49
Harper's Monthly, 108; publishes WDH's "Editor's Easy Chair" (on Piatt), 27; "Editor's Study" (on C. Kinney), 43; "Editor's Study" (on J. G. Nicolay and Hay), 75; "Editor's Study" (the series), 397; "Overland to Venice," 88; "The Royal Portraits," 115, 126, 229, 231; "Saint Christopher," 158, 160, 161, 162, 172, 173, 176; "Sweet Clover," 126, 231; "A Young Venetian Friend," 215; a Dickens novel, 196; rejects WDH's "Forlorn," 180; "A Visit to Petrarch's House at Arquà," 229
Harper's Weekly, publishes L. G. Mead, Jr., drawings, 179, 183
*Hart, John S., *376*
Hart, Mary E. *See* Loomis, Mary E. H. (Mrs. G.).
*Harte, Bret, "Concepcion de Arguello," 398; *The Luck of Roaring Camp*, 354, 355; *Overland Monthly* (ed.), 354, 355; will not succeed J. T. Fields, 363–64; seen in New York, 397
Harte, Bret, family, visits WDHs, 246, 363, 365–66
Hartford *Courant*, 397
Harvard Magazine, 62, 64, 65, 66, 70
*Harvard College (or University), 257, 274, 282, 284, 295, 402; attended by C. M. Sturgis, 84, 85; Class-day, 263; WDH lectures at, 333–34, 345, 350, 357; Emerson's course, 342
Harvard College Library, 265
Hassaurek, F., *Four Years Among Spanish Americans* (reviewed by WDH), 291
Hawthorne, Julian, 382
Hawthorne, Nathaniel, letter from Lowell cited, 58, 61; *The Blithedale Romance*, 363; *Our Old Home*, 267, 268; *The Scarlet Letter*, 380, 385; *Septimius Felton*, 380, 382, 385; visited by WDH, 4, 60; his analytical fiction, 66; death, 199; compared with WDH, 289, 362; compared with James, 331
Hawthorne, Sophia (Mrs. N.), 382
Hawthorne, Una, 382
*Hay, John, *81*, 82, 205, 206, 215; *Abraham Lincoln: A History* (with J. G. Nicolay; reviewed by WDH), 75; early friendship, 4, 246; seen in New York, 397, 398
Hayes, Rutherford B., 340, *341*
Haynes, 314
Hazewell, Charles C., 279
Hecker, Matilda, 248
Hedge, Frederick H., *The Primeval World . . .*, 349, 350
Heine, Betty, 46, 47
Heine, Heinrich, 134, 275; "Nachtgedanken," 46, 47; *Reisebilder*, 10, 13, 34, 35; *Romantische Schule*, 44, 45, 62; *Salon II: Zur Geschichte der Religion . . .* (noticed by WDH), 67; "Der Traum," 45; unnamed book, 33; influence on WDH, 4, 26, 41, 42, 107, 145, 195, 226, 276; lecture on by WDH, 68, 70; attitudes of WDH and Lowell, 71, 72, 197; sentimentality of, 342
Hendry, William, 54, 55
Hicks, Mr. and Mrs., 163, 164
Higginson, Anna, 289, *290*
Higginson, Laura, 270
*Higginson, Thomas W., 245, 290, 339, 349, 402; *Malbone*, 318; "On an Old Latin Text-Book," 369; review of H.

Hunt's *Verses*, 362, 363; review of *Memoir... of Margaret Fuller Ossoli*, 349; review of E. S. Phelps's *Hedged In*, 356; "A Shadow," 356

Hilen, Andrew, 74

*Hillard, George S., *Six Months in Italy*, 265, *291*

Hildreth, Arthur, 153

Hildreth, Richard, 128, *129*, 137, 153, *212*; *History of the United States*, 129; *The Slave: or Memoirs of Archy Moore*, 129

Hinton, Richard J., *83*, 104, 303, 379

Hinton, Mrs. Richard J., 104

Hoar, Ebenezer R., 320, *321*

Holland, Josiah G., *Bitter-Sweet*, 226, 227; *Miss Gilbert's Career* (reviewed by W. P. Garrison), 70

Holman, Ellen, 12, 29, 30

Holmes, John, 283, *284*, 341, 392

*Holmes, Oliver W., 59, 194, 195, 228, 246, 284, 341, 392; *The Autocrat of the Breakfast Table*, 17, 18, 57; *Elsie Venner* ("The Professor's Story" noticed by WDH), 64, 65; "Nearing the Snow-Line," 237; "The Poet at the Breakfast Table," 385; volume by, 134; meetings with WDH, 4, 61; at Parker House, 57, 58, 69, 84, 224; at Dante Club, 256; at Saturday Club, 281; his analytical fiction, 66; believes in H. B. Stowe article, 335, 336, 337; parodied by B. Taylor, 388

*Holmes, Oliver W., Jr., *62*, 78, 79, 84; "Notes on Albert Durer," 64, 65, 66; "Plato," 64, 65, 69, 70

Home, Daniel D., 319, *320*

Homer, 323

Hood, Thomas (1799–1845), *403*

Hood, Tom (1835–1874), *403*

Hook, James, "Morning," 33, 35; "Night," 33, 35; "Noon," 33, 35

Hoppin, Augustus, 368, 380, 384, 389

Horton, Edwin J., *295*, 303, 305

Hoskins, Noah, 36, *38*

Houghton, Henry O., 268

Howe, Mark A. DeW., 70, 79, 299, 305

Howell, James, ...*Signorie of Venice*, 174, 176, 409

Howells, Anne Cooper (WDH's aunt), 15

*Howells, Anne T. (WDH's sister), 5, 287; letter from Elinor cited, 378; "Frightened Eyes," 286, 307; Chatauqua letter (unpublished), 381; "Jaunty" (MS?), 285, 286, 292, 307; "The Jefferson Light Artillery," 200, 201; "Lame Turkey's Tragedy" (MS?), 290; "Letters from a Country Post Office" (unpublished), 395–96; "Notes of a Quick Trip," 387; "A Tour in a Basket" (unpublished), 387; "A Visit to Put-in-Bay Island," 378–79; Washington letter (unpublished), 381; education, 28, 76, 173; described, 166; soldier fiancé, 207, 208, 209; writing criticized and encouraged by WDH, 285–86, 315, 361, 384; visits with WDHs, 272, 274, 278, 396; as Washington correspondent, 376, 379, 381, 382, 383, 385–86; model for WDH character, 387. *See also* Fréchette, Anne H. (Mrs. A.).

Howells, Anne Thomas (WDH's grandmother), visit by WDH, 76, 77, 84; illness, 118, 119; death, 169, 170, 172; in W. C. Howells' memoir, 366

*Howells, Aurelia H. (WDH's sister), 5, 104, 205, 359; invited to Venice, 169, 184–85, 199; visits WDHs, 250, 322, 324, 333; described, 364

Howells, Charles E. (WDH's cousin), 87, 88, 106, 108, 239, 240

Howells, Edward (WDH's cousin), visit to Venice, *193*, 199, 208, 209

*Howells, Elinor M. (WDH's wife), 122–26 passim, 146–51 passim, 157, 159, 253, 341, 393; letter to W. C. Howells cited, 206; letter to Anne T. Howells cited, 378; "Diary, Venetian" (MS), 204–5, 210, 212; meeting WDH and engagement, 5, 58, 76, 77, 85, 119–20, 121; marriage, 93–94, 130, 132; early months in Venice, 138, 139, 140, 141; illustrations for *No Love Lost* and "Saint Christopher," 137–87 passim; sketches and illustrations, 137, 142; copy of painting, 153, 158, 161, 168, 173, 193, 316; of Mary D. Howells, 386; health, 149, 171, 218–19, 286, 404; Winifred born, 171; relatives visit in Venice, 190, 191; entertains Harte family, 246, 366; religious interests, 141, 247, 390; visits to Brattleboro, 278, 309, 328, 330; gift of peacock, 279–80; John born, 297, 298; her miscarriage, 319; Mildred born, 400, 401; praises James story, 404

Howells, Eliza W. (Mrs. J. A.; WDH's sister-in-law), 10, 157, 169, 220; has son, 8; has child(?), 340

Howells, Florence B. (Mrs. S. D.; WDH's sister-in-law), marriage, 300, 302; has child(?), 340

INDEX

Howells, Henry C. (WDH's uncle), 88, 157, 193, 273, 274, 384; dentist, 77; sees WDH in New York, 240

Howells, Henry C., Jr. (WDH's cousin), 99, 100, 102, 126, 229, 240; WDH visits in New York, 87, 88, 89; WDH's attitude toward, 169, 170, 227; return from Europe, 248, 249

Howells, Mr. and Mrs. Henry C., Jr., 5, 306; visited by WDH, 397, 398

Howells, Henry I. (WDH's brother), head injury, 33; Victoria's devotion to, 76; fluctuations in condition, 149, 286, 319; described, 167

Howells, Howard (WDH's cousin), 384

Howells, Israel (WDH's uncle), 89

Howells, J. A., & Co., 185, 212, 218

*Howells, John B. (WDH's brother), 5, 197, 203, 204, 205; illness, 20, 21; hunting, 25; death, 94, 188; death commented upon, 190, 191, 192, 198, 213, 214

Howells, John M. (WDH's son), 306, 307; birth, 235, 246, 297–98, 302; described, 304, 305; temperament, 309, 310, 313, 340, 356; illness, 314, 353; WDH's affection for, 323, 330, 331; activities, 349, 360, 361, 394

Howells, Joseph (WDH's grandfather), 77, 366

Howells, Joseph, Jr. (WDH's uncle), 15

Howells, Joseph (WDH's cousin), 14, 15

*Howells, Joseph A. (WDH's brother), 5, 10, 15, 280, 289, 290; Hamilton sketch (partly written), 321; letters about New England, 296, 297; "The Metis Disaster," 400, 401; printing interests, 6, 7, 32; has son, 8; visits to WDH in Columbus and to WCHs, 33–34, 306, 400, 401; money and WDH, 38, 102; suggests poem on rafting, 118; and draft, 123, 124, 196, 197, 198, 199; publishing ventures, 169, 170, 192, 219, 224, 225; trips, 218, 287; similarity to B. Harte, 266; post-office appointment, 216–17, 322

Howells, Martha (WDH's cousin), 157

*Howells, Mary D. (WDH's mother), trip to Washington, 56, 57; visits WDHs, 261, 278, 280; poor health and death, 246, 301, 302; WDH keeps her relics, 306, 307; thought and dreamed of by WDH, 310, 311, 319, 321, 322–23, 325; monument for, 312–13, 317; crayon of by Elinor, 274, 386; Pennsylvania-German descent, 375; financial propriety, 381

Howells, Mary E. (WDH's niece), 219, 220, 290

Howells, Mildred (WDH's daughter), 85; *Life in Letters*, 15, 42, 69, 77, 80, 112, 132, 144, 157, 170, 225, 261, 278, 285, 287, 327, 332, 343, 363, 366, 387, 397, 405; birth, 246, 392, 400, 401; named, 404

*Howells, Samuel D. (WDH's brother), 5; early employment, 6, 7, 29, 30; encouraged by WDH, 35–36, 37, 50, 51; as dentist, 77, 87, 89, 118, 119; as soldier, 77, 123, 166, 167, 191, 192; compared with Selden Day, 79; sickness and invitation to Venice, 196, 197, 200; second marriage, 300, 301, 302

*Howells, Theodora (WDH's cousin), 89

*Howells, Victoria M. (WDH's sister), 5, 29, 287, 288; early travel, 12, 14, 17; first to learn of WDH's engagement, 119, 120, 121; own engagement and death of fiancé, 204, 205, 208; WDH recalls early Christmas, 239; visit to WDHs, 350

*Howells, William C. (WDH's father), 15, 87, 113, 280; letter to B. F. Wade cited, 74, 75; letter from H. M. Ticknor cited, 115; letter from Elinor cited, 206; Address before Lake County Agricultural Society, 165, 166; "The Byron Scandal"(?), 340; "Camp-Meetings in the West Fifty Years Ago," 319, 320, 386, 387; defense of religious faith, 370, 371; "Dress of Women, Etc.," 387; editorial on franking, 112; introduction to "Letter from Europe," 112; letters on Washington trip, 57; memoir (MS), 366; "Mrs. Woodhull and Her Set," 387; "Ohio Fifty Years Ago," 314, 315, 316, 317, 319, 321, 323, 324, 384; "The State Convention," 280, 281; "Women and Politics," 386, 387; earlier political career, 3, 104, 105, 165, 166, 168; antislavery activities, 37, 38, 48, 49; trip to Washington, 56, 57; exporting oars to Venice, 148; asked to Venice, 200; visits to WDHs, 278, 286, 322, 324, 333, 363, 392, 394, 396, 397; governorship campaign, 278, 280, 281; at wife's death, 302, 303; Welsh descent, 375

*Howells, William C., family.

Howells, W. D.:

INDEX 483

WORKS:
"Among the Ruins," 408
"Andenken," 4, 22, 147, 276; acceptance of, 41, 42, 44, 45
The Atlantic Almanac for 1870 (contr.), 67
"At Padua," 191
The Battle in the Clouds, 185, 192, 193
"Bereft" (MS), 86
"The Bird Song," 19, 27
"Das blaugekleidste Mädchen" (MS), 65
"Bobby," 20, 21, 24
"A Book Read Yesterday" (review of Aldrich's *Ballad of Babie Bell*), 43
"Bopeep: A Pastoral" (MS version), comments on to O. W. Holmes, Jr., 64, 66, 67, 69, 70, 72, 74; a failure, 76, 77; revision considered, 148
"Bopeep: A Pastoral" (published version), 67
"Boston Notions" (lecture delivered?), 70
A Boy's Town, 3, 4, 56, 112, 362
"Bubbles," 68, 69, 147, 276
"By Horse-Car to Boston," 252, 348–49
"By the Sea," 145, 146
[Catholic Orphan's Home], 38
A Chance Acquaintance, beginnings, 380, 386, 387, 393, 394; Quebec material and illustrations, 378; revisions, 401, 402; first chapter in proof, 404, 405; comment by Boyesen, Parton, and New York *Evening Mail* reviewer, 410, 411
"Charles Eliot Norton: A Reminiscence," 238
"Clement," 164, 228
"Consolation," 233
Consular Report, *Letter of the Secretary of State* (1863, 1865), 201, 202
"Courtesy in the Cars," 232
"Dante as Philosopher, Patriot, and Poet," 227, 228, 231, 232
"Day in Pompeii," 237
"A Day's Pleasure," 331, 332, 338, 339
"Desultoria" (projected essays), 18, 19
"Diary about Winifred" (MS), 175
"Diary, 1851" (MS), 32
"Diary of 1852" (MS), 7
"Diary, Venetian" (MS), 15, 105, 113, 115, 129, 153
"The Discomforts of New York and Their Remedies," 233–34

"Disillusion." *See No Love Lost*.
"Doorstep Acquaintance," 310, 311, 312, 328, 332
"The Doubt," 18
"The Drama, the New Play at Wallack's," 234, 235
"The Dream" (*Ohio Farmer*), 45
"The Dream" (trans.), 44
"Drowsihed" (MS), 71, 72
"Drum Taps" (review of Whitman's *Drum-Taps*), 236, 237
"Ducal Mantua," 289; preparation for, 190, 191, 195, 196; nearly completed, 200, 201; sent to Lowell, 225; accepted, 233, 238, 239, 240, 241
"Editor's Easy Chair" (on Piatt), 27
"Editor's Study" (on C. Kinney), 43
"Editor's Study" (on J. G. Nicolay and Hay), 75
"Editor's Study" (series), 397
"The Empty House," 69, 72, 147, 279. See also "The Old Homestead."
"En Passant," 62
"The Faithful of the Gonzaga," 212, 240; composition, 185, 192; rejection by *Atlantic* and acceptance by New York *Ledger*, 195, 210, 211
"Fast and Firm...," 164
A Fearful Responsibility, 160
"Flitting," 361
A Foregone Conclusion, 261, 291
"Forlorn," 86, 180, 257, 270
"For One of the Killed," 138, 140
"Forza Maggiore," 272, 273
"From Europe," 116, 119, 121, 123
"From Ohio," 78
"From Venice to Florence and Back Again," 152, 153
"Gallipolis" (projected essay), 303, 305, 313, 317, 318
"Garfield," 75
"Geoffrey Winter" (MS), 66, 67, 76, 77
"A Glimpse of Genoa," 274
"Glimpses of Summer Travel," 59, 62
"Gnadenhütten," 301, 302, 303; deprecated by WDH, 308, 310, 322
"Gone," 18, 27
"A Great New York Journalist" (Godkin), 232
A Hazard of New Fortunes, 47
Heine lecture (undelivered), 68, 70
"Henry Wadsworth Longfellow," 272, 273, 274
Heroines of Fiction, 131
"Italian Brigandage," 208, 209, 218, 232

Italian Journeys, 290, 301, 302, 355, 375, 376; events and sketches leading to, 115, 121, 191, 205, 206; revision and printing, 272, 273, 274; WDH hurried by, 281, 282; praised by James, 284; now ready, 287; favorable notices, 288; praised by Holmes, 289; and by G. S. Hillard, 291; reviewed in New York *Evening Post*, 291; reviewed in *Saturday Review*, 299; 1872 edition, 156, 389. See also titles of individual sketches.
"Italian Poets of Our Century" (Lowell Institute lectures), 358, 359, 360
"The Jenkins of Tragedy," 231, 232
"John Butler Howells," 188, 193
"John Hay in Literature," 81
"Jubilee Days," 327, 328, 330, 332
The Lady of the Aroostook, 160
Lazarillo de Tormes (projected trans.), 30
lectures on lyceum circuit (projected), 158, 159
"Letter from Columbus," 3, 8, 9, 18
"Letters from Europe" and "From Europe," on voyage and England, 85, 97, 102, 105, 112; on Italy, 114, 115, 116, 119, 121, 123
"Letters from Venice," 85, 94, 123, 135, 269; Letter I cited, 140; continues writing, 144, 161; contractual arrangements, 153, 154, 173, 173–74, 211; some titles proposed, 162–64; sends Letters VIII and IX, 164, 165; liked by father, Lowell, 166, 194, 197
Literary Friends and Acquaintance (as background information), 42–299 passim, 347, 378
"Literary Gossip," 55, 67, 82
"A Little German Capital," 123, 125, 130, 131, 164
Lives and Speeches of Abraham Lincoln . . . , 3, 75, 279, 375
"Louis LeBeau's Conversion," 94, 147, 194; composition, 81, 82, 104, 105, 109; submitted to *Atlantic,* 111, 112, 124; father's corrections, 113, 115, 116, 119; and Conway, 145, 276; to be in proposed "Rhythmic Ballads," 228
"Lost Beliefs," 53–54, 147, 276
"Marriage Among the Italian Priesthood," 233–34
Memoirs of Carlo Goldoni (ed.), 143
"Minor Italian Travels," 279
"Minor Italian Travels: II. Como," 121

"Minor Topics," 238, 250
A Modern Instance, 112, 378
"Modern Italian Poetry and Comedy" (Harvard lecture, 1871), 246, 334
"Modern Italian Poets" (articles), 215, 218; composition of October number, 226, 227, 241, 256, 257; praised by Stedman, 271; composition of April number, 272, 273, 274; discontinuance, 281, 282
"Mr. Francis Bret Harte," 365
"Mr. Longfellow's Translation of the Divine Comedy," 283, 284
"The Mulberries," 125, 126, 130, 229
My Literary Passions, 9, 13, 30, 131, 287
"New Arcady Mills." See *New Leaf Mills.*
"New Italian Literature" (Harvard lecture, 1870), invitation, 331, 333, 334, 345; preparations, 339, 345, 350; delivery, 357
New Leaf Mills, 40; five chapters written, 290
"News and Humors of the Mails," 19, 27, 41, 47
"The New Taste in Theatricals," 389; composition, 313, 317; wants authorship withheld, 321; widely discussed, praised in *Nation,* 325, 326
"The Next President," 245
No Love Lost, 188, 245, 376; F. E. Foster negotiations, 94, 158–87 passim; summary of publication history, 137; Foster denounced, 192, 193, 219, 220; M. M. Hurd negotiations, 227, 228, 272, 273; and Norton, James, and Lowell, 240, 241, 310; Putnam publication, 291, 301; reviewed in *Nation,* 308
"Not a Love Story," 25, 39
"The Old and the New Year," 20, 21
"Old Brown," 54, 55
"The Old Homestead," 69, 72, 74. See also "The Empty House."
"An Old Venetian Friend," 112
"Ordeals" (MS), 169, 170, 172, 173
"Out-Door Beauty of Florence" (projected book with L. G. Mead, Jr.), 179–80
"Our Last Year in Venice," 389
"Overland to Venice," 88, 97
"A Pedestrian Tour," 331, 332, 335, 341, 346, 352
"A Perfect Goose," 39

"A Pilgrimage to Petrarch's House at Arquà," 155, 156, 229, 230, 231
"The Pilot's Story," 147, 228, 276; corrections, 58, 59; notice in New York *World* (by Stedman), 58, 59; by others, 60; praise from Lowell, 68; from O. W. Holmes, Jr., 74
"Pleasure-Pain," 45–46, 47, 52–53, 147, 276
Poems (1873), 47, 67, 74, 140, 173
Poems of Two Friends (with Piatt), 4, 27, 72, 74, 82, 147, 375; inception and publication, 43, 44, 47, 48; reviewed in *Saturday Press* (by Henry Clapp), 51–52; in *National Era* (by Mary A. Dodge), 52–53; in *Atlantic* (by Lowell), 54; reception discussed with Piatt, 81
Poems (rejected in London), 174–75, 176
"A Poet," 143
"A Poetical Lot," 335
Poets and Poetry of the West (contr.), 21, 43, 53, 54
"The Poet's Friends," 42, 43, 147, 276
Quebec article (unpublished), 378
"Question of Monuments," 255
rafting poem (projected), 118, 124
"Recent Italian Comedy," 143, 201, 208, 209, 210, 226; composition, 185, 187; acceptance by Lowell, 193, 196, 199; reputation in Italy, 220, 221, 237; Godkin's opinion, 232
"Recent Literature" (passage on Hawthorne), 382
"Recent Travels," 335, 336

REVIEWS and NOTICES:
About, E., *King of the Mountains*, 70
Aldrich, T. B., *Ballad of Babie Bell* ("A Book Read Yesterday"), 43; *The Story of a Bad Boy*, 318
Atlantic, Nov. 1860, 64, 65
Bjornson, B., *Arne, A Happy Boy, The Fisher-Maiden*, 355
Botta, V., *Dante*, 228
Cantù, C., *Della letteratura italiana*, 275
Clemens, S. L., *The Innocents Abroad*, 335, 336
Cobbe, F. P., *Italics*, 217, 218
Colvil, E., *Fifteen Days*, 256, 258, 259
Craven, H. T., *The Needful* ("The Drama, the New Play at Wallack's"), 234, 235

Dall'Ongaro, F., *Poesie* and *Stornelli italiani*, 249, 250
Davis, Mrs. S. M. H., ... *Sir Philip Sidney*, 26, 27
De Forest, J. W., *Miss Ravenel's Conversion*, 397
Dickinson, A. E., *What Answer?*, 306, 307
Emerson, R. W., *May-Day and Other Pieces*, 279, 281, 282, 284
Fisher, G. P., *Life of Benjamin Silliman*, 259, 260
Greek literature (1859, 1861), 112
Hassaurek, F., *Four Years Among Spanish Americans*, 291
Heine, H., *Salon II*, 67
Holmes, O. W., *Elsie Venner*, 64, 65
Ingelow, J., *A Story of Doom*, 282
James, Henry, Sr., *The Secret of Swedenborg*, 335, 336, 339
Longfellow, H. W., *The Divine Comedy*, 284; *The New England Tragedies*, 307
Lowell, J. R., "The Cathedral," 347; *Under the Willows*, 307, 309
Mansel, H. I., "The Limits of Religious Thought," 67
"Neo-Christianity," 66, 67
Nicolay, J. G., and J. Hay, *Abraham Lincoln*, 75
O'Connor, W. D., *Harrington*, 87, 88
Parkman, F., *The Discovery of the Great West*, 411
Piatt, J. J., *Poems in Sunshine and Firelight*, 254, 255
Porter, J. L., *The Giant Cities of Bashan*, 259, 260
Putnam, M. L., *Fifteen Days*, 256, 258, 259
Scudder, H. H., *Stories from My Attic*, 335, 336
Taylor, B., *By-Ways of Europe*, 327; *Faust*, 363; *The Picture of St. John*, 269, 270; *The Story of Kennett*, 254, 255
Upham, C. W., *Salem Witchcraft and Cotton Mather* (MS), 338
Whitman, W., *Drum-Taps* ("Drum Taps"), 236, 237
Whittier, J. G., *Ballads of New England*, 335, 336
Young, J., *The Province of Reason*, 67

"The Revival of Mosaic Painting in Venice," 148, 176

"Rhythmic Ballads" (projected book), 228, 229, 231
"A Romance of Real Life," 352, 353
"The Road to Rome and Home Again," 212, 213, 219, 220
"Romance of the Crossing," 39
"The Royal Portraits," 229; submitted to *Atlantic* and rejected, 113, 115, 125, 164; accepted by *Harper's Monthly*, 126, 231
"Saint Christopher," 158, 160, 161, 162, 172, 173, 176
miscellaneous items in *Saturday Press*, 46, 47
"Scene," 363
Soldini Masses (MS), 158, 160
"Some Islands of the Lagoons," 123
"Some Lessons from the School of Morals," 389
"Spanish-Italian Amity," 231, 232
Suburban Sketches, 245, 376, 389; suggested by M. M. Hurd, 332; response to magazine articles, 347, 352; revisions for book, 350; publication, 361; comments of Hay, 362; and Higginson, 363; reviewed in *Nation* (by J. R. Dennett), 364. See also titles of individual sketches.
"Summer Sunday in a Country Village," 39
"Sweet Clover," submitted to *Atlantic* and rejected, 125, 164; accepted by *Harper's Monthly*, 126, 229, 231
"Thanksgiving," 238, 239
Their Wedding Journey, 246, 389; composition, 360, 360–61, 362, 370, 371; illustrations by A. Hoppin, 367–68, 380, 384; use of trip, 371–74; completion, 377, 378, 380; publication and sales, 386, 387, 393; praised by Longfellow, 386; and Parton, 410–11
"Tonelli's Marriage," 245
Venetian histories (projected), 212, 310, 316, 317
Venetian Life, 94, 115, 173, 245, 273, 274, 289, 301, 302, 346, 375, 376; relation to "Letters from Venice," 123, 135–36, 154, 176; beginnings, 166, 167, 192, 193, 194; completion, 197, 199, 201, 203, 205, 206; submission to Trübner & Co. with further negotiations, 205, 208, 209, 214–15, 220; negotiations in U.S. with M. M. Hurd accepting, 224, 225, 227, 228, 231; announced and advertised in England, 237, 238, 239; reviews by *London Review*, *Examiner* (London), *Athenaeum* (London), *Review* (London), *North American Review* (by Norton), *Nation* (by Lowell), 258, 259; negotiations on errors, 260, 266–67; review in Columbus *Morning Journal*, 263–64; in *Round Table* (by J. Windsor), *Christian Examiner* (?), *Westminster Review* (London), 264, 265; praised by B. Taylor and Longfellow, 266–67; proposal of 2nd ed., 267–68; reviews in Boston *Transcript* (by E. P. Whipple), 269; in *Pall Mall Gazette* (London) and *Fortnightly Review* (London, by Conway), 276; comparison with J. A. Howells' New England letters, 296; 1867 edition, 202; 1872 edition, 140, 146, 160, 389
"Venice Come True," 158, 160
Venice. Her Art-Treasures . . . (trans.), 139, 140, 141, 144
"A Visit to Pompeii," 237
"A Year in a Venetian Palace," 389
Years of My Youth (as background information), 3–140 passim, 157, 287
"A Young Venetian Friend," 215

TOPICS:

Culture, aspects of: *art* studied with Elinor, 141–42; *Hellenism*, 61, 62; *propriety*, theatrical license, 313; sister as correspondent, 376; B. Taylor's parodies, 388
Culture, national: *America vs. Europe*, 101, 103, 106–7, 114–15; *Italian*, 93; *Swiss*, 223; *Western American*, 68
Family: *children*, effect of first child, 158, 172, 263; household celebrations, 279–80, 349–50; advice to daughter, 300; *parents*, affection for, 5, 36, 88, 302–3, 323; effect of engagement, 119–20, 121; advice offered, 150, 205–6, 261; *siblings*, relation with Victoria, 21, 24–25, 76; with Joe, 40; with Anne, 63, 289–90; with John, 151–52, 156–57; with Sam, 189; in Venice, 172; *wife*, marriage plans and marriage, 93–94, 130, 132; early years with, 135, 138
Financial affairs: *contracts* with Trübner, 185–86; with Hurd & Houghton, 278; *editorships* with *Ohio State Journal*, 19, 25, 47; with *Nation*, 237; with *Atlantic*, 245, 249, 250,

293, 294; *expenses* in Columbus, 38–39; in Venice, 110–11, 184–85; *income* in Venice, 113, 153, 173, 174; *loans* at outset of consulship, 102

Health: *mental,* hypochondria in youth and early manhood, 3, 31–32, 55, 116; unhappiness in Jefferson, 11; visits Dr. S. M. Smith, 40; homesickness, 56, 202–3; recollection of an Ohio summer, 296; *physical,* variety of illnesses, 15, 20, 110, 111, 173, 350, 353, 371

Languages: *French,* studied in Venice, 118; *German,* lessons in Jefferson and Columbus, 10, 11, 46; *Italian,* improved in Venice, 93, 103, 106, 132; *Spanish,* in youth, 4; *various,* 113, 375

Literary movements: *bohemianism,* 54, 55, 178, 344; *realism,* 377, 395–96

Literature, forms of: *criticism,* 308; *fiction,* 30, 66, 366–67; *poetry,* 60, 66, 177, 368, 369, 408

Literature, national: *American* (western), 226; *English,* 4; *German,* 10, 27, 34, 71, 177, 226; *Italian,* 64, 65, 93, 177, 214, 217; *Spanish,* 30

Politics: *consulships,* in Venice, 2, 83–231 passim; applications or offerings, 74–83 passim; ethics of office, 111, 112, 127, 221–22; recommendation of Piatt, 209; consideration of renewal, 230, 231; *democracy,* 370; *parties,* 47, 49, 125, 399; *war,* 1861 attitudes, 71, 77, 78, 94, 99; 1862 attitudes, 122, 125, 130; 1863 attitudes, 135, 147, 160, 162; in 1864 hopeful, 200; at end rejoices, 213

Reform: *antislavery,* his father's views, 3, 37, 38; on John Brown, 48–49, 50; family activity, 89; emancipation, 117–18

Religion: *agnosticism,* 56, 66–67; *Christianity,* 141, 247, 370; *Episcopalianism,* 306, 312; *Methodism,* 316; *Moravians,* 301; *Presbyterianism,* 20; *Roman Catholicism,* 32, 36, 37, 62; *Shakerism,* 319; *spiritualism,* 381, 384, 391; *Swedenborgianism,* among family and friends, 3, 23, 33, 89, 141, 272–73; reading, 30, 141, 304, 390; concepts, 311, 314, 319, 386; *Unitarianism,* 312, 314, 383

Residences: early, 3; Jefferson, 4–85 passim; Cincinnati, 8–9; Columbus (Starling Medical College), 4, 19–82 passim; Venice (on Campo San Bartolomeo, in Casa Falier, in Palazzo Giustiniani), 93, 94, 99, 114–221 passim, 375; New York City, 227–51 passim; Cambridge (41 Sacramento St.), 246, 252, 253, 260 et passim; 3 Berkeley St., 367 et passim; 37 Concord Ave., 274, 401, 402

Self-conceptualization: *abilities,* 168–69; *aging,* 272; *ambition,* 14, 22, 48, 130; *appearance,* 86, 103–4; *career,* 23, 118; as of 1861–1865, 209–10; plans in 1865, 211, 214, 218; dissatisfactions, 309; outline, 375; *death,* 73–74, 190, 204, 213, 329–30; *friendships,* 4, 106, 210, 387, 405; *immortality,* 288, 304, 392, 394; *purpose,* 113, 154, 184, 198; *shortcomings,* in Jefferson, 11, 13–14, 197; indolence, 72; in Venice, 145, 178, 195, 196, 295, 321

Society: *Boston,* 58, 70; *Cambridge,* 84, 329; *Columbus,* 23, 24, 33, 295; *Newport,* 338–39; *New York City,* 60; *Venice,* 114

Travels: New England and New York (1860), 4, 57–58; St. Paul (?), 16; New York, Washington, and Boston, 82–83, 84; England and London, 95–96; England to Venice, 97–99, 107; Italian trips, 120–21, 149, 153, 155, 156, 178, 181–82, 187, 199, 203–4, 210, 219, 351; Boston via London, 220, 222–23; Brattleboro, 282–85; Niagara tour, 360–61; Ohio tour, 370, 371; Quebec, 378, 380; New York (1872), 396–97

Writing: *editing,* 263; *illustrations,* 389; *proofreading,* 343; *publishing,* 94, 155–56, 194, 252; *reviewing,* 348, 391; *revisions,* 378–79

Howells, W. D. II (WDH's nephew), 8, 12; gifts from WDH, 157, 169, 170, 239; New York journal, 287

*Howells, Winifred, 184; birth, 94, 171; descriptions in Venice, 171–72, 175, 178, 189; development and life in Venice, 187, 191, 193, 198–99, 203; as traveler, 223; illness, 229, 287, 313, 314; later development, 248, 250; later activities, 260, 279–80, 301, 304, 310, 349, 350; later descriptions, 262, 296; education, 286, 288, 340, 345; and race, 290; at church, 306; threatened by Bridget, 324; kissed by U. S. Grant,

331; future treatment by S. W. Mitchell, 406
Hugalde y Mollinedo, Nicolas, *Historia de la literatura española*, 275
Humphrey, Mr., 160, 162
Hunt, Helen, *Bits of Travel* (review withdrawn by Higginson), 391; *Verses* (reviewed by Higginson), 362, 363
Hunt, Leigh, *Autobiography*, 64
Hunter, David, 118, 119
*Hunter, William, 222, 231
Huntington, Frederick D., 312, *313*
Hurd & Houghton, 228, 229, 252, 290, 291, 352, 375, 376; may publish *No Love Lost* and book of poems, 137, 231; publishes *Venetian Life*, 264; plans second ed. of *Venetian Life*, 269; to publish *Italian Journeys*, 274; suggests *Suburban Sketches*, 332. See also Hurd, Melanchthon M.
*Hurd, Melanchthon M., 169, 170, 278; meetings with WDH, 227, *228*, 231; on correcting London ed. of *Venetian Life*, 266; on *Suburban Sketches*, 361
Hurd, William T., 50, 51
Hurtt, F. H., 80, 264
Hutchins, John, *49*
Hutchins, Uriah, *49*
Hutchinson family, "Excelsior" (comp.), 33, 35
Huxley, Thomas, 402
Hyde, Mrs., 299
Hyde Park, 96

Idiot Asylum, Columbus, 31
Illinois Staats-Anzeiger, 100
Independent, 364
Ingelow, Jean, 226, 227; *A Story of Doom* (reviewed by WDH), 282
Irish, 329, 345
Irving, Washington, 362
Isaac, 16

*Jackson, Mrs. Frances M.
James, Alice, 351
James, Garth W., 332
*James, Henry, Jr., "Gabriele de Bergerac," 328, 330–31, 332, 335, 337; "Guest's Confession," 404; "A Light Man," 328, 332; "The Madonna of the Future," 404, 405; "My Friend Bingham," 273; "Poor Richard" (reviewed in *Nation*), 271, 272, 283, 284; "The Romance of Old Clothes," 283–84; WDH's enthusiasm for, 246, 283, 353; talks with WDH, 271; opinion of *No Love Lost*, 310; and Norton, 346; return from Europe, 358; friendship with WDH, 404–5
James, Henry, Sr., 330, 331, 339; "Is Marriage Holy?" (based on lecture), 311, 312; review of J. R. Seeley's book, 259, 260; *The Secret of Swedenborg* (reviewed by WDH), 335, 336, 339, 347; "Spiritualism New and Old" (review of R. D. Owen's book), 392; *Substance and Shadow*, 273, 274; "The Woman Thou Gavest with Me" (based on lecture), 311, 312, 352, 355; talks with WDH, 303, 305; on Swedenborg, 319, 320
James, Mr. and Mrs. Henry, Sr., 347, 350–51
James, Mrs. Henry, Sr., 352–53
James, William, 328, 404; review of J. Morley's *Voltaire*, 402
Jarvis, Edward, "The Increase of Human Life," 335, 336
Janney, John J., 75
Jefferson, Joseph, 354, *355*
Jerrold, Douglas, 17, 18
*Jewett, Sarah O., 246; "Mr. Bruce," 337; "The Shore House," 366–67
Johannes, Count, 134, 136, 147
John (messenger boy), 283, 284
Johnny Stephen (animal or toy), 306, 307
John the Baptist, 153, 319
John Swinton's Paper, 100
Jones, George, 231, 232
Jones, Kate. See Ensign, Kate A. J. (Mrs. J. D.).
Jones, Mollie, 25
Jones, Publius V., 25–26
Jones, Mrs. Publius V., 25
Jones, Stiles, 16, 17
Jones, Thomas D., 20, 26, 27, 31, 33, 35
Johnson, John, 315
Johnson, Samuel, *The Rambler*, 118
Joseph, 46, 47

Karr, Jean B. A., *The Alain Family*, 71, 72; *A Tour Round My Garden*, 71, 72
Katy, 253
Kaufmann, H., 13, 35, 45, 62
Keats, John, 204
*Keeler, Ralph, 246, 377, *378*, 407
Keene, Edmund, 251, 252
Keene, Laura, 251, 252
Keller, M., *The Battle in the Clouds* (comp.), 185
Kellogg, Abner, *191*
Kellogg (son of Abner), 190, 191

INDEX 489

Kellogg, Mr. and Mrs. Miner K., 175, *176*
Kelty, G. L. & J. B., 100, 102
Kensington Gardens, 96
Kimball, C. W., 328
King, Clarence, 246; "Mountaineering in the Sierra Nevada," 335, 366
King's College, Dublin, 24
Kinney, Coates, 42; *Ke-u-ka & Other Poems, 43*
Kirk, 335, 336, 337
Kirk, Clara M. and Rudolf, 47, 140
Kirk, John F., 386, *387*
Knickerbocker Club, New York, 397
Krum, Abel, *40*, 105
Kügler, Franz T., *Kügler's Handbook of Painting*, 144, 145, 146

Lake Erie, Battle of, 378, 379
Lamartine, Alphonse de, 342
Lamb, Charles, 294
Landor, Walter S., article on by Stedman, 403, 406
Lane, G. M., 341
*Larcom, Lucy, *274*, 315; "Phebe," 398
La Salle, Robert C. de, 411
Lazarillo de Tormes, 29, 30
Lazarus, Emma, *Admetus and Other Poems*, 342; "Admetus" (rejected by WDH), 341, *342*
Lee, Mother Ann, 319, 320
Lee, Robert E., 213, 214
Leland, Charles G., 109
Leslie, Frank, 354, *356*
Lessing, Gotthold E., 234
Lévis, Duc de, 139
Lewis, Dio, *The New Gymnastics...*, 287, 289
Library of Congress, 313, 411
Lie, Jonas, *Den Fremsyute* (reviewed by Boyesen), 392, 393
Limbeck, Otto, 89, 90; tutors WDH in German, 10, 11, *13*; to bind WDH's Atlantic poems, 87, 88
Lincoln, Abraham, 184, 205, 206, 222, 252; letter from J. A. Garfield cited, 74, 75; letter to T. Canisius cited, 100; sculptures of by T. A. Jones, L. G. Mead, Jr., and cast of hand, 20, 227, 228, 231, 234; and WDH consulship, 74, 75, 81; and emancipation, 117–18, 119, 130, 131, 132, 139; comments on by WDH, 123–24, 200; death and mourning, 94, 215, 216, 216–17, 218
Linton, Ethel L., "The Channel Islands,"

335, 337; "Let Us Be Cheerful," 335, 337
Lippincott, Sarah Jane (Clarke), "The Children of Today..." (lecture), 23, *24*; *Greenwood Leaves*, 24
Lippincott's Magazine, 320, 386, 387
Little Miami Railroad, 29
Liverpool Line, 89
Locke-Ober Café, 378
Lockwood, Charles, and Son, 275
London *Daily News*, 158, 159
London *Review*, reviews *Venetian Life*, 258, 259, 263
*Longfellow, Henry W., 246, 281, 294, 357, 391; *Alcuna Poesie di Enrico W. Longfellow*, 218; "The Black Knight" (trans. of Uhland), 42, 43; "The Castle by the Sea" (trans. of Uhland), 42, 43; "The Cumberland," 137; *The Divine Comedy* (trans.), 256, 257, 258; (reviewed by Norton), 281, 282, 283; (reviewed by WDH), 284; *Evangeline*, 37, 73, 74, 161; "Excelsior," 33, 35; "Footsteps of Angels," 304, 305; *Hyperion*, 43; *The New England Tragedies* (reviewed by WDH), 307; "On Translating the Divina Commedia: Second Sonnet," 263, 264; first meets WDH, 251; and Dante Club, 253, 256–61 passim, 272; visits, 262, 362, 401; on *Venetian Life*, 267; and Dickens, 287, 293; and B. Taylor, 362, 388; and Harte, 366; on *Their Wedding Journey*, 386
Longfellow, Samuel, *287*
Longhi, Pietro, "The Dancing Master" (painting), 134
Loomis, George M., 13, *15*
Loomis, Mary E. H. (Mrs. G. M.), 13, 15, 16, 17
Louisville *Journal*, reprints WDH's "Gone" and "The Birdsong," 27; publishes Piatt's poems and articles, 40, 326
Louvre, Hôtel du, Paris, 132
Low, Walter, 187
Lowell, Frances D. (Mrs. J. R.), 84, 85
Lowell Institute, 358, 359
*Lowell, James R., 59, 119, 201, 246, 255, 311–12, 358, 387, 394, 409; letter to N. Hawthorne cited, 58, 61; *The Bigelow Papers*, 236, 237; "The Footpath," 299; "The Cathedral" (reviewed and commented on by WDH), 334–48 passim, 352; "A Good Word for Winter" (praised by WDH), 342–43; *North*

American Review (ed.), 238, 239; "On a Certain Condescension in Foreigners" (praised by WDH), 305; review of *Poems of Two Friends*, 54; review of *Venetian Life*, 94, 258, 259, 264, 265; "Rousseau and the Sentimentalists," 281, 282; *Under the Willows* (reviewed and commented on by WDH), 307, 308, 309; meets WDH, 4; on Heine, 4, 197; at Parker House, 57; visits and walks, 84, 256, 257, 262, 283, 330, 341, 345, 392; advice to WDH, 196–97, 233–34; gifts from WDH, 233, 392; at Dante Club, 256, 258; on *Venetian Life*, 260; on WDH's "Forlorn," 270; and Dickens, 287, 294; on *No Love Lost*, 310; urged as U.S. minister by WDH, 320; on children, 323; and Harvard lectures, 331, 333, 334; on WDH's "A Poetical Lot," 335; on H. B. Stowe's article, 335; and Cornell, 359; and Piatt, 361
Lowell, Mr. and Mrs. James R., 351
*Lowell, John A.
Lowell, Mabel, 84, 85. *See also* Burnett, Mabel L. (Mrs. E.).
Lowell, Maria W. (Mrs. James R.), 85
Luke, 68, 69
Lynch, Isaac, 22
Lynn, Kenneth S., 5, 15, 55, 406

McClellan, George B., 162, 179
McClintock, John, 132, *133*
McIntyre, P. W., 87
McIntyre, Stephen, 87
Macmillan & Co., 155, 156
Macmillan's Magazine, 340, 341; rejects "Geoffrey Winter," 67; offered *No Love Lost*, 137
McMillen, Dr. and Mrs. William L., 85
Manassas, Second Battle of, 125, 126
Mann, Mrs. Horace, 304
Mansel, Henry L., "The Limits of Religious Thought" (Bampton Lecture; noticed by WDH), 67
Manzoni, Alessandro, "Il Cinque maggio," *241*; *I Promessi sposi*, 241, 275
Margry, Pierre, 411
Marvel, Ik (pseud.). *See* Mitchell, Donald G.
Mary, Virgin, 182
Mason, James M., 156, 159
*Masson, David.
Mather, Cotton, 338
Matthews, Stanley, 165, *167*

Mead, Albert, 304, 305
Mead, Charles L., 235, 303, 305, 333
Mead, Elinor G. *See* Howells, Elinor M.
Mead, Frederick G., 392
Mead, Larkin G., Jr., 90, 137, 141, 282; "Echo" (statue), 147; Lincoln monument (sculpture), 227, 228; "Out-Door Beauty of Florence" (projected with WDH), 179–80; "The Recording Angel" (snow sculpture), 343; at marriage in Paris of Elinor, 94, 132, *133*, 134; artist for *Harper's Weekly*, 179, 183; as vice and acting consul, 207, 215, 231; help in early career by WDH, 230, 231, 232, 261; visit to WDHs and sketch for Mary D. Howells monument, 312–13, 317
Mead, Mr. and Mrs. Larkin G., Jr., 298
*Mead, Larkin G., Sr., *132*, 162, 184, 196, 248, 252, 282, 285, 289; illness and death, 328, 329, 333, 336
*Mead, Mary J. N. (Mrs. L. G., Sr.), 261, 282, 285, 289; visit to New York, 235, 238, 240; visits with WDHs, 329, 383; may live with WDHs, 355, 356; visited by WDH, 397, 398
Mead, Mary N., 184; visit with WDHs in Venice, 165, 166, 169, 210; dinner with Mr. and Mrs. James, Sr., 351; may live with WDHs, 355, 356; visit with Mrs. J. M. Shepard, 360
Medical College of Ohio, Cincinnati, 26
Medina *Gazette*, 9, 303, 322
Meissner, Alfred, *Heinrich Heine: Erinnerungen*, 41, 42, 47
Mercato Nuevo, boar at the fountain, Florence, 179
Messadaglia, Angelo, 202; *Alcuna Poesie di Enrico W. Longfellow* (trans.), 218; review of work on Mississippi, 202; translation of Longfellow (MS), 218
Methodism, 32. *See also* WDH: Religion.
Methodism, German, 100
Methodist Seamen's Bethel, 316, 317
Metis (ship), 400–401
Mill, John S., 402
Michelangelo, statue by, Florence, 179
Milton, John, 64, 229
Mitchell, Donald G., 222, 223
Mitchell, John G., *102*, 340
Mitchell, Gen. and Mrs. John G., 206, 233, 234
Mitchell, Laura P. (Mrs. J. G.), 100, *102*, 115, 166, 289, 304, 305
Mitchell, Margaret J., 147, *148*

INDEX

*Mitchell, S. Weir, 339; "The Case of George Dedlow," 263, 264; "Miss Helen," 405, *406*
Mohammed, 335
Monroe, James, 75
Montaigne, Michel E. de, *Essays*, 41
Monti, Vicenzo, 256, 257
Moodie, Isabella E., 34, *35*
Moore, Clement C., "A Visit from St. Nicholas," 304, 305
Moorhead, William G., *162*
Moravian Church. *See* WDH: Religion.
Morley, John, *Voltaire* (reviewed by W. James), 402
Mormonism, 16
Morphy, Paul C., 228, *229*
Morris, William, 341, 403, 406; "May Grown A-Cold," 335, 337; "Rhyme Slayeth Shame," 335, 337
Morton, Mr., 398, 399
Mother Goose's Tales, 248
*Motley, John L., 200, *201*, 321; "Florentine Mosaics," 17, 18; *The Rise of the Dutch Republic*, 201
Mould, Jane, 359, 360
Moulton, Ellen L. C., *395*
Mt. Auburn Cemetery, Cambridge, 262
Mowatt, Mrs., 152
Mowatt-Ritchie, Mrs. Anna C., 141, *143*
Müller, Adalbert, *Venice. Her Art-Treasures...* (trans. WDH), 139, 140, 141, 144
Müller, Mr., 343
Muigs, Frank, 54

Napoleon I, of France, 219, 241
Napoleon III, of France, 313
Nast, Condé, *100*
Nast, William, *100*
Nast, William F., 98, *100*
Nation, 255, 298–99, 331, 346, 354, 370, 378; WDH's connection with and contributions to, 86, 123, 126, 156, 220, 231–52 passim, 256, 272, 375, 384; reviews *Venetian Life*, 258, 259, 264, 265; reviews James's "Poor Richard," 283, 284; perhaps reviews A. E. Dickinson's novel, 306; reviews *No Love Lost*, 308; notices WDH's "New Taste in Theatricals," 325, 326; reviews *Suburban Sketches*, 364; publishes Boyesen's review, 407, 408
National Bank Note Co., 228
National Era, 46; publishes WDH's "The Doubt" and "Gone," 18; "The Bird Song," 27; reviews *Poems of Two Friends*, 53
"Neo-Christianity" (notice by WDH), 66, 67
Nevins, Allen, 232
Neil House, Columbus, 26, 27
New Church Magazine, 273
New York Bar Association, 230
New York *Evening Mail*, 365; notices *A Chance Acquaintance*, 410
New York *Evening Post*, 46, 139, 163, 192, 232, 395; WDH applies for work, 58, 59; reviews Stedman's poems, 176, 178; reviews *Italian Journeys*, 291
New York *Ledger*, 313; publishes WDH's "The Faithful of the Gonzaga," 185, 211, 212
New York *Mail and Express*, 230
New York *Sun*, 100
New York *Times*, 99, 100, 102, 130, 139, 245; European letters offered by WDH, 84, 85; negotiations with WDH for job, 229, 230; publishes WDH's "The Jenkins of Tragedy," "Spanish-American Amity," "Courtesy in Cars," 231, 232; "Marriage Among the Italian Priesthood," "The Discomforts of New York....," 233, 234
New York *Tribune*, 139, 212, 387; and Reid, 255, 395; and H. B. Stowe, 334; and Hay, 362; published WDH's review of Lowell's "The Cathedral," 347
New York *World*, 87, 128; notices WDH's "The Pilot's Story," 58, 59; publishes "From Ohio," 78
*Nicolay, John G., 205, 206; *Abraham Lincoln: A History* (with Hay; reviewed by WDH), 75; secures consulate for WDH, 83
Nile (statue at Vatican), 206
Nina, 149
North American Review, 67, 291, 352, 389; publication of WDH's essays, reviews, and other connections, 93, 143–323 passim; "John Hay in Literature" (1905), 81; "A Great New York Journalist" (1907), 232; "Charles Eliot Norton" (1913), 238; review of *Venetian Life*, 258, 259, 264, 265; reviews and articles by Norton, John Dryden, Lowell, Godkin, 281, 282; and J. G. Palfrey, 347; and E. W. Gurney, 355; articles by C. F. Wingate, 365; and T. S. Perry, 404, 405
Northway, Benas A., 205
*Norton, Charles E., 232, 246, 284, 291,

294, 351, 355; *Lowell Letters*, 58, 61, 68, 72, 196, 237; Memoir in A. H. Clough's *Poems*, 240, 241; review of Longfellow's *The Divine Comedy*, 281, 282; review of *Venetian Life*, 258, 259, 264, 265; first meeting with WDH, *238*, *239*; assistance with WDH's Cambridge house, 251, 252, 254; entertains Dante Club, 274; illness in Europe, 307, 310, 312

Norton, Mr. and Mrs. Charles E., 278, 332

Norton, Elizabeth G., 262, 263

Norton, Grace, 332, 351, 355

Norton, Rupert, 281, 282

Norton, Susan S. (Mrs. C. E.), 253, 262, 263

Noyes, John H., *374*

O'Connor, William D., 106, 108; *Harrington* (reviewed by WDH), 87, 88

Odd-Fellows' Casket, 19, 20, 39, 51; publishes WDH's "Not a Love Story" and others, 21, 22, 25

Oglesby, Richard J., 231

Ohio Farmer, 9, 10; publishes WDH's "The Dream," 45

Ohio Republican Press, 50

Ohio Register, 314, 315

Ohio State Journal, 139; W. C. French 1852 foreman, 7; WDH as an editor and contributor, 19–85 passim, 97–112 passim, 375; after 1865 J. M. Comly as editor, 32; Oran Follett as former editor, 32; publishes WDH review of W. D. O'Connor's novel, 88; H. M. Gangewar's 1856-1858 association with, 109; W. C. Howells considers joining, 200, 201; rival paper to employ WDH, 229; reprints WDH review of Piatt's poems, 255; name changed to Columbus *Morning Journal*, 264; WDH requests 1858-1861 files, 294, 295

Ohio State Library, 46

Ohio State Weekly Journal, 65

Old and New, 352

Oliver, James L., 31, 32

Oliver, Thomas, 31, 32

Ollendorf, Henri G., *Ollendorf's New Method ... for Italian Language*, 118, 119

Olmstead, Miss, 340, 341, 345

Oneida Community, 373, 374

"One, two, three, four..." (counting rhyme), 63

Orion, 134

Orsini, Palazzo, Venice, 409

*Osgood, James R., 393, 395; visits WDH, 248, *249*; advises WDH, 333, 342; on future editorship, 363, 364; on Stedman, 369; entertains WDH in New York, 396. See also Osgood, James R., & Co.

Osgood, James R., & Co., and Harte, 366; publishes *Every Saturday*, 377; Woolman's *Journal*, 381; *Septimius Felton*, 382

Ossoli, Margaret Fuller, *Memoir* (reviewed by Higginson), 349

Our Young Folks, 274, 315; ed. by Mary A. Dodge, 53; ed. by H. M. Ticknor, 59; and Anne T. Howells, 286, 292; publishes Aldrich's book, 318

Overland Monthly, 354, 355

Owen, Robert D., 391; "A Chapter of Autobiography," 401, 402; *The Debatable Land* (reviewed by James, Sr.), *381*, 384, 392

Oxford University, 323, 402

Padovanino. See Varotari, Allessandro.

Padua, University of, 202

Paine, R. F., 87

Palfrey, Mr. and Mrs. James G., 347

Pall Mall Gazette, reviews *Venetian Life*, 276

Palmer, J. W., "My Heathen at Home," 269, 270

Parish, Francis D., 47, *48*

*Parker, Benjamin S., 252

Parker House, 84, 405; dinner for WDH, 57, 194

Parker, Theodore, 314, *315*

Parkman, Francis, *The Discovery of the Great West* (reviewed by WDH), 411; on Pierre Margry documents, 411

Parliament, Houses of, 96

Parma, Duchess of, 139, 140

Parnell, Thomas, "The Hermit," 83, 85

Parrott, Ed A., 75

Parsons, H. E., 75

Parsons, R. C., 75

Parsons, Samuel, *35*

Parsons, Mrs. Samuel, 34, 35

Parsons, Theophilus, 273, 274, 402; *Deus-Homo*, 390

*Parton, James, *410*–11; articles on Washington politics, 335, 337

*Payne, Daniel C.

Peace Jubilee, Boston, 327, 338, 331

Pelton, 150

Peninsular Campaign, 179

INDEX 493

Pennington, William S., 132, *133*
Perry, Thomas, *Reliques of Ancient English Poetry*, 42
Perry, John T., 52
Perry, Oliver H., 378, 379
Perry, Thomas S., 404, *405*
Peruvian attaché at Torin, 192–93
Peterson, Charles J., *339*
Peterson, Mrs. Charles J., 338, *339*
Peterson, G. J. P., *A Norwegian-Danish Grammar* ... (reviewed by Boyesen), 407, 408
Peterson's Magazine, 338, 339, 374
Petrarch, Francisco, 155, 156, 229, 230, 231; book on, 283, 284
Phelps, Elizabeth S., *The Gates Ajar*, 356; *Hedged In* (reviewed by Higginson), 354, *356*
Phillips, Wendell, "Harper's Ferry," 48, 49, 50; "Letter to the Tribune," 125, 126
*Piatt, John J., 4, 27, 132, 139, 169, 179, 218, 219; "Ada," 43; "After Mrs. Hemans's 'Bended Bow,'" 27; "The Church Path," 27; "The Ghosts," 45, 47; *The Hesperian Tree* (ed.), 109; "In Autumn" (also as "In the Orchard"), 45, 47; "Living and Dead," 45; "The Morning Street," 26, 27; *Nests at Washington*, 187; "The Night Train," 40, 41; "Parting and Meeting," 27; *Poems of Two Friends* (with WDH), 27, 43, 44, 47; reviewed by Lowell, 54, 147, 375; *Poems in Sunshine and Firelight* (reviewed by WDH), 254, 255; *Poets and Poetry of the West* (contributor), 43; "The Unmended Bow," 27; poems reprinted in *Ohio State Journal*, 26; poems defended by WDH, 51; visits to WDH, 68, 326, 360; clerkship and marriage, 83; recommended by WDH, 233; on WDH review, 254, 255; tasteless reporting, 361
Piatt, Mrs. Emily S., 53
Piatt, Sarah M. B. (Mrs. J. J.), 53, 83, 179, 187; "A Voyage to the Fortunate Isles" (also book), 360; *A Woman's Poems*, 360
Pickering, Basil M., *137*
Pickering, William, 137
Pillsbury, Parker, 370, *371*
Pine and Palm, 116, 119
Pioneer, 387
Pius IX, Pope, 123
Plato, 64, 65, 69, 70

Platt, Laura. *See* Mitchell, Laura P. (Mrs. J. G.).
Polish Revolution of 1863, 139
Ponti, Carlo, 160, *162*, 167
Pope, Alexander, 177, 346, 347; *Odyssey* (trans.), 106, 109
Porter, J. L., *The Giant Cities of Bashan* (reviewed by WDH), 259, 260
Porter's Station, Cambridge, 346, 355
Porter's store, Cambridge, 349
Porter's Tavern, Cambridge, 340
*Potter, Martin D., *19*
Potter, Thomas B., *188*
Powers, Hiram, 141, *143*
Prentice, Noyes B., 9, *10*
Presbyterianism. *See* WDH: Religion.
Preterre, Eugene and A., 89, *90*
*Price, Samuel, 4, 79, 100, 126, 130, 139; a fellow editor, 65, 67; seeks state clerkship, 165; little correspondence with WDH, 170; suggested by WDH as *Sentinel* editor, 198; recalled by WDH, 294, 295
Princeton Theological Seminary, 54
Princeton University, 376
Procter, Bryan W., *403*
Prometheus, 334
Protestant Cemetery, Rome, 205
Przemysl, Miss, 175, *176*
Putnam, George P., *291*
Putnam, G. P. [& Son], 137, 291, 376
Putnam, Mary L., *Fifteen Days* (reviewed by WDH), 256, 258, 259
Putnam's Magazine, 18, 137, 291, 301, 354
Putnam's Monthly Magazine, 17, 18, 153
Putnam, Samuel, 69

Radcliffe College, 282
Randall & Aston, 22, 26, 27
Ransom, Caroline L., 31, *32*, 64, 65, 66
Raymond, Henry J., 229, *230*, 231
Reade, Charles, 411; *Christy Johnston*, 130, 131
Redpath, J., *Echoes of Harper's Ferry* (ed.), 54, 55; *The Pine and Palm* (ed.), 116, 119
Reed, James, 31, *32*, 165, 166
Reed, Samuel R., 4, *24*, 112; advises WDH, 23, 35; companionship with WDH, 37, 50; on John Brown, 48, 49; goes to Cincinnati *Gazette*, 54, 55
Reed, Thomas B., 281, *282*
Reeves, John K., 67, 72, 160, 170
Register of Officers and Agents (Department of State), 80, 81, 87

*Reid, Whitelaw, 255, 385, 386, 395, 398
Rellstab, Ludwig, "Serenade," 33, 35
The Retina, 273, 274
Review (London), reviews *Venetian Life*, 258, 259
Rialto Bridge, 115, 189
Richardson, Benjamin, 117, *119*
Richardson boy, 326
Richmond, Battle of, 213, 214
Richmond, B. W., 16, *17*
Riley, James, *An Authentic Narrative* ..., 55, 56
Riverside Magazine for Young People, 290, 292
Riverside Press, 43
R., Madame, 20, 32, 33, 35
Roberts Brothers, 322
Robertson, Frederick W., *Sermons Preached*..., 141, 143
Rogers, Samuel, *Italy*, "Ginevra," 182, 183; *Italy*, "Venice," 101, 102
Roman Catholicism. *See* WDH: Religion.
Romano, Eccelino de, 187, *188*
Rossetti, Dante G., 403
Rossini, Antonio, *Otello*, 159, 160
Rossini, Gioacchino A., *The Barber of Seville*, 377, 378
Round Table, ed. by Stedman et al., 176–77, 178; publishes WDH's "Dante ...," 227, 228, 231, 232; considers other WDH contributions, 229, 231, 235, 245; publishes WDH's "Drum Taps," 236, 237; and *Nation* contract with WDH, 237; publishes Stedman poem, 255; control of, 255; reviews *Venetian Life*, 264, 265, 266
Ruess, Herman, *50*
Russell, Addison P., *48*, 49, 75, 249
Ruskin, John, 146, 160, 162

St. James's Palace, 96
St. James's Park, 96
St. John's Church, Worthington, Ohio, 7
Salviati, Antonio, 174, *176*
Salviati, Signora Antonio, 174
Sampson, Low & Co., 187
San Francisco Bulletin, 119
San Francisco Chronicle, 407
San Diego Herald, 335
Sandusky Register, 37
San Marco, Cathedral of, Venice, 108, 142, 177
San Marco, Library of, Venice, 190, 195, 201
San Stefano, Church of, Venice, 139
*Sanborn, Franklin B., Boston *Commonwealth* (co-ed.), 143; "Politics," 398; Springfield *Republican* (ed.), *399*
Saturday Club, 281, 365
Saturday Press, 82, 177, 226, 239; publishes WDH's review of Aldrich's *Ballad of Babie Bell*, 43; other WDH contributions, 46, 47, 55, 147; reviews *Poems of Two Friends*, 51, 52, 53; publishes WDH's "Consolation," 233
Saturday Review (London), reviews *Italian Journeys*, 299; *Suburban Sketches*, 376
Scarbro, Elizabetta, 171, 173. *See also* Bettina.
Schiller Casino, Venice, 103
Schiller, Johann C. von, 50, 98, 107; *Gedichte*, 26, 27; "Das Lied von der Glocke," 26, 27
Scottish American Journal, 102, 105
Schubert, Franz, "Serenade" (comp.), 33, 35
Schwartz, Marie S., *Birth and Education*, 394, 395; *Gold and Name*, 394, 395; *The Wife of a Vain Man*, 394, 395
Schweinitz, Edmund de, 301, 302
Scott, Gamaliel, 7
Scudder, Horace E., *James Russell Lowell*, 119; *Riverside Magazine for Young People* (ed.), 290; *Stories from My Attic* (reviewed by WDH), 335, 336
Sedgwick, Arthur G., 332; "Politics," 404, 405; sees WDH, 298, *299*; visited by WDH, 345, 346, 370
Sedgwick, Theodora, 298
Seeley, J. R., *Ecce Homo* (reviewed by James, Sr.), 259, 260
Servant (hired through Freedman's Bureau), 290
Sewall, Francis, 385, 393, 410, 411
Sewall, Mr. and Mrs. Francis, 408, 409
*Seward, Frederick W., *128*, 205, 212, 214, 222; at time of Lincoln assassination, 215, 216; attitude toward WDH, 230
*Seward, William H., 86, 222, 297, 373, 374; letter from Charles Sumner cited, 112; and Conway, 155, 156; attack on, 216
Seward, William H., Jr., 373, 374
Shakerism. *See* WDH: Religion.
Shakespeare, William, 62, 347; *Antony and Cleopatra*, 158, 160; *Hamlet*, 36, 38, 354; *Henry IV, Part I*, 104, 105, 117, 119; *Julius Caesar*, 46, 47; *Macbeth*, 251; *The Merchant of Venice*, 223, 224; *A Midsummer Night's Dream*,

INDEX

258, 259; *Othello,* 138, 140, 159; *Romeo and Juliet,* 181, 183; *Two Gentlemen of Verona,* 181
Shaler, Nathaniel S., articles on earthquakes, 335, 336
Shaw, Henry W., *Josh Billings' Farmers' Allminax,* 397
Sheldon, Frederick S., "The Dead Level," 334, 336
Shelley, Percy B., 204
Shepard, Augustus D., 227, *228,* 230
Shepard, Mr. and Mrs. Augustus D., 393, 397–98
Shepard, Augustus D., family, 232
Shepard, Elinor, 235, 240
Shepard, Elliott F., 229, *230*
Shepard, Mr. and Mrs. Elliott F., 397, 398
Shepard, Fitch, 227, *228*
Shepard, Joanna M. (Mrs. A. D.), 185, 228, 235, 240, 248, 249, 360, 398
Shepard, Margaret L. V. (Mrs. E. F.), 230
Sheppard, William L., *378*
Sherman, William T., 187, *188,* 189
Shock, Samuel, 125, *126*
Sidney, Sir Philip, 26
Silliman, Benjamin, 259
Sinks, Olive, 295
Sister Felicitas, 37
*Smith, Azariah, *321*
*Smith, Ellen, 29
Smith, Fanny, 84, 85
Smith, Goldwin, 323, *324,* 335
Smith, John, "Lines of Life," 46, 47
*Smith, Samuel M., 4, *32, 33,* 37, 239; loan to WDH, 83–84, 85, 102, 124; comment recalled by WDH, 263
Smith, Dr. and Mrs. Samuel M., 34, 50
*Smith, Mrs. Samuel M., 4, 30, 32, 34, 116, 128
*Smith, William H., 19, *51,* 201, 212, 229, 230; buys "Not a Love Story," 21
Socrates, 69
Soldini Masses, 158, 160
Solomon, 283
South Carolina secession crisis, 65
*Speck, W. A.
Spencer, Herbert, 255, 402
Spenser, Edmund, 177
Spofford, Ainsworth R., *411*
Spofford, Harriet P., 354, *356*
Sprague, Katherine C. (Mrs. W.), 22, 23
Sprague, William, 22
Sprenger, John J., 221, 231; WDH's predecessor at Venice, 99, *100,* 112; WDH on his consulship, 127, 128

Springfield *Republican,* 193, 365, 399
Standard of the Cross, 7
Starling, Lyne, 30
Starling Medical College, 295; WDH rooms in, 20, 24, 30, 32, 34; landscape, 39
*State, Department of.
*Stedman, Edmund C., 4, 86, 246, 265; *Alice of Monmouth,* 176, 178; "Anonyma," 254, 255; "Edmund Booth," 251; "The Feast of the Harvest" (criticized by WDH), 284, 285; "The Mountain," 254, 255; notice of "The Pilot's Story," 59; "Pan in Wall Street," 269, 270, 271; review of *Venetian Life,* 266; "Spoken at Sea," 254, 255; "Tennyson and Theocritus," 369; *Victorian Poets,* 403; W. S. Landor essay (rejected by WDH), 403; in Washington, 87, 106; leaves New York *World,* 128, 129; entertains WDH, 397; WDH on poem and article submitted, 403, 406
Stedman, Laura, 78
Stillman, William J., 298, *299*
Stoackel, 313, 325
*Stoddard, Charles W., "Behind the Scenes," *407;* "Over the Footlights," *407;* "A Prodigal in Buskins," *407;* "A Prodigal in Tahiti," *407*
*Stoddard, Elizabeth D. B. (Mrs. R. H.), 128, 129; *Temple House,* 266, 267; *Two Men,* 179
Stoddard, Richard H., 4, 128, 129, 179, 246, 254, 265, 266, 271; *The King's Bell,* 134, 144; meets WDH, 102, *105;* and J. L. Graham, Jr., 133, 134, 228; illness, 144; and *Round Table,* 177; on WDH's Italian translations, 230; and *Nation,* 255
Stoddard, Richard H., family, 251
Story, Charles W., 341
Stowe, Harriet B., "The True Story of Lady Byron's Life," 245; sensation of, 334, 335–36, 337; WDH's part explained, 339–40; controversy continues, 344; *Uncle Tom's Cabin,* 18
Strodtmann, Adolf, 133, *134*
Strozzi Palace, Florence, 179
Sturgis, Charles M., 84, *85*
Sullivant, Miss, 36, 38
Sullivant, William S., 36; *Icones Muscorum, 38*
Sumner, Charles, 111, 112, 281, 282; letter to W. H. Seward cited, 112; "Prophetic Voices about America," 279
Sunday-School Times, 376

Sutliff, 314
Swan, Annie, 84, 85
Swan, Joseph R., 34, *35*, 85
Swayne, Mary L., 28, 30, 34
Swayne, Noah H., 28, *30*
Swedenborg, Emanuel, 319; *The Divine Love and Wisdom*, 304; *Heaven and Hell*, 304, 305, 390; *Spiritual Diary*, 303–4, 305; subject of James, Sr., book, 336, 339, 347; as understood by WDH, 391–92
Swedenborgianism. *See* WDH: Religion.
Sweeney, Gerald M., 112
Swinburne, Algernon C., 102, 105, 388, 403, 406; *A Song of Italy*, 281, 282
Swinton, John, 99, 100, 102, 105; encourages WDH for New York *Times* job, 229, 230, 231, 232
Swinton, William, 315

Tasso, Torquato, 103
Tautphoeus, Baroness Jemina (M.) von, *The Initials*, 33, 35
*Taylor, Bayard, *129*, 136, 246, 251, 265; "The Accolade" (rejected by WDH), 388; "An August Pastoral," 334, 336; *By-Ways of Europe* (reviewed by WDH), 327; "Diversions of the Echo Club": "The Ballad of Hiram Hoover" (parody of Whittier), "The Lay of the Macaroni" (Swinburne), "Nauvoo" (Longfellow), "Palabras Grandiosas" (Aldrich), "The Psycho-Physical Muse" (Holmes), "The Sewing-Machine" (Longfellow), 388; *Faust* (trans., reviewed by WDH), 129, 362; "The Haunted Shanty," 84, 85; "In My Vineyard," 334, 336; *The Picture of St. John* (reviewed by WDH), 269, 270; "Sheik Ahnaf's Letter from Bagdad" (rejected by WDH), 326, 327; *The Story of Kennett* (reviewed by WDH), 254, 255; return from Russia, 179; on WDH review, 254; on *Venetian Life*, 266–67; visit to WDH, 307–8
Taylor, Edward T., 316, *317*
Taylor, R. W., 75
Té, Palazzo del, Mantua, 182
Tennyson, Alfred, 95, 275, 341, 403; "The Daisy," 178; "The Dying Swan," 95, 97; *Idylls of the King*, 41, 177; "The Lady of Shalott," 135, 136; "Locksley Hall," 56, 57, 58, 59; "The Lotos-Eaters," 120; "Love and Duty," 224; "Marianna in the South," 178, 283, 284; "The Miller's Daughter," 11, 329, 332; *The Princess, A Medley*, 39, 57; WDH reads, 37; O. W. Holmes, Jr., on imitating, 74; cast of hand, 234
Thackeray, William M., 41, 66, 396; *Early and Late Papers* (reviewed in *Atlantic*), 279
Thaxter, Celia, "Among the Isles of Shoals," 327, 335, 336
Thayer, Alexander W., 134; Beethoven biography, *136*
Thayer & Eldridge, publishes *Leaves of Grass* (1860 ed.), 87, 88
Thompson, Lawrence, 35
Thoreau, Henry D., 48–49, 55; *Walden*, 49; *The Writings of...* (1906), 49
Thorpe, Father, 304, 305
Thrall, W. B., 75
The Three Principal Objections Against ...Swedenborg..., 30, 32
Tiberius, Palace of, Capri, 351
*Ticknor & Fields, 59, 245, 252, 260, 274, 277, 283, 284, 293, 314; WDH neglected by, 224; represented by Osgood, 248, 249; WDH visits office, 251; H. M. Ticknor leaves, 304. *See also* Ticknor, Howard M., and Fields, James T.
*Ticknor, Howard M., 59, 125; letter to W. C. Howells cited, 115; accepts WDH's "The Empty House," 69; rejects WDH's "A Little German Capital," 121–22; and Anne T. Howells, 286, 292; leaves Ticknor & Fields, 304
Tintoretto, 108, 142, 298
Titian, 108, 142
Toggenburg, Count, 122, *123*
Toledo *Commercial*, 67, 130, 139
Toledo *Journal*, 32
Torcello, Cathedral at, 149
Tortorini, G. A., *121*; befriends WDH, 93; lends WDH money, 102, 124; nurses WDH, 110, 111, *112*; gift from WDH, 111, 114; WDHs visit, 219
*Treasury, Secretary of.
Trinity Chapel, Brighton, 141, 143
*Trollope, Anthony, 219, 220
*Trübner & Co., 205, 225, 239, 375; rejection of WDH's poems, 158, 160; further negotiations through Conway, 176, 185, 186, 187, 188; nonagreement on terms, 192, 193; submission of *Venetian Life*, 208, 209; provisional rejection, 214–15; publication through Hurd, 227; announcement of publication, 237; negotiations on errors, 260, 266–67
Tubbs, Captain and Mrs., 133–34

INDEX

Tuckerman, Henry D., *305*
Tupper, Martin, *Proverbial Philosophy*, 17, 18
Twain, Mark (pseud.). See Clemens, Samuel L.
Tweed Ring, 365, 370, 371
Tweed, William M., 365
Tyndall, John, *402*

Uhland, Johann L., 107, 226; *Gedichte*, 42, 43; "Love of the Singers" (trans. of "Sängerliebe"), 46, 47; "Der Schäfer," 44, 45; "Das Schloss am Meere," 43; "Der Schwarze Ritter," 43; "Der Traum" (*see also* Heine), 44, 45
Union College, 246, 300–301
Union League Club, New York, 396
Unitarianism, 354. *See also* WDH: Religion.
University Press, Cambridge, 260, 335
University Quarterly, 65, 69, 70
Upham, Charles W., *Salem Witchcraft and Cotton Mather* (reviewed in MS by WDH), 338
Urbana University, 23, 55, 385, 408, 409

Van Buren, Martin, 211
Vanderbilt, Cornelius, 230
Vanderbilt, relatives of Margaret L. V. Shepard (Mrs. E. F.), 397, 398
Vanity Fair, 99, 108, 128, 129
Varotari, Alessandro, 161, *162*
Vasari, Giorgio, *Lives of the Most Eminent Painters*, 144, 145
Verdi, Giuseppe, "Anvil Chorus," 328
Vere, Aubrey de, 362, *363*
Veronese, 146
Victor Emanuel II, of Italy, 182
Victoria Magazine, 160
Victoria, of Great Britain, 141
Vittoria, Hotel, Venice, 409
Volksbücher, German, 27
Voltaire, 64, 65, 402; *Philosophical Dictionary*, 70

Wade, Benjamin F., 36, 37, 111, 112, 126; letter from W. C. Howells cited, 74, 75; supports WDH for consulship, 3, 74, 75; considers governorship, 370
Wade, Decius S., 125, *126*
Wallack's Theatre, New York, 234, 235
Wallingford Community, 383
Ward, Artemus (pseud.). See Browne, Charles F.
Ward, Herbert D., *256*

Ward, John Q. A., WDH stays with in New York, 87, *88*; WDH likes Ward's work, 378; meets in New York, 397
Ward, Samuel, 256, 257
Warden, Robert B., lives of S. A. Douglas and S. P. Chase, 277
Waring, George E., Jr., *363*
Warner, Charles D., *The Gilded Age* (with Clemens), 397
Webster, Franklin, 208, *209*
Weiss, John, 314, *315*
Wessen, Ernest J., 75
Westermann & Co., 275
Westminster Abbey, 96
Westminster Review, 64, 65; publishes "Neo-Christianity," 66, 67; and Conway, 158; reviews *Venetian Life*, 265
Wheeler and Wilson sewing machine, 280
*Whipple, Edwin P., *Character and Characteristic Men* (reviewed in *Atlantic*), 269, 270; review of *Venetian Life*, 269
White, Andrew D., 357, *358*
Whitman, Walt, "A Carol of Harvest for 1867," 285; *Drum-Taps* (reviewed by WDH), 236, 237; *Leaves of Grass* (1860 and 1867 eds.), 88, 271–72; "The Return of the Heroes," 285
Whitney, William D., 331, 333
Whittier, John G., 55, 388; *Ballads of New England* (reviewed by WDH), 335, 336; *Journal . . . of John Woolman* (ed.), 381
Wilder, Burt G., articles on science, 335, 336
William I, of Württemberg, 105, 106
Williams, Jim (James E.), 4, 10, 30, 32
Williams, John S., 317
Williams, Walter F., 232
Williams, William F., 232
Williston, Mrs. Samuel, 370, *371*
Willson, Forceythe, 257, 258
Wimsatt, William K., 347
Wing, Miss, 33, 35
Wingate, Charles F., "The History of the Tweed Ring," 365
Winsor, Justin, review of *Venetian Life*, 264, 265
*Winter, William, 55, 177
Wolcott, C. P., 75
"The Woman Question," 387
Wood, George, *Future Life, or Scenes in Another World*, 26, 27; *Peter Schlemihl in America*, 26
Woodhull, Victoria C., 387
Woodress, James, 106, 115, 134, 136, 137, 154, 156, 173, 176, 215

Woodward, 346
Woolman, John, *Journal*, 381
Worcester, Joseph E., *Comprehensive ... Dictionary ...*, 357
World's Fair, London, 96
Wordsworth, William, 342, 343; "The Idiot Boy," 28, 29
Wright, Francis M., *24*
Wright, Miss, 23

*Wyman, Don L., 275; "Onion and the Dolphin," 225; "Only a Year," *226*, 275

Yale College (or University), 35
Young, John, *The Province of Reason ...* (noticed by WDH), 67

Zaccaria (or Zaccharia), 128
Zanchi, Antonio, 159, 160, 161
Zona, Antonio, 174